PARADISE

PARADISE

Reflections on Chiara Lubich's Mystical Journey

Foreword
Peter Casarella

Preface
Piero Coda

Edited and with an Introduction by
Donald W. Mitchell

Published in the United States by New City Press
202 Comforter Blvd., Hyde Park, NY 12538
www.newcitypress.com
©2020 New City Press

Editorial and translation work by Thomas Masters

Most articles included in this book were published by:
Purdue University Press in *Claritas: Journal of Dialogue and Culture* from 2012 until 2019.
© Purdue University Press.

Cover design and typesetting by Miguel Tejerina

Library of Congress Control Number: 2020939914

Includes bibliographical references and index.

ISBN: 978-1-56548-401-6 (paperback)
ISBN: 978-1-56548-409-2 e-book

Contents

Foreword 9

Preface 19

Introduction 29

1. **The Mystical Experience of Chiara Lubich: Paradise '49** 41

   Piero Coda, Donald W. Mitchell, and Judith Povilus,
   Contextualizing "Paradise '49" 43

   Chiara Lubich, *Paradise '49* (1961) 58

   Chiara Lubich, *Paradise '49* (1969) 69

   Gérard Rossé, *Entry into the Paradise of '49
   and Biblical Revelation* 87

2. **The Pact and Paradise '49** 111

   Chiara Lubich, *The Pact* 113

   Anna Pelli, *Going from the Pact to the Soul:
   Exploring a Metaphysical Journey* 116

3. **Implications of Paradise '49 for Theology** 137

   Piero Coda, *Chiara Lubich and the Theology of Jesus:
   The Trinity as Place, Method, and Object of Thinking* 139

   Piero Coda, *A Charism in History as a View from the Center* 154

   Piero Coda, *God and Creation:
   Trinity and Creation Out of Nothing* 167

   Piero Coda, *Creation in Christ and the New Creation
   in the Mysticism of Chiara Lubich* 186

Thomas Norris, *A Spirituality that Inspires Ontology:
The Discovery of God-Love and the Renewal of Ontology* 197

David L. Schindler, *The "Yes" Under Every "No"* 206

Brian K. Reynolds, *The Virgin Mary, Creation, Incarnation,
and Redemption: From the Church Fathers to Chiara Lubich* 214

4. Implications of Paradise '49 for Biblical Studies 239

Gérard Rossé, *Revisiting Chiara Lubich's Paradise '49
in Light of the Letter to the Ephesians* 241

Gérard Rossé, *Revisiting Chiara Lubich's Paradise '49
in Light of the Letter to the Ephesians:
Divine Adoption and Divine Design* 262

Gérard Rossé, *Revisiting Chiara Lubich's Paradise '49
in Light of the Letter to the Ephesians:
The Holy Spirit, the Son of God, and the Cosmos* 280

Gérard Rossé, *Revisiting Chiara Lubich's Paradise '49
in Light of the Letter to the Ephesians:
Jesus Forsaken, the Church, and Agape-Love* 300

5. Implications of Paradise '49 for Humanity and the Church 329

Callan Slipper, *Towards an Understanding of the Human Person
According to the Mystical Experience of Chiara Lubich
in the Paradise of '49* 331

Callan Slipper, *Towards a New Kind of Cognition* 362

Chiara Lubich, *Look at All the Flowers* 371

Jesús Morán, *Transferring Self to Other:
Radicalizing Human Being* 374

Hubertus Blaumeiser and Brendan Leahy,
*"When the tree will have blossomed fully..."
Reflections on the Church* 384

6. **Implications of Paradise '49 for Society and Culture** 393

    Maria Voce, *The Charism of Unity in Dialogue with Contemporary Culture and the Paradigm of Fraternity* 395

    Antonio Maria Baggio, *Love of All Loves: Politics and Fraternity in the Charismatic Vision of Chiara Lubich* 404

    Luigino Bruni, *The Economy of Communion: A Project for a Sustainable and Happy Socioeconomic Future* 422

    Bernard Callebaut, *Economy of Communion: A Sociological Inquiry on a Contemporary Charismatic: Inspiration in Economy and Social Life* 435

7. **Implications of Paradise '49 for Interreligious Dialogue** 451

    Donald W. Mitchell, *The Mystical Theology of Chiara Lubich: A Foundation for Interreligious Dialogue in Asia* 453

    Donald W. Mitchell, *Dazzling Darkness: Buddhism and Chiara Lubich's Mystical Writings* 472

    Cherylanne Menezes, *Christian and Hindu Dialogue on the Charism of Unity* 481

    Roberto Catalano, *Spiritual Friendship and Interreligious Dialogue: The Experience of Chiara Lubich and Nikkyo Niwano* 498

    Cinto Busquet, *A Buddhist-Catholic Dialogue of Life in Japan: Finding Shared Values for Global Collaboration for the Common Good* 515

Authors 533

Foreword

One does not usually think of a Catholic mystic in the guise of a mid-twentieth century lay woman who emerged from the rubble of post-war bombardment. In fact, there were eighty incursions by the Allied troops into Chiara Lubich's native city of Trent between 1943-45 with a total of 400 fatalities and 1,792 injured. The Lubich home, for example, was rendered completely uninhabitable. The end of the war also meant the end of Fascism, but the way forward for the people who had suffered under this authoritarian regime still needed to be charted. Igino Giordani, who Lubich later would call her "co-founder" of the Focolare Movement, arranged for the release from prison by Mussolini of the Tridentine Social Democrat and later Italian Prime Minister Alcide De Gasperi.[1] The reconstruction of life and society after Fascist repression and a bloody Nazi occupation was slow and filled with concerns that might have appeared more pressing than devotion to one's spiritual life. Yet the illumination of Paradise '49, the subject of the essays in this remarkable volume, began precisely in this milieu. Moreover, the war had shattered the illusion of a God who aided in the divisive expansion of either fascist or socialist might. Chiara Lubich was not seeking a balm from God that would free her and her companions from the misery and confusion they now faced. She and her companion "Foco" (Igino Giordani) opened their hearts to a God who could make sense of the rubble, well aware that Jesus Christ had emptied himself on a cross and thereby entered into the midst of human fragility. When the thirty-four year old French philosopher and exiled Vichy opponent Simone Weil redacted *L'Enracinement* ("The Need for Roots") in 1943, she too realized that the needs of the vanquished and spiritually arid soul could not be a mere addendum to post-war reconstruction.[2] Jesus was in the midst of the community of Chiara and her companions, huddled together in their Mount Tabor in the Dolomites, to help them build new "edifices" out of the rubble for the soul and for society.

---

1. De Gasperi later visited Chiara at the Mariapolis as the Italian Prime Minister.
2. Simone Weil, *The Need for Roots: Prelude to a Declaration of Duties toward Mankind*, tr. Arthur Wills (New York: Routledge, 2002). The first edition of the original French appeared in 1949, the same year that Chiara Lubich began to record her visions.

Chiara eventually came down from the mountain and began life anew. These essays explain exactly what is meant by "a mystic on a journey." Chiara Lubich was certainly an itinerant mystic on fire with the love of God and no less eager to transmit that illumination to others who joined her on this path. She recounts *never* to have experienced a blinding vision or a fall from a horse. Her mystical experience was "a sweet engrafting," an experience of the unitive presence of Divine Love.[3] The dramatic *chiaroscuro* of Caravaggio's *Calling of St. Matthew* was replaced by the quiet still life with her eight companions that transpired in a mountain cabin that was little more than a cowshed.[4] The everydayness of this scene is deceptive. God was working through her *de arriba* ("from above"), in the words of St. Ignatius of Loyola, but the effects of God's work were palpably evident on the ground and in the midst of the humble women who were sharing their lives and scarce material goods together.[5]

Chiara also narrates an experience of beauty. The environment of the Dolomites contributes a natural beauty, but she was responding to a divine beauty that was, in the words of St. Augustine, both ancient and new.[6] Why is hearkening to divine beauty so urgent and important in our day and especially in the midst of the manifold social and political problems that beset our world? Theologian Brendan Sammon has written about the relevance today of being called to the attractiveness of God.[7] Young adults are often just as befuddled by the numbing indifference of the world to faith as by the opponents of the Church. They need to be awakened by the power of God's beauty and the beauty that irradiates from the lives of holy women and men. Even more concretely, the mosaicist Marko Ivan Rupnik has argued convincingly that the vocation to beauty and the new evangelization go hand in hand.[8] Such beauty is never sanitized or precious. Beauty is the irruption of an unforeseen reality that beckons a call to a new way of life. Beauty penetrates the core of a person and unifies the forces of creative energy that must be harnessed if one wishes to face the harsh realities of life.

---

3. Chiara Lubich, "Paradise 1949 told by Chiara in 1969," *Claritas: Journal of Dialogue and Culture* 8,1 (2919): 8.
4. Chiara Lubich, "Paradise 1949 told by Chiara in 1969," 9.
5. On *de arriba*, see Hugo Rahner, *Ignatius the Theologian*, 3-10.
6. St. Augustine, *Confessions*, Book 10, 26, 37.
7. Brendan Sammon, *Called to Attraction: An Introduction to the Theology of Beauty* (Eugene, Oregon: Cascade Books, 2012).
8. Marko Ivan Rupnik, *In the Fire of the Burning Bush: An Initiation to the Spiritual Life* (Grand Rapids, Michigan: Eerdmans, 2004).

From the outset, Chiara Lubich pursued a mysticism in the Church. This included but went beyond the sacramental life. The ecclesial dimension of her mysticism was a function of the communal relationship with Christ. The mystical marriage that she undertook in the wake of her pact with Foco was unique. It was not between her individual soul and God, as in the much-revered traditional female spirituality of the Middle Ages. But it was also not a union between a social body and a non-localizable and utopian Absolute Spirit, as in the ideology of secular progress. In the concrete place of the Father's bosom, Chiara saw one Soul that embraced the "we" of her own soul and that of her companions.[9] Seen from the vantage point of paradise, God's own unfathomable love was now *da noi*, dwelling among us and beckoning us to greater discipleship.

Gerard Rossé has written elegantly about how the ecclesial origins of Focolare can be likened to the Church in the Letter to the Ephesians.[10] Chiara does not just interpret the ecclesiology of Ephesians. She shows her companions how daily life can be lived in imitation of the revelation of the divine love in the Word of God. St. Thomas Aquinas had a similar inspiration regarding the catechetical pedagogy of communicating the eternity of paradise into the midst of time.[11] Regarding the unity encountered in the body of Christ, Aquinas exegetes Eph. 4:15-6 as follows:[12]

> a connecting and binding force emanates from Christ, the head, into his body, the Church, since whatever is united must be held together or bound by some nexus or bond. On this account he says fitly joined together, by what every joint supplieth, that is,

---

9. Chiara Lubich, "Paradise 1949 told by Chiara in 1969," 11: ""I saw in the bosom of the Father a small company: that's us."
10. Gerard Rossé, "Chiara Lubich's Paradise '49 in Light of the Letter to the Ephesians: Jesus Crucified and Forsaken, the Church, and Agape-Love," *Claritas* 6, 1 (March 2017): 4-24. This piece as well as the three other installments on Ephesians are reproduced in this volume.
11. Aquinas writes in *Summa theologiae* II-II, 171, 6c: "Prophecy is a type of knowledge impressed on the prophet's intellect from a divine revelation, this happens after the manner of education. Now the truth of knowledge is the same in both the student and the teacher since the student's knowledge is a likeness of the teacher's knowledge, just as in natural matters the form of what is generated is a certain likeness of the form of the generator."
12. "Rather, living the truth in love, we should grow in every way into him who is the head, Christ, from whom the whole body, joined and held together by every supporting ligament, with the proper functioning of each part, brings about the body's growth and builds itself up in love."

through the faith and charity which unite and knit the members of the mystical body to one another for their mutual support. "All the works of the Lord are good: and he will furnish every work in due time" (Eccles. 39:39). Thus, the Apostle himself, confident of this mutual being-of-service (*mutua subadministratione*) which reigns among the members of the Church due to the divine unifying action, had said: "I know that this shall happen to me unto salvation, through your prayer and the assistance of the Spirit of Jesus Christ" (Phil. 1:19).[13]

Chiara too sees faith combined with charity infusing the members with a new spirit of unity. Her ethics of Paschal unity and spirituality of communion have vast repercussions for how we can think about the field hospital of the Church in itself and in its service to the woundedness of the world.

Accordingly, she also connects this unity of Agape-Love to Jesus Crucified and Forsaken.[14] Chiara and Foco had a vocation to make their own the experience of Jesus' forsakenness. As she herself recalled saying to Foco at that time:

> Look, it might be that what you feel is really from God. But not two one, all one. But it may really be that it is from God so we shouldn't waste it. . . . You know my life, it is to be nothing, because I live Jesus Forsaken, and so I exist if I am nothing. He is everything, I am the nothingness. So, if I want to be what I truly am, I have to be nothing, and in this way I exist. And you are nothing, because you too are Jesus Forsaken. We have to live this nothingness. If we are this nothingness, then we are what we are, because we put ourselves in our true being. As Saint Catherine said: 'I am nothing, you are Everything.'"[15]

Il nulla ("nothingness") is not a mere metaphor; it is a form of existence. How can we exist seeking to share in the fullness of life if we are called to imitate Christ's self-emptying to the utmost? There are implications here that extend far beyond a secure spirituality for the most dedicated of Chris-

---

13. St. Thomas Aquinas, *Commentary on St. Paul's Epistle to the Ephesians*, Translation and Introduction by Matthew L. Lamb, O.C.S.O. (Albany, N.Y.: Magi Books, 1966), cited here following on-line version at https://isidore.co/aquinas/Eph4.htm#7.
14. Fabio Ciardi, "Traveling Paradise," *Claritas* 8:1 (2019): 11.
15. Chiara Lubich, "Paradise 1949 told by Chiara in 1969," 10.

tians. It is the adventure that remains attentive to God's presence and absence in multiple contexts and sets of beliefs. Through communion with her "Almighty Spouse" the sin and even "the hell" that Christ undergoes is made her own.[16] When humanity experiences God in God's absence, the heart that is wedded to the Forsaken One embraces this very emptiness out of a firm faith in his being resurrected on the third day.

Chiara's spirituality of an "exterior castle" is also a vision for humanity.[17] Others have recognized its breadth of application to contemporary life. In 1977, for example, she was awarded in London a Templeton Prize for Progress in Religion. In the context of this translation of her founding experience into English, it is interesting to reflect on her experiences of entering, like Mother Cabrini (whose actual tomb she visited in 1997) arriving from a distant shore, to the "castle" of these shores. According to Donald W. Mitchell, Chiara made seven trips to the United States:

- 1964: First trip to USA to visit the Focolare in New York City.
- 1965: Visit to New York City and founding of New City Press.
- 1966: At invitation of Cardinal Richard Cushing, she founded the Focolare in Boston.
- 1968: Visit to New York and inauguration of the Mariapolis Center in Chicago.
- 1990: Visit to Mariapolis Luminosa in Hyde Park, New York, one of thirty-two "little cities" operated by the Focolare around the world.
- 1997: Received Honorary Degree in Humane Letters from Sacred Heart University in Fairfield, Connecticut and made a presentation at Malcolm Shabazz Mosque in Harlem.
- 2000: Received Honorary Doctorate in Education from Catholic University of America, and went with W.D. Muhammad to the "Faith Communities Together" event at the Washington DC Conference Center with Focolare members and with African American Muslims.

Each of these engagements pointed to building up a new civilization on the North American landscape. She knew that practical culture wanted

---

16. Chiara Lubich, *The Cry of Jesus Crucified and Forsaken* (Hyde Park, New York: New City Press, 2001), 62.
17. On this point, see, for example, Piero Coda, *Dalla Trinità: l'avvento di Dio tra storia e profezia* (Rome: Città Nuova, 2012, 2nd ed.), 493-512.

concrete answers to the problems people face. The experience of the Dolomites was not meant to be replicated in the Hudson River Valley of the State of New York or anywhere else that she visited. From the challenges of race relations and religious pluralism to the invigoration of the Christian's task of education, Chiara was prepared to share her gift from the triune God with peoples of many lands, including here in the United States. The Focolarine and Focolarini in the United States represent a culturally diverse communion spread throughout many regions of this land, endowed with diverse professional talents. More importantly, they are the recipients of the gift of Chiara's seven initiatives on U.S. soil to build a new culture of encounter in ecclesial settings and beyond.

The pact that Chiara made in 1949 with Foco had no marketing plan. It transpired in its own distinct socio-political milieu but was never intended to spread the social Gospel of De Gasperi's Christian Democracy throughout the globe.[18] It was a pact with the Trinity that was designed to let the fruits of their new life grow organically in new and hitherto unexplored fields. The readers of this volume will thus be astonished at the newness of Chiara's experience. Chiara even writes about her mystical experience as a revolution:

> It is necessary to make God be reborn in us, to keep him alive and make him overflow onto others as torrents of Life and resurrect the dead. And keep him alive among us by loving one another.... Then everything is revolutionized: politics and art, school and religion, private life and entertainment. Everything.[19]

No sphere of existence is excluded. The nurturing of an inner flame expands from the interior castle to an exterior one. From that socially inclusive but spiritually well-fortified rampart, even politics and economics need to be assessed in a new light. Her social vision recapitulates an insight that G. K. Chesterton once made with regard to the social vision of Charles Dickens. The novels of Dickens, Chesterton said, reclaimed the forgotten third ideal that was used by Robespierre as a rallying cry after the French Revolution, namely, the principle of fraternity.[20]

---

18. Chiara Lubich, *Essential Writings: Spirituality, Dialogue, Culture* (Hyde Park: New York: New City Press, 2007), 238.
19. *Paradise '49*, as cited in Fabio Ciardi, "Traveling Paradise," 17.
20. See G.K. Chesterson, "Preface," to Charles Dickens, *Hard Times*, available on-line at https://documents.uow.edu.au/~nillsen/Chesterton_on_Dickens.html.

What does fraternity look like in the Americas today and how is it linked to the original experience of 1949? Chilean social scientists Rodrigo Mardones and Alejandra Marinovic have argued that fraternity has a suppressed but nonetheless identifiable semantic domain in the North American socio-political consciousness.[21] This hidden undercurrent in North American politics represents both a more subtle and a more viable political theory than a poorly defined communitarianism. This impetus for a new ethos of political unity thus merits a great deal of further study. A small band of women were the nucleus, to which Chiara added the pact with Foco. The Focolare thus included a complementarity of the Marian and Petrine profiles virtually from its very founding. Mardones and Marinovic remind us that the sociologist and jurist Georges Gurvitch long ago defended fraternity in the domain of law to show that there is a legal foundation for criticizing the juridical rights only of an isolated individual and that feminists have put forwarded the notion of civic friendship (solidarity between women and between women and men) as an alternative to the male dominated discourse that inevitably accompanies the English word "fraternity." The Jewish philosopher Emanuel Levinas likewise argues that fraternity is not just a biological reality like filiality but a genuine social fruit of an ethical monotheism.[22] For Levinas intersubjective encounters between strangers that are dialogical and thus genuinely fraternal are one primary alternative to monolithic totalities, but he controversially claims that such fraternal bonds only flow out of the monotheistic view of human kinship standing before God, not from a merely secular ethic. Levinas also reminds us that the Good Samaritan is a prime Biblical example of the politics of fraternity. These starting points for a new politics of fraternity could certainly be explored further in the light of the unique encounter with God in *Paradise '49* that Chiara extended as an offering both to the members of Focolare and to the world.

To the English-speaking audience, the essays dealing with the significance of Paradise '49 for the dialogues with Buddhism, Gulen, and non-Western religious traditions will be particularly noteworthy. The Focolarini who par-

---

21. Rodrigo Mardones and Alejandra Marinovic, "Tracing Fraternity in the Social Sciences and in Catholic Social Teaching," *Logos: A Journal of Catholic Thought and Culture* 19, 2 (Spring 2016): 53-80, especially 55-61.
22. Emmanuel Levinas, *Totality and Infinity: An Essay on Exteriority* (Pittsburgh: Duquesne University Press, 1969), 214 and 278-280 and also his *Otherwise than Being* (Pittsburgh: Duquesne University Press, 1978), 159. Cf. John Llewelyn, *Emmanuel Levinas: The Genealogy of Ethics* (London and New York: Routledge, 1995), 125-7.

ticipated in these encounters are offering a homecoming to the adherents of non-Christian traditions. Far from proselytizing, these are opportunities to transform the gift of love into a dialogue.[23] As Mitchell notes, Chiara's search for the right balance between personal and communal experiences of the fruits of contemplation can find unexpected echoes in other traditions.[24] The barriers between religions easily become social barriers, even where violence in the name of God has never been an issue. Chiara's dialogical, agapic-kenotic method has attracted admirers because of its insights into the unique form of human relationality that results from a commitment to transcendence in our fast-paced and atomizing world. These encounters have engendered both religious and social bonds that are especially important in the face of the present and future crises that we face and will face as a planet. Likewise, the Holy Father in an *Urbi et Orbi* message during the Easter season of 2020 asked Catholics around the world to promote "a contagion of hope" in the midst of the global pandemic caused by the coronavirus.[25]

The international headquarters for Chiara's ecclesial movement is located in the Diocese of Frascati, and Chiara's tomb can also be found there in the Focolare's International Center (together with the tombs of the original companions Igino Giordani and Pasquale Foresi). The first phase of the beatification process of servant of God Chiara Lubich was completed in November of 2019 by the local ordinary, Bishop Raffaello Martinelli. The devotion to her continues today with pilgrimages to the tomb, but her spirituality of unity goes far beyond the ecclesial movement that she founded. It is a gift for the Church and for the world. The overwhelming illumination given by divine beauty that first irradiated itself in the midst of rubble is now refracted through many lenses on every continent. The reports in the pages of this volume testify to the hope that this light is engendering in our world today. The remarkable fact is not the vision's vastness but its continuity with the origins. Jesus in his forsakenness gives birth to a new unity that is received through the Spirit from within the bosom of the Father. The Mount Tabor of the Dolomites was the original source of this espousal to the Word and

---

23. Donald Mitchell, "The Mystical Theology of Chiara Lubich: A Foundation for Dialogue in East Asia," *Claritas* 3,2 (October 2014): 45.
24. Donald Mitchell, "The Mystical Theology of Chiara Lubich: A Foundation for Dialogue in East Asia," 46.
25. Pope Francis, *Urbi et Orbi* Message, Easter Season, 2020, available on-line at: http://www.vatican.va/content/francesco/en/messages/urbi/documents/papa-francesco_20200412_urbi-et-orbi-pasqua.html.

the communal activity of witnessing that it generated. This volume makes it possible to explore the Trinitarian spirituality of Paradise '49 in a new and exciting way. It will surely contribute to spreading the contagion of hope proclaimed by Pope Francis, and for that I am deeply grateful.

Peter Casarella
Professor of Theology
Duke Divinity School

Preface

What is the meaning of Chiara Lubich's "mystical journey"? How does its original and unprecedented significance change the way we act? How does it change the way we see the future? At first sight, it does not seem easy to answer these questions. This becomes possible and fruitful when we reread the breadth and variety of the whole arc of Chiara's mystical journey, looked at in all simplicity, in light of the experience of Jesus which is delivered to us through the pages of the New Testament. This rereading will allow us, then, to evaluate how Jesus' experience has leavened the history of Christian experience throughout the ages.

Because one thing is sure: Chiara's existential—spiritual and social—journey, and that of her charism, are undoubtedly mystical in the deepest and truest sense of the term. In fact, it is connected directly with the experience of God given by Jesus with the outpouring of his Spirit "without limit" to humankind. But this is precisely why it has all the exceptional dimensions of Jesus' experience together with all that is related to our ordinary social life. In the sense that it is not something uprooted from the bodily drama of earth and history in order to be lived in an ethereal region of pure spirit, but precisely in following Jesus, it is the experience—as Chiara loved to repeat—of having one's feet firmly on the ground while the heart and mind are immersed in Heaven, in God. "On earth as it is in heaven," as Jesus taught us to pray in the Our Father. Yes, it is indeed mystical, but it is Jesus' mysticism. Chiara herself writes it in a note from September 29, 1950:

> Ours is the mysticism of Jesus and of Mary themselves: the mysticism of the *new* Testament, the new commandment, the mysticism of the Church, by which the Church is truly Church, because it is *Unity*, Mystical Body, Love, because in it there circulates the Holy Spirit who makes it Christ's Bride.
>
> It is the mysticism of Jesus, of a complete Jesus and not of another Jesus; yes, of another Jesus, but only if a complete Jesus: the Human Being, not a human being. And Jesus is "where two or more." Hence [it is] the mysticism of those who love one another as he has loved us, of a unity of souls that mirrors, while on earth, the Trinity on High: *while on earth*, because here below we are to witness to the God-who-is-Man and here below is the Church.

In these few words is summed up the whole meaning of Chiara's mystical journey. They invite us to look at it from two complementary points of view—the point of view looking upon the self-awareness, expressed by Chiara, of the gift of God that she received and experienced; and a point of view that looks upon the teaching of gospel life that she herself obtained in order to transmit it to all those called to follow this new spiritual way which in the end is as old as the gospel itself. But it is to be transmitted to all those thirsting for the full meaning of existence. I will try to explore in depth both of these dimensions.

Chiara's Self-Awareness

Let's consider the spoken and written testimony Chiara left us about the steps and nature of her mystical journey. We must clarify right away that even though this is eminently personal, just as each mission in the Church's life is personal, it is not something individual, elitist, or even esoteric. It blossoms from the fertile soil of tradition and ecclesial experience, and therefore it is subject to the Church's reception and discernment. Bearing in mind that within this framework, encompassing Chiara's adventure from beginning to the end, three steps can easily be distinguished; they are deeply expressed one in the other.

First is seen the natural, but clearly defined, progressive kindling of the charismatic inspiration guiding Chiara to become the pioneer of a specific form of Christian discipleship It goes from the beginning of the 1900's (Chiara was born in 1920 in Trent) until the summer of 1949. Two facts among many leap into view during this first period.

On one hand, there is the fact that with an unusually open soul, Chiara absorbed the most precious essence of Christian faith—an essence transmitted to her by a Christian community like that of Trent where she lived and was formed. Trent had solid and rich traditions: catechesis, preaching, the parish's spiritual guidance; formation in the ranks of Catholic Action; an encounter with the charism of St. Francis and St. Clare of Assisi; and active participation in the life of the Franciscan Third Order. On the other hand, Chiara soon sensed the inspiration and interior guidance of a Light, Jesus' Light, gift of his Spirit, urging her like the Spouse in the Song of Songs to seek her Spouse above everything and in each thing, embracing his infinitely loving will for her and for everyone. By reconstructing the noteworthy episodes of this Light's gradual manifestation, it is not difficult to recognize how a new charism is taking form in the Church: beginning especially with Chiara's consecration to God on December 7, 1943; the coming to light of the cardinal points of an original spiritual way; the gathering of a number of people around her who wish to follow her way of gospel life; and the accompaniment and approval by the diocesan bishop.

What we can highlight in the gospel experience being profiled here is a focus on Jesus' message, pivoting around two points: on one hand the unity Jesus requested of the Father at the last supper for his followers (see Jn 17); on the other hand the key to accomplishing it—the abandonment Jesus experienced on the cross. Looking closely, it is already possible to find here the white-hot core of Chiara's mystical journey. In fact, it is a matter of entering—with Jesus through the gift of the Holy Spirit—into the same unity lived by the Father, the Son, and the Holy Spirit in the Holy Trinity, not individually but as a body, as a people. And this—to be perceived through divine inspiration—is made possible and viable in Jesus' experience transmitted by the church, by participating in that death to self in order to live in God, a way indicated by Jesus' abandonment on the cross. Indeed it is Jesus Forsaken—as he is known and called, a name until this point unknown in Christian spirituality and doctrine—who is the "living way" of that unity which is a true, real participation in the life of the Holy Trinity.

The Christian adventure that begins from this point and develops and rapidly spreads is, in truth, already a first step in Chiara's mystical journey. This is because the presence of the risen Jesus (ascended to the right hand of the Father) in the church and in history comes to be perceived by the senses of the soul of Chiara, and is also sensed by her community in its everyday life. It is perhaps not by chance that the year of Chiara's consecration to God, 1943, which she herself recognized as the date when the Focolare Movement began, coincides with the year of Pius XII's promulgation of the encyclical *Mystici Corporis*. In the gospel experience lived by Chiara and the community forming around her, the presence of Jesus where two or more are gathered in his name (see Mt 18:20) becomes possible. With that, the reality of the church as Christ's mystical body enters into history in those who love one another as he loved them himself, in accordance with the commandment Jesus calls "his" and "new" (see Jn 13:34 and 15:12). Chiara herself noted a "qualitative leap" she and her first companions experienced as they became aware that their Christian life was reaching a new level of intensity when they strove to live a pact of mutual love among themselves. Because of the effects—joy, peace, freedom, ardor, strength, perseverance—

they could recognize that the risen Jesus was truly in their midst. He imbued their existence and sent them to everyone to bear witness to this new life. This is the experience, almost a discovery by experiment, of that presence of Jesus which Chiara calls "Jesus in the midst." It was the manifestation of the risen Jesus in person, making it possible for the senses of the soul to perceive him in their mutual love, in their love for all as disciples, in his presence in the church through his Word and the sacraments—the height being the Eucharist—and in the ordained ministry.

We must pay close attention to this experience and the self-awareness in Chiara which is its confirmation, because it is something unprecedented. In this case the "spiritual senses," well known in the Christian mystical tradition, are not activated by perceiving God's presence in Christ, through the Holy Spirit, in the interior of the single soul, but by perceiving the presence of Jesus present among "two or more," in other words in the community and in history. This highlights that here, truly, something new is happening, although it has always been held deep within the Christian event.

Paradise '49

At this point it is possible *a posteriori* to sense something about the divine logic—humanly unexpected and totally gratuitous—that sheds light upon what happens in the second step of Chiara's mystical journey, which is referred to as "Paradise '49." The qualitative leap in this second step is a mystical experience with all the characteristics of classical doctrine. This is because the originating and fundamental element in each authentic mystical experience, including this one, is that the direction of the experience is completely in God's hands. Precisely because he is the protagonist, God raises the person in grace to an experience of himself far exceeding the possibilities of a creature by introducing such a one into the depth of his own divine life in Christ by means of the Spirit.

But Chiara's experience of "Paradise '49" in the bosom of the Father has a distinctive element: it is established upon the foundation of a pact that she proposes and lives with Igino Giordani. It is not merely the "pact of reciprocal love" which she was already living with her first companions—women and men—but a "pact of unity," meaning offering together their own "nothingness of love," as Chiara explains it to Giordani. In other words, on the measure of Jesus Forsaken, they completely open their own existence to Jesus really present in the Eucharist. In this way Jesus is the one generating that unity among them which in him corresponds to the Father's plan of love: the unity of the Trinity itself. The narration of what happens mystically as the unforeseeable fruit (grace!) of the "pact of unity," is what comprises the testimony of the mystical journey along which God guides Chiara, starting from this pact and on the abiding foundation of it. It is not a matter of an event occurring on July 16, 1949 to then be spent in a past which is no longer, but an event opening up to a new kind of mystical experience.

What is new is that the subject of this mystical journey is not only Chiara, but in her and with her there are Igino Giordani, her first companions—women and men—who with her participate in the experience. And later there are also all those who along the way came and come to be associated with the pact of unity. In her account of the mystical journey, Chiara speaks in first person because she is its witness. But she also speaks on behalf of being "one heart and one soul" in Jesus which is born from the pact. On this basis, Chiara defines this "we" as "the Soul," which is "being one" in Christ. In "the Soul" everyone, with his or her own unique identity, is present in Jesus, in each other. In this way they share in the life of the Trinity. That is how Chiara, using a fortunate neologism, speaks of "trinitization" in Jesus, of those who participate in the grace of God that comes about in the pact of unity.

But what is the essential content of the "mystical journey" of "Paradise '49"? It is clearly not possible to answer this with a few quick comments, because Paradise '49 narrates a very rich experience of God with manifold spiritual, doctrinal, scriptural, cultural, interreligious, and social implications. What is present in this book are the beginning of the study of these implications. I will only highlight some of the great themes so important for theology in Chiara's account: her vision of God-Trinity as Love; Mary, in whom the whole of creation is redeemed and transfigured, as "fourth in the Trinity"; creation as an event of love; Jesus Forsaken as the key to understanding the mystery of God-Trinity and all reality in God; creation's vocation to participate in Trinitarian life as "trinitization"; a new interpretation of evil and hell. As Chiara's mystical journey unfolds, these themes come back in perfect consistency with what was announced right from the beginning, but in ever new forms that gradually are explored further as they are penetrated, while sharing in the depths of the life of God-Trinity. It is a matter of a theo-cosmic-anthropic vision which is amazingly held together and in which everything is unfolded in the Light of *ut unum sint*, of the cry of abandonment, of Mary's *fiat*.

I will make only two short remarks. First of all, it should be noted that Chiara's mystical journey is not so much an intellectual contemplation of some eternal truths from God's revelation, but participation in the unfolding of the "*mystérion*," to use Paul's expression, always hidden in and disclosed in the fullness of time in Jesus Christ. As happens in the deepest, most authentic mystical experiences therefore, it is a matter of the mysteries of Christ's life and mission being shared with his church, his Spouse. This is so much the case that Chiara uses a densely ontological term, "reality," to define each of the moments experienced along her mystical journey. And it is even more realistic because of the fact that it involves a participation in the mystery of salvation which happens as a group, and therefore which must have ecclesial, social, and historical significance.

A second remark concerns the specific Marian profile that the mystical journey takes on from the beginning, then gradually opens up the whole of its meaning. This is so much the case that Chiara ends up giving the name "Work of Mary" to the spiritual and social movement that takes form, a name subsequently approved by the church. This name is not merely a devotional fact, but something deeper. If in fact the essential mission of Jesus is to bring the life of heaven on earth, if this is the life of Jesus himself communicated to his Body which is the church (and through the church to all of humanity), then it follows that the exercise of Mary's divine maternity is a fundamental and indispensable dimension of salvation history. She is the mother of Christ, true God and true man, and due to this divine maternity, in him she is the mother of everyone. God gradually introduces Chiara into this experience in her mystical journey. Mary's divine maternity exercised with respect to the historical Jesus was mystically widened at the foot of the cross with respect to all those who called on him, the first born again to become sons and daughters of the one Father in the Holy Spirit. This divine maternity is found precisely in the charism entrusted to Chiara—the charism of "where two or more," the charism of "unity"—an effective ecclesial and historical expression in the maternity of the church with respect to the building up of Christ's mystical body with respect to the "trinitization" of humanity in Christ. As Chiara later explained, and as it is specified in the outline of the Focolare Movement's profile as approved by the Catholic Church in the Movement's Statutes, this is why the Work of Mary is nothing other than Mary's presence and work in the Holy Spirit for humankind and for the accomplishment of salvation history in the church. Here is how Chiara explained it in 1964:

When Mary was on earth, her work was not, for example, to found a religious order, or a convent. Her work was Jesus. The work that Mary does in the Work of Mary is Jesus in the midst. Therefore, Jesus in our midst makes us Mary, makes us be Mary. . . . He is the work that Mary produces, or better, the Work of Mary produces the fruit of making *us* a work of Mary, making us Mary. . . . Our part is to give Jesus to the world. (*Chiara to the Women's School of Formation*, Grottaferrata, February 26, 1964)

Final Perspective on the Mysticism of Chiara Lubich

And so we reach the third and last step in the mystical journey described in Chiara's gospel adventure. This third step is precisely what allows us to obtain with a brief glance another perspective of the interpretation of Jesus' mysticism that Chiara lived and that we outlined at the beginning of our itinerary. It is a perspective of the communication and transmission of her mystical experience as leaven for transforming the church's mission and the history of the human family.

If we ask when Chiara's mystical journey ended, we have to recognize that, based on Chiara's own testimony, there certainly is a precise date that at first glance seems to conclude her experience of "Paradise '49." We are referring to September 20, 1949, when she had to abandon the places where she had lived her mystical journey during the summer spent in the mountains around Trent and return to everyday life in the city. Chiara wrote the famous passage, "I have only one Spouse on earth: Jesus Forsaken. I have no other God but him. In him is the whole of Paradise with the Trinity and the whole of earth with Humanity."

This passage is dizzying—from heaven to the earth. Perceiving that here God does not identify himself with the Light he has given, but with Jesus Forsaken who lives in humanity, Chiara lives this moment readily. As a consequence, she chooses him alone and follows him wherever he is to be found. This is the *magna carta* of Chiara's mystical journey, and in her that of the Work of Mary. Through Jesus Forsaken, Chiara entered as "Soul" into the bosom of the Father. Then she returned to humanity out of love for Jesus Forsaken without leaving that "place," the Paradise to which Jesus had brought her. Because of Jesus Forsaken, the heart of God is in humankind, in anyone who is seeking, desiring, suffering, crying, being disoriented, and despairing. The divine-human "law" Chiara discovered in the bosom of the Trinity is that the more one enters into God, the more one goes out toward human persons.

So we are in a new stage. Chiara recognizes that her mission is to communicate the Light she had received, not just to those living the experience of Paradise with her as she had done until then, but to everyone. It is a matter of "trinitizing," or inserting God's life into relationships among human beings in our common home wherever and however these relationships are manifested. It is prolonging the Incarnation of Jesus, the Word of the Father who is Love, culminating in Jesus Forsaken, extending into the world through the church and the Holy Spirit's universal action. Chiara understood that this is the summing up and the legacy of the mystical journey God had her live.

From this comes the joyous pressing urgency to communicate the Light—forming and shaping new life on an anthropological, social, and cultural level—received so that Jesus would be born, would grow, and would bear fruit in hearts, minds, and human works. This is to be communicated where God is already to be found—through and in Jesus Forsaken. To put this "evangelical revolution" into action, God pushed Chiara to focus on two realities: the newness and evangelical power of the way and life Jesus had shown her, and the theological, cultural, and social meaning and significance of the doctrine that had been communicated to her.

As for the first of these two realities, little by little Chiara drew the outline of what by now stands out fully as a spiritual way as ancient as the gospel, and yet very new and pertinent today. This task entailed a fascinating and creative actualization in the history of Christian spirituality that involved a "trinitarian" synergy with the principal charisms of the past and the ways of discipleship they have laid out. This task defined the role Chiara's charism of unity can play with them today. In correlation with this task, there is also an awareness and study of what is new in the doctrine produced this way.

It is at this point that Chiara emphasizes the humanistic range and the cultural and social commitment which must characterize the incarnation of the Light received in "Paradise '49":

> [A]part from a new theology (because it is based on the trinitarian life lived in the mystical Body of Christ) [it] must give rise also to a new science, a new sociology, a new art, a new politics, and so on – *new* because they are of Christ, renewed by his Spirit. This School will set in motion a new humanism, where humanity is

really at the center, that humanity which before all else is Christ and Christ in human beings.

Incarnation of Light: this, therefore, is the key word for the third step of Chiara's mystical journey which gives orientation toward the purpose and goal of "travelling Paradise" that Chiara, and the "Soul" in her, lived and experienced in "Paradise '49." The Work of Mary was forged in Paradise, beginning with the pact of unity. Now the Reality communicated by God in Paradise has to become leaven and salt for a new humanity. In fact, Chiara wrote on November 8, 1950, "The Lord has called me to found a Movement as a new wineskin in which is put the new wine, that is, the new Spirit that he has given rise to on earth. From the wineskin it must be poured out upon the whole world." Many essays in this book discuss this incarnation in the different fields of today's global culture.

In light of the itinerary followed to this point, it is possible to sense the deep reason why, at the end of the second step of Chiara's mystical journey, "Paradise '49" seems to be extended indefinitely. I believe this is an indication that the contemplated Reality is in the process of being incarnated. There is a humble, discreet, though active and fruitful unfolding that is produced along the way in the dynamic of the incarnation of the charism of unity in history and in dialogue with all positive inspirations of life and of love. This book is the first publication to present both the experience of Paradise '49 and interpretations of its context and meaning, and implications for the many fields of the culture of our times. It also prepares readers for the eventual publication of Paradise '49, and perhaps will inspire readers to contribute to a culture of unity for the good of humanity and the world in which we live.

Piero Coda
Sophia University Institute

Introduction

When just a young woman in her twenties, Chiara Lubich, founder of the Focolare Movement—also known in the Catholic Church as the Work of Mary—had been meeting with a group of young women in Trent as the leader of the local Franciscan Third Order. Then, during World War II, their city was heavily bombed. During the air raids she and her companions would go to the shelters carrying only a book containing the four gospels. In pauses between the bombings, they began to live what they found in the gospels by serving the wounded, the poor, and the displaced. Others joined them in what came to be a new way of life based on a charism Chiara was receiving, a way that became the spiritual life of the Focolare. After the war, living together in a simple apartment, they continued their work. During the summer of 1949 their bishop recommended that they go to the Dolomites to rest for few months. During that time in her early life, Chiara experienced a mystical period that later came to be called "Paradise '49." Throughout that summer and afterward until 1951, she wrote about her mystical experiences in her journal.

In 1990, the German bishop Klaus Hemmerle, a well-known theologian, worked with Chiara to establish the Abba School, which until her death in 2008 met with Chiara to study the Paradise '49 texts. The name for this group comes from the word Chiara prayed in 1949 that began her mystical experiences. Eventually, as the members realized that the mystical experiences of Paradise '49 had implications for many fields other than spirituality, the Abba School grew to include twenty-four scholars from a range of disciplines: theology, philosophy, the social sciences, economics, mathematics, psychology, and the arts. The Abba School has published its studies in books and in the Italian-language journal, *Nuova Umanità* (http://www.rivistanuovaumanita.it).

In November 2010, scholars from around the world met at the Focolare conference center on the grounds of the Papal Palace in Castel Gandolfo for the Abba School's international conference for academics. A group of us took this opportunity to discuss the possibility of founding an English-language journal for articles related to the mystical writings of Chiara Lubich. Scholars who research and publish in English, as well as the leaders of the Abba School itself, welcomed the idea. During 2011, a staff of editors and an editorial board was established to publish an open-access academic journal: *Claritas: Journal of Dialogue and Culture*. I was chosen to be editor and it was published at Purdue University, where I was a professor.

The first issue came out in 2012, and the final issue at Purdue University was published in 2019. The articles in this book come from those issues of *Claritas*. In 2020, the journal moved to Sophia University Institute, a Pontifical university located on the grounds of Loppinao, Italy, the Focolare's school of formation. The articles are organized into six sections.

The Mystical Experience of Chiara Lubich: Paradise '49

The first section presents articles concerning the mystical experiences of Chiara Lubich. It contains a contextualizing article, two of Chiara Lubich's presentations of her experience of Paradise, and a biblical commentary on her experience. "Contextualizing Paradise '49" introduces readers to Chiara Lubich's talks about her mystical experience that began during the summer of 1949 and continued to 1951. The authors are Giuseppe Zanghi, Piero Coda, Judith Povilus, and myself. Zanghi, Coda, and Povilus are all members of the Abba School. The essay locates Lubich in the history of Christian spirituality. Then, by examining her letters, it explores the history of her spirituality from the founding of the Focolare in 1943 to the summer of 1949. Finally, it looks at the text of the 1961 talk in order to help clarify the meaning of Lubich's experiences.

"Paradise '49 (1961)" is a translation of Lubich's remarks about those mystical experiences that began during the summer of 1949. This talk was presented at Oberiberg, Switzerland, on the Feast of St. Paul, June 30, 1961. "Paradise '49 (1969)" was published for the first time recently in Italian. It is her second presentation about her experience, this time to members of the Focolare in Rome. She clarifies some of the statements she made in 1961.

In "Entry into the Paradise of '49 and Biblical Revelation," Gérard Rossé explores some of the beginning passages from Lubich's 1961 talk about Paradise '49. Rossé seeks to explain these passages in the light of biblical revelation, in particular Pauline and Johannine theology. He focuses on two aspects: The first concerns how living the Word of God led up to Chiara's experience. The second concentrates on what she wrote about the special circumstances in which the mystical experience began, particularly the "Pact" she made with Igino Giordani, a noted Catholic writer and politician. This section of the essay serves to introduce the second sets of essays, which focus on this Pact.

The Pact and Paradise '49

The second section includes Chiara Lubich's talk concerning her Pact with Igino Giordani in 1949, a Pact that opened the door to Paradise '49. In sections 19-38 of this document, Chiara tells of Giordani's arrival in the mountains near Trent and how his request to take a vow of obedience to her led to making a pact of unity together when they would receive the Eucharist on the following day. This pact led to Chiara's first mystical experience of the Trinity, which she shared first with Giordani and then also with her other companions. Her companions joined Chiara and Giordani in the pact. This pact led them all into a new relationship of unity, the collective birth of what Chiara called the "Soul." The final sections (38-42) describe the very first moments of what they experienced collectively as the Soul when together they felt they were entering the life of the Trinity.

In "Going from the Pact to the Soul: Exploring a Metaphysical Journey," Anna Pelli explains how the Pact led to something new: the Soul. Chiara describes the Soul as "the bond between us," the "space" where the multiplication of the one and the unification of the many is actualized. This article explores the conceptual development of thought about this issue. Pelli looks at the One-many relationship emblematic of the cultural and spiritual history of the West. Tracing its development from the pre-Socratics then to Plato, Nicholas of Cusa, and Leibniz, Pelli arrives at Lubich's contribution based on Uni-Trinitarian Love, the intimate mystery of God.

Implications of Paradise '49 for Theology

In the third section, noted scholars address the theological implications of Paradise '49. It begins with two articles by Piero Coda. The first is entitled: "Chiara Lubich and the Theology of Jesus: The Trinity as Place, Method, and Object of Thinking." By outlining the variety of forms theology takes, Coda illustrates how the key to knowing God theologically is by participation in Jesus' knowledge of God. By exploring scripture and theological tradition, Coda argues that, for all its advances, the modern theological method must regain awareness of participating, through Christ, in God's self-knowledge. Coda also presents the charisms, the different gifts of the Spirit throughout history, with particular attention upon Chiara Lubich's charism of unity. He explains how this charism, via the experience of humans united in God, provides a participatory knowledge of God in which knowing and loving coincide. This participation has a variety of significant consequences. Coda then turns to the basis for this knowledge, namely, the forsakenness of Christ upon the cross, to show how the crucified intellect goes beyond its natural limitations to share in the intellect, the mind (*nous*), of Christ. Coda concludes by pointing out the implications of this way of knowing for theological practice and suggests possibilities for a fresh approach that respects contemporary needs.

In his second article, "A Charism in History as a View from the Center," Coda provides an "interpretative key" for understanding Chiara Lubich's charism. Like all charisms, its light illuminates the revelation of the Word made flesh in ways that guide and enrich all humanity. Chiara's charism, Coda argues, provides a convergent guide that includes all cultures for the mutual enrichment of humankind. Since we live in a bewildered, wounded, and fluid world today, Chiara's charism, light coming from the darkness of World War II, has its center in the hidden wound on Christ's soul when he cried, "My God, my God, why have you forsaken me?" The author points out that this is not a center to be looked upon, but from which to observe the world in order to help all persons find themselves in mutual relatedness—each as gift for the others on the pattern of the Trinity.

Coda's third article is entitled "God and Creation: Trinity and Creation out of Nothing." Using the fundamental and specifically Christian theological stance that begins from *creatio ex nihilo*, the author shows how Chiara Lubich, on the basis of her charism of unity, develops an original understanding of the creation event in which God gives being to nonbeing, constantly creating historically and preserving in being what is created, and, at the same time, making what is created evolve. This understanding is based upon reading creation out of nothing in light of a radical understanding of divine love that, as a result of its own dynamic, is both One and Three. This vision of reality implicitly contains a Trinitarian metaphysics that reinterprets the *vestigia trinitatis* in creation and gives a fresh understanding of creation's vocation to share in the divine life.

Coda's fourth and final article, "Creation in Christ and the New Creation in the Mysticism of Chiara Lubich," expands upon the meaning of "creation out of nothing" from the point of view of a Trinitarian ontology of love. He focuses more precisely upon creation in Christ, taking a closer look at the "new creation" in Christ crucified and risen and at our participation in it.

The next article in this section, by Thomas Norris, is "Creation in Christ and the New Creation in the Mysticism of Chiara Lubich." Norris points out that charisms lie at the root of great spiritualities, and great spiritualities not only provide ways of living the gospel in harmony with the tradition of the church but also inspire and renew cultures. Chiara Lubich and her companions made many discoveries under the bombs that pulverized Trent between 1943 and 1945: God-Love, the pearl of the gospels in the new commandment, and the reality of Jesus' presence among those united in his name. This article reflects on the insights that those discoveries provide for a Trinitarian ontology centered upon relationship.

The fifth article in this section is David L. Schindler's "The 'Yes' Under Every 'No.'" Based upon the charism of Chiara Lubich, this article proposes that in all those places and ways in which the world, at least on its surface, appears to be saying "no," we must penetrate to the "yes" that is straining to come out into being.

In the last article in this section, "The Virgin Mary, Creation, Incarnation, and Redemption: From the Church Fathers to Chiara Lubich," Brian K. Reynolds discusses a series of texts in "Paradise '49" regarding the Virgin Mary. After discussing Mary as *Theotokos* and the *Desolata*, he considers Lubich's mystical vision of Mary in relation to the Trinity, humanity, and creation. He shows how Lubich partakes entirely in the tradition of the Church Fathers, then argues that Lubich's insights add something new, particularly with regard to understanding the relationship between Jesus' cry of forsakenness on the cross and Mary's desolation as she participates in the agony of her Son and assents to the loss of her divine motherhood. Reynolds argues that Lubich's new understanding of these events has implications for a variety of doctrinal matters concerning Mary. But more important than this, he claims that Lubich shows how in her desolation Mary most fully mirrors the *kenosis* at the heart of the perichoretic relations of the Trinity, providing a model of how we may live Trinitarian love on earth in the renewal and transformation of creation.

Implications of Paradise '49 for Biblical Studies

The next section contains a four-part series of articles on the significance of Chiara's mystical experience for biblical studies. In this series, Gérard Rossé, a biblical scholar and member of the Abba School, presents similarities between Paradise '49 and the Letter to the Ephesians, with particular focus on the themes of God, Christ, the Word, ecclesiology, faith, and ethics. The first article, "Revisiting Chiara Lubich's Paradise '49 in Light of the Letter to the Ephesians," begins with the proposition that genuine Christian mysticism and the thought it produces is never separated from faith. Rather, it produces a faith lived with greater clarity and intensity. This forms the basis for comparing the Letter to the Ephesians with some of Lubich's notes on her contemplative experience in 1949. Her mystical experience, Rossé emphasizes, was born from an experience of communion, of church. In a personal way, Chiara lived the reality of church in its profound identity with the Body of Christ. This reality can be described as participation in the Trinitarian life of God by being inserted into the Son's relationship with the Father. This study is particularly significant given that the principal concern of the Letter to the Ephesians is the identity of the church and its vocation to unity.

Rossé's second article, "Revising Chiara Lubich's Paradise '49 in Light of the Letter to the Ephesians: Divine Adoption and Divine Design," explores the initial blessing of divine adoption as children of God in Christ as expressed in Ephesians and in Chiara's Trinitarian experience of adoption in the design of God. Rossé then discusses how the divine design is fulfilled according to a Trinitarian dynamic in both Ephesians and Chiara's experience. Finally, he looks more deeply into the source of this design, namely, the glory of God from which everything radiates and to which everything converges as it is expressed in Ephesians and in Chiara's Trinitarian-ecclesial-cosmic vision of the light and splendor of Divine Love. Rossé concludes that in this glory or splendor within the heart of the Trinity itself divine adoption is fulfilled.

In the third article of the series, "Revising Chiara Lubich's Paradise '49 in Light of the Letter to the Ephesians: The Holy Spirit, the Son of God, and the Cosmos," Rossé focuses on the Holy Spirit, the Risen Christ, the church, and the cosmos. The Holy Spirit is seen as creating the conditions for unity between persons in the church and throughout the cosmos, according to the pattern of the Trinity that shows the "mothering face of God." The Risen Christ is presented in his cosmic dimension, bringing creation to its eschatological recapitulation, a "marriage of the Uncreated and the created." The Risen Christ is presented in terms of his upward movement to the church's fulfilment (*pleroma*) in God, bringing humankind and all creation into its fullness of life.

The fourth and final article is "Revisiting Chiara Lubich's Paradise '49 in Light of the Letter to the Ephesians: Jesus Forsaken, the Church, and

Agape-Love." Rossé explores these three themes. First is the meaning of the death of Jesus Christ on the cross for the church, humanity, history, and the cosmos. He then turns to the mystical writings of Chiara Lubich about Jesus Forsaken's role in the life of the Christian, the church, and the destiny of humanity and creation. Second, Rossé reflects on the understanding, found in Ephesians, of church as the Body of Christ brought about by the cross, by which new human persons are transformed and fulfilled in Christ. He explores Chiara Lubich's collective experience of being a cell of the church, and of living both Mary and Jesus to further the mission of Christ in the church and the world. Finally, Rossé explores the role of love—*agape*—both in Ephesians and in Chiara Lubich's spirituality of unity.

Implications of Paradise '49 for Humanity and the Church

The fifth section explores the implications of Chiara Lubich's experience of the Trinity for humanity and the church. In the first article, "Towards an Understanding of the Human Person According to the Mystical Experience of Chiara Lubich in the Paradise of '49," Callan Slipper maintains that the category of the person is a pillar of Chiara Lubich's experience and thought. It is fundamental to the philosophical and theological anthropology at the basis of the culture that is in the process of developing from her inspiration. To understand this category, however, it is necessary to see the person in the context of the whole architecture of her thinking. Looking at Lubich's experience of Paradise '49, Slipper outlines this architecture in four sections. He begins with an overview of created reality in relation to uncreated reality, showing how all things are the creaturely expression of Trinitarian Love. Then he looks at the specific characteristic of humanity that recapitulates creation and lives in a personal manner. Next, he demonstrates how this specific characteristic is focused in Mary the Theotokos, the perfect example of a human person. This leads, finally, to presenting how the individual person is fulfilled when human persons together partake of the presence of Jesus among them.

The second article, also by Callan Slipper, is entitled "Towards a New Kind of Cognition." Using a phenomenological and interdisciplinary approach, he offers insight into the experience of cognition and provides a basis for understanding it within the context of human development. Based upon a schematic outline of childhood development, the article presents three modes of human cognition. These modes are then examined from an evolutionary perspective to show how human cognition, from the arrival of representational thought, has developed under the influence of culture more than of biology. This provides instruments for understanding the patterns of cognition within Lubich's text "Look upon All the Flowers," showing its historical continuity with other forms of cognition and indicating the significant new elements that it contains.

Slipper's article provides a basis for the third item in this section, Chiara Lubich's "Look upon All the Flowers." This article includes an introduction that deals with the setting, a presentation about the text itself, and its implications. The introduction is followed by "Look upon All the Flowers," dated November 6, 1949.

The fourth article is Jesús Morán's "Transferring Self to Other: Radicalizing Human Being." This article begins by recounting recent developments in philosophical anthropology that provide background for understanding the key elements concerning what it is to be human that underlie "Look upon All the Flowers." Morán begins by examining self-transcendence, noting how Chiara Lubich's context of mutuality, her reciprocal transfer of self to the other, is a shift from the starting point of previous spiritualities. He then looks at the metaphysical structure that supports this way of being and explores three core categories: transcendence, relationality, and corporeality. These underpin relationships according to the pattern of the Trinity that take people beyond individual relationships, and at the same time beyond their mutual relatedness.

The fifth article, by Hubertus Blaumeiser and Brendan Leahy, is "When the Tree has Blossomed Fully: Reflections on the Church." The authors discuss "Look upon All the Flowers" as a seminal text and suggest that the Second Vatican Council's vision of the church can be realized through mutual personal relationships that reflect the very life of the Trinity. The model of such relationships, and therefore of the Christian community and of the church itself, is Mary at the foot of the cross, who "lost" God with her for the God who is present in every human being. "Look upon All the Flowers" demonstrates how that Marian profile can be lived out individually, in local communities, and in the church so as to generate living cells of the Mystical Body, renewing both church and society.

Implications of Paradise '49 for Society and Culture

This section contains five articles. The first, by Maria Voce, is "The Charism of Unity in Dialogue with Contemporary Culture and the Paradigm of Fraternity." Voce begins by asking: Does Chiara Lubich's charism of unity have something to say to contemporary culture? She presents Lubich's experience of unity and her vision for contributing to a more united and peaceful world based on Paradise '49. Voce presents the difficult cultural situations in Europe and Latin America and the positive social, economic, and political changes that have recently taken place as well as the challenges that remain. She presents Lubich's 1998 visit to Latin America that led her to propose an international interreligious and intercultural "360 degree dialogue" based on fraternity. Voce explains what fraternity meant to Lubich in the history of her own experience, in the Focolare spirituality of unity, and how it can be a paradigm for cultural development that addresses the challenges of the global community today.

The second article, by Antonio Maria Baggio, is "Love of All Loves: Politics and Fraternity in the Charismatic Vision of Chiara Lubich." Baggio presents the original meaning that Chiara gave to fraternity based on her mystical life. He points out that there is a "logic" of fraternity that arises from her Trinitarian experience. While the concept of fraternity is found in the scriptural and religious background of Christian faith, Chiara's thought on fraternity is expressed in the context of the Focolare's social outreach, such as in the Movement for Unity in Politics and the Economy of Communion. Baggio proposes that Chiara's notion of fraternity, given its universal human dimension as well as its religious affiliations, is relevant to all societies and cultures.

The third article is Luigino Bruni's "The Economy of Communion: A Project for a Sustainable and Happy Socioeconomic Future." Bruni begins by presenting a picture of today's global economic changes and the issues that have arisen as a consequence: the widening inequality and income gap, as well as the greater correlation between inequality and quality of life than between income (GDP) and quality of life. Inequality, he argues, is a major obstacle to socioeconomic development. Therefore, companies need to expand their range of action to include social and community activities as opportunities for enhancing economic success and the well-being of employees and of the community. Bruni then turns to the Economy of Communion founded by the Focolare, giving its background and its approaches to healing poverty through relational community changes and concrete productive inclusion. As a consequence, workers are partners and thus happier and more effective citizens. Bruni concludes with reflections on the nature and purpose of communion formed within business and community life.

The fourth article, by Bernard Callebaut, is "Economy of Communion: A Sociological Inquiry on a Contemporary Charismatic Inspiration in Economy and Social Life." Callebaut asks: Is Chiara Lubich's initiative, the Economy of Communion (EoC), an example of a "sudden invention" in the field of the economic activity? EoC, proposed by Lubich, does have some charismatic aspects. Her initiative brings together two functions of society: the economic and the social, symbolically represented by the figures of the entrepreneur and the poor. Callebaut relies on the interpretive framework of Max Weber and his analysis of charismatic leadership, as well as other authors working directly on the relationship between economy and charism. Ultimately, this article discusses the relevance for the contemporary world of the input EoC gives not only at the level of the economic rationality, but to a "culture of communion."

Implications of Paradise '49 for Interreligious Dialogue

The first article in the final section is Donald W. Mitchell's "The Mystical Theology of Chiara Lubich: A Foundation for Interreligious Dialogue in Asia." Mitchell begins with the assumption that Chiara Lubich received a charism that is embodied in her spirituality of unity and that the Trinitarian source of this gift was revealed in the mystical experience of "Paradise '49." The first part of the article reflects on the charism of Chiara's spirituality of unity as lived out in interreligious dialogue. The second part reflects on what has been published about Chiara's mystical illuminations, which Mitchell believes can serve as new sources for dialogue with the East Asian traditions of Buddhism and Confucianism. In the third and final section, he presents his views on how such a dialogue could contribute to a more global Catholic philosophy.

The second article, also by Donald W. Mitchell, is entitled: "Dazzling Darkness: Buddhism and Chiara Lubich's Mystical Writings." Mitchell begins by presenting two experiences of what he terms "dazzling darkness," one in a Christian context and the other in a Buddhist context. He then proposes an explanation for the experience in the context of Buddhist traditions in India and China. In so doing, he connects darkness to suffering and light to Nirvana and Buddha-nature. He then turns to the mystical writings of Chiara Lubich to propose an explanation for the Christian experience and its relation to suffering and the luminosity of God in suffering through Jesus Forsaken. In discussing Lubich's writings, Mitchell also explores her experiences of the relational arising and mutual indwelling of all beings, and the indwelling of the light and love of God in the darkness of suffering. He then compares these insights to the experiences of Buddha-nature, dependent arising, mutual indwelling, and the identity of Nirvana and suffering in Buddhism.

In the third article, "Christian and Hindu Dialogue on the Charism of Unity," Cherylanne Menezes provides an historical introduction to Chiara Lubich and the Focolare Movement's work in interreligious dialogue, with special attention to Christian-Hindu dialogue. It introduces the various personalities and encounters, as well as the spirit that informs this unique experience of dialogue. It makes particular use of Lubich's diary entries that recount her own discovery of dialogue as "one of the most beautiful expressions of love." At one point, Menezes discusses how Chiara shared some of her experiences from Paradise '49 with Hindu scholars, and their positive response from a Hindu point of view. Finally, Menezes introduces the innovative and fruitful experience of Christian-Hindu symposiums organized between Indian scholars and those associated with the Focolare Movement in India.

The fourth article is Roberto Catalano's "Spiritual Friendship and Interreligious Dialogue: The Experience of Chiara Lubich and Nikkyo Niwano." Catalano introduces the spiritual friendship between Chiara Lubich and Rev. Nikkyō Niwano, founders and longtime presidents, respectively, of the Focolare Movement and of the Risshō Kōsei-kai. The two movements, though founded in completely different geographical, social, and religious contexts, developed strong ties and collaborations based on friendship and dialogue. Catalano also evaluates the role each of the two spiritual leaders played with respect to their religious experiences.

In the final article, "A Buddhist-Catholic Dialogue of Life in Japan: Finding Shared Values for Global Collaboration for the Common Good," Cinto Busquet article analyzes the global dialogues between members of the Risshō Kōsei-kai and the Focolare Movement. This unique relationship, Busquet points out, is founded on friendship and a deep spiritual unity based on their own scriptural and spiritual foundations. From their dialogues of life and collaboration these Christians and Buddhists have discovered common values based on worldviews that, in some cases, are quite different. Their shared values have provided the basis for their interreligious projects that seek solutions to the global issues we all face today.

Part One

The Mystical Experience of Chiara Lubich: Paradise '49

Chapter One

Contextualizing "Paradise '49"

Piero Coda, Donald W. Mitchell, Judith Povilus

Most who recognize the name Chiara Lubich (1920– 2008) know her as the founder of the Focolare Movement.[1] Her writings reflect her deep spiritual experience and her charism that is the source of the life of the Focolare. It is also clear from the beginning that this life has had a marked communitarian dimension shared by her first companions and then by those who chose to follow in their footsteps. At the core of this communal dimension of the Focolare spirituality is a strong experience of unity. During World War II, Lubich and her companions would often go into the bomb shelters in Trent, taking with them only a book containing the Gospels. As they read them together, "Certain phrases stood out for us from the very beginning, especially those that spoke of love of God, of love of neighbor and of unity."[2] Lubich says that when they read John 17, it was as if the words "lit up from within."[3] They sensed that God was calling them to work for the ideal for which Jesus prays in that chapter, namely, that "all may be one." Lubich writes: "Conscious of the difficulty, if not impossibility, of putting such a program into practice, we felt the urge to ask Jesus for the favor of teaching us the way to live unity. Kneeling around an altar, we offered our lives to Him, that—if He wishes to and trusts us—He may use us to bring it to pass."[4]

Chiara Lubich's writings from these early years reveal the development of a strong mystical Trinitarian element in her community's collective and lived experience of unity. While this is true concerning her writings from

---

1. For a biography of Chiara Lubich's life see Jim Gallagher, *A Woman's Work: Chiara Lubich; A Biography of the Focolare Movement and Its Founder* (London: HarperCollinsPublishers, 1996; Canada: New City Press, 1997; New York: New City Press, 2002). For a compendium of her work see Chiara Lubich, *Essential Writings: Spirituality, Dialogue, Culture* (New York: New City Press, 2007).
2. Chiara Lubich, May They All Be One: Origins and Life of the Focolare Movement (New York: New City Press, 1995), 16–17.
3. Piero Coda, "A Gift of the Spirit and a Work of God," in Lubich, *Essential Writings*, xiii.
4. Chiara Lubich, *Unity and Jesus Forsaken* (New York: New City Press, 1985), 25.

the founding of the Focolare, it was not until the summer of 1949 that the fullness of this mystical life of unity was experienced and understood during a period that came to be called Paradise '49. While taking a rest from their demanding activities after the war for two months during that summer, Lubich experienced "intense illuminations" that she shared with her closest companions. Although she communicated some of these experiences to members of the Focolare in the years following 1949, Lubich usually did not talk about them in public.[5]

While this mystical period of Chiara Lubich's life is called Paradise '49, the illuminations actually continued into 1951. In 1992, the noted German theologian Klaus Hemmerle urged Lubich to begin reexamining her mystical writings and opening them to study. She formed an interdisciplinary study group to meet with her in this task that eventually expanded and became known as the Abba School. Some years after its founding, scholars in all fields of study from around the world were invited to meet in Rome on a regular basis to discuss the work of the Abba School in a broader venue.

Nuova Umanità, the Italian journal of the Focolare, publishes select papers written by members of the Abba School. Some of these articles have been translated into English and published in *New Humanity Review* by the Focolare in the United States. In 2002, *An Introduction to the Abba School: Conversations from the Focolare's Interdisciplinary Study Center* was published.[6] After the passing of Klaus Hemmerle and Chiara Lubich, the Abba School continues to meet in Rome and its members continue to publish their works in *Nuova Umanità*. We have chosen to publish in this first issue of *Claritas* an English translation of a private talk about Paradise '49 given by Lubich in 1961 that was originally published in *Nuova Umanità* only after her death.[7] The first part of the text describes the first few days of Paradise '49 during which her mystical experiences gave her and her companions a more complete understanding of the Trinitarian life, of the charism of unity and of the Movement that would be born from it. The

---

5. Chiara Lubich gives the following reason for not talking about her experiences: "Because we were aware, as we are even now, that it is a grace of God, special gifts of the Holy Spirit, that are not usually spoken of until the person who received them has gone to heaven. . We always considered them as being reserved, confidential" (Chiara Lubich, Talk at Castel Gandolfo, February 23, 2001).
6. Hyde Park, NY: New City Press(hereafter referred to as *Abba School*).
7. Chiara Lubich, "Paradiso '49," *Nuova Umanità* 177 (2008): 285–96. The translation for *Claritas* is by Callan Slipper.

second part goes on to present a few "pictures" from experiences Lubich had during the rest of the two months. We will focus in this essay on the first part since it deals more directly with her experience of the life of the Trinity.

In order to contextualize this important text, we will first discuss an article by Piero Coda, a noted Italian theologian and member of the Abba School, that situates Chiara Lubich's mystical experiences of the Trinity in the history of Christian spirituality. Next, drawing on the scholarship of Judith Povilus, who is another member of the Abba School, we will present Lubich's early writings about unity dated from 1944 to 1949. Given this background, we will then present clarifying remarks on the text itself. It is important to note, however, that since the full text of notes on Paradise '49 has yet to be published, and the present work of the Abba School is precisely to clarify its substance and implications, we can only make limited contextualizing remarks in this essay.

Chiara Lubich and the Church's Developing Experience of the Trinity

In a recent article, Piero Coda traces the history of Christian mystical experiences of the Trinity from Augustine to Chiara Lubich.[8] He notes that in *De Trinitate*, Augustine looks for a "place" where the Trinity can be experienced. Augustine first discusses the place of love drawing on 1 John 4:16: "God is Love, and those who abide in love abide in God, and God abides in them." In love, according to Augustine, there is the lover, the beloved and the love in which they abide. This love is greater than one's own creation and therefore is itself a relational place where the triune God can be experienced. In a moment of confession, however, Augustine says that he could not find the Trinity in love: "But when we came to love . . . the glimmerings of a Trinity began to appear, namely, that lover and what is loved, and love. However, that inexpressible light beat back our gaze and somehow convinced us that the weakness of our mind could not yet be attuned to it."[9] Given this "inexpressible light" that blocked his gaze into the place of love, Augustine turned to a place with which he was more familiar, namely, the inner life of the soul.

---

8. Piero Coda, "L'esperienza e l'intelligenza della fede in dio trinità da sant'Agostino a Chiara Lubich," *Nuova Umanità* 167 (2006): 527–52.
9. Augustine, *De Trinitate*, XV, 6, 10.

According to Coda, for centuries this interior step from a relational place to an internal place would determine where contemplatives searched for the Trinity. Coda mentions that Dionysius the Areopagite described the triune God as an ineffable fountain of being found only by an inner journey through darkness, silence, and "unknowing" into what is inconceivable and unspeakable mystery. Coda also describes how two new places for experiencing the Trinity were later found by the mendicant orders. St. Thomas Aquinas describes creation as based on the relational dimension of the Trinity. For Thomas, it is in the Word that God the Father knows creatures and through the Word that creation takes place. The Holy Spirit is the breath of God's love both within the Trinity and within creation through the Word. Therefore, creation is seen as a place where the Trinity can be found. According to Coda, St. Francis of Assisi discovered another place where one can find access to the Trinity, namely, in Jesus crucified. As Bonaventure commented: "To God there is no access except through the Crucified."[10]

Coda then turns to the Carmelite mysticism of John of the Cross. For John, one reaches the inner place where the Trinity is found through the dark nights of ascetic and graced *kenosis*.[11] In describing this union with God, John says that "it seems to [the person] that the entire universe is a sea of love in which it is engulfed, for, conscious of the living point or center of love within itself, it is unable to catch sight of the boundaries of this love."[12] In other words, one discovers in his or her inner center the Trinitarian love of God penetrating all creation. Coda concludes that Carmelite mysticism brings to a kind of fulfillment the interior spiritual journey to the center of the soul by adding the two other places where the Trinity can be found, namely, creation and Jesus crucified. Coda then raises the question about the first place Augustine looked for the Trinity. Coda asks: "[W]hat happens with the other intuition of Augustine: that of the mutual love 'as the place' from which we can fly up to the contemplation of the Trinity?"[13]

Coda answers this question by proposing that Chiara Lubich's mystical experiences of the Trinity came from two unions. First was an inner personal union with Jesus forsaken, seen as the apex of the kenotic love of Jesus cru-

---

10. Bonaventure, Itinerarum mentis in Deum, 3.
11. See Donald W. Mitchell, "Christian Kenosis," *Pro Dialogo* 100 (1999): 148–51.
12. John of the Cross, *The Living Flame of Love*, 2, 10.
13. Coda, 33.

cified. Second was a union with the Risen Christ within the collective unity of mutual love between her and her companions. It was these two unions that enabled Lubich's companions to share in her experiences. That unity of kenotic mutual love lived with Jesus forsaken within each of them and the Risen Christ among them became the collective place of love wherein Lubich and her companions communally experienced the Trinity. This communal experience of the Trinity also embraced a new awareness of the Trinity in creation. It is important to note that Lubich and her companions were prepared for this collective discovery of the Trinity during the five previous years of living their spirituality of unity.

Chiara Lubich's Early Experience of Unity: Writings from 1943 to 1948

By 1943, a group of young women had joined with Chiara Lubich in the city of Trent as war raged around them. When they went into the bomb shelters, they took only a book of the Gospels with them. Lubich writes,

> One day I found myself with my new companions in a dark, candle-lit cellar, a book of the gospels in my hand. I opened it. There was Jesus' prayer before he died: "Father may they all be one" (John 17:11, 21). It was not an easy text to start with but one by one those words seemed to come to life, giving us the conviction that we were born for that page of the gospel. On the feast of Christ the King, we gathered around an altar. We said to Jesus: "You know the way to achieve unity. Here we are. If you so desire, use us."[14]

Following this prayer, Lubich experienced God showing her and her companions the way to achieve unity.

In the middle of destruction and death caused by the war, Lubich and her companions felt that everything is passing, so they chose God as the one thing that does not pass away to be the Ideal of their lives. God responded by manifesting himself as Love, as "God-Love." They were deeply moved by this love of God for each one of them and desired to respond in some way. The following verse of the gospel gave them the way to respond: "Not everyone who says to me 'Lord, Lord' will enter the kingdom of heaven, but

---

14. Lubich, *Essential Writings*, 4.

only the one who does the will of my Father in Heaven" (Matthew 7:21). Another verse from Matthew gave them a particular will of the Father to do: "Love your neighbor as yourself" (Matthew 19:19). This path of love that opened up to Lubich and her companions would lead to the unity for which they felt they were born.

Lubich and her companions put into practice the passages of the gospels that they read together. She gives examples of how they loved their neighbors during the war:

> Where is my neighbor? There beside us. In that old lady barely able to drag herself each time to the shelter. We must love her as ourselves; we must help her each time and then support her. The neighbor was there in those five frightened children alongside their mother. We must take them in our arms and help them home. The neighbor was there in that sick person confined to home, unable to go to the shelter, but in need of care. We must go there and get him medicine.... People around us were in terrible conditions—hungry, thirsty, injured, without clothing, without shelter. So we cooked big pots of soup and distributed it to them.[15]

At one point, another question came to Lubich and her companions. As they were facing death each day, they asked: "Is there a will of God especially pleasing to him?"[16] The gospels gave them the answer in a commandment that is Jesus': "This is my commandment, that you love one another as I have loved you. No one has greater love than this, to lay down one's life for one's friends" (John 15:12–13). So, they declared that they were ready to give their lives for each other. Lubich says that when they began to love with this intensity, "We saw our lives take a qualitative leap forward. Someone came into our group, silently, an invisible Friend, giving us security, a more experiential joy, a new peace, a fullness of life, an inextinguishable light."[17]

---

15. Lubich, *Essential Writings*, 5.
16. Lubich, *Essential Writings*, 6.
17. Lubich, *Essential Writings*, 6.

Unity and Jesus in the Midst

Judith M. Povilus has written a groundbreaking work on Lubich's writings concerning unity.[18] Povilus says that in putting the New Commandment into practice, they discovered that when their love was mutual they experienced a oneness or unity that was new to them and totally out of proportion to their own efforts. She goes on to say that this unity involved a divine presence of light, peace, joy and a fullness of life. In January 1945, Lubich wrote a letter about their experience of the presence of God among them when they lived mutual love: "Then God will live among you. You will sense it, you will enjoy his presence; he will give you his light; he will enflame you with his love."[19] In a note from 1946, she writes:

> Persons who want to be a channel for unity must maintain themselves constantly in an abyss of humility so that they lose their own soul for the benefit and service of God in their neighbor. . . . [I]f our neighbor is loved this way, mutual love (unity) is achieved and the Testament of Jesus [that all be one] will be fulfilled. . . . That is the goal for which we were born, the purpose for which He raised us up. [20]

In notes from 1946, Lubich writes the following about the difficulty of loving to the degree that contributes to unity:

> Feeling in ourselves what our neighbors feel. Dealing with their feelings as if they were our own, making them our own through our concern. *Be them*, doing this for the love of Jesus in our neighbor. . . . To be able to love our neighbors [in this way], we've got to undo the strings around this hard and stony heart of ours and get a heart of flesh.[21]

She would later comment about this difficulty: "It's no easy thing. We have to be empty in ourselves: chase our own ideas out of our heads, our own affections out of our hearts, everything out of our wills, to identify ourselves with the other person."[22] Her statement reveals a kind of asceti-

---

18. Judith M. Povilus, *United in his Name: Jesus in Our Midst in the Experience and Thought of Chiara Lubich* (New York: New City Press, 1992).
19. Povilus, *United in his Name*, 14.
20. Povilus, *United in his Name*, 27, 28, 29.
21. Povilus, *United in his Name*, 25, 60.
22. Povilus, *United in his Name*, 32.

cism contributing to a "copenetration," as she puts it, between two or more persons who love one another in this way. However in another letter from 1946, she points out that while an individual's efforts contribute to the goal of unity, it is really Christ who causes it: "Only Christ can make two into one; it is because his love is the emptying of self . . . that allows us to reach the depths of others' hearts."[23]

Povilus explains the importance of Lubich's discovery of the gospel passage, "For where two or three are gathered in my name, I am in the midst of them" (Matthew 18:21). This, for Lubich, was a fuller explanation of what they were experiencing. When she and her companions were together loving one another as Jesus loved them, that is, being willing to give their lives for each other, Jesus was in their midst giving them the grace to reach that oneness or unity for which he had prayed. Povilus notes that only in 1947 does Lubich begin to refer to what she calls "Jesus in the midst" when discussing unity. In a letter from 1948, she rejoices over this discovery:

> Unity . . . who could dare speak about it? It is as ineffable as God. You can sense it, see it, enjoy it; but it is ineffable! All enjoy its presence, all suffer its absence. It is peace, joy, love, ardor, an atmosphere of heroism and unlimited generosity. It is Jesus among us![24]

Here, Lubich affirms that unity is ultimately a gift of Jesus in their midst understood to be the Risen Christ. She sees this gift as part of the charism given to her and her companions as well as to those who choose to follow in their footsteps. Discussing this gift of the presence of the Risen Christ, she says that it is not as if Jesus occupies a space among persons uniting them with his love. Rather, she writes in 1948: "When two persons meet in the name of Christ, Christ is born among them; that is, *in them*. In maintaining this unity, they can sincerely say: 'It is no longer I who live but Christ who lives in me.'"[25] Jesus in the midst means to Lubich the Risen Christ uniting people by his inner presence and bringing them together united in himself, in his new life of light and love.

---

23. Povilus, *United in his Name*, 15.
24. Povilus, *United in his Name*, 18.
25. Povilus, *United in his Name*, 51.

Unity and Jesus Forsaken

Chiara Lubich writes: "What happiness, new discoveries, graces and victories! That is the gospel. But from the beginning we understood that it had another side too, that the tree has its roots . . . . Loving Christ crucified in every suffering is another focus of this spirituality."[26] Coda comments about this focus:

> So Chiara was guided to discover and to choose, among the sufferings of Jesus, the one most hidden and interior, yet the deepest and most tragic. . . . It is the cry of the ninth hour: "My God, my God, why have you forsaken me?" (Mt 27:46). . . . Chiara Lubich's spirituality springs from the free, exclusive choice of Jesus forsaken that allows Jesus himself to pour into her heart those streams of living water and light that, as the Word of the Father made man, he brings down from heaven to earth to communicate in their fullness to all.[27]

We need to go back to the beginnings of the Focolare during World War II in order to understand this fundamental role of Jesus forsaken. The date given for the founding of the Focolare was the day of Chiara Lubich's personal consecration to God, namely, December 7, 1943. Just six weeks later, on January, 24, 1944, a Capuchin priest had brought communion to one of Lubich's first companions who had fallen ill. He asked Lubich when she thought that Jesus suffered the most. She answered that perhaps it was in the Garden of Gethsemane. But the priest responded that he thought it was when Jesus cried: "My God, my God, why have you forsaken me."[28] Hearing these words, Lubich and her companions were moved to choose Jesus crucified at the moment of his forsakenness as their spouse. By "spouse," they meant that Jesus forsaken would be not only their model for loving others through self-giving, but would be, in Lubich's words, "*the* living personality in our lives."[29]

From her letters written during 1944 and 1945, Lubich seems completely taken by her new relation to Jesus forsaken. Just one week after discovering him, she writes: "You will be the recipient of joys . . . if you will make

---

26. Lubich, *Essential Writings*, 7–8.
27. Lubich, *Essential Writings*. xviii.
28. Lubich, *Unity and Jesus Forsaken*, 45.
29. Lubich, *Unity and Jesus Forsaken*, 46.

an effort to see Jesus in the way I have presented Him to you . . . at the culmination of His pain, that is the culmination of His love."[30] Five months later, she writes that nothing "gives my soul such strength and above all so much love as Jesus Crucified. . . ."[31] Then she suggests to "Forget everything . . . even the most sublime things: let yourself be ruled by a single Ideal, by God, who must penetrate every fiber of your being: Jesus Crucified."[32] She writes in a profound piece from 1944:

> He who has told me—from the height of His cross: "I have given up everything that is mine . . . everything. I am not beautiful any more; I am no longer strong; I have no peace here; up here, justice is dead; I am ignorant of science; what was truth for me has vanished. All I have left is my Love, this love that wanted *for your sake* to empty all the riches I possessed *as God*. . ."[33]

A question arises here about the relationship between Jesus in the midst as the Risen Christ on the one hand, and Jesus forsaken as the spouse of souls on the other. Lubich describes her experience in the following way: "We began to understand how dynamically divine the Christian life is, in that . . . it gives us a taste of life in its fullness, that is to say: the experience of resurrection, light and hope, even in the midst of tribulation."[34] In other words, by embracing Jesus forsaken, their sufferings were transformed such that Jesus was not only sharing the burden of suffering but sharing the love of his suffering and its fruits, namely, the life of the resurrection. Lubich discovered that Jesus forsaken was not only the "key" to union with God but also to unity with others: "We must *be nothing* (Jesus forsaken) in the presence of each of our neighbors in order to embrace Jesus in him or her."[35] With Jesus in oneself embracing Jesus in others, one finds the Risen Christ among them.

In addressing this point, Lubich wrote in 1948: "The book of light that God is writing in my soul has two aspects: a luminous page of mysterious love: Unity. A luminous page of mysterious suffering: Jesus forsaken. They are two faces of the same coin."[36] Elsewhere Lubich explains: "It is Jesus in

---

30. Lubich, *Unity and Jesus Forsaken*, 51.
31. Lubich, *Unity and Jesus Forsaken*, 48.
32. Lubich, *Unity and Jesus Forsaken*, 47.
33. Lubich, *Unity and Jesus Forsaken*, 53.
34. Lubich, *May They all be One*, 62–63.
35. Povilus, *United in his Name*, 73.
36. Lubich, *Essential Writings*, 25.

his deepest suffering! Infinite disunity . . . to give us perfect unity that we will reach only relatively here on earth, and then perfectly in heaven. . . ."³⁷ She clarifies later: "As Jesus in his abandonment has redeemed humanity, in the sense that he reunited us his children to the Father (he was the means that brought about unity), so too Jesus forsaken, when loved, brings about Jesus in our midst."³⁸ Thus, Chiara and her companions embraced Jesus forsaken within and in others and found the Risen Christ among them bringing about the unity for which they had given their lives.

We find in Lubich's writings just before 1949 descriptions of her experiences of Jesus forsaken, unity, love, light, the Risen Christ, and the Father. For example, a letter from 1948 states:

> This presence [Jesus forsaken] . . . very soon becomes *felt*, so that throwing ourselves into a sea of suffering we discover ourselves in a sea of love, of complete joy. . . . and the soul feels itself refilled with the Holy Spirit, who is joy, peace, serenity.³⁹

She describes this dynamic of being filled by the Holy Spirit as "a sort of Easter," a "Passover" that to her resembled "the triumphal entry of God into the soul."⁴⁰ Another letter refers to this dynamic as a movement "beyond his wound":

> [H]aving embraced Jesus forsaken totally, so that we found ourselves beyond pain, in love we felt like we were contemplating the immense love that God has poured out over the world . . . we were merged with love and shared in its light: the light of Love.⁴¹

And after 1949, Lubich would write even more clearly:

> Unity among us is achieved if each of us is well united to God, following our charism. It is written in fact, "As you, Father, are in me, and I in you that they also may be in us." (John 17: 21). . . . by loving Jesus forsaken and going faster and faster "beyond the wound". . . . It is the Risen Lord who lives within us and in our midst and He gives us the Holy Spirit.⁴²

---

37. Lubich, *Essential Writings*, 24.
38. Povilus, *United in his Name*, 74.
39. Lubich, *Unity and Jesus Forsaken*, 67.
40. Lubich, *Unity and Jesus Forsaken*, 69.
41. Lubich, *Unity and Jesus Forsaken*, 70–71.
42. Chiara Lubich, Talk to the Secretariats for the Men Religious, January 30, 1990.

These passages prepare the way for our understanding the experiences of Paradise '49. It seems as if she too was being prepared for a fuller understanding of the immense love, light, and oneness of God.

Chiara Lubich's Trinitarian Experience: Paradise '49

Chiara Lubich's 1961 talk begins with a description of what led to what she titles "Entrance into the Father." For five years, she and her companions had been living the fundamental principles of their spirituality with emphasis on the gospels lived in each present moment, on mutual love and on receiving Jesus in the Eucharist. In doing so, they were living what she calls three "communions": with the Word of God, with their neighbor and with Jesus in the Eucharist. They realized that the communion with the Word that they experienced in actually living each of the words of the Gospels always had the same effect, namely, growth in love. Lubich would later say that each word entered them and became a "flame" of love that burned away their old life, bringing the new life of the kingdom of God.[43] She compares this five-year process to a kind of novitiate at the end of which it seemed that the love found in Jesus forsaken was the pinnacle of the love they had found piece-by-piece in the words of Jesus. It was as if all the words of God were, so to speak, in substance summarized in this one cry of the abandonment. As they went on vacation in the Dolomites during the summer of 1949, they were living the gospel passage: "My God, my God, why have you forsaken me?"

Their first experience before entering Paradise was of a supernatural sun that saturated nature, linking all created things in a "bond of love" so that nature seemed to be all love. Lubich writes that in this "red-hot atmosphere," it seemed as if within her the words of God were fused in Jesus forsaken. This "red-hot atmosphere" of love brings to mind the reason for Augustine's failure to contemplate the Trinity in love, namely, that its "inexpressible light beat back our gaze." How could Lubich and her companions penetrate this overwhelming supernatural sun?

Igino Giordani, a noted politician and Catholic scholar, proved to be a key figure in the Entrance into the Father. Lubich describes how she and Giordani—whom she called Foco, meaning "Fire"—prayed to Jesus in the Eucharist asking him in each of them to make a pact of unity between them.

---

43. Chiara Lubich, Talk on Paradise '49 given in 1969.

When Lubich went back into the church to pray before the Blessed Sacrament, she was unable to say the word "Jesus" because she experienced Jesus as being one with her. In the next moment, she had the impression of finding herself "on the peak of a very high mountain" without love. In that instant, the word "Father" came to her lips and she found communion again. Lubich then entered into the bosom of the Father which she experienced "as the inside of a sun." Lubich tells of how she asked her companions to join Foco and herself in the pact. When they did so, she saw a "little company in the sun" to which she gave the name "Soul." In this collective Soul, Lubich and her companions had together entered the oneness for which they had prayed "May they all be one."

In the bosom of the Father, they went on to discover a series of what Lubich calls "Realities" that they both "felt" and "lived" together. It seemed that a special grace enabled them to live by participation the relationality of the Trinity, as much as it was possible for them as human beings, and to experience the realities therein. John of the Cross said that in union with God a person becomes God by participation. But unlike John's, this was a communal participation in the life of the Trinity. For Lubich and her companions the Trinitarian indwelling in love became a lived experience of unity. Thus, they came more fully to understand the unity they had been experiencing for years.

Lubich goes on to describe visions[44] and impressions of the Son as the Word that is all Love of the Father, splendor of the Father. She also describes how they experienced creation in light of the Word in the bosom of the Father. Their previous experience just prior to entering Paradise was of a bond of love uniting creation. Now they experienced the luminous Word, the one divine Wisdom, bringing about order and harmony in ever new scenarios of creation.

This section of Lubich's talk concludes with two reflections about their experience of the Son. First, after seeing creation from the standpoint of the uncreated, they found that in the Trinity all that had been previously manifested remained just as it was. The transcendent Trinity subsisted as it always is even as the dynamic of the economic Trinity was at work in the drama of

---

44. By "vision" Chiara Lubich means an "intellectual vision," in the technical sense of the term, that imprinted her soul. She said that the images of what was revealed to her intellect were given to her so she could convey her experience to others. It is not that what she saw is exactly the way things are—but expressed in a human way what she experienced and then possessed in her soul.

creation. Second, reflecting on the rays of the sun, they realized that before entering into the Trinity their lives had been an "ascent" in fulfilling God's will each in his or her own ray. But with the graced fusion in Jesus, they had become the One Soul that enabled their collective entrance into the house of the Father.

On the following day, Lubich unexpectedly experienced Mary. About this surprise Lubich says that it seemed like the Word wanted to present the Soul to Mary before marrying it. In fact, Lubich says that after this they experienced a new relationship with the Word in which they felt the Soul was "Church." Following this experience, as Lubich and her companions sat in meditation before a statue of Mary in the chapel where they would go each day, Lubich experienced the Holy Spirit. She characterized the Holy Spirit as the "atmosphere" in the bosom of the Father. Indeed, from this time on, Lubich would often speak of the Holy Spirit as the atmosphere of unity, of Jesus in the midst. Jesus in the midst brought on earth the very atmosphere of heaven, a taste of Paradise. In a later writing, Lubich says:

> [This] atmosphere and its effects are the fruits of the Spirit of Jesus, which is the Holy Spirit himself. And the Spirit of the Risen Jesus in our midst makes us Jesus, that makes us appear to others as his continuation, the Body of Christ, the Church.[45]

In the second part of her talk, Lubich presents what she calls "pictures" of a few of their 150 or so experiences that took place during the rest of the two months she and her companions were together in the mountains. Lubich says that it was as if the Soul-Church was led on the "divine honeymoon" to see the realities of heaven. After the consecration of the Soul to Mary, she understood that their destiny was to be "other Marys," as it were. Many years later the Catholic Church would officially name the Focolare the Work of Mary. The infinite Sun also opened up into a "heavenly landscape" within the bosom of God. They had visions of the "new Heavens and new earths" and of hell, understood in terms of the cosmic reality of Jesus forsaken.[46] Finally, she refers to what it was like to leave the mountains after two months in "that Heaven," and return to the ordinary world. One has the sense that she is here giving glimpses of different experiences that add theologically en-

---

45. Lubich, *Essential Writings*, 147.
46. For a discussion of Chiara Lubich's experience of hell, see: Hubertus Blaumeiser, "Forever Toward Disunity: Reflections on Hell in the Thought of Chiara Lubich," *Abba School*, 72–88.

riching dimensions to the fundamental Trinitarian experiences presented in the first part of the talk. We will not attempt to comment on these pictures, but look forward to future contributions in our journal and elsewhere for fuller explanations of these realities and others as well as their implications for theology and other fields of study.

Concluding Comments

In providing a short contextualization of Chiara Lubich's 1961 talk on Paradise '49, this essay can only scratch the surface of this fundamental event in her life and defining point for her thought. This is especially the case since the full text of Lubich's notes on Paradise '49 have yet to be published. At this time only pieces of the picture are available for examination.

Finally, we should note that Lubich's experience of Paradise '49 strengthened her conviction that in today's world it is important to give primary emphasis to a collective spirituality where God is in oneself and also among persons generating a communal reflection of the Trinity in order to bring humanity to a civilization of love. In this way, all aspects of human life and culture can be transformed.[47] The Second Vatican Council stressed how the Holy Spirit sends charisms to guide and help the church and humanity on the journey of history. Given the emergence of multiculturalism, globalization, ecumenism, and interreligious dialogue in our times, one could expect a charism of unity that gives guidance and hope as humankind seeks to build a more united and peaceful world. This path forward must avoid any over-simplified uniformity on the one hand, or any relativizing multiplicity on the other. Chiara Lubich presents a life of unity that celebrates diversity, a communal contemplation that generates collective action, a oneness with the divine that embraces all persons as brothers and sisters and discovers a "golden thread" linking humankind with nature. This life of unity expresses itself through dialogue in many aspects of contemporary cultures and human endeavors. *Claritas* is committed to exploring the foundations, initiatives, and implications of this life at the beginning of the third millennium.

---

47. Lubich, *Essential Writings*, 173–76.

Chapter Two

Paradise '49 (1961)

Chiara Lubich

Entrance into the Father

We had been trying with great intensity to live the main points of our spirituality: the present moment, mutual love, the Word of God.

We had been trying to become identified with the Word of God with which we made our communion constantly in the present moment.

There were three compulsory communions for us: with Jesus in the Eucharist, with our brother or sister, with the Word of God.

For about five years we had been meditating in our life upon the Word of Scripture and, in the Spring of 1949, I realized that the effects in our life of its various words were more or less the same, if not exactly the same, as if the substance of each word were "love."

For years we had thought that, just as the whole of Jesus is in the sacred Host and likewise in each piece of it, so also the whole of Jesus is in the Gospel and likewise in each Word of it, in each complete idea.

But now we were experiencing this.

As a consequence the desire to continue this practice was gradually fading in me, not because it was not useful or out of negligence, but because it had, as it were, achieved its goal.[1]

I do not remember the way things happened exactly, but deep within me the conviction was taking root, with the practice that went with it, that *Jesus forsaken* effectively summed up the whole of the Gospel. And that, in loving Him, all the virtues would blossom.

---

1. Saying this, Chiara does not mean to devalue putting the Word into practice, but simply to underline the centrality of Jesus forsaken who, in that moment, became "Everything" for her. In a note written at a later date, taking into account the whole experience of that summer of 1949, she wrote: "It is wonderful that even the highest mystical experience we live never stops us from contemplating the Word, but urges us to live it with always greater intensity."

He seemed to us to be the summary of the ascetic practice God was proposing to us and that, by living Him, we would be able to live Christ in us.

In Jesus forsaken there were all sufferings, all loves, all virtues, all sins (since He had made Himself "sin") and in Him we all found ourselves in every instant of our lives.

He was the summary of physical sufferings, because he was dying, and of moral and spiritual sufferings.

He was the summary of all loves: He was "father" for having regenerated us; He was "mother" in the labor pains of our divine birth; He was brother, friend.

He was the summary of the virtues: *the pure one*, to the point of being detached from every divine consolation, He who was God; *the poor one*, poor of everything. even of the sense of His divinity; He was *the obedient one*, because He was losing everything in the Father, who was Authority for Him.

In fact, in that cry He appeared to us as suffering and love together.

He had made Himself "sin" for us sinners, rebellion, division, excommunication, and so forth, out of love. I don't know how to link these two terms: love and suffering that in Jesus forsaken appeared to us to be a single thing, so that one would not exist without the other.

By living Jesus forsaken we had come to understand that He had *made Himself nothing* and that in this *nothingness* was our life. To be like Him out of love for Him, that nothingness that we really are.

We nothing, He all.

At that time there took place an extremely profound meeting of soul with Foco,[2] when he came to Fiera;[3] when I spoke with him I found in him a soul like none I had ever met. Unlike the *pope*,[4] he had a special grace to understand this Ideal that God had given to me, giving it the importance it deserved.

---

2. Igino Giordani was a distinguished writer, student of Christianity, and politician of great moral stature.
3. Fiera di Primiero is a small center in the area surrounding Trent where Chiara went for a short period of rest.
4. This is a word in the Trent dialect, here in its feminine form, meaning "children," which Chiara used to refer to the focolarine. The term recalls the "little ones," the "children" of the gospel.

In his own person, he clearly brought a particular presence of Jesus in our midst, that made my soul rejoice in celebration and made me to see things in a way I had not seen them before.

Every meeting, every conversation I had with him, I then repeated to the *pope* in detail and with all the warmth I felt so as to make them participate in everything and because it seemed to me that whatever is not useful to humanity, or at least to others, has no value. I also communicated it so as to conserve its divine transparency and so that no "human"[5] elements would be added and ruin everything.

I remember that during those days, nature seemed to me to be enveloped totally by the sun; it already was physically, but it seemed to me that an even stronger sun enveloped it, saturated it, so that the whole of nature appeared to me as being "in love." I saw things, rivers, plants, meadows, grass as linked to one another by a bond of love in which each one had a meaning of love with regard to the others.

It was something similar, but universalized, to what I had experienced while walking down from the Franciscan Institute[6] when I was twenty years old, singing the Hail Marys of the rosary. I had seemed to see the blossom of a horse chestnut tree alive with a higher life that sustained it from beneath so that it seemed to be coming out towards me.

In this red-hot atmosphere in which the Words of God within me were being fused into Jesus forsaken, the greatest "expression"—for us—of Jesus, of the Savior—and it appeared to me that nature was given substance by love—there came about the entrance into the Father.

Foco, taken by the desire to serve God, proposed making a vow of obedience to me.

I did not see any need for this, nor was this desire in harmony with my Ideal that was "to live according to the Mystical Body" (for me the greatest expression of Christian life). But so as not to waste this act of love of his that he wanted to make for the Lord, I proposed to change it.

The following morning, during Holy Communion, both of us would pray to Jesus-Eucharist that, on *our nothingness*, He should make a pact of unity.

---

5. Human is used here in the sense of something that flattens the mystical experience into something banal, neither open to nor informed by the divine.
6. The Opera Serafica where Chiara taught as a young woman.

We did this with full faith and with love.

While Foco then went to visit the fathers of the monastery next to the church, I went before the Blessed Sacrament to pray to Jesus. But I found it impossible. I could not utter the word *Jesus*, because it would have been calling upon Someone I realized had become identified with me, One who in that moment I was.

I had the impression of finding myself on the peak of a very high mountain, seemingly the highest one possible, that came to a point, the point of a pin: *one* therefore and high, but *not love* (and from this came my instant torment), so much that it seemed to me that even *being God, but not threefold*, would be a hell.

And in that instant, on my lips blossomed the word "Father" and I found communion again in the midst of amazement and joy.

I told Foco about this and, I do not know in which moment of that day, I found myself again, as in a vision seen with the eyes of the soul, having come *into the Bosom of the Father*, who showed me, as it were, the inside of a sun that was all gold or flames of gold, infinite, but not frightening.

I remember well that this vision—let's call it—only became clear to me when I asked the *pope*, on the nothingness of themselves, to make the same pact with Jesus-Eucharist, so as to be united with us.

And I saw this little company of persons in the sun.

From that moment, I called "Soul" that One which united all of us. And for two months, while there was a succession of intellectual and imaginary visions (as it seems to me they were, though I could be grossly mistaken),[7] we always spoke of the Soul.

Within it we had the impression of finding ourselves in Heaven. Above all there was space to breathe that was infinite, ample, utterly new, and our souls found themselves at ease.

In the Communions we received on the following days, the "Soul" was aware of being in communion with God and therefore of taking steps forward in the divine. And during the day these "Realities," as we called them

---

7. Using the theological language of the time, Chiara indicates the ways in which God discloses himself in mystical experience, either by "visions" created by God in the imagination or by "communications" in the intellect.

and felt them to be, were lived by all of us united in a rather unique way, perhaps as a result of these special graces.

In the evening, at our meditation that lasted about half an hour, we were careful to place the whole of our souls in the most absolute passivity, so that the Lord, if he wished, could communicate Himself. And my companions silenced everything in them, even what could have been inspirations, so that unity with me would be perfect.

And during the meditation new manifestations followed one after another. I was always intent upon communicating them at once to the other *pope*, because I felt them to be our common heritage and because we could then all place ourselves in those Realities.

The Son

Perhaps on the third day, as we remained in the Bosom of the Father, we had the manifestation of the Son. I remember that it had an extraordinary light, but maybe I lack now all the elements to be able to describe it.

I only know that from the walls inside the Sun, the Father pronounced the word: *Love*, and this Word, concentrated in the heart of the Father, was his Son.

Outside in the evening, a majestic sunset displayed by nature, rendered more beautiful by the enormous Sun shining in us, seemed to confirm this "vision." And so far as I now recall, if I recall it correctly, the long rays of the sun, that like arrows of light caressed the blue sky after the sun's disk had gone down, gave us an idea of the Word, *as the light of the Father*, the splendor of the Father.

Everything in those days worked together to build "Paradise" inside and outside us, almost as if the elements, people and events were themselves actors in the divine drama that for a long time transfixed our soul—as if the one, divine Wisdom ordered all things with ever new scenes and scenery.

At the point that the Son was made manifest, we had an experience full of meaning for us and in keeping with the Truth.

We *entered* into the Most Holy Trinity, and what had already been manifested remained, subsisted.

If now it was the hour of the Son, in our soul the Father remained in His place as God, present.

And life before this "entrance" appeared to us rather like an "ascent" fulfilling the divine will, each one on our own ray, until the hour came for our "fusion" in Jesus and for being admitted together into the house of the Father.

Mary

We were convinced that if there were to be another manifestation, it could only be of the Holy Spirit. Before going into church all of us wanted in some way to guess what the Lord would do. And we said this as a fruit of our own reasoning, of a human logic. But we said it convinced that it would not be like this because [what took place was] not the work of human beings but of God, whose logic transcends us. Communion with Him is not a human calculation or composition.

And thus it was always.

On that day I understood Mary, perhaps through an intellectual vision, *as I had never seen her before*. And now twelve years have passed since that day, but I still have the clear impression of the unexpected "greatness" that this discovery of the Mother of God in the Bosom of the Father made on me.

As the blue of the sky contains sun and moon and stars, so Mary appeared to me, made by God so great as to contain God Himself in the Word.

I had never had such a notion of Mary, but there her divine[8] greatness was impressed upon my soul in such a way that I do not know how to say it again.

I can say only that no human reasoning would be able to render the idea.

That vision produced conviction.

And we thought that perhaps the Holy Spirit would have given His place to Mary in the sequence of divine pictures, because she is His Spouse. And it appeared to us that the Word wanted to present the "Soul" to Mary before "marrying it." And this it seems to me is what happened, when the "Soul" felt it was no longer "Soul" but "Church": that small company of souls immersed in the Bosom of the Father felt it was *Church*.

---

8. Divine by participation in the divinity of God.

The Holy Spirit

It must have been the fourth day when, as usual, we were all recollected in meditation in front of the beautiful little statue of Mary,[9] when it seemed to me that a light wind, like a gentle breeze, came out from the tabernacle and brushed my face.

I had great doubts about this physical fact, but many years later I checked that no window opens up next to the tabernacle. That "air" was, as it were, Jesus' breath, as it were, the atmosphere of His Heart.

Then I saw—in an imaginary vision—coming from the tabernacle a white dove with its wings spread open, and it moved to the height of Mary's face [on the statue] and circled several times above us and then stopped in an attitude as if about to illuminate, but it did not illuminate.

> I understood that the Holy Spirit is the atmosphere of Heaven, in the Bosom of the Father.
>
> Going outside, I did not have the courage to tell my companions what had happened, but looking at a fiery red sky, I saw on the electric-light wires three little birds. And one came out from behind the church and flew above us. Still caught up with what had happened inside the church, I mustered the courage to speak, as it seemed to me that those three were a tiny symbol that each Person of the Trinity is God and that the Holy Spirit is God.

* * *

> This is how the first chapter of this story came to a close, the part I most remember.

The rest I remember with a certain disorder without the [thread of the] succession of pictures that were, we said, about a hundred and fifty.

They made us understand the Kingdom of the *Heavens* because it was a matter of different Heavens, one more beautiful than another, always linked to our life of union with God—in that Reality where the Soul-Church found itself—to perfect communion among us and, above all, with Jesus Eucharist.

At that time, I was convinced that the Lord was going to draw the "Soul" into the Heavenly Kingdom as on a divine honeymoon and that the *whole* of the *Word* would be revealed to me, naturally as much as my capacities could "understand."

---

9. A wooden statue of the Virgin Mary in the church of Tonadico di Pimiero.

Other Pictures

In the divine abyss of love and of light where we walked, I expected now to be presented with the *saints*. But it was not like that. I am not sure, but it seems to me that the only saint I saw "intellectually" was St Joseph.

Another time we decided to "consecrate"—I think it was on a feast day of Our Lady—the "Soul" to Mary.

We came back from church with the impression that the "Soul" was somehow "sacred" with Mary. It had been made Mary, as if our destiny were to "be Mary."

I do not know if it was that time, but I know that I understood that we had to be like a small reproduction of Mary, as Chiaretta, my niece who at that time looked very much like me, appeared more my daughter than her mother's.

We had to be perfectly Mary, daughters only of Mary, other Marys.

Another time I saw Mary in Heaven in the position of, so to speak, *the handmaid of the Lord*: a speck in the infinite, as if she were all recollected on her knees, in adoration.

Another picture I remember is what seemed to me to be *my place in Heaven*. I seemed to be in the center of a living amphitheater made up of my companions (around me), of young people, behind whom, like radiating rays, were the religious orders. I *set the tone* and I felt as if I were covered, I do not know how to express myself, as if I were veiled.

This picture filled me with joy, but it did not exalt me. I said it had the effect there was for St. Teresa when she saw her place in hell (if she did not mend her ways). I saw my place in Paradise (if I lived up to what was asked of me). It seemed logical to me that in a "Mystical Body" type of spirituality, where there is Christ among us, we should see the positive.

Another time, after the Consecration to Mary, I sensed a word in my soul that to me meant "bearing within" and it seemed to me that God wanted to repeat mystically an incarnation with the Soul consecrated as "Mary."

Heaven and earth, exulting in unspeakable joy, were celebrating the event and, as I was going up to St Victor's[10] these words sang in my soul: "Hushed one day I know not on what slopes." At the same time, unusually,

---

10. Another church in Tonadico.

in church the Magnificat was being sung, and Archangela[11] was locking up the cemetery. That underlined for us a richer presence of Jesus on earth, of life against death, of the One who is Risen.

One day in the Bosom of the Father, that for us was always like the inside of an infinite Sun, a great change took place; we found ourselves in a *heavenly landscape* made up of all the elements that make up the earth, in color.

I remember trees, paths, springs and, I think, flowers and birds, and I understood that there Above, it will be as here, but in God. Before this new vision that finally revealed the inside of Paradise to me, I thought that we would have had to suffer a little at not seeing anything. But instead it was not like that. Heaven is always Heaven and even if it is immense, in it you do not feel alone.

There Above it seemed to us that every time souls meet, they form between them a new spiritual heaven that is continually different and various and heavenly through participation in the Trinitarian life that is always new.

From Paradise I saw creation. The Father, looking into the Son, had created, and from the Center of the Sun what seemed to be like divergent rays were going out beyond the Sun.

At the end of time, God would have drawn back those rays that from being divergent would have become convergent, and in the bosom of God we would have had new Heavens and new earths.

On earth there was not the *idea* of the pine tree, for example, for it was in the Word, because the plants have their being in humankind and humankind in Christ who leads creation back into the Bosom of the Father.

In Heaven I understood that created nature had the stamp of the Trinity: matter like the Father; its law like the Word; its Life like the Holy Spirit.

By contrast, I do not remember when, I seemed to understand something of hell.

It appeared to me that Jesus forsaken, in that cry that was the salvation of the redeemed, was the justice of the damned.

And that He, I do not know in what way, eternalized hell.

From Heaven, however, hell—through Jesus forsaken—would be seen upside-down, in the sense that, for the blessed, every disunity would appear

---

11. The sacristan.

as unity and that in Jesus forsaken hell would turn out to be the Paradise of Paradise.

Jesus forsaken having made himself "sin" had made himself hell. But He is God and in Paradise one sees God.

It seemed to me that through Jesus forsaken the duality of the Afterlife was wiped out and that Jesus forsaken was the solution, the contact between the two realms where in one Eternal Life is lived and in the other Eternal Death.

In hell nothing would have made unity because love does not exist. In hell one is in the impossibility to love.

Hell was thus like the corpse of nature, where there are eyes to see but do not see, ears to hear but do not hear, and so forth. All are constructed to tend to God Whom eternally it can no longer reach. And every meeting between souls was in order to become more separated in an always more tragic division.

Hot would not make unity with cold and there would never be lukewarm. Only hot or only cold. Fire and gnashing of teeth.

* * *

I remember that in the final "realities" of Paradise we were the "Mystical Body of Christ."

And I remember the last "vision" was this: all those Heavens that we had seen and lived and possessed as if they were the most sacred—tremendously sacred—thing, as a result of an intervention like a new dimension, disappeared. But it was not a matter of being extinguished, but of *being sublimated*, because each one of us felt that he or she bore in himself or herself distinctly that which until that moment had been our common heritage.

And we came down from Fiera with this treasure in our heart.

I did not want to leave Paradise. I could not reconcile myself to having to go away from that Heaven where, for about two months, we had been living. I did not see the reason and I did not understand it, not because of attachment or a whim, but because of the *inability* to adapt myself to earth after having become accustomed to Heaven. I believed that God could not want it.

It was Foco who gave me courage by opening my eyes when he reminded me that Jesus forsaken was my Ideal and that I should love Him in the humanity that awaited me. It was then in my pain and tears that I wrote: "I have only one Spouse on earth: Jesus Forsaken. I have no other God but him. In him there is the whole of humanity, in Him is the Trinity. What hurts me is mine. I will go through the world [seeking it in every instant of my life]. . ."[12]

---

12. This refers to a meditation that can be found in Chiara Lubich, *Essential Writings* (New York: New City Press, 2007), 95.

Chapter Three

Paradise '49 (1969)

Chiara Lubich

First of all, I'd like to make it clear what 1949 was. It was a gift from God. It wasn't God. So, however great it was, we have to make it clear that it was a gift of God, and not God himself. So, the God whom we have chosen is something much greater than what God has given us. On the other hand, we can't deny that God does give gifts and we shouldn't despise these gifts from God. We can also qualify the various gifts of God, give a particular weight to some of these gifts, a different weight to others. . . .

So now I am seeing the significance of what happened, of this particular gift of God. And I am seeing that it is important not just for us focolarini, but for the world and for the church, and that there is a patrimony there that will take centuries to understand. I am also seeing that maybe, if I manage to rewrite it, it will be the greatest gift that the Work of Mary will leave to the church and the world.

The Vision from God's Point of View

The impression I have this morning is that what happened to me is like what happened immediately after the conversion of St. Ignatius. This was not because of some merit on his part, and the same is true of me: it was not because of my merit or that of anyone else.

It was truly the religious vision of the universe, the religious vision of the world. That is, the way God sees the world, how God sees things, how God sees creatures, how God sees Paradise.

The other day I spoke to you about '43; that is when the Movement began. But at a certain point, this Movement had to be consolidated as an Opera.[1] Up to that point, it was a simple Movement and we had no inten-

---

1. The word "opera," which literally means "work," was used in Catholic environments to refer to what came to be called ecclesial movements. Chiara distinguishes

tion, as I have said on other occasions, to make a rule, because I couldn't understand why approval was needed to be Christians.

But at a certain point, God wanted these Christians also to be a particular Opera in the church. This reminded us of Mary, who, although she is but one particular of the whole, is nevertheless everything that she is.

And since at the time Loppiano[2] didn't exist yet, there was no formation. What I understood was that the Lord needed us focolarine to have a kind of novitiate. At the time I had been living the Ideal for five years. The others came later, so they would have had two or three years of Ideal.

Since there was no Loppiano and no school of formation therefore, it was the Teacher, Jesus, [who intervened] and he brought Paradise. And the Trinity was our school, where we learned. What did we learn? Who God is and what the Opera is.

This was the thing that I understood this morning. I had been wondering, "Did I see the Opera?" or "Did I see Paradise?" This morning I understood that I saw both. And so, if I saw Paradise, I saw the vision of the world from God's standpoint. And if I saw the Opera, I saw the Opera and the function that the Opera has in the church. So, just to have an idea . . .

A Gift of God

If I can recount this to you today, it is like a mother on a feast day, who gathers all the children together and tells them about the wonderful things of the past, those things that never pass, because they keep coming back. Just like a mother who opens up the jewelry box, shows the children what's inside, and then closes it again quickly so that the child doesn't take anything away from it, so that the child doesn't become too curious. I do the same myself. I open the casket and then I close it up again immediately. Because this is not the moment to show everything. It is not God's will, because God has to make me see everything again, because I was a little disoriented by these first impressions. But then everything else will be told. Maybe not everything, but much will be told.

So, how will we proceed?

"Movement" from "Opera" and sees the experience of the Pact and the experience of Paradise as a transition from the first to the second.

2. Loppiano is a little town belonging to the Focolare Movement where in the 1960s the school of formation of the focolarini and focolarine was established.

That's the thing. It was a gift. And a gift is not God himself. Nevertheless, it was God's gift. And while it is true that in the future this thing will truly be the church's patrimony, it is also true that it is first of all your patrimony, and so it is right that you should have it.

So, how did this thing happen?

In reality, it was also very simple. Indeed, to me it was extremely simple. At the same time, I have such great gratitude to God for what he has done for this Opera that I cannot quantify it.

I said that we *pope*[3] had already done our "external formation."[4] And how did we do this? With great commitment, because it is God who is bringing you ahead. And when he wants something, he doesn't have brakes. So, he had made us live these years in a particularly and perhaps uniquely intense way. So, it is only now, with this little group that is learning to live the present moment that we may take up this race again. And we had learned many things. Already in the first moments, the first months, we had understood the fundamental ideas of the Ideal as a spirituality: Jesus in the midst, Jesus Forsaken, charity, everything.

A Change of Mentality

Where the Lord had focused our attention was especially on the Word of Life and on living it. I remember that we knew the gospel, almost by heart. It is not like now where every month we try to live a Word as best we can and then we do other things. At that time, we did nothing other than living the Word, because we didn't have other particular activities to do. So the Word of God truly entered into us. And if today the Ideal has become the way in which many people think, even outside the Movement, it is because we lived with such intensity that the mentality of that first group of people changed. This mentality, since it was light, moves by itself and is seen by many, if they take it and make it their own.

---

3. Chiara uses the word "pope" affectionately to refer to her female companions with whom she shared the experience of the Focolare. It is a word taken from the dialect of Trent, meaning "girls."
4. The "external formation" is a period of formation for focolarini. This period, which comes before the school of formation occurs in Loppiano, is deemed "external" because the candidates are usually not yet integrated into the focolare houses. Above, Chiara references a kind of novitiate. This corresponds to the "external" formation.

And it meant putting the whole worldly mentality into question. A divine protest, because it was a divine mentality that was entering a human mentality. But not just the mentality; it was entering our will, entering our affective life, into the whole of our humanity. So, we were being re-evangelized.

And among us *pope* we had had a unique experience, and in this we were directed only by Jesus in the midst, which has never been repeated in such an intense way in the Movement.

This was: you live one Word of Life, a second Word of Life, a third Word of Life, a fourth Word of Life. . . . We understood at a certain point that whatever Word of Life we lived, the practical external effects were the same. So, living "blessed are the pure of heart" or "the poor in spirit" or "the meek" came to the same thing. Living "love your neighbor as yourself" or "don't do unto others what you would not want done unto you." . . . Whatever Word of Life we lived we reached the same conclusion, that is, we were being called to act in the same way. So everything came to coincide.

And we had discovered that the Word of God was truly the Word of God, even if it was expressed in human terms. And being the Word of God, it was charity. In this way, we had discovered beneath the Word of God the essence that lies beneath, that is God, that is: love.

The Fire of the Word of God

In this way, everything became progressively simpler. So much so that in the final months, prior to '49, when one of these Words of God fell into my soul it became fire, flame, and charity. And I lived them with an elasticity that had become like a vortex, a bit like the earth that rotates so much that it appears to be still.

So as soon as the Word of God entered, even before we had time to think about it, it had already become charity.

You might say: "What is this charity?" It is the voice, the voice of God. Yes, the Word of God helped me to amplify what we call the inner voice that guides you and brings you ahead. And this voice had become like a loudspeaker when compared to how we felt it when we were younger, when I used to speak of listening to "that voice" as in the Scripture. And so we heard this voice among the thousands of sounds of the world. And by living the Word of God, this Word entered. And so what were we other than Word and this voice? So inside of me, as soon as a Word came into me it was already flame. So, I felt that inside of me was only love.

We had discovered many other things. For example, how every complete-in-itself Word of God is God, and therefore beneath each is the Trinity. And it was marvelous, because we could see how in every Word of God that we lived, there was a negative aspect and a positive aspect. The "poor" was the negative aspect, while "they shall inherit the kingdom" was the positive aspect. Similarly, the "pure" is the negative aspect, while "they will see God" is the positive aspect. And it was always a purity that was charity, and so it was positive, and a kingdom of God that was charity, and so it was positive. And so, in every Word we had discovered the life of the Most Holy Trinity. So, we had penetrated it not just with contemplation but also with this effect of spiritual life, so that it was the voice of God inside us that guided us.

So we had arrived more or less at this point. Naturally, the first focolarine and focolarini[5] were with me in everything. And whatever I experienced immediately became the experience of everyone. It wasn't that we could live the Word: he had to live the Word. That was the Ideal; it was living. Perhaps in me this thing was even more accentuated, because I was the guide, but we all had this same experience. And so, within us everything was love.

The impression of our soul was the impression of rising, rising, rising, rising as if along a ray—we used to say it this way—of the will of God. But to speak in this way diminishes it. It was a getting ever closer to the sun, ever closer to God. What does this "rising" mean? It means that the further up you go, the more you leave below the things beneath. They are lost. In fact, my new life, the new life that I had in me, the God who lived in me, had in itself the God of yesterday and of the previous day, and the God of a year ago. So, whatever was behind me collapsed into nothing, because it was all *in* me. So, the impression we had was the impression of climbing, so to speak, of rising ever closer to God.

Vacation in the Mountains

That's when 1949 happened. It seems that I had worn myself out a little and was a bit tired. So, the doctor suggested that I take a break in the mountains and leave behind the life of the Movement. And my companions said that I shouldn't go alone and that they would come with me too. So, I agreed of course. But I had no idea what would happen up there. So, having left

---

5. Focolarine (also referred to here as *pope*) are female members of the focolare houses or communities and Focolarini (also referred to here as *popi*) are male members of those communities.

the Movement behind, we went up into the mountains. I remember—and Father Spiazzi says it too—that Wisdom often uses little external details to communicate with souls and especially inexperienced souls like us. So, I remember the impression that a poster for a film made on us: "Amidst the peaks I'll bear you away." But this was just one sign among many, because God uses many means.

So, when we arrived up in the mountains, I noticed a second phenomenon: that this kind of fire that was inside me—because the Word had become fire as well as Word—was also a voice and that, as soon as it entered into us, the gospel flamed up And I found myself saying: "I have just finished a first phase of living the Word of God; later I will live it again in a different way, because here everything is becoming fire, everything is becoming God." So if, inside me—and inside the *pope*, I think—things were like this; outside us there was something else. The Lord, through an extraordinary grace, showed me all of nature differently from how I see it now, or how you see it now, or how I myself had seen it previously.

A Spiritual Sun

So, the vision of God beneath all things was very strong—obviously a special grace of God. So, if the pine trees were gilded by the sun, if the streams ran down in their waterfalls glistening in the sunlight, and so on, if the daisies, the other flowers, the sky . . . beneath every created thing that I saw there was a spiritual sun—not the sun—but stronger, and I saw it.

You might ask me: "What did you see, Chiara?"

With the soul.

"But what did you see?"

God who sustains all things. God who holds everything up.

"But how did you see it?"

So, I saw that God beneath things made them be not as we see them; they were all linked among themselves by love, all in love with one another.

So if the stream flowed into the sea, it was out of love. If one pine tree rose up beside another, it was out of love. Saying "out of love" is unclear. I saw love, which is God, beneath things, which bound all things together. And this was a blinding sun. And so, the vision of this unity that God gave us or, even better, the vision of God who united everything in creation, was stronger than the things themselves.

I was at this point in the spiritual life when, at a certain moment, Foco came to the mountains. Until that point, I had felt the need to meet someone who . . . , because I felt that the Ideal wasn't a common thing. The *pope* who were with me, in contrast, believed that everything was normal.

A Sweet Engrafting

This was because the Lord hadn't treated me in a rough way. What he did was he called me and I followed. But he didn't give me visions. He didn't throw me off a horse. Instead he gently engrafted himself onto my nature. So much so that in the first moments, when I explained the Ideal to the *pope*, I explained it in philosophical terms, because that was the language that I knew, having studied philosophy. And so I didn't have other terms with which to say these things, but they weighed me down, they seemed unpleasant to me. So, I said, I should have other words to say these things. But I didn't have other words; my language was philosophical.

So, this light, which also had many episodes in the earlier times of my spiritual life, gradually engrafted itself onto my nature and my life, the life of grace engrafted itself gently, and so we arrived at this point in a sweet way, without violent shifts.

The *pope* believed that this was the Christian life. So much so that Giosi [one of my companions], was amazed that others didn't live in the same way. She said: "How come the members of Catholic Action don't live in the same way?" And the same with the other *pope*; they were like children who drank the same milk. And they thought that everyone drank the same milk. But they didn't understand what the Ideal was, while I had a sense that there was something different from Christianity as normally understood. Deep down inside, I felt the need for someone who would confirm this for me.

An Important Personality

And so, I met Foco, who was older than me. He was twenty-five years older than me. He was, and is, a well-known personality in the church. He knew the church well, had fought for the church, had known the saints, had written many biographies of saints—he was a hagiographer—he was the one who had a kind of divine plan or design not to be behind me, following, but ahead of me, helping me to understand what the Ideal was. And this then justified what I felt; that someone could tell me that it was something new. But we needed someone like him to do it.

Throughout his life—his vocation is a splendid thing—Foco had sought a virgin he could follow and bring him to God. He was in love with Saint Catherine and was her follower, and he had sought her and was obviously called to do so. When Foco encountered this spirit [i.e., Chiara herself], there was this great understanding between them immediately. And for me too, in front of him, only 28 years old, like a child . . . he was such an important personality, and I was just a provincial girl. But none of this made much impression on me. What impressed me was the beauty of Foco's soul. He was the Christian, the open Christian, highly intelligent and learned, of great culture, but that culture that is capable of making itself really nothing. That's how Foco was.

So, I met him. He was immediately taken with me. He came up to see us, to meet me in Fiera di Primiero, where I was with the *pope* in that mountain cabin. Actually, it wasn't really much more than a cowshed at the time. It didn't have windows or anything. Eight of us slept there in the same room.

One day something apparently simple happened. Foco comes to me. I don't remember exactly, but it seems that I had already been speaking with him about the Word of God and, above all, what I had been saying was how everything had gone up in flames for me, and how the Word par excellence was "My God, My God, why . . . ," that is, it was Jesus Forsaken, which for me was Jesus in his fullest expression—final in the sense of redeemer—the way he had really annihilated himself, made himself nothing. . . . And so I said, "All the Words of God basically amount to this: nothingness and everything. On the nothing that we are, there is the everything that is God."

As I remember, I was explaining Jesus Forsaken in this way, as the Word of God. Because if Jesus is the Word, he is the Word of God; Jesus in his dereliction is the Word unfurled, fully open and explained. Jesus, who took the nothingness upon himself and filled it up: the vanity of all things and filled them up and divinized them. And it's him: God. . . . So, Jesus Forsaken was everything, he was the Word. I explained these things to Foco, and he followed and understood. And I explained them to the *pope* too, and they followed and understood.

A Special Pact

One day, Foco called me aside; he felt called to say this to me: "Listen, I want to become a saint. So, I want to bind myself tightly, as Saint Catherine says, and so I would like to make a vow of obedience to you, Chiara. Because I have the impression that God has chosen you, and all of my life I have sought a virgin to be able to follow her. And I think I have found her. I want to do your will, Chiara, and I think it is God's will that I do so." He said, "In this way, Chiara, we will become saints." And he gave me an example: Saint Francis de Sales and Saint Jane de Chantal, who had become saints together.

I listened, but I didn't like the idea. Something within me reacted negatively to the idea. I had two feelings together. One said, "Here Foco is under the action of a grace; we shouldn't waste this grace." The other feeling said, "No, not just two of us. All should be one, not just two being one. That, 'all might be one' (Jn 17:21), not two might be one. Yes, Saint Francis de Sales might have become a saint in that way, but this is not my path: all, all one." And I didn't understand the part about obedience either. I said: "A vow to me? Why? One with me and with everyone.[6] Why obedience to me?" The Opera didn't exist at the time. But I didn't say these things to him at the time, because it would have been like a mortification. . . .

So I said to Foco, "Look, it might be that what you feel is really from God. But not two one, all one. But it may really be that it is from God so we shouldn't waste it. . . . You know my life, it is to be nothing, because I live Jesus Forsaken, and so I exist if I am nothing. He is everything, I am the nothingness. So, if I want to be what I truly am, I have to be nothing, and in this way I exist. And you are nothing, because you too are Jesus Forsaken. We have to live this nothingness. If we are this nothingness, then we are what we are, because we put ourselves in our true being. As Saint Catherine said: 'I am nothing, you are Everything.'"

And I had learned this following Jesus Forsaken, and Foco had understood it. So I said, "Let's do this. Tomorrow, when we go to Mass and there, when Jesus-Eucharist enters into me and when Jesus-Eucharist enters into you, he will enter into an empty chalice because there is nothing there. So we, who are nothing, will say to him . . . I will say, 'Jesus, make unity with Jesus-Eucharist in him, and bring about that unity that you want with [Foco's] soul.'"

So, we went to the church, to Mass, and at Communion, Jesus entered our heart. At Communion I really made this pact and said to Jesus: "On the nothingness of me, which I am, I ask you to make this pact of unity with you on the nothingness of Foco who is there."

---

6. She means that the unity that was her ideal was a unity between all people, and not between two individuals.

In the Bosom of the Trinity

We left the church. Foco had to go back in through the sacristy to give a talk to the Capuchin Fathers. I felt urged to return to the church itself. I entered the church and went in front of the tabernacle. And, in front of the tabernacle I was about to begin a prayer to Jesus-Eucharist, beginning, "Jesus . . ." But I couldn't say it because Jesus was here. I too was him. It was me. I was one with him. I was him. I couldn't call myself. And I found myself as a person on the peak of a very, very high mountain, as though I was on a very fine point, fine like a needle. And one.

So [I was on] a very high mountain, but incapable of calling out to the one whom I was. The Eucharist doesn't call out to itself. And there I heard a word emerge from my mouth: "Father."

And in that moment, I found myself in the bosom of the Most Holy Trinity.

You might ask me: "How did it happen? What did you see?"

It was as if I had entered into an immense abyss, like the universe, but even greater. I saw it, not with these eyes, but with the eyes of the soul. I almost didn't have these eyes, didn't have these eyes. And to the eyes of my soul it appeared to be all made of gold, all flames. And I found myself there. And I realized that the one who had put the word "*Abba*, Father" on my lips had been the Holy Spirit. And that Jesus-Eucharist, the bond of unity, had been truly the bond of unity between me and Foco. And that he alone remained on these two nothingnesses. And that our two rays had arrived at the point where they converge in the sun. And it was as if I had arrived in this infinite sun. And that outside of me had remained created reality. And I understood that I had entered into the uncreated: into God, into the bosom of the Father. I didn't see what was in Paradise. I couldn't distinguish anything, but this did not disturb me. It was infinite, but I felt very much at home.

Foco came out from his meeting with the Fathers. "Come," I said to him. We went around the church and walked over and sat on a bench. I said, "Listen to what happened to me. Do you know where we are?" And I explained. Foco listened.

Then I went home. And I loved the *pope*. And the *pope* had followed me to that point, and I wanted to tell them everything. So I gathered them together and told them. I said what was happening to me and what I saw. I said, "Listen, come with us. On your own tomorrow, ask Jesus-Eucharist in you to make the pact of unity on the nothingness of you with Jesus-Eucharist in me and in Foco."

A "Small Company" in the Bosom of the Father

The following day, the *pope* went to church. I remember that they were in the pew behind me and they did as I had suggested. Then they came out from the church and said to me, "Chiara, what do you see?" I answered, "I saw in the bosom of the Father a small company: that's us." So, the *pope* were so taken because I communicated these things to them, and as I was telling them these things, I was also giving them these things. And the *pope* saw the things with my eyes. And they too felt themselves to be in the bosom of the Father. And they too saw these things.

I said, "Something new is beginning here. Where will we end up? I don't know. Now, tomorrow we will renew our communion with God—what will happen? I don't know." We entered the church and received Communion. And then we were accustomed to doing the following: we lived that reality, so that even though we were doing our various jobs, even though we continued doing the normal things, our walks and so on, we were there. And at 6:00 in the evening, we went in front of that statue of Our Lady there, in Tonadico, to have meditation.

And I said something very strange to the *pope*, that was not at all common. The meditation was quite different from the normal one. I said, "Don't think about anything, anything at all." Because I had understood, in Paradise, that this little company, even though in a certain way I did see it made up of a group of persons. . . . I didn't call it a group any more, since the warmth of the Trinity and God's Spirit, which was stronger than any of our individual spirits, had fused us into one, and I called this the "Soul," with a capital S. We were the Soul.

And I told them: "The Soul has a center." Years later, I learned that Saint Teresa of Avila says that the soul has a center. Only that, in her case, it was an individual spirituality, while here it was a collective spirituality. And it was evident that the center of the Soul was here.[7]

---

7. Chiara uses the word "here" to refer to herself.

So I said to the *pope*, "Come, adore Jesus during meditation, but while adoring him, become nothing. You have to be nothing, so that he can tell us what he has brought about through the new communion." So the *pope* made this effort to not think, to not be. So this was the maximum meditation, right? And I did the very same, while waiting for God to help me understand what the new communion had brought about. Because there were two communions: the daily Communion with him, and the communion with the *pope*, among us. I gave everything to them. And then we went to Jesus to receive whatever he would have given us and then I communicated this to the *pope* and then we went back to him.

The Word of God

So, that evening, we go for the meditation. I gather myself in the Trinity, within. . . . On television the other day, I saw the photograph of the earth seen from the moon, where you can see a part of the moon, and the earth far beyond. And you might say, "Was it something like that Chiara?" Yes, it was also something like that. Because God adapted these visions to my eyes. But it was infinitely [more]. . . . I can't explain it.

So anyway, in the meditation that evening, I went to the meditation and I spent a moment recollected with Jesus, without a thought, and I felt that from all . . .—if I can express it like this—from all of the infinite walls of the bosom of the Father, there was a single word pronounced, but in an infinite number of ways: "Love." And it came to be concentrated in the bosom of the Father. And it was the Son.

And there the Lord had me understand that the Father, expressing himself, who is charity, who is love, generates the Son, the light: himself. And there I understood an infinite number of things. I understood . . .—ah, I can't explain it.

Then I went out with the *pope*. And they said to me: "Where are we? What do we see?" I said, "I saw the Word of God."

"What's that?"

I remember that I was up near a little church, in Tonadico, and there was a wonderful sunset, and the sun had just disappeared behind the mountain, and rays of light were shooting up. I told them: "There, that's how it is. The Word is the splendor of the Father—the Father is the sun—he is the splendor of the Father."

But then I understood, and it was he who helped me to understand it, that if the Trinity, the Father, in his bosom generates the Word, who is God, it's like, using a human illustration, the converging rays of the sun. In creation he created all things, while looking at the Son, as if by diverging rays. And through the Son all things had been made. And there was the footprint of the Word in all things. And of all things, there were many that at the end of the world, having returned to the bosom of the Father, would have returned like many Word [*sic*] in one Word.[8] In the created world there were many plants, in the Word was the plant. Many flowers, but in the Word was the flower. Many mountains, but in the Word was the mountain. Many stars, but in the Word. . . . And that at the end of the world these rays would have been drawn back into the bosom of the Father, and they would have constituted new heavens and a new earth.

Then, among us *pope*, we asked ourselves: "What's going to happen next?"

A Portion of Church

And so we wanted to prove to ourselves how incapable humanity is of understanding God's mind, and we said, "Let's see if we can guess what we will see next, so that later, when it's something entirely different, we will see God's triumph over the human." So I said, "Logically now we're going to see the Holy Spirit, no? That's how it's going to be. You will see, you will see." And, so, all of us together, all of us inside the Trinity—the Soul was in the Trinity—went to the new Communion, and the *pope* consistently lived that new reality that was there on the basis of their nothingness, their silence.

And in this new reality we understood something. During the meditation in the evening—then the *pope* were waiting for me outside—we understood that the Word was marrying the Soul, and that the Soul was Church, was a little piece of Church. I don't know how to say it.

Then we understood, and I felt it, as if the Word was saying to the Soul—which was nothing other than Jesus in our midst, "You are my beloved Son." And I understood that he was going to tell me everything, that the Word would explain everything to me: all of creation and all of the Uncreated.

---

8. Chiara says, "many Word [sic] in one Word," presumably to emphasize the radical unity of the many when they converge in the Word who is in the bosom of the Father.

At the End of the World

Then I understood how at the end of the world there will be Paradise and Hell. And I understood that these rays, that had diverged from the center of Paradise in creation bringing order, love, and life to creation, would be withdrawn from creation at the end of the world, leaving whatever remained without order, love, and life. That what remained would be Hell. And that in what remained there would be no unity. Such that fire would not make unity with cold. There would not be anything lukewarm. Rather, there would be "fire and gnashing of teeth." And I understood that whatever remained outside the Trinity would have been like a corpse. It will have eyes made for seeing but which no longer see; a breast made to rise and breathe but which would no longer rise; a heart made for loving but which would no longer be able to love. I understood that the men and women who remained outside, outside of Paradise, would have tried to meet one another, but that every meeting would have become a fight and that forever they would move from disunity to disunity, from disunity to disunity, from disunity to disunity. And that either one would continue running and the other would always be still, because there wasn't unity, because order will have been withdrawn.

Meanwhile, in heaven I saw the opposite. That the meetings of souls, that every soul who had returned to heaven by their own will, would have been a Word of God that, lost—as we had tried to do ourselves—making themselves nothing in the Word, would have been Word in the Word. And that [if] I had not returned to Paradise, he would not have lost anything of me, nor would the blessed in heaven be missing anything of me, since they would see me in the Word of God, from which I had come forth. They would see the Idea of me. And that Paradise would not suffer because of my absence. And that even those things that might have been in the future would have been seen in God. In that case, the blessed would have gained, because they would have participated, as free and immortal, in the joy of God himself. They would have been God in God, Word in Word.

Ever New Meetings

And I understood that every Word would have been God. And that the meeting of two creatures up there would have been a song of songs. And that if we go up there, for example, at a certain point we would all be together like a rosebud. Then, in a different moment—because of the distinction which is intrinsic to the trinitarian life—we would have distinguished ourselves . . . , and each one of us would have been a rose, and that this would have then opened up into many petals, but that each one of these was Word and that therefore it would open up into many petals. Then, many meetings, then dances, then different forms of musics;[9] then Paradise, blessedness, happiness, God.

Then I understood that Jesus Forsaken had made the nothingness his own. He had become sin, which means nothingness: *the* nothing. And that he had incarnated the word: "All is vanity of vanities"; and another: "The heavens and the earth will pass away." He had incarnated this emptiness when he made himself forsaken. He had also made himself that word then: "The heavens and the earth will pass away," and he had divinized this word bringing it into heaven. And that the thought of the existence of Hell would not be disgusting in heaven. Because Hell. . . . Jesus in his dereliction, made himself sin, and therefore nothingness, and therefore Hell. So, for those who were in Paradise, looking at Hell they would have seen Jesus Forsaken.

And I understood therefore that for Paradise, Hell would have been Paradise. And that Jesus Forsaken's cry, which was his final cry on the cross, was like a swan song of the Son of God on earth. And that for Paradise, Hell would have been super-Paradise, the Paradise of Paradise. And that in the other life there would not have been that division, disunity, that lack of harmony. Instead, everything would have been made harmonious by Jesus Forsaken.

Then I explained all of these things to the *pope*, even though I did not see all of this in heaven. I just saw this infinite abyss in which the Soul did not feel disoriented even though we were so small. As if everything was full, and as if everything was home, and it was infinite.

A Blue Sky Containing the Sun

Then we went back to the communion, after having explained these things and lived them. And we said: "What will we see next?" But we didn't know the answer.

So, we went back to Communion. And the Lord helped me understand Mary, using my imagination but also my reason. I had never understood her in this way. I discovered that I hadn't really known Mary at all. And he

---

9. Chiara writes "musiche," which is the plural of "musica." Music is uncountable in English, but in this case the translator has preferred to preserve the plural.

showed her to me when we were in the bosom of the Trinity. And he gave me this concept: as the blue sky contains the sun, so Mary had been made so great as to contain God himself. I had not had this sense of the measure of Mary. And I was stunned. And I said to the *pope* that I used to have another concept of Mary, like . . . I thought of her as a Christian first, like a little statue, like one of those little statues of Our Lady. I had never had the idea of Mary in all her greatness, as I had seen her in Paradise. And I explained it to the *pope*. And it was then that the first understanding of Mary was born. It was as if he was saying to me: "I made Mary great, even greater than myself—but it is he who had made her so great—because she contained me."

And so, I go to the *pope* and say: "What's going on! We are in the Trinity, the Soul has married the Word, the Word has married the Soul, we are Church. Now he has introduced Mary to us: Why? Why not the Holy Spirit?" Then I understood. The third, fourth, and fifth day had come; I don't know exactly; and we went back to Communion. And at Communion. . . . We were always ready for anything unexpected, but it is as though I didn't expect it, because I wasn't the kind of person that these things happened to, except that these also had a powerful influence, weighing down my body, to the extent that I felt as though I was going to explode as soon as the illumination came to me sometimes in the pew, where I was amidst the *pope*.

The Atmosphere of Heaven

And we went before the statue of Mary. And at a certain moment we begin adoring Jesus in the Eucharist, in the tabernacle. And I become aware—and this was the strangest thing yet—of something like a little breeze coming out of the tabernacle, like a waft of air, like a waft of air. I looked, and later I checked to see if the windows were open or closed. But they were sealed windows.

I didn't understand what it was, but I understood that something was coming out from the tabernacle and was coming toward me. And without having ever, ever thought about it, I saw a dove—it was probably about 20 centimeters across—come out of the tabernacle. And I realized that it was the Holy Spirit. And that the soul of the tabernacle, the air . . . I realized that the Holy Spirit was in the heart of Jesus in the tabernacle. And it came out. It came out, and came toward me. It positioned itself above my head and those of the *pope*, and slowly circled in very, very, very slow circles. And then it stopped as if in the position to shed light. But it didn't shed light.

And there in the Trinity, I understood that the Holy Spirit, spouse of the Virgin Mary, closed the Trinity. He had allowed his spouse to come first, set as a jewel in the Trinity. And that the Son, the Word, having wed the Soul, had shown his Mother to it. And that he was conducting us on a honeymoon voyage, showing us all of his treasures. These were just the first of many. The treasures of the uncreated and of creation. And I realized that within, in the bosom of the Father, the atmosphere of the Father, the atmosphere of Paradise, was the Holy Spirit: it was the Holy Spirit.

A Kaleidoscope of Visions

Things kept happening. Every day a new vision. And after a few days there was more than one vision a day. And it was the Soul that saw all of these things, the little Church that God then consecrated to Mary, as it had to become another Mary in the world, in the church. And how we were destined to be a little Mary. That was another vision that I had.

I saw the Opera as it would be and as it now is. I was at the heart of this Opera, in the center, veiled. Then later I understood that it was the presence of someone else who, together with me, had as a vocation in this Opera—as I used to say—to set the tone in the Opera. And that person who was "veiled"—at the time I didn't know who it was so I couldn't understand it—would be an assistant, someone who would represent the church for me. Maybe it was Father Foresi,[10] who was not yet there. And around me, as in a semicircle, the *pope*. And then the first *popi*. And behind them, the religious orders and all of the church.

Then, for example, at a certain moment in this immense sea, ocean, indeed universe, that I was telling you about, that I had seen made of gold and flames, I don't know, at a certain moment there was like a leap forward, as when from the light, the seven colors [of the rainbow] emerge, and I saw a majestic landscape, as the new heavens and new earth will be. And there were trees and there were birds and there were flowers.

That which previously had been uniform was all of a sudden full of colors. And I saw heaven within, as it will be. And then many things, then many more things. More than a hundred and eighty of these visions that the Lord gave me.

---

10. This is Pasquale Foresi, one of the first focolarini and considered by Chiara a cofounder of the Movement. He became the first focolarino to be ordained a priest in 1954 and became the Movement's first copresident.

And at the end, he made me understand: "What you have seen is not this way. I adapted the vision of the Trinity to your eyes, to your three dimensions. Because you are a creature and you can't see with God's eyes. It is not how you have seen it, but you have it this way. What you have seen is true. But I have shown it to you in a human way, so that you can see it."

The Evolution of an Opera

But I felt that everything that I had seen, I had seen within. Indeed, I felt myself more sublimated than ever after more than a hundred and eighty visions rather than feeling lost. It was as if everything that I had seen had evaporated, as if it had been sublimated, as if it had been undone. And the Lord made me understand, "Yes, because I adapted things that your eyes of this world, and even your soul, cannot see. But they are true." What I felt, he didn't tell me, but I felt it and it remained within me. And in these one hundred and eighty visions, I saw all of the evolution of the Opera, all of the evolution of the Opera, all of the evolution of the Opera.

And after twenty years now, because now it is 1969, and that was 1949, I saw—and I can say it now—that many, almost all of those things—you can't imagine it—are being realized. Many have already come about, and many more will come about. And the last one will be when we reach the *ut omnes*.[11] And I understood that this Paradise that I saw, this heaven that was in us, in our midst, would be in each of us, in all of those who will form the heavenly Jerusalem: unity, the *ut omnes*.

---

11. The expression *ut omnes* is drawn from the Latin translation of John 17:21 and refers to the prayer "That all may be one."

Chapter Four

Entry into the Paradise of '49 and Biblical Revelation

Gérard Rossé

Introduction

This study examines texts written by Chiara Lubich in response to a singular mystical experience that took place in the Dolomite Mountains during the summer of 1949. This period of illumination is known as "Paradise '49."[1] My intention is to come to an understanding of these texts based upon biblical revelation, particularly in the light of Pauline and Johannine theology. Since that time, thanks to the Second Vatican Council, the church has changed direction, and in a more precise way has renewed its awareness of the mystery of communion rooted in the mystery of the Blessed Trinity. Keeping in mind the date of Chiara's writings, her intuitions, whose prophetic riches even today have not been fully examined, can be seen as precursors to the insights of the Council.

As she herself has noted, the experience of 1949 was preceded by and prepared for through an intense Christian life, nourished by the words of the gospel and lived with a group of her first companions. It was with a commitment like this that they went to the Dolomites for a period of rest. With them went also a writer and political figure, Igino Giordani—known familiarly to them as "Foco."

This is how Chiara recalls the initial moment: "Foco, fascinated by St. Catherine of Siena, had always sought in his life a virgin like her whom he could follow. And now he had the impression that he had found such a figure in us." He proposed to Chiara, therefore, that he take a vow of obedi-

---

1. A translation of a talk given by Chiara Lubich in 1961 about her mystical experiences that began in the summer of 1949 was published in the first issue of *Claritas*: Chiara Lubich, "Paradise '49," *Claritas: Journal of Dialogue and Culture*, 1 (2012): 4-12. With this translation is an editorial essay that contextualizes the talk: "Editorial Essay: Contextualizing 'Paradise '49'," *Claritas: Journal of Dialogue and Culture*, 1 (2012): 13-23. The talk and the essay are also contained in this volume, pages 43 to 68.

ence to her. Although she didn't share his idea of a vow of obedience, Chiara accepted the proposal, modifying it in this fashion: "Very well, tomorrow we will go to church and to Jesus-Eucharist who will come into my heart, as into an empty chalice, I will say, 'Upon the nothingness of me, you make a pact of unity with Jesus-Eucharist in the heart of Foco. And do things in such a way, Jesus, that there come forth that bond between us that you know.' Then I added, 'And you, Foco, do likewise.'"[2]

They made this "pact of unity" and, as Chiara writes, "In that moment I found myself in the Bosom of the Father." It was the beginning of a mystical experience that lasted for months. Concerning it, we will examine in the light of biblical revelation two aspects: the role of the Word of God, and the entrance into "the Bosom of the Father."

The Word of Life

"For some time," recalled Chiara, referring to the period that led up to 1949, "we had been concentrating on the Word of Life, which we were living with a very particular intensity." We must not forget the originality of such an approach to the gospel in that place and time. Catholics were not in the habit of going directly to the "source" to nourish themselves with the words of Jesus. Religious formation and spiritual nourishment, given by priests, was based largely on hagiographies and upon the edifying thoughts proposed by authors who wished to cultivate souls in asceticism, virtue, and devotion. Certainly with biblical renewal and with the Second Vatican Council within the Catholic Church there spread groups that engaged in biblical meditation and Bible study groups. Nevertheless, the first focolarine[3] were approaching the word of God not primarily to meditate upon it or to study it, but to put it into practice, to incarnate it in their lives.

The words of the gospel were not only to be contemplated, but to be put into action. Spontaneously, therefore, the first focolarine had assumed before the word of God the attitude that the gospel itself requires of a believer. We recall the exhortation, expressed as a question, in Luke: "Why do you call me 'Lord, Lord,' and do not do what I tell you?" (Lk 6:46). In Matthew this appeal becomes a general rule: "Not everyone who says to me, 'Lord,

---

2. These passages are taken from unpublished texts written by Chiara about her experience of Paradise '49. If not otherwise noted, all quotations from Chiara Lubich are from these yet unpublished documents.
3. This term refers to women who live in focolare houses.

Lord,' will enter the kingdom of heaven, but only the one who does the will of my Father in heaven" (Mt 7:21). It is not enough, therefore, to proclaim the authority of Christ, to acknowledge his sovereignty. One must put into practice that which, in Matthew's Gospel, comes to be called "the will of the Father who is in heaven" and which is identified with the Word and with the requirements that Jesus lays out in the Sermon on the Mount, and of which the previous passage (7:21) forms the conclusion. To live completely in accordance with the choice of God, it is necessary, therefore, not only to know certain truths of the faith or nourish a relationship with the Lord by doing devotions, but to live the demands explicitly expressed in that choice. The experience of the first focolarine, then, follows the same line. They sought in the Gospels a way of loving God as God wants to be loved, and the gospels replied: by doing God's will.

The written text of the gospels offers the criterion of authentic discipleship: *hearing and doing*. Recognizing the sovereignty of Christ and fulfilling his words are inseparable. This bond between hearing and doing is described in the metaphor in Matthew's Gospel concerning the house built upon rock or sand: "Everyone then who hears these words of mine and acts on them will be like a wise man who built his house on rock" (7:24). Living the words of Jesus, then, is the sign of *wise* persons who found their existence on what is solid, what does not crumble. For a biblical audience, the word "rock" brings to mind several psalms that speak of YHWH as the Rock (see Psalms 18, 3:32, 31, 4, etc.). Putting into practice the words of Jesus means basing one's life upon God, the Faithful One. Those who do not live the words of God build on sand and demonstrate their foolishness. The trials come, the sufferings, the difficulties, the false teachings, but only those who listen to the gospel and put it into practice are able to resist. That same Word lived out will be for believers the rock that will save them. The wise demonstrate intelligence, good sense, and spiritual maturity, unlike the foolish, who show themselves to be shortsighted.

The nuance is a bit different in the parable in Luke (see Lk 6:47-49). The evangelist contrasts the one "listening to the word," that is, having an obedience that lasts, one who perseveres ("listening" is a present participle), to the one who "listens" (the verb is in the aorist form) for the moment only and therefore in a superficial sense. Moreover, the man in Luke demonstrates prudence in constructing a house with a foundation, therefore "digging deep": to build on rock requires strength, commitment to a life lived according to the Word. This man is the opposite of someone who is lazy and does not dig. How could such a person resist when crises arise?

Concerning the importance of putting the words of the gospels into practice, the letter of James is quite clear:

> Welcome with meekness the implanted word that has the power to save your souls. But be doers of the word, and not merely hearers who deceive themselves. For if any are hearers of the word and not doers, they are like those who look at themselves in a mirror; for they look at themselves and, upon going away, immediately forget what they were like. But those who look into the perfect law, the law of liberty, and persevere, being not hearers who forget but doers who act—they will be blessed in their doing. (Jas 1: 21-25)

The comparison with the mirror may be surprising. The writer criticizes the superficiality of those who content themselves with hearing the words of the gospels without allowing them to bud into life. Listening to the Word without putting it into practice is an illusion. Certainly, it is easy to glace at oneself quickly in a mirror; but listening to the Word demands a bending down, a submission to it, a careful examination of it and a lasting commitment. The Word indeed requires action, decision. It is a constant theme in biblical thought: the Word, an expression of the will of God, is communicated in order to be done. Following this line of thought, James distinguishes the steps—hearing the Word, making it one's own, and putting it into practice. This is "the perfect law," that is, the realized expression (with Jesus) of the divine will.

The experience of the first focolarine, expressed in the following comment of Chiara, corresponds closely to the positive part of James's text. We find the dual attitude required as one faces the Word: listening and doing. Listening is fundamental. It signifies openness to God who takes the initiative, who comes close to believers and communicates his will to them. It is an essential dimension of biblical faith. Such openness to God who speaks allows God to penetrate a person's life effectively and transform it. In Chiara's words: "The Word of God entered so deeply into us that it changed our way of thinking . . . it called forth in us a re-evangelization."

For the first focolarine, the words of the gospels no longer conveyed only a notional understanding of truth, or of a certain number of laws to be observed, but a living encounter with God who speaks and whose Word is divine self-communication. The Word lived out became an "event" in them, in accord with the meaning of the Hebrew word *dabar*, which does mean "word," but also can convey the sense of "something done, an event, an episode," insofar as it always maintains to some extent the aspect of activity as expressed by the voice of the verb in Hebrew.[4]

Listening to the words of God is, therefore, fundamental; but as the words of God constantly remind us, listening cannot be separated from putting it into practice. Listening certainly suggests that the initiative is left to God; but this does not reduce it to a merely passive acceptance of what God is doing. A Christian's behavior must be in accordance with the gospel. "Doing" therefore is necessary, but a doing characterized by "letting oneself be determined by the will of God"; therefore, an active passivity, an active attitude of receptivity typical of a "Marian" style of faith. Listening is inseparable from "doing," and therefore from fulfilling the will of God. Not by chance, in scripture, "to listen" can be synonymous with "to obey" understood as openness to the Word in the sense of putting it into practice. Only then is God's protective presence guaranteed to the people. In the covenant theology that runs through the Old Testament,[5] listening means observing the divine commandments, being able to live in the presence of YHWH and to rejoice in his love and under his protection. The same line is followed by Jesus' statement in John 14:21: "They who have my commandments and keep them are those who love me; and those who love me will be loved by my Father, and I will love them and reveal myself to them." This passage gives rise to further reflection.

Obedience to the words of the gospels does not consist only in attention turned toward an outer word, but corresponds to listening to a "voice" already present in the believer's heart. Chiara suggests this when she says:

---

4. See "DABAR," in Ernst Jenni and Claus Westedmann, eds., *Dizionario teologico dell'Antico Testamento* (Turin: Matiett, 2000).

5. The covenant structure is characteristic of the relationship that God established with the Chosen People when the Israelites were brought out of slavery in Egypt, forming them into a people and giving them the Law of Moses on Mt. Sinai. Israel made this relationship with God effective through the characteristic formulation of a pact or treaty. The covenant structure is as follows: the proclamation of an action by God on behalf of the people—the gift of the Law—the promise of obedience as a condition for remaining in God's presence—blessings or curses. For further reference, see: Gérard Rossé, "L'esperienza di Israele con Dio alla luce dell'alleanza sinaitica," *Nuova Umanità* IX (1987): 9ff; by the same author, "Relazioni tra l'amore di Dio e l'amore del prossimo alla luce dell'alleanza: Spunti biblici de una spiritualita de communione," *Nuova Umanità* XVII (1995): 101ff.

Since God is Love, every word is Charity. . . . This charity amplified, furthermore, within us what we called "the voice." The Word lived out made it effective as a loudspeaker, so we could clearly distinguish it among the thousand noises of the world.

Listening actively to the words of the gospel, as it were, awakens the Word, that is, the Holy Spirit, already present in the heart of the believer. Paul also presents the Holy Spirit, this great gift that is there at the beginning of the new life of the believer, as the "Law" placed deep in the Christian (see Rom 8:2). Such a person, then, has received into his or her very being an inner law, the Holy Spirit, able to give life. The new Law that is the Holy Spirit that works within the heart of the believer is not to be understood as a series of precepts to be observed, but as the strength of God internalized and made to work effectively, capable of opening up the human person to love-*agape* as a personal imperative. Love, the fullness of the Law, is precisely the Spirit's gift, as Paul teaches (see Rom 5:5). James also points out to his readers the truth that has been communicated to them in baptism: "the word sown in you."

This teaching runs through the entire New Testament. The applications of the parable of the sower call attention to the various dangers that threaten believers who accept badly "the seed sown in them" (Mk 4:15). Its usefulness can be neutralized by the actions of Satan, who plucks the words of the gospel from a heart full of things that alienate human beings from God. Also, the word of God accepted with joy runs the risk of being canceled out by the lack of perseverance—the trials of life can make the Christian crumble . . . just like that house built upon sand. Finally, the parable mentions another obstacle to the development of the words sown in the heart of the believer—preoccupations, riches, the pleasures of life, smothering the Word. These dangers smother also the authenticity of the believer.

There are also certain conditions by which the sown Word can bear fruit, can develop its power of salvation. Luke speaks of:

- "an honest and good heart," one that is open and therefore ready to accept the Word;
- the effort to "hold fast," to not let the Word of God slip away;
- and finally the "endurance" typical of the true disciple, in the inevitable trials of Christian existence (see Lk 8:11-15).

There is no lack of texts that underscore the positive effects of the "word of God living and eternal," that "undying seed" that regenerates (see 1 Pt 1:23), that makes one "born of God" (see 1 Jn 3:9). John also speaks about the "anointing" received by Christ (see 1 Jn 2: 20-27), which is the strength of sanctification. It is the Word of God that dwells in believers makes them strong, able to conquer the Evil One (see 1 Jn 2:14), illuminates them, making them penetrate the understanding of the divine reality (see 1 Jn 4:2), creates a connaturality with the divine Persons (see 1 Jn 2:24, 4:6).

There exists in fact a close link between the Word and the Holy Spirit. It is precisely the task of the Spirit to internalize God's words in believers: "When the Spirit of truth comes, he will guide you into all the truth" (Jn 16:13; see Jn 16:13-15; 14:26). This is a process of internalization that transforms a believer more and more into a being-who-loves (see Jn 15:9-10). As already pointed out, it is the same Spirit of God who becomes the new Law that acts in the hearts of believers. The Spirit is the complete divine will placed in the deepest parts of the human being who makes believers able to understand this divine will—that is, to love—as a *personal imperative.*

Living God's words, therefore, made the latent potential in every believer spring forth in the first focolarine; that is, the power of the Holy Spirit, the life placed by the same Spirit in the hearts of Christians and identified with *agape*. There exists, therefore, an intimate bond between God's Word, the Holy Spirit, and love, as the inner reality of Christians who live such faith, drawing out its full potential through contact with the words of the gospel. Living the Word, therefore, becomes a truly mystical experience of communion with God, source of light and love. Chiara describes its effect:

> We realized that putting into practice any one of the Words of God, the effects, in the end, were the same. . . . The fact is that every Word, although expressed in human terms and in different ways, is Word of God. But, since God is Love, every word is Charity. . . . And when one of these Words fell into our soul, it seemed to us that it was transformed into fire, into flames, it was transformed into love. It could be affirmed that our inner life was all love.

We can understand, then, what Chiara meant when she writes, "every Word is charity." It might seem to be a logical deduction from the fact that God is love; thus every word is an expression of God's love for human beings. This would be correct, but too weak. Another possibility: certainly the New Testament throughout affirms that, for Jesus and the Christian tradition, love of neighbor is the soul of the whole of the Law. Paul said that love is the fullness of the Law (see Gal 5: 14; Rom 13: 8-10); in John, there is significance in going from the plural ("my commandments") to the singular ("my commandment") which then is made specific: "that you love one another as I have loved you" (Jn 15: 10-12).

The experience that Chiara records in this text, however, does not refer so much to the fact that love sums up the content of the precepts of the Law, but more deeply that the Word lived out leads to an experience with God in the reality of God as Love. Putting into practice the words of the Gospel, so to speak, moves the Holy Spirit who lives in the depths of the believer; and the Spirit makes the believer experience love, as an experience of God-Love, as an imperative of life. God who dwells in every human heart gives, in the Word lived out, the experience of who God is in God's very being, that is, Love. It is clear that this includes the experience of a Word which, as Chiara writes, is transformed into fire, into flames . . . into love in our souls. Here, one can think of the experience of the disciples of Emmaus: opening the scriptures, the risen Jesus had made "their hearts burn" within them. "Opening the scriptures" becomes a source of light and love.

Pauline Theology

To appreciate this deeper understanding, it is necessary to go to theological thought such as that of Paul or of John, and translate the twofold expression "listen-do" into "believe-love." Turning to Paul's theology, he never fails to refer to the sayings of Jesus or to the tradition concerning Jesus in order to specify a certain behavior to his communities (see 1 Cor 7:10, 11, 23ff; and 1 Cor 15:3ff). But above all for the great apostle, the Word par excellence is Jesus crucified, that is, Jesus in the act of his greatest love (and not so much Jesus as the teacher who speaks words). He, in his obedience even unto death on the wood of condemnation, is the criterion of every way of acting. What Paul paradoxically calls "the law of Christ" (Gal 6:2) is not a rule given by Jesus, but the behavior of Jesus taken as the norm of Christian life, which is love understood and lived out in the light and to the measure of the cross. For Chiara, too, Jesus forsaken "appeared as the Word par excellence, the Word totally explained, the Word completely open. It is enough, then, to live Him."

Consequently Paul, more than giving a specified number of precepts to follow, presents to believers a principle that must give shape to the entire

Christian existence. Believers then do not find themselves subject to a system of precepts to observe, but are placed into the possibility of seeking out and living God's will that presents itself to them moment by moment. They know that they ought to love, but *how* to love they must discover, one instance after another. God leaves to every believer the task of discovering in his or her own particular life the way of behaving according to a particular principle—love to the measure of Jesus crucified. The apostle thus can sum up Christian ethics: "In Christ Jesus . . . the only thing that counts is faith working through love [agape]" (Gal 5:6).[6] Faith seen as openness to God who communicates God's own self is alive in love. Faith, therefore, uses love to be active and thus lead to unity.

Therefore, the principle received by Christians that ought to direct and animate their behavior is not an external criterion, but is divine love—that love revealed by Jesus crucified—placed in believers' hearts together with the gift of the Holy Spirit: "God's love has been poured into our hearts through the Holy Spirit that has been given to us" (Rom 5:5). Paul is thinking of the love that comes from God, closely related to the activity of the Holy Spirit in believers. Love then has its origin in the very life of God: it is the gift of *divine life* that should circulate among the believers, a sign of being inserted intimately within the Trinity. And because it has been placed within the hearts of Christians, they can love as a personal imperative, and not because they are subject to an obligation imposed from without. Love, therefore, as the "fullness of the Law" becomes an imperative of life and at the same time an experience of God-Love.

Before moving on to the teaching of John that will serve as an introduction to the entry into the bosom of the Father, I would like to emphasize once again certain characteristics of the Word lived out, demonstrated in the text of Chiara (and in line with Paul): "When one of these Words fell into our soul, it seemed to us that it was transformed into fire, into flames, it was

---

6. To be sure, the apostle does not intend to say that the commandments, the Decalogue in particular, no longer have value; on the contrary, they are the thousand faces of love which gives them life. "If I give away all my possessions, and if I hand over my body so that I may boast, but do not have *agape*, I gain nothing" (1 Cor 13:3). The new life expressed thanks to the inner gift of the Holy Spirit does not take away the commandments, but situates the life of believers on a higher level of relationship with God and neighbor, where the commandments are, so to speak, sublimated; believers not only do not steal, but are ready to place their goods in common; not only do they not kill, but they are ready to give their lives; not only do they not covet, but they "see Christ" in their neighbors, and so forth.

transformed into love. It could be affirmed that our inner life was all love." The experience of the Word lived out was manifested as a genuine experience of the Spirit; and precisely because it was so, the experience was not identified with sentimental feelings or a sense of exaltation. The experience of the Word as an experience of the Spirit is simultaneously one of divine Love and openness to relationship, to communion.

Being nourished by the Word of God gives life to the activity of the Holy Spirit present within believers. It gives rise to that dynamic of the Spirit which urges them toward unity within the group and to spread it to others. When Chiara asserts that the Word of God changed "our mentality" and "brought about a re-evangelization," we can conclude the focolarine did not limit the demands of the Word to their personal religious space, but it permeated all of their existence, hence also what is "profane." It is the discovery of the "non-religiosity" of the Word of God, of a God who wants to reveal the divine presence in all human situations. This is to say that genuine communion with God does not need a special environment, but can develop anywhere, in all sectors of secular life. It is the discovery that holiness is not reserved to martyrs, virgins and celibates, and bishops, but is open to all. It is found in simply living the ordinary things of daily life, with its problems, its joys, and its sorrows.

Chiara and her companions, understanding that the words of the Gospels had to shape human behavior in *everyday* life, saw that the practice of the gospel had to be not just in convents and monasteries, but along the streets, in the towns, in families. The gospel was not only something to do with the individual and private religious sphere, as a certain mentality thought or still thinks, but with life in society. As a consequence, the logic of the gospel incarnated into life will give life to the conviction that such logic should inspire every sector of existence and of human activity—the words of economics, culture, politics, science, education, the arts, etc.

Another characteristic that comes to light in Chiara's text is that the words of the Gospels were lived out *as a group*, not only privately. This fact carries a certain importance: as will emerge, particularly in the teaching of John, the saving will of God—communion with God—achieves its true end in mutual love and therefore in the gospel lived out as an expression of fraternal communion. Communicating to one another the experience that one has lived does not mean only relating edifying stories, but giving to the other and receiving from the other one's personal relationship with God. It was, therefore, a growing together in the journey toward sanctity; in other words, it was living communion with God in fraternal love. Personal relationship with God emerged from the sphere of a private relationship in order to be lived out as a community. It gave value again to a spirituality of communion as lived in the early church, consistent with the ecclesiology of communion later proposed by the Second Vatican Council.

In this way, the first focolarine turned to the words of scripture following an eminently biblical pattern, strongly present in the prophets as well as in Jesus, Paul, and John. It deals with the logic and the structure of covenant (in the terms Chiara habitually used: according to what has been called the "collective spirituality").[7] Believers live within communion with God (who takes the initiative) observing God's commandments that can be summed up in love for one's brothers and sisters. A genuine relationship with God, within the covenant, cannot take place other than through behavior that is moral and socially adequate. Only mutual love, as the lived expression of the divine will, guarantees the presence of God (of Jesus as "God-with-us") according to the logic of covenant, and that is according to how God, throughout the whole of salvation history, wants a relationship with God to be lived out.

It is upon the basis of this kind of logic that there came about the mystical experience of the entrance into the bosom of the Father. Before exploring these texts, however, it may be helpful to turn our attention to the teachings of John. Johannine mysticism, in fact, sheds light upon this experience. In greater detail than others, John presents the connection between observing the commandments (living the Word), communion with the Risen Jesus, and the entrance into the bosom of the Father.

Johannine Theology

Even if developed in different theological categories, John's thought corresponds closely with that of Paul; they are the two pillars of church theology. In practice, John's entire Gospel is based on the theme "believe-love," the logical conclusion of "listen-do." "Believe," in fact, is one of the principal themes of the first part of his Gospel (chapters 1-12) just as "love" is the theme that comes into view in the second part (chapters 13-17). What becomes evident is the Fourth Gospel's overall structure: from the faith, to which all are called, to fraternal love, as obedience to God's will (and so an

---

7. See fn. 5.

expression of love for Jesus). The call to believe (the first part of the Gospel) is made concrete in the communion of the disciples around Jesus (the second part), an expression of the new people of God, a prefiguring of the *perichoresis* (mutual indwelling) that comes to be among the Risen One and believers, in the church.

Like Paul, John can then summarize God's command to human beings as *believe and love:* "And this is his commandment, that we should believe in the name of his Son Jesus Christ and love one another, just as he has commanded us" (1 Jn 3:23). There is an intrinsic link between "believing" and observing the commandment of Jesus. Believing in Jesus expressed the actual will of God for human beings. This is not about—as it also is throughout scripture—a generic belief in the existence of God, but precisely about a belief in *Jesus*. To the Jews who asked what they should do so as to perform "the works of God," Jesus replies, "This is the work of God, that you believe in him whom he has sent" (Jn 6:29). Believing replaces zeal for the Law of Moses (in the Jewish sense of performing the works of God) not because it stands in opposition, but because Jesus fulfills and overcomes it: "The law indeed was given through Moses; grace and truth came through Jesus Christ" (Jn 1:17).

Believing is also more than a store of truth to which one adheres intellectually. The act of total and personal attachment to the person of Christ, then, implies the gift of self to God, openness to God's word, and the duty to fulfill God's will. For John, believing involves listening, conversion, seeing and contemplating, understanding and knowing, and doing. It is relational, something living and dynamic that takes up the entire person. It is no accident that in his Gospel, John uses the verb *believe* ninety-six times, but never the noun *faith*! Believing, therefore, is seen as adherence to Jesus; it is welcoming and accepting and so knowing his divine origin, the reality of his being the Son sent by the Father and, as a consequence, opening oneself to the inner life of the divine Persons. Believing creates a living bond with Christ, develops a knowledge that is communion with Jesus, and in him with the Father.

Consequently, the evangelist can use phrases that are synonymous with "believe in Jesus," such as "go/come to Jesus" (Jn 5:40, 6:35-37, and so forth), "receive/accept Jesus" (Jn 1:23, 5: 43, 13:20); "follow Jesus" (Jn 1:37f, 4:44, and so forth), "love Jesus" (Jn 8:42, 14:15: 21, 23, 28; 16:27). Believing thus implies both "loving Jesus" and "observing his word." This bond is expressed in Jn 14:15: "If you love me, you will keep my commandments." Believing—

that is, "loving Jesus"—does not remain as a sentiment but requires total adherence to his person that comes about by living faithfully according to his requirements. Believing, then, involves two things that are intimately linked: entering into a deep perichoretic relationship with Christ, and observing his commandments. The first requires the second as a response.

John uses the word "commandments" in the plural without defining or listing them. As with Paul, he does not discuss a catalogue of precepts to be observed, but "the commandments" are the completed expression of the Will of the Father (and of the Son) that must be carried out in the concrete details of life. The "commandments" are God's words oriented completely toward the commandment par excellence, mutual love, a commandment that brings to life, penetrates, and gives direction to the total behavior of believers (see Jn 15:10-12).

Such a connection between "believing" and observing the commandments demonstrates by itself that welcoming God's words is not limited to the initial act of openness to the Gospels through which human beings welcome the Word and adhere to Jesus. It implies a relationship that lasts throughout their existence. And this relationship, in turn, cannot be reduced to the formal observance of a particular number of precepts; but is lived as a perichoretic relationship between the Word that is communicated (in the Gospels) and believers through a process of internalization that the evangelist expresses with formulations like these: "My words abide in you" (Jn 15:7), the word has a "place" in human beings (see Jn 8:37), in particular, "abide in my word/my words abide in you" (Jn 8:31 [KJV]; 15:1ff). "Abiding" or "dwelling" convey the notion of habitation, of permanence, of faithfulness. It is necessary then to persevere in the relationship with Christ created by the Word. Observing his commandments, therefore, is the necessary condition for "abiding in Jesus," for realizing this bond that is so deep that there is a mutual indwelling of Christ and the believer (the other bond, as we shall see, is in the Eucharist: Jn 6:53ff).

Characteristic of John's language in speaking of a deep communion between believers and Jesus is the use of the expression "I in them, they in me." The phraseology of abiding within or mutual indwelling is used often in the allegory of the vine and the branches to express the relationship between the disciples and Jesus. We can note the evangelist's theological consistency. John uses the same phraseology for the relationship of Jesus with the Father and for the relationship between Jesus and the disciples, but never for that between the Father and believers or for the disciples among themselves, not to deny such a relationship, but because it is mediated through Christ.[8] This mediation is the meeting place between the Father and the disciples, as it is among the believers themselves. Jesus is the Mediator in each case. Jesus explains it to Thomas at the Last Supper: the one who sees Christ sees the Father (see Jn 14:5-11).

Because Jesus in his humanity is the Revelation of the Father—that is, the Truth—and he possesses fully the Life of the Father, he is the Way that leads to the Father (see Jn 14:6). Jesus is the one Mediator in a dual sense: as Revelation of the Father and as Way to the Father. Communion with him, then, is fundamental: united to him at the point of receiving his relationship as Son, the disciple becomes one with the Father, as Jesus is, and thus is brought into the life of the Trinity. Believers are "children of God" (Jn 1:12; 11:52; 1 Jn 3:1, 2:10, 5:2); they live out the same relationship that the only-begotten Son sustains with the Father. Obviously, John always safeguards the distinction, as shown by his use of the words *teknon* (solely for the disciples, meaning *child*) and *hyios* (only for Jesus, meaning *son*).

One can see what sort of "divine adventure" comes from observing the commandments, which is to say, living the Word. Believers find themselves in a current of love, something like Jacob's ladder that links heaven and earth. Everything comes from the Father and returns to the Father, mediated by the incarnate Son: "As the Father has loved me, so I have loved you; abide in my love. If you keep my commandments, you will abide in my love, just as I have kept my Father's commandments and abide in his love" (Jn 15:9-10).

The everlasting and generative love of the Father for the Son is poured upon me personally, mediated by the personal love of Jesus for me, to become the source and imperative of love for my neighbor; in turn, it is the condition for abiding in the love of Christ and thus for participating in the love with which the Father loves the Son. Mutual love, the heart of Jesus' commandment, makes the Father's love attain its purpose: the life of unity of the human community in the life of unity among the divine Persons (see 1 Jn 4:11-13; Jn 17).

---

8. Except in 1 Jn 3:24, 4:13-16: "All who obey his commandments abide in him, and he abides in them;" "Those who abide in love abide in God, and God abides in them." These speak of God (not of the Father) perhaps in reference to an indwelling that has already come about. Christ as mediator is implicit.

In the light of the Johannine vision, we can understand how the intense experience of the Word of life called forth in the focolarine a kind of inner theophany: "When one of these Words fell into our soul, it seemed to us that it was transformed into fire, into flames, it was transformed into love. It could be affirmed that our inner life was all love." And so we come back to what, in the New Testament, constitutes the core, the fullness of the commandments: love.

It becomes clear that for John, love could not be reduced to one precept among many others. Love has a divine origin; it is the love of the Father that generates, that transforms disciples into children of God, raises them to the life of God, makes them "be." The first letter of John contains some weighty statements: "God is love, and those who abide in love abide in God, and God abides in them" (1 Jn 4:16). In believers, divine love becomes the source of permanent love toward their brothers and sisters, a love that as a consequence becomes the sign and guarantee of communion with God. "No one has ever seen God; if we love one another, God lives in us, and his love is perfected in us" (1 Jn 4:12f). The sacred author emphasizes anew the tight link between love for God and concrete love for one's brothers and sisters. Genuine Christian mysticism is summed up in these words. To see God directly is not possible on this earth, a certainty often stated in the Bible. Communion with God, however, is possible even now. It is attained not through ascetic practices, but it is God who is self-revealing and reaches us; God comes to live in our midst when we love one another. John remains faithful to the logic of revelation; it is not love among believers that calls forth the presence of God, but mutual love is the proof and the sign that the divine *agape*, which has always dwelt in the church, lies at the source of our love: "Beloved, let us love one another, because love is from God; everyone who loves is born of God and knows God" (1 Jn 4:7).

One cannot affirm more forcefully the kinship that exists between God and those who live the Word. It becomes clear that love for one's brothers and sisters is, so to speak, an imperative of nature, given the "connaturality" with God that we have received. Since they are generated by God, the life of disciples comes from the divine *agape* that makes them "lovers." They love as a personal imperative. Professing to love God without loving one's brothers and sisters is simply a contradiction in nature. In fact, one cannot separate cause and effect; one cannot separate mutual love from its source: divine *agape*. Consequently a "collective" spirituality is not only one possible way among others, but is the true way because it corresponds to a necessity of nature. The "ascent of the mountain," the union with God of classical mysticism, takes place in mutual love—only it is God who descends and dwells among the disciples.

We ought to bear in mind that the love of the Son communicated to believers is not just that of the pre-existent Logos turned toward the bosom of the Father (see Jn 1:1), but a love lived and revealed by Jesus crucified and forsaken. And therefore the Crucified One is the way of the divine *agape* toward human beings, and therefore he is the way to the Father. On the other hand, precisely for this reason, love for one's brothers and sisters has the characteristic of radicality: "We know love by this, that he laid down his life for us—and we ought to lay down our lives for one another" (1 Jn 5:16), as well as the characteristic of concreteness: "Little children, let us love, not in word or speech, but in truth and action" (1 Jn 3:18).

The entire spirituality of John carries a forceful thrust to loving our brothers and sisters, and therefore lies far from an individualistic or sentimentally inward spirituality. Certainly, to live the Word is to obey a word communicated from without; but such openness allows the Spirit to place in the heart love as the fulfillment of the Law. Moreover, such love urges a turn toward the other, brings about an exodus that develops a constantly deepening internalization and a growth toward the Source of love. Having become children of God, believers turn their filial love toward the Father. But on the other hand, they cannot do other than love as does the Father, and, consequently, cannot but love all those whom the Father—in the Son—has generated as children and who thereby are their brothers and sisters: "Everyone who believes that Jesus is the Christ has been born of God, and everyone who loves the parent loves the child" (1 Jn 5:1).

And the Holy Spirit? In John's work too the Spirit's presence is discreet and silent (although certainly not in the life this work gives rise to) because it often is not mentioned explicitly. The Spirit is called the Paraclete in the Farewell Discourses, which emphasize the role of the Spirit in enlightening the disciples after Easter. Given the task to "guide you [the disciples] into all the truth" (Jn 16:13), the Spirit conveys the post-Easter understanding of redemption, of the mystery of Jesus as Son, and therefore of the life of communion between the Father and the Son. This understanding is not only intellectual, but living, putting believers into contact with the richness of life hidden in Christ, a richness that is everything Jesus as Son has received from the Father and that he communicates to the disciples (see

Jn 16:15)—the experience of the Father's generative love lived out in the experience of Jesus' love for his own.

The first letter of John mentions the Holy Spirit in relationship to the indwelling of God in believers who love: "All who obey his commandments abide in him, and he abides in them. And by this we know that he abides in us, by the Spirit that he has given us" (1 Jn 3:24; 4:13). Those who observe God's commandments, and who therefore live the Word that directs of the whole of their existence to the fulfillment of mutual love, live in perfect communion with God. This is not a logical deduction, but an inner certainty that comes from the Holy Spirit.

Revelation, John's writings in particular, discloses the quality of intimacy with God given by living the words of Jesus. The experience of the word of life practiced intensely by the first focolarine can be considered an ideal example because it involves the elements that John emphasizes: opening oneself to the words of Jesus, putting into effect his commandment of mutual love, and the experience of love as a divine experience. The mystical experience of the entrance into the bosom of the Father makes manifest our standing before the Father through Christ in the Holy Spirit. The core of the text concerning the entrance into the bosom of the Father can be read in the words of the "pact" between Chiara and Igino Giordani:

> "On the nothingness of me may you seal a pact of unity with Jesus-Eucharist in Foco's heart. And, Jesus, bring about between us the bond which is known to you." Then I added: "And you, Foco, do the same."

I believe that the request Chiara addresses to Jesus is significant: "you seal a pact of unity" Jesus himself is asked to bring about the unity for which he prayed to the Father. What will follow is, as it were, a tangible experience of what, in fact, unity brings about, the fulfillment of the prayer of unity: being carried within the life of the divine Persons, being able to live in God, in the way God does, the law of the Persons' communal being. On "the nothingness" as the perfect expression of mutual love, Jesus can bring about unity not only between the two, but as a being brought into God, as an entering into that divine space which is the bosom of the Father, where Jesus lives his filial relationship—"I in them and you in me"—making them find their relationship with Jesus in a new way: "I made your name known to them, and I will make it known, so that the love with which you have loved me may be in them, and *I in them*" (Jn 17:26).

The Eucharist

In the passage by Chiara cited above, the founding elements of the entrance into the bosom of the Father come into light immediately, and the first among these is *the Eucharist*. Chiara's mystical experience regularly came about on the basis of this sacrament: a concentrated moment of church, a moment that in itself already says that the gift of God is prior, and it is mediated within the church. This gift is none other than Christ himself at the height of his love (crucified and risen), who makes himself present in the community and in each individual, and present as a gift from the Father to humankind.

In the Eucharist is signified (actualized) the love of the Father for the Son communicated by the Son in the moment of his greatest offering. The Eucharist is a sign that everything comes from God who takes the initiative. And Chiara respects such a priority because she asks Jesus himself to "make a pact of unity," to bring about, therefore, the reality of which the Eucharist is the efficacious sign. The mystical experience that comes from the Eucharist at the same time speaks of the divine origin of such an experience and its presence within the church that makes the Eucharist.

Let us examine more closely the effects of the Eucharist made tangible in the entrance into the bosom of the Father. *The Eucharist is the sacrament that identifies us with Christ.* In John's Gospel, this "being Jesus" is affirmed through the language of mutual indwelling. It appears for the first time in his Gospel precisely at the moment of the discourse on the bread of life and does not appear elsewhere in the first part of the work (chapters 1 – 12). "Those who eat my flesh and drink my blood abide in me, and I in them" (Jn 6:56). Chiara experienced this first effect of the Eucharist and expresses it in these words:

> I was about to pray to Jesus-Eucharist, to say to Him, "Jesus." But I could not. That Jesus, in fact, who was in the tabernacle, was also here in me, was me, too was me, identified with Him. I could not therefore call out to myself.

Chiara was living, therefore, the relationship of identity of the Christian with Christ in a way that could be sensed. The Eucharist brings about, nourishes, and makes grow the baptismal reality. "As many of you as were baptized into Christ have clothed yourselves with Christ" (Gal 3:27). Being clothed in Christ has nothing exterior about it, but signifies being determined entirely by that with which one is clothed. In other words, Jesus communicates what most characterizes him: his filial relationship with the Father.

To make of us true children of God at the same level as the only-begotten Son, God, as Paul says, sent into our hearts "the Spirit of his Son" (Gal 4:4ff). It is not a matter of the Spirit as sent by the Son, but of the Spirit insofar as the Spirit is characteristic of the Son as son, which constitutes the depth of the Son's being. And the presence of the Spirit of the Son deep within the baptized brings about the experience through "connaturality" with the Fatherhood of the Father. "Being Jesus" is the experience of identification with what constitutes the Son as Son turned toward the bosom of the Father (see Jn 1:1). Therefore Chiara continues, "And there I noticed coming spontaneously from my mouth the word: Father."

Chiara, then, also had the experience of distinction from Jesus. The Christ-identity signified by the Eucharist does not, in fact, involve fusion:

> It seemed to me at that point that my religious life . . . should not consist so much in being turned toward Jesus, as in placing myself beside him, our Brother, and turned toward the Father.

In this context, Jesus, "our Brother," does not suggest Jesus' solidarity with the human condition, but the elevation of believers to Jesus' divine filiation, which reaches its fulfillment in the bosom of the Father.

As a Eucharistic gift, therefore, "being Jesus" does not take away a personal relationship with Christ. John's Gospel proceeds in the same direction: "Those who love me will be loved by my Father, and I will love them and reveal myself to them" (Jn 14:21; see also Jn 17:26, and 1 Jn 1:3). Jesus, as Mediator, places the disciples, having become one with him, in direct communion with the Father. But once placed in the bosom of the Father, they also meet Jesus as a distinct You in a personal relationship, experiencing ever more His presence. This staying "at His side, our Brother, turned toward the Father" comprehends the whole of God's plan for humankind. In fact, Chiara suggests that this relationship with Jesus must not be lived out as a devotional concern for self, but as a being sent on mission.

Another characteristic of the Eucharist that comes to light in Chiara's mystical experience is its ecclesial dimension as the sacrament of unity. This is clearly affirmed by Paul writing to the Corinthians:

> The cup of blessing that we bless, is it not a sharing in the blood of Christ? The bread that we break, is it not a sharing in the body

of Christ? Because there is one bread, we who are many are one body, for we all partake of the one bread. (1 Cor 10:16-17)

Here, the apostle begins by emphasizing the communion with Christ effected by the Eucharist. Drinking the Eucharistic wine is having a share in the blood of Christ, that is, having a part in the death of Jesus and in the salvation it brings about. In the same fashion, *koinonia* with Christ's body is entering into communion with the Lord who is present and therefore partaking of the saving actions of the One who died on the cross for his own.

At this point Paul reverses the order of the Last Supper so as to insist upon the unity that such *koinonia* establishes among the participants (v. 17). Receiving the Eucharistic bread that is the body of Christ, the many become One, that is, Christ in His Body. In the Eucharist the apostle sees the everlasting source of *koinonia* among believers, giving it its Christological foundation: communion with the Crucified-Risen One. For Paul, unity conveys the true nature of the church that, as such, is identified with Christ, is the dwelling-place of His presence, prompting the realization in historical time of the eschatological goal already fulfilled in the paschal event: the unity of humanity in God. Here, Chiara experiences the whole of this dimension of the church in its Christ-identity. She explains this further with this affirmation: "We became 'Church' when on the nothingness of ourselves (Jesus Forsaken) two Jesus-Eucharists made a pact of unity."

Before speaking of the Pact itself as a response of love, I would like to point out another characteristic of the Eucharist that comes into effect in Chiara's mystical experience: its *eschatological dimension*. The Eucharist brings participants into Christ crucified-risen, who is the final fullness, the One who brings about universal recapitulation. It roots the church, therefore, although continuing its journey through history, in the eschatological fulfillment of all things. The Christ who makes the many One is present also as the One from whom everything proceeds and to whom everything is directed as its end (see Col 1:15-17). He is present as the Alpha and the Omega of creation and of history. The eschatological dimension of Chiara's mystical experience must also be considered a fruit of the Eucharist: anchored in the final fullness, she ranges across the entire created universe.

Mutual Love

Another foundational element in the text of the entrance into the bosom of the Father is *mutual love*, fruit of the Eucharist and the ideal way of responding to it so as to enjoy its effects. Two things should be taken into consideration: love itself and the communitarian dimension of this love, and this in close relation with the Eucharist. Love is the gift of divine life, and the love of the Father for the Son communicated bestows this love upon his own, open to his Word.[9] Mutual love makes real in actual experience what Christ has already brought about in his gift of himself and is represented in the Eucharist: namely, the gathering into one of the scattered children of God (see Jn 12:51ff), the unity generated by communion in the one Body of Christ that is the church, the perfecting of the *agape* that comes from the Father (see 1 Jn 4:12).

The relationship between the Eucharist and mutual love as the visible expression of the unity represented by the sacrament has been emphasized from the very beginning in the tradition of the church, because it has always been known as constitutive of the church itself. This link is present in Luke's Gospel, which to the institution of the Eucharist adds exhortations to love and to service within the community (see Lk 22:24ff), a theme then expanded upon in the Farewell Discourses in John's Gospel. The link is also present in the common meals that the first century Christian community shared in the context of the Eucharistic celebration, which not accidentally were called *Agape*, just as in the "fraternal kiss" that, in the Mass, precedes Communion. Who does not recall Paul's severe admonition to the Christians of Corinth in this regard? They were taking food and drink just for themselves (see 1 Cor 11:17ff) and so the fraternal meal was doubly scorned. It became a sign of inequality and the poor were offended because of the non-division of goods. They were sinning both against the unity of the church and against fraternal love, a complete contradiction to the meaning of the Eucharist.

The Pact and the Trinity

This link between the Eucharist and mutual love was lived out to the full in the Pact, on the threshold of this mystical experience, the entrance into the bosom of the Father. The Pact did not generate directly a charitable institution, nor did it deepen one particular virtue; but something was lived that

---

9. The Word of the gospel lived out and communicated obviously remained the constant "rock" throughout those months of contemplation, and was not only a preliminary step to the entrance into the bosom of the Father. Chiara recalls this in an unpublished document from 1986: "Three, then, were our communions: that with Jesus-Eucharist, the one with his Word, and the one among us."

is constitutive of the church. The Eucharist gives mutual love its theological-ecclesial value. It does not achieve solely interpersonal harmony in the community, but raises this harmony to be within the divine intimacy, making it the Presence of God. Chiara's mystical experience has made tangible the deepest aspect of faith, which St. Athanasius summed up in these words:

> For since the Word is in the Father, and the Spirit is given from the Word, He wills that we should receive the Spirit, that, when we receive It, thus having the Spirit of the Word which is in the Father, we too may be found on account of the Spirit to become One in the Word, and through Him in the Father.[10]

In the text of the Pact, it is true, Chiara does not speak explicitly of "mutual love," but of *nothingness*; of a "nothingness," however, that expresses the quality of love. As a consequence, it is not about extreme mortification, nor is it an ascetic ideal, nor is it even the effort aimed at putting the ego to death. "Nothingness" characterizes the life of *agape* in its dynamic of not-being/being, where not-being—according to the logic of a "collective" spirituality and not of an individual asceticism—lies in *relationship* (to another) and becomes the space where God is present and can be manifested. It follows Paul's way of thinking: when I am weak, then I am strong; thus in the logic of the paschal reality of being dead together with Christ. A passage from Chiara puts this into evidence:

> The awareness of our nothingness must be infinite so that God may dwell in us. We must have the nothingness of Jesus Forsaken, which is infinite nothingness. So in us will rest the Holy Spirit.

In the logic of a collective spirituality, "being nothing" is inherent in the very act of turning toward and opening oneself to the brother or sister; it is an act of self-dispossession possible for those who know they are accepted totally by God. Chiara's originality, however, does not lie so much in "being nothing" because the dimension of "non-being" is part of the dynamic of every genuine love. Its originality lies in perceiving in this "nothingness" the face of Jesus forsaken, who is its quality and measure: losing God for God. It is therefore a love that rips the temple veil, overcomes the boundary between sacred and profane, gives space to God in the not-God, and therefore corresponds to the most genuine soteriology, as it is for Paul. In Jesus crucified, God saves sinful human beings . . . and opens them to the consequent ethics.

---

10. Athanasius, Discourses Against the Arians, III, 25.

This "being nothing" as the highest expression of love, in turn, is not lived out individually as a private relationship with Jesus-Eucharist, but is realized in reciprocity. Love lived out in this way creates the space where the one Christ can come forth from the two made One. Chiara explains it in these words: "Here nothing, there nothing, then Jesus-Eucharist linking them. What remains? Zero plus zero plus Jesus: Jesus remains."

In the space of mutual nothingness, the Eucharist as effective sign has made explicit its potential as sacrament of unity; it makes actual our being "one in Christ Jesus" (Gal 3:28) in its Christological ("being Jesus") and ecclesial significance (the community as Body of Christ). In this being One, the self receives from Christ its own personality as "new man," through the mediation of the brother or sister; and on the other hand the self is enriched by the wealth of the brother or sister through Christ's mediation.

At this point Chiara is able to give full ecclesial value to the words of Paul: "It is no longer we who live; it is truly Christ who lives in us" (see Gal 2:20), giving to the adverb "truly" the full weight of authenticity and of fulfillment. The "nothingness" of the Pact reveals, in one cell of the church, the church itself in its mystery as Body of Christ, as Spouse of Christ, as Icon of the Trinity, as the fulfillment of creation and of humanity. God now makes visible all of the eschatological greatness of the church—expressed in Marian typology—in the form of mystical experience.

It is true that in the text itself about the Pact, Chiara does not mention the Holy Spirit, but the Spirit is present and at work in this experience, as the God who comes forth in "mutual nothingness." This is evident in a later moment on November 9, 1949, where she mentions how the working of the Holy Spirit was spelled out to her explicitly: "'Why do you not live your Reality, that one I brought about in you through the care given by the divine Spirit in the bosom of the Father? Why do you not live as a daughter of God . . . ?'" The Spirit is manifested as "the Spirit of his Son" (Gal 4: 6) who has brought about filial identification with Jesus; she is daughter in the One who is Son. The Spirit made Chiara experience connaturality with Jesus to the point of no longer being able to speak to him. Hence it is the Holy Spirit who has placed Chiara (that is, the believer) "existentially" into the relationship of the Son with the Father.

On the following day, November 10, the Holy Spirit continued to reveal himself as the source of supernatural "understanding" of communion with God (see 1 Jn 3:24). Chiara writes, "When Jesus came into my nothingness

I clearly heard the voice of the Spirit speaking to my Soul: 'What? I have to seal a pact with myself? *I* am in your nothingness . . .'"

The experience of the Pact is thus an experience of the Holy Spirit. It is fitting that the same Spirit recalls that the Eucharistic Christ's gift is the Holy Spirit who creates and nourishes connaturality with the Risen Lord, so making unity, the link that makes of two, One: Jesus. The mystical experience of the entrance into the bosom of the Father was truly an experience of the Trinity, an experience of entering into the intimacy of the divine Persons.

Part Two

The Pact and Paradise '49

Chapter Five

The Pact

Chiara Lubich

19. We were living these experiences when Foco[1] came to the mountains.

20. Throughout his life Foco, who had a deep love for St Catherine, had sought a virgin he could follow. And now he had the impression of having found her among us. One day, therefore, he suggested something: to make a vow of obedience to me, believing that in doing so he would be obeying God. He added that like this we could become saints as did St Francis de Sales and St Jane de Chantal.

21. I did not understand at that moment either the reason for obedience or this two-person unity. The Movement did not yet exist and there was not much talk among us of vows. And I did not understand a two-person unity because I felt called to live "that they may *all* be one."

22. At the same time, however, it seemed to me that Foco was moved by a grace that ought not be lost.

23. And so I said something like this to him: "It may really be that what you feel comes from God. So we ought to consider it. I, though, don't feel this two-person unity because all should be one."

24. And I added: "You know my life: I am nothing. I want to live, indeed, like Jesus Forsaken, who annihilated himself completely. You too are nothing because you live in the same way.

25. "So then, we will go to church tomorrow and I will say to Jesus-Eucharist who will come into my heart, as into an empty chalice: 'On the nothingness of me may you seal a pact of unity with Jesus-Eucharist in Foco's heart. And, Jesus, bring about between us the bond which is known to you.'" Then I added: "And you, Foco, do the same."

---

1. Foco is Igino Giordani (1894-1980), an Italian intellectual who was a writer, journalist and politician. At that moment he was a member of parliament. (Editorial note)

26. This is what we did, and we stepped out of the church. Foco had to go through the sacristy to give a talk to the friars. I felt urged to go back into church. I entered and went before the tabernacle. And there I was about to pray to Jesus-Eucharist and say to him: "Jesus." But I could not. In fact, that Jesus who was in the tabernacle was also here in me, was me too, was me, identified with him. Therefore I could not call out to myself. And there I felt coming spontaneously from my lips the word: "Father." And in that moment I found myself within the bosom of the Father.

27. From that point it seemed to me that my religious life needed to change from how I had lived it till then. It should not consist so much in being turned toward Jesus, as in placing myself beside him, our Brother, and turned toward the Father.

28. I had, therefore, entered into the Bosom of the Father, which appeared to the eyes of my soul (but it was as if I saw it with my physical eyes) as an abyss that was immense, cosmic. And it was all gold and flames above, below, to the right and to the left.

29. Outside of us remained what is created. We had entered into the Uncreated.

30. I could not distinguish what was in Paradise but that did not disturb me. It was infinite, but I felt at home.

31. I seemed to understand that the one who had put upon my lips the word "Father" was the Holy Spirit. And that Jesus-Eucharist had acted truly as a bond of unity between me and Foco, because upon the two nothings we were, only he remained.

32. Foco, meanwhile, had come out of the friary and I invited him to sit with me on a bench next to a stream. And I said to him: "Do you know where we are?" And I explained to him what had happened to me.

33. Then I went home where I met the focolarine, who I loved so much, and I felt urged to bring them up to date on everything. And so I invited them to come with us to church the next day and to ask Jesus, who entered their hearts, to make the same pact with Jesus who entered ours. And they did so. After that I had the impression of seeing in the Bosom of the Father a small company: it was us. I communicated this to the focolarine who made such a great unity with me that they too had the impression of seeing each thing.

34. In the meantime we did not cease *living*, living with intensity, amid our jobs about the house, the reality that we were, living the Word of Life.

35. Every morning we received Communion, letting Jesus bring about what he desired, while in the evening at six o'clock in church, before the altar of Our Lady, which was to the right of the main altar, we meditated in a rather original fashion. Thinking that Jesus wanted to communicate something of what he had brought about by the new Communion we had received, I invited the focolarine and myself not to think of anything, to nullify every thought so that he could enlighten us.

36. In the fire of the Trinity we had, in fact, been so fused into one that I called our company "Soul." We were the Soul. Now the Lord, if he wished, could enlighten this Soul (through me because I was like its center) about the new realities and so it seemed necessary for us to have the deepest inner silence.

37. Then I communicated what I had understood to Foco and the focolarine. Our communions, therefore, were three: with Jesus-Eucharist, with his Word, and among us.

Day One of the Paradise

38. Before our entrance into Paradise we always spoke of the rays of the sun and we felt that each of us should walk along the ray of the divine will that lay before us, different for everyone and yet one, like the substance of the sun is one in the multiplicity of its rays.

39. And each of us felt his or her self clothed in light, the light of the ray, clothed in that one divine will that made us another Jesus.

40. We were Chiara-Jesus, Grazia-Jesus, Giosi-Jesus, and so on.

41. But when two of us, knowing ourselves to be nothing, prompted Jesus-Eucharist to seal a pact of *unity* upon our two souls, I became aware that I was Jesus. I felt the impossibility of communicating with Jesus in the tabernacle. I experienced the elation of being at the peak of the pyramid of all creation, as on the point of a pin; at the point where the two rays meet, where the two who are God (so to speak) seal a pact of unity, becoming trinitized where, having been made Son in the Son, it is impossible to communicate with anyone except the *Father*, just as the Son communicates with him alone.

42. It is the point where the created dies into the Uncreated, where nothingness is lost in the Bosom of the Father, where the Spirit pronounces with our lips: Abba-Father.

Chapter Six

Going from the Pact to the Soul: Exploring a Metaphysical Journey

Anna Pelli

The account of the pact of unity between Chiara Lubich and Igino Giordani—a pact that is the prelude to the whole of Chiara's mystical experience during the summer of 1949 and that began with the entrance into the Bosom of the Father[1]—closes with a sober and meaningful hint of the reality that the pact was about to produce. "In the fire of the Trinity," writes Chiara, "we had been, in fact, so fused into one that I called our company 'Soul.' We were the Soul." It was a unique and unrepeatable mystical event, something truly new in the history of spirituality, and Chiara immediately put it in common with those who shared her spiritual path. This gave shape to a new subject: the Soul.[2] It was a subject that, bit by bit, took form, not as a kind of entity with clear edges, nor as a simple, single center, but as an infinite process of becoming one. From the source of the mystery of God, this subject drew triune Love, which gave it dynamism and life and was the key to its interpretation. Thus the Soul was an encounter, a relationship perpetually bringing it into being.

The Soul, then, as that "relationship among us," that "space"[3] where we are at once drawn together and opened out in distinction, is the multipli-

---

1. The event, which took place on July 16, 1949, was proclaimed by Chiara Lubich on April 8, 1986 as the premise of the entire text of Paradise '49. A careful study of the event can be found in *Il Patto del '49 nell'esperienza di Chiara Lubich: Percorsi interdisciplinari* (Rome: Città Nuova, 2012).
2. Two studies, one of philosophical anthropology and the other sociological, explore the fundamental characteristics of the new subject. They are in the volume cited earlier, *Il Patto del '49 nell'esperienza di Chiara Lubich*: Jesús Moran's "Il Patto di unità e il 'riceversi' come esistenziale: Un'icona tra fenomenologia e antropologia," and Vera Araujo's "Un inedito legame sociale."
3. It is significant that Chiara, commenting on the passage cited above, speaks of the mystical event having taken place not only as a "being the Soul" but as a "living in the Soul," alluding implicitly therefore to a "spatiality" where such an event can continue to happen.

cation of the one in the many and the unification of the many in the one.[4] This particular way of existing together, still more, of belonging to one another in the merging of the many (the company) in unity (the Soul), allows, significantly, the penetration of what is perhaps the most challenging question of philosophy, one that to human reason seems to face the ultimate metaphysical depths. This is the question of the relationship between the One and the many and, as a consequence, of the relationship between the infinite and finite, between the universal and the particular.

The long history of Western thought could be seen as a constant effort to work out the thorny problem of the reciprocal relationship between these two terms: unity and multiplicity. Sometimes they have been thought of as so divergent as to be irreconcilable and sometimes, through being given excessive value, one has prevailed over the other with obvious existential, historico-political and cultural repercussions. This story, articulated around the issue of the One and the many, has been decisive for the Western soul, to the extent that Hegel claimed "all of philosophy is nothing other than the study of the meanings of unity," or, more precisely, it is nothing other than "determining in different ways the relationship between unity (understood as Principle) and multiplicity." What is determined, in the view of one contemporary scholar, gives "a common metaphysical basis to the different forms of philosophy."[5]

Many have grappled with the vastness of the One: mystics full of wonder and philosophers in the vigor of their thought. These have included figures such as Plotinus and, later, Meister Eckhart and Jakob Böhme, Nicholas of Cusa and Leibniz, Schelling and Hegel. Each one glimpsed in his own way that unity is, in essence, a marvelous interweaving of relationships and so, as it were, inhabited by multiplicity.[6] We can now begin to explore this story of centuries and indicate some of its most significant moments. We will see

---

4. Thus the author offers an important gloss on the passage cited above: "The term 'company' expresses more multiplicity, the term 'Soul' more unity. There were several of us there, but we were one. Distinctly then each one of us was the Soul."

5. Walter Beierwaltes, "Unità e identità come cammino del pensiero," in *L'Uno e i molti*, ed., Virgilio Melchiorre (Milan: Vita e Pensiero, 1990), 31-32. When titles of works are cited in Italian, all translations are the work of the editors.

6. Hegel's affirmation in his *Einleitung in die geschichte der philosophie* (Hamburg: Felix Meiner, 1959) can speak for all of them, "We are no longer atomists; the atomistic principle has been refuted. Certainly the spirit is also a One, but no longer is it the One in abstract terms. The simple One is a concept and definition of the spirit that is too poor to draw out all that it is" (128). Cited in *L'Uno e i molti*, 419.

emerge an approach to the fundamental and creative nucleus of the one in the many and the many in the one.

An Outline of the Question of the One and the Many: The One as Structurally Multiple Origin . . . . "and from all things One and from One all things."[7]

The question of the relationship of the One and the many emerges in a significant fashion at the very beginning of philosophical thought. Thinking about the origins of things, the first philosophers began to discover the notion of a *first principle*, pictured as the root of all things from with they are derived and to which they tend. As a fragment from Anaximander says: "The principle . . . encompass[es] all and steer[s] all."[8] These were the first outlines of a vision of the real as the unity of all, sustained by a law that gives order to the many, the multitude of things, and forms reality as a structure of universal connectedness. "It is wise for those who hear, not me but the universal Reason," states Heraclitus, "to confess that all things are one."[9] And it is in looking at this all-one that the penetrating gaze of Heraclitus discerns the intimate relationship of unity and multiplicity not as a simple movement of one thing deriving from another, but as their mutual implication and connection to one another. As a marvelous fragment affirms, "There is one wisdom, to understand the intelligent will by which all things are governed through all."[10]

There thus began to take form the concept of the One as ungenerated and indestructible *Origin*, infinite and unlimited, immutable and immobile, and yet, in itself, *structurally multiple*, as demonstrated later by Anaxagoras and Empedocles, precisely because it is capable of generating the multiplicity of things and hence to justify the infinite differences present in the universe. Obviously, in considering the multiple that is constitutive of the One, these philosophers were not referring to empirical multiplicity, known through the senses, but to a universal capable of containing in itself and of giving meaning to all particular things, unifying them, hence to a further multiplicity that in itself is undifferentiated and imperceptible, and

---

7. Heraclitus, *Fragment* 22 B 10.
8. Ananximander, *Fragment* 12 A 15.
9. Heraclitus, *Fragment* 22 B 50.
10. Heraclitus, *Fragment* 22 B 50.

which nonetheless is the basis and *raison d'être* of the very multiplicity of phenomena, in their qualitative differences.

Indeed, from the perspective of various Greek thinkers, the multiplicity of things is explained as the result of the refraction of the *One-Being* into an infinite number of one-beings, that is, of single beings, seeking to maintain as much as possible the characteristics of the One-Being. In a well-known fragment, Melissus of Samos says, "If there were many things they would have to be such as I say the one is."[11] Leucippus, turning upside down Melissus's attempt to reduce *ad absurdum* the pluralism commonly believed in, responded that in reality the many exist because they can be as the One, and hence are eternal and immutable. And therein lies the value of each of them. Nevertheless, in the context of the philosophy of origins, it is not the value of single things that is dominant so much as the absolute affirmation of the value of the One, since true multiplicity is that which is comprehended within the One, or, in other words, true multiplicity is the first Principle insofar as it is equivalent to the One.

Plato and the Concept of the One as that which is above Being. . . . "These problems of the one and the many . . . that cause real difficulties if ill decided, and the right determination of them is very helpful."[12]

In a similar fashion, but with much greater theoretical depth, Plato makes the question of the One and the many the axis of his thought. The point of departure is his well-known theory of the Ideas, which marks a turning point in the history of Western thought because it opens it up to that which is beyond the senses, discovered to be a new dimension of being, one where the truth of things resides.[13] Indeed if things are many, the Idea—of Beauty,

---

11. Melissus of Samos: *Fragment* 6.
12. Plato, *Philebus*, 15c.
13. Hegel does not hesitate to affirm that Plato's "true speculative greatness" lies in his teaching about the Ideas "thanks to which he marks a milestone in the history of philosophy and therefore in the general history of thought" (*Lezioni sulla Storia della Filosofia*, vol. 2 [Florence: La Nuova Italia, 1932], 209). It can be seen to be so because this teaching has given rise to the greatest number of theoretical revisions, to such an extent that it could be said that a history of its interpretation "would cover a huge area of the history of Western philosophy in one of its key points" (Giovanni Reale, *Per una nuova interpretazione di Platone: Rilettura della metafisica dei grandi dialoghi alla luce delle "dottrine non scritte"* [Milan: Vita e Pensiero, 1997], 161).

Goodness, and Greatness—is only one, inasmuch as it unifies the multiplicity by reducing it, so to speak, to its true being. It is, according to Plato's rich intuition, a unified multiplicity. And it is, as Aristotle was to say later, "the one which is absolutely many."[14]

But Plato's metaphysical penetration goes further. The Ideas themselves are, in fact, many. Therefore in order to overcome this further multiplicity, also manifest at the level of the intelligible, it is necessary to reach another level, to proceed to a further unification, to go to the sphere that is supreme and primary in an absolute sense and which can give an account of the multiplicity of the Ideas and provide the ultimate explanation for the totality of things that exist. Plato thus arrives at identifying the sphere of the first Principles that are the *Supreme One* and the *indeterminate Dyad* or *Duality of the small and great*. Like this he gives a reason for multiplicity by using a bipolar metaphysical scheme, inasmuch as each Principle structurally calls for the other.[15]

Indeed, if the One is the Principle of being as such and therefore absolutely without multiplicity, indeterminate Duality is the Principle and root of the multiplicity of beings. And, as such, it is conceived to be a Duality of the small and great, in the sense that it is *infinite smallness and infinite greatness, the tendency to infinite smallness and to infinite greatness*. It is a kind of "intelligible matter," of indeterminate multiplicity, which, acting as a substratum beneath the action of the One, produces the multiplicity of things in all its forms. And these, participating in the original One, bring about value and beauty, order and harmony—that harmony which is unity in multiplicity.

---

14. Aristotle, *Metaphysics,* Book XIV, Part 1.
15. "The polar form of thought sees, conceives, models, and organizes the world, as a unity, in pairs of opposites. They are the form in which the world presents itself to the Greek spirit, in which it transforms and conceives the multiplicity of the world in patterns of order and as patterns of order. These pairs of opposites in polar thought are fundamentally different from the pairs of opposites in monist or dualistic thought, in the context of which they exclude each other, or, in struggling with each other, are destroyed, or, finally, are reconciled and cease to exist as opposites.... Instead in polar thought not only are the opposites in a pair indissolubly bound, as the poles of the axes in a sphere, but they, in the innermost logic of their existence, precisely because they are polar, are conditioned to exist in opposition: losing the opposite pole, they would lose their meaning" (Paula Philippson, *Origini e forme del mito greco* [Turin: Boringhieri, 1983], 65-66).

It follows from this that the two Principles are not in themselves being, but, insofar as they are constitutive of every being, they are *prior* to being, so that the One, as a principle of determination, is *above* being—the "Nothingness of all" as Proclus was to call it—while the indeterminate material principle, as non-being, is *below* being.[16] It is at this level that, for Plato, the concept of the *One* takes on the features of the *Good*, so much so that it can be said that the highest measure of every form of multiplicity, which is precisely the One, constitutes the very essence of the Good. From a Platonic perspective, indeed, the greatest good is "that which binds and makes one," while the worst evil is that which divides and produces disintegrative multiplicity.

This produces a clear notion of human nature: the perfect person is one who harmonizes his or her various faculties so as to become "one out of many," so that "wisdom and understanding consist in making unity out of the multiplicity that lies within" and, as a consequence, of that which lies outside as well. A human being, therefore, is called to introduce into human society a network of harmonious relationships, which means bringing order to disorder, proportion to excess, unity to multiplicity, "assimilating" them in this way, as much as possible, to the Good, the One, the Divine. For, Plato affirms, it is God who "possesses the knowledge and power needed to combine many things into one and again dissolve the one into many. But no human being could possess either of these in the present or the future."[17] Nevertheless, he adds, "and if I believe that someone is able to discern a one that is by nature also many, I will follow behind him, and walk in his footsteps as if he were a god."[18]

Thus, in this surprising trust in the "knowledge" and "power" of God, Plato gives a glimpse of the final form of the solution to the problem of the relationship between the One and the many. And understanding what this means is, for him, to arrive after a long journey at that place where "for these paths lead at last to that place that is our final rest."[19] It is a place that, in Plotinus' reworking of the same themes, would take the form of a unity that, risking itself, shows itself to be an intense, relational web, so much so that it seems that, if it is impossible to see the One, it is also impossible to see without the One. Plotinus writes, "There everything is transparent,

---

16. See Giovanni Reale, *Per una nuova interpretazione di Platone* (Rome: Center for Metaphysical Research, 1987), 214-227; 265-280; 341-388.
17. Plato, *Timaeus*, 68d.
18. Plato, *Phaedrus*, 266b.
19. Plato, *Republic*, 532d-e.

nothing is dark and impenetrable, everyone everywhere is manifest in depth to everyone, because the light is manifest to the light. And indeed everyone bears all in self and every other sees all. Hence each thing is everywhere, each thing is all and each one is all and the splendor is infinite."[20] Charting this unfolding of the One into the many, Plotinus suggests the fundamental features of a metaphysics that was to be decisive for subsequent reflection within Christianity. These features would emerge always more clearly as an echo of the trinitarian unity, of the self-disclosure of the divine Being in its threefold Persons which will give rise, in the way of absolute otherness, to the most intense form of unity.

Nicholas of Cusa and the Philosophy of Unity as the Unity of Unity and Multiplicity. . . . "If you have [mentally] removed all other things and behold oneness alone, you understand that oneness never was anything else or never is anything else or never can be made to be anything else, and if you [mentally] remove all plurality and every respect and enter only into most simple oneness . . . then you will have penetrated all things secret."[21]

Nicholas of Cusa, one of the most important contributors to Humanism and the Renaissance, should be acknowledged as starting a philosophy of unity understood as "the unity of unity and multiplicity." [22] This philosophy of unity refers explicitly to the image of the One who is God recognized as Absolute Being transcending all beings, as the absolute reflection upon itself within the Trinitarian process—a process which, giving itself and manifesting itself in the creation of the world, makes the world its theophany.

At the same time, Nicholas's philosophy could be called a philosophy of the Infinite which, in its absoluteness and otherness, cannot be grasped by human reason. For reason proceeds by finite definitions based on the criterion of proportionality, which allows it to determine, for example, that one thing is greater or smaller than another. But the Infinite, by its very nature, cannot be captured by any proposition and thus remains unknown.

---

20. Plotinus, *Enneads*, V, 8, 4.
21. Nicholas of Cusa, *De Coniecturis* I, 5, 18.
22. Kurt Flasch, *Die Metaphysik des einen bei Nikolaus von Kues* (Leiden: E.J. Brill, 1973), 254-255. See also Aldo Bonetti, "La filosofia dell'unità nel pensiero di Nicolò Cusano," in *L'Uno e i molti*, 283-318; Ernst Cassirer, *Storia della filosofia moderna*, vol. 1 (Milan: Mondadori, 1968), 39-96.

Nevertheless, the very thing the human mind seeks is the knowledge of the Infinite, since the mind is itself a participation in the Infinite: it is a finite reality that subsists as otherness in the act of the Infinite. And this allows it to cast its gaze always more deeply into the unattainable infinity of the true.

How does the Infinite manifest itself to this gaze? Nicholas's reply is unequivocal: in its most proper meaning, the Infinite is *Absolute Unity*, without any limits or distinctions, and hence it is "absolutely simple," so much so that the opposites of maximum and minimum are the same thing. Let's consider, for instance, a maximum quantity and a minimum quantity. If our minds abstract themselves from the notion of quantity, that if we set aside the great and small, what remains is the coincidence of the maximum and the minimum, "for maximum is a superlative just as minimum is a superlative."[23] Therefore, Nicholas writes, "it is not the case that absolute quantity is maximum quantity rather than minimum quantity; for in it the minimum is the maximum coincidingly."[24]

In this sense, the Absolute Maximum, which is God, "is beyond both all affirmation and all negation. . . . [I]t is a given thing in such way that it is all things; and it is all things in such way that it is no thing; and it is maximally a given thing in such way that it is it minimally. . . . For Absolute Maximality could not be actually all possible things unless it were infinite and were the boundary of all things and were unable to be bounded by any of these things."[25] As a result of its maximality, the Maximum is thus, for Nicholas, the *coincidentia oppositorum*, the coinciding of the minimum with the maximum: "Therefore, we see incomprehensibly, beyond all rational inference, that Absolute Maximality (*to which nothing is opposed and with which the Minimum coincides*) is infinite."[26]

This "coinciding" results in a vision of transcendence that is not opposed to immanence, but contains it and raises it to an extraordinary intensity.[27] We can glimpse here a new avenue of research to express the fundamental metaphysical relationship between the One and the many, between the

---

23. Nicholas of Cusa, *De docta ignorantia* I, 4,11.
24. Nicholas of Cusa, *De docta ignorantia* I, 4,11.
25. Nicholas of Cusa, *De docta ignorantia* I, 4, ,12.
26. Nicholas of Cusa, *De docta ignorantia* I, 4,12 (editor's italics).
27. There are well-known examples of the coincidence of opposites in the infinite (the point and the line, the circle and the straight line) which Nicholas uses when drawing on geometry. Indeed he understood mathematics "as an eminently speculative science, able to supply effective symbols to represent the deepest core of reality." See

absolutely simple and the complexity of the multiple. It is a question of studying and focusing upon the One in its unfolding within the world of plurality, while remaining distinct in a dimension that does not participate in this variation, but that precedes it and makes it possible.

With this intention Nicholas developed his thought regarding the genesis of the multiple from the One and its subsistence within it, in the light of three key concepts, in which it is possible to recognize a kind of Trinitarian rhythm, a reflection of the eternal divine intra-trinitarian relationship.[28] His argument goes thus: inasmuch as God is the Maximum of all maximums, all things are contained in God. It can be said that God, in God's identity and simplicity, includes them, *makes them complex*, in such a way that all things, in their necessity and truth, are God, are God in God. But God is also the *explication* of all things, in the sense that the divine identity is unfolded in diversity, God's unity in divisibility. God is the eternal living seed that stretches out to compose itself in a multiplicity of forms. Giving origin thus to the multiplicity of the finite, in all things God is what they are, although remaining absolutely beyond them in God's unmultipliable unity.

Derived from this is the third key concept: that of *contraction*. God is "contracted" in the universe, as unity is "contracted" in plurality, the simple in the composite, stillness in movement, eternity in temporal succession, and so on. God, who is the absolute essence of the world, is "contracted" in the world seen in its unity, and the universe, understood as the contracted essence of things, is determined, that is, is "contracted," in the multiplicity of things. Each being is thus the "contraction" of the universe, as, in its turn, the universe is the "contraction" of God. This means that each being sums up the whole of the universe and God. The whole universe, therefore, is sun in the sun, moon in the moon, flower in the flower, wind in the wind, water in water. "It follows," Nicholas says echoing the ancient maxim of Anaxagoras,[29] "that *all* is *in all* and each in each."[30] "[I]n each created thing the

---

Ludovico Geymonat, *Storia del pensiero filosofico e scientifico*, vol. 2 (Milan: Garzanti, 1970), 38.

28. See Nicholas of Cusa, *De docta ignorantia* I, 9,24 to I, 10, 29.
29. Anaxagoras, in fact, should be credited with having introduced the important idea of the mutual containing of things and of a mutual influence among the parts: "All things are in everything" and "all things have a portion of everything" (*Fragment*, 59 B 4; B 11).
30. Nicholas of Cusa, *De docta ignorantia* II, 5,117.

universe is this created thing; and each thing receives all things in such way that in a given thing all things are, contractedly, this thing."[31]

Now, since the universe is contracted in each actually existing thing:

> [I]t is evident that God, who is in the universe, is in each thing and that each actually existing thing is immediately in God, as is also the universe. Therefore, to say that each thing is in each thing is not other than [to say] that through all things God is in all things and that through all things all things are in God.[32]

If therefore God is the *unitas absoluta* who precedes and conditions the multiplicity of being, any inquiry into reality can be undertaken only in the light of the divine unity, since any reality is only conceivable or thinkable as existing in its relation to the divine unity.

Alternatively, the *unitas absoluta*, in which every multiplicity subsists, has no need to be demonstrated, since it is the foundation of every reality and fundamental to its knowability. From this it follows that, if the *unitas absoluta* precedes every opposition, it would be more accurate to deny the opposites in it rather than regard it as the coincidence of opposites. Nicholas therefore defines absolute being as *non aliud*, "not other," meaning, on the one hand, that the absolute is not separated and divided from what is empirically observable, from which it constitutes immanent being and, on the other hand, that, insofar as it is the supreme unity, it cannot be understood and determined as "this" or "that," like an individual thing. God "[i]n all things . . . is all things, and in nothing He is nothing"[33] is the unequivocal antinomy that concludes Nicholas's metaphysics.

Therefore, the metaphysics of unity he proposes, placing the need for a rigorous distinction between the absolute unity of the One and the unity of the multiplicity which is proper to the sphere of being, brings as a consequence the abandonment of the notion of God as *coincidentia oppositorum* so as to achieve, in its final outcome, a notion of Unity as that which lies beyond not only multiplicity and its opposite, but the very coincidence of opposites. As such, God is not "the foundation of contradiction" but is "Simplicity, which is prior to every foundation."[34] God is that ineffable unity which lies "above

---

31. Nicholas of Cusa, *De docta ignorantia* II, 5,117
32. Nicholas of Cusa, *De docta ignorantia* II, 5, 118.
33. Nicholas of Cusa, *De li non aliud*, 14,65.
34. Nicholas of Cusa, *De deo abscondito*, 10.

nothing and something,"³⁵ where, since every opposition is eliminated, also the dialectic of being and non-being loses any force.

In this way, Nicholas's solution resolves the question of the relationship between unity and multiplicity by privileging oneness. It restores, certainly more than he intended, a renewed form of abstract unity, which, on closer inspection, does not allow the many, the different, to stand out in its specific identity, albeit in the context of a unitary Principle. Therefore, in the end, in all its elevated and lucid speculation, the *coincidentia oppositorum* remains a pointer to a place where the opposites, in the words of Beierwaltes, "do not coexist... but are overcome." It is a place dominated by "absolute difference without difference."³⁶

Leibniz and the Universe as "Infinity of Infinities"...."The universe in some way multiplies itself as many times as there are substances, and in the same way the glory of God is magnified by so many quite different representations of his work."³⁷

About two centuries later, another German philosopher, Gottfried Wilhelm Leibniz, addressed with particular speculative skill the relationship of the infinite and the finite, of unity and multiplicity, beginning, however, not from a Platonic metaphysical One, nor from a *unitas divina* as did Nicholas of Cusa, but from the multidimensional nature of the real in which he sees an infinite perspective, through which everything, according to different viewpoints, can be perceived more clearly. Leibniz thus reaches a notion where the world, in the words of Ludwig Feuerbach, looks like "crystal that refracts the light (of divinity) into a rich spectrum of infinite colors."³⁸

Leibniz's thought is that reality is constituted in its multiple aspects and in its ultimate foundations by original principles of force, indivisible and therefore simple (the "substances" of classical metaphysics). He uses the term *monad* (from the Greek *monas*, "unity") to designate them.³⁹ A monad,

---

35. Nicholas of Cusa, *De deo abscondito*, 9.
36. Walter Beierwaltes, *Identità e differenza* (Milan: Vita e Pensiero, 1989), 152.
37. G. W. Leibniz, *Discourse on Metaphysics*, 9.
38. Giovanni Reale and Dario Antiseri, *Il pensiero occidentale dalle origini ad oggi*, vol. 2 (Brescia: La Scuola, 1989), 289.
39. Leibniz, *La Monadologie* I, 1-3 (Brescia: La Scuola, 1938), 38. This term, which originates in Neoplatonism, was later revived by Giordano Bruno. It was also used by the Dutch natural philosopher Franciscus Mercurius van Helmont, who Leibniz

then, is a substance or a substantial form (an Aristotelian *entelechy* as Leibniz himself called it),[40] a center of original force, of metaphysical order, which has in itself its own determination and essential perfection, and together, its own inner finality. Everything that exists, Leibniz maintains, is either a simple monad or a complex of monads. Consequently they constitute the "elements of all things," such that by coming to know the nature of the monad, we come to know also the nature of all reality.

What, then, it the nature of a monad? Leibniz's reply is highly significant: "The simplicity of a substance does not exclude the multiplicity of modifications that must be found together in that same simple substance, and that must be composed of the variety of relations with external things. Thus in a center or a point, although simple, there is found an infinite number of angles, formed by the lines that intersect there."[41] Every monad, consequently, can be conceived as *expressio multorum in uno*, the expression of a multiplicity in unity, in that all others converge in it, which it therefore represents. Every monad is a point of view upon the world and is therefore *all* the world from a specific point of view, such that each becomes the expression of the whole, of the totality.[42]

It could be said that from the perspective of its conceptual structure such a teaching, where every monad represents all the others, is a variant of what the Greeks called "the conspiring of all things among them," which the Renaissance thinkers saw as *omnia ubique*, that is, the presence and echo of all things in all. But in his re-reading of this, Leibniz introduces a new and significant perspective. The presence of "all in all" is not only one of the basic points of his metaphysics, but it is also the key to unlocking his thought and to overcoming its apparently contradictory nature. As he says, "every substance exactly ex-

---

      knew personally and from whom he borrowed it. *Monadology* sets forth Leibniz's basic concepts, centered on the themes of unity, individuality and the uniqueness of each entity its relationship with the universe and with the original unity. Christian Woolf considered this metaphysical text the point of departure for eighteenth century German scholasticism.

40. Leibniz, *La Monadologie*, 18.
41. Reale and Antiseri, *Il pensiero occidentale*, 340.
42. "And just as the same city looked at from different sides appears completely different, and thus appears multiplied by perspective, so it is that the infinite multitude of simple substances create the appearance of many different universes, which nevertheless are only perspectives on a single universe, according to the points of view which differ in each monad." (G. W. Leibniz, *Monadology*, 57)

presses all others through the relations it has with them,"[43] so that "each created monad represents the whole universe,"[44] which in this way manifests itself, in its infinite richness, as an "infinity of infinities." "The wonderful thing is that sovereign wisdom has found the means, via representative substances, of varying the world itself and of doing so in infinite ways. The world, already having an infinite variety in itself, and being varied and expressed diversely in an infinity of different representations, receives an infinity of infinities."[45]

A passage from *Discourse on Metaphysics* explains this notion clearly:

> Every substance is like a complete world, and like a mirror of God, or of the whole universe, which each one expresses in its own way—rather like the same city looks different due to the positions from which it is viewed. The universe is multiplied as many times as there are substances, and in the same way the glory of God is multiplied by as many quite different representations of his work.[46]

In other words, every monad represents the world from a different perspective and it is precisely this perspective that makes each monad different from all the others. Each perspective, therefore, possesses its own essential importance, which is revealed however in a relative manner. Because of this it refers intrinsically to another—that of God—which is superior to it and resolves it in itself. The passage cited above continues:

> It can even be said that each substance bears in some way the character of God's infinite wisdom and omnipotence, and imitates him as much as it is capable. For it expresses, though confusedly, everything that happens in the universe—past, present, or future—this resembles in some way an infinite perception or knowledge. And as all the other substances express this substance and accommodate themselves to it—that is, they are as they are *because* it is as it is—it can be said to extend its power over all the others, in imitation of the creator's omnipotence.[47]

It follows from this that the complex content of reality is revealed only through the totality of perspectives. Only in the interconnectedness and

---

43. Leibniz, *Monadology*, 59.
44. Leibniz, *Monadology*, 62.
45. Reale and Antiseri, *Il pensiero occidentale*, 343.
46. Leibniz, *Discourse on Metaphysics*, 9.
47. Leibniz, *Discourse on Metaphysics*, 9.

stratification of perspectives does being acquire ever-richer content. This vision is reflected, for Leibniz, in the constitution of corporeality. For him everything is alive because each monad is alive. Moreover, since every aggregate is made up of innumerable monads, it is possible to imagine in each of them a series of ever smaller aggregates, which infinitesimally reproduce the same characteristics, in a kind of fugue to infinity of increasing smallness. As we read in an emblematic passage of *Monadology*:

> Each portion of matter can be conceived as a garden full of plants or a pond full of fish. But each branch of the plant, each limb of an animal, each drop of its humors, is also such a garden or such a pond.[48]

This principle is one that, in Leibniz's hermeneutic revival, expands to include the chronological succession of the multiplicity of events. In fact if every monad is a "perpetual living mirror of the universe,"[49] it is also of all the events of the universe, so that in the smallest monad (such as in the soul of each of them) we can perceive all that has happened, that happens and that will happen, that which is distant in time and space, and so the whole of history, the entire "connection" of the universe.[50] Leibniz can say therefore, in a deeply attractive expression, that "the present is pregnant with what is to come," meaning that in each instant the totality of time and of temporal events is present, just as in each substance the totality is present: "the present is pregnant with the future."[51]

This interrelationship of substances and things gives the entire universe a tone of harmony. Given that Leibniz emblematically defines substances or

---

48. Leibniz, *Monadology*, 67.
49. Leibniz, *Monadology*, 56.
50. Leibniz, *Monadology*, 61-62. With far-sighted intuition, which distances him decisively from his rationalist predecessors, Decartes and Spinoza, and makes him the harbinger of the coming Kantian revolution, Leibniz comes to a conception of space and time not as independent substances subsisting in themselves, but as ideal orderings of phenomena resolved in the "truth of relations." Therefore they too are part of the phenomenal order, but of the *phaenomenon bene fundatum*, since they are based on the effective relations among things (space) and upon the effective succession of things (time), presupposing therefore the existence of other realities. As he writes with great insight, "Space is the order that makes it possible to situate bodies, and by which they, existing together, have a position relative to each other. In a similar way, time is an analogous order, in relation to the position of things in their succession. But if creatures did not exist, space and time would not be among God's ideas." (Reale and Antiseri, *Il pensiero occidentale*, 338)
51. Leibniz, *Principles of Nature and Grace Based on Reason*, 13.

monads as having "no windows, through which anything could come in or out,"[52] which indicates that each one of them "is like a separate world, independent of all other thing, except for God,"[53] it also true that he conceives of substances as structured in such a way that each of them is in perfect correspondence and harmony with each of the others, since what each of them draws from within itself coincides with what each other, in perfect correspondence, draws from what is within itself. Nor is this all. Harmony also means agreement among the different and mutually conditioned perspectives by which reality can be represented and clarified.

This is what Leibniz calls "my system of *pre-established harmony*,"[54] which is "the most exalted and most divine among the works of God."[55] It is what the Creator has established. God, then, is the true bond of communication among the substances and it is through him that the phenomena of one monad are in harmony with one another.[56] "*Harmonia universalis, id est Deus*," Leibniz affirms, recognizing God as the foundation and, the same time, the point of view of his own metaphysical vision.[57]

Chiara Lubich and the Trinitization of Love. . . . "It happens as in those mirrors that, facing one another, project images of each other infinitely and are re-contained in each other through the returning reflection."[58]

The intuition of the One as structurally multiple Origin, the highest measure of every form of multiplicity; the notion of the One as the coincidence of maximum and minimum, as the unity of unity and multiplicity; the vision of the One as that which makes it possible to understand the inner affinity placing the many in mutual relationship, giving life and connection to the real as the "infinity of infinities": these are a few of the notable theoretical advances that we have seen punctuate the progress of philosophical

---

52. Leibniz, *Monadology*, 7.
53. Leibniz, *Discourse on Metaphysics*, 14.
54. Leibniz, *Monadology*, 80.
55. Leibniz, *Monadology*, 86.
56. Leibniz, *Discourse on Metaphysics*, 32.
57. For further discussion see Emerich Coreth, *Dio nel pensiero filosofico* (Brescia: Queriniana, 2004), 218-229.
58. Chiara Lubich, unpublished passage, September 8, 1949.

thought about the metaphysical problem of the relationship between the One and the many.

Chiara Lubich's thought is located within this progress with its moments of darkness and its abundant light. She looks at the question of the One and the many from a perspective that, while it presupposes and values what has gone before, displays something truly new because it finds its focal point in a "principle that is unifying, and therefore active," which is "love."[59] Such love does not overcome the One-many duality by canceling it out. Rather this love interiorizes the duality by including it in itself and, in the process, it becomes the metaphysical key for an explanation of the origin and structure of the multiple.[60]

While it is indeed true that love is absolute "simplicity,"[61] it is equally true that love does not consider what is distinct as foreign to itself because it treasures that distinction in its inner self as the immanent secret of its life. It is precisely the nature of love to create space in itself for that which is other than self, so much so that it can be said that real diversity, real plurality is intrinsically part of love. This can be seen in the following passage from Chiara in which, going into that "unoriginated origin of love"[62] which is the inner self of the triune God, we see coming together the apparently irreconcilable extremes of unity and multiplicity: "The Father says 'Love' in infinite tones and generates the Word, who is love, within Himself, the Son, and the Son as Son, who is echo of the Father, says 'Love' and returns to the Father!"[63]

In this light, love is manifested as something that can explain the contraposition of categories because the *one* Word-Love (i.e., "God in the infinitely small") treasuring within himself infinite richness (i.e., "the infinitely Great") can be uttered in "infinite tones" and so summon into existence the *many*. An examination of this kind, from the point of view of metaphysics,

---

59. Lubich, "Gesù in mezzo a noi. Rendere visibile la presenza del Risorto nella Chiesa," *Nuova Umanità* 27 (2005): 414.
60. For an earlier reflection on love's semantic depths, see my article, "'Solo l'amore è': Alcuni tratti sull'essere come amore negli scritti di Chiara Lubich," in *L'essere come amore:Percorsi di ricerca*, Anna Pelli, ed. (Rome: Città Nuova, 2010), 91-115.
61. I interpret the meaning of absolute simplicity, which Chiara Lubich relates explicitly to love, as the absence of complexity. See Gérard Rossé, "Aspetti dell'etica cristiana nella luce dell'ideale dell'unità," *Nuova Umanità* 19 (1997): 56.
62. Walter Kasper, *Il Dio di Gesù Cristo* (Brescia: Queriniana, 1984), 410.
63. Lubich, cited in Piero Coda, "Sulla teologia che scaturisce dal carisma dell'unità," *Nuova Umanità* 18 (1996): 160.

means that the ultimate depths of the Principle-Love, that is, of that One which displays itself intrinsically in a multiple plurality, allows us to see in the reality it originates[64] the very same dynamic it signifies in its existence. This dynamic is defined by Chiara, in a highly effective turn of phrase, as "trinitizing itself." She does not mean by this a multiplication of individuals but a distinguishing of persons, where each one, being consumed in the One, is wholly the One, and hence the expression of the One.[65]

Significantly, the term "trinitizing" appears for the first time in a passage from December 8, 1949, where Chiara Lubich, in a reflection that recalls what happened in the Pact, describes this uni-trinitarian dynamism, which

---

64. To illustrate this springing of the many from the One, Chiara Lubich often turns to an image pregnant with meaning—the irradiating of the love of the Father outside of himself, revisiting thereby the Platonic doctrine of Ideas. She writes a passage cited in Hubertus Blaumeiser, "All'infinito verso la disunità: Considerazioni sull'inferno alla luce del pensiero di Chiara Lubich," in *Nuova Umanità* 19 (1997):563; and in Piero Coda, "'Viaggiare' il Paradiso," *Nuova Umanita* 19 (1997): 224-225: "I understood that from the Father emerged those divergent rays when he created all things and that those rays gave Order which is Life and Love and Truth; the Ideas of things were in the Word and the Father projected them outside of Himself," thus summoning them into existence in a new and different dimension: the created dimension. And Chiara points to the ultimate form of the solution of the question of the One-many relationship when she outlines the final fulfillment of us and of all creation. This is shown as the return into the Idea, who is the Word, of the Ideas. These returning ideas are the reality of us and created things that were made actual in historical existence, but now purified, transfigured, that is, made completely love. She writes, "Now, in the end, the Father will draw back those rays which from being divergent become convergent and they will meet one another in his Bosom. And the meeting will generate the Idea of the Ideas: the Idea of the Flower, the Idea of the sea, the Idea of the stars . . . and that Idea will be the Word whence it came and Paradise will be the Word: the substance of love where the flowers and the stars and the roads and the seas will be Love and therefore immortal: immortal in the eternal Word, eternal contemplation of the Father and of the children of the Father." At the end, then, "there will not be pieces of music, but the Music. Not poems, but the Poem. Not flowers, but the Flower." But such music will be "The Music of musics (= which too will be musics of musics) . . . Poetry of poetry . . . Flower of flowers . . ." And so "The ideas of things (the reality of things, in fact) . . . will also be opened up fanlike into many ideas; but each one will be of the same value as the Idea. They will be one and be many of each. And all, many, but one: the Word, who is the beauty, that is, the expression of God."

65. In an unpublished passage Chiara says, "God-One is the Three, Father, Son and Holy Spirit, consummated as one. And God-One is wholly in each of the Three, as, analogously, in the Mystical Body of Christ, precisely because of participating in the trinitarian life, the whole is present in each individual."

requires the unfathomable mystery of "making oneself nothing" for love,[66] as the experience that gave rise to the Soul. She writes:

> But when two of us, knowing ourselves to be nothing, prompted Jesus-Eucharist to seal a pact of *unity* upon our two souls, I became aware that I was Jesus. I felt the impossibility of communicating with Jesus in the tabernacle. I experienced the elation of being at the peak of the pyramid of all creation, as on the point of a pin; at the point where the two rays meet, where the two who are God (so to speak) seal a pact of unity, becoming trinitized.[67]

What does this "trinitizing" mean? Chiara explains it like this: trinitizing "means that, because we make a pact of unity, we are one, but that each, becoming distinct," is the one: "We are, that is, on the pattern of the Trinity." Therefore "trinitizing themselves" is like a mutual indwelling of subjects, *on the pattern of the Trinity*, in a continuous mutual self-giving of one to another—to the point of experiencing one's being nothing. This leads to refinding oneself in the mirror-like presence of otherness, in a being-more that does not simply exceed these things (as taught by the Platonic and Aristotelian lesson of the One beyond the many) but that, while it contains them, is, at the same time, contained by them. In other words, losing oneself to find oneself in that One which now makes itself known not only as something that is ultra-subjective or even only as inter-subjective, but as the One that treasures in itself and forms intra-subjectivity.

This is the origin and locus of the experience of the Soul, that mysterious but real identity of a "subject" modulated according to the rhythm of the Trinitarian life. This life is such that—as Chiara boldly maintains—it is possible to say that in an analogous way, in the Soul each one is Soul. The individual is the whole, the whole is the individuals. In other words, each one (the particular, the finite) attains the value of the all (the universal), be-

---

66. In another unpublished passage Chiara says, "The Three, in the Trinity, are One by mutual indwelling. But to be One it is necessary that each of the Three be truly nothing, a great nothing, a divine nothing, with regard to their being One. We ought to penetrate this being nothing of theirs, this total inexistence of theirs. Without doubt it remains a mystery how in the Trinity the Word is nothing and at the same time is the Son, and likewise for the Father and the Spirit. Certainly God, being Love, is able to make himself nothing."

67. Lubich, cited in Hubertus Blaumeiser, "Il patto d'unità come accesso esistenziale e metodo della teologia: Alcune riflessioni alla luce dell'esperienza della 'Scuola Abbà,'" *Nuova Umanità* 22 (2000): 782-83 (translation revised).

cause each one bears in self the reality of the all, of the one ("If the infinite is 'broken up,'" Chiara notes, "there remain 'many' infinites").

But who, in the created order, allows us to see in the particular the value of the all, of the universal? It is the Word-Love who, in a climax of Love, was able to make himself Other in what is other than himself. Out of All Nothing, out of universal particular, he realizes thus an unimaginable *coincidentia oppositorum*, where finite and infinite, far from excluding one another, are reciprocally manifested and give space to one another—even though it is a reciprocity that nevertheless rests on an asymmetry—in their shared origin and vocation: Love. It is the Word-Love who has assumed the face of Jesus Forsaken, "the Love concentrated in the infinitely small . . . but [that] is the whole of Love" and therefore "infinitely great."[68]

It is the Infinite that has made itself finite, revealing to our eyes the unheard-of mystery of a Unity—the Unity of the divine—capable of shattering, in a sense, its own self to give space to a new and also unheard-of fullness of unity. It is the Infinite that makes itself finite while preserving its infinity, so that the finite makes itself infinite and, participating in the Infinite, may be. Chiara explains:

> Never was Jesus so much a human being as when he was Jesus Forsaken. In fact, whereas before then he was indeed seen as the Human Being, now he is a human being.
>
> In fact, as he was – because God – the universal Human Being, having been detached from God, he remained a particular human being. But, not ceasing to be God, he divinized the particular.
>
> So he, being God, made divine the *particular* and shows how in a particular human being there can be contained the Universal[69]

She concludes:

> Participating in the divine Life, therefore, does not mean our receiving a part, but our having the whole of it in us, we who are particulars

---

68. Jesus forsaken "is all the most contrary things: beginning and end; the infinitely great and small . . ." (Chiara Lubich, cited in Anna Pelli, "L'apporto di un carisma all'approfondimento teologico dell'abbandono di Gesù," *Nuova Umanità* 18 [1996]: 333) (translation revised).

69. Lubich, cited in Silvano Cola, "Morte e resurrezione: la dinamica del 'saper perdere' per lo sviluppo integrale della persona," *Nuova Umanità* 23 (2001): 235 (translation revised).

Each one of us will be a Word, but, since each Word is the whole Word, each one of us will be the Word, will be a harmony = a unity. The new song is the harmony of harmonies![70]

Something new, therefore, that is infinitely reproduced and generates "designs" and "harmonies" that are "perennially new." Chiara Lubich describes this with the evocative image of the "mystical rose," which is an image of the Soul at whose center converge many souls, like many petals, so that they form a complete oneness among them, just as in a rosebud. "Then," she continues:

> [T]hey will become distinct, detach themselves . . . as it were into many petals, each of which will take the form of a rose, of a rosebud with other petals subdividing themselves, unfolding and in turn forming other buds . . . The whole then will return to the heart bud . . . Then the rose will open up in other ways, according to other relationships among the souls, and the patterns and the harmonies will be perennially new.[71]

Unity, indeed, Chiara comments, "is not static; it is a beauty on the move, it is a dynamism." It is the vital trinitizing of the Soul as that oneness which shatters itself and makes itself reverberate, distinctly and singly, in each of the many, in the togetherness of which it then comes back to be recollected and expressed in unity, in a dynamic process, as Leibniz would say, of an "infinity of infinities."

In the light of the uni-trinitarian dynamic, briefly outlined, the many are not thus thought of as foreign to one another and in a dialectical relationship among them, but rather as tending to enter into relation with one another, to "interpenetrate" one another "to bring about a new beauty of love." "Make one of all and in all the One."[72] And this can be done by love, as Chiara illustrates in a novel passage where she explains the infinite refraction of the One in the many as a mutual containing of the Infinite in the finite and of the finite in the Infinite:

> When a ray of light meets a drop of water suspended in the air, it opens out into a rainbow and in the array of 7 colors are collected

---

70. Lubich, cited in Maria Therese Henderson, "Gli infiniti toni della voce del Padre," *Nuova Umanità* 25 (2003):. 374 (translation revised).
71. Lubich, cited in Piero Coda, "Viaggiare' il Paradiso," *Nuova Umanità* 19 (1997): 110 (translation revised).
72. Lubich, *Essential Writings* (London: New City and New York: New City Press, 2007), 102.

all the nuances of every color. The one therefore becomes 7 and the 7 becomes 70 x 7 and so on to infinity. It is the finite that becomes infinite, having in itself the Infinite.[73]

Finite and Infinite are manifested here in their intrinsically perichoretic nature, by which the finite does not appear as the outcome of a limiting of the Infinite, nor does the Infinite appear as the most extreme expansion of the finite, according to a logic that, in the end, imprisons and dissolves one into the other, as Hegelianism and nihilism would teach. Here, rather, everything goes back to their mutual indwelling, their mirror-like illumination of one another, and this allows the finite not only to maintain its identity, but to intensify and expand it to the measure of Unity. This, Chiara says, is done by "the Light of God" which opening out "like a fan:"

> ... penetrated into each soul (that made itself open) in a way that was varied but one, as colors are varied and of the same substance of light. It did not illuminate two souls in the same way (as the Three in the Trinity are not the same but distinct Persons) and gave to each their beauty so that they would be desirable and loveable by others and in love (the common substance in which the souls recognized themselves as one and themselves in each other) would recompose themselves in the One who had recreated them by his Light which is himself.[74]

This unique explication of the logic of trinitization characterizes the experience of the Soul. Here trinitization finds its own spatial-temporal reflection as an experience that originates and founds a new ontological framework, with its consequent vision of what it is to be human. The nature of this is to expand further as a paradigm for all that is real. And this leads to the recognition that in the process of "trinitizing" there is that "fundamental agreement" in which, as Heidegger would say, "every thought vibrates" and in which, at the same time, it is established "in this origin and its breadth."[75] The most luminous and convincing evidence for such a claim, formulated according to this fundamental agreement, is in the pages of *Paradise '49* where Chiara Lubich passes on the full extent of her mystical experience.

---

73. Lubich, unpublished passage, October 15, 1949.
74. Lubich, cited in Hubertus Blaumeiser, "Un mediatore che è nulla," *Nuova Umanità* 22 (1998): 406-407 (translation revised).
75. Martin Heidegger, *Introduzione alla filosofia:Pensare e poetare* (Milan: Bompiani, 2009), 55.

Part Three

Implications of Paradise '49 for Theology

Chapter Seven

Chiara Lubich and the Theology of Jesus: The Trinity as Place, Method, and Object of Thinking

Piero Coda

1. Theology takes many forms. There is critical-scientific theology, symbolic and wisdom theology, and also mystical theology. These theologies have many faces: Augustine is not Thomas Aquinas, Maximus the Confessor is not Luther. Yet, there is something essential that defines theology as theology. We can say that it is *to know God in God, and all things in God, by participating in the being and existence of Jesus in the inspiration of his Spirit.*

I tend to avoid speaking of knowing God. I believe it risks thinking of God as merely an "object" outside of us. Instead we can refer to knowing *God in God*, in order to express the specific participation given to us in Jesus, through the gift of his Spirit, in the knowledge that God has *of* Godself, and *in* Godself, of all that exists. This, furthermore, emphasizes that theology is most of all about "being" or "dwelling" in God, which naturally leads to and expresses itself in a knowledge corresponding to that condition.

As the *Dogmatic Constitution on Divine Revelation* of the Second Vatican Council (*Dei Verbum*) explains, the Church receives in Christ Jesus the full and definitive Word of God about God. It is precisely for this reason that "as the centuries succeed one another, the Church constantly moves forward toward the fullness of divine truth until the words of God reach their complete fulfillment in her" (n. 8). It is in this unceasing journey in the light of the truth given us in Jesus Christ that the Holy Spirit guides the Church "toward the whole truth" (Jn 16:13). *Dei Verbum* teaches that this occurs:

> through the contemplation and study made by believers, who treasure these things [the words of God] in their hearts (see Lk 2:19, 51) through a penetrating understanding of the spiritual realities which they experience, and through the preaching of those who have received through Episcopal succession the sure gift of truth.

As Hans Urs von Balthasar explains, great experiences of God in Jesus, like those of Augustine, Francis of Assisi, and Ignatius of Loyola, can give rise to glimpses, provided by the Spirit, into the center of revelation, glimpses that enrich the Church in unexpected ways and with permanent meaning.[1]

The charism of unity, I am convinced, is one of these charisms of the Holy Spirit that open our gaze toward the center of revelation and thus allow for the "deposit of faith," of which the Church is custodian and dispenser, to be understood and lived with incisiveness and new light. In fact, a particular characteristic that, according to von Balthasar, is typical of the action of the Spirit is found also in this charism: "He infuses the divine fullness of the infinite, but only always so as to unify it again and again and always more."[2] According to Chiara Lubich, unity and Jesus Forsaken, both central to her charism, are two sides of the same coin. They contain the gift of light and life of the charism of unity, and they illustrate the universalizing and unifying dynamic of the Spirit of Truth in a manner that is both unprecedented and faithful to the tradition of the church. In this way, Chiara says that the Word of revelation becomes ever more "one" and ever more "three."

2. It is significant that Chiara Lubich, when describing Christian existence in the experience manifested by the charism of unity, speaks of being already "in the bosom of the Father." This is so by virtue of the living presence of the Risen Lord among those who are united in his name (Mt 18:20). And she speaks of a new way of knowing on the basis of this particular kind of existence.

The Christian faith is concentrated in this promise of knowing God in God: "And this is eternal life, that they may know you, the only true God, and Jesus Christ whom you have sent" (Jn 17:3). In fact, this is the greatest tension within human knowledge: the awareness, on the one hand, of our inability to attain such knowledge on our own; and the yearning, on the other hand, to realize ourselves beyond ourselves, in God. All religious traditions and all the great seekers of God bear witness to this tension.

The fact is that precisely because the human person, in one way or another, perceives him or herself as a creature that is willed and loved by Someone who is infinitely Other, humans are aware of being known by this Someone

---

1. Hans Urs von Balthasar, *Teo-logica*, vol. 3 (Milan: Jaca Book, 1992), 22.
2. Hans Urs von Balthasar, *Teo-logica*, 22.

in the core of their being and in the hidden meaning of their existence. In turn they therefore desire to know that Someone just as they themselves are known: to know the One who knows them and to know themselves just as they are known by that One. Augustine writes in the *Confessions*: "I shall know thee, O my Knower; I shall know thee even as I am known (1 Cor 13:12)."[3] There is an urge toward reciprocity in the desire a human has to know God. Likewise, there is a deep desire to love just as one is loved.

In Jesus, the object of this desire becomes a reality: "All things have been handed over to me by my Father. No one knows the Son except the Father, and no one knows the Father except the Son and anyone to whom the Son wishes to reveal him" (Mt 11:27). Jesus exclaims this in the Gospel of Matthew and in the parallel passage in Luke, while the whole Gospel of John seems to revolve around this truth. Jesus knows the Father just as he is known by Him and wants to communicate *this* knowledge to us. This is because Jesus, according to the Christian faith, is the Son, the God-Son, the Word made flesh. As Son and Word of the Father, he lives in full communion with the Father in every moment of his existence. This does not mean that Jesus, while truly human in all things except sin (Heb 4:15), was exempt from "growing" and "learning" to know the Father and, through the Father, persons, events, and even the dramatic unfolding of the plan of salvation. Luke, in fact, notes that "Jesus grew in wisdom, age and grace" (2:52), and the letter to the Hebrews says that "Son though he was, he learned obedience from what he suffered" (5:8).

Jesus, as a man, grows in his knowledge of the Father and paradoxically comes to know him in the form and with the measure by which he is known by him: as totally and only *agape*. The Father knows Jesus as a free and total gift of self only through the abandonment and death he suffered on the cross. The paradox is that the Father knows Jesus *in full measure* when Jesus entrusts himself to the One who knows him in the moment in which, humanly, he no longer knows anything about him: "My God, my God, why have you forsaken me?" (Mk 15:34; Mt 27:46). Jesus' knowledge brought about through the wound of being forsaken is made manifest in the resurrection. In his being human, the Risen Lord, thanks to the Holy Spirit, is the event of perfect union with the Father. This reciprocity is expressed in the "face to face" knowledge (1 Cor 13:12) that the Father has of the Son,

---

3. *Confessions*, X, 1.1: "Cognoscam te, cognitor meus, cognoscam, sicut et cognitus sum."

and that the Son, even as a human being, has of the Father. Glorified by the Spirit, Jesus appears to the disciples gathered together on the first day after the Sabbath (Jn 20:19), attesting to and infusing with grace this knowledge that humanity may share in.

This dynamic is, for Chiara, *the theology "of" Jesus*; it is the knowledge of God lived by Jesus two thousand years ago, today, and always, inasmuch as Jesus has risen, with his humanity, to the bosom of the Father, from where he embraces and contains all time and space. This is the knowledge of God that Jesus offers us and transmits to us in faith: "And because you are children, God has sent the Spirit of his Son into our hearts, crying, 'Abba! Father!'" (Gal 4:6). This knowledge is simultaneously *already* and *not yet*. *Already*, because human existence—through faith, baptism, and the Eucharist—is truly and once and for all grafted into the event of the crucified and risen Christ, who introduces us into the bosom of the Abba. Thus, we can participate in the knowledge of God in God, which is the Risen Christ. At the same time it is *not yet* because humanity, whose existence unfolds in time and space, is subject both to growth and to limits and must await our freely given fulfillment from God in Jesus, who will come at the end of times.

If we take seriously what the incarnation and death/resurrection of the Son of God, his ascension to the Father, and the effusion of the Holy Spirit has ontologically introduced into creation, then we cannot underestimate the importance of this event for the knowledge we can now have of God-in-Christ, thanks to the gift of the Holy Spirit "without measure" (Jn 3:34). Here is how Paul describes this new possibility:

> "What no eye has seen, nor ear heard, nor the human heart conceived, what God has prepared for those who love him"— these things God has revealed to us through the Spirit; for the Spirit searches everything, even the depths of God. For what human being knows what is truly human except the human spirit that is within? So also no one comprehends what is truly God's except the Spirit of God. Now we have received not the spirit of the world, but the Spirit that is from God, so that we may understand the gifts bestowed on us by God. . . . "For who has known the mind of the Lord so as to instruct him?" But we have the mind (*nous*) of Christ. (1 Cor 2:9-12,16)

3. "We have the mind of Christ." Christian theology has always recognized this extraordinary reality. Thomas Aquinas says, "Faith is assimilation to divine knowledge, in that by faith infused in us we are united to the first truth itself, and thus immersed in divine knowledge we know everything as if with the eye of God."[4] When it comes to defining theology, Aquinas affirms that "God is the Subject of this science" because "in sacred science, all things are treated of *sub ratione Dei* [which we could translate: "in the light of God," "according to what belongs to God as God"] either because they are God himself or because they refer to God as their beginning and end."[5] It is in this sense that the object of theology in and of Jesus is God in himself and God "all in all" (1 Cor 15:28): in other words, all reality as seen by God and in God.

It would be instructive to go through the history of theology to see how this awareness has been expressed, albeit with different words and emphases. And it would be interesting to outline the paths of its development, its crises, and its coming to maturity. But suffice it to say that for all the great theologians, in every period, it is clear that if we are grafted onto Jesus as branches onto the vine (Jn 15:5), we participate in the knowledge that he has of the Father through faith, baptism, the Eucharist, the gifts of the Spirit, and the life of love. And yet, even though the Fathers of the Church—from Irenaeus to John Damascene—and the great Scholastics—from Anselm to Duns Scotus—have no problem subscribing to Aquinas's definition, albeit in different words, things seem to change greatly in modern times. The rift between reason and faith, on the one hand, and between speculative theology and mystical theology, on the other, has led in the West to a preference for theology in either its rational-doctrinal form or in its historical-critical and scientific-critical form.

There is something positive in this modern approach to doing theology. It is in conformity with the very dynamism of the incarnation of the divine in the human that occurred once and for all in Jesus Christ and that progressively penetrates into the consciousness and praxis of humanity. Attention has been drawn to historicity, to the human subject, to social and cultural perspectives and issues, to contemporary science, and to critical and philosophical modes of thought. While all of these approaches to theology are positive, some have been treated as absolute and thus are destined to lead us into a blind alley.

---

4. In *Boetium de Trinitate*, q. III, a 1.
5. *Summa Theologiae* I, q. I, a 7.

Beginning in the late 1800s and developing especially in the last century, the need to return to the great theology of tradition, while accounting for the positive perspectives of modern times so as to avoid seeking refuge in the past, became urgent. Many of the "new theologies" take as their inspiration following Jesus in that unprecedented "dark night and trial of faith" (as John Paul II called it) that is also expressed as "the death of God." It is fascinating to reread the pages of these prophets of the "new theology": Anthony Rosmini and John Henry Newman, Pavel Florenskij and Sergej Bulgakov, Karl Barth and Dietrich Bonhoeffer, Maurice Blondel and Karl Rahner, Henri De Lubac and Hans Urs von Balthasar, along with such witnesses of life and thought as Thérèse of Lisieux, Edith Stein, and Simone Weil. Collaborations with the great religious traditions of Asia, especially in the last decades, also require being open to new horizons. And it is against this background of historic change that the theological contribution of the charism of unity is situated.

4. The event inaugurated by this charism of unity is the experience of our being one in Jesus Christ, actualized in the here and now of history according to the prayer of Jesus to the Father: "That they may all be one. As you, Father, are in me and I am in you, may they also be in us" (Jn 17:21). Since the beginning of her Christian journey, and in a foundational way during the period of intense mystical light she lived in 1949, Chiara together with her first companions experienced that being one in Jesus, and by extension being one in the Father, can become a tangible reality that transforms and clarifies one's knowledge of all existence. How? The intentional commitment to live Jesus' new commandment of mutual love (Jn 13:34), to be ready to give all of one's self as Jesus did in his forsakenness, making a Pact of Unity in Jesus-Eucharist, and in him among us, so that he may accomplish all that he offers, allows us to be one *in* him and *through* him, and thereby we can become one *in* the Father. In this way Chiara experienced and understood—by a special grace from God—a reality that is at the same time both simple and crucial. She describes it with these words:

> We understood that being consummated in one and basing our life's journey on *unity*, we were Jesus who journeyed. He who is Way in us became Wayfarer. And we were no longer ourselves, but he in us. . . .

Let us reflect for a moment upon the intellectual meaning of this reality, that is, upon its implications in terms of knowledge *in* God for theology.

What happens when we live our knowledge of God in faith based on our being one *in* Jesus? Knowledge becomes permeated by love and becomes one with love in two ways.

First, our knowledge *becomes all listening and reception*. We listen to God, who reaches us through his Word, but we also listen to our brothers and sisters. Christ is present in our neighbor so that their hearts and minds, each in its particular and original way, resound with the Word of God. In this loving receptivity before God and neighbor, I "lose" my thought, I "set it aside," I "silence" it in order to receive in me the thought of Jesus.

Second, my knowledge *becomes a gift and self-communication* to others. By formulating and expressing the thought that takes shape in me based on Jesus who dwells in unity, I act out of love. I act in order to communicate Jesus in me (what I have understood *in* Jesus) to Jesus in my brother or sister. And this happens in reciprocity, because if there is unity, my brother or sister is also approaching me in the same manner.

The event of unity lived at the level of knowledge makes us, by the grace of God that is actualized in reciprocal love, *one with Jesus in each of us, one with Jesus in the other, and one with Jesus among us*. In this way, our being becomes totally love, totally concentrated—to use an image dear to mystics—in that Still Point, that Center, in which it receives itself as love from God and gives itself back as love to God and to our brothers and sisters. This occurs *in* Jesus in whom we are "one" (Gal 3:28) by the gift of the Holy Spirit. We then become in *praxis* what we already are in essence by grace in Jesus. We each become another Jesus while remaining ourselves because we are "clothed" with him. Living this unity makes our being, as individuals and as a community, an event *in Christ Jesus*.

Therefore, we can say, with Paul, "We have the mind of Christ." That is, we can know God *in* Jesus because in unity we are born together with and in him by the Father in the Holy Spirit as sons and daughters in the Son. About us in Jesus, the Father can say: "You are my Son, today I have begotten you" (Acts 13:33; Heb 1:5). Obviously, this state of being in Jesus depends on us and on others, on the transparency and the truth of our doing our part so that God—through the grace of being grafted in Jesus through faith, the Eucharist, and mutual love—may grant us the grace of unity that makes us fully Jesus.

Theology rediscovers its true "home" in this experience of unity lived in knowledge. In theology, we traditionally speak of "theological sources" (*loci theologici*) from which the truth of revelation can be drawn. The event of unity focuses upon and realizes the "theological source" (*locus theologicus*) par excellence: Jesus himself, alive and in our midst, who leads us to the bosom of the Abba where he is and dwells. It is just as he promised: "On that day you will know that I am in my Father, and you in me, and I in you" (Jn 14:20).

It is significant that to express the originality of this theology, we must define it as theology "in" or "of" Jesus. Not of the historical Jesus, of course, but of the Risen Lord who lives today in the Christian community, who actuates unity, and as a result who also lives in everyone vitally participating in this event. It is a reality given in our unity in Jesus that allows for and urges toward this definition. There is nothing presumptuous or overenthusiastic about it, because to say "theology of/in Jesus" does not equate with wanting fundamentally to possess Jesus or to reduce him to our measure. Rather, it means emphasizing that in unity we tend with all our being toward a total emptying of ourselves, even in our thoughts, in order to receive and exercise together, as Paul says, "the mind of Christ."

In the event of unity, therefore, theology can rediscover its most profound identity and vocation to be a theology "of" and "in" Jesus with the clarity and equilibrium that springs from the center of revelation. Such a theology is in line with the great tradition of the church's spiritual and intellectual journey while speaking to the fundamental dimensions of historicity and intersubjectivity brought to light in modern times.

5. I feel at this point compelled to underscore that the event of unity outlines a specific theological methodology. It can be summarized as a rediscovery of Jesus himself, of the "dwelling" in him through unity, that provides the *mēth-odos* as the "living way" (Heb 10:20) *to know God in God*. Allow me to mention some of the resulting implications.

First, living unity enables us to be church, which is the only basis for a theology of and in Jesus that draws out its potential. To be church as a Catholic theologian does not mean simply to live the faith, to know the scripture and tradition, to be faithful to the magisterium, and to account for the charisms and the sense of the faithful (*sensus fidelium*). It means also to receive, through one's own being crucified with Christ and living mutual love, the grace of unity that is the church in act. Through this grace of unity, all aspects find their place and their authentic meaning as "bearers of the Word of God" in the relation of reciprocity.

Second, by living unity, being in Jesus, and "putting on" Christ, our person becomes unified in itself. It becomes unified not only in the sense that it achieves a vital bond between existence and knowledge and therefore between spirituality and theology but also in the sense that knowledge imbibes love and love becomes contemplation. It is the depth of my being, my true "self" already "hidden with Christ in God" (Col 3:3) that is progressively made capable of knowing by loving and of loving by knowing.

Third, knowledge of God, by living unity in Jesus, does not draw me out of the world but places me through my relationship with others at the heart of the world where the Word of God took its place in the incarnation. It brings me to the wounds and to the most radical questions of humanity today with which Jesus identified himself in his forsakenness. It is true that to know God in Jesus one must go beyond this world to "enter" the bosom of the Father. Yet that does not mean to forsake the world but to know the world in God and God in the world. In other words, the theology of and in Jesus pushes me outside any enclosure toward God, bearing the reproach he bore, as the letter to the Hebrews (13:13) invites us to do. Thus, we leave behind us all that is sheltered and confined in order to visit the existential peripheries of the world, just as Pope Francis has recently encouraged us to do.

Finally, this theology in Jesus is one and yet multiple, just as God is One and Three. It is true that there are as many theologies as there are theologians; but it is just as true that Christian theology is one because Jesus is one. And this becomes especially clear in a unity that embraces diversity. True theological pluralism does not clash with the identity of a single theology. In every theology forged by unity, we should be able to hear the one and only Word pronounced—as Chiara would say—"in infinite tones." This is because it is the one and only Christ who has "clothed" each one of us in different ways and who expresses through us the one/multiple knowledge of God *in* God. In this way, we can all say, like Peter, James, and John on Mount Tabor: "It is good for us to be here!" (Mk 9:2-5).

6. We have thus far touched on only one side of the coin that describes the charism of unity and its mark on the theology that emerges from it. But this discussion of unity leads us to the second side, which is in fact the key to the first side. The second side, that of *Jesus Forsaken*, is necessary for the first to be understood and lived. In Chiara's innovative lexicon, this expression refers to Jesus who pushes his obedience to the Father and his love for humanity to the point of suffering on the cross the tragic absence of God to whom he entrusts himself with his whole being.

In the spiritual experience and the theological perspective that emerge from the charism of unity, Jesus Forsaken is not just an aspect of Jesus alongside others. Rather, it expresses the ultimate meaning of his life, and therefore the meaning of the revelation that he is of God and of creation. I would like here to draw from one of Chiara's texts that is like a flash of light illuminating unexpected scenery:

> Jesus is Jesus Forsaken. Because Jesus is the Savior, the Redeemer, and he redeems when he pours the Divine upon humanity through the Wound of his Forsakenness which is the pupil of the Eye of God upon the world: an infinite Void through which God looks upon us, the window of God thrown open upon the world and the window of humanity through which we see God.
>
> The Eye of God upon the world is the Heart of Christ, but its pupil is that Wound.
>
> The eye is the heart because even though the eye is the organ for seeing (in the Trinity the Eye of God is the Word), God who is Love cannot see but with the Heart. In him Love and Light make unity.

The image of the eye is symbolic both of being known by God and of knowing him as we are known by him. This imagery is typical of the mystical tradition, where it is said that the human person, enraptured to know God in God, becomes "all eye." It is a striking expression for communicating what it means to know oneself and all other things *in* God just as one is known *by* God. Even Aquinas, who is usually so moderate in his language, affirms that faith is knowing "as if with the eye of God." And Catherine of Siena even more boldly defines faith as "the pupil of the eye of intelligence."[6]

Chiara's imagery goes further. First, it reiterates the reciprocity that is constitutive of knowing God. We know God because God knows us first. If the Word is indeed the "Eye" through which God knows, then Jesus Forsaken, the incarnate Word in his being and mission laid completely bare, is "the pupil of eye of God upon the world." God therefore knows the world with a knowledge that is completely one with love in Jesus Forsaken. And only because God, who in the "fullness of time" reaches every time and gathers all

---

6. Catherine of Siena, *Dialogue*, c. 45.

time to himself, knows us in Jesus Forsaken, we, on our side and as a reply, can know God as he knows us "in" Jesus Forsaken.

Yet, Chiara emphasizes another aspect. It is evident that to know God in the manner of God's knowing, to know *in* God, it is necessary to go beyond the merely human way of knowing. It is necessary to lose God and enter the forsakenness of God in order to find God anew and be transfigured by God. Only God as God knows God. This is what the mystics know and what the greatest theologians say when they put the "theology of the cross" at the center of doing theology. When they speak of the importance of apophatic theology, they mean not simply negating with one's own intellect one's merely partial and provisory knowledge so far gained about God but rather negating intelligence itself so as to know God not "in a human way" but "in a divine way." This is done with one's own intelligence, obviously, but an intelligence "lost" and "found" anew in Christ.

Bonaventure, for example, in the last phase of the *Itinerarium mentis in Deum*, teaches that at the peak of the journey to know God, it is necessary to pass, on an exodus from this world to the Father, through Christ crucified.[7] He wrote these pages on Mount La Verna, where he contemplated what happened to Saint Francis when he received the gift of the stigmata to be truly crucified with Christ. The same is taught by John of the Cross.

Chiara contemplates the depths of *this* crucified Jesus in Jesus Forsaken, who—as she explains—"loses God for God." He loses, in terms of the topic at hand, the knowledge that he has of the Father for love of him and us and thus makes himself an "absolute Void," as empty as the pupil of the eye. He comes to know fully the Father precisely as he is known by the Father, and also as man, in the shining Light of the Holy Spirit effused "without measure" in the resurrection. In this sense, Chiara affirms, Jesus Forsaken is not only the "window of God opened upon the world" but also "the window of humanity through which we see God." Therefore, Jesus Forsaken, more than just a topic of theology, is theological knowledge itself brought to its roots and lived at its most dynamic. When Paul speaks of knowing nothing "except Jesus Christ, and him crucified" (1 Cor 2:2), I think he was referring to this decisive and unique dimension of knowledge by faith.

By concentrating on Jesus Forsaken, the charism of unity emphasizes that what is important is not so much the individual act of intellectual ascet-

---

7. Bonaventure, *Itinerarium mentis in Deum* VII, 6.

icism in "losing" even our own intelligence in order to know God in the way God knows. Rather, it is an act of love by which I become one with Jesus Forsaken in loving the Father and all brothers and sisters "as" Christ does (Jn 15:12-13). Only through this act, lived out in daily life, can my intelligence be resurrected as imbued with the Holy Spirit in the Risen Christ who lives in the bosom of the Father.

Earlier, in describing the experience of unity, we explored how intelligence and love might become one. This oneness constitutes and expresses the center of our being as it is received from God and given back to God. We now see that this oneness occurs in Jesus Forsaken when we make ourselves one with him because he has made himself and makes himself one with us. Then, in a single act, we know and we are born, born again, together, from his "wound," as sons and daughters in the Son who knows the Father in the Spirit, just as they are known by the Father.

7. At this point, I would like to make an important clarification. Jesus Forsaken, as the identity and mission of Jesus completely disclosed, is the full revelation of who God is and who humankind is. Chiara affirms this in an often quoted text that is rich in meaning: "Jesus Forsaken, because he is not, is we are, if we are not."

What is meant by this affirmation? It signifies a new and profound interpretation of reality, a new ontology that emerges from Chiara's vision of Jesus Forsaken, and thus "from the depths of revelation," as Anthony Rosmini would say. Theologically, this is one of the most original points to spring from the charism of unity. Among other things, it builds a bridge in the light of revelation between the vision of being that is typical of Western classical philosophy and the intuition of nonbeing that is typical of the great wisdom traditions of the East. Precisely for this reason, it is a delicate point that requires proper understanding and expression in conformity with the vision of the charism. I will try to say only a few words about this.

First, this language of nonbeing/being as the inner rhythm of love in terms of Jesus Forsaken not only shows itself to be completely legitimate but also offers insight into expressing the nature of the divine Persons in the Holy Trinity. In fact, as the theological tradition (Augustine and Aquinas in particular) explains, the divine Persons subsist only *in* relation, or rather *as* relation, which, being love, means total and real self-giving to the Other.

Looking to Jesus Forsaken, we can go even further and say that in God, each Person is himself because he is not fixed and closed in self. The Father, for example, is Father because he generates the Son. In generating the Son, the Father communicates all that he is, sharing with him all the divine life that he has in himself. He does so—to use human language—by completely emptying himself of self; yet precisely in this way he is himself, Father.

This absolute rhythm of love, which at the same time "is" and "is not," belongs to God and to God alone, because "God is love." Created persons in themselves cannot achieve this act of absolute love for the very reason that they are created. As creatures, they receive their being from God and do not enjoy the possibility of giving it away by emptying themselves of it ontologically. At most, they can give or offer themselves intentionally on the level of an act of knowledge, of will, and of love—but never to the point of totally emptying their own being. Only death permits such emptying into the hands of God one's own being as creature.[8]

But Jesus Forsaken accomplishes a "new creation" that fulfills what the "first creation" was destined for by grace. He is the Word who became man and who lives a Trinitarian relationship with the Father by the Holy Spirit in his humanity. His humanity is so united to the Word that he can experience in being forsaken, and in death accepted out of love, that extreme annulment of self in love by which he is fully inserted in the Trinitarian life.

Therefore, it is only by being grafted into Jesus Forsaken, taken on and lived through grace by our own freedom, that the created person can participate in this reality. We recall what Paul says about "dying" and "rising" with Christ (Rom 6:4-5). This is not just a way of speaking, but a reality. This is so even if our conscious minds can understand it only partially and even if its full ontological depth will be disclosed only in its eschatological completion.

---

8. Hans Urs von Balthasar explains: "In creatural reality there cannot be such absolute surrender, because man cannot dispose of his own existence and, therefore, of his real self, and 'he cannot give what is not at his own disposition to give' (Emil Brunner, *Dreifaltigkeit* [Einsiedeln: Johannes, 1976], 24). But when it comes to the absolute being who has total possession of self, it is possible to arrive at the extreme concept that 'the divine self-possession expresses itself in the perfect gift of self and reciprocal self-surrender, which at the same time includes the existence of self, that which is not at the creature's disposition as creature' (Brunner, 25). The self-surrender of the Father, who gives not only something of what he *has* but all that he *is* . . . . passes on completely to the generated Son. . . . This total gift of self, that the Son and the Spirit repeat in reply, signifies a kind of a 'death,' a first radical 'kenosis,' if you will: a super-death." (Author's translation from *Teodrammatica*, vol. 5 [Milan: Jaca Book, 1986],71–72).

It is therefore justifiable, and even necessary, to use the language of *not being/being* to express the rhythm of love not only in reference to God the Trinity, but also, through Jesus Forsaken, in reference to human persons. As Klaus Hemmerle perceived and had begun to outline in his *Thesen zu einer trinitarischen ontologie*, this leads to an ontology radically considered in Christ that is charged with new implications for both Western thought and Eastern thought.

8. In our discussion of theology in the light of the charism of unity, we have touched upon two concepts: unity and Jesus Forsaken. We have seen how when considered as the pattern or *form* of theological knowledge prior to its being the *content* of that knowledge, these concepts correspond to the profound vocation of theology and have extremely contemporary implications. The horizons that this form of theology opens up for ecumenical and interreligious dialogue, as well as for dialogue with modern thought, are revealing this potential.

To use an image from Chiara, theology based on unity and Jesus Forsaken is like the blossoming of a tree that has grown for centuries. Such blossoming requires a remodeling of theological knowledge in how it is practiced. The history of theology has had many models and organizing patterns in the course of the centuries that extend from the biblical commentaries of the Church Fathers to the medieval *Summae* to treatises in the form of manuals. What form or pattern can be hypothesized for a theology inspired and nourished by the charism of unity? I would venture two words: *journeying* and *trinitizing*.

Journeying. If theology is knowledge *in* God as we have described, then by nature it is an event. If it is a theology *of* Jesus that occurs *in* him, and *in* Jesus Forsaken as the way to the Father, then theology becomes a *"viam agre,"* a being "on the way," a journeying. It becomes what the Fourth Gospel speaks of as "doing the truth" (Jn 3:21), and what the Paul refers to as "doing the truth in love" (Eph 4:15). A new, dynamic unity can thus be found between exegesis and systematic theology, dogmatic and moral theology, and the mystical approach and the critical-scientific approach, while allowing for each of them to remain distinct and necessary at their own level.

Trinitizing. If one is in Jesus, and if one is in him in the bosom of the Father, all things are known as God knows them. And God knows them in himself, in the One who is Three. And God knows them at the same time in the incarnate, crucified, and risen Word, in whom God and the human creature are united and distinct: "without confusion and without separation," as defined by the Council of Chalcedon. God knows them from the eschatological point of view, when being "all in all" (1 Cor 15:28), everything in God will be everything else. Chiara uses a neologism to define this participation in the divine-human knowledge of the Risen Christ: "*Trinitizing.*" That is, *knowledge in the Trinitarian rhythm of the One who is Three*. This means that every reality can be known in truth only when it is known as containing within itself all other realities in a Trinitarian relation. Here is how Chiara describes it:

> The mystery of God is in a way like that of a sacred host in that every tiny piece contains the whole of Christ. If you break apart the great mystery of Christian life you find the entire mystery in every detail. Why is this so? Because we, all of us and all creation as well, are destined to become God. So every detail contains the whole. This is a new view of theology.

One can sense what fascinating and demanding methodological possibilities are disclosed by this vision. In such "a new view of theology," one discovers in theology itself the necessary relation between theology and all the other disciplines that tend toward knowledge as the expression of love that makes us human. And theology can come to the knowledge that everything that matters and remains is contained already in every act of simple and true love because, by this action, God enters and dwells in our lives.

Chapter Eight

A Charism in History as a View from the Center

Piero Coda

Chiara Lubich was a bearer and witness of a charism, that is, of a gift of light and life for humanity in our times.

We cannot but sincerely and, we hope, responsibly be grateful in the midst of our amazement at Chiara's personal witness. Also a matter of amazement is what came about so abundantly from the gift of light and fire that she received and that so soon reached the ends of the earth. This gift has touched the hearts and minds of men and women of every faith and conviction through nothing more than the strength of love and the persuasive force of wisdom, overcoming everything put in its way.

Chiara's charism is recognized both by persons with a secular worldview and by persons guided by faithfulness to religious inspiration who have eyes to see and value the ideal stirrings at work for what is positive and just. They see her charism affecting human events and encouraging history in the direction of future prospects that foster a more mature and united humanity. It is a charism that has been studied and accepted as new and fruitful by the Catholic Church in which it was born. But it has also been studied and accepted by other Christian churches searching for that full and free unity desired by Jesus.

But what is a charism[1] and what is the original gift that *this charism* brings: the charism that defines itself and can be recognized in a few meaningful words: the *charism of unity*? I do not presume to give an adequate response in this brief article. I intend simply to offer an interpretive key that could suggest a wider, more detailed dialogue enriched by a host of voices that would make it more precise and useful.

---

1. In light of Catholic theology, see Fabio Ciardi, Carismi: *Vangelo che si fa storia* (Rome: Città Nuova, 2011); and Marc Ouellet, *La sfida dell'unità: I carismi e la Trinità*, (Rome: Città Nuova, 2011).

Let us begin with a quote from Hans Urs von Balthasar, one of the giants of twentieth-century theology.

Von Balthasar considers in his *Theo-logic* the great charisms that through the work of the Holy Spirit throughout the centuries illustrate and detail the light of Jesus Christ in which, according to Christian faith, the Word of God "made flesh" (Jn 1:14) shines forth in the world. Von Balthasar describes these charisms as lucid insights "*into* the heart of Revelation."[2] Thanks to these charisms, the eyes of the heart and of the mind are able to see more clearly, drawing out from what they perceive ever new and more effective energies for life and engagement with history, all within the original and progressive gift through which God communicates his own life, which is light for all (see Jn 1:4).

In the wake of the Second Vatican Council, John Paul II[3] highlighted the fact that this definition of a charism holds true for every ray of understanding that has enriched the life of humanity throughout history. An eloquent icon of this generous and hope-filled vision is the World Day of Prayer for Peace in Assisi in 1986. Pope John Paul II organized the event and invited representatives of different faiths to attend. This vision was further enriched twenty-five years later by Pope Benedict XVI through the added presence

---

2. Hans Urs von Balthasar, *Theo-logic*, Vol. III: *The Spirit of Truth*, (Milan: Jaca Book, 1992), 22: "Great charisms such as that of Augustine, Francis and Ignatius can receive from the Holy Spirit glimpses into the heart of revelation, glimpses that enrich the Church in a totally unexpected but lasting way. Each time, they are charisms in which intelligence, love and imitation are inseparable. From this we can recognize that the Spirit of understanding is at once divine wisdom and divine love, and in no case pure theory, but always a living praxis. A last trait is typical of the Spirit: he infuses the divine fullness of the infinite, but only always so as to unify it again and always more."

3. See *Gaudium et Spes*, n. 22: "for all men of good will in whose hearts grace works in an unseen way. For, since Christ died for all men, and since the ultimate vocation of man is in fact one, and divine, we ought to believe that the Holy Spirit in a manner known only to God offers to every man the possibility of being associated with this paschal mystery." On the other hand, John Paul II, illustrating in his preparatory catechesis for the Jubilee Year 2000 the unceasing and universal action of the Holy Spirit at the heart of the cultures of humanity, underlined, "It must first be kept in mind that every quest of the human spirit for truth and goodness, and in the last analysis for God, is inspired by the Holy Spirit. The various religions arose precisely from this primordial human openness to God. At their origins we often find founders who, with the help of God's Spirit, achieved a deeper religious experience. Handed on to others, this experience took form in the doctrines, rites and precepts of the various religions." (General Audience, September 9, 1998, n. 2)

at a similar day of "pilgrims of truth and peace."⁴ Assisi renewed the vision that Vatican II had brought back into focus with prophecy and vigor. The event, in a spirit of fraternity and peace, gathered around Jesus, the new and universal Man, charisms from the many paths of history that include us all and that, at first sight, have often appeared to be truncated and divergent.

Therefore, it is a matter of looking "*towards* the center" together with everyone else as a sign of justice and peace. In this way, the views and insights, energies, and practical methods used and promoted by each in his or her search for truth and goodness can circulate among everyone. This is the *identity and the mission of a charism*. Charisms are called to stand out clearly in their particular and highest meaning. This is needed above all and in a new way in the world today. Even in the midst of the world's agonizing and painful contradictions, the idea of a free and diverse family of peoples and nations has become both urgent and practicable. Indeed, we can see in our times, albeit in a radically different way, a movement that corresponds to what Karl Jaspers has identified as an "axial period" of civilization, such as can be seen in the centuries before the coming of Jesus Christ with the appearance of figures such as the Buddha, Lao-Tzu, Socrates, Zarathustra, and Isaiah.⁵

In fact, the direction of history evident in the precious seeds of life and rays of light⁶ guiding the development of peoples in the axial age was a *centrifugal* force. It aimed at defining the identities and richness of different societies, starting with their ideal aspirations. Today many signs suggest that there is a call to go in the opposite direction, that is, from *centrifugal*

---

4. See talk by Benedict XVI, October 27, 2011, at the *Day of Reflection, Dialogue and Prayer for Peace and Justice in the World: "Pilgrims of Truth, Pilgrims of Peace"*: "In addition to the two phenomena of religion and anti-religion, a further basic orientation is found in the growing world of agnosticism: people to whom the gift of faith has not been given, but who are nevertheless on the lookout for truth, searching for God. Such people do not simply assert: 'There is no God.' They suffer from his absence and yet are inwardly making their way towards him, inasmuch as they seek truth and goodness. They are 'pilgrims of truth, pilgrims of peace.' They ask questions of both sides."

5. See Karl Jaspers, *The Origin and Goal of History* (New Haven: Yale University Press, 1953); Arnold Toynbee, *Mankind and Mother Earth: A Narrative History of the World* (Oxford: Oxford University Press, 1976); Antonio Rizzi, "*Periodo assiale e universalità*," in *Gesù e la salvezza: Tra fede, religioni e laicità*, (Rome: Città Nuova, 2001), 158–65; Ewert Cousins, *Christ of the 21st Century* (Rockport: Element Books, 1992).

6. This is the language, taken from biblical writings and the tradition of the church, used by Vatican II in *Nostra Aetate* on the church's relations with other faiths.

to *centripetal,* from *divergent* to *convergent,* so as to favor an encounter and an exchange of the gifts among societies. At the same time, the identity and mission of each society must also be safeguarded and promoted precisely with a view to the mutual enrichment of all.

Yet, what often seems lost, if not irreparably destroyed, today is a shared sense of what can credibly and usefully guide our personal and social lives.

Today, it is often as though the eyes of the soul cannot see the inner core that anchors it and gives direction. As a consequence, we cannot find the focal point for our projects and actions, the point around which and for which they orbit with liberated creativity.[7] It is what the madman in Friedrich Nietzsche's parable of "The Madman" penetratingly, provocatively, and prophetically foretold:

> What did we do when we loosened this earth from its sun? Whither does it now move? Whither do we move? Away from all suns? Do we not dash on unceasingly? Backwards, sideways, forwards, in all directions? Is there still an above and below? Do we not stray, as through infinite nothingness? Does not empty space breathe upon us? Has it not become colder? Does not night come on continually, darker and darker?[8]

It is true that today the perception of nothingness, of an emptiness of meaning, of the darkness in which the world seems to float, no longer takes on the tragic and final tone that Martin Heidegger gave it in the parable of nihilism that had reached its fulfilment.[9] But what profoundly remains, as Zygmunt Bauman observes,[10] is the sad bewilderment of the self in the tempting but insidious space of a fluid society and globalized world. It is a

---

7. See the lucid historical-theoretical phenomenology offered by Giuseppe Maria Zanghì in *La notte della cultura europea: Agonia della terra del tramonto?* (Rome: Città Nuova, 2007).
8. Fredrick Nietzsche, *The Gay Science,* ed. Walter Kaufman (New York: Vintage Books, 1974), 181.
9. Martin Heidegger, "Nietsche's Word: 'God is Dead,'" in *Martin Heigegger off the Beaten Track,* ed. Julian Young, trans. Kenneth Hayes, (Cambridge: Cambridge University Press, 2002), 157–200.
10. See Zygmunt Bauman, *Liquid Modernity* (New York: Blackwell Publishers, Inc., 2000).

bewilderment that may not know the painful consequences of desperation but it is nourished nevertheless with equal bitterness by daily uncertainties and a sense of resignation. While it does not satisfy, it suppresses the sincere desire for transformation, for constructiveness, and indeed for revolution dwelling in the consciousness of the coming generations in every region of the world, urging them on often in passionate and prophetic tones.

Chiara Lubich, in the darkest moment of the World War II, grasped this situation and allowed herself to be shaped inwardly by the particular ray of light and life that is the charism of unity.

She immediately shared this charism with those around her and thus gave life to the first Focolare community.[11] This event takes on symbolic and even universal meaning, as attested by the rapid, though always rather measured, spread of the Focolare and its vast impact in the world. All of this took place at a moment when the disintegration of the spiritual, cultural, and social balance, which until then had grounded human life in common, became an agonized openness with a heart-felt longing for the arrival of a charism of truth, love, and unity. Thus it was that in that openness there blossomed and swiftly took form from Chiara an Ideal of life and thought that was clearly centered on the gospel as its origin and purpose. At the same time, it was an Ideal that was immediately and wholly universal: *ut unum sint*, "*May they all be one, as you, Father, are in me and I in you*" (Jn 17:21).

For Chiara, in the context of the "historic" and "collective" dark night[12] into which humanity had plummeted in those years, this Ideal of hers did

---

11. See the studies of Bernard Callebaut, *Tradition, charisme et prophétie dans le mouvement international des Focolari: Analyse sociologique* (Bruyères-le-Châtel: Nouvelle Cité, 2010) and Lucia Abignente, *Memoria e presente: La spiritualità del Movimenti dei Focolari in prospettiva storica* (Rome: Città Nuova, 2010). Also significant is the delineation, in a number of voices and under a number of profiles, of the ecclesial and social context of the time (with reference above all to the city of Trent) in Andrea Leonardi, ed., *Comunione e innovazione sociale: Il contributo di Chiara Lubich* (Rome: Città Nuova, 2012).

12. John Paul II described in these very terms the spiritual and cultural quality of our time. He, re-evoking in Spain the figure and doctrine of Saint John of the Cross ("doctor of the Church because a great teacher of the living truth on God and on the human person") and referring to the interpretation given by the latter to the cry of abandonment launched by Christ to the Father while on the cross, said: "The dark night, the trial that makes us touch the mystery of evil and demands the openness of faith, acquires at times epochal dimensions and collective proportions," and he outlined a similar epochal and collective dark night "in the abyss of abandon-

not remain a purely spiritual event, nor did it turn into a mere utopia. Rather, it became the *start of a new chapter of history*, born as it was from a radical sharing of the dizzying wound into which the whole story of humanity in the depths of war and hatred seemed to have been taken. The longing was to turn things upside down in their deepest depths, by entering fully into them out of love. Indeed Chiara sought to immerse herself in the woundedness of things, to take it on and pass through it, passionately following the example of Jesus who, believing in the Father and out of love for his brothers and sisters, immersed himself not only in the living flesh of human history but also in the painful darkness of the absence of every meaning. She did this to rekindle within it the light of hope.

It was in January 1944, as though for the first time in two thousand years of Christian history, that she discovered the hidden wound inflicted on Christ's soul when, nailed on the wood of the cross, he gave voice to the "why?" of every human being. He launched *this* anguished cry: "*My God, my God, why have you forsaken me?*" (see Mk 15:34; Mt 27:46). It is the same wound that in those years secretly attracted other men and women's inner desires for justice and truth. I am thinking of Dietrich Bonhoeffer, Edith Stein, Simone Weil, and Pavel Florenskij, to name just a few. They all experienced the ruthless cruelty, the consequences of that death of God that were poured out inevitably in the agony and death of humanity.

In the wound and the cry of Jesus, which contains all the wounds and cries that arise from "the reversal of history,"[13] Chiara rediscovered not so much the center *toward which* to turn her gaze but rather the center *from which* to open her eyes to a vision capable of starting history afresh. Just a

---

ment, in the temptation of nihilism, in the absurdity of many physical, moral and spiritual sufferings" that wound today's humanity. For this reason, he concluded, "also the Christian and the very Church can feel identified with the Christ of Saint John of the Cross, at the height of his suffering and of his abandonment," in order to reveal to the world today in faith, in hope, and above all in love, from within this very dark night, the dawn of a new resurrection. (Homily, Segovia, November 4, 1982, n. 7) Chiara, referring to this talk, used a similar expression during the last years of her life to describe the trial that we are called to go through today in order to rekindle the light of the resurrection in the living flesh of today's culture. See Chiara Lubich, "Jesus Forsaken and the Cultural and Collective Night," *Charisms in Unity* 4 (2007): 5-11.

13. The formula expresses the story of suffering, injustice, and misery of many from which, all too often, was built and is still built the story of success, promise, and wealth of a few. See Gustavo Gutiérrez, *The Power of the Poor in History*, trans. Robert R. Barr (Eugene, OR: Wipf and Stock, 2004).

few years after the end of World War II, in the summer of 1949,[14] she wrote a passage where she described the *focus* of this new vision of reality with clarity and force:

> I have only one Spouse on earth: Jesus Forsaken; I have no other God but Him. In Him is the whole of Paradise with the Trinity and the whole of earth with humanity.[15]

Here is the center!

It is found again in that it was freely received and resolutely embraced by Chiara. When she wrote these words, she had just finished living through an intense period of light (in the summer of 1949) where she had contemplated and lived in her heart the wonders of God's plan of love for the whole of humanity revealed to her by Jesus and shared with her companions. Then, in returning to everyday life, she saw the new life and light born from the love of God for humanity concentrated in Jesus, who on the cross suffered forsakenness to the very depths, thereby identifying himself with each person whatever their situation. It is passing through *this* wound, together with every other person, that a new human history begins to unfold. It is not by chance that the one to accompany her on this "divine adventure," in those key years of postwar moral and civil reconstruction, was a man of a vast and open culture, a man of conviction and generous political action, namely, Igino Giordani.[16]

Chiara, therefore, had found the center in which to dwell. But it was not a calm retreat or an impenetrable fortress. Rather, it was a tent open to pilgrims, destined to welcome in whoever thirsts for truth and hungers for justice. The

---

14. On the meaning of the summer of 1949 in Chiara's story and that of the Focolare, we see in particular the fruit of the work of the Abba School in publishing Chiara's original writing from those times along with commentaries by Abba School members in *Clartias: Journal of Dialogue and Culture* 2 (2013): 4–31. This event is narrated, in a full synthesis, by Chiara herself in the story published in *Claritas: Journal of Dialogue and Culture* 1 (2012): 5–12.

15. Chiara Lubich, *Essential Writings: Spirituality, Dialogue, Culture* (Hyde Park, NY: New City Press, 2007), 95 (translation revised).

16. For a brief but rigorous and well-documented introduction, see Tommaso Sorgi, *Giordani: Segno di tempi nuovi* (Rome: Città Nuova, 1994). Nor can we forget the decisive contribution that, starting from those years, Pasquale Foresi would give to the incarnation of the charism of unity. He, like Giordani, was considered by Chiara to be a co-founder of the Focolare Movement.

wound of the Forsakenness is term new and original to Chiara and is a "sign of the [new] times" beginning to appear.[17] It was for Chiara the point of entry to the house where all can live freely. By together crossing the threshold of the experience of love received, returned, and generously spread everywhere, people can experience the conviviality and joy of a reconciled life. They regain hope and re-find meaning and direction in life. Because of its inner roots in the Spirit of God, coupled with an original "unchurchy" and non-ideological approach that addresses the various issues of the human condition, the charism of unity opens hearts and minds to a vision where *all* can feel at home. This includes those who are in any way wounded and marginalized by the harsh trials of life and the heartless processes of history. It is a vision shared by *all together* on the basis of their living tradition's experience and thought.

In the wound of the Forsaken One is summed up the history of humanity and of civilizations in their immense diversity and in the magnificence and drama of actual events, not only *diachronically*, in history's unfolding over time, but also *synchronically*, in the dialogical encounters, in the exchanges, and in the synergy to which the many expressions of human experience are called. Jesus Forsaken is for Chiara the face *before which* and the space *in which* people can re-find themselves as part of a mutual relationship with every other person. He is, for her, the Teacher[18] of that full dialogue that Pope Paul VI proclaimed with prophetic vigor in his encyclical *Ecclesiam Suam* (1964). There, he proposed the following to the conscience of humanity as the imperative and the *immense opportunity* of our time:

> The Church must enter into dialogue with the world in which it lives. It has something to say, a message to give, a communication to make. (n. 67)
>
> Indeed, the whole history of man's salvation is one long, varied dialogue, which marvellously begins with God and which He prolongs with men in so many different ways. In Christ's "conversation" with men, God reveals something of Himself, of the mystery of His own life, of His own unique essence and trinity

---

17. See *The Cry of Jesus Crucified and Forsaken* (Hyde Park, NY: New City Press, 2001). For a biblical understanding, Gérard Rossé, "Entry into the Paradise of '49 and Biblical Revelation," *Claritas: Journal of Dialogue and Culture* 2 (2012): 4–21. For a theological understanding, see Stefan Tobler, *Jesu Gottverlassenheit als Heilsereignis in der Spiritualität Chiara Lubichs* (Berlin: Walter de Gruyter, 2003).

18. Above all, see the penetrating essays of G. M. Zanghì, *Gesù Abbandonato maestro di pensiero* (Rome: Città Nuova, 2008).

of persons. At the same time He tells us how He wishes to be known: as Love pure and simple; and how He wishes to be honoured and served: His supreme commandment is love. (n. 72)

Wherever men are striving to understand themselves and the world, we are able to communicate with them. (n. 101)

For it becomes obvious in a dialogue that there are various ways of coming to the light of faith and it is possible to make them all converge on the same goal. However divergent these ways may be, they can often serve to complete each other. They encourage us to think on different lines. They force us to go more deeply into the subject of our investigations and to find better ways of expressing ourselves. It will be a slow process of thought, but it will result in the discovery of elements of truth in the opinion of others and make us want to express our teaching with great fairness. It will be set to our credit that we expound our doctrine in such a way that others can respond to it, if they will, and assimilate it gradually. (n. 86)

Chiara, during that decisive summer of 1949, wrote:

To take into self the All it is necessary to be nothingness like Jesus Forsaken.

And on nothingness everyone can write . . . It is necessary to put ourselves before everyone in an attitude of learning, for we really have something to learn. And only nothingness gathers all into itself and clasps to itself each thing in unity: it is necessary to be nothing (Jesus Forsaken) before each brother or sister in order to clasp *Jesus* to ourselves in them: "Whatever you do . . ."[19]

In a word, Chiara discovered in Jesus Forsaken a surprising metaphor that seems to sum up the intuition of the charism:

[T]he pupil of the Eye of God upon the world: an infinite Void through which God looks upon us, the window of God thrown open upon the world and the window of humanity through which we see God.[20]

---

19. Chiara Lubich, Unpublished Writing, August 1949.
20. Chiara Lubich, Unpublished Writing, August 28, 1949.

In Chiara's intuition, our view of the world insofar as it is correct, beautiful, and productive is born from God's view of us. Jesus Forsaken is its form and *focus*. This is because we are dealing with a view (the eye) that passes through the emptiness of self[21] (the pupil) to welcome the other and be regenerated together with the other in love.

But this is not only a religious or spiritual intuition. Rather, it is the principle and the *theor-ethical*[22] key that is doctrinal and practical at the same time. It is the key to an amazing ferment of cultural renewal that is offered and proposed to us.[23] It is a matter of looking to God (for believers), to the human person and the cosmos (for everyone), with the eyes with which Jesus looks at them in his forsakenness: that is, from and in that unconditional and infinite love that is "the" life and "the" destiny of us all. Fascinating, unforeseen future prospects thus emerge. They respond to the nostalgia that can be found in every genuine culture urging it towards the attainment, achieved with huge effort and foretasted in history, of the goal to which we all aspire. Indeed, I recently heard at the Sophia University Institute a student from a war-torn country say, "Certain things can be seen only by eyes that have cried." Indeed. The prospects that the window of Jesus forsaken opens before us are of a different vision, one that is performative. It welcomes and transforms what it perceives and contemplates in the tears it shares with those who weep and in the longings of those who search.

This vision contemplates God, in the first place, as the One who is all and always agape.[24]

Agape here means a gift and communication of Self so that the other can be and become fully what the other is. This, for Chiara, is the deep meaning enclosed in faith in a God who is Father, Son, and Holy Spirit. Contemplating God as a Trinity of love means not only that God says with deeds,

---

21. Such an "emptying of oneself" recalls the *kenosis* (emptying) that the apostle Paul refers to in the letter to the Philippians (2:7) to describe the act with which the Son of God stripped himself of his equality with God to become in all aspects similar to humans and to thus share with them, through this poverty, his richness (2 Cor 8:9).
22. See Adriano Fabris, *TeorEtica: Filosofia della relazione* (Brescia: Morcelliana, 2009).
23. An account of it is given in the book referred to above, that is, a compendium of some of Chiara's most significant writings: Chiara Lubich, *Essential Writings*.
24. See Marisa Cerini, *God Who is Love in the Experience and Thought of Chiara Lubich* (New York: New City Press, 1992).

"*it is absolutely good for the other to be,*"[25] but also that he wants the other to become, in a freely given gift, "*his or her other self.*" God, in Chiara's intuition, is the first to live with human beings the key commandment he gave us: "love your neighbor *as* yourself." This is precisely because God is Love, and to love is to want *to bring the other to the height of self*[26]—into the freedom and the joy of sharing all one is and all one has.

This is the life of God, the Trinity of love,[27] communicated to the world in Jesus forsaken. We can look at people, at history, at the cosmos with this vision and in all discern and advance the grammar and the syntax of *this* love. This is a love that is human and social, a love that lives and grows within the rhythm of Trinitarian love. It is a love that loves, is loved, and makes us one in that life, which is freedom and joy. It is a love that still loves where meaning has been lost, distorted, even rejected—precisely where relationships have been damaged by conflict, indifference, or hatred. For God himself, in his Son who shared the human condition to the point of his cry of forsakenness, immersed himself in our condition, in everything so as to rekindle meaning and life.

---

25. As noted by Hans Urs von Balthasar in his *Theo-drama*, Vol. V, (Milan: Jaca Book, 1996), 70.
26. "All that God does," explains Chiara in an unpublished document on Paradise '49, "is *perfect work, perfect like God,* and so Trinitarian, which means: Love-filled, that is: bringing the brother or sister, the other to the height of self by communicating self to the other." About this passage, she commented: "Love, in fact, cannot be but Trinitarian."
27. For an illustration of Chiara's Trinitarian vision at its roots in the dogmatic and theological tradition and in the ray of light traced out by the great charisms, see my essay: "L'esperienza e l'intelligenza della fede in Dio Trinità: Da Sant'Agostino a Chiara Lubich," *Nuova Umanità* 167 (2006): 527–52. A summary of my arguments appears in *Claritas: Journal of Dialogue and Culture* 1 (2012): 15–16. This essay developed into *Dio che dice Amore: Lezioni di teologia* (Rome: Città Nuova, 2007); *Dalla Trinità: L'avvento di Dio tra storia e profezia* (Rome: Città Nuova, 2011); and *La Trinità e il destino d'Europa* (Rome: Città Nuova, 2013). In this regard, of particular interest is the work of Klaus Hemmerle, who took part in the Abba School since its inception, from *Tesi di ontologia trinitaria: Per un rinnovamento della filosofia cristiana* (Rome: Città Nuova, 1986) to his last book, published posthumously, *Partire dall'unità: La Trinità come stile di vita e forma di pensiero* (Rome: Città Nuova, 1998); and Giuseppi Maria Zanghì, *Dio che è Amore: Trinità e vita in Cristo* (Rome: Città Nuova, 1991). Worthy of attention is the fact that the great social encyclical of Benedict XVI, *Caritas in Veritate* (2009), published to commemorate the *Populorum Progressio* of Paul VI, indicates in the mystery of the Trinitarian God the focus, in the Christian vision, of that "new thrust in thinking" necessary today to face the crisis of the current world, revealing a utilizable horizon of transformation (nos. 54–5).

All this is true even though what it provokes and often demands can only be believed in and hoped for with trust and perseverance, even as we do not see it accomplished in fact and cannot guess how and when it will happen. Chiara once wrote:

> I felt that I have been created as a gift for the one next to me and the one next to me has been created by God as a gift for me. As the Father in the Trinity is all for the Son and the Son is all for the Father.
>
> On earth all is in relationship of love with all: each thing with each thing. It is necessary to be Love to find the thread of gold among beings.[28]

The humanism to which we all aspire is expressed in these simple words full of light.

What we have to do is wake up and make effective in historical praxis the logic of gift that dwells in our consciences and enlightens our minds. It is this logic that makes us men and women who are responsible for each other in the concreteness of social, cultural, economic, and political life. And all the time we must keep our attention on the "who" of each person in his or her extraordinary dignity and extraordinary destiny.

In Jesus' vision, this is the humanism of "on earth as it is in heaven." In the "Our Father," which he gave to his disciples (see Mt 6:10), he invites us to ask for this humanism with trust and to pursue it with determination. It is a humanism that, in the wonder of the gift received in this way, builds up through human acts and time not only the *interior castle*, which cares for and contemplates the presence of God in the heart of the individualal, but it also builds up the *exterior castle*,[29] in which "love that is true and truth that

---

28. See Callan Slipper, "Toward an Understanding of the Human Person According to the Mystical Experience of Chiara Lubich in the Paradise of '49," *Claritas: Journal of Dialogue and Culture* 1 (2012): 29 (translation revised).
29. The expression is from Chiara herself and already appears in her writings of 1949. It recalls the symbol of the "interior castle" that Teresa of Avila used to describe the mysticism aimed at collecting within one's soul—aptly seen as an "interior castle"—the presence of God Trinity promised by Jesus (Jn 14:23). With the symbol of the "exterior castle," Chiara intends to express the originality of the mysticism that is proper to the charism of unity where God Trinity does not come to dwell only in the soul of each one, but among those who, also according to Jesus' promise,

is love" comes to live not only in the heart of *each one of us*, but also *among us*, as men and women who believe in the greatness of our common destiny.

Certainly, and Chiara was aware of this, such a faith becomes incarnate in the here and now of the unfinishedness and provisionality that characterize the course of our lives, with their ever-present tentativeness and riskiness in time. And these lives, for the one who believes, are accompanied by the presence of the love of the Father and destined, in Jesus, to conclude in "new heavens and new earth."

The course of our lives asks of all of us not so much to *manage* what we are and live and do but to *generate* it together with others. This means to give birth in reciprocity of intentions and action, step-by-step, meeting after meeting, project after project, to the growth of each one of us, excluding none, into the mature and perfect stature of the complete Person (see Eph 4:13). And this, according to the charism of unity of which Chiara became for us the incomparable interpreter and guide, is *the style and the work of Mary*. She gave her body and her life to the seed of a new humanity.

---

are united in His name (Mt 18:20). Chiara explains that this unity extends from the God in oneself to the God in the neighbor. This has important implications on the cultural and social levels. On this subject, see Chiara's own meditation, "A Spirituality of Communion," in *Essential Writings*, 31–2. See also the dense synthesis by Zanghì, "Il castello esteriore," *Nuova Umanità* 26 (2004): 371–76; and the essays by Jesús Castellano Cervera, *Il castello esteriore: Il "nuovo" nella spiritualità di Chiara Lubich*, ed. Fabio Ciardi (Rome: Città Nuova, 2011).

Chapter Nine

God and Creation: Trinity and Creation Out of Nothing

Piero Coda

The approach in this essay on God and creation is not purely biblical but theological while obviously proceeding constantly from and in the light that comes to us from the Word of God.

Current Relevance and Implications

A basic theological reflection on the relationship between God and creation is of great topical relevance nowadays. It involves a question that, even if only rarely asked explicitly, provides the backdrop for so many of the issues and problems that contemporary culture is facing.[1] One need only think of the pressing questions to which the Christian doctrine of creation has been subjected by physicists (with the Big Bang theory),[2] by cosmology (with its anthropic principle),[3] and by the new ecological and holistic awareness that is marking the passage from modernity to postmodernity.[4]

---

1. Evidence of this renewed interest in the subject of the beginning (the Greek philosophers' *archē*) can be found, for example, in Massimo Cacciari's tour de force, significantly entitled *Dell'Inizio* (Milan: Adelphi, 1990).
2. See Brendan Purcell, *From Big Bang to Big Mystery: Human Origins in Light of Creation and Evolution* (Hyde Park, NY: New City Press, 2012).
3. See John Polkinghorne, *Faith, Science, and Understanding* (New Haven, Conn.: Yale University Press, 2001).
4. With regard to these themes in general, see: in Italy, the documentation from the Conference of the Italian Theological Association entitled *Futuro del cosmo: Futuro dell'uomo* (Padua: EMP, 1997); in France, the wide-ranging and accurate review by Jean-Michel Maldamé, "Science et foi: Conditions nouvelles du dialogue," *Revue Thomiste* (1997): 525–62, the work of the astrophysicist Michel Cassé, *Du vide et de la création* (Paris: O. Jacob, 1996), and that of the theologian Adolphe Gesché, *Dieu pour penser: Le cosmos* (Paris: Cerf, 1994); in Germany, the volume by Alexandre Ganoczy, *Suche nach Gott auf den wegen der natur: Theologie, mystik, naturwissenschaften; Ein kritischer versuch* (Dusseldorf: Patmos, 1992), and Max Seckler's essay "Was heisst eigentlich 'schöpfung?' Zugleich ein beitrag zum dialog zwischen

But interreligious dialogue also seems to be calling the concept of creation into question. For example, the Buddhist interpretation of the universe has difficulty not only in accepting but also in understanding the sort of God-world duality that the creation principle would seem to postulate, at least in some of its simplistic and reductive interpretations.[5] This is to say nothing of a whole vein of modern philosophy—starting with Nietzsche and passing through Heidegger—that sees the interweaving of the Christian doctrine of creation out of nothing with the Greek metaphysics of being versus becoming as the cause of the nihilism into which the history of Western culture has fatally slipped. Some authors argue that a mysterious obfuscation of the perception of God's creative presence seems to be casting its shadow over our era: If everything is born of nothing, then everything is also irreparably destined to return to nothing.[6]

This field of research requiring further in-depth analysis is thus vast and the need to do it is pressing. This field extends from exegesis on the teaching that

---

    theologie und naturwissenschaft," *Theologische Quartalschrift* (1997): 161–88; in English, Keith Ward, *Religion and Creation* (Oxford: OUP, 1996).

5. Here is evidence from two well-known thinkers from the Kyoto School in Japan, who have opened a dialogue with Christian thought regarding the creation theme. Kitaro Nishida writes: "God has created the world out of love. And this entails the self-negation of the absolute—that *God is love* . . . the absolute affirmation through the self-negation of God, and this is the true meaning of creation" (*The Logic of Place and a Religious Worldview* [Honolulu: University of Hawaii Press, 1987]a, 100, 86–87). Masao Abe writes: "The Christian God ought to be understood not as a God who is far from non-being and negativity, but as a God who willingly takes on a non-being and a self-denial. . . . Although self-sufficient, God denies Himself out of love and creates the world as different from Himself" ("Buddhism and Christianity as a Problem of Today," *Japanese Religions* [1963]: l0). For a full comparison of the Kyoto School and Christianity, see Donald W. Mitchell, *Spirituality and Emptiness: The Dynamics of the Spiritual Life in Buddhism and Christianity* (New York: Paulist Press, 1991).

6. In an interview, Emanuele Severino summarized this point of view thus: "At the root of Western culture there now lies the persuasion that the real things we have to deal with are ephemeral. We can certainly try to grab and hold onto the greatest possible number of them but the undisputed fact remains that the great, unchanging gods conferring a stable sense of the world no longer exist. The message that our culture gives to contemporary humanity is that everything is nothing, in the sense that everything comes out of nothing and goes back into nothing. So, I wonder whether those who assume psychologically deviant attitudes—the mad, the depressed and those we consider not to be normal—may not, in reality, be far-sighted. Far-sighted because through their behavior they are drawing the conclusion that must inevitably be drawn from a vision of the nullity of things" (*l'Unità*, July 21, 1997, 2).

comes to us from scripture and the revisiting of assertions of dogma acquired through tradition to more systematic theological reflections, all of which have secured important results over the last decades. In this context, Chiara Lubich's theological vision of the relationship between God and creation shows a pithy relevance and an equally incisive originality. It is this vision that I would seek to explore here, offering no more than a sort of reasoned indication of some of the subjects on which her perspective sheds light.

Regarding the Meaning of the Concept of Creation

Before we get to the heart of our subject, it seems essential to make a preliminary, methodological remark that may allow us to get off to a good start. What does the word "creation" mean? And how are we to understand the concept if we are to keep as close as possible to the perspective of revelation? As it is generally used in our cultural context, the term "creation" has three distinct meanings.

The first is typical of biblical revelation and has been defined with the precision of dogma through the reflection of Church Fathers and medieval theologians. It indicates that *act* of God and God alone through which God freely gives being to that which is not. In this sense, the word "creation" has a primarily verbal meaning insofar as it indicates "creating" as an action that is specifically God's and no one else's.

A second meaning, one obviously closely linked to and deriving from the first, indicates that *being* is distinct from God and is the fruit of God's creative act. This is creation as a noun, that is, as "that which has been created," of which—in the light of Christian revelation—the cosmos and humanity must be seen as its culmination and fullest meaning.

But there is also a third, deeper, and broader meaning. Already present in the Old Testament, it is most clearly expressed in the New Testament, gaining ground in Christian self-awareness in the light of an understanding of Jesus Christ as the heart of God's salvation plan. Here, creation means *relationship* between God and that to which God freely makes the gift of existence. Creation is so as to introduce it into full communion with Godself. Thus creation has the meaning of a dynamic *event*, of *history*: the history of God's relationship with humanity and through the latter with the cosmos. Paul illustrates this meaning in his letter to the Ephesians (Eph 1:3-10), where he gives a panoramic view of the plan always known and desired by God the Father in Jesus Christ, in whom "we were chosen before the world was created." This plan was implemented in the fullness of time through the incarnation of the Son of God and is destined to come to its fulfilment in the recapitulation of all things in him.

In this perspective, the biblical scholar Giuseppe Barbaglio can justifiably formulate the following thesis:

> Creation is the whole range of divine action, from the forming of the world and the birth of humanity to the end of the kingdom, passing through the historical phases of the People of Israel's salvation adventure, the existence of Jesus Christ Who died and rose again and the experience of the community of believers.[7]

Chiara Lubich's Perspective

Chiara opts decisively for this last perspective, but she does not neglect the other meanings of the concept of creation, especially not the first: that of creation as an act of God. As we shall see, this meaning has a huge metaphysical importance. It helps us understand the meaning of all that is.[8] I am thinking, in particular, of a passage of hers that has, for me, shed much light on our subject: "God creates all things just as he develops the Heavens: the Heaven coming after supersedes the one before with infinite beauty, and sums it up."[9]

In Chiara's language, "Heaven" is the Reality that God enables her to live unity with her brothers and sisters sealed by the Eucharist. God gives Himself to her in ever new ways, so that the Reality that follows supersedes

---

7. Giuseppe Barbaglio, "Creazione: Messaggio biblico," *Nuovo Dizionario di Teologia*, ed. Giuseppe Barbaglio and Severino Dianich (Alba: Edizioni Paoline, 1977), 185.
8. In reality, in order to be understood correctly from the Christian revelation viewpoint, the abovementioned concept of creation as an event must be related to that which emphasizes the novelty and freedom of the creative act by which God brings into being that which is not. This in order to safeguard the ontological difference between God and that which is created, insofar as only God is through Himself and in Himself. Even when that which has been created is brought (through Christ and in the Spirit) to participate in God's Being, God remains, precisely, the permanent origin of the absolutely free gift of His Being to the created being (which, by itself, is not).
9. All quotations that do not have footnote references are from Chiara's unpublished writings from her mystical period called "Paradise '49." For a translation of the beginning of this text and a contextualization of the full text, see *Claritas: Journal of Dialogue and Culture* 1, no. 1 (2012): 5–23.

the preceding Reality and contains it within itself. Reading creation in this perspective, Chiara explains:

> First God created the whole universe. Then humankind. The universe without humankind would have appeared an absurdity, and humankind was its crown. Humankind was its crown and its synthesis: it is the head of the universe and hence contains it During creation, however, humankind did not appear absurd since humankind, the last thing created, was the head of all the rest and its crowning.

However, she then states more specifically, "All creatures and humankind are summed up in Jesus."

Thus Chiara emphasizes that creation is precisely an "event": God brings that which is created into being, thereby beginning a story. So creation stretches over time and develops. It is not simply a specific act that is realized once and for all in the beginning. In this way, the conflict between nature and history that has marked Western culture is overcome. We normally say that there is the cosmos, on the one hand, and there is human history born of freedom, on the other. In reality, things are simpler and at the same time more profound. While not denying that the human being gifted with intelligence and freedom is original and distinct from the other created beings, Chiara says that it is also necessary to emphasize humanity's communion with nature. Indeed, Paul demonstrates this communion in his letter to the Romans when he states that "the whole creation is eagerly waiting for God to reveal his sons" and "still retains the hope of being freed from its slavery to decadence, to enjoy the same freedom and glory as the children of God" (Rom 8:19-21).

The schematic distinction between creation and redemption became established in theology after the patristic period. Thus it became necessary to pose the question whether the incarnation of the Son of God would have been necessary had there been no original sin.[10] For Chiara, this must be profoundly re-understood in a unitary and dynamic perspective. Because

---

10. This problem is overcome in the theology of Franciscan inspiration that, being decidedly Christocentric, intuits the unity of the divine salvation plan. In this respect, the theological vision of Duns Scotus is emblematic. He writes, "I say therefore that the fall was not the cause of Christ's predestination and that if no one had fallen, neither the angel nor man, in this hypothesis, Christ would still have been predestined in this way" (*Reportatio Pariensis in III Sent.* D. 7, q. 4) (translation revised).

just as the human being sums up the cosmos insofar as the cosmos finds its meaning in humanity, so Jesus sums up humanity and the meaning of humanity's history.[11]

Creation must therefore be conceived of as an event: a unitary event that is fully realized in Jesus Christ and that strains toward its eschatological consummation. This is the basic perspective that stands out clearly in Chiara's thinking. More specifically, she sees creation from the perspective of the "One" that is at the same time its Origin (the One and Triune God) and its eschatological point of arrival ("God all in all"). It is not a question of creation as only a matter of causing being to spring out of the nothing "outside" God. Rather, creation is a causing of being to spring out of the nothing outside God so that God, through Jesus and in the Holy Spirit, may give God's own Being to created being.[12]

A Trinitarian and Creational Metaphysics of Love

In Chiara's thinking, this unitary and dynamic vision is totally imbued with all that is most original in what the New Testament tells us about God's being and acting: "God is *Agape*" (1 Jn 4:8, 16). With a radical and also intellectual faithfulness to this confession of faith that summarizes the Christological revelation, Chiara sees in *agape* not only one in the variety of God's attributes but also that which expresses God's very Being. For this reason, one can and one must say that the Being of God is Love. This allows us to penetrate the mystery of God in Godself. Precisely because God is Love, God is One and Three: Father, Son, and Holy Spirit, or as Augustine explains, the Lover, the Beloved, and their reciprocal Love.[13] It also allows us to penetrate the mystery of creation, its most profound raison d'être, its

---

11. Contemporary theology is moving in this direction. Karl Rahner emphasizes that "the human being . . . is the true primary intention of creation understood as the pre-condition of the divine self-communication," and thus "a theological doctrine of creation . . . must have a Christological orientation" (*Schöpfungslehre*, in LThK, IX [Freiburg: I.B., 1963], 472).
12. Giuseppe Colombo writes, "Jesus Christ is the revelation of creation's meaning. That is, he reveals that creation is the action God takes in order to communicate the Trinitarian existence ad extra and, more precisely, in order to generate sons and daughters of God ad extra" ("Creazione: Riflessione teologica," *Nuovo Dizionario di Teologia*, 201).
13. St. Augustine, *De Trinitate*, VIII, 8, 12: "Embrace the love of God, and by love embrace God . . . 'God is love; and he that dwells in love, dwells in God'; but when I see love, I do not see in it the Trinity. Nay, but you see the Trinity if you see love.

dynamic and its purpose.¹⁴ Chiara writes: "All that *is* in Creation is God's creature, creature of that God who cannot give what he does not have, what he *is not*."

To put it positively: God, being Love, cannot not but want to share everything God has and is with His creatures. So, the key to casting light on the mystery of creation—on the being that is created by God—is precisely this: the fact that God, because God is Love, wants to give His very Being to that which is not Godself. In another text, Chiara develops this perspective further:

> All that God does is *perfect* work, *perfect like God*, and so trinitarian, which means: Love-filled, that is: bringing the brother or sister, the other to the height of self by communicating self to the other.

The first person to live the commandment to love one's neighbor—"love your neighbor *as* yourself"—is God. Indeed, God creates the other (God's neighbor) from Godself, so as to make him or her become like Godself, another Self. This is because God is Love; God is Trinity. Were God not to love His creature to that extent, God would not be totally and only Love. Chiara writes:

> The Father, loving the Son, loves himself. Loving us as the Son, *he loves us as himself*. Hence he lives the Gospel. He loves his neighbor (and we are God's neighbors) as himself.

In light of this, I will now try, in a few rapid brushstrokes, to depict the main phases of the creation event in the perspective of what we could call Chiara's Trinitarian and creation metaphysics of love. The phases are consecutive if considered in terms of temporal development. This is because God first creates the cosmos, then human beings appear and then, in the

---

But if I can, I will put you in mind, that you may see that you see it." St. Augustine, *De Trinitate*, VIII, 10, 14: "Behold, then, there are three things: he that loves, and that which is loved, and love. What, then, is love, except a certain life which couples or seeks to couple together some two things, namely, him that loves and that which is loved?"

14. In reality, traces of this vision are present in the whole of the church's great theological and mystical tradition. For example, Catherine of Siena writes, "For what reason would you have elevated man to such great dignity? Of course, it was the unfathomable love with which you looked upon your creature within yourself and you fell in love with that creature" (*Dialogo della Divina Provvidenza*, chapter 13).

fullness of time, there is the event of Jesus: his incarnation, his forsakenness, his resurrection, his ascent to the bosom of the Father. But at the same time, while the phases are chronologically distinct and follow one after the other, they are also—if seen from the perspective of the One—dimensions that bit by bit begin to constitute the creation event in its final meaning and its eschatological point of arrival, revealing and realizing God's final project. So the cosmos is recapitulated in humanity, humanity is recapitulated in Jesus, and Jesus carries everything with Him to the bosom of the Father.[15]

Creation out of God the Trinity

Creation out of Nothing

The first point for development here concerns the initial act through which God creates and the permanent act through which God supports that which he has created, keeps it in being, and makes it evolve. Following the perspective of biblical revelation, Christian theology has developed a concept that is characteristically its own and original to it: the concept of *creatio ex nihilo* (creation out of nothing).[16] This precise formula is intended to emphasize two things of the utmost importance. On the one hand, that God alone is and has always been and that every being other than God has its origin in God, without the contribution of anything else. On the other hand, that the origin of things in God is the fruit of freedom, a newness that is rooted solely in God's freely made and gratuitous choice

---

15. After all, this is Paul's perspective when he states succinctly, "all belong to you, and you belong to Christ, and Christ belongs to God" (1 Cor 3: 21-23).

16. This doctrine of the faith was formulated by the IV Lateran Council (1215): DS 800; by the Council of Florence (1442): DS 1333; and by the First Vatican Council (1870): DS 3002. Thomas Aquinas explains, "If the emanation of the whole universal being from the first principle be considered, it is impossible that any being should be presupposed before this emanation. For *nothing* is the same as no being. . . . So creation, which is the emanation of all being, is from the 'not-being' which is 'nothing'" (*Summa Theologiae* I, 45, 1, c). As regards the genesis of this formula during the patristic period as the updating extension of the doctrine contained in the Hebrew-Christian revelation, see Jacques Fantino, "L'origine de la doctrine del la création ex nihilo," *Revue des Sciences philosophiques et théologiques* (1996): 589–602, which enters into a dialogue with a book on the same subject by Gerhard May, *Creation ex nihilo: The Doctrine of "Creation out of Nothing" in Early Christian Thought* (Edinburgh: T. & T. Clark Ltd, 1994).

to love. "The newness of the world," writes Aquinas, "cannot be demonstrated on the part of the world itself."[17]

Within the perspective of a Trinitarian metaphysics of love, it is possible to penetrate more deeply into the reason for, and the dynamics of, the event of creation "out of nothing." This is a path of reflection that contemporary theologians are beginning to follow. One may think of Hans Urs von Balthasar[18] in the Catholic tradition; even more so of Sergei Bulgakov[19] in the Orthodox tradition; and of Jürgen Moltmann[20] in the Protestant tradition. As far as the philosophical field is concerned, one can think of Maurice Blondel.[21] Chiara herself writes:

> When God created, he created all things from nothing because he created them from himself – from nothing means that they did not pre-exist because he alone pre-existed (but this way of speaking is inexact because in God there is no before and after). He, however, drew them out from himself because in creating them he died (of love), he died in love, he loved and so he created.[22]

---

17. Thomas Aquinas, *Summa Theologiae* I, 46, 2 c.
18. See Hans U. von Balthasar, *Theo-Drama: Theological Dramatic Theory*, vol. 5: *The Last Act*, trans. Graham Harrison (San Francisco: Ignatius Press, 1998).
19. See, above all, Bulgakov's *Bride of the Lamb* (Grand Rapids: W. B. Eerdmans, 2002).
20. See Moltmann's *God in Creation: An Ecological Doctrine of Creation* (London: SCM Press, 1985).
21. Having observed that "the idea of nothing is a pseudo-idea," Blondel states, "God most certainly does not leave outside Himself absolutely anything that one may imagine empty or call positive nothingness. But in that case, it will be said, where are we to place the potential or existing creatures, then, in this integrally compact monism? . . . I have already remembered, by having recourse (like Ravaissan) to St. Paul's sublime expression, *Deus semetipsum exinanivit*: God, in order to create, has not produced a new fullness or at least a semi-fullness, some ontological nebula, outside and alongside Himself (which would be absurd). . . . It is less deceptive to start from the premise of a wholly merciful intention on the part of the Creator, Who prepares the possibility of life, happiness and a transforming union for other Selves not in space, not in His substantive fullness but in His fruitful love" (*L'Être et les êtres* [Paris: *PUF*, 1963], 311–12; see Santino Cavaciuti, "Naturale e soprannaturale nell'ontologia di Blondel," in *Attualità del pensiero di M. Blondel*, ed. Romeo Crippa and Peter Henrici (Milan: Massimo, 1976), 103–8.
22. Of the authors referred to, it seems particularly meaningful to quote some of the statements Bulgakov makes in his book *Bride of the Lamb*: "Absolute nothing, *ouk on*, simply does not exist; it is a 'conditional reflex' of our thought, not more. And if we believe that the world is created out of nothing, then, in the positive sense, this can mean only that God created the world out of Himself" (44). He then explains, "God is love, and the creation of the world is the action of God's love, its self-rev-

Chiara sees creation as a "death," as God's loving *kenosis*: the leaving room for the other or indeed, from our perspective here, the making oneself the other. This is analogous to what happens between the divine Persons in the Trinity, where the Father generates the Son through love, loses Himself in the Son, and "dies" in the Son; the Son hands Himself back to the Father through love, loses Himself in the Father, and "dies" in Him; and the Holy Spirit proceeds from both through love and fuses them into One through love, loses Himself and "dies" in Them; so that each one of the Three is through, with, and in the Other Two. The only difference is that in creation, this happens on God's part in relation to that which is not God, or better still, in relation to that which of itself simply is not.

In the perspective of charity, we could therefore reformulate the *creatio ex nihilo* principle by speaking of an *ex nihilo amoris*[23] in the sense that the "nothing" out of which God creates is that loving nothing that God freely becomes in the moment when God gives being to that which is not. Indeed, in a certain sense, loving always means dying to oneself in order to let the other "be." Infinitely more than we experience in human existence, however, in God this gift, this loving "death," is wholly and only positive: it is the expression of the infinite freedom and super-abundance of God's Being, which is Love.

Scholastic theology clarifies the concept of *creatio ex nihilo* still further by speaking of an *ex nihilo sui et subiecti*, meaning that the "stuff" (the being) of which the creation is made comes totally and only from God. The *ex nihilo "sui"* emphasizes that the creation's being does not derive from God as if the creation were a part or a necessary expression of Godself. The *ex nihilo*

---

elation" (48). And just as the Trinitarian love between the divine Hypostases is a "supra-eternal *kenosis*, but a *kenosis* that has overcome for each of the hypostases in joint Trinitarian love, in the all-blissfulness of this love" (49), so it is in the creation, where "the Holy Trinity in Unity, or the Unity in Trinity, renounces, as it were, in its sacrificially kenotic love the possession of the divine world for itself and allows this world to have its own being. The Trinity in Unity has, or posits, this world outside itself, in separateness from itself, precisely as the world, as non-hypostatic being" (50). Thus "the world is the alter-being of the Principle, the creaturely mode of the divine being" (53).

23. The formula *ex amore* ("by love") can be found in the Second Vatican Council's *Pastoral Constitution on the Church in the Modern World* (No. 19), as can its analogy in the previously cited work by Bulgakov. As regards *Gaudium et Spes*, No. 19, see Andrés Arteuga Manieu, *"Creatio ex amore": Hacia una consideración teológica del misterio de la creación en el Concilio Vaticano II* (Santiago: Pontifical Catholic University of Chile, 1995).

"subiecti" emphasizes that the creation derives nothing from some element of the creation that in some way existed before God's creative act (such as the prime matter [*prote hule*] or empty space [*chora*] that Aristotle and Plato spoke of, respectively). But this formula does not say positively *how* the creation's being derives from God's Being. Nor does it intend to deny that the creation's being—as Aquinas explains—comes from God's Being through "emanation" or "participation," two concepts that are intended to refer to that mystery wherein it is God's Being that is the sole Principle of every other being.

It is precisely through looking at the Trinity that the Trinitarian perspective of love can help us to penetrate the creation dynamic more deeply. The Father gives Being to the Son by generating Him and, in this way, gives the Son all the Father's (divine) Being except His paternity. Thus God in giving being to the creation and in Christ Jesus, through the Spirit, gives it all His Being, except His Being God in and through Himself. Therefore, just as the Son—in the Trinity—is God without being the Father, so the creation—in Christ—participates in God's Being without being God in and through Himself. Creation is, rather, made to participate fully in God's Being only and always by way of a gift.[24]

Trinity and Creation

The understanding of creation is thus indissolubly linked to the mystery of God who is One and Three. This is an article of faith that belongs to the church's traditional doctrine. St. Augustine, for example, has already stated succinctly, *unus mundus factus est a Patre per Filium in Spiritu Sancto* (the one world was made by the Father through the Son in the Holy Spirit).[25] Developing this thought further, Aquinas reached the conclu-

---

24. Obviously, such a revisiting of the traditional doctrine of creation also requires two of the tradition's other "givens" to be thematically modified and analyzed in greater depth. The first is the ontological status of the "divine ideas" in the Word, and the second is the hypostatic union in Jesus Christ, the Word made flesh, true God and true man, and the participation of other human persons in Him, as His Body, through grace.
25. Augustine, *In Joannis Evangelium* 20, 9: PL 35, 1561; C.f. *De Vera Religione* 55, 113: PL 34, 172; and *De Trinitate* 1, 6, 12: PL 42, 827.

sion that "the causation of creatures belongs to the Persons according to processions and relations."[26]

Chiara's thinking contains an echo of this patristic and scholastic tradition regarding creation as "the work of the Trinity *ad extra*" in light of her own understanding of the One, love, and *kenosis*. We could express her vision more or less in the following terms: God is One and Three because God is Love: Father, Word, and Holy Spirit. The Word is the expression of the Father within Himself, in which the Father contemplates Himself and expresses Himself as infinite tones of Love that converge in One, in the Word that is Love. The Father contemplates in the Word the infinite expressions of Himself—which the classical tradition calls the "divine ideas"—that constitute the Word and, out of love, "dying" out of love, He projects these expressions outside Himself to bring into being another, the creation, that is distinct from Himself and make it freely become another Self.[27] Hence, seen in this light, creation is, we could say, a created God.

---

26. Thomas Aquinas, *Summa Theologiae* I, 45, 6 ad 2um. He calls the divine processions not only the creation's *ratio*, but also its *causa*, *exemplar*, and *origo*; see Gilles Emery O. P., *La Trinité créatrice* (Paris: Vrin, 1995). Here is one of Aquinas's strong statements about the intimate relationship between the creation and the life of the Trinity: "Hence, as the Father speaks Himself and every creature by His begotten Word, inasmuch as the Word 'begotten' adequately represents the Father and every creature; so He loves Himself and every creature by the Holy Ghost, inasmuch as the Holy Ghost proceeds as the love of the primal goodness whereby the Father loves Himself and every creature" (*Summa Theologiae* I, 37, 2 ad 3um).

27. The subject of the divine ideas would require a separate treatment, which is not possible here. Although it appears necessary for an understanding of the creation mystery in a Trinitarian perspective, this subject has fallen into oblivion in modern times after having been widely examined by the Church Fathers and the medieval theologians. This may be primarily because it could lead people to think of a duplication between the two levels or situations of being that the divine ideas have "in" God and "outside" God. For a historical-systematic presentation in contemporary theology, see, in the Catholic Church, Hans Urs von Balthasar, *Theodramatik, Bd. 4: Das Endspiel*; in the Orthodox Church, Bulgakov, *Bride of the Lamb*; and, in the Protestant churches, Wolfhart Pannenberg, *Systematische Theologie* (Göttingen: Vandenhoek and Ruprecht, 1991). In what Chiara says of the "ideas" that are "in" the Word (and are the Word) projected "outside" God during creation, there is the suggestion of the unity of these two levels of the being of the ideas. Going more deeply into this difficult and delicate theological and metaphysical problem in the nineteenth century, Antonio Rosmini gave the following explanation that, while maintaining the essence of the classical tradition, seems to develop it more precisely and in a manner that may be more widely shared: "If one compares the procession of the two divine hypostases from the Trinity's originating Principle, and the procession of the world, one finds an analogy that demonstrates the same con-

What is created is called to become God. This is the reason, in particular, why God creates humanity. Here is a magnificent passage of Chiara's:

> Humankind therefore is creation and, when redeemed, all is redeemed. And then it is the human being who is the one destined to be *another God*. It is the human being who is the masterpiece of God "in process," God's Recreation, his Image and Likeness, which means: another him. And God directed his gaze here above all so he could *live* as a human creature as well as in his divine Nature and could experience loving "according to nature" as well as "according to supernature," in summary, so that he, the Creator, could make himself creature and live the life he had brought about, wed the creation he himself had created making himself *one* with it: *One, Unity inseparable*.

It is important to stress that in this text of Chiara's are present two themes which are closely connected with the central one of creation and humanity's destiny as "another God." First is that of the spousal relationship between Creator and creature thanks to Christ. Second is that of creation as a possibility for God to be not only in Himself (in "the divine nature" as traditional language puts it) but also in/as a creature. There is an important Christolog-

---

stant law of divine operation, a law founded in the same divine essence: (1) Both in the procession of the Persons and in the procession of the world, one finds the distinctive note of *giving* and *producing* an *other* in which lies the actualization of the divine essence insofar as it is what makes up the first hypostasis; (2) Both in the former procession and in the latter one, the *other* that has been produced *remains in the Principle* from which it proceeds and, insofar as it remains in the Principle, it renders it perfect as a principle, it renders it totally actual; but, at the same time, the other that has been produced also exists in itself, as something other than the Principle that has produced it, and this *otherness* does not diminish the Principle: on the contrary, it is a necessary condition of the latter's act and perfection, which lies in giving and producing. Up to this point there exists an analogy and shared law by virtue of which the divine Word is called by St Paul the 'Firstborn of all the creatures,' being also their Principle or cause" (*Teosofia* IV, Book III, Section VI, Cha IV, art. I, 1319, 165 of the Rome 1938 edition). In this perspective, it is not metaphysically contradictory to speak both of the "divine ideas" in God and of the "divine ideas" projected "outside" God. In God, they are one in the Word, being the Word; "outside" God, they are distinct and ontologically autonomous, but their true, full being is nothing other than that which, from the beginning, is to be found in God. "Reaching" or "re-joining" it (figuratively speaking) is due to the recapitulation in Christ where the "created ideas" are realized in God while remaining distinct from God. For a lucid, in-depth examination of the question in a Christological-Trinitarian key, see Giuseppe M. Zanghi, *Dio che è Amore* (Rome: Città Nuova, 1991), 139–40.

ical theme in this second case, too. It reminds us of three things. First is the novelty that the event of the Son's Incarnation constitutes for God because, thanks to that, God can live a new experience as God "in a creature." In this regard, Bernard of Clairvaux uses an expression that Klaus Hemmerle often liked to repeat: the Word *quod ab aeterno sciebat per divinitatem, hoc aliter didicit experimentum per carnem.* Second is creation's calling, in Christ, to participate in the life of God Himself. And third is that the unity is thus deeper and more comprehensive than the distinction (or duality) that nevertheless remains between Creator and creature. One should also note the use of the felicitous expression that calls humanity "God's Recreation." This means, in the first place, that humanity is God's possibility to "create" by participation another Self (re-create = create again). However, it also means, in a figurative sense, that humanity is what gives joy and "renews" God since "recreation" also means play, rest, and enjoyment.[28]

This way of understanding the event of creation by God the Trinity has certain consequences for how nature and the destiny of what has been created are interpreted. Some interpretations confirm the tradition. Others are more markedly original, which makes them suited to a dialogue with the claims of contemporary philosophical and scientific thought.

The Trinitarian Imprint on Creation

Here is a first consequence. Precisely because it occurs as an extension of the divine processions within the heart of the Trinity (as Aquinas would say), creation itself bears the Trinity's imprint. Not only as far as the ontological structure of every single thing is concerned, as the Christian theological and mystical traditions well know,[29] but also as far as the relationship *between* things is concerned. Chiara explains:

> In Creation all is Trinity: Trinity, things in themselves because their *Being* is Love, is Father; the Law in them is Light, is Son, Word; the Life in them is Love, is Holy Spirit. The All given through participation to the Nothing. And they are Trinity among themselves, for the one is Son and Father to the other,

---

28. Here, there is perhaps a reference to the figure of Wisdom "rejoicing in his inhabited world and delighting in the human race" (Prv 8: 31).

29. This is a theme that became central in medieval theology, following the line inaugurated by Augustine in his *De Trinitate*; one need only think of Bonaventure's doctrine of the *vestigia Trinitatis* in the cosmos and the *imago Trinitatis* in humanity.

and all draw together, loving one another, to the *One*, whence they came.[30]

This simple statement has important repercussions for our understanding of the world that cannot go unnoticed. For example, it has much to add to our understanding at a scientific and cosmological level, where there is a tendency nowadays to highlight the fact that all phenomena are structurally interrelated. But also at a philosophical level,[31] it can contribute to the question of the one and the many. In Chiara's vision, the root of the multiplicity of created realities is their unity of being (*esse*) in God, in the Word, from Whom they spring and toward Whom they are orientated. In a well-known text, she uses an enlightening image:

> The Father has an expression of himself outside himself, made as it were of diverging rays, and an expression within Himself, made of rays that converge in the center, in a point that is Love: God in the infinitely small: the Nothing-All of Love! The Word.[32]

This, obviously, is a view from the One, from the perspective of eschatological fulfilment. Indeed, the realization of the Trinitarian structure that

---

30. It is Chiara herself who emphasizes this, commenting on the above text as follows: "Here we see things as they will be: God all in all (see 1 Cor 15:28). And, as Trinity, the Father will be better seen in the being of things, the Son in the law that is in them, the Holy Spirit in the life running through them. Indeed, the text says later, things "all draw together, loving one another, to the One," and so they are on the way to self-realization, to divinization."

31. Joseph Ratzinger, for example, writes that in the Trinitarian conception of God, "lies concealed a revolution in man's view of the world: the sole dominion of thinking in terms of substance is ended; relation is discovered as an equally valid primordial mode of reality. It becomes possible to surmount what we call today 'objectifying thought'; a new plane of being comes into view. It is probably true to say that the task imposed on philosophy as a result of these facts is far from being completed—so much does modern thought depend on the possibilities thus disclosed, without which it would be inconceivable" (Joseph Ratzinger, *Introduction to Christianity* [San Francisco: Ignatius Press, 2004], 184). See also Klaus Hemmerle's theses for a Trinitarian ontology, *Thesen zu einer trinitarischen Ontologie* (Einsiedeln: Johannes Verlag, 1976). For a closer examination of the various perspectives, see the essays in Andreas Tapken and Piero Coda, eds., *La Trinità e il pensare* (Rome: Città Nuova, 1997) and Lubomir Zak and Piero Coda, eds., *Abitando la Trinità* (Rome: Città Nuova, 1998).

32. For a closer examination of the ontological meaning of the multiplicity of the beings created in the light of the One Being of God as tripersonal Love, see the penetrating work by Giuseppe M. Zanghí, "Trinità e creazione," in *Dio che è Amore*, 123–27.

is already present (as an imprint and a calling) from the beginning in what is created requires the completion of the plan in Christ and humanity's free and creative obedience to it in practice. It is Chiara herself who emphasizes this, commenting on the above text as follows: "Here we see things as they will be: God all in all (see 1 Cor 15:28). And, as Trinity, the Father will be better seen in the being of things, the Son in the law that is in them, the Holy Spirit in the life running through them. Indeed, the text says later, things 'all draw together, loving one another, to the One,' and so they are on the way to self-realization, to divinization."

All of this is the work of Jesus Forsaken who (as Chiara explains in another context) "redeemed all that is created, in which the trinitarian trace and life (there we found being and law and life, and all is Love: Father, Son, Holy Spirit) is borne by Jesus Forsaken to the full and complete Trinity."

In God, everything is One, in a Unity that, being Love, is expressed in the Trinity of Persons. Even the "rays" that express the infinite richness of the Father-Love are, in God, Word in the Word. "Outside God," on the other hand, the "rays" are manifold. They are distinct and particularized. But by their nature, they tend toward the One who is the Word, from whom they come. After returning within the Word—through Jesus and Jesus Forsaken—they are One: Word in the Word. In humanity's case, however, they are also distinct one from the other and from God, as occurs in the Trinity,[33] where Father, Son, and Holy Spirit are One and distinct.

This same image of the diverging rays that come back to converge through Jesus Forsaken suggests the importance of another of the fundamental dimensions of creation: time. Nowadays, science talks about (creative) "operative time" as "an immanent component of the universe." Now, it is clear that in this dynamic vision of the creation event, time appears to be an inherent reality of the very multiplicity of created things, which need time both to become distinct and to become one according to God's original plan.

Creation, Conservation, and Evolution

There is another consequence that can only be barely mentioned here. As Pierre Teilhard de Chardin (among others) intuited and tried to explain, there is no insuperable contradiction between the concept of creation and

---

33. As regards the eschatological dimension of the relationship between God and creation, see Piero Coda, "Viaggiare il Paradiso," *Nuova Umanità* (1997): 211–29.

that of evolution when these are properly understood. The fact is that the concept of creation must not be reduced to the anthropomorphic concept of causality as producing things. Adolphe Gesché writes, "Manufacturing is the act of making a thing that is completely determined by and geared towards its own utility. Creating, on the other hand, is making in such a way that the other exists for itself." In this way God "is not the watchmaker intent on making a watch, but the beginner of an adventure." Seen properly, God has created a "creative becoming."[34]

So God not only sustains what God has created and keeps it continually in being (or, to put it better, continually infuses it with being) but also makes what is created in such a way that in some way it "creates itself," it develops itself thanks to God's relationship with it that is always new and always giving rise to new things. There is a very beautiful passage of Chiara's that highlights this. It emphasizes, in particular, that the dynamic key to creation's development is that same *kenosis* of love that creation carries within itself like an imprint. This imprint derives its very origin from the love that comes from God:

> The plant that grows this year from the seed is born from a death: therefore from a nothing. But this nothing is positive in the sense that it is a created nothing. In fact, the plant could not be born from a nothing that is not created. It needs the dead seed.

On the one hand, bringing into being is an act of God; on the other hand, once the creature has been brought into being, it develops the dynamic of its existence. The latter is a dynamic of self-annulment that differs according to the various beings.[35] That allows creation's further temporal and evolutionary development. In this sense, Chiara says: "There was a single creation and God creates continuously."

At the end of this passage, Chiara also talks about human beings and the unique part they are called to play in the history of creation, thanks to their freedom: "Likewise God is born from our willed nothingness for, if I were not, God could not be in me." In this case, too, humanity is brought into being by God so that humanity, as it develops the act of its existence, freely recognizes its own nothingness (i.e., that everything it is, has, and does

---

34. Gesché, *Dieu pour penser*, 75.
35. The self-annulment dynamic that characterizes the creation ultimately derives from the latter's being imprinted with the Being of God, Who, being Love, a Trinity of Persons in the unity of Being, "is because He is not."

comes from God) and thus may welcome God in itself, make space for God in itself, so that God lives in His creation through it.

But let us return to the subject of the relationship between creatures by virtue of which one creature is called to annul itself so that the other may be. According to Chiara, this "law" does not only hold for the relationship of temporal development between things belonging to the same species, by virtue of which the new plant springs from the "dead" seed and so on. It also holds good for the whole cosmic drama, in the harmonious hierarchy ordering the different species of beings. Thus the Trinitarian imprint is also reflected in cosmic evolution as a whole, in accordance with the principle that I described at the beginning of this reflection. Chiara writes:

> Every lower creature serves the one that is higher and says (because the whole universe is a living Gospel): "The Father is greater than I," that is, "the higher being is greater than I am." And each created thing has worth to the extent of its behavior in relation to the higher, like Jesus in relation to the Father: "My food is to do the will of my Father." Jesus was nothing but the living will of the Father: they were a single will because Jesus used his own human-divine will to do his Father's. And he denied his own will, he hated it: "Not my will but yours be done," because he hated himself, loving himself only for the sake of the Father.

Thus the whole drama of the universe is a drama of love that is hate. All things are distinct from one another and destined for communion, for unity. And so each thing is consumed in the one superior to it (hates itself) and loves the one superior to it in which it loses itself and finds itself again, new.

He who loses his life will find it.

So every human being must lose self in God to become God; each must be pure *will of God* to be manifestation of God here below—that is, love of God.

The universe's created beings are marching towards Unity, towards God, to be made God and they are made God through humankind: a little creation in miniature with a kingdom and a king.

This vision could appear overoptimistic. "Where is the suffering?" one might wonder. "Where are the struggle and conflict?" In reality, everything is viewed here from the vantage point of the One. It is already transformed into its point of arrival. That point is what Teilhard de Chardin, taking up the language found in Revelation, used to call the *omega* point, that is, the Risen Jesus Christ Who has ascended to the bosom of the Father. But it is precisely from this point of arrival that everything acquires its true place and its true meaning.

Chapter Ten

Creation in Christ and the New Creation in the Mysticism of Chiara Lubich

Piero Coda

Jesus Christ: The Oneness of the Uncreated and the Created

From Paul's letters[1] to John's Gospel,[2] from the Letter to the Hebrews[3] to the book of Revelation,[4] the New Testament witness is unanimous about the doctrine (undoubtedly original to the Christian faith) of creation "in Christ." In the Letter to the Colossians, to give just one example, Jesus is not only said to be "the image of the invisible God" but also "the firstborn of all creation," and it is emphasized that all things were created in Him, through Him, and for Him. Scholastic theology, taking up and transforming the language of Greek philosophy, would later speak about Jesus' role in creation as its exemplary, efficient, and final cause. The world, therefore, was created by God in view of Christ, indeed, "in" Christ. Outside of Him no created thing is thinkable and nothing can exist.

It should be noted, furthermore, that the New Testament does not just speak about the Word but about Jesus, the Word incarnate. Therefore it is Jesus (true God and true man) who is the center of God's project in creation. This is the vision that Chiara expresses with great clarity in 1949:

> The Kingdom of Heaven is in the bosom of the Father. The Father has an expression of himself outside himself, made as it were of diverging rays, and an expression within himself, made of rays that converge in the center, in a point that is Love: God in the infinitely small: the "Nothing-All" of Love! The Word. The diverging rays are Jesus.

---

1. See, e.g., 1 Cor 8:6; Col 1:15-17.
2. Jn 1:1-14.
3. Heb 1:1-3.
4. Rv 3:14.

By means of Jesus the Father reaches all his children outside Himself in whatever point they are to be found.[5]

And again, echoing the New Testament:

> "Through him all things were made" (See Col 1:16.). All that is created is but Jesus unfurled, as the spectrum is the fanning out of the colors that make up the white. The stars, the plants, the sun, the moon, the sea, the mountains, the birds, all creatures and humankind are summed up in Jesus.

In the first of these quotations, thanks to the spatial symbolism of "within" and "outside" and of rays that "converge" and are "divergent," two levels can be distinguished: the life of God in Godself, on the one hand, and creation, eternity, and time, on the other. It should be noted that with reference to the "diverging rays," that is, of the expression of God "outside Himself," Jesus is spoken about in time. Bearing this mind, it can be said that what Chiara writes is set within the perspective of the New Testament and the church's dogmatic tradition. According to this perspective, to be precise we must speak of the pre-existence (at the level of the life of God) of the Person of the Word who forever (in eternity) is in relation with the wholly free event of creation—even though, from the point of view of time, the Word was incarnate only in "the fullness of time."

It is in this perspective that Paul affirms, as has already been noted, that "in him all things in heaven and on earth were created . . . and in him all things hold together" (Col 1:16-17). This does not refer simply to the Word, but to the Word incarnate. God in creating, in fact, aims at Jesus Christ as the meaning and goal of creation ("Christ as all and in all"; see Col 3:11). This means that every created thing bears in itself, as an openness, a longing, a tension, the inchoate "form" of Jesus Christ, which the historical person of Jesus, in the event of his Incarnation and death/resurrection/pouring out of the Holy Spirit, will actualize and fulfill with his fullness.

The final cause of creation thus exercises its own specific and powerful effect. Hans Urs von Balthasar, looking at things more from above, speaks of the "Christo-typical" form of every creature. Karl Rahner, looking at things more from below, speaks of a "supernatural existential" form inherent in

---

5. From an unpublished text of 1949. Unless otherwise indicated, all quotations from Chiara Lubich are taken from unpublished texts written in 1949.

every human person, even "before" and "outside" coming within the explicitly experienced (categorical, as Rahner puts it) influence of Jesus Christ.

We must therefore recognize the presence and the salvific effect of the event of Jesus Christ, which is extended to the whole of time. As Chiara writes: "By means of Jesus the Father reaches all his children outside Himself *in whatever point* they are to be found." The presence and the action of God "outside Himself" are always mediated—mysteriously but really—by Jesus Christ crucified and risen in his Spirit. Jesus, the Word incarnate crucified and risen, is the point where God's "internal" and "external" (to use a spatial metaphor), the eternal and the temporal, touch and join together while remaining distinct. God, so to speak, "goes out of Godself" in Jesus and we enter into God in Jesus.

Therefore, from the point of view of temporality, a mysterious but real efficacy is given to the Jesus Christ event, which is located historically, as stated above, in "the fullness of time," not only *after* Jesus (as an event that takes place in time) but also *before* him. It is an efficacy that is not only eschatological and anticipatory (reaching forward) but also protological and retroactive (reaching back). At the same time, it is also necessary—so as not to render vain the reality of temporal succession—to distinguish between the efficacy he exercises before the historical-eschatological event of his Incarnation from the efficacy he exercises after it.

It seems to me that the article of faith of Jesus' descent into Hell, in particular, should be interpreted in this way. Jesus in his death reaches also those who lived before him, to communicate redemption to them and freely guide them with his Risen Self into the bosom of the Father. In this way, as the Word incarnate, crucified and risen, he realizes in himself the contemporaneous reality of all times. Hence all human beings, before and after him, participate in the salvation that comes from him. Did not Jesus exclaim: "Your ancestor Abraham rejoiced that he would see my day; he saw it and was glad" (Jn 8:56)?[6] The dogma of the Immaculate Conception of Mary, in my opinion, should also be interpreted in this light as we shall see. Mary was preserved from original sin *intuitu meritorum Christi*, in consideration of the merits of Christ. It is not some kind of ideal foretaste of the redemption that will take place by means of Christ but the mysterious and unique retroactive efficacy of the death/resurrection of Jesus that makes possible

---

6. See Giovanni Ancona, *Disceso agli inferi: Storia e interpretazione di un articolo di fede* (Rome: Città Nuova, 1999).

Mary's divine maternity, which, in terms of time, takes place before the death/resurrection of Jesus.

It is a mystery that will have to be studied in depth. And this demands, in particular, a new understanding of the relationship between eternity and time and of the very meaning of eternity and time in the light of the Jesus Christ event. Jesus, indeed, is presented by Chiara as the Oneness of the Uncreated and the Created; or, in terms well known to theological and mystical tradition, as the "consummated marriage" between God and creation.[7]

Mary, Creation in Synthesis that Marries the Creator

But for the Jesus event to be possible and actually to happen, it is necessary to have, through the free necessity of love, the presence and the *fiat* of Mary. The intrinsically Marian dimension of creation is rooted precisely here—and so in reference to and, as we shall see, in dependence upon the Christological mystery. While not unknown to tradition,[8] this dimension acquires in Chiara's understanding a particular power as part of an overall understanding of God's creative and salvific plan. Mary, seen in her essential role within the event of the Incarnation, is presented as in fact "the whole of creation in synthesis at the apex of its beauty, when she is presented as bride to her Creator" (and this by a retroactive action of the Redemption).

Picking up again the nuptial image recalled previously, if Jesus is the fruit of the marriage of God and humanity, then Mary is the creation that gives itself as the bride of the Creator, offering her immaculate flesh to God the Father so that he can beget, in the Holy Spirit, his Son as man. In reality, if Jesus is the Oneness of the Uncreated and the Created, it is necessary not only that God should give Godself—through the Word in the Spirit—to creation but also that creation, in a free response, should give itself to God. This happens by means of Mary.

On the other hand, as Chiara notes, this is only possible retroactively. It is a result of the redemption wrought by Christ, as is affirmed by the dog-

---

7. I will not look further into the central theme in this context of Jesus the Mediator, because it has already been studied by Hubertus Blaumeiser in "Un mediatore che è nulla," *Nuova Umanità* 20 (1998): 385–407.
8. This is a theme that is currently being reconsidered theologically, especially in an Orthodox context from point of view of "Sophiology" (see Sergei Bulgakov, *Bride of the Lamb* [Grand Rapids: W. B. Eerdmans, 2002]).

ma of the Immaculate Conception.[9] This becomes at least to some extent comprehensible if we think of the centrality of the Christ in the event of creation, which makes ontologically possible various temporally distinct and successive phases and dimensions.

Jesus Forsaken and the New Creation

In addition Chiara has an original understanding of Jesus Forsaken as the climax and expression in synthesis of the mystery of Jesus and, as a result, of the entire event of creation.[10] All of this is deeply in accord with the biblical witness. The concept of "new creation" that we find in the New Testament, especially in the Pauline corpus (see 2 Cor 5:17; Gal 6:15), indicates that Jesus Christ is the new humanity who is created in conformity with God's project that is fully realized in the paschal event and who, through faith and baptism, clothes the human person with himself (see 1 Cor 15:45-49; Eph 2:14-16, 4:22-24).

Now, Jesus Forsaken, for Chiara, is Jesus who fully actualizes the pattern of his being, God's plan for him, his "design," as he makes real in himself the unity of the Uncreated and the Created, and out of himself gives rise to the new creation. Chiara sees this central event of the mystery of creation that is made actual in Jesus Forsaken under two complementary and interrelated dimensions that are rich in meaning and future possibilities.

In the first, Jesus Forsaken is described as the one by whom God the Father in the Holy Spirit makes his creature participate in his very own Being. Chiara writes:

> [Jesus Forsaken] is the Creator who makes himself Non-Being, he, Being, to give himself through participation to Creation. . . .
> He is the Creator of the Creator given through participation to Creation that thereby becomes Creator.

---

9. Pius IX's Bull, *Ineffabilis Deus* (December 8, 1854) declared as revealed by God that "the Most Blessed Virgin Mary at the first moment of her conception was, by singular grace and privilege of the Omnipotent God, in virtue of the merits of Jesus Christ [*intuitu meritorum Christi Jesu*], Savior of the Human race, preserved from all stains of original sin." See Piero Coda, "Maria e la Trinità: A 150 anni dal dogma dell'Immacolata Concezione," *PATH* 3 (2004): 589–605.

10. See Stefan Tobler, *Tutto il vangelo in quel grido: Gesù abbandonato nei testi di Chiara Lubich* (Rome: Città Nuova, 2009); Florence Gillet, *La scelta di Gesù Abbandonato: Nella prospettiva teologica di Chiara Lubich* (Rome: Città Nuova, 2009).

What happens in Jesus' forsakenness? Jesus, out of love for the Father and for human beings, feeling himself detached from the Father, out of love "loses" the divine link making him one with the Father, namely, the Holy Spirit. But in this very way not only does he find this link again in himself (in the event of the resurrection where his humanity is also glorified by the Spirit) but he also makes human beings participate in it. Thus, thanks to the gift of the Holy Spirit, Jesus Forsaken makes creation participate in the Being of the Creator.

Here, the other dimension (that of salvation) comes into play, and it allows us to go still further in an understanding of the dynamism of this event. The Church Fathers, and following them the great thinkers of the Middle Ages, had the insight that the Word of God in becoming man assumed human nature in its universality even though this took place, as explained also by Saint Thomas, by means of a particular individual. For this reason he could exercise a redemptive influence upon all humans of all times.[11] An echo of this teaching can be found in the Second Vatican Council, where

---

11. The Fathers of the Church emphasized how the event of the incarnation of the Word recapitulated the universe. Among the Greek Fathers, Cyril of Alexandria states that "all human nature was in Christ through the fact of his being human" (*Commentary on John*, 24; PL 10, 66). Among the Latin Fathers, Hilary of Poiters said he was born of Virgin and the Holy Spirit so that "He might take to Himself from the Virgin the fleshly nature, and that through this commingling there might come into being one hallowed Body of all humanity" (*On the Trinity*, 2, 24; PL 10, 66). At the close of the patristic age, Maximus the Confessor gave a highly meaningful summary, saying that God wishes "that the multitude of beings, separated one from the other by their natures, come toward unity, converging with each other in the one nature of man, and that he himself in this way might become all in all," which takes place, indeed, through the incarnation of the Word (*Ambigua*; PG 91, 1092C). On the other hand, it should never be forgotten that the incarnation, for the Fathers too, is always understood in a dynamic relation to the paschal event. On this important theme see Marcello Bordoni "L'evento dell'incarnazione e la sua funzione salvifica universale nell'intera umanità," in *Gesù di Nazaret Signore e Cristo*, 3 (Rome: Herder-PUL 1986), 862-871; Bernard Sesboué, "Incarnazione e/o mistero pasquale," in *Gesù Cristo: l'unico mediatore* (Cinisello Balsamo: Ed. Paoline, 1991), 242ff. While he was within this same tradition, Saint Thomas gave a further and more precise explanation of this insight, saying that "The incarnate Son of God is the common Savior of all, not by a generic or specific community, such as is attributed to the nature separated from the individuals, but by a community of cause, whereby the incarnate Son of God is the universal cause of human salvation" (*Summa Theologica*, III, q. 4., a. 5, ad 1).

Gaudium et Spes affirms that "by His incarnation the Son of God has united Himself in some fashion with every man."[12]

The mystery of Jesus Forsaken allows us to penetrate the dynamic of the mysterious but real communion of the Word with every human being, not just by means of the universality of the human nature he assumes in the incarnation—a dimension to which past culture until Medieval times was particularly sensitive. But we also see the Word in the particularity of the concrete existence of each individual human being that Jesus reached with his forsakenness. This is a dimension that, beginning with the "critique of the universals" at the end of the Medieval period, has become increasingly important through the centuries of modernity—an approach that is typical of Judeo-Christian revelation. Chiara explains:

> Never was Jesus so much a human being as when he was Jesus Forsaken. In fact, whereas previously he saw himself as the Human Being, now he is a human being. In fact, as he was – because God – the universal Human Being, having been detached from God, he remained a particular human being. But, not ceasing to be God, he divinized the particular. So he, being God, made divine the *particular* and shows how in a particular human being there can be contained the Universal. Participating in the divine Life, therefore, does not mean our receiving a part, but our having the whole of it in us, we who are particulars.

This explanation links to what has already been said about the "diverging" rays in creation that return to being "converging" in the bosom of the Father by means of Jesus. We could say that it is precisely by means of Jesus Forsaken's becoming one with each human being in his or her particularity that the diverging rays can converge, because they are gathered into one by him and in him. They do not lose their identity but become one in their distinction, because they are, each one, fully clothed with the one Christ. In this sense, Jesus Forsaken is the decisive "turning point" of the history of creation, so much so that he can be called, in Chiara's words, "the Mother of Creation."

None of this sets aside the fact that Jesus Forsaken is also the key to understanding the meaning of suffering in creation's process of becoming and to humanity's redemption from sin. A consideration of these issues would

---

12. *Gaudium et Spes*, 22.

demand a separate investigation.[13] Here, we will conclude by examining the last point we said we would consider.

Creation "in" God the Trinity

The reality of the new creation, fruit of Jesus Forsaken, is made manifest in the resurrection of Jesus. It is then manifested in us through our being grafted into the life of the Risen Lord by means of faith in him and of baptism.

The Eucharist and the Divinization of Creation

We participate in the fullest way in the life of the Risen Christ in history by means of the Eucharist. It, in fact, makes us concorporeal and consanguineal with Him, sharing with us the gift of the Holy Spirit. By means of the Eucharist, already in this world creation experiences the fruit of the redemption and of the divinization brought about by Jesus. The philosopher Maurice Blondel, with reference to the ontological meaning of the Eucharist for the realization in Christ of the event of creation, wrote:

> We must all give ourselves birth by giving birth to God in us. . . . The gift which religious life brings [a man] is so closely incorporated into his substance that human nature becomes capable of producing and creating in some way the One from whom it has everything, as if at one and the same time the donor wanted to have everything from the donee, as if man, summoned finally to satisfy the excess of his willing, became, according to the expression of Saint Thomas, "the God of his God."[14]

In some way, the Eucharist is shown as a real foretaste and a prophetic and effective sign of what the whole creation is destined to become by means of Jesus and human beings nourished on Him-Eucharist, to become indeed the created expression of God. As Chiara explains it, creation, which is the work of God who is Love, cannot but also be made Love and so be Eucharist: the expression of God that has the value of God. The Eucharist

---

13. There are some remarks in my contribution to the Assocazione Teologica Italiana (the Association of Italian Theologians), "Il Cristo crocifisso e abbandonato: Redenzione della libertà e nuova creazione," Saturnino Muratore (ed.), *Futuro del cosmo: Futuro dell'uomo* (Padua: Messaggero 1997), 191-232.

14. Maurice Blondel, *Action: Essay on a Critique of Life and a Science of Pratice* (South Bend, Indiana: Notre Dame University Press, 2003), 386.

has, therefore, a cosmic destiny, or, better, the whole cosmos has a Eucharistic vocation.[15] This is one of the great insights of Teilhard de Chardin:

> As our humanity assimilates the material world, and as the Host assimilates our humanity, the eucharistic transformation goes beyond and completes the transubstantiation of the bread on the altar. Step by step it irresistibly invades the universe. . . . In a secondary and generalized sense, but in a true sense, the sacramental Species are formed by the totality of the world, and the duration of the creation is the time needed for its consecration.[16]

The Life of Unity and "Trinitization"

What the Eucharist produces as grace in creation, by means of the humanity that is Christified by it, is fully actualized in the life of unity. Being one with God and among created persons, the fruit of Jesus Forsaken participated in through the Eucharist, becomes a lived experience for us in the life of unity. This life of unity means living "trinitarian relationships," in the sense that created persons, grafted into Christ, are called to live according to the pattern of the Trinity, living out mutual love though the total gift of self in Jesus Forsaken. But, more profoundly still, at its root it means participating

---

15. In the words of the Orthodox theologian John Zizioulas: "[T]he Eucharist . . . is the most dramatic evidence of a meeting in human existence here and now between the eschaton and history, between the perfect and the relative. . . . This eschatological invasion is not an historical development that one can comprehend logically and by experience; it is the descent of the Holy Spirit, by epiclesis—this epiclesis that is so fundamental and so characteristic of the Orthodox Eucharist—that transfigures the 'present age' and transforms it in Christ into 'a new creation'. This descent from heaven to earth, which makes possible the ascent of the earth to the heavenly throne, fills the earth with light, with grace and with joy, and makes the feast of the Liturgy a solemn celebration from which the faithful return to the world full of joy and charism. . . . Therefore the Eucharist will always open the way not to the dream of a gradual perfection of the world, but to the demand for heroic ascesis, an experience of kenosis and of the cross, the only way in which it is possible to live the Eucharist in the world until the victory of the Resurrection at the end of time. At the same time, the Eucharist offers the world the experience of this eschatological dimension that penetrates history in the eucharistic communion and makes possible our deification in space and time" (John D. Zizioulas, *The Eucharistic Communion and the World* [London and New York: T & T Clark, 2011], 117-18).
16. Pierre Teilhard de Chardin, *The Divine Milieu: An Essay on the Interior Life* (New York: Harper and Row, 1960),125-6. See also Franco Bisio, "Cristogenesi: Croce e Trinità in Teilhard de Chardin," in Piero Coda and Andreas Tapken (eds), *La Trinità e il pensare* (Rome: Città Nuova, 1997), 229-57.

in the very dynamism of God, who is Three and One. This is "trinitization": being made one in Jesus and being made distinct as other Jesuses if we are united and insofar as we are united. As Chiara explains:

> Our Ideal: Jesus Forsaken gives us the possibility to be *perfect like the Father* even while being particular human beings. . . . But this because at the base we put *unity* – "ante omnia" [before all]– and we distinguish ourselves from one another after we have been united, that is, we distinguish ourselves: *Jesus*, and hence *God*, distinct from God, God by participation.

Trinitization, clearly, is not only a matter of the relations of each created person with God and in God with other created persons, but it is also a matter of the Trinitarian relationship that, through Jesus and Jesus Forsaken, is established between the Creator and the creation seen as "one."[17] In Jesus Forsaken, in fact, there comes about the marriage of the Creator with the created, that marriage which will be consummated in the Parousia:

> The Church is Bride of Christ because through participation he has given her his Spirit. Creation is Bride of the Creator because the Creator[18] has given it his *Being*: Love.

Thus "between the two is the Love *of the Trinity*, and God loves Creation and is loved back in the *Perfection of Unity*[19] as was the Testament of Jesus. They love one another as God loves Himself."

This Trinitarian relation between the Creator and creation finds its eschatological icon already realized in Mary, whom the faith of the Roman Catholic Church contemplates as Assumed in Heaven.[20] More could be said here. But following the vision of faith that Mary is the Mother of God, Chiara says that she "does not reassume in Herself only the Creation, but the uncreated and the created universe." Even though her role in the history of salvation remains unique and unrepeatable, She, by means of her divine maternity, through the grace of the Holy Spirit giving birth in her bodiliness

---

17. See Piero Coda, "Creatio ex nihilo amoris: Per una lettura trinitaria del principio di creazione," Stefano Moriggi and Elio Sindoni (eds), *Perché esiste qualcosa invece di nulla? Vuoto, Nulla, Zero* (Castel Bolognese: ITACA, 2004), 29-40.
18. "That is, God through Jesus," Chiara explains.
19. "Because creation is divinized by him" (in terms Chiara uses).
20. See "Discorso tenuto da Chiara Lubich all'Università San Tommaso di Manila il 14 gennaio 1997 in occasione del conferimento del *dottorato honoris* causa in Sacra Teologia," *Nuova Umanità*, XIX (1997): 17-29, es, 26-7.

to the One who created her, shows us the vocation of all: created by God in order to give birth to God in us – a created God.

Trinitarian Eschaton: "God all in all"

The event of creation reaches therefore its fulfilment. And it is possible to glimpse the meaning of Paul's striking and wonderful eschatological vision of God as "all in all" (1 Cor 15:28). This is not the pantheistic effect of a God who cancels creation in the divine self, but the fulfilment of the prayer of Jesus to the Father: "As you, Father, are in me and I am in you, may they also be in us" (Jn 17:21). As Chiara concludes:

> In this unity each thing is in the Bosom of the Father and each thing is outside the Father and contains the Father. Indeed, as each thing is in the Son, in the Word, it is with the Word in the Bosom of the Father ("I in you") and embraces the Father ("you in me"). ("I in them and you in me"). Thus in the end all was *God*: God in himself and God in the created. Two yet made one by the Mediator, Jesus. In creating, therefore, God did not do anything other than clothe nothingness with himself, giving himself through participation to nothingness. God is he who is. All that is, is God – God: Creator, God: Creation.

Chapter Eleven

A Spirituality that Inspires Ontology: The Discovery of God-Love and the Renewal of Ontology

Thomas Norris

Catholic priests will readily admit that the Sunday which most challenges them is Trinity Sunday. Most dread the preparation and the delivery of the homily on that day. The paradox is that the Trinity is the central mystery of our faith. St. Thomas Aquinas stresses the point and explains: "The Son of God came and he caused the hidden rivers to gush forth, making known the hidden name of the Trinity."[1] Yes, it is true that Augustine required sixteen years to write his famous work on the Trinity. It is also the case that he wrote that there is no comparable subject "in which study is more arduous, discovery more valuable, and error more dangerous."[2] He knew well what he was talking about, and he knew it from experience. Yet, like St. Benedict Joseph Labre many centuries later, he felt drawn into the mystery that the church in the *New Catechism* calls the summit and foundation of all faith.

The paradox of the central mystery of faith being the one most dreaded by the pastors of the church stands out even more strikingly when one looks at the liturgy of Holy Week, itself the summit of the whole liturgical year. The mystery of the cross on Good Friday and the resurrection on Easter Sunday are clearly events involving the three divine Persons. This is what the scriptures say and what the liturgy of that week insinuates. The liturgy aims at doing so in a most explicit manner. A quick look is enough to remind ourselves of this fact.

As to Good Friday, there is the fact that "the Father did not spare his own Son but gave him up for us all" (Rom 8:32), that "the Son loved me and gave himself up for me" (Gal 2:20), and that "Jesus bowed his head and

---

1. Thomas Aquinas, *In Sententias*, I, Prologue.
2. Augustine, *De Trinitate*, I, 2, 5.

handed over the Spirit" (Jn 19:30).³ The Father, the Son and the Holy Spirit are the three actors in the drama of Good Friday where to a non-Christian it seems that it is a case of Jesus of Nazareth being the victim of betrayal by the Twelve, of intrigue on the part of Caiaphas, and of the cruel temporizing of a Roman governor. But God the Holy Trinity writes straight on the crooked lines of humanity. The three divine protagonists on Calvary act together and they do so "for us." They conspire, it could be said, in our favor. The cross, or rather the Crucified One, is the living icon of the Triune God who saves us. And as Jean-Luc Marion observes, icons function by drawing us by means of what is visible toward what is invisible and mysterious, which then sheds its light and splendor on the beholder.⁴

As to the resurrection, a similar pattern is clearly observable. It is the Father who "will not let his holy One see corruption" (Acts 2:27) but who "raised him up, having freed him from death" (Acts 2:24, 32). The crucified and dead Christ "rose again on the third day" (1 Cor 15:3), while the Holy Spirit acts as the agent of the Father in raising and in glorifying the crucified Lord of glory (1 Cor 2:8). Good Friday and Easter Sunday focus on the divine three who conspire together in a divine project on behalf of humanity. Watching this drama shown to us on the stage of the church's summit liturgical celebrations might have coaxed us closer, as it were, enabling us in the process to "perceive what is revealed" (Eph 1:17), making the mystery of the Trinity fascinating and intriguing, even if always more mysterious. In the words of Augustine: "*Si comprehendis non est Deus*" (If you understand, it is not God that you have understood).⁵ Still, the God and Father of our Lord Jesus Christ together with the Holy Spirit advance toward us as eternal truth and true love and loving eternity.⁶ "God is love" (1 Jn 4:8, 16), writes John; but he immediately describes the kind of love he is naming: "This is the love I mean, not our love for God, but God's love for us when he sent his Son to be the atoning sacrifice for our sins" (1 Jn 4:10). God is love and God is Trinity. Here we encounter the first point of the spirituality manifested to Chiara Lubich as described by Maria Voce.

---

3. In each case, the Greek text employs the same verb, *paradidonai*.
4. Jean-Luc Marion, *God without Being* (Chicago: University of Chicago Press), 1991.
5. St. Augustine, *Sermon* 52, 16.
6. See St. Augustine, *Confessions*, 7, 10.

The Neoplatonic One, Not the Trinitarian One

What amazes us, then, is that we should arrive into the twentieth century and find ourselves more monotheists than Trinitarian theists. Karl Rahner was of the view that if the doctrine of the Trinity were deleted from the Creed that deletion would have little or no bearing on the way in which Christians thought about God. Other great theologians such as Hans Urs von Balthasar wrote along these very lines. The Italian theologian Bruno Forte wonders if "the God of Christians is a Christian God."[7]

And yet, in spite of this state of affairs, the Trinity has made an amazing return to center stage. In fact, it is now center stage where it belonged. An Italian theologian, Nicola Ciolo, is of the view that the Blessed Trinity is now the grammar of all theology.[8] A rapid recovery has happened. Many factors are responsible for this happy *ressourcement*. One of these factors has to be the biblical, patristic, liturgical, and theological renewals that began in the nineteenth century and flowered in the last century. The Second Vatican Council saw the final flowering of these sources of faith and of faith-life. Another factor, however, has to be the emergence of spiritualities such as that of Chiara Lubich and the Focolare. That contention does require a little teasing out and perhaps some justification.

Chiara Lubich's Discovery of God-Love

As soon as Chiara Lubich and her first companions discovered that God is love, they quickly went on to discover further gospel truths such as Jesus dwelling in each person we meet, mutual love between people to the point of that unity for which Jesus suffered and prayed, and Jesus crucified and forsaken as the measure and the method of the love required. One might see in all of these points the presence, the dynamic, and the laws of New Testament love, or *agape*. Maria Voce notes that by living these points all drawn from the pages of the gospels, Chiara and her companions discovered a spirituality flowing from the pure wellspring of divine revelation. However, what was particularly striking was the immediate link that Chiara observed from the beginning between the emerging spirituality and the mystery of the Trinity. In her words: "Wherever this spirituality is put into practice, it

---

7. Bruno Forte, *Trinità come storia* (Milano: San Paolo, 1988), 13.
8. Nicola Ciolo, "L'avanzare di nuovi orizzonti," in *Teologia trinitari: Storia—metodo—prospettive* (Bologna: EDB, 1996), 157–97.

generates and fosters a life modeled on the life of the Holy Trinity, the life Jesus brought on earth."⁹

The lifestyle inspired by the spirituality, however, provided a ready and, let it be said, accessible entry to discoveries relating to the first mystery of the faith. We understand by living. "God is Love" is the first point of the spirituality of unity. Because God *is* love, love is much more than an attribute of God. Rather, love is God's very being, it is his life. Now this makes us think at once of God's reality as consisting in the life of loving. However, there cannot be love without someone who loves, someone who is loved, the beloved, and the love uniting the lover and the beloved.

Now this is precisely the way Augustine accessed the Trinity in Book VIII of his great study. Whoever reads this masterpiece will immediately notice that Augustine had been seeking like a competent mountaineer for a firm foothold in order to climb toward some understanding of the God of Jesus Christ. He found that foothold in the experience of *caritas* in the church into which he had entered. Augustine found a point of access to the great mystery precisely in the church's practice of *caritas*. A phenomenology of love then enabled him to grasp something of the great mystery, something that drew him and fascinated him. Augustine could then write these words:

> In truth, you see the Trinity if you see love. . . . They are three: the lover, the loved, and the love. . . . And not more than three: one who loves the one who comes from him, one who loves the one from whom he came, and love itself.¹⁰

At this point I remember vividly the experience of a young German priest who attended a Mariapolis of the Focolare in his native country.¹¹ Initially very suspicious as to what he saw going on around him, he asked a young girl, "What are you doing here?" only to receive the answer, "We're living the Trinity." The name of that priest was Klaus Hemmerle, later to become the bishop of Aachen as well as a renowned theologian and philosopher. "Chiara," he wrote many decades later, "has conveyed to us a school of life. This school of life, however, is also a school for theology.

---

9. Chiara Lubich, "The Spirituality of Unity and Trinitarian Life," *New Humanity Review* 9 (2004): 6.
10. St. Augustine, *De Trinitate*, VIII, 8, 12; VIII, 10, 14; VI, 5, 7.
11. A Mariapolis ("City of Mary") is a gathering where the emphasis is placed upon mutual love as the pearl of the gospel.

The result is not so much an improvement of theology, as a living theology that originates from revelation."[12]

Love of Neighbor in Each Present Moment

The second point of the spirituality presented by Maria Voce is that of love for each brother and sister. This love is not generic in character but specific. It does not remain on the level of a vague benevolence but descends to action and concrete help Chiara and her companions always tried to recall that the neighbor is the person you or I am with in the present moment. Relationships based on concrete loving of each neighbor became their very lifestyle, and all that under the bombs falling daily on their city. In the unfolding discovery of the gospel as the most practical of all spiritual guides, they put a central emphasis on their own relationships and on relationships with each brother and sister they encountered on the streets and in the airraid shelters of Trent.

Now it is fascinating to notice that Augustine in Book V of his treatise on the Trinity made the "discovery" that each of the divine Persons is a relationship: "At times one speaks of God according to relation. Thus the Father bespeaks a relation to the Son, and the Son to the Father. Now this relation is not accidental, since the one is always the Father, the other always the Son."[13] This discovery opened the way for him to advance his understanding of the great mystery of the Trinity. Of this discovery, Joseph Ratzinger writes in his now famous *Introduction to Christianity*:

> In this simple affirmation [each divine Person is a relation] there is evident a genuine revolution in the form of the world: the absolute supremacy of a thinking focused on substance is displaced in as much as relation is discovered to be an equal and original modality of the real . . . and a new thinking about being emerges in reaction.[14]

---

12. Klaus Hemmerle, "Tell Me about Your God," *Being One* 1 (1996): 20.
13. St Augustine, *De Trinitate*, VIII, 5, 6.
14. Joseph Ratzinger, *Introduction to Christianity* (San Francisco: Ignatius Press, 1990), 135–36.

Walter Kasper sees in this breakthrough of Augustine a veritable "revolution in the understanding of being . . . the ultimate and highest reality is not substance but relation."[15]

However, in the history of theology there was an entirely opposite idea of the person that was destined to gain the ascendancy, the person, namely, as individual. The definition of Boethius from the eighth century omitted entirely the dimension of relation, replacing it with that of individual: "The person is the individual substance of rational nature."[16] Perhaps this notion or definition of person is what has most contributed to the anxiety of people in recent centuries even to think about the first mystery of the faith. The reason is obvious: if person is individual and not relation, then all mention of three Persons in the one God threatens the believer with three divine Individuals, and that is the very definition of Tritheism. Three distinct divine centers of consciousness and action must entail three distinct beings. And believers are obliged to shy away from any such insinuation.

Mutual Love to the Point of Unity

The third major point of the spirituality of the Focolare that Maria Voce explores is that of mutual love to the point of unity. Pope John Paul II calls the new commandment (Jn 13:34; 15:12) the "pearl of the Gospel." It is the necessary prelude to the unity for which Jesus prayed on the night before he died (Jn 17:21f) and which is a summit chapter of John's Gospel, perhaps the summit of the whole of sacred scripture. When we live this way, the church becomes, both effectively and affectively, "a people made one from the unity of the Father, the Son and the Holy Spirit."[17] The fruit of living this mutual love at this measure (note the "as" in the text of the new commandment) is also the gift of Jesus coming to live in our midst (Mt 18:20).

Now this experience of gospel living, particularly of living out the mutual relationship of the new commandment in the measure of the love that went all the way to the cross and the abandonment, is a fountainhead of insight. It led Chiara and her companions to a vivid realization of the classical language of Trinitarian theology. She writes:

---

15. Walter Kasper, *The God of Jesus Christ* (New York: Crossroads Publishing Company, 1986), 154.
16. Boethius, *Liber de persona et duabus naturis*, 3: PL 64, 1343; see St. Thomas, *Summa theologica*, I, q. 29, a.1.
17. *Lumen Gentium*, 4.

> The Father generates the Son out of love. Going completely out of himself, so to speak, he makes himself, in a certain sense, "non-being" out of love and for this reason he is Father. The Son, in turn, as an echo of the Father, returns to the Father out of love, making himself, too, in a certain sense, "non-being" out of love and for this reason he is Son. The Holy Spirit who is the mutual love between the Father and the Son, their bond of unity, also makes himself, in a certain sense, "non-being" out of love—that "non-being" and "emptiness of love" in which the Father and the Son meet and are one. And for this very reason he is Holy Spirit.[18]

This explanation not only does not damage the unity of God, it actually enhances that very unity. In a passage of exceptional ontological clarity, Chiara explains:

> If we consider the Son in the Father, we must think of the Son as a nothingness (a nothingness of love) in order to think of God as One. And if we consider the Father in the Son, we must think of the Father as nothing (a nothingness of love) in order to think of God as One. There are three Persons in the Most Holy Trinity and yet they are One because Love *is not* and *is* at the same time. . . . In the relationship of the three divine Persons, therefore, each one is Love, each one *is* completely by not being, because each one is wholly by indwelling in the other Person, in an eternal self-giving.[19]

Chiara's was a theology following upon life, and never otherwise. This explains her concern, particularly during the first decades of the movement, lest Paris would destroy Assisi.

Jesus Crucified and Abandoned

We will recall that the fourth point presented by Maria Voce is that of Jesus crucified and abandoned. The cry of forsakenness is now recognized as a key moment of Jesus' passion and death. This recognition has led to a convergence of theologians from the churches: in the Orthodox Church one could mention Sergei Bulgakov; in the Lutheran Church, Jürgen Moltmann; and

---

18. Lubich, "Spirituality of Unity and Trinitarian Life," 9.
19. Lubich, "Spirituality of Unity and Trinitarian Life," 9–10.

in the Catholic Church, Hans Urs von Balthasar. All focus very much on this dimension of the passion. The fruit of this happy convergence is an area of special growth in the dialogue between the theologians of the churches. In the magisterium of Pope John Paul II, the topic played a role that was profound, prominent, and proleptic. For Chiara, the cry of abandonment provides "the most luminous explanation of the meaning of love: to empty oneself, to 'not be,' to disappear, so as to be love in action."[20]

At the beginning of the second century, Ignatius of Antioch described himself as "an imitator of the passion of my God."[21] Perhaps the key reason why this cry was overlooked in the church since the early centuries when it was associated with the widespread and sustained phenomenon of martyrdom and persecution lay in the fact that it could be employed to suggest a denial of the divinity of the Lord. The discovery of the cry of abandonment in the Focolare spirituality, far from threatening any heresy, actually threw light on the mysterious and eternal loving that is the eternal event of the Blessed Trinity. In that way, it connects the redeeming Son's loss of his Father in his human soul at the summit moment of his loving us with the eternal self-emptying of the Son before the Father in the Trinity.

The Christ who comes among us reveals and communicates to us the life of the Trinity. It is impossible to read the Gospels and not perceive that Jesus has one and only one mission in mind: to reveal the love of the God who had sent him: "Father, you have loved them as much as you have loved me" (Jn 17:23). His very existence is not only a pro-existence "for us" (Mk 10:45; Mt 26:28; 1 Cor 11:24), it is above all a pro-existence for his Father: "For this reason the Father loves me, because I lay down my life in order to take it up again. . . . I have received this command from my Father" (Jn 10:17, 18). He makes himself a sacrifice for us, going to the cross. In that way he empties himself out totally. This *kenosis* is a form of non-being, but it is the non-being of love. The self-emptying redeeming Christ as Son of the eternal Father "lays down his life for us" and so he coaxes us toward a perception of his Trinitarian homeland where the Father and the Spirit and the Son live for and in each other.

This insinuates the great truth that each divine Person is a relationship of love for the others. Each person is when that person is not out of love for the others. In the words of Chiara:

---

20. Lubich, "Spirituality of Unity and Trinitarian Life," 8.
21. St. Ignatius of Antioch, *Letter to the Romans*, 6.

In the light of the Trinity as revealed by Jesus forsaken, God who is Being reveals himself, we could say, as safe-keeping in his most inner recesses the non-being of self-giving: not the non-being which negates being, but the non-being which reveals Being as Love.[22]

Theology in the twelfth and thirteenth centuries had arrived at a philosophy that was its instrument, its *ancilla*. That Christian philosophy saw in the idea of the act of being, *esse*, that which is most profound in things. It then advanced further to see God as the pure act of Being. However, in the words of one of the founding members of the Abba School that Maria Voce discusses:

> This act of being did not reach as far as being-love as God is Being-Love. *Philosophy*, in other words, did not reach as far as a *Trinitarian ontology*, which would be required by a being who is love. In fact, *it is only the Cross that could lead so far*.
>
> But it must be the cross understood at the very heart of the Trinity and as the summit of humanity in its very thinking: *the Cross as a cultural event*.[23]
>
> This is perceptible only if the believer allows himself or herself to be led into the night by Jesus forsaken, that is, by his life and *the thinking that radiates from it*, with its absolutely original categories.[24]

The truth is that "it depends on Christ whether we dare to address being as love, and thus all beings as worthy of love, an idea to which the face of the world would otherwise have hardly brought us."[24]

---

22. Lubich, "Spirituality of Unity and Trinitarian Life," 10; see Piero Coda, "L'unità e la trinità di Dio nel ritmo di una ontologia trinitaria," *Sophia: Ricerche su i fondamenti e la correlazione dei saperi*, 2 (2010): 174–89.
23. Giuseppe Maria Zanghi, *Notte della cultura europea* (Rome: Città Nuova, 2007), 59–60. 24, 61.
24. Hans Urs von Balthasar, *The von Balthasar Reader*, Medard Kehl and Werner Loeser, eds. (Edinburgh: T. and T. Clark, 1982), 113.

Chapter Twelve

The "Yes" Under Every "No"

David L. Schindler

The charism of the Focolare is one of love. Of course in today's culture reference to love can seem vague and unrealistic. But as noted by Maria Voce, Focolare recuperates love in a new key: it recapitulates love in its wholeness—in its radicality and comprehensiveness—in a way that goes to the heart of the peculiar problems of our time. Indeed, the wholeness of love is just the point. We live in a time characterized above all by a new—indeed, one might say unprecedented—brokenness and fragmentation. To quote the words of Chiara: "The groaning of creation, of which St. Paul speaks (Rm 8:22), seems no longer to be heard. It has been covered by what Heidegger called the 'idle chatter of existence' and therefore of an 'inauthentic culture.'"[1] In this regard, Chiara says:

> We no longer understand how God can fill the world with himself. For people of Western societies, the world has gradually become empty of meaning. . . . Gone is the intelligence of love capable of grasping the truth and beauty of creation *from its origins*, from God who contains it and nourishes it with himself. Instead, it has been replaced by a skeptical and cold rationality that moves *among* things without penetrating into their deepest roots.[2]

Chiara's statements here, of course, do not at all imply that the world of today does not contain an abundance of achievements signaling the greatness of the human spirit. Indeed, to linger in the negative would belie the very burden of her lifework. Thus, she goes on, following the statements just cited, to ask whether we are "up against an irreversible crisis," or rather whether there is hope for the "slow coming to birth of a new world."[3] As we know, she directs us emphatically toward such hope. The ground for this hope lies hidden in the very words with which she describes the culture's

---

1. Chiara Lubich, *Essential Writings* (Hyde Park, NY: New City Press, 2007), 213.
2. Lubich, *Essential Writings*, 213.
3. Lubich, *Essential Writings*, 213.

central problem, that is, in her reference to a "rationality that moves *among* things without penetrating into their deepest roots," and that thus fragments itself, for example, in the interests of power or endless bits of information or technical efficiency. What is needed, then, is a rationality that unifies—and hence integrates. We need a rationality that sees things from their origin and destiny in the God who sustains and, indeed, somehow contains all things, thereby establishing humanity and the whole of creation in a fundamental unity or community.[4]

An excellent way of framing the problem of an intelligence of love and depth and current cultural problems is indicated by Thomas Norris and the other authors of the introduction to Chiara's recently published *Essential Writings*, in which they cite the words of the twentieth-century American poet, Wallace Stevens:

> The tragedy, however, may have begun,
> Again, in the imagination's new beginning,
> In the yes of the realist spoken because he must
> Say yes, spoken because under every no
> Lay a passion for yes that had never been broken.[5]

These words seem to take us to the heart of Chiara: we must penetrate to the yes that is straining to come into being in all of those places and ways in which the world, at least on its surfaces, appears to be saying no. It is this penetration that enables us to recuperate the meaning and authentic human culture that otherwise can remain buried within the often idle and distracted chatter of the dominant culture. It is in terms of the realist passion noted by Stevens—and I emphasize *realist*—for recovering the yes that is never completely broken, even in the uttering of the most desperate and would-be nihilistic no,[6] on which I wish to focus the key to what Chiara and Focolare call "the spirituality of unity, or communion."

---

4. See also in this connection Pope Benedict XVI's lecture at Regensburg, in which he urged, with respect to Western science and the Western academy, an opening up of reason to the *Logos* of God.
5. Lubich, *Essential Writings*, xxviii; from *Esthétique du mal*, in *The Collected Poems of Wallace Stevens* (New York: Alfred A. Knopf, 1954), 320.
6. In the metaphysical terms of Thomism, the truth of these assertions is rooted in the understanding of evil as a privation of the good. Thus, even the strongest negations remain in their depths affirming passions for the good, however badly distorted.

Jesus Forsaken and Mary's Fiat

As is well known, this communion for Chiara begins and ends with the love of God revealed to us in Jesus Christ as a Trinity. Further, in the words of John Paul II cited by Chiara, Mary is "an integral part of the economy of communicating" this love. Let me say a brief word about how both Jesus and Mary each disclose the shape of this love—and thus the most radical way of bringing to light the yes hidden inside every no.

First of all, love, says Chiara, is not merely an attribute of God, but God's very being, One and Triune at the same time: Father, Son, and Holy Spirit. This unity of God that is thus revealed to us as a communion of persons indicates the ultimate nature and measure of the love to which we are called. In the words of Jesus' prayer as recorded in the Gospel of John: "As you, Father, are in me and I in you, may they also be in us, so that the world may believe that you sent me" (Jn 17:21). What does this prayer of Jesus reveal about the nature of God's love?

Chiara says that in his abandonment Jesus made himself "sin" (2 Cor 5:21), "cursed" (Gal 3:13), in order to make himself one with those who were far from God. Jesus' separation from the Father on our behalf is the way to our unity with him in the Father. What this abandonment—suffering, crucifixion, and death—of Jesus means is beautifully expressed by Joseph Cardinal Ratzinger in his Lenten retreat of several years ago to John Paul II and the papal household. I would like to draw on his profound words that seem to me very appropriate for the present context:

> It becomes clear that the abasement of the Incarnation . . . is in profound inner correspondence with the mystery of the Son: *the Son by his essence is the gift and giving back of himself: this is what is meant by "being son"* [emphasis added]. The Incarnation of the Son means from the beginning: "he became obedient unto death" (Phil. 2:8).[7]

The significance of Ratzinger's emphasis on sonship becomes clearer when he points out that the sin of Adam lay not in wanting to become like God but in Adam's casting off of the childhood-like character proper to his being *as a creature*. That is, we image God, according to Ratzinger, not when we set ourselves up as self-sufficient (and, so to speak, adult-like), but "by sharing in the action of the Son, . . . and thus in the measure that we

---

7. Joseph Ratzinger, *Journey towards Easter* (New York: Crossroads, 1987), 69.

become children."⁸ "It is only by preserving the innermost heart of infancy, the existence of Son as lived by Jesus, that humanity enters with the Son into divinity."⁹ It is as gifts—and thus as *receivers*—that we image the generous creative activity—the *giving*—of God the Father.

It is important to see here the entire arc and richness of Ratzinger's idea of the creature's participation *in the sonship* of Jesus, and thus as it were in the *divine childlikeness*. There is in the child an original "letting be" of the other—a childlike *fiat* that takes the form of wonder before the other. Ratzinger mentions the ancient Greeks who stood at the origins of Western civilization, who, he says, wanted "to be a people of philosophers and not technocrats, that is, eternal children, apt to wonder in amazement" at reality in all its depths and openness to the transcendent.¹⁰ This *fiat* that takes the form of wonder before the other is completed only in the giving of oneself entirely to the other, to the point of being willing to die for the other. Jesus shows us the divine and human depth of this *fiat*—this original yes before the Father and all of creation—that goes to the end for the sake of the Father and of all creation.

Second, regarding Mary, Ratzinger says that this childlike yes of Jesus is in a significant sense learned from his mother's yes, her yes that, as Ratzinger says, "*goes on always without wearying*" [emphasis added].¹¹ And thus we come to the important further meaning of Focolare as the "Work of Mary," indeed to what Chiara (and Ratzinger and John Paul II) understand as the "Marian profile" of the church.

The key to understanding Mary lies in her *fiat*, expressed in her *magnificat* and in turn in her reality as *Theotokos*, as God-bearer, the bearer of Jesus in and all the way through his forsakenness:

- *Fiat:* Letting be, humble wonder before the Lord, making space for the reality of the other inside oneself. The fiat that goes on without wearying, remaining with the other to the end.

- *Magnificat:* Through the *fiat*, Mary magnifies the Lord, and also herself now as Mother of the Lord, becoming creative with the power of

---

8. Ratzinger, *Journey towards Easter*, 69
9. Ratzinger, *Journey towards Easter*, 72.
10. Ratzinger, *Journey towards Easter*, 73.
11. Ratzinger, *Journey towards Easter*, 74.

God. Letting the other be inside me enables me to magnify the other, to extend the power of the other—and myself—through our unity.

- *Theotokos:* This creativity becomes fruitful in bearing God into existence, in and with the power of God. In the letting be that enables unity between myself and the other, I am able to bear the other into a new form of existence: I liberate the other into a new fruitfulness.

The *fiat* that goes on without wearying, creativity, fruitfulness: these together indicate the unique way toward, and true nature of, unity. It is in Mary's *fiat*, *magnificat*, and *Theotokos* that we find the archetypal meaning, supernatural and natural, of this way.

As all of this clearly indicates, the *fiat* is not passivity or inactivity. On the contrary, the *fiat* presupposes the interior silence that alone permits the depths of the presence of the other. "Be still and know that I am God," says the Psalmist (Ps. 46:10). Without this interior stillness enabling true presence, we can, in the words of Job, know God—and the other—"only by hearsay" (42:1–6).

Indeed, the resonance of this truth disclosed in Mary, of the truth that the *fiat* is not uncreative activity nor a matter of an unrealistic Christian piety, can be confirmed by statements by two thinkers who can scarcely be accused of lacking in creative energy or of too much Christian piety: Friedrich Nietzsche and Jacques Derrida. Nietzsche states:

> Is there a more sacred state than pregnancy? . . . Our child must be born from all that is best and gentlest. . . . "Something greater than we are is growing here"—such is our most secret hope; we prepare everything with a view to his birth and prosperity—not merely everything that is useful, but also the noblest gifts of our souls. We should, and can, live under the influence of such a blessed inspiration! Whether what we are looking forward to is a thought or a deed, our relationship to every essential achievement is none other than that of pregnancy, and all our vainglorious boasting about "willing" and "creating" should be cast to the winds! True and ideal selfishness consists in always watching over and restraining the soul, so that our productiveness may come to a beautiful termination.[12]

---

12. Friedrich Nietzsche, *Daybreak: Thoughts on the Prejudices of Morality*, Maudemarie Clark and Brian Leiter eds., R. J. Hallingdale, trans., (Cambridge: Cambridge

And in the words of Derrida:

> [A]ffirmation [is] anterior to any question and more proper to thought than any question. . . . The remnant of the *Aufklärung* [Enlightenment] . . . slumber[s] in the privilege of the question. . . . The question is . . . not the last word in language. First, because it is not the first word. At any rate, before the word, there is this sometimes wordless word which we name the "yes." A sort of pre-ordinary pledge [*gage*] which precedes any other engagement in language or action.[13]

The summary point here, then, is that, in the thought of Chiara and the "spirituality of unity, or communion," the privilege of the question, or of the "no," bequeathed to modernity by the Enlightenment is taken over and transformed by Jesus' forsakenness and Mary's unwearying *fiat*: by the affirmations of Jesus and Mary that bear death into life, and thereby all "noes" into "yeses."

The Abba School

The Focolare's Abba School is an important expression of Chiara's "spirituality of unity" as sketched by Maria Voce. It is described in the words of Piero Coda as a "group of academics and scholars . . . in a variety of disciplines [who] have gathered around Chiara with the idea of making explicit the cultural dimensions of Jesus forsaken and of unity."[14] The new life and experience indicated in the spirituality of unity, in other words, is tied to a new doctrine, giving rise to a new theology and a new philosophy, and opening up a new sense of unity and integration among the disciplines. The key to this unity lies in the very term "Abba." Abba, the prayer of Jesus to the Father in the garden of Gethsemane: the prayer of Jesus, that is, which is the inmost expression of the reality of Jesus as *Son*. It is in the reality of creation in Jesus as the Son of God, and thus in the image of his divine childlikeness, that we discover reality, the reality of humanity and of all that is, as a gift-meant-for-giving-back. Here we should cite the well-known text of *Gaudium et Spes*, 22: "Christ the Lord, Christ the new Adam, in the very revelation of the mystery of the Father

---

University Press, 1997), 522.
13. Jacques Derrida, *Of Spirit: Heidegger and the Question*, Geoffrey Bennington and Rachel Bowlby, trans., (Chicago: University of Chicago Press, 1989), 130-31.
14. Lubich, *Essential Writings*, xxiii.

and of his love, fully reveals man to himself and brings to light his most high calling." We should also say, he thereby fully reveals, in and though man, the meaning of all "flesh," of the entire cosmos.[15]

What Chiara began in the "spirituality of unity," and what she developed in the Abba School, and what is now taking concrete form in Sophia University Institute in Italy can thus be seen both to anticipate and to express what, according to both John Paul II and Benedict XVI, indicates the central teaching of the Second Vatican Council as expressed in *Gaudium et Spes*. The task of the Abba School, in and through the lived experience of the love revealed in Jesus, the Son of God who loved to the end, is thus to show how the whole of reality is open to the logic of Jesus' prayer as the Son. This task does not deny the legitimate autonomy of the academic disciplines. Rather, it shows how this autonomy is itself best understood in terms of the form and activity of filial love as revealed in Jesus (in both its supernatural and its natural meaning) in terms of a love that is first received as a gift. "In this is love, not that we have loved God, but that he has first loved us" (1 Jn 4:10).

The point is to see all things in light of their origin in God and, thus, as Chiara says, not as one perspective "side by side with other perspectives" but rather as the perspective that, in giving other perspectives their unity, opens "new horizons for them."[16] Rooted in Jesus, "in whom all realities are recapitulated, [this perspective] sheds light on the various sciences, making them truer and more genuine."[17] Again, the world has its own value in itself as creaturely, and its own autonomy, but, as Chiara says, the world from its origin is destined for "eschatological fulfillment in the Person of the Word Incarnate . . . who recapitulates all in himself."[18] She adds:

> Through the Holy Spirit we intuit the existence of a spousal relationship between the Uncreated and creation, because by becoming flesh, the Word aligned himself with creation thereby divinizing it and recapitulating it in himself. This wide and majestic vision makes us think of the entrance of all creation one day into the bosom of the Father. . . . Certainly, these new heavens and the new earth are still far from their full realization, but we can

---

15. See John Paul II, *Dominus Vivificantem*, 50.
16. Lubich, *Essential Writings*, 209.
17. Lubich, *Essential Writings*, 209.
18. *An Introduction to the Abba School: Conversations from the Focolare's Interdisciplinary Study Group* (Hyde Park, NY: New City Press, 2002), 34–35.

already see them developing in the heart of creation if we look at it with the eyes of the Risen One who lives in us and among us.[19]

Conclusion

I would like to conclude, then, simply by citing Chiara's poem, "Give Me All t Lonely," as well as what she termed her "last wish," which concretely express the depths and catholicity of her vision:

> Lord, give me all the lonely. . . I have felt in my heart the passion that fills your heart for all the forsakenness in which the whole world is drifting.
> I love every being that is sick and alone: even plants in distress cause me pain . . . even animals left alone.
> Who consoles their weeping?
> Who mourns their slow death?
> And who clasps to their own the heart in despair?
> Grant me, my God, to be in this world the tangible sacrament of your Love, of your being Love: to be your arms that clasp to themselves and consume in love all the loneliness of the world.[20]

And thus her "last wish" as she expresses it, using the words of Belgian theologian Jacques Leclerq: "On your day, my God, I shall come to you . . . , I shall come to you, my God . . . with my wildest dream: to bring you the world in my arms."[21]

These words, I would say, harbor an ontological vision at the heart of which lies the Christ-l ike, Marian, and human truth of the words of Stevens, so necessary for the global culture of today, which I quote again:

> . . .in the imagination's new beginning,
> In the yes of the realist spoken because he must
> Say yes, spoken because under every no
> Lay a passion for yes that had never been broken.

It is in this passion for the yes hidden inside every no, the passion for yes that must never be broken, that we discover the testament of Chiara.

---

19. *Introduction to the Abba School,* 36–37.
20. Lubich, *Essential Writings,* 81–82 (translation revised).
21. Lubich, *Essential Writings,* 369 (cited by Chiara).

Chapter Thirteen

The Virgin Mary, Creation, Incarnation, and Redemption: From the Church Fathers to Chiara Lubich

Brian K. Reynolds

Among the considerable body of writings by Chiara Lubich known as "Paradise '49," which describe the mystical illuminations she experienced between 1949 and 1951, shortly after the birth of the Focolare Movement, are a series of passages on Mary. In this paper, I discuss a selection of these passages in light of some fundamental texts of the Church Fathers and medieval theologians. Anyone familiar with the enormously rich Marian heritage of the patristic and medieval periods who reads Lubich's '49 writings about Mary will, in some respects, find themselves on familiar ground. This is true not only with regard to the fundamental theological categories within which she operates, which are profoundly rooted in the tradition, but also because the language is strongly reminiscent of the imagery the Church Fathers employed to extol Mary's beauty and virtue and to explain her role in the economy of salvation. Nevertheless, it would be an error to think that Lubich's writings simply reconnect with an ancient tradition that had been obscured by the sometimes excessive Marian pietism that arose in medieval Europe. At the heart of Paradise '49 is a profound paradigm shift in our understanding of the relationship between God and humanity, which necessarily involves Mary. That paradigm shift involves understanding everything from the viewpoint of the Trinitarian logic of unity ("May they all be one," Jn 17:21) and Jesus Forsaken ("My God, my God, why have you forsaken me?" Mt 27:46), who (re)generates unity in creation, returning it to its original telos, which is to participate "in the ever-new and unending dynamism of the Trinitarian relationships."[1]

---

1. Chiara Lubich, "Toward a Theology and Philosophy of Unity: The Principal Cornerstones," in *An Introduction to the Abba School: Conversations from the Focolare's Interdisciplinary Study Centre* (Hyde Park, New York: New City Press, 2002), 28.

First a few words by way of introduction to Paradise '49 are in order, since it is important to understand that the experience itself, and not just the content of the illuminations, diverged from the established pattern for mystical events.[2] The experience that began in July 1949, when Chiara went for a period of rest to the Dolomite mountains near her hometown of Trent together with some of her first companions, did not emerge from a vacuum. It was the culmination of intense years of living the Word by putting the gospels into practice. This practice had begun in 1943, when Chiara consecrated herself to God and was joined by the first small group

2. A summarized version of the "Paradise," as recalled by Lubich in June 1961, was published in *Nuova Umanità*, in Italian, and in *Claritas: Journal of Dialogue and Culture*, in English (see note 4; it is also contained in this volume). As yet, only parts of the full text have been published in scattered sources, mainly in articles of *Nuova Umanità* and *Claritas*. Some extracts appear in English in Chiara Lubich et al., *An Introduction to the Abba School: Conversations from the Focolare's Interdisciplinary Study Centre* (Hyde Park, NY: New City Press, 2002) (with important passages regarding Mary on pages 9 and 27–28). Chiara cited from and alluded to the "Paradise" frequently in her talks and writings, the most important of which are gathered together in Chiara Lubich, *La dottrina spirituale* (Rome: Città Nuova, 2006) and published in English as *Essential Writings: Spirituality Dialogue Culture* (Hyde Park, N.Y.: New City Press, 2007). On Mary in the "Paradise," there are three articles by Gerard Rossé in *Nuova Umanità*: "Maria, la realtà dell' 'Anima' alla luce del mistero di Maria nell'esperienza mistica di Chiara Lubich: I. I primi giorni," *Nuova umanità* 195, no. 3 (2011): 291–314; "La realtà dell' 'Anima' alla luce del mistero di Maria nell'esperienza mistica di Chiara Lubich: II. La Desolata," *Nuova umanità* 196-97, no. 4-5 (2011): 437–58; "La realtà dell' 'Anima' alla luce del mistero di Maria nell'esperienza mistica di Chiara Lubich: III," *Nuova umanità* 198, no. 6 (2011): 597–610; (hereinafter referred to as "Maria I," "Maria II," and "Maria III"). In addition there are articles by Marisa Cerini, "Aspetti della mariologia nella luce dell'insegnamento di Chiara Lubich," *Nuova umanità* 121, no. 1 (1999): 19–28, Brendan Leahy, "Il Dio di Maria." *Nuova umanità* 151, no. 1 (2004): 59–70, and Alba Scariglia, "Maria soltanto Parola di Dio," *Nuova umanità* 200, no. 2 (2012): 189–98. A number of key texts by Chiara on Mary, including some that refer to the "Paradise," appear in the volume *Maria: Trasparenza di Dio* (Rome: Città Nuova, 2003), published in English as *Mary: The Transparency of God* (Hyde Park, New York: New City Press: 2003). I quote from the Italian version. Crucial to an understanding of Mary's role in the charism of unity is the talk "Maria nell'esperienza del Movimento dei Focolari," given to a group of bishops in 1987, which appears in a reworked form in *Maria: Trasparenza di Dio*, 15–43. Another useful resource is the dissertation of Leonar Maria Salierno,"Maria" negli scritti di Chiara Lubich (Rome: Marianum, 1993), which gathers together nearly all the significant talks and writings of Lubich on Mary up to the year 1993. Translations of the Paradise not previously appearing in English are, in the spirit of the Paradise, the fruit of a collaboration between Callan Slipper, Thomas Masters, Fr. Fabrizio Tosolini, and myself. All translations of other Latin and Italian texts cited are mine unless otherwise stated.

of women who were to become the foundational columns of the Focolare Movement. During these years, as they nourished themselves on the Word, on the Eucharist, and on love of their brothers and sisters, the key points of the Focolare spirituality began to clarify, especially the concepts of unity and Jesus Forsaken. Chiara tells us that there came a point when all the words of the gospels seemed to express the same thing: love, which culminated in Jesus Forsaken.[3]

It was at this time that a key encounter occurred with Igino Giordani, a man of deep faith, a renowned politician, a writer, and a patristic scholar. It was he who recognized the import of the charism that Chiara had received in a way that her companions, who were young women like herself, could not. Giordani was also to play a key role in the '49 illuminations. Chiara described these circumstances in the following way. Giordani, who had joined Chiara and her companions in the Dolomites, told her that he would like to make a vow of obedience to her in the manner of the followers of Catherine of Siena. Chiara, feeling that this could be an inspiration of the Holy Spirit but not quite comfortable with the idea of someone vowing obedience to her, said to him:

> It could really be that what you are feeling comes from God. . . . So tomorrow in church, when Jesus in the Eucharist comes into my heart, as into an empty chalice, I will say to him: "on my nothingness, make a pact of unity with Jesus in the Eucharist in Foco's[4] heart. And bring about that bond between us as you see it should be." Then I added, "And Foco, you do the same."

After they had made this Pact of Unity, Giordani had to leave for a speaking engagement. But Chiara felt urged to go back into the church:

> I was about to pray to Jesus in the Eucharist, to call his name, Jesus. But I couldn't. That Jesus who was in the tabernacle was also in me. I was still myself, but made another him. Therefore,

---

3. What I recount here verbatim is drawn from various accounts of Chiara of the events of 1949, in particular "Paradise" as recalled by Chiara in 1961, published as Chiara Lubich, "Paradise," *Nuova umanità* 30, no. 3 (2008): 285–96, and in English as "Paradise '49," *Claritas: Journal of Dialogue and Culture* 1, no. 1 (2012): 4–12, accessed August 5, 2014, http://docs.lib.purdue.edu/cgi/viewcontent.cgi?article=1003&context=claritas. The quotes of Chiara are taken from an unpublished talk by Eli Folonari to the Volunteers of the Focolare Movement, entitled "Il patto di unità" (The Pact of Unity), Castelgandolfo, February 6, 2010.
4. Foco, meaning "fire," was the name Chiara gave to Giordani.

I could not call myself. And then I was aware of a word spontaneously coming from my mouth, "Father (Abba)," and in that moment I found myself in the bosom of the Father.

And so, on July 16, the series of illuminations known as "Paradise '49" began. They continued all that summer and, sporadically, over the next two years. Chiara shared them intensively with Giordani and her first companions, whom she called the "*Anima*," or Soul. It is important to understand that what was happening was much more than Chiara receiving illuminations that she then passed on to the others. The *Anima* was the protagonist of the illuminations, so they entered as a group into the "Paradise." This collective entering was possible because of the Pact of Unity they had made (first between Foco and Chiara, and then between Chiara and the others) to love each other to the degree that Jesus had loved in his forsakenness on the Cross, a pact sealed by the Eucharist. The fact that "Paradise '49" was an experience of communion in which the collective "Soul" participated in the life of the Trinity has important implications for Mary, too. Mary, like all the other realities they experienced, is understood above all in a "collective" (one could say ecclesial) sense.[5]

But let us turn now to the passages themselves. I divide them into two sections. The first deals largely with illuminations on Mary's role as Theotokos, the Mother or Bearer of God. The second concerns the part she plays in the Redemption as the *Desolata*.[6] I conclude with some remarks about Chiara's vision of Mary in relation to the Trinity, humanity, and creation (of which Mary is the synthesis, par excellence).

First Illuminations

Having entered the bosom of the Father, the *Anima* (Chiara and her companions "united in an infinite abyss of Love"[7]) was the subject of a "mystical marriage" ("And so the Word wedded the Soul in mystical marriage"). It is to this Soul that the Word first presents Mary just two days into the vision-

---

5. This is a subject that Gérard Rossé discusses extensively in his three articles on Mary in the "Paradise."
6. I have chosen to maintain the original Italian term, which means "Desolate One," since it is impossible to render into English with a single word. Where appropriate, I translate it as "Mary Desolate." It should also be pointed out that the term "*Desolata*" was in common use in Italian and was by no means original to Chiara.
7. Rossé, "Maria I," 291–92.

ary experience, on July 18, 1949: "The Word, having wed the Soul clothed as Church, now in his home (in Paradise) was introducing first Mary, his Mother."[8] The fact that the Word presents Mary to the Soul as church is significant, since she is immediately seen not simply as the mother of Jesus but in her relationship to the Mystical Body of Christ (thus anticipating Vatican II). This will be true throughout the Marian illuminations of the "Paradise," where Mary is never understood in isolation, as is natural for a communitarian spirituality whose core message is unity.

Moreover, Mary does not present herself; rather, it is the Word who presents her to his spouse, the Soul, so that she is part of a single chain, the Word-Mary-Soul-Church-Humanity chain. If we ignore this collective aspect, it is not possible to appreciate the full meaning of this first encounter with Mary, which Chiara explains at length the next day:

> And then I looked above me, where there was a beautiful statue of our Mother,[9] and I understood that She is only Word of God and I saw Her as beautiful beyond telling: all clothed in the Word of God who is the Beauty of the Father; hidden guardian of the Spirit within.
>
> And, as soon as I loved Her, she loved me and with the clarity of Heaven showed me all of her beauty: the Mother of God! ["My God, I said within myself, but is She the Mother of that God the Father and of that Spouse who I came to know in these last few days? She is truly the Queen of Heaven? And it seemed impossible that She could be so great, even greater than Her Son who She contains in Herself. She is truly the Queen of Heaven and earth!
>
> "Yes, it is true that She is contained by the Trinity, but yesterday I saw Her, because the Son showed Her to me, as containing within Herself the whole of Heaven."]
>
> Outside the sky was of a blue never seen before. . . . And so I understood. The sky contains the sun! Mary contains God! God loved Her so much as to make her His Mother and his Love made Him become small before Her.[10]

---

8. Rossé, "Maria I," 293 (translation revised).
9. The term she uses in Italian is "Mamma."
10. July 19, 1949, *Maria: Trasparenza di Dio*, 88 (translation revised). The section in square brackets was omitted by Lubich in her talk but is in the original text of the "Paradise."

This passage perfectly encapsulates both the novelty of Chiara's vision and her rootedness in the tradition. One might ask, why is Chiara so amazed? Did she not already know that Mary was the mother of God? Did she not know that Mary had contained God and that God had made himself small, had bowed down in an act of kenosis so as to take on our human nature? After all, Mary had already been definitively proclaimed Theotokos at the Council of Ephesus (431),[11] and from the very earliest times the church had recognized God's extraordinary condescension in taking on human nature. This is evident, for instance, in the motif—found frequently in the textual tradition from the time of Ephrem the Syrian (†c. 373) onward—of expressing amazement at Mary's capacity to contain the uncontainable God.[12] Even the idea of Mary having been "all clothed in the Word" is not entirely new. Andrew of Crete (†c. 740), for instance, writes of her as the "living book in which the spiritual word has been silently inscribed by the living pen of the Spirit."[13] Bernard of Clairvaux († 1153) imagines Mary praying for the living Word to come and dwell in her, the Word who will speak, not through the words on a page

11. For a summary of the main debates and the politics surrounding the Christological disputes, see Leo D. Davis, *The First Seven Ecumenical Councils* (Collegeville, Minn.: Liturgical Press, 1983). See also David F. Wright, "From 'God-Bearer' to 'Mother of God' in the Later Fathers," in *The Church and Mary*, ed. Robert N. Swanson, 22–30 (Woodenbridge: Boydell, 2004); Richard Price, "The *Theotokos* and the Council of Ephesus," in *The Origins of the Cult of the Virgin Mary*, ed. Chris Maunder, 89–103 (London: Burns & Oates, 2008) and "Theotokos: The Title and its Significance in Doctrine and Devotion," in *Mary: The Complete Resource*, ed. Sarah Jane Boss, 56–74 (Oxford and New York: Oxford University Press 2007). Also see my *Gateway to Heaven: Marian Doctrine and Devotion, Image and Typology in the Patristic and Medieval Periods*. Vol. 1 (Hyde Park, NY: New City Press, 2012), 25–30.

12. See, for instance, *Hymns on the Nativity*, 21, 6–8, in Ephrem the Syrian, *Bride of Light: Hymns on Mary from the Syriac Churches*, trans. Sebastian Brock (Piscataway, N.J.: Gorgias Press, 2010). Cyril of Alexandria († 444) greets the Virgin as "you who have contained the Uncontainable in the holy matrix of your virginal womb" and calls her "the location for the One who is uncontainable"; *Homily* 4, which was delivered at Ephesus, and *Homily* 11 (Reynolds, *Gateway*, I, 24). Proclus of Constantinople († 446) writes: "Come then, let us admire the Virgin's womb, a womb wider than the world. For she, without difficulty, enclosed within her him who cannot be contained in anyone, and he who carries everyone in his hands, including his Mother, was carried by her in her womb"; *Fourth Homily on the Birth of the Lord*, 1. *Patrologia Graeca*, ed. Jacques-Paul Migne (Paris: Migne, 1857-66), 65 (1862), col. 708C–709B (henceforth *PG*).

13. Third Homily on the Dormition, 7, in *On the Dormition of Mary: Early Patristic Homilies*, ed. Brian E. Daley, 142 (Crestwood, N.Y.: St. Vladimir's, 1998).

or even through the inspired words of a prophet, but in person, because he will be born of her.[14] It was also commonly held from patristic times onward that Mary was thoroughly familiar with the scriptures.[15] This idea later manifested itself in art, with the Virgin at the Annunciation often shown reading a scroll or a book, usually the Bible open at the prophecy of Isaiah 7:14, that foretold a virgin giving birth.[16]

What, then, is novel about Chiara's intuition? In the first place, the main purpose of the patristic Church's declarations of wonder that the finite Mary could contain the infinite God was to proclaim belief in the dual human and divine natures in the one person of Christ. Heated disputes over the person of Christ dominated much of the patristic period. Chiara's amazement, however, derives from a new illumination, namely, on the greatness of God's design for Mary, which reaches truly cosmic dimensions. The majesty of Mary's calling—to be contained by God (the Trinity) and also to contain God—is extended to her containing Heaven. Now Heaven is humanity and the whole of God's creation glorified, so that Mary represents the eschatological fulfilment of God's plan for the cosmos. In her we see that the perichoretic telos of every human being is to contain God as he contains us and for each of us contain within ourselves the entirety of creation.

As to Mary being "clothed in the Word," it is not simply that she was familiar with scripture, as we have seen in the passages of the Church Fathers I have quoted, but also that she had so emptied herself that she was, in a certain sense, already all Word of God before he came to dwell in her physically. Lubich expands and deepens the traditional understanding of what attracted God to Mary, namely, her being, which was filled with grace, and her virtue, especially her virginity and humility. Chiara's vision offers a new perspective on Mary's being endowed with grace and virtue, and on her being without sin, or spotless, as she is frequently called in the marvellous

---

14. See the *Fourth Sermon on the Glories of the Virgin Mother*, in *St. Bernard's Sermons on the Blessed Virgin Mary*, a priest of Mount Mellary Abbey, trans., 76–7 (Devon: Augustine Publishing Company, 1984) (hereafter *SBS*).

15. In fact, in the very early apocryphal tradition one finds the story that Mary lived in the Temple from the age of three, where she would have been thoroughly educated in the Scriptures, while the *Gospel of the Pseudo-Matthew*, a medieval Latin infancy narrative dating from between the sixth and the eighth centuries that builds on the earlier *Protoevangelium*, describes Mary reading a psalter at the time of the Annunciation.

16. See Jean Fournée, "Les orientations doctrinales de l'iconographie mariale à la fin de l'époque romane," *Centre international d'études romanes* 1 (1971): 53.

panegyric tradition of the East. Her beauty consists in being entirely clothed in the Word, and it is this that attracts God to her: for in her is mirrored the Word who is the beauty of the Father. Only a creature who was entirely Word, and therefore completely in conformity with God's original design for creation, could contain the Word: "He could not descend into sin and so he 'invented' Mary, who, summing up the entire beauty of creation in herself, 'fooled' God and attracted him to the earth."[17]

What is more, in presenting Mary to the Soul, the Word was also revealing the Soul's identity to itself, because the experience of the Soul since 1943 had, in a certain sense, mirrored that of the Virgin: They also had lived the Word to the point that they were clothed only in the Word and the Word had mystically married the Soul. In a way, Chiara's amazement in looking on Mary is a form of self-amazement, of discovering what she, the Soul, is called to be: the Work of Mary, which is the official title of the Focolare Movement.[18]

---

17. "Flower of Humanity," July 9, 1950, *Maria: Trasparenza di Dio*, 87. Chiara's understanding that Mary's beauty consists in her being clothed in the Word is an important contribution to studies on Mary's beauty, which were given new impetus by Pope Paul VI's 1975 advocacy of the Marian *via pulchritudinis*. See Paul VI, "Allocutio: In auditorio Pontificii Athenaei a Sancto Antonio in Urbe ob coactos Conventus, VII Mariologicum atque XIV Marianum, 16 maii 1975," *Marianum* 37 (1975): 491–94, and Johann G. Roten, "Mary and the Way of Beauty," *Marian Studies* 49 (1998): 109–27. Since patristic times Psalms 44:10-12, "And the king shall greatly desire thy beauty; for he is the Lord thy God, and him thou shalt adore," had been interpreted in a Marian key, while the Fathers, and even more so medieval theologians, found myriad reasons for her beauty, most of which boiled down to her freedom from sin, her virginity (and from the Middle Ages, her humility), and, after the Incarnation, her Motherhood of God, and finally her assumption into Heaven. Athanasius of Alexandria († 373), in what is one of the first readings of Psalm 44 in a Marian key, believes that because God foreknew the Virgin would be beautiful and pleasing to him proves that he truly became incarnate from her, rather than simply passing through her, as the Docetists maintained (*Letter to Marcellinus*, 6, (*PG* 27, 16B-C). The *Life of Mary* attributed to Maximus the Confessor († 662), Stephen Shoemaker trans., (New Haven and London: Yale University Press, 2012), dedicates almost a whole chapter (chapter 7) to Mary's beauty, while the thirteenth-century *Mariale super missus est*, vol. 37, ed. Emile Borgnet (Paris: Vivès, 1898), 62–246, long attributed to Albert the Great († 1280), offers fully 150 reasons for Mary being beautiful. Bonaventure († 1274) names "beautifying grace" among the seven graces that Mary received. See his *Fifth Sermon on the Annunciation* in *Testi mariani del secondo millennio*, ed. Angelo Amato et al., 8 vols. (Rome: Città Nuova, 1996-2011) (henceforth *TMSM*), IV, 268–9.

18. That the calling of the Focolare is to "repeat" Mary, in a certain sense, both individually and collectively, is confirmed many times by Chiara. In particular see her

Now to the second part of the description, where Chiara speaks of Mary being like the sky that contains the Sun. Here, too, she is drawing, perhaps unconsciously, on the tradition, both theologically, as we have already seen in terms of the uncontainable God being contained within Mary's womb, and typologically, since Christ had long been identified with the Sun of Justice (Mal 4:2) while Mary was the dawn sky that announced his arrival.[19] But here the vision is more cosmic and hints at later illuminations where Mary is revealed in her relationship to the whole of creation.

The breadth of this vision is beautifully interpreted in a stained-glass window in the Church of the Theotokos in Loppiano, Italy, designed by Dina Figueiredo.[20] Here, at one level, we have in abstract form the same concept as a Byzantine icon of the Theotokos or a medieval portrait of the Madonna and Child. The blue glass symbolizes Mary, while the yellow circle in the center at the bottom represents the Christ child. All icons of Mary in some way invoke the relationship between herself and the Christ child and convey some message about him to the faithful. The Hodigitria tells us to look to him for guidance, the Panakranta and the medieval *sedes sapientiae* tell us that he is Wisdom, and so on.

What do we learn from Chiara's illumination as interpreted in this window? First and foremost, we learn that Mary is the Theotokos, she who contained the infinite God. But the blue expanse also tells us that Mary is the synthesis of the cosmos,[21] who is apparently greater than the Sun. Chiara says in her unpublished writings from Paradise '49 that like the blue sky, Mary is the background of creation and heaven, "as if she had her feet on earth and her head in Heaven." But it is from the Sun that she receives her Light-Life. Moreover, we understand that it is because she makes herself nothing that she can be a silent background, colored with the infinite shades

---

meditation, "I want to see her again in you," published in *Meditations* (London: New City, 1989), 52–53.

19. Already in the Fathers we find the motif of the sun and the dawn, for instance, Chrysippus of Jerusalem († 479), *Homily on the Holy Mother of God, Testi mariani del primo millennio*, ed. Georges Gharib et al., 4 vols. (Rome: Città Nuova, 1988–1991), I, 603 (henceforth *TMPM*), and Jacob of Serug († 521), *Homily on the Blessed Virgin Mary Generatrix of God. TMPM*, IV, 155–56.

20. Numerous images of the window are available online, including this one: https://c1.staticflickr.com/3/2066/2334119426_ac6fa89a56.jpg.

21. In a later note, dated July 9, 1950, Chiara writes: "Mary, although she is just one [person] is the whole creation in synthesis at the apex of its beauty, when she is presented as bride to its Creator," *Trasparenza*, 85 (translation revised).

of the Word, allowing the Sun to shine all the more, and truly magnifying the Lord. And at yet another level, the yellow disc can represent the Eucharist, the flesh of Christ, which he received from his mother. This is another rich vein of Mariology on which Chiara sheds new light, though we do not have the space to explore it here.[22]

The Second "Fiat": The Desolation

Already in the intuitions of July 18–19 it was implicit that Mary's greatness lay above all in her "nothingness," since it was only by being completely empty of herself and "clothing" herself in the Word that she had "attracted" God to herself and the events of the Incarnation had been set in motion. The nature of Mary's nothingness clarifies when we move to the second stage of the illuminations, which begins on July 27. Here, Chiara understands that Mary's first "fiat"[23] (Luke 1:38) at the Annunciation is not the only, or even the highest, moment of assent. Instead, it is at the cross, when she endures a "desolation" that corresponds to Jesus' forsakenness, that the full majesty of Mary's design in the economy of salvation is revealed:

---

22. See Chiara Lubich, *The Eucharist* (Hyde Park, NY: New City Press, 2005). Of particular interest is the section where she deals with the Eucharist and the transformation of the cosmos, which can be related to the eschatological role of Mary's bodily assumption into heaven.
23. *Fiat mihi secundum verbum tuum*; Be it done unto me according to thy word.

> But to be Mary it is necessary to be Jesus Forsaken or, indeed, the Virgin desolate: offer oneself to suffer the loss of the Son: rejoice in being without Peace, Joy, Health . . . all that she is: feel ourselves Mary desolate . . .[24]
>
> ". . . because you are desolate": that is, be *only*: Word of God. Hold within yourself only the Word of God.
>
> ". . . and blessed is the fruit of your womb, Jesus . . ."
>
> Giving birth to *Jesus* in oneself (becoming holy for the others = living the Word of God that gives birth to Christ in the entire Soul) for oneself and for the souls.[25]

Our first observation is that Mary has taken on a new measure: No longer is she the young woman assenting to the Incarnation. Now she is saying a "yes" of a far higher order. In one sense, it seems that Chiara is not saying anything new, given that it has long been believed that Mary endured unspeakable suffering in witnessing her Son's death on the cross. In the West many writers follow Ambrose († 397), who movingly evokes her stoic martyrdom as she witnessed the agony and death of her Son,[26] while in the patristic East harrowing portrayals of Mary's distress on Calvary exist from at least the fifth century[27] and give rise to dramatic poems known as Planctus Mariae, among which the earliest and best is by Romanos the Melodist († c. 560).[28] By the seventh century, in Maximus the Confessor († 662), who

---

24. In other words, we have to be like Mary, who is truly herself when she is desolate, when she experiences herself as desolated.
25. July 27, 1949; Rossé, "Maria II," 441 (translation revised).
26. *De institutione virginis*, 49; *Patrologia Latina*, 221 vols., ed. Jacques-Paul Migne (Paris: Migne, 1844-65), 16 (1841), col. 333 (henceforth *PL*).
27. See, for instance, the apocryphal *Acta Pilati B* known as the *Gospel of Nicodemus*, and Sandro Sticca, *The Planctus Mariae in the Dramatic Tradition*, Joseph Berrigan trans. (Athens: University of Georgia Press, 1988), 34.
28. The main purpose was to encourage the faithful to dwell on Christ's suffering and its meaning through the eyes of the Virgin. On Romanos' plaint, see Elisabeth Catafygiotou-Topping, "Mary at the Cross: St. Romanos Kontakion for Holy Friday," *Byzantine Studies / Études Byzantines* 4 (1977): 18–37; Gregory Dobrov, "A Dialogue with Death: Ritual Lament and the θρῆνος Θεοτόκου of Romanos Melodes," *Greek, Roman and Byzantine Studies* 35 (1994): 385–405; and Niki Tsironis, "The Lament of the Virgin Mary from Romanos the Melode to George of Nicodemia," Ph.D. diss., University of London, 1998.

speaks of the sword of Simeon (Lk 2:34-35) piercing Mary on Calvary,[29] we already see a recognition that she shared in an extraordinary way in Christ's suffering, while by the ninth century, when Fathers such as Andrew of Crete and John of Damascus († 749) speak of Mary suffering the pangs of birth at the foot of the cross that she avoided at the birth of Jesus, there is at least an implicit recognition that, fully aware now of the awful implications, she is being asked to repeat the "yes" that she spoke at the Incarnation.[30]

But if Jesus' cry on the cross, "My God, my God, why have you forsaken me," is the moment of his greatest suffering—rather than his night in Gethsemane, as most held at that time—when he emptied himself and "lost" his relationship with the Father out of love, then Mary Desolate takes on a whole new significance, because her self-emptying and the loss of her relationship with the Son, also out of love, directly correspond to the experience of Jesus. This correspondence is entirely new in the history of Mariology. It is clear from Chiara's text that she understands Mary Desolate to be, in one sense, the same as Jesus Forsaken. Indeed, she says that to be Mary one can be either Jesus Forsaken or Mary Desolate because of the absolute identification that the *Desolata* experiences with the forsaken Jesus. And so, just as Chiara has said of Jesus Forsaken that every negative adjective in the dictionary could be applied to him,[31] the same could be said of Mary Desolate. To be Mary means to embrace everything negative and transform it through Jesus Forsaken into love.

But there is something more. Because the *Desolata*, through the grace of her love for Jesus Forsaken, generates Jesus in herself but not for herself, we, too, should imitate her so that he can be present in us as he was in the Soul. One does not sanctify oneself for oneself but for the sanctification of others.[32] The Jesus that is generated by this process is not the Incarnate Jesus

---

29. From the time of Origen (*In Lucam*, 6, 3–4, and 17, 6-7, *PG* 13, 1814–15 and 1845), the sword has been connected with the suffering of Calvary in the Eastern Church, but in a negative sense of a prophecy that Mary, like all the disciples, would suffer a loss of faith. Maximus is possibly the first Eastern Father to put an entirely positive spin on it.
30. See, respectively, *Triodion for Palm Sunday*, *Theotokion*, Ode VIII, *TMPM*, II, 464, and *Exposition on the Orthodox Faith*, 6, 14, *TMPM*, II, 493–94.
31. Unpublished talk, "The Clothes of Jesus Forsaken," Rocca di Papa, June 1, 1972.
32. This may be better understood by a recent experience of a dear friend of mine. Having been diagnosed with a very serious cancer, his first thought was to prepare well for death, looking upon this as what God wanted for him. But then, having received many messages of concern from people, he thought of the pain his death

of the Annunciation but the Risen Jesus of Easter whom Chiara and her companions found present in the Soul-Church ("Where two or three are gathered in my name, there am I in the midst of them," Mt 18:20).

Once again we see how the experience of Paradise '49 was collective and how it emphasizes how the understood realities transfer into the life of the collective Soul, not the individual soul or just the souls of those who are participating in the event. The lesson learned from Mary Desolate is that the individual must not remain transfixed in some sort of mystical transport, contemplating the wounds of Christ, but needs to "go beyond the wound," as Chiara puts it elsewhere, to love others.[33] One must not content oneself with generating Christ in one's own soul but instead should imitate Mary Desolate in losing Jesus in oneself so as to generate the Risen Christ in the souls of others and in the midst of the Soul.

In a passage written about a month after this first intuition of Mary Desolate, Chiara returns to the same theme, this time adding some extra elements:

> The Desolate too has a Wound.[34] And entering into that Wound inflicted upon her in her heart by the forsakenness of Jesus: "Woman, here is your Son" (the silence around the One replaced by John was the peak of her pain and was comparable to the silence of God in the forsakenness of Jesus) there came John and with him Humanity. Into Mary's most pure Womb, whence came the Son of God, go back the sons and daughters of humankind to be brought into Godhead via their immaculatization in Mary.[35]

---

would cause them, and therefore vowed that he would do all he could to get better out of love for them, not for himself.

33. See "Maria nell'esperienza del Movimento dei Focolari," *Trasparenza*, 34: "It was necessary to go decisively beyond the wound, it was necessary to embrace the Forsaken One so that the Risen One would always shine forth in us, the new creature. Only in this way would we be like Mary."

34. We can understand what Chiara means by wound in another passage: "Now Jesus is making me understand that we too have to be *Wounded*: to have a void in our hearts and in the void the whole of Heaven and earth with all the children of God and all of creation." Rossé, "Maria II," 447.

35. The term Chiara uses is *"indiarsi,"* literally "to ingod," which to the best of my knowledge first occurs in Dante's *Paradiso* 4, 28. It is almost never found thereafter, although its Latin equivalent is to be found elsewhere. This is one of several terms that Chiara uses that may have been inspired by the *Commedia*, which she would have known well.

The Virgin Mary, Creation, Incarnation, and Redemption

> She is the Gate of Heaven. One is not Christian if one is not Marian. One is not divine if not immaculate. One does not go to Jesus if not through Mary. One does not possess the Forsaken but through the Desolate.[36]

Here Chiara uses a series of traditional motifs but not their traditional meanings. When the Fathers spoke of Mary as the Gate of Heaven, it was to affirm her virginity or that through her had come the salvation of the world.[37] Later on, beginning with the likes of Andrew of Crete and Germanus of Constantinople († 733), the epithet was understood primarily in terms of her mediatory role in Heaven, where she intervened constantly on behalf of sinners.[38] The motto, "*ad Iesum per Mariam*" (To Jesus through Mary), which was popularized in the eleventh century by Peter Damien († 1072) and which Chiara adopts here, also had essentially the same meaning: that as it was through Mary that Jesus became incarnate, so it is through her that sinners can receive the grace to reach heaven.[39] Chiara instead sees Mary's mediation entirely in terms of the relationship between the *Desolata* and Jesus Forsaken. Here, she is closer to the tradition of Marian plaints we mentioned earlier, whose purpose was to allow the faithful to participate vicariously in the Passion of Christ by experiencing the emotions of Mary. But the identification that we can experience with Jesus Forsaken through Mary Desolate is far deeper than mere empathy.

Chiara identifies the *Desolata* for the first time in this passage specifically with John 19:26-27, the moment when Jesus tells his mother that from now on the apostle John is her son. In traditional Mariology, Mary's presence at

---

36. "Gate of Heaven," September 28, 1949, *Trasparenza*, 93 (translation revised).
37. The typological interpretation of Mary as the closed gate (see Ez 44.1-3) who remains a virgin and gives admittance only to God goes back at least as far as Ephrem the Syrian, and in the West is already found in Jerome († 419).
38. By the fifth century the gate was also being interpreted in terms of Mary's mediation, as is evident from the *Akathistos Hymn*, where she is addressed thus: "Hail, key to the gates of Paradise" (7, 9), "Hail, gate of hallowed mystery" (15, 7), "Hail, through whom Paradise is opened; / Hail, key to the kingdom of Christ" (15, 15, 16), cited from the translation of the *Akathistos* by Leena Peltomaa, *The Image of the Virgin Mary in the Akathistos Hymn* (Leiden: Brill, 2001). The epithet is widely found in medieval texts, especially hymns.
39. Damien's precise words from which the motto is believed to have been coined were: "Since it was through you that the Son of God deigned to descend to us, so it is through you that we may attain communion with him" (*Sermon for the Nativity of the BVM*, 46, 7, *PL* 144, 761B).

the cross is interpreted in terms of two moments. The first is John 19:25, which describes Mary standing by the cross together with Mary, the wife of Clopas, and Mary Magdalene. This moment, in the Western tradition, has been interpreted since the time of Ambrose as an indication of Mary's dignified and recollected grief throughout the Passion and death of Jesus (an attitude portrayed most beautifully in Michelangelo's *Pietà*). The second is the moment when Jesus addresses his mother and consigns her into the care of the John. For most of the patristic period very little attention was paid to this event. It served only as a proof that Mary did not have any other children, since Jesus would hardly have handed her over to John if he had had siblings who could have taken care of her. The act was taken at face value as an act of filial piety, albeit an impressive one given Jesus' extreme agony. In the ninth century, however, George of Nicodemia († after 880) offered a new interpretation of these lines, identifying this as the moment when Mary passes from being the mother of Jesus to the universal mother: "Now I constitute her not only as your Mother, but of all the others too. I place her as guide to the disciples and I absolutely desire that she be honoured because of her privilege as Mother."[40]

It would take several centuries for Western commentators to posit such a clear link between John 19:26-27 and Mary's universal motherhood of humanity. Anselm of Lucca († 1086), writing on the Presentation in the Temple (Luke 2:22-38), is perhaps the first to do so.[41] Chiara's words are particularly reminiscent of two twelfth-century theologians: Eadmer of Canterbury († c.1124) states that he believes the moment of greatest suffering for Mary was when Jesus gave her into the care of John, depriving her, in a certain sense, of her divine motherhood. Rupert of Deutz († 1130) affirms that with the role Christ assigned her of being the mother of John, Mary becomes the mother of all humanity.[42]

On the surface, then, we are in the presence of a fairly orthodox restatement of traditional Catholic belief. But Lubich's understanding goes further than this because Mary's loss of divine motherhood is intimately linked to her being the *Desolata* who leads on to Jesus Forsaken. This link becomes

---

40. Homily 8, *TMPM*, II, 756.
41. See his *Oratio ad suscipiendum corpus Christi* 1, Henri Barré, *Prières anciennes de l'Occident à la Mère du Sauveu: Des origines à saint Anselme* (Paris: Lethielleux, 1963), 227.
42. Respectively, *De excellentia Virginis Mariae* liber, 5, PL 159, 567A-B, and *Commentaria in Evangelium S. Joannis*, 13, PL 169, 790A-B.

clearer if we read another note dated October 2, 1949, which goes under the title "Today in the Glory of the Trinity we are the *Desolata*-Creation":

> It is a "fiat" that is different from her first: with the first she gave up her virginity (apparently); with the second she gives up her Motherhood (also apparently). Only like this is she Mother of all. She acquires the *divine* Motherhood of an infinite number of souls by giving up the divine Motherhood of her First Son. And this too is done according to the economy of God. She gives one and gets a hundred.
>
> But how much pain she felt at Jesus' cry of forsakenness cannot be imagined. It was the hour when she would have wanted to stay closest to him. But by this point she had been removed by him from her place as his Mother. She had had no right to be his Mother and, in the face of the shift to another Motherhood pointed out to her by Jesus, she could neither complain nor lose her composure. In that moment, therefore, Jesus had neither Mother nor Father. He was nothingness born of nothingness.
>
> And Mary too was suspended in nothingness. Her greatness had been her divine Motherhood. Now it was taken from her.
>
> So in that moment the Desolate, through God's will, did not participate in the Redemption. She was excluded by her Son who alone offered himself for all, including her. And at the same time, she participated in it with infinite intensity because, precisely there, she was made our Mother.
>
> Now, divine Motherhood was hers, hence a Mother not human, but *divine*, infinite. And therefore producing God. Because she was a *divine Mother* she can be Mother of us *all*.[43]

Now the full extent of Chiara's illumination becomes clear: Mary's desolation is a two-stage process, but not in the sense it had been understood before. First comes her acceptance of the loss of any rights of maternity over her divine Son, in exchange for which she receives John.[44] Here she is

---

43. This passage appears in sections in Rossé, "Maria II," 450–53 (translation revised).
44. Origen already recognizes that Mary finds Christ in John on the basis of the Pauline affirmation that it is not he who lives but Christ in him, In *Johannes*, 1, 6, PG, 14.32.

giving up the entire beauty of her personal relationship with Jesus, all the riches and fruits of the years she had lived in intimate contact with him, all the wonder and beauty of the last three years of his life, when he had revealed himself publicly. And for what? So that she may love him in John, who represents each brother and sister, now that her maternity has become collective. In other words, she is losing God in herself in order to love him in the other; this is the mirror image of what Jesus will do, but at an entirely different level because he is the Second Person of the Trinity, when he "loses" the Father in his cry of forsakenness. The second moment cannot happen without this initial loss of divine maternity. Now Mary does not just lose Jesus in herself but, excluded from the moment of Redemption, as is the whole of creation (since only God can redeem), her loss takes on a universal, one could even say cosmic, dimension in that she experiences the absence of God in everything. Even her Son is at this moment, in a certain sense, without God ("my God, my God"). It is because of that loss of God that she, too, like the rest of humanity, is in need of redemption. And yet, because she has lost God, emptied herself of him out of love, just as Jesus Forsaken did on a divine scale, Mary paradoxically participated in the Redemption to such a degree that she became the universal mother.

This entirely new way of understanding Mary's participation in the Passion casts in new light the question of the Marian coredemption, a notion that remains a source of controversy and debate in the Catholic Church because it bridges the divide between those who deny the possibility of Mary having in any way contributed to the Redemption and those who affirm that she did in some way co-operate in it.[45]

That Christ alone objectively brought about the Redemption is the unequivocal teaching of the church. Paul affirms that there is only one me-

---

45. The discussion that follows draws on my chapter on the immediate co-redemption in Reynolds, *Gateway to Heaven*, 1, especially 272–75. Older works that deal with the immediate co-redemption include: E. Druwé, "La médiation universelle de Marie," in *Maria: Études sur la Sainte Vierge*. 8 vols., ed. Hubert du Manoir, 417–600 (Paris: Beauchesne, 1949-71), vol. I; Juniper Carol, *De Corredemptione Beatae Virginis Mariae: Disquisitio Positiva* (Vatican City: Typis Polyglottis Vaticanis, 1950); and Gabriele M. Roschini, *Problematica sulla Corredenzione* (Rome: Edizioni Marianum, 1969). Two more recent studies that support the doctrine are Brunero Gherardini, *La corredentrice nel mistero di Cristo e della Chiesa* (Monopoli: Vivere In, 1998), and Mark Miravalle, *"With Jesus": The Story of Mary Co-Redemptrix* (Goleta, Calif.: Queenship Publishing, 2003). See also the collection of articles in *Theotokos*, 72 (1999).

diator between God and humanity (1 Tim. 2:5), and the Church Fathers, most notably Augustine, also confirm this teaching.[46] What is at question is whether Mary could have subjectively associated herself with the Redemption. Most of the Fathers did not even raise the question of Mary's participation in the Redemption, other than to recognize her more indirect role of incarnating the Word. An exception is Ambrose, but he does so only to exclude the possibility.[47] In the medieval West, however, following on from the new awareness of Mary's universal motherhood, which we have already discussed, theologians began to consider the question of her contribution to the Redemption. Bernard of Clairvaux seems to suggest that Mary plays an active role in the Redemption by offering Jesus to the Father as a victim for the reconciliation of the world.[48] Although he does not explicitly state that she co-operated in the Passion, he does use the term "compassion" (*compassio*) when he speaks of the sword that pierced her heart at her Son's death (Luke 2:38) and states that she was fully aware of the purpose of Christ's sacrifice, sharing in it as she did to a degree greater than any other creature.[49] But the first fully worked out justification of the coredemption was by Arnold of Bonneval († after 1156), a disciple of Bernard of Clairvaux.[50] Building on the Irenaean principle of recapitulation,[51] he affirms that the New Eve not only shared in the process of reversing original sin through giving birth to the new Adam but also freely chose to share in the Passion of her Son. Thus the Passion and co-passion, which are the free act of a man and a woman, became a counterparallel to Adam and Eve's rejection of God. As a creature, Mary cannot contribute anything to Christ's redemptive act, but because her Son accepts her self-offering and presents it to the Father,

---

46. See *De Trinitate*, 4, 14, 19, and *De peccatorum meritis et remissione*, 1, 28, 56, Sant'Agostino, *Augustinus Hipponensis*, accessed June 15, 2014, http://www.augustinus.it/links/inglese/index.htm
47. *De institutione virginis*, 49; PL 16, 318B–319A, [333].
48. *Third Sermon on the Purification*, PL 183, 370.
49. See "Sermon for the Sunday within the Octave of the Assumption," SBS, 226–27.
50. See Ricardo Struve Haker, "Arnoldo de Bonavalle: Primer teólogo de la Corredención mariana," *Regina mundi* 7 (1963): 48–75.
51. See Matthew C. Steenberg, "The Role of Mary as co-Recapitulator in St. Irenaeus of Lyons," *Vigiliae Christianae* 58 (2004): 117–13, and my discussion in *Gateway*, 110–13.

she participates in the Redemption through her Son and thus contributes to the restoration of creation.[52]

Chiara's understanding fits with this explanation but goes further. The paradox of the logic of Jesus Forsaken (which is also the logic of the Trinity) means that by the very fact of not being (of being out of love), one is both lost and found:

> Jesus lost the Father or, rather, God ("My God, my God, why have you forsaken me") and he found Him again in Himself ("whoever gives up his life . . ."). Mary lost Jesus and found Him again in Herself, in fact She became Jesus in the Upper Room among the

---

52. "Lord, where are thy ancient mercies" (Psalms 88:50). "What are you waiting for? The time has already come: before you are your Mother and John, whom you love. You speak to the thief but do not speak to your Mother? She who is blessed amongst women looks at you and, with her eyes fixed upon you, she contemplates your wounds with maternal pity. And although she is not unaware of the good that your Passion is procuring for the world, she nevertheless feels that she is dying with you in her maternal affection while her Mother's heart is crushed by an unspeakable suffering. She sighs within herself and holds back the tears that want to burst forth; and the more her anguish swells, the more is she forbidden from showing it and from relieving her feelings with cries and laments. Every now and again sobs slipped out, but they were controlled and stifled so that they went back into the depths of the mind from which they had come out where they clashed against each other. In her soul a strong storm blew up while violent emotions assailed her. . . . Do not marvel if in that tabernacle you could see two altars: one in the heart of Mary, the other in the body of Christ. Christ immolated his flesh, Mary her soul. She truly wished to add the blood of her heart to the blood of her soul, and, raising her hands to the Cross [she wished] to celebrate the vespertine sacrifice with her Son, and with the Lord Jesus, to consummate the mystery of our Redemption, through her mortal body. But this was the exclusive task of the High Priest, to bring, that is, the offering of his own blood to the sanctuary, and he could not let anyone else participate in this dignity. Indeed, in the Redemption of man, no angel and no other man had or could have this power in common with him. Nevertheless, that affection of his Mother, according to her capacity, cooperated greatly in placating God, because the love of Christ presented both his own offering and that of his Mother to the Father, given that what the Mother asked the Son confirmed and the Father granted. The Father loved the Son and the Son the Father; and after the two of them came the Mother in the ardour of her charity, and if the functions were different the objective, which the good Father, the pious Son and the holy Mother sought and which love caused them to work out together, was the same. Contemporaneously, piety, charity and goodness compenetrated each other: the Mother beseeched, the Son interceded and the Father forgave." *De septem verbis Domini in cruce*, 3, PL 189, 1693A–1695A.

disciples and the Holy Spirit descended to make Her truly Jesus, because Jesus gained Him[53] for Her in His Forsakenness.

Mary lost Jesus to find Him again in Herself and in the others. . . . The Spirit descended on her and on the disciples. So Jesus, in His Forsakenness lost God in order to find Him in Himself and in his brothers.

Therefore: if Jesus gave God, he will find God again (other than in Himself in the Mystical Body of Christ).

This is the justice of the divine economy.

If Mary gave Jesus she will find Him again in her children: the mystical body of Mary is justice.[54]

And so it is that Mary, by not being what she was (the mother of God), becomes his mother in us. In exchange for the loss of the divine maternity of Jesus she receives the divine maternity of humanity. Moreover, since Mary Desolate corresponds perfectly to Jesus Forsaken, she is perfectly redeemed. In fact, Jesus Forsaken had need of someone in whom his redemptive sacrifice would bear perfect fruit,[55] and this someone is Mary Desolate, in whom humanity and creation are made new and through whom the Church is generated. In "losing" the Father, Jesus abandoned himself to the Father, through whom he rises again, his humanity divinized. Mary Desolate, in losing Jesus, rediscovers him through the Spirit as the Risen Lord present in her children, all the members of the church and of humanity. No longer is she just immaculate, but, like the Risen Jesus, she too is divinized:

---

53. In the sense that it was through his forsakenness that Jesus "breathed" the Spirit.
54. September 28, 1949; Rossé, "Maria II," 447. Chiara here capitalizes the pronouns of Mary to emphasise how she has been divinized, has become totally Jesus through her emptiness of self. By "justice" Lubich means the law of the divine economy, namely, that it is in not being that one is, in losing that one finds.
55. This is one of the arguments of John Scotus in favor of the Immaculate Conception: if Jesus had not saved at least one person perfectly, he would not be the perfect Redeemer. Indeed, Mary was especially in need of the merits of the Passion, which were anticipated in her case (*praeredemptio*), so that she would never be inhabited by sin, which would have closed off the means of Redemption. See *Questiones disputatae de Immaculata Conceptione BMV, TMSM*, IV, 438–48. For further discussion and a bibliography, see my chapter in *Gateway to Heaven* on the Immaculate Conception, especially 367–69.

When in her Desolation our Mother, at the foot of the Cross ("Woman, here is your Son . . ."), lost the divine commission of her human-divine Motherhood of Jesus and became, with the descent of the Holy Spirit, Jesus, she changed her immaculate flesh into divine flesh: she became Jesus in soul and in *body*. She became true Daughter of God, Daughter of her Son, of Jesus Forsaken to whom she had given immaculate flesh. And she equaled Jesus[56] and was able to preside in the Upper Room and to become Jesus among the Apostles who also, through her sacrifice, had become Jesus – through her sacrifice and hence by her having given Jesus and having received a hundred: Jesus in her and Jesus in them. Hence the Apostles were immaculatized, that is, they had the *flesh of Mary*. They were her children in soul and in body.[57]

Mary Desolate, having lost Jesus, becomes the Risen, divinized Jesus through the descent of the Holy Spirit, whom Jesus breathes forth on the cross. This leads us to the final step in Chiara's understanding of Mary's coredemption, which consists in her gathering the fruits of her Son's Redemption. Having emptied herself of her Son out of love (just as he emptied himself of himself out of love) she now rediscovers him in the universal love that she has for all humanity, as the mother of all: "How beautiful the Desolate in this turning of herself towards humanity to gather up the fruit of her Son's death – truly co-redeemer in this collaboration for the redemption of all."[58]

---

56. Here Chiara is not saying that Mary has become a goddess but that as a result of her complete identification with Jesus' act of Redemption in his forsakenness, and the consequent breathing forth of the Holy Spirit, she has been divinized, so that she now partakes in the divine nature of her Son. As in the passage above, this is why Mary is designated with capitals here. *Theosis*, or divinization is a central notion in patristic theology, particularly in the Eastern tradition, in such writers as Justin Martyr, Irenaeus, Clement of Alexandria, Origen, Athanasius, Gregory of Nyssa, Gregory of Nazianzus, and Maximus the Confessor. It is also present in the West, where it is termed *deificatio*, for instance in Augustine and Thomas Aquinas. See, for example, *Theōsis: Deification in Christian Theology*, ed. Stephen Finlan and Vladimir Kharlamov, 2 vols. (Cambridge: Clarke, 2006), and *Partakers of the Divine Nature: The History and Development of Deification in the Christian Traditions*, Michael J. Christensen and Jeffrey A. Wittung, ed. (Grand Rapids: Baker, 2007).
57. October 10, 1949: Rossé, "Maria III," 601.
58. October 2, 1949: Rossé, "Maria II," 455 (translation revised).

Mary, Humanity, and Creation

It is important to remember that the experience of Paradise '49 is not an end in itself. The entrance of the Soul into the bosom of the Father and the many illuminations on Mary that we have discussed should not be treated merely as some sort of intellectual exercise but must be understood in terms of their implications for the world in which we live. Chiara's illuminations on Mary Desolate have very real consequences in the here and now, both in the way we live our lives and in our understanding of the relationship between creation and Creator.

In each of the illuminations on Mary (and this is also true of other illuminations in Paradise '49), the realities that Chiara sees in the bosom of the Father become life in the experience of the Soul, which is destined to "incarnate itself" in the Work of Mary, in the church, and more generally in humanity. Jesus Forsaken and Mary Desolate are the highest expressions of how humanity can repeat the life of the Trinity on earth and bring about that unity that is at the core of the charism Chiara received. We, too, like Chiara and her companions who formed the Soul, can repeat this experience in our own lives:

> And we too who are on this journey – along this narrow road (so narrow that it is full of God, of the Trinity, and through it passes only Pure Spirit, Love, which is Simplicity) – we must be wounded, that is to say, absolutely empty of ourselves, even of God in us (and this is loving in the style of the Trinity!): must be, that is, nothingness, which means Jesus Forsaken: that is, the brother or sister who is to be lived in us (and nothingness is capable of welcoming him or her into itself), Mary Desolate, Jesus Forsaken.[59]

And again, some days later:

> We must be the living Desolate who gives up her Son, who is Father and Brother and All for her, for the Jesus to be built up in others. For her it is being forsaken by *God*. But woe if she had not done it!
>
> Her very "fiat" at the Incarnation would have been worthless because she would have impeded the Redemption. The Blood of

---

59. October 10, 1949: Rossé, "Maria III," 603 (translation revised).

Jesus which is the Holy Spirit (Blood of God!) would not have been passed on to his brothers and sisters.

The whole work of Jesus depended upon Mary.[60]

At first glance, this statement would seem almost heretical. How could Mary have impeded the Redemption, since only a refusal by Jesus himself could have done so? However, there is a long tradition in the church of saying that the Incarnation depended on Mary's assent, so why not the Redemption?[61] Lubich's insight is that for the Redemption to come about in the way that it did required Mary to become nothing, to empty herself, and to exclude herself from it. Being nothing she did not add anything to the nothingness of Jesus Forsaken, so that he alone brought about our Redemption. Moreover, if Mary had not completely emptied herself, by losing God in Jesus for God in humanity, the Redemption would have had no perfect object upon which it could act, as we have already pointed out, and therefore it would have been impeded. So what we should understand here is that Chiara is not saying that Mary could objectively impede the Redemption, any more than she could objectively contribute to it, but that by refusing to assent to it she would have been an obstacle to the flowing forth onto humanity of the grace that the Redemption unleashed. It is in this sense that she is co-operator in the Redemption, or coredemptrix.

And the same is true for us: Without the co-operation of humanity, salvation is merely a theory. Woe to us, too, then, if we do not learn from Mary Desolate that we must lose God in ourselves for God in our fellows! Like Mary we must "run towards humanity"[62] in order to generate it anew in the Risen Christ, and in this sense we can become "co-creators" alongside

---

60. October 15, 1949: Rossé, "Maria III," 603 (translation revised).
61. Of course God could have chosen to bring about the Redemption in another way, but he did not, so in this sense Mary could have prevented it, as Anselm of Canterbury († 1109), says in his *Oratio* 7 (51), PL 158, 955A–956B. Bernard of Clairvaux makes a similar point in his *Sermon for the Sunday within the Octave of the Assumption* (*SBS*, 206) and famously portrays the whole of Creation, the angels in heaven, the patriarchs and prophets, even God himself, waiting with bated breath for Mary to give her assent to the Incarnation (*Fourth Sermon on the Glories of the Virgin Mother, SBS*, 70–71).
62. "I see her with him running towards humankind who have become their God out of love for God! Both ready to leave everything for us. We too, like them, must leave God for human beings, must leave Unity for the Jesus Forsakens scattered throughout the world. Must make of Unity our springboard towards humanity." October 2, 1949: Rossé, "Maria II," 445 (translation revised).

her of the "new heavens and new earth" (Is 65:17; Rv 21:1) to which Jesus Forsaken gave life in an act of re-creation:

> Mary's originality was—although in her unique perfection—the same as it should be for every Christian: to repeat Christ, the Truth, the Word, with the personality that God has given to each of us. Just as the leaves of a tree are all the same and yet each is different from the other, so it is of Christians,—and, indeed, all people—: all are equal yet different. In fact, each of us recapitulates the whole of creation within ourselves. Therefore, each person, being "a creation" is the same as the others but different at the same time.[63]

Finally, since it is through Mary that "all of creation [is] purified and redeemed" and it is through her that creation returns to God,[64] we must look to her if we are to understand the telos of humanity, the eschatological destiny of creation, which is to return to the bosom of the Father, where she already is:

> Because there is in God a perfect perichoresis between the three divine Persons, and because, through Christ, in the Spirit, there is also a perichoresis between the Trinity and humanity, apex and synthesis of creation (You loved them even as you loved me [Jn

---

63. *Trasparenza*, 23.
64. See *Trasparenza*, 32. In so stating, Chiara is placing herself in a long line of commentators stretching back to Irenaeus, who sees Mary as the recapitulator of Eve, restoring the damage she did through original sin (see *Adversus Haereses*, 3, 22, 4, and 5, 19, 1); Proclus of Constantinople sees her as the locus where the whole Trinity has acted so that creation might be remade and human nature returned again to its divine image and likeness (*First Sermon on Mary, the Mother of God*, 1, TMPM, I, 557). A homily attributed to Modestus of Jerusalem († 634) links not just the Incarnation but the bodily Assumption with the restoration of creation for the first time (*Homily on the Dormition of the Mother of God*, 7, TMPM, II, 129). For Germanus of Constantinople, the Assumption completes the process begun in the Incarnation, since it was necessary for Mary to pass through death and then be assumed into heaven in order that she should fully become the Mother of Life, cancelling out the corruption of death caused by Eve (*First Homily on the Dormition*, 6, Daley, *On the Dormition*, 158–59). For Anselm of Canterbury Mary's *fiat* unleashes a re-creation of the whole of God's original creation, and she herself, in some way, contains all of this new creation within herself, not only because she bore the Creator in her womb but also because she herself is the synthesis of nature perfected and redeemed, through her absolute conformity to the divine blueprint. *Oratio* 7 (51), 4–7, *Gateway*, 136–37.

17:23]), all creation, recapitulated in Christ, is also destined to be, as Mary already is, eternally set into the Trinity: that is to live and rejoice infinitely in the intimate life of God, in the ever new and unending dynamism of the Trinitarian relationships.[65]

This is why Chiara, in a message addressed to a branch of the Focolare Movement that concerns itself with the incarnation of the spirituality in the world's different activities, presents the glorified Mary, assumed into heaven body and soul, as the model to whom one should look in seeking to transform humanity and return it to the Father:

> It [Mary's glorified body] is the symbol of that human part which God created and which has to return to him, completely transformed. It is the symbol of all the expressions of humanity in the world, of that incarnation in society, in the economy, in art, in education, in health, etc. It is in this [incarnation] that you see traced out the luminous path that will lead you to God, bringing with you society which has been transfigured.[66]

I leave the last word to Chiara, who says: "Just as Mary brought Creation into Paradise in her body, so you too must not aspire to enter [Paradise] without a world renewed."[67]

---

65. "Toward a Theology and Philosophy of Unity," *An Introduction to the Abba School*, 28.
66. Message for the Feast of the Assumption, August 15, 1980.
67. Unpublished "Message of the 40th Anniversary of the Birth of the 'Volunteers,'" Meeting of the Volunteers of God, Rocca di Papa, November 6, 1996.

Part Four

Implication of Paradise '49
for Biblical Studies

Chapter Fourteen

Revisiting Chiara Lubich's Paradise '49 In Light of the Letter to the Ephesians[1]

Gérard Rossé

The Letter to the Ephesians

The Letter to the Ephesians is a unique text and in many ways a mysterious one. We do not know to whom it was addressed. Maybe this was a circular letter addressed to various Christian communities including the one in Ephesus.[2] Furthermore, the letter does not seem to have been written in response to specific internal or external dangers, such as the seduction of "philosophies" or persecutions, although scholars try to find them. Rather, the letter written in the years 80–90 CE stems from a time when the church needed to reflect on its own identity, its mission, and its place in the world during a time of transition. It was in fact a time in which the first generation, the generation of the apostles and especially of Paul, was passing away while the church was spreading throughout the Roman Empire and the future seemed open.

Taking the Letter to the Colossians as a starting point, the author of Ephesians offers a broad vision of the magnificent design of God on humanity and creation—which was already taking place in the church—and invites and encourages the church and Christians to become aware of God's design in a new way, namely, to join in it as protagonists and to bring it about. This perspective helps explain why the fundamental argument of the letter is that the

---

1. This article and the other three published in *Claritas*, and are included as chapters fourteen, fifteen sixteen, and seventeen in this volume, are considered classic publications on the mysticism of Chiara Lubich. This article was first published in *Nuova Umanità* XXXI (2009): 351–75. It has been translated by Giovanna Czander, Dominican College, in Blauvelt, New York. The four Rossé articles are contained in Section 4 of this volume, "Implications of Paradise '49 for Biblical Studies," pages 241-328.
2. The name "Ephesus" at the beginning of the letter (Eph 1:1) does not appear in the earliest manuscript (before the second century) or in the most important codexes (Vaticanus, Sinaiticus).

church must rediscover and bring about its own identity, ideal, and mission in unity. Unity is actually "the specific theme of Ephesians more than any other canonical writing and it can be found both in its most doctrinal section (2:14-18; 3:6) and in its most parenthetic section (4:3-6, 16)."[3]

We do not even know the identity of the author of the letter. Looking at the context of the letter, we are led to believe that he must have been a "theologian with a broad vision and unique intellectual and contemplative abilities."[4] He can be considered a mystic, even though what he writes does not come from an extraordinary mystical experience, as Chiara Lubich's did, but "from a vision of faith."[5]

Mystical Experience and Vision of Faith

The intrinsic relationship between mysticism and a life of faith should always be kept in mind. Incorporated in Christ through baptism, Christians are already introduced as members of the Body of Christ into God's life, into the bosom of the Father. They have, right from the start, the Holy Spirit and divine *agape* (see Rm 5:5). Each baptized individual is therefore potentially a mystic, because he or she can experience in his or her own existence a communion with God who lives in the depths of his or her heart. The baptized individual, if malleable in the hands of the Holy Spirit, can be transformed and become increasingly more similar to Christ (see 2 Cor 3:18). Through the gift of the Spirit, which introduces the person to the knowledge of God's secrets (see 1 Cor 2:13), each believer is called to live as "normal" the extraordinary experience of communion with God within his or her own lifetime.

The mystical experience of the life of faith requires only that we put God in the first place in our lives and live out the gift of *agape*. The goal of a life of faith is not to achieve a personal contemplation of God in the desert but, according to the symbolism of the Book of Revelation, for the heavenly Jerusalem, made up of all peoples among whom God dwells, to descend to

---

3. Romano Penna, *Atti del III Simposio di Efeso su Giovanni Apostolo*, ed. Luigi Padovese (Rome: Istituto Francescano di Spiritualità, Pontifical University Antonianum, 1993), 145.
4. Romano Penna, *Lettera agli Efesini* (Bologna: EDB, 1988), 62.
5. This is demonstrated in the fact that the author does not describe his own experience but makes use of other Pauline writings, in particular the Letter to the Colossians, to write from its point of view.

earth. This reality is already possible in the fraternal communion lived out in the midst of the world.

Christian mysticism, even if it can benefit from extraordinary insights, does not stray from faith. Authentic mysticism, as a unique phenomenon, is not different from the vision of faith (given from Revelation) but is this very same faith experienced with greater clarity and intensity. In the revealed texts (and especially in Paul and John) there is consistency between faith and mysticism. This is an invitation not to separate the life of faith and mystical experiences, because the two share the same root: the indwelling of the Holy Trinity in the deepest recesses of each member of the Body of Christ.

In light of the fundamental consistency between the light of faith and the light coming from mystical experience, it is legitimate to embark on a comparative study of the Letter to the Ephesians and Chiara Lubich's writings from 1949. This is possible also because Lubich's enlightening illuminations originated from an experience of communion, an "ecclesial" experience. Chiara experienced personally the reality of the church in its deepest identity as the Body of Christ, which resulted in her participation in the Trinitarian life of God by being inserted in the very relationship of the Father and the Son. A comparative study is even more intriguing because the main topic of the Letter to the Ephesians is the church in its identity and calling to unity.

Approach

I would like to introduce a more external approach before comparing the content of the Letter to the Ephesians and of Chiara's writings. I wish to look at circumstances and conditions that reveal commonalities between the two writings and therefore to underscore God's consistent way of working throughout the history of the church.

The "Mystery"

The author of the letter uses the term "mystery" (Eph 1:9; 3:3, 4, 9; 6:19) to speak of the design of salvation, in all its cosmic-eschatological breadth, that had always been present in God's mind but was hidden for centuries and is now being revealed. The letter calls it more specifically the "mystery of Christ" (Eph 3:4) because the "the wisdom of God in its rich variety" (Eph 3:10) is completely given, brought about, and revealed in the Christ event and is expressed in the "boundless riches of Christ" (Eph 3:8). Christ is the alpha and the omega of the Father's design on the world. In Christ everything is recapitulated (see Eph 1:10). The mystery is also "the mystery of the gospel" (Eph 6:19). It is a mystery because it is the unique content of the gospel message that in Paul has its privileged, though not exclusive, mediator.

God Reveals through Charisms

The knowledge of this mystery, of the project of God's love in all its cosmic-eschatological dimension, cannot be the result only of proper human reasoning nor of mere intellectual reflection on the truths of faith. Knowledge of the mystery manifested to the apostle can be received essentially through revelation, that is, through God's initiative: "The mystery was made known to me by revelation," writes the author, speaking of Paul (Eph 3:3). According to the author of the letter, Paul was the recipient of a personal revelation (Eph 3:3, 18). Shortly after (Eph 3:5), he associates Paul with the "holy apostles and prophets." According to this letter, the way the mystery is communicated follows a divine logic. Knowledge of the mystery is not given directly to everyone; rather, God chooses specific individuals whom we could call "charismatic." These chosen individuals experience a certain light, as the letter attests. Paul, we read, received a grace from God, a revelation (Eph 3:2-3) that had at first overwhelmed him. The author reminds the reader of the historical experience of the apostle on the way to Damascus. In Paul's own words, "God said, 'Let light shine out of darkness'" (2 Cor 4:6). The revelation of the Son was certainly for the apostle an experience of light, which enveloped him and reached the most intimate depths of his being, shining within him as on a new day of creation. As written in the Letter to the Ephesians, God is "the Father of glory" (Eph 1:17). The splendor of his Love is reflected on the face of his Son, and the Father communicates glory as inheritance to his children (Eph 1:18).

Now, the glory of the Father, his communicated splendor, is not only for the future. It emanates from the unity witnessed by the church, where two groups of peoples, Jewish and Gentile, up to this point a sign of division, live together in unity. The mystery that was communicated already bears fruit. As Romano Penna writes:

> This is the abundant glory of the mystery among the peoples (Col 1:27) not only in the sense that the mystery of God is

brought to the Gentiles, but rather because the Gentiles' access to the mystery makes it shine in all its splendor, emphasizing the shining overcoming every division in a perfect mutual communion with God.[6]

Chiara expresses this aspect of light with the term "claritas," an essential aspect of her contemplative experience in 1949.

Light Needs to Be Communicated

This light communicated by God to Paul and others is of the same nature as the light of faith: insight about the things of God coming from the Holy Spirit to the believer who is open to encountering Christ. Yet, it also has a unique feature: a touch of "novelty" because of God's initiative. It is a light aligned with faith, but it has a "charismatic" nature. As such, this light, unlike faith understood as the believer's supernatural intelligence (Eph 1:8), *needs* to be communicated to the whole church. It is a gift for the person who has a charism, but it is also a mission.

For the author of the letter, therefore, "the holy apostles and prophets" (Eph 3:5), and especially Paul, are the recipients of a revelation that is hidden from the world and that now, through them, is being communicated to everyone and becomes an "event" in history. The author, however, does not consider these individuals as the first charismatics in a long chain that continues throughout the history of the church. Their charism is unrepeatable and unique. For the author, "the holy apostles and prophets" are an eternal foundation for the church (Eph 2:20). As Bouttier writes, "The revelation of the *mystery* is not a permanent process. The great act of God has two stages: the first is its messianic implementation and the second its apostolic manifestation."[7]

So can there be new insights in the church? Of course, but these subsequent revelations will reveal in more depth the meaning and realization of the message of these apostles and prophets. Our author confirms this because he too is aware of having been invested with a new light—reinterpreting the work of the great apostle more than twenty years after the fact.

---

6. Penna, *Lettera agli Efesini*, 62.
7. Michel Bouttier, *L'Epitre de Saint Paul aux Ephésiens* (Geneva: Labor et Fides, 1991), 143.

In the beginning, Paul had the grace of understanding the importance of the Crucified Jesus as related to overcoming the Law and beginning the mission to the Gentiles. By the time the Letter to the Ephesians was written, what Paul had to fight for was already widely accepted, that is, the existence of a church made up by the unity of peoples who up to that point had been divided. Such unity is seen as a sign of the actualization of God's plan on the cosmos: the recapitulation of all things in Christ. This is a new insight, though one in continuity with the apostolic message.

The mystery therefore is God's great design on humanity and creation, hidden throughout the centuries, brought to fruition in the risen Crucified One, and revealed by God to the apostles—that it may be communicated to everyone. Christian faith has not fallen into the errors of mystery cults or Gnosticism that talk about a "mystery" communicated but then reduce it to secret revelations addressed only to initiates and not to be shared. In the Letter to the Ephesians (and in the whole New Testament) even if the mystery is communicated to a few chosen people, it is destined to be shared with everyone. The author has written the letter precisely to communicate to the church a new light that, by a gift of the Holy Spirit, he has received. The grace that the apostle has received is "for you" (Eph 3:2), a grace to be given to the ecclesial "us." The author's prayer to God (Eph 1:18) is done in order that "the eyes of your heart [be] enlightened" to welcome and understand this new light.

Chiara Lubich's charism should be understood from this perspective and in this context. She received a charism of light in 1949 but did not keep it all to herself as if it were something addressed to her alone. Rather, she immediately shared it with her companions. This points to two features: The mystical experience of *Paradise '49* is an integral part of a "charism" and therefore is to be communicated. The "ecclesial" character of the visions means that they are addressed to the "we" that is the church.

Participation in the Charism

The author of the Letter to the Ephesians certainly desires to communicate to his Christian audience the light that has touched his inner being, his new understanding of the mystery. However, he is not satisfied with just informing his readers. Their knowledge of God is not simply the acquisition of concepts about God. It is not enough for one merely to receive information; rather one needs to have the experience of knowing God, an experience that is at the same time contemplative and incarnational. The author wishes to bring his readers into the experience of light that he himself experienced: The same Spirit who enlightened him needs to enlighten also the faithful. Therefore, we can ask: What are the conditions for this collective experience? What does the author do in order to bring it about?

A feature of the letter is the relevance given to prayer. The first part (which is the doctrinal part) begins with a prayer (blessing and thanksgiving, followed by a prayer of petition: Eph 1:3-14, 15-23) and concludes in reverse order with a prayer of petition followed by praise (Eph 3:14-10, 20-21). The revelation that the author wishes to communicate is therefore addressed to "us" gathered in the church at/in the presence of God. Enveloped in prayer, the addressees become part of a movement that starts from God (blessing makes them aware of God's working) and through the question and the praise returns to God as the human answer for/to the glory of God. The prevailing liturgical context in the letter, where "we" experience the church, is the perfect place where they can participate in the gift of the light. In the prayer that involves the whole assembly, the believers live out their Christian identity and become more keenly aware of their own mission.

It cannot be a coincidence that in *Paradise '49* we find a very similar context. Chiara felt prompted to share with her companions her experience of entering into the bosom of the Father. This is why she "then invited them to come with us to church the next day."[8] This behavior happened regularly. Chiara writes, "I went into church for the usual meditation with the souls who made up the Soul,[9] and looking at the tabernacle I waited, upon the emptiness of myself, for God to send his light."[10] This example could be generalized.

However, gathering in church is not sufficient to participate with one's life in the light to the charism. People need to *be* church. This need is expressed in the Letter to the Ephesians:

> I have heard of your faith in the Lord Jesus and your love towards all the saints, and for this reason I do not cease to give thanks for you . . . that the God of our Lord Jesus Christ, the Father of glory, may give you a spirit of wisdom and revelation as you

---

8. Bouttier, *L'Epitre de Saint Paul aux Ephésiens*, 143.
9. Chiara uses the word "Soul" to refer to what she calls "that One which united all of us."
10. Unpublished note from 1949.

come to know him, so that, with the eyes of your heart enlightened, you may know what is the hope to which he has called you. (Eph 1:15-18)

For the Spirit to communicate the wisdom and light that allow us to become intimate with God (see 1 Cor 2:6-10), faith is needed that places us under the vital influence of God as well as love lived out among the "saints"—the members of the community.

Faith and love, which characterize the church as human-divine communion, are therefore indispensable to experiencing light in a vital way, to sharing in the charism. The following text by Chiara is the best commentary. After the Pact with Foco and the experience of entering into the bosom of the Father, we read the following:

> Then I went home where I met the focolarine [her companions], who I loved so much, and I felt urged to bring them up to date on everything. I then invited them to come with us to church the next day and to pray Jesus, who entered their hearts, to make the same pact with Jesus who entered ours. And they did so. After that I had the impression of seeing in the Bosom of the Father a small band: it was us. I communicated this to the focolarine who made such a great unity with me that they too had the impression of seeing each thing.[11]

A life of a "collective" mystical experience (expressed in *Paradise '49*) and a life of faith lived out as church (expressed in the Letter to the Ephesians) are the same if the following conditions are present: gathering in prayer, faith, and mutual love. Specific to Chiara and her companions were also the Eucharist and the Pact of Unity. In light of this, the prayer we read in Ephesians 3:14-19 is particularly compelling:

> For this reason I bow my knees before the Father, from whom every family in heaven and on earth is named, that according to the riches of his Glory he may grant you to be strengthened with might through his Spirit in the inner self, and that Christ may dwell in your hearts through faith; that you, being rooted and grounded in love, may have power to comprehend with all the saints what is the breadth and length and height and depth, and

---

11. Unpublished note from 1949.

to know the love of Christ which surpasses all knowledge, that you may be filled with all the fullness of God.

In spite of the difficult phrasing, which is typical of the author's style, this prayer shows an overall movement: the design of the Father has been realized in Christ, and to achieve the "fullness of God" in Christ it needs to be comprehended and incarnated thanks to the Spirit in a life rooted in love.

The three divine Persons work within this design, which is to bring the "fullness of God" to human beings. What dominates is the theme of light. The Holy Spirit is requested in order to be able to "comprehend with all the saints what is the breadth and length and height and depth, and to know the love of Christ which surpasses all knowledge." The author is inspired by Paul's cry of admiration (in Rm 11:33-36; see Rm 8:38-39) and has an eye on Colossians 2:2, which is even clearer: "I want their hearts to be encouraged and united in love, so that they may have all the riches of assured understanding and have the knowledge of God's mystery, that is, Christ himself."

"To be rooted in love, with all the saints" is the source of a knowledge that goes beyond ordinary knowledge. Knowledge then has an ecclesial dimension. It is experienced together with all the saints, not in the sense of sharing the same doctrine but of having together the vital experience of light. From unity a light shines forth that is not the sum total of the lights of the individual persons. As Michel Bouttier argues, "We essentially need others, in time and space, to approach what is in Christ and beyond us. We don't do this by collecting the tiny sparks in each one but because the truth to be comprehended is a truth made of love. Without a relationship based on love, the truth remains ungraspable."[12] Knowledge that comes from love and is a gift of the Spirit becomes realized in a light that goes beyond knowledge. It is a light that stems from having become Christ-like, and Christ leads to the "fullness of God."

Growing in the "fullness of God" is lived "together with all the saints." It could not be otherwise, because the splendor of the glory of God shines precisely in unity, that is, in the realization of the divine plan of reconciling all things. This universal reconciliation that manifests the glory of the Father is already at work in unity lived out; it is not only something to hope for. It is a process in progress, a growth that tends toward fulfillment, as the author

---

12. Bouttier, *L'Epitre de Saint Paul aux Ephésiens*, 143.

says, "that you may be filled with (*eis*) all the fullness of God." The choice of the preposition *eis* entails a "movement toward," a journey from light to light, from fullness to fullness.

I maintain that this prayer in the Letter to the Ephesians is like a condensed version of the reality of faith experienced mystically by Chiara. It is seen especially in the Pact of Unity, in her having entered into the bosom of the Father, and in her visions of the various "Realities."

Unity as Cosmic Eschatological Design

Unity may be approached from different viewpoints. Paul emphasizes its Christological and ecclesial reality in his concept of the Body of Christ, of "being one in Jesus Christ." John explores its Trinitarian (being one as the Son and the Father are one) and Christological-ecclesial (allegory of the vine and the branches, etc.) dimensions. In the understanding of faith according to Ephesians (and Colossians), which has continued by the great tradition of the church and also in the mystical experience of Chiara, unity is inscribed in a great divine design with cosmic, eschatological, and Trinitarian dimensions as a Christological-ecclesial reality.

In the Letter to the Ephesians

Unity does not simply appear to be a part of this great universal design but coincides with this plan of God for creation and humanity. It is a plan that originates in God and is projected toward its fulfillment in God, having Christ as its center. Furthermore, in the Letter to the Ephesians, as well as in Chiara's writings, the interest concerning the cosmic greatness of the divine design is not purely speculative but arrives at inserting each person's daily life into it. Even the behavior of just one believer is part of the cosmic design. This reality is all-encompassing and embraces the cosmic dimension all the way to interpersonal relationships, as shown by the link between the beginning (doctrinal) section and the exhortative section of the Letter to the Ephesians.

Let us give a quick overview of the divine design. Here is a summary of this vision in the letter: the design starts from the Father, is mediated by Christ, and reaches out to humanity and creation in order to return in Christ to the Father (see Eph 3:14-19). This is only an outline of the description but should be enough to call attention to an important point not always evident in past theology: the uniqueness of the divine design does not separate creation and humanity or redemption and eschatology.

In the initial blessing we read that God the Father "chose us in Christ before the foundation of the world" (Eph 1:4-5). God created the world with God's children in mind! The connection between human beings and creation is constantly present in the Bible. In God's mind, the human being precedes creation and the goal of creation is humanity. Furthermore, as will be explained shortly, the creation of which human beings are the pinnacle participates in the eschatological destiny of human beings.

Creation and eschatological salvation are therefore part of the same divine plan: This truth is expressed in a condensed way in Ephesians 3:9, which speaks of "the mystery hidden." As Bouttier writes, "The economy of salvation and the economy of creation, far from being foreign to one another, are contained in one another. At the heart of the creating inspiration there is already the collection in the universe of Christ."[13]

For the author of the letter, those who are prechosen, predestined, are the ecclesial "we"[14] who already experience the reconciliation brought about by Christ in the unity of the church. In the church, the recapitulation of the cosmos brought about in Christ becomes visible. Unity lived out is the visible sign that the divine design of recapitulating the universe in Christ is already being realized in our history as the effect of unity already eschatologically fulfilled in the Risen One.

Creation, in its own way, takes part in the design of the unity of humanity and is called to share in the Risen Christ in the eschatological destiny. The letter summarizes the Messianic design of God: "to gather up all things in him" (Eph 1:10). By rising, the Crucified One is put at the head, therefore as king of the cosmos. All things are unified through Christ. The whole of creation finds in Christ cohesion and ultimate meaning. Montagnini writes that through and in Christ, God wants to "gather the scattered parts and put them together so that they form a harmonious united reality."[15]

Based on this vision of the design of God, let us summarize the vision of Ephesians:

---

13. Bouttier, *L'Epitre de Saint Paul aux Ephésiens*, 143.
14. Note: "election" does not mean "selection."
15. Felice Montagnini, *Lettera agli Efesini* (Brescia: Queriniana, 1994), 104.

- Redemption through Christ is not merely the salvation of human beings but includes the universe: Therefore, it has a cosmic dimension.

- Redemption, that is the incarnation of the Son, has the function not only of healing from evil but also of fulfilling the eternal design of the Father.

- This design is a project of unity forever present in the mind of the Creator.

- Eschatology is the completion both of the creative act and of the redemptive act.

It is not by chance that in a context that talks about the eternal design realized by Christ for the sake of humanity (Eph 3:8-12), the author gives to God the title of "the one who created all things" (Eph 3:9). God is the origin and cause of creation and salvation: These realities are connected, destined from eternity to be fulfilled in the "new creation." Creation, destined to be recapitulated in Christ, finds its meaning in the Eschaton begun by the crucified-risen one. Therefore the laws of the universe, the relationship between things and living beings, will be beauty, harmony, cohesion: It will be "peace" (Eph 1:2), a term that includes the eschatological good *par excellence.*

The recapitulation of all things has already happened through the resurrection of Christ (the verb is in the aorist). But what is reality for God in our world needs time to be fulfilled. In the church, where Jews and Gentiles already are living united in order to form one and the same "new humanity" (Eph 2:15), God's project to recapitulate all things in Christ takes shape on earth. This deep connection between creation and humanity in the design of God, the cosmic role of Christ, creation-salvation-Eschaton as the design of God toward unity: all of these aspects of the theology of Ephesians (and Colossians) certainly were not ignored, but they were emphasized very little in classical mysticism and in theology before the Second Vatican Council. The unitarian character of the divine design, contemplated under these various aspects, is certainly one of the most unique themes of the mystical vision of Chiara.[16]

---

16. This, however, should not be seen in isolation, as if the Spirit did not manifest itself in the whole Church. So Teilhard de Chardin expressed his Christian vision of the world. His own thinking, which encountered opposition at the time, is beginning

In Chiara's Writings

The connection of creation with humanity redeemed in Christ is constantly present in Chiara's mystical vision. Since the beginning, when she had the mystical experience of entering into the bosom of the Father, creation was present. In the Pact of Unity with Foco, made after having received the Eucharist, Chiara says,

> I became aware that I was Jesus. I felt the impossibility of communicating with Jesus in the tabernacle. I experienced the elation of being at the peak of the pyramid of all creation, as on the point of pin; at the point where the two rays meet, where the two who are God (so to speak) seal a pact of unity, becoming trinitized where, having been made Son in the Son, it is impossible to communicate with anyone except the *Father*.[17]

This is not just about the place of human beings within creation. From the Eschaton, Chiara contemplates the place of redeemed humanity. In unity, having become Son in the Son, the believer finds him-or herself where Christ is, the one who recapitulates all things. It is there, in the Recapitulator, that creation has access to the Father through humanity. Creation therefore is associated with human destiny and belongs to the divine design toward the fulfillment of humanity.

In Chiara's vision as reported in her writings from 1949, one name expresses this connection between creation and humanity in the unifying design of universal recapaitulation: Mary. Mary is the creation that culminates in humanity, that culminates in the people of God, that culminates in the church, that culminates in unity: the point in which the Uncreated weds creation in an eschatological marriage. Chiara cannot hide her surprise before the greatness of Mary, a cosmic greatness that makes Mary similar to the woman in the book of Revelation (Rv 12) because she contains within herself the "sun and moon and stars. All was in her."[18]

This is not all. Mary is so great that she contains God within her. "Mary contains God! God loved Her so much as to make her His Mother and his

---

to have an impact. The renewed impetus in biblical studies is also linked to this field in modern theology.
17. Chiara Lubich, unpublished note from 1949.
18. Lubich, unpublished note from 1949.

Love made Him become small before Her!"[19] The greatness of Mary, which Chiara found very surprising, is manifested especially in two aspects that are not to be separated:

- Mary, enclosed by the Holy Spirit, is the fourth within the Trinity.
- Mary is the Mother of God.

The first aspect cannot be understood separately from a text that gives an interpretive key and confirms this interpretation of Mary: "The whole creation returns, through Mary, into God. Mary is the entire Creation purified, redeemed. And as she is the fourth in the Trinity, in Mary Creation is fourth, so to speak."[20] Mary represents all of creation that, through the redeemed humanity, has achieved eschatological maturity.

Creation takes part, because of its connections with human beings, in the relationship of humanity with the Father. Mary is seen as humanity that has become Christ and participates by "co-naturality" in the father-son relationship because of having received the Spirit. Therefore she is inserted in the Trinitarian Community. Though inserted into the Trinity, Mary-Creation does not cease to be a creature. Though "divinized," that is, being relocated transfigured into the bosom of the Father and participating in the Trinitarian Life, Mary-humanity-creation is not dissolved into the Trinity. She is the fourth one in the Trinity. Here, we are far from a Gnostic vision.

On the other hand, Mary's greatness is also that of being the "Mother of God." The interpretive key has not changed. The expression "Mother of God," which was solidly rooted in the Christian tradition by the Council of Ephesus, is now explained in a totally surprising way. Mary, in her maternal womb, contains God. She is greater than God just as the "sky which contains the sun."

Mary's motherly womb represents the value of the Incarnation. It becomes the revelation of divine love, a real symbol of a love so great that it makes itself smaller to the point of fitting into the limitations of the human condition, of taking the last place "to serve and give life." In this act, God

---

19. Lubich, unpublished note from 1949.
20. Lubich, unpublished note from 1949.

makes humanity greater,[21] a greatness that becomes even more astonishing for Chiara, who only a little earlier has experienced God's greatness.

Fourth in the Trinity and Mother of God should not be separated in Chiara's vision. Entering into the bosom of the Father is not a negation of created reality but is made possible thanks to God descending into creation, "becoming smaller" within humanity. To enter into God, one does not need to be detached from creation in order to find God somewhere far away. The resurrection of Jesus does not send Christ far from creation but brings to an end the descending movement of Incarnation. The resurrection confirms that the true maternity of Mary, Mother of God, is finally fulfilled in the church, in the redeemed humanity: offering to the world a Jesus "made perfect" (that is, "divinized") also in his humanity. Mother of God and fourth in the Trinity explain also the wonder of a mystic who contemplates the greatness of God's design in this descending of God into the heart of creation and humanity in order to raise humanity in the intimacy of God's life.

The greatness of Mary contemplated by Chiara at the beginning of *Paradise '49* was not an isolated vision. While in the bosom of the Father, the visions continued, month after month, and always with that cosmic scale. Chiara called them "Realities."

> Today we are *Mary-the Creation*:
>
> the Creation which is synthesis of created and Uncreated.
>
> Our nothingness is clothed with this dignity before the eyes of God, the Angels and whoever understands.
>
> It was necessary to pass through Immaculatization to arrive at Divinization and – made God (keeping ourselves so with Jesus Forsaken) – to be renewed each day in the Gospel which, begun here below, will last forever there Above.
>
> Mary, the Creation!
>
> In our eyes, in our face, in our every member are, in the eyes of God, all the created beauties in the mineral kingdom, the plant

---

21. The same idea is in 2 Cor 8:9: "Though he was rich, yet for your sakes he became poor, so that by his poverty you might become rich."

kingdom, the animal kingdom . . . and in the soul, everything is God. There the Trinity rests, has come to dwell.[22]

As in her initial vision, Mary-Creation is still seen as humanity, synthesis of the universe, open to God. Again this vision contemplates not humanity in general but a redeemed, united humanity, represented by Mary with her "immaculatized flesh." Immaculatization, in Chiara's mind, brings to completion the baptismal virginization (see Eph 5:16-17). It happens in the life of unity, in the "nothingness" of mutual love, that is purifying by its excellence, where God can find room for our divinization, and that, nourished by the gospel, gives this "being *one*" the face of Mary who welcomes God within her. A humanity thus fulfilled enjoys the presence of the indwelling Trinity. Such humanity is not only the synthesis of creation but the goal of creation, in which God can contemplate all the beauty of creation.

One vision follows another and each contains and deepens the previous one. From vision to vision, it is a journey through Paradise. For example:

> Today is Saturday and in the Glory of the Trinity we are *Mary the Trinity*.
>
> Therefore all that is, is Trinity and is Mary, who is identified with the Trinity, and we ourselves are united in Claritas and we, each of us, if we are united, become distinct from one another like the Three in the Trinity, like Mary who, though being Trinity, is perfectly distinct from it as creature participating in all the Glory of the Creator.
>
> And here we see how the finite and the infinite merge and the finite becomes infinite and the Infinite becomes finite. It is a continuous incarnation. Today is the incarnation of the Trinity in Mary so that the Trinity becomes Marian, clothes itself with Mary [23]

This is a new contemplation of "Mary" always from the viewpoint of the Eschaton. And as always, it is a mystical perspective that tends toward the identification between God and creation to express the sublime greatness of divine love, which was contemplated. Again, Mary is the creation that, through redeemed humanity, lives in full communion with God. However,

---

22. Chiara Lubich, unpublished note from 1949.
23. Lubich, unpublished note from 1949.

living in communion with God means to live according to the pattern of the Trinity—by living full unity, which maintains full distinction, that is, the identity of each one—in a constantly new dynamic, in order to participate in the life of Communion of the Divine Persons. Mary identified with the Trinity means the complete participation of humanity in the life of the Divine Persons. Jesus' prayer "as you and I" (Jn 17) is thus fulfilled. In Paradise, the eternal wedding feast is fulfilled: the love that from God's perspective is descent (incarnation) into humanity and that from humanity's perspective is ascent of the humanity-creation in God becomes a reality.

Going back to Ephesians, this "wedding feast" is fulfilled in the Crucified Jesus (for Chiara, in Jesus Forsaken, as we will see later), who creates communion (Eph 2:13-22). As Risen Lord, Jesus is placed at the head of the cosmos and of the church and extends his position to all of creation. Chiara summarizes this concept succinctly, in the style typical of mystical language, which attempts to embrace everything and express what is ineffable:

> Today in the Glory of the Trinity we are *Jesus*: Universal King, the One in whom is the Trinity of Trinity.
>
> In him
>
> - is God Uncreated-Trinity
>
> - is the One divine Person of the Word who is trinity (the Unity of human nature and divine Nature by the work of the Holy Spirit)
>
> - is Humanity (= the Creation) participating in the Divine, and hence trinity (in its Being-Law-Life [= how it already is by nature], supernaturalized by its marriage with the divine Nature of the Word made incarnate in Mary).[24]

The Word incarnate (in the ultimate fullness of the Crucified-Risen Jesus) is seen as the marriage between God (in the richness typical of the Divine Persons who give themselves to each other in love) and creation made "in the image of the Trinity," that is, bearing in itself the Trinitarian stamp of the Creator: Being, Law, Life. As I will discuss later about Chiara's mystical experience, "Being" refers to the Father, who gives being to all things in creation; "Law" refers to the Word, which contains all the "divine ideas"

---

24. Lubich, unpublished note from 1949.

that give form to all things in creation; "Life" refers to the Holy Spirit, who gives life to all living things in creation.

So far, I have emphasized the similarities/consistencies between the Letter to the Ephesians and Chiara's vision concerning the cosmic dimensions of the redemption. It is true that Chiara's vision of creation goes beyond a reflection on the letter, which does not touch on topics that were developed later in the history of the church. Does creation have existence in the bosom of the Father? St. Thomas Aquinas denies it (only the four elements remain), even though according to part of revelation this is undeniable. Chiara wrote about this, still as part of her mystical experience of entering into the bosom of the Father:

> I was expecting you to show me the saints one by one, yet I saw instead the whole of Paradise in its attire, abloom and starry and many-hued, with seas, with mountains, with lakes, with stars, with the sun, with the moon, with broad avenues and the whole of Paradise. . .[25]

Therefore, creation too—impacted by the work of human beings—is found wherever humanity is found in Christ. However, Chiara noted the difference in "existence" in Paradise:

> At the end of time, therefore, life will be drawn back from the universe and the diverging rays will return and converge in the Word. All the ideas of the plants will converge in the Idea of the plant that will be in the mind of God and will become again Word, even while having been always in the Word . . . thus all that is in nature and is not immortal will return to the love of God that gave rise to it, but without being distinct from that love, that is, from the mind of God which is the Word.[26]

This follows the logic of traditional theology: unlike other creatures, each human being exists in him-or herself because his or her soul is created immortal.

However, the mystical vision cannot be grasped by philosophical thinking. So, when Chiara writes that things "will return to the love of God," this means not that things will become abstract and vanish but that they will be

---

25. Lubich, unpublished note from 1949.
26. Lubich, unpublished note from 1949.

even more "real" because they will have become "God," therefore "always alive and always new," though unlike human beings. The universe finds in the Word, the risen Christ, its original beauty and harmony as conceived before creation by the "the wisdom of God in its rich variety" (Eph 3:10). Therefore: "Paradise will be the Word: substance of love in which the flowers and the stars and the roads and the seas will be Love and so immortal—immortal in the eternal Word."[27] This conviction corresponds to revelation: see Romans 8:19-25; Ephesians 1:10; Revelation 21.

A Closer Look at "Recapitulation" (see Eph 1:10)

With respect to creation, the central statement of the letter appears in Ephesians 1:9-10: the mystery of the Father's will "according to his purpose which he set forth in Christ as a plan for the fullness of time, to unite all things in him, things in heaven and things on earth." Prepositions are important: They express the role of Christ as mediator (to unite all things) and his protological and eschatological position ("in him" as beginning and end of the movement). The divine design, rooted and originated "in the Love of God," was never conceived outside of Christ. Therefore, it is "in Christ" that God wishes to fulfill this project: to recapitulate all things "through Christ and in Christ."

Chiara's texts emphasize that the cosmic role of the Risen Lord is also an eschatological role (present at the Beginning). "At the end of time, therefore, life will be drawn back from the universe and the diverging rays will return and converge in the Word."[28] In God's eternity, protology and Eschaton reconnect with each other: Christ recapitulates "the wisdom of God in its rich variety" (Eph 3:10) which was always present in God's project. In other words, the goal of creation is already inscribed in its nature, in the law that governs it, as potentiality open to the "new creation."

There are other texts by Chiara that can be helpful in this regard:

> The Father has an expression of Himself outside Himself, made as it were of diverging rays, and an expression within Himself, made of rays that converge in the center, in a point that is Love: God in the infinitely small: the Nothing-All of Love! The Word.[29]

---

27. Lubich, unpublished note from 1949.
28. Lubich, unpublished note from 1949.
29. Lubich, unpublished note from 1949.

Later, Chiara explains:

> The convergent rays in the heart of the Sun, which is the Father, are Word of God; they are Word converging in the Word. . . .
>
> The Father says: "Love" in infinite tones and begets the Word, who is love, within Himself, the Son, and the Son being the Son, echo of the Father, says "Love" and returns to the Father![30]

And she adds:

> I understood that from the Father those diverging rays went out when he created all things and those rays gave Order that is Life and Love and Truth.[31]

These texts are consistent with Christian thinking rooted in biblical wisdom and in the Jewish tradition (Prov 8:26-31; Wis 7:26, etc.). Creation is not chaos but is permeated by Wisdom, order, and harmony, as reflections of God. Later, Christian Wisdom literature (see Colossians and Ephesians) attributed wisdom traits to Christ: the world has meaning and direction, revealed through faith in Christ, who is an "image of the invisible God" (Col 1:15). And later, Christian reflection becomes enhanced by the doctrine of the Trinity: creation is understood as originating from the divine depths, stemming from the love among the three divine Persons. As a work of the Trinity, creation is born *ad extra* but within the dynamics of life among the three divine Persons, where the Father loves the Son in the Spirit.

From the heart of the Father, from the Word who expresses the Father, depart diverging rays: that which is created. In the Son, the "wisdom of God in its rich variety" (Eph 3:10) is present and becomes concrete in creation. Creation is not only characterized by a rich variety of wisdom and diversity, but it is already aiming toward being recapitulated in Christ, converging its rays in the Word as the final and full manifestation of the "unsearchable richness of the Divine wisdom."

Creation is born from the heart of the Father, from the Word. It is therefore rooted in the eternal generation of the Father. It is not born outside the Fatherhood of the Father, "the Father of our Lord Jesus Christ" (Eph 1:3), who is also "one God and Father of us all, who is above all and through all and in all" (Eph 4:6). This latter statement, where the term "all" is found

---

30. Lubich, unpublished note from 1949.
31. Lubich, unpublished note from 1949.

four times (both in the masculine and neuter gender) should be understood in a universal, cosmic way. The fatherhood of the Father is the "first principle" of unity, from whom everything radiates and in whom everything converges. What is created, therefore, is in a filial relationship not just because of being adopted but because of being created from the Fatherhood of the Father. The world has always been "in Christ" (Eph 1:9) and has always had filial traits, "the Order which is Life, and Love, and Truth."

What is created, destined to be recapitulated, reveals already the hidden divine law that is at the foundation of the relationships among things beyond mathematical and physical laws: love. The universal recapitulation in Christ, which is the eschatological fulfillment of the universe, will make shine forth this law of love hidden within and among creatures. It will also require a sort of death and resurrection of the cosmos ("life will be drawn back from the universe"[32]). In order to become what has always been in the Word, creation needs to follow Jesus Crucified and be joined to his death. Jesus Forsaken is exactly "the point . . . where the nothingness is lost in the bosom of the Father."[33] In the universal recapitulation by the Father in Christ, human beings will inherit a world reconciled, transformed, and freed from any separation and disharmony, a world therefore fit for the new condition of the children of God.

---

32. Lubich, unpublished note from 1949.
33. Lubich, unpublished note from 1949.

Chapter Fifteen

Revisiting Chiara Lubich's Paradise '49 in Light of the Letter to the Ephesians: Divine Adoption and Divine Design[1]

Gérard Rossé

Divine Adoption

In the Letter to the Ephesians

Since it deals with God's design on humanity, it is normal that the very beginning of the Letter to the Ephesians emphasizes what is considered most important: our divine adoption. In the initial blessing and in a very condensed way, the author associates the election before creation with the final result, namely, the adoption as children through Jesus Christ:

> Just as he chose us in Christ before the foundation of the world to be holy and blameless before him in love. He destined us for adoption as his children through Jesus Christ. (Eph 1:4-5a)

Before such greatness of God's love, the letter breaks out into praises of God: "Blessed be the God and Father of our Lord Jesus Christ" (Eph 1:3). God blesses us with God's overabundance and we bless God in reply with praises that return to God. We should notice a movement here: God's love receives in reply the love of God's children.

From all eternity, God created human beings to be God's children, so they were created "toward" God. On the other hand, God never thought of human beings outside of Christ. Christ is present at the beginning and at the end of the divine design.

---

1. This article is the second in a four-part exploration entitled "Revisiting Chiara Lubich's Paradise 1949 in the Light of the Letter to the Ephesians." They are considered classic publications on the mysticism of Chiara Lubich. This article was first published in *Nuova Umanità* XXXI (2009): 499–520. It has been translated by Giovanna Czander, Dominican College, Blauvelt, New York. The four Rossé articles are contained in Section 4 of this volume, "Implications of Paradise '49 for Biblical Studies," pages 241-328.

The author of the letter is most likely thinking about Paul's text on the adoption as children[2] that entails not only a privileged relationship with YHWH in light of a mission but also receiving the "Spirit of the Son," which is the very close relationship between the only-begotten Son and the Father.

The Christian experience of adoption is then lived out in the communion with Christ ("in him"). Humanity created with Christ as its goal is ultimately inserted into communion with the Father. The letter expresses it a little later with a formula that will become a classic: "Through him [that is, the church made up of the unity of Jews and gentiles] both of us have access in one Spirit to the Father" (Eph 2:18).

The divine Persons are at work in the design for the good of humanity. And humanity can experience this eschatological reality already actualized in the present.

Being in the presence of the Father is actualized as church, in a unity made of love. The letter suggests it in the initial blessing: "Be holy and blameless in his sight in love" (Eph 1:4).[3] Living in the presence of the Father requires being holy and blameless or immaculate. This is cultic terminology referring to an animal that is without blemish and therefore fit for sacrifice. This perfection is given "in love." In God's sight, human beings can exist only by loving, as their ultimate way of being "made immaculate or without blemish" that stems from living in unity.

The theme of the adoption as children introduces another theme that appears shortly after in the letter: inheritance. In Paul's letters (Gal 4; Rom 8) the idea of being adopted as children is linked to the theme of their being heirs. The Letter to the Ephesians continues Paul's theme and also asserts that the Holy Spirit has been received as a down payment (Eph 1:14); it is not something borrowed that needs to be given back but a permanent advance that will conclude in our complete possession of the inheritance.

However, the author does not define what that inheritance is. In Ephesians 5:5 he identifies it with the Kingdom of God and of Christ. In the context of Ephesians 1:14, we can think that inheritance is connected to adop-

---

2. In fact, in the New Testament the Greek term for "adoption as children" used in Ephesians is found only in the letters that are definitely written by Paul (see Rom 8:15, 23 and 9:4; Gal 4:5).
3. I here depart from the NRSV version, to be closer to the Italian translation used by the author (Translator's comment).

tion, as its fulfillment. In Ephesians 1:18, inheritance is identified with God's "treasure of glory," that is, with the divine splendor manifested in God's love. In any event, this inheritance is received by those who are "holy" together (Eph 1:18), as an inheritance enjoyed with humanity made one (Eph 3:6).[4]

In Chiara's Mystical Experience

The Letter to the Ephesians confirms in its own way the centrality of the mystical experience of divine adoption made by Chiara at the very beginning of her mystical experience in 1949. Adoption as a child is the goal of the whole design of God for humanity—a design that includes creation and is brought about by Christ. This reality summarizes the Christian vision of humanity's destiny of salvation. It is not by chance that Chiara's initial experience is the experience of divine adoption: not only is it an opening to the contemplation of Paradise, but it is also the very same Paradise that will be disclosed. Here is her text:

> I was about to pray to Jesus-Eucharist and say to Him: "Jesus." But I could not. That Jesus who was in the tabernacle was also here in me, was me too, was me, identified with Him. Therefore I could not call to myself. And there I discovered coming spontaneously from my lips the word: "Father." And in that moment I found myself within the bosom of the Father.[5]

A little further in the text, we read:

> I seemed to understand that the one who had put upon my lips the word "Father" was the Holy Spirit. And that Jesus-Eucharist had acted truly as a bond of unity between me and Foco, because upon the two nothings we were only He remained.

This experience is extraordinary not because of the exceptional revelation that up to this point had not been disclosed but, paradoxically, because it is

---

4. Ephesians 1:13-14: "In him *you* also, when you had heard the word of truth, . . . were marked with the seal of the promised Holy Spirit; this is the pledge of *our* inheritance." Note that the passage moves from "you" to "we." The "we" who receive the inheritance are no longer separated from "you"; it is a united "we" that cannot be divided because we have been joined permanently by the Holy Spirit. See Romano Penna, *Lettera agli Efesini* (Bologna: EDB, 1988).
5. From the unpublished Paradise '49 document: all subsequent citations that are from this document will not have footnotes and pages 58-68 in this volume.

a "sensible" experience of what makes up the identity of each baptized individual, that is, the normalcy of the faith experience: being a child of God. What is described as a mystical experience in the Letter to the Ephesians and in the constant teaching of revelation is typical of God's project understood and lived out in faith.

Consistently is the reality of Christ's mediation not only in his historical work of salvation but also in the communion-incorporation in him that is necessary to remain in the presence of the Father. However, the originality of Chiara's experience remains and consists in the fact that since the beginning, as a point of departure, this experience has an ecclesial dimension. This aspect of church is precisely the condition for Chiara's entering into the bosom of the Father. The mutual "nothing" as (paschal) expression of mutual love creates, so to speak, a cell of the Body of Christ. It expresses among the faithful the one Christ who dwells within each one, as the true subject emerging from their unity.[6]

What Paul says to the Corinthians concerning the Eucharist as food of unity becomes true: "Because there is one loaf, we who are many, are one body, for we all share the one loaf" (1 Cor 10:17). The total openness lived out in the mutual "nothing" made it possible for Jesus-Eucharist to best express his potential of communion (of being Recapitulator): the two bring about the church as the Body of Christ; that is, according to Paul, in the unity achieved, they are their most authentic identity, the person of the Christ, the Risen one made visible, his emerging into existence and history.

The identification with Jesus experienced mystically was an experience of church that Chiara personally lived out. The One who makes the two into One raises each one to the adopted fullness that only the ecclesial "we" as church possesses. "It is no longer we who live; it is Christ, *truly*, who lives in us," wrote Chiara, interpreting what Paul had said in ecclesial terms.

Chiara's experience is closely linked to what Paul wrote to the Galatians and the Romans, which is known also to the author of the Letter to the Ephesians: "Because you are sons, God sent the Spirit of his Son into our hearts, the Spirit who calls out, 'Abba! Father!' So you are no longer a slave but God's child, and since you are his child, God has made you also an heir" (Gal 4:6-7). The identification with the Son (through his Spirit) opens one up to "com-

---

6. Here, Rossè makes reference to the "Pact" between Chiara and Igino Giordani, which paved the way for the experience of 1949. See Chiara Lubich, "Paradise '49," *Claritas: Journal of Dialogue and Culture* 1, no. 1 (2012): 5–12.

munication," to a relationship with the Father, and therefore to the Love that constantly brings about the reality of the Son of God as self-donation.[7]

The identification with Jesus—expressed elsewhere as "having being made Son in the Son, it is impossible to communicate with anyone except the Father"—came about through "the Spirit of the Son," and therefore by communication of the relationship that the Son has with the Father. It is an identification based on a shared nature but always respectful of the distinction thanks to the Spirit who is the Third and at the same time makes One.[8] We should note here that the expression chosen by Chiara is not "sons in the Son" but "Son [singular] in the Son," meaning what each one is when, because of a life of unity, he or she acquires the richness of Christ in relationship with the Father.

As already mentioned, Paul (in the letters to the Galatians and Romans and followed by the Letter to the Ephesians) links another theme to the believer's identity as child: the theme of inheritance. It seems to me that the same relationship exists in the mystical experience of Chiara. If her experience of Abbà expresses the fulfillment of the divine design on humanity, then this same experience also leads into the bosom of the Father, a populated divine space: "Within the Bosom of the Father we come to know all the inhabitants of heaven and we understand the work God does in us, clothing us bit by bit in the divine." So Chiara expresses the mystical experience of entering into communion with those who populate heaven in the bosom of the Father: "My sweetest Spouse . . . show me your possessions which are mine!" In Paradise, "where each thing is seen in the Father," Chiara moves from one reality to the next but in a way in which the previous reality is not erased but persists in the following one and in which the relationship is experienced in "the pattern of the Trinity": unity as fullness of distinction.

Chiara often uses spousal symbolism between Christ and the church; the inheritance is synonymous with "dowry." In a very rich text, Chiara states

---

7. In a following note from 1949, Chiara adds these suggestive words: "The impossibility of communicating that I experienced here (in that fraction of a second before the 'Abba Father') made me realize that being God by participation but without being love and so unable to communicate (given that God, being Love, is the highest Communion among the divine Persons) was hell."

8. Immediately following the experience of identification with Jesus, Chiara adds, "It seemed to me that my religious life . . . should not consist so much in being turned toward Jesus, as in placing myself beside Him, our Brother." This means to be Jesus next to Jesus-brother: unity and distinction!

that the wedding between the church and Christ brings about the wedding between created and uncreated:

> A soul made Jesus, which enters into the Father and weds (as Church) the Son, bears within itself the whole of creation and this is its dowry! Without this dowry Jesus does not wed it. Then Jesus gives it the whole of Paradise. And this is the dowry he brings!

Chiara suggests that the mystical experience of Paradise can be expressed with other poignant expressions such as "travelling Paradise" rather than "journeying through Paradise." Paradise is seen not so much as a place within which one can walk and move around as it is an encounter of communion ("on the pattern of the Trinity") with the various realities that are part of it. In the mystical vision related in Chiara's texts, the "inheritance" promised in revelation unfolds and appears in its colorful richness.

The Design of God: Work of the Trinity

The Letter to the Ephesians and Chiara's text have another aspect in common that has been mentioned above: the importance and role of the divine Persons in relationship to the design of God on humanity and creation. In its first few lines, the letter addresses a personal God, the Father. It moves with a sense of familiarity with the working of a God that has opened up and revealed communion as God's manner of working on behalf of humanity. The divine design is conceived according to a Trinitarian dynamic.

In the Letter to the Ephesians

In the New Testament, there is no doubt that the Letter to the Ephesians expresses most evidently the Trinitarian reality of God. Together with the Johannine writings, the Letter to the Ephesians is the work that most contributed to the Christian doctrine of the Trinity elaborated by the Fathers of the church and the Councils. However, the letter does not explicitly address the inner mystery of God, the relationship among the three divine Persons, as takes place in Chiara's mystical insights, which makes use of the great tradition of the church.

In the Letter to the Ephesians, multiple texts refer to the Trinity (see Eph 1:13-14; 2:18-22; 3:14-19; 4:4-6; 5:18-20), and it is plausible to think that the author understands God and God's design in a Trinitarian way. Ephesians 1:13-14 concludes the beautiful initial blessing: the Holy Spirit brings to fulfillment the communion between the Father and those who are in Christ. For the author, the personal relationship with God is never without the ecclesial "we." It is this "we" that has access to the Father, as stated also in Ephesians 2:18, a particularly compelling synthesis that became a formula used to refer to the divine work of salvation: "Through him [Christ] both of us have access in one Spirit to the Father."

Another Trinitarian expression is found in Ephesians 4:4-6, which follows and grounds the exhortation to unity in verses 1-3: the monotheistic confession of the one God becomes Trinitarian doxology, only one Spirit, one Lord, one God and Father. The divine Persons, each in a unique way, contribute to the great design of unity.

Other passages from the Letter to the Ephesians, and the letter as a whole, emphasize the dynamic aspect of the Trinity: unity is not a static reality. Ephesians 2:22 makes this Trinitarian dynamic explicit: The believers are formed together in the Lord in order to become God's dwelling in the Spirit. The church is a stable reality because it has Christ as cornerstone and the apostles and prophets as foundations. However, the church is also constantly developing toward becoming ever more the place of God's presence (Eph 2:20-21).

The church has access to the Father and lives in God's Presence to the measure in which it realizes its deepest identity: Christ. The Holy Spirit works toward making this come about, as mentioned in Ephesians 2:22, by supporting and permeating the whole communion process. Even in the great blessing in chapter 1, the Holy Spirit is mentioned last as the One who brings to fulfillment the whole divine design.

In Chiara's Mystical Experience

In light of these statements of faith, Chiara's mystical experience of entering into the bosom of the Father is meaningful: It is not the result of a solitary search for God in the depths of her soul, nor of the mystical wedding of the soul with Christ as in traditional mysticism. This experience is at the same time ecclesial and Trinitarian: being *Jesus*, calling out "Abbà," put "on our lips," Chiara explains, by the *Spirit*. This Trinitarian dimension is consistently present in Chiara's texts.

Therefore, I find great similarity between what was mentioned above from the Letter to the Ephesians and Chiara's words: "We did not yet know the Holy Spirit. He had given place to his Bride and then, by his manifestation, enclosed her, fourth in the Trinity." The Holy Spirit "encloses." Chiara's mystical experience suggests the pericohretic character of God's communion in the church. This communion can be understood as entering into the bosom of the Father (Eph = access to the Father, or "in the fullness of God," Eph 3:19) and also as the presence of God and Christ among his own (Eph = becoming a "holy temple," which means the place of God's indwelling).

In unity, we enter into God and God enters into us. In the sight of the wonders performed by God, a prayer of praise is the answer that bursts forth from the human heart. The Letter to the Ephesians is also permeated by this prayer. The author asks the addressees to have the same attitude:

> Be filled with the Spirit, speaking to one another with psalms, hymns, and songs from the Spirit. Sing and make music from your heart to the Lord, always giving thanks to God the Father for everything in the name of our Lord Jesus Christ (Eph 5:18b-20).

Mystics have a similar reaction, but their praise, rather than being sung, is experienced as admiration and as a "dying for love." The "mystic" Paul comes to mind, when he is filled with awe before the divine design: "O the depth of the riches of the wisdom and knowledge of God!" (Rm 11:33). In Chiara's writings, we read, "Silence, new revelations of Above would make me die." We also find a declaration of love of the "Bride": "All that is left for me is to swoon into You, to die again upon your Heart, consumed by your love! My God, but why? Why so much for me? Why so much Light and so much Love?"

Divine Love

In the Letter to the Ephesians

Ten times in the letter God is called "Father." This was the name given by the early church to YHWH. Ancient Israel had certainly experienced God as Father through experiencing a close relationship, God's saving acts, love, and faithfulness. Now the God of Israel is revealed in a new way as "Father of our Lord Jesus Christ" (Eph 1:3). The solemn formula was already a traditional one, but there is something original about it that should not be overlooked. God is revealed as Father in a unique sense, in the way in which Jesus, during his life on earth and especially in his death, lived out his sonshi

As we read in the beginning (Eph 1:2), God is also *our* Father: God is revealed as the One who opened his fatherhood to all human beings, to the believers who know that their reality as children of God is rooted in the uniqueness of the Son. In God's design, everything begins and ends in the foundational experience of the divine fatherhood. The experience of the Abbà was also the first of Chiara's mystical experiences as fulfillment of God's design.

The letter is also familiar with a cosmic divine fatherhood, which envelops everything and everyone. The prayer in Ephesians 3:14-19 addresses the "Father, from whom every family in heaven and on earth derives its name." The author addresses God as Father of all beings existing in the cosmos. The author is faithful to the biblical idea that God is Father of all things not because he generates, as in the ancient cosmogonies, but because "he names them," that is, as Creator, makes them exist. Whoever and whatever exists is called by God.

Moving on to Ephesians 4:6, we find the acclamation (Eph 4:4-6) in which the Father is listed at the end, as the apex of the acclamation: "one God and Father of all, who is over all and through all and in all." This formula is reminiscent of the philosophy of the times. The Greek expression *Patêr pantôn* (Father of all things) is not found elsewhere in the Bible. However, the context (Eph 4:1-3, as the exhortation to unity) suggests that such divine fatherhood is to be understood first of all as a principle of unity in the church and then extended to all the realities in the world. In the letter, the claim that God the Father is the only God is not made to counteract the widespread polytheism of the time but refers to God as the principle of unity from whom everything irradiates and to whom everything converges.

The Father is therefore the principle and final destination of the mystery that is the great divine design on the world and on humanity. This reality is expressed also by emphasizing the *eternal* character of God's design. The letter mentions an "eternal purpose (literally: a "deliberation of the centuries, an expression influenced by the Hebrew language) which he realized in Christ Jesus" (Eph 3:11) of the "mystery of his will . . . which he purposed in Christ" (Eph 1:9), of the election of the believers in Christ "before the foundation of the world" (Eph 1:4).

In all these texts, God's plan for the church and the world emerges as something that was never conceived outside of Christ, who is the one bringing it about in history (Eph 3:11) and in the Eschaton (Eph 1:10; 2:20). The reading assumes the text of Colossians 1:16, which mentions the pre-existing Christ "in whom everything has been created." However, the author of Ephesians goes even deeper: the action starts from the Father (who is the explicit subject of the verb in Eph 1:4: "the Father . . . who has blessed us in Christ"). Everything begins from the Father but starting from the center, which is Christ. As Bouttier notes, the gaze of the Letter to the Ephesians penetrates "into the divine origin of everything that exists, in the presence of Christ with the Father."[9]

I would like to point out the terminology used by the author of the letter to express the divine qualities of the Father's work reflected in his own Being. On the one hand, we find terms such as "grace" and "power," and on the other hand, "wisdom" and "glory." Eph 1:6 praises the glory of God, his divine splendor that consists in his grace, that is, in his unconditional love (in Hebrew *hesed*) toward humanity, in his self-giving as Father. Ephesians 1:19 is remarkable in that it contains terminology connected to "power." The verse talks about the "immeasurable greatness of his power in us who believe, according to the working of his great might." The author uses four terms: *dynamis* (power in itself), *energeia* (energy), *kratos* (power in action), and *ischys* (strength). These terms convey the idea of the extraordinary greatness and efficacy of the Father's power present in the history of salvation since the beginning and exploding at the resurrection of Jesus (v 20). This is a power that is capable of making death die and generating fullness of life.

In Ephesians 3:10, the "mystery," that is, the great divine design, is identified with "the wisdom of God in its rich variety." The author uses a term that appears only this time in the Bible and that literally describes wisdom as being "many-hued." The term conveys the idea of richness, variety, things produced, and things creatively organized. In this context, the masterpiece of the many-hued wisdom of the Father is unity realized among the parts of humanity that up to this point were divided, in a sole New Human Being. This many-hued wisdom of God manifested in the church should be made known to the cosmic powers. In other words, the church is entrusted with a mission of liberation: to promote universal reconciliation, freeing human beings from hidden forces that oppress them.

---

9. Michel Bouttier, *L'Epitre de Saint Paul aux Ephésiens* (Geneva: Labor et Fides, 1991), 62.

The Father reveals his glory by operating through his grace, which is goodness, power, and wisdom. He is *the* "Father of glory" (Eph 1:17): a Love that permeates the entire creation, works in salvation history, and manifests fully its strength in the resurrection of Jesus. The glory of the Father communicates a gift to his children, as the "riches of his glorious inheritance" (Eph 1:18). Believers are called to the immeasurable glory of God.

God works according to "the riches of his glory" (Eph 3:16) and this prompts a spontaneous "praise to his glory" (see Eph 3:21) in a movement involving the whole being turning toward God, who manifested Godself in all God's splendor. The answer of the believer "is not just a duty but the irresistible thrust of a child's heart."[10] God has revealed himself as *Divine Love* in all his actions, manifesting the greatness of his glory.

There is a particularly poignant passage about this in the letter. In a context (Eph 2:1-3) in which the author reminds readers of their past condition of death, that is, of being far from God and God's people, Divine Love brims with all its force and splendor:

> But God, who is rich in mercy, out of the great love with which he loved us even when we were dead through our trespasses . . . and raised us up with him and seated us with him in the heavenly places in Christ Jesus, so that in the ages to come he might show the immeasurable riches of his grace in kindness towards us in Christ Jesus. (Eph 2:4-7)

Here, one can note the piling up of terms where again the themes of overabundance and unconditional love are used to express the immeasurable riches of the divine *Agape*: mercy, grace, and kindness. All this is part of God's "great love" for us. The entire divine work bears the mark of merciful and unconditional love. Whatever is at the beginning is also at the end: revealing to everyone that everything is love, centered in the Christ-event. This reality is not only present in the church but also tends toward being fulfilled in the "ages to come."

Divine Love, experienced now by the believers already co-risen with Christ reveals the plan of reconciling the whole universe:

> By associating his own to the enthronement of the Messiah, God makes his plan of reconciling the whole universe to himself ex-

---

10. Robert Baulès, *L'Insondable Richesse du Christ: Lectio Divina 66* (Paris: Cerf, 1971), 23.

plode ahead of time. The goodness God uses toward us shows the goal God is pursuing in the coming ages, which seem to be the instruments God uses.[11]

In Chiara's Writings

The Letter to the Ephesians offers a vision of faith that the author has received mostly from tradition but that he was able to explore with creativity in light of his charism. Chiara's mystical language is different. It expresses also a vision of the Father using intellectual images with symbolic value. The comparison though is still valid and is even more intriguing because Chiara's mystical experience exists on the same Trinitarian-ecclesial-cosmic level. This experience, as we have seen, begins as an experience of a child calling out "Abbà" and being introduced into the bosom of the Father. This relationship is immediately transformed into a vision:

> I had, therefore, entered the Bosom of the Father, which appeared to the eyes of my soul (but it was as if I saw it with my physical eyes) as an abyss that was immense, cosmic. And it was all gold and flames above, below, to the right and to the left.

The same vision of the Father was also recounted in different words: the Soul (Chiara and her companions) "had the clear impression of being immersed in the sun. It saw sun everywhere: beneath, above, about." And also, "In heaven, where each thing is seen in the Father, where the Sun, which is the Father, is at midday, everything becomes *God:* both the Moon, which is Her, and the stars and first of all the Son."

While the author of the letter tends to use terms expressing overabundance and glory, Chiara's vision uses terms related to light and splendor, such as gold, flames, sun, and moon. It is a traditional theophanic phenomenon of a human being coming into contact with divine splendor. For Paul, the revelation of the Risen Lord by the Father is described as an experience of light: "God who said, 'Let light shine out of darkness,' who has shone in our hearts to give the light of the knowledge of the glory of God in the face of Jesus Christ" (2 Cor 4:6). In this text, "light" is synonymous with "glory," which is characteristic of the Father reflected onto the Risen One.

---

11. Bouttier, *L'Epitre de Saint Paul aux Ephésiens*, 105.

The book of Acts of the Apostles talks about Saul's encounter with Jesus as an experience involving light. The author of the book had his reasons for doing so (to distinguish the apparition to Paul from the apparitions of the Risen Jesus to the Apostles). This insistence on the theme of light is interesting especially the text in Acts 26:12-13, "at midday . . . I saw a light from heaven, brighter than the sun." Again, we find the typical ingredients—light, sun, midday—in a vision of the divine.

As in the Letter to the Ephesians, the experience of Abbà by Chiara does not stop at the level of a private and intimate relationship between child and Father but spills over into the universal Fatherhood of God. It is in this sense that the images of the "abyss that was cosmic" and the sun that could be seen "above, below, about," where each thing "is seen in the Father," should be understood.

The claim of universal Fatherhood in Ephesians is more philosophic: "God and Father of all, who is above all and through all and in all" (Eph 4:6). The Father as Creator transcending and enveloping everything has profound implications for understanding God's design: creation itself as child of the Father is destined to unity, of which the Father is the origin and ultimate destination. As repeated in the letter, everything takes place "in Christ." The Father works through a mediator, the Risen Christ, present in Him, at the origin and fulfillment of everything.

In light of this, we can examine the following text by Chiara, a text that summarizes the images related to the Father that emerge in the Letter to the Ephesians, in the doctrine of the church (especially of the Trinity), and in the typical symbolic language of mystics:

> The Father has an expression of Himself outside Himself, made as it were of diverging rays, and an expression within Himself, made of rays that converge in the center, in a point that is Love: God in the infinitely small: the "Nothing-All" of Love! The Word.
>
> The diverging rays are Jesus. By means of Jesus the Father reaches all his children outside Himself in whatever point they are to be found.
>
> As bit by bit these come closer to God, walking along the will of God (being Jesus), they come closer to one another.
>
> The converging rays in the heart of the Sun, which is the Father, are Word of God; they are Word converging in the Word . . .

The Father says: "Love" in infinite tones and begets the Word, who is love, within himself, the Son, and the Son being the Son, echo of the Father, says "Love" and returns to the Father!

But all the souls who are in the Bosom of the Father (who have arrived there by walking along the external ray, being "Jesus") respond to the echo of the Father [= respond to the Father]; indeed they too are Word of the Father, who responds to the Father . . .

Thus the whole of Paradise is a song that rings out from every part: "Love, love, love, love, love, love . . ."

Later, Chiara further explains the reality of the diverging rays:

The rays that go out from the Father (from the heart of the Father), and are diverging, also reach the whole of creation, matter, to which they give Order, which is Love, Life, the Idea: the Word.

In the end the Ideas will return by their rays to the one who generated them and, passing into the sun, their diverging will become converging and their meeting will form Paradise all made from the substance of love. Of each thing there will be the Idea as it was, before creation, "ab aeterno," in the Word.

And again,

I understood that from the Father those diverging rays went out when he created all things and those rays gave Order that is Life and Love and Truth; the Ideas of things were in the Word and the Father projected them outside Himself.

Now, at the end, the Father will draw back those rays that from being divergent will become convergent and they will meet in his Bosom.

Here, I cite Chiara's notes extensively to offer a more comprehensive vision and to understand the similarities between her vision and the vision of faith in the Letter to the Ephesians.

First, we notice that everything comes from the Father and goes back to the Father. By posing the Father as the subject of the action, Beginning and End of everything, the Letter to the Ephesians also transcended the Christocentric view emphasized by the hymn in Colossians 1:15-20.

Second, the Father's work takes place "in Christ" and "through Christ." As in Colossians 1:15 ("He is the image of the invisible God"), Chiara's statement "The Father has an expression of himself outside of himself" comes from Christian wisdom tradition. Chiara's statement includes two truths: the distinction of the divine Persons within God and the Word's mediating and revealing function (the Word as the point within the bosom of the Father who is the heart of the Father where the rays converge and from which they diverge). Chiara's concept goes beyond the one in Colossians and Ephesians and focuses on the intra-Trinitarian relationship between Father and Son. The latter is called "Word"[12] with regard to creation and incarnation. One finds a Johannine influence in these theological concepts.

The Word is the "Nothing-All" of Love, the Mirror of God ("Echo of the Father"). This expresses divine intimacy in its purest form. Chiara's mystical insight becomes more explicit in another text: "The Father in the Trinity is Father by being (begetting) the Son and hence *not* Father. And here we see how Being and Non-Being . . . coincide in God." This is a bold statement, especially by scholastic theological standards, because it assumes non-being within Godself. However, it is consistent with the inner dynamics of love and with the definition of God as Love. Within the dynamics of being and non-being, Love is fully lived out in God: the Nothing manifests the Fullness of Being, Love (= the Spirit). The Nothing of the Father is identified with the loving act of generating the Son. In that act, the Father gives all of himself; in a certain sense, he "dies" so that the Son may be, and it is precisely in this act that he is fully Father, therefore God. If this were not so, at this point there would be two gods.

As for the Son, he is the "Echo of the Father," the "Nothing-All," the perfect transparency of the Father, Love lived out, and therefore the irradiation of the Father's infinite riches. The "Nothing-All of Love" turns out to be the Law of the life of the three divine Persons, Law that is deeply impressed in creation, in the relationships among things and beings. This is a theologically deep exploration of the Trinity, in line with Johannine theology (the Holy Spirit is presupposed), which the Letter to the Ephesians has not made explicit. However, it opened the way for it.

---

12. Ephesians speaks of "Christ." Its perspective is more markedly eschatological; that of Chiara is more protological.

Third, the divine design, the revealed "Mystery" mediated and brought about by Christ, is described with the image of the rays, in a movement of going outward and inward that includes protology and eschatology in the one design of unity. The vision of the Letter to the Ephesians and the mystical vision of Chiara are essentially in agreement.

The image of the rays is compelling but should not be misunderstood. If it is misunderstood, it could recall ideas emanating from God or the divine spark fallen onto human beings (as in Neoplatonism). In spite of what appears, Chiara's thought remains faithful to revelation. Even if coming from the heart of God and reflected in God's life, in his Law, creation is "nothing" or "vanity." In the mystical understanding this does not mean that creation is a ghost, a shadow without essence, or that creation is evil (as in the Gnostic view); rather, it emphasizes most of all the radical difference between creation and God. Creation is non-God.

The mystical insight perceives in that "created nothing" also the positive mark of love infused by God into creation as an eternal link with the Creator and the openness to eschatological transformation. The image of the divergent and convergent rays also offers a dynamic way to understand that even in the diversity that expresses the "divine design" on each one, all are called to unity as "Word of God."

As in the Letter to the Colossians, the Letter to the Ephesians speaks about *Christ*, that is, of the risen Christ as the beginning and the end, as the Recapitulator of everything. In some of Chiara's expressions, the Word is identified with Jesus; Chiara, in other texts, makes a distinction between the Word and Jesus. In some of her notes, the Word tends to be understood as the expression of God in relationship to creation, while Jesus, upon whom the believer is modeled, is the Word incarnated in the eschatological function of the Recapitulator who leads to the Father. Overall, Chiara's thought emphasizes the importance of incarnation, while the resurrection event (as eschatological event) does not explicitly have the relevance it is given in contemporary theology

As in the Letter to the Ephesians, Chiara's vision emphasizes the universal Fatherhood of God. The Father is the Beginning of everything and permeates and envelops the whole of creation. In Chiara's writings the function of Christ as mediator becomes more explicit given the fact that creation is born and rooted in the intra-Trinitarian relationship of Father-Son. Creation is not originated outside of the Father's fatherhood toward the Son. The

Father "exudes of many beings the love which generates the Son, enveloping them into the same mystery."[13]

The universe is generated within God, where the Father loves the Son (from "the heart" within the bosom of the Father) and communicates everything to Him. "The generating and creation work of the Father is focused first and above all on Christ. It is the one that makes him the beginning of all things."[14] As a consequence, there is a unique affinity between what is created and the Son. Creation, as Chiara underscores, has within itself the traits of the Word: "Order that is Life and Love and Truth," that gives meaning, authenticity, and cohesion to the universe of human beings (see Col 1:17). Therefore, the world is adopted because it was created, because it was born from the Fatherhood of the Father. The world is "in Christ" since its origin before time (see Col 1:15; Eph 1:4). It bears forever, as its own trait, the relationship with Christ, and it is destined to become increasingly in unity a united world. This adopted mark of the universal Fatherhood of God/Creator entails an eschatological destiny of unity, revealed and inaugurated in the Christ-event.

Concerning universal Fatherhood, I would like to cite a mystical text by Chiara about a woman who lives this adopted mark so perfectly that she actually contains universal Fatherhood. It is a difficult text because it is rich, deep, and new. The vision expresses the ultimate fruit, in the Eschaton, of the design of God, of the impenetrable wisdom of God, on humanity-creation actually incarnated in Mary. Fatherhood is understood as law of Unity seen among the various beings as the fullest relationship in the pattern of, and within, the Trinity: that "all may be one *as* we are one, as you Father are in me and I in you" (Jn 17:21). Mary, as redeemed creature, lives to the fullest the "Nothing-All of Love" typical of the relationship between the Son and the Father. This is the fullest expression of God's Fatherhood that makes the Other be in that "Nothingness of Love:"

> Today I am Mary, the Mother of God, as Mother of Universal Fatherhood.[15] had discovered that all that is, is *Fatherhood* because all that is, is God and God is Father, is Love.
>
> Fatherhood thus is God.

---

13. François-Xavier Durrwell, *Il Padre* (Rome: Città Nuova, 1995), 101.
14. Durrwell, *Il Padre*, 107.
15. This means that Mary, being Mother of God, contains universal Fatherhood. Mary's greatness is to be *Theotōkos*. If she were not *Theotōkos*, she would not contain universal Fatherhood.

Fatherhood, the Three in the Trinity.[16]

Fatherhood, the Three in the Trinity.[17] Fatherhood all that is outside the Trinity: that to which God through participation gives *Being*.

Because all that *is* in Creation is God's creature, creature of that God who cannot give what he does not have, what he *is not*.[18]

In fact in Creation all is Trinity: Trinity, things in themselves because their *Being* is Love, is Father; the Law in them is Light, is Son, Word; the Life in them is Love, is Holy Spirit.[19] The All given through participation to the Nothing.

And they are Trinity among themselves, for the one is Son and Father to the other, and all draw together, loving one another, to the *One*, whence they came.

And this by means of humankind who are brought into Godhead by Holy Communion.

The whole Creation returns, through Mary, into God. Mary is the entire Creation purified, redeemed. And as she is fourth in the Trinity, in Mary Creation is fourth, so to speak.

Mary represents humanity saved, the entire creation arrived, through the redeemed ones, in eschatological maturity. Being the "fourth" in the Trinity means that humanity, having become, in unity, adopted children in the Son, is perfectly inserted into the Trinitarian communion, though without losing its rich diversity or its identity as creatures. Although "divinized," that is, located in the bosom of the Father, participating in life of the Trinity, humanity-creation becomes fourth in the Trinity.

---

16. Each of the Three in the Trinity is Love, is the one God.
17. Mary, because already divinized, apart from God's amazing design for her, participates in the Fatherhood of God more than any other created being.
18. This would be His intention, precisely because He is Love. But He can bring it about only if persons welcome and accept His love, and He will bring it about definitively at the end of the world.
19. Here we see things as they will be: God all in all (see 1 Cor 15:28). And, as Trinity, the Father will be better seen in the being of things, the Son in the law of them, the Holy Spirit in the life running through them. Indeed, the text says later, things "pull together, loving one another," and so they are on the way to self-realization, to divinization.

Chapter Sixteen

Revisiting Chiara Lubich's Paradise '49 in Light of the Letter to the Ephesians: The Holy Spirit, the Son of God, and the Cosmos[1]

Gérard Rossé

The Holy Spirit

The fact that the Letter to the Ephesians mentions the Holy Spirit is remarkable, especially since the Letter to the Colossians, which comes right after it, does not mention the Holy Spirit at all. Unlike the Letter to the Colossians, the Letter to the Ephesians emphasizes the function of the Holy Spirit and expresses a truly "Trinitarian" perspective.

The Holy Spirit and God's Design

The author of the letter does not reflect directly on the Third Divine Person and the Holy Spirit's role within the Trinity. In this regard, Chiara's writing is a witness to the richness of a whole doctrinal tradition that has developed in the church. Furthermore, since it is a mystical experience, the Holy Spirit becomes "alive," is experienced, and thus avoids the risk of being an abstract concept in the doctrine on God.

For example, consider the experience of the kiss (with which other mystics such as St. Bernard or William of Saint-Thierry are familiar): "I was touched anew by the Holy Spirit, at whose kiss I felt a sharp pain in

---

1. This article constitutes the third part of a now famous study, in four parts, entitled "Revisiting Chiara Lubich's Paradise'49 in Light of the Letter to the Ephesians." It proposes to collect the points of contact between Lubich's Paradise '49 and the Letter to the Ephesians, and to explore the grand themes of faith that emerged from both of these writings, in particular God, the Word, ecclesiology, and ethics. This third article by Rossé was first published in Italian in *Nuova Umanità* 31 (2009): 691–713. The four Rossé articles are contained in Section 4 of this volume, "Implications of Paradise '49 for Biblical Studies," pages 241-328.

my heart."[2] The Holy Spirit's kiss expresses direct contact with the Divine, just as marriage expresses the fullness of a relationship, experienced by the Church-Bride (Eph 5:21-33). Shortly before this experience, Chiara writes: "We did not yet know the Holy Spirit. He had given place to his Bride and then, by his manifestation, enclosed her, fourth in the Trinity."

Chiara talks clearly about a "felt," experienced knowledge of the Holy Spirit. Her remarkable expression should be noted: "The Holy Spirit *closes the circle*" within the Trinity. The Holy Spirit is understood as the manifestation more *ad extra* of God, as the One who brings to completion God's action. The Holy Spirit is "the ultimate expression of God; the Holy Spirit closes the circle." The Holy Spirit is "third" not because the Spirit is inferior to the other divine Persons but because in the Holy Spirit, Father and Son love each other. The Holy Spirit brings about unity between them. At the beginning and at the end, the Third Person is the eternal perfection of the Trinitarian movement.

The Holy Spirit has the same function in salvation history: It is the Spirit who inserts believers into the Communion between the Father and the Son. From this perspective, the ideas in Ephesians are not so different. In fact, the Holy Spirit is mentioned last both in the conclusion of the great benediction in the first chapter and in the final part of the central section of the letter (Eph 2:22). The Holy Spirit is like the place where the Trinitarian action toward humanity happens and is completed.

In the Letter to the Ephesians, we find relevant concepts that are found also in Chiara's experience. The introduction of the Holy Spirit as "down payment of our inheritance" (Eph 1:14) comes from Paul (2 Cor 1:22; 5:5). The concept of a down payment is taken from the business world and here indicates a payment that guarantees and provides a foretaste of Paradise. As mentioned previously, it is not a sum borrowed to later be returned but a free installment, given permanently, that accompanies the believer until the final completion.

Therefore, a Christian can live the future in the present time of history: The "mystical" grace brings about in the experience of the senses what is believed by faith, an installment of Paradise. It is the Holy Spirit who made

---

2. From Chiara Lubich's notes. Unless otherwise stated, all references to Chiara's writings are to these notes from 1949, which are as yet unpublished. Translations of all texts from 1949, which are provisional, have been done by Callan Slipper and Thomas Masters.

possible and brought about the mystical vision of the whole Paradise '49. He anticipates the Eschaton both as faith experience and, thanks to a special grace, as mystical experience. As a consequence, Chiara recognizes that the Holy Spirit has the function of making known, of enlightening human beings, and sees the Spirit at work in the Light (*Claritas*) that the Father gives to the Word and is communicated to the seer (see Jn 17:22).

This is consistent with our understanding of the letter: The Holy Spirit enlightens the apostle on the "mystery of Christ," the divine plan concealed up to that point that needs to be shared with the ecclesial "us" (Eph 3:5f). The author prays from the start, "the God of our Lord Jesus Christ . . . may give you a spirit of wisdom and revelation as you come to know him" (Eph 1:17). The author asks for Christians the gift of the Spirit. This gift is given with baptism but is a Presence that needs to remain active during the whole existence of believers in order to allow them to penetrate more deeply the existential understanding of God and of God's presence behind things (wisdom). But in Christian existence there may be some powerful moments, such as the encounter with a charism of light and therefore also a powerful experience of the Holy Spirit.

In the Divine Design of bringing humanity to God, into the bosom of the Father, the Holy Spirit has a specific role. It is "in the Holy Spirit" and through the mediation of Christ that we have access to the Father (Eph 2:18). The Spirit is the space of our encounter with God, the One who "closes the circle," to use Chiara's term. So it is the Holy Spirit who makes one experience the Abba as a child, as Paul says (Gal 4:6).

Chiara writes of the experience of entering into the bosom of the Father: "And from my lips came forth expressed by the Spirit a single Word: Father! And everything was accomplished. Nothing lacking at all." Nothing is lacking here: "The circle is closed," but now it includes humanity and creation. This more cosmic vision is made explicit in the following text: "I experienced the elation of being at the peak of the pyramid of all creation . . . . where the Spirit pronounces with our lips: *Abba*-Father." The Holy Spirit appears at the end of the "recapitulation of everything in Christ."

From a different perspective, and always related to the experience of entering into the bosom of the Father, the Letter to the Ephesians confirms that the Holy Spirit, being "the Spirit of the Son" (Gal 4:6), as Paul writes, assimilates Christians to Christ from within. The Spirit is the inner power that works in the depths of a baptized person (Eph 3:16), where Christ dwells (Eph 3:17).

The Holy Spirit in Relation to the Church and the Life of Unity

With respect to the church, the Letter reminds us of the image of the holy temple (in Paul: 1 Cor 3:16f) "in whom you also are built together spiritually into a dwelling place for God in the Spirit" (Eph 2:22).[3*] It is a live temple, permeated by the Spirit of the Risen One who unites and distinguishes; it is the link of continuity and the power of growth. In the Spirit, the Trinity opened its intimate life of Communion in order to "close the circle," bringing the church, and with it humanity, within the Communion.

This teaching belongs to the doctrinal heritage of the church and is not missing in Chiara's mystical reflection: "It is with the descent of the Holy Spirit . . . that Mary became Jesus." In more general terms, "Whoever is born again in the Spirit is *another Jesus*" (remembering that for Chiara "being Jesus" is lived as "church," that is, in actualized unity). Therefore, the role of the Holy Spirit as bond of unity is of central importance to Chiara:

> God is interested in the divine bond, the Holy Spirit, that makes us children of God and brothers and sisters of one another, the sole bond of fraternity; for us to have this bond we need to break the others that hinder: to break, that is to say, to burn them with the Holy Spirit, who is a consuming Fire. He, wishing to work a second birth in us (the birth that makes us children of God in perfect unity between the human being and grace, God given through participation), consumes all in Himself, divinizing, setting all ablaze, translating all into Fire, into God, into true children of God as Jesus.

This is an essential text for understanding how Chiara sees the role of the Holy Spirit with regard to the life of unity. It is on the "nothingness" of mutual love that the Spirit can best perform his divine role. This is deeply consistent with Paul's thoughts: God revealed Godself as the one "who gives life to the dead and calls into existence the things that do not exist" (Rm 4:17).

God can only "create" out of "nothingness" as the space in which the Holy Spirit works. Only the Holy Spirit creates perfect unity, on the pattern

---

3 * "In the Spirit" is missing in the NRSV but present in the Greek text followed by Rossé. [Translator's note]

of the Trinity (being *One* in the fullness of distinction) and in communion with the Trinity (divinization). Where there is unity, the "new creation" is being realized. It is possible now to interpret some of Chiara's writings and to find in them a recurring concept: "The Holy Spirit is only there where nothing else is," that is, whenever reciprocity is fully lived, unity is perfect, divine, without falling into uniformity, without exiting the human sphere where God has entered, and without escaping from daily life. Another passage of Chiara's in this regard reads:

> Love is to be distilled to the point of being only Holy Spirit. It is distilled by passing it through Jesus Forsaken. Jesus Forsaken is nothingness, is the point and through the point (= Love reduced to the extreme, having given everything) passes only Simplicity that is God: Love.

Distilling Love, reducing it to extreme nothingness, does not mean lessening it, or calculating what is owed, but making it go through one's brothers and sisters, being open to them as "non-being" that takes away as much as possible of the pollution caused by one's ways of seeing, acting, and thinking.

> Our most important task is to maintain the chastity of God, that is to say: maintain love in our hearts as purely and solely Holy Spirit. The Holy Spirit in the Trinity is the Relationship of the Two, hence their Love and Purification . . . He is the fire that burns, purifying. Hence, to be pure we need not deprive our heart and repress the love in it. We need to enlarge it to the measure of the Heart of Jesus and love everyone.[4]

The "chastity of God" is love lived out in the measure of Jesus Forsaken. This entails a love that is completely open to the other, to all others, and therefore "purified" from one's own self-centeredness. Giving "everything" to God means giving the God we have within (the "distilled" love that is the Holy Spirit) to the other. Therefore, *agape*-love can give to each one what eros-love (though good) is not capable of giving: the richness that quenches the thirst for the infinite present in each heart and mediates God's love for all brothers and sisters.

---

4. Chiara explains: "In the sense of being 'their Distinction.' In the Trinity the Holy Spirit is Love, in which there is the maximum unity and the maximum distinction among the divine Persons."

I would like to conclude with a page from Chiara, an experience rich in content that she had on July 26, 1949:

> I went into church for the usual meditation with the souls who made up the Soul with me, and looking at the tabernacle I waited, upon the emptiness of myself, for God to send his Light. I had the impression that in the tabernacle Jesus was breathing and that this breath, almost a waft of air, came toward me. I lifted up my head to receive it on my face. (It was not something physical.) When this waft of air, rising up above me was between me and the statue of Mary most holy that stood in a niche on the right of the high altar, it took form – to the eyes of my soul – as a dove, about twenty centimeters across, with its wings outspread. It circled a few times above my head and it was in place to give illumination. But it did not illuminate. Confused, I understood it to be the Holy Spirit and as the Holy Spirit it was the whole breath of Jesus, all his Warmth, his Life and, as it were, *it formed the atmosphere of Heaven*, with which the whole of Heaven is pregnant, and that it was a zephyr and a gentle breeze.

In this vision, we see a rich teaching on the Holy Spirit: in the Christian tradition[5] the dove has always been considered a symbol of the Holy Spirit (as in the baptism of Jesus); the metaphor of the "wind" is often linked to the Holy Spirit,[6] as in the powerful wind at Pentecost (Acts 2:2); there is also the saying "the Spirit blows where it chooses" (Jn 3:8). The gentle breeze brings to mind God's self-revelation to the prophet Elijah (1 Kgs 19:12). The Holy Spirit as "the whole breath of Jesus," that is, as *ruach* or *pneuma* coming from Christ, recalls the Risen Jesus breathing on his disciples: "Receive the Holy Spirit" (Jn 20:22).

The Holy Spirit is also the Warmth and Life of Christ: Here the motherly face of God appears. He is also like "the air in Heaven": He is not seen but brings about life, just like the space that "closes the circle" within the Trinity, the bosom of the Father, images that recall the formula *in one Spirit* in Ephesians 2:18.

---

5. In the Old Testament the Spirit of God is never presented in the form of a dove.
6. Compare to the Hebrew word *ruach* and the Greek *pneuma*, whose meaning is "puff" or "wind."

The Son of God

I do not intend to illustrate the whole Christology present in the Letter to the Ephesians but would like to focus on the place and eschatological role that Christ has in it.

The Risen Jesus: Head of the Church and the Cosmos

For the author of the letter, Christ Jesus or Christ or the Lord Jesus Christ[7] is always the Risen Jesus, the One whom resurrection has set above all things and in relationship with each thing. The resurrection is the divine glorification of Jesus, an event that is very personal but has repercussions throughout the whole universe. Jesus is the One who, from eternity in which the Father lives, reveals, brings about, and brings to completion the loving Design that the Father has conceived in him, in favor of humanity and creation. Through the resurrection, therefore, Jesus has become the eschatological Sovereign of the world: This is the cosmic dimension that is typical of Colossians and Ephesians. The letter is familiar with the term "the Lord" and the image of "seating at the right hand of God," which were already church traditions that indicated this sovereignty.

After the Letter to the Colossians, to express the Lordness of Christ, the author also uses the metaphor of "Head": God gave Christ as the Head of the Church, which is his Body. This is stated in Ephesians 1:20-22:

> God put this power to work in Christ when he raised him from the dead and seated him at his right hand in the heavenly places, far above all rule and authority and power and dominion, and above every name that is named, not only in this age but also in the age to come. And he has put all things under his feet and has made him the head over all things for the church.

The text emphasizes the royal enthronement, through the resurrection, that gives Christ power over the cosmic powers. The mythological language should not overpower the value of the statement. Set "in the heavenly places," Christ belongs to the realm of the Divine, where the Father is. The relationship he has with the universe is the same as God's. Therefore Christ rules

---

7. Only once, in Eph 4:13, is he called "Son of God"; in Eph 1:6, "the Beloved."

also the hidden powers.[8] At the time, this sounded like a true liberation from a world perceived as hostile, in which human beings saw themselves as dominated by fate, by absurdity, and by hatred. These cosmic powers now can no longer be an obstacle to a direct relationship with God, which is granted by the only Mediator. These invisible powers exist on earth even today, hiding under different names. These powers aim to take possession of human beings: They are materialism, consumerism, scientism, various ideologies, and so on. Proclaiming the Sovereignty of the Risen Christ over these powers—the author repeats it in Ephesians 6:12—means giving back to the world its true essence of "creation" oriented toward a goal, and giving back to human beings their place, willed by God, in creation.

As the abovementioned text (Eph 1:20-22) states, it is as universal Sovereign, as ruler of the cosmic powers, that Christ is given by God to the church as its Head. There is a close relationship between the church and the cosmos in Christ. In him, the cosmic reality and the ecclesial reality are in a relationship: not only at the level of creation (humanity as the synthesis of creation) but also at the eschatological level.

The privileged relationship with the Head is given to the church, which is his only Body. As Head of his Body, Christ exerts his Sovereignty not only by dominating the cosmic powers and freeing humanity from them but also by taking care of and nourishing his Body, the church (Eph 4:15). The Head is therefore also the source of life and cohesion. From the Head comes the vital force that runs through the whole Body, gives it life, holds it together, and makes it grow. The sovereignty of the Risen Christ entails also Christ's omnipresence in time and space. Resurrection puts him at the beginning ("he chose us *in Christ* before the foundation of the world" Eph 1:4) and at the conclusion as recapitulation of creation (Eph 1:10). The author applies an eschatological exegesis of Psalm 68:19 and concludes: "He who descended is the same one who ascended far above the heavens, so that he might fill all things" (Eph 4:10, see also vv 7-10).

By stating that the one who descended "into the lower parts of the earth" (v 9) is the same one who ascended "far above the heavens," he means that Christ went from one extreme end of the universe to the other, occupying

---

8. According to Eph 2:2, these occupy the air, thus making an obstacle to the relationship of human beings with Heaven. The language is mystical but expresses a religious-existential reality: a person controlled by evil who cannot succeed in bringing about communion.

all the space that up to that point had been occupied by the cosmic powers. Another reading is possible. The extreme ends touched by Jesus hint at his solidarity with humanity to the very end (the cross) and his exaltation in the reality of God (according to the pattern annihilation-glorification: see Phil 2:6-11). The extreme ends then are humanity far from God, on the one hand, and the bosom of the Father, on the other. Jesus crucified and risen envelops everything with his presence: He is capable of bringing ahead God's plan of bringing everything in unity with God.

The Function of Recapitulating

After this introduction on the resurrection of Jesus according to the perspective of Ephesians, we can look at the eschatological function of recapitulation given by the Father to the Risen Christ.[9] Let me go back to the double meaning of the verb *recapitulate*: "to put under the same head" and "to gather, collect things together." This implies the convergence of multiplicity toward Christ as the center of unity. The author of the letter talks about recapitulation only in Ephesians 1:10, and therefore this seems like an isolated topic. Furthermore, since the author does not explain it nor share his understanding of the verb, Ephesians 1:10 can have various interpretations, including creative ones. However, the author clarifies his perspective little by little, by explaining the steps in his argument. In the end the cosmic recapitulation will appear to be the reconciliation of the universe—already brought about in the Risen Christ—and cannot be separated from the reality and mission of the church and of the believers. We will see this further on.

For her part, Chiara returned to the idea of recapitulation, which has become traditional within the church, and shed light on it with *claritas* that comes from the charism of unity. Chiara expresses this reality by using the image of rays converging in the center of the Sun.[10] Here is a very deep text in which she summarizes her mystical experience:

> In showing me Paradise with all that is beyond this life and all that is created the Lord was truly a teacher.

---

9. This topic was already touched on in the first part of this study: see Gérard Rossé (2016) "Revisiting Chiara Lubich's Paradise '49 in Light of the Letter to the Ephesians," pages 241-61 in this volume.
10. Gérard Rossé (2016) "Revisiting Chiara Lubich's Paradise'49 in Light of the Letter to the Ephesians: Divine Adoption and Divine Design," pages 262-79 in this volume.

At first he made me experience the nothingness of all that is created, that is, its being non-being, in itself.

Having arrived within the Father, I felt to be concrete (Being) only him and all that is contained in his Bosom.

Then, unfolding created reality to me with analogies (like that of the sun) that are inadequate yet useful for a first understanding, he filled each thing for me with concreteness. Indeed, he showed to my mind Heaven as the inside of the Sun. The projection of the Father within himself is the Word and all that in him is contained. And the created, instead, was the Sun's projection outside itself.

At the end of all these illuminations, I felt the projection of the Father, which is Love's projection outside itself, and Love's projection within itself to have equal concreteness.

And this because the Father sent his Son to earth to be intermingled with created things, to sum up and divinize them. Jesus, the Mediator, was the cause of the marriage between the Uncreated and the created, of the unity between the created and the Uncreated, equal to the unity between the Word and the Father.

We could say that Chiara, in the span of her mystical experience, goes through God's design on creation from the extreme distance from God (the "nothingness" of creation) up to the "marriage between the Uncreated and the created," thanks to the incarnate Son who "synthesizes."

We can also look at another text, a type of allegory that sheds light on the phrase, "what is created . . . was the Sun's projection outside of itself":

When I see the water of a lake projected upon the wall by the sun, and see the play of the water upon the wall trembling in accord with the quivering of the true water, I think of creation.

The Father is the true sun. The Word is the true water. The reflected lake is what is created. What is created is nothingness clothed in the Word. It is the Word reflected. Therefore, what has "being" in the created is nothing but God. Except that, while the lake on the walls is false, in creation the Word is present and alive: "I am . . . the Life."

In the created there is unity between God and nothingness. In the Uncreated, between God and God.

Everything begins from the sun, the sun who is reflected in the lake (the Word) but who sends, from the lake, his rays onto the walls, a wall on which the sun (Father) models the reality of creation on the Word, projecting in creation the various and multicolored richness contained within the Word (the image of trembling water). However, there is a difference between the image and reality. The image on the wall does not have a separate existence because there is no real lake on the wall, while in creation the presence of the Word is real and He gives creation his own identity: "nothingness clothed in the Word."

Since always what is created is nothingness (a radical distinction from God) but clothed in the Word, therefore, it has the mark of a child and bears within itself its own future destiny in God. For Chiara, recapitulation is therefore the *parousia* of creation; its "divinization" (which is not fusion) is the glorious manifestation of the connection with God and the divine law that from eternity carries in itself: the "marriage" of the Uncreated with the created that entails a relationship of love between God and creation.

Chiara continues from the passage cited above:

> And in this unity[11] each thing is in the Bosom of the Father and each thing is outside the Father and contains the Father. Indeed, as each thing is in the Son, in the Word, it is with the Word in the Bosom of the Father ("I in you") and embraces the Father ("You in me").... Thus in the end all was God: God in himself and God in the created.

. . .

Two, yet made one by the Mediator, Jesus. In creating, therefore, God did not do anything other than clothe nothingness with himself, giving himself through participation to nothingness. God is he who is. All that is, is God—God: Creator, God: Creation.

---

11. That is, the "wedding" between the Uncreated and what is created.

In this passage, the "nothingness created" is perceived in its positive value: the potential to be open to the divine, space where God can enter, where the constant relationship between creation and God exists. On the other hand, if in the language of mystics God is said to be also creation, this does not mean that there is a fusion of divine and creation: the two realities are distinct and remain that way, in every aspect. However, the reality of *divine density* underneath everything comes to the fore: it is final—eschatological—reality already present at the moment of creation that the mystic takes in with one gaze.[12] If God is Being and, as such, expresses his relationship with creation (truth of the "continuing creation"), then God is the real truth of creation. Matter does not have true existence without God. The cosmic function of the Risen One is to bring this relationship to fulfillment.

Going back to Ephesians 1:10 (on the "recapitulation"), we need to keep in mind the value of the expression "in Christ," which is emphasized. The chosen preposition "in," which expresses the Hebrew b^e in the Letter to the Ephesians, often means "in" and "through," that is, of instrumental (mediation) and inclusion or participation meanings. Therefore, the phrase "recapitulating all things in Christ . . . in him" shows that Christ is not only the mediator of recapitulation, that is, in the act of recapitulating (dynamic aspect of his function), but also the end of the Father's acting: Christ is also the perpetual place of the fulfilled recapitulation.

This truth is well illustrated in Chiara's text "Each thing is in the Son," which is the wisdom perspective (Word, mirror of God's creative project: see Wis 7:26; Heb 1:2f; in Chiara, "He is the Word in whom the Father sees all he made when he created") and finds its natural eschatological conclusion. In other words, the world, though created *ad extra* and destined to fullness, never existed outside of Christ but has always been rooted in the depth of God, where the Father loves the Son and communicates everything to him.

Link between Creation and Fulfillment: in Christ

This reflection leads us to another concept mentioned earlier that needs to be developed. If the universe is created "in Christ" and finds its fulfillment "in Christ," then it has within itself from the beginning the filial mark, and recapitulation does nothing else but shed full light—even in a completely

---

12. It is always important to keep in mind the language of mystics, outside of which a syllogism like "God is the One who is. All that is is God" would seem to be a mistake.

new fullness—on a law that has always been inscribed in nature. This is how Chiara illustrates this recapitulation: "I understood that from the Father those divergent rays went out when he created all things and those rays gave Order that is Life and Love and Truth."

Creation has within itself the relationship with the Word. The varied richness of creation given by the diverging rays is as held within the One, in the Word from whom it comes. In other words, behind everything, behind multiplicity, there is the hidden presence of the One. This One present underneath everything ensures that creation is not a disorderly and chaotic multiplicity, an absurd juxtaposition of things. The One behind things creates harmony, relationships, beauty, and cohesion and gives meaning to the individual in relation to the whole. Each thing is as if sustained in its deepest meaning by an invisible reality that gives it true consistency and its place within the whole of creation. The Word behind things gives them meaning because it sets them in a relationship of mutual love. One of Chiara's powerful mystical experiences shows this well:

> I had the impression of seeing, perhaps through a special grace of God, the presence of God beneath things. So, if the pine trees were gilded by the sun, if the streams ran down in their glistening waterfalls, if the daisies and the other flowers and the sky were festive because of the summer, stronger yet was the vision of a sun that lay beneath all that is created. I saw, in a certain way, I think, God who sustains, who upholds things.
>
> And God beneath things made them be not as we see them; they were all linked among themselves by love, all, so to speak, in love with one another. So if the stream flowed into the lake, it was for love. If one pine tree rose beside another, it was for love.
>
> And the vision of God beneath things, which gave unity to creation, was stronger than the things themselves; the unity of the whole was stronger than the distinction among the things.

The following text is a summary: "On earth all is relationship of love with all, each thing with each thing. It is necessary to be Love to find the golden thread that connects all beings." This is not a utopian vision but a mystical perception that sees, beyond the "laws of the jungle" that seem to dominate our world, a hidden reality that will be manifested in the Eschaton. In order for us to perceive the positive within the negative, to discover the golden thread behind a law of death that is prevalent in the current conditions of creation, an event is needed to change the direction of our vision entirely and reveal and realize in history this total change of direction. The event is Jesus crucified and forsaken.

For now, let us keep this in mind: The Word, the One who sustains the multiplicity in creation, does not absorb, does not eliminate diversity but creates, as the law of creation, relationality among things. For one thing, recapitulation is possible because the law of the Word has been in creation since the beginning and because creation is not chaos but has inscribed within itself relationships among all things. If the Crucified One reveals the law of the Word in history and in the world, there has begun the journey toward unity as manifestation and realization of love among things.

Several of Chiara's writings express this link between protology and eschatology. "At the end of times (everything) will turn again into the Word, though it had always been in the Word." I find a thought-provoking application of this link in Chiara's critique of the thought of the seventeenth-century theologian Olier, whose spiritual books were very popular before the Second Vatican Council.

> Comparing the condition of Christians to that of Adam in his innocence, Olier writes that there is a great difference between the two. Adam sought God, served him and adored him in creatures; Christians instead are obliged to seek God through faith, to serve him and adore him drawn away into himself and in his holiness, separate from every creature, and that the grace of baptism lies in this.
>
> If we were to think like this, we would say that Jesus, dying on the cross, did not re-establish the order broken by sin on earth. While I believe that everything has been done by him in such a way that whoever takes advantage of his Redemption to the full, implementing the Gospel entirely (as it is implemented in our Unity, where other than the first rebirth with water there is also rebirth in the Spirit),[13] discovers the pristine order of things, in the fullness of joy.

---

13. Chiara explains, "With the expression 'rebirth in the Spirit,' I mean to refer to all that the charism works in us and in our life."

In reaction to a Christian spirituality focused on the individual that thinks God can be found in searching far from things (a dualistic risk of classic mystics stemming from Hellenistic philosophy), Chiara sets the Christian within the logic of redemption, where Christ "has re-established the order broken by sin." Whoever lives the gospels becomes part of this direction, infuses love where there is none, and participates in the "recapitulation." Recapitulation is brought about in history not by isolating oneself from the rest of the world but by living in a relationship of love with everyone and everything. Thus, one "discovers the pristine order of things in the fullness of joy." Chiara's thought is consistent with the core of Revelation: Redemption does not distance humanity from the world to allow humanity to reach God. On the contrary, redemption makes God enter fully into the world so that human beings can encounter God.

Intimate Relationship between Christ and the Church

Through the resurrection, God set Christ above cosmic powers and gave him, as the Head, also to the church. This is a privileged relationship with the church, which is his Body. Let us keep in mind the unbreakable relationship between Christ and the church, represented by the image Head-Body, that expresses a deep shared identity while preserving their distinction, as well as the vital role of the Head toward the entire Body. In the Letter to the Ephesians, the reader is constantly reminded of the relationship between the church and Christ with the phrase "in Christ," which emphasizes the mediating function of the Risen Christ and the ultimate end/purpose of the Father's actions. We read "in Christ" at least twelve times in the initial blessing (Eph 1:3-13): "In Christ" God chose us, we have adoption as children, redemption, universal recapitulation, inheritance, and so on.

In a non-Pauline way, but consistently with Colossians 2:12, the author states that "in Christ" we are already co-vivified, co-risen, and God has already made us co-seated in heaven where Christ lives (Eph 2:5-6). Since we are members of his Body, we already participate in His Easter, and we are where He is: in God. The author of the Letter to the Ephesians contemplates Christian life starting from its fulfillment.

When the author states that we are "created in Christ" (Eph 2:10) he has in mind (clearly, from the context) the eschatological function of the Lord: it is God who made "the new creation" uniting us to Christ as our mediator and ultimate end/purpose. "In Christ" we are close to one another

(Eph 2:13) and have access to the Father (Eph 2:18). Therefore, humanity is called to live "in Christ." Christ is the destiny of human beings, the place in which to dwell (that is, in a relationship that brings about being). In Christ, human beings are constituted as His Body and become Children who live in the presence of the Father.

The relationship with the Risen Jesus is described again with additional images: The image of the Spouse underscores the loving relationship. Christ is also the cornerstone of the building that is the church: The whole building is kept together by this stone, which is Christ. Furthermore, this building is alive and *grows* toward the Risen Christ in a process of development that makes the church increasingly more similar to Christ (Eph 2:21; see 4:13, 15-16). It is the Risen Jesus who envelops the whole growth process from its beginning to the end. The growth of the church toward Christ is not primarily seen as a growth in time, a journey toward the future, but rather an upward movement toward the Head that has always been present in the church, which makes it possible to grow toward the church in each person's daily life, as toward the One who is the true identity of the church itself (Eph 4:15).

One last concept: the *Pleroma*. The letter talks about Christ as the Head, given to the church "which is His Body, the Fullness (*pleroma*) of the one who fills all in all" (Eph 1:23). Here, I translate a sentence that is ambiguous and can be rendered in multiple ways and therefore can yield many interpretations. The following are two of the possible interpretations: (1) the church, Body of Christ, is the *pleroma* (the fullness) of the One (Christ) who is filled (he himself) completely (with God); (2) the church, Body of Christ, is the *pleroma* of Him (Christ) who brings to fullness everything in every part (or: in all).

The Letter to the Colossians says that the fullness (*pleroma*) of God dwells in Christ (Col 1:19). The Letter to the Ephesians is inspired by Colossians but has a more ecclesial perspective: Now it is the church that is the fullness (*pleroma*) of Christ who brings everything to fullness. Christ fills the church with his presence. Therefore, the church is rich with the divine fullness of Christ who dwells in her. The Risen Jesus who received everything from the Father communicates his richness to the church. As a consequence, the church is introduced into the divine fullness that Christ received from the Father. The church, in turn, becomes the place where Christ wants to irradiate his unifying force in creation: "The Letter to the Colossians designated

Christ, who is filled with God and fills us with God; Ephesians continues along the same line and brings up the Church, fullness of Christ, filled with Him in order to fill the universe, while waiting that the same universe, filled by the divine presence, become the expression of glory."[14]

The letter then underscores that for the church filled with his presence Christ is all. The relationship of the Risen Lord with the church never achieves a complete identification. Such "identification" and the terminology to express it should be carefully avoided. Christ, in his deep—I would say natural—relationship with the church remains always the Head, distinct from the Body, the Bridegroom, distinct from the Bride, the cornerstone. Christ always remains in a relationship of transcendence and unification.

In authentic Christian mystical language, though recognizing as obvious the distinction between Christ and the church, the emphasis is on the identification: It is the experience of the radical transformation in Christ, the experience of "no longer I but Christ in me" (Gal 2:20). In Chiara's mystical writings, there are frequent expressions such as "I was that Jesus," "Today we are Jesus," "We are each truly destined to be another Jesus," and so on. These are mystical expressions that emphasize the reality of union experienced as identity. However, they should not be understood as an experience of "fusion" or "de-personalization." Furthermore, the originality of Chiara's experience should always be kept in mind even if the usual mystical expressions are used. When we read in Chiara's writings "I am Jesus" or "my neighbor is Jesus" or "we are Jesus," we are not encountering someone who withdraws from the "world," goes up a mountain, and lives full union with God (Christ). The experience of "being Jesus" is essentially the result of "being church" and therefore of the charism of unity.

Whatever Chiara experiences in a mystical way personally is the unity as constitutive of the church, Body of Christ. "Being Jesus" that stems from it expresses the *full* presence of Christ, which characterizes his *Pleroma* in the "mutual nothingness" that brings about the church. Therefore, between two individuals who are made church, there is no temptation to fusion in this ecclesial vision whereby the neighbor becomes mediator of the Risen One. Therefore, Chiara can answer Paul's statement to the Galatians in which he wants to emphasize the Christian novelty compared to the Mosaic Law (Gal

---

14. Michel Bouttier, *L'Epître de Saint Paul aux Ephésiens* (Geneva: Labor et Fides, 1991), 293.

2:20) by giving to it a markedly ecclesial interpretation: "It is no longer we who live; it is Christ, truly, who lives in us"

More than ever in the relationship of unity, the church reflects in the best way the Mystery dwelling in her, and it is its *Pleroma* (fullness). In mutual love, Christ, whose *Pleroma* is the church, becomes present within each individual. I will talk more later about the importance of love (as implementation of the cosmic "recapitulation" in history). For the time being, it is important to emphasize the deep relationship between Christ and the church in this comparison between the Letter to the Ephesians and Chiara's mystical writings.

Christ – Church – Cosmos

We are now going to consider the relationship existing "in Christ" between the church and creation. As previously mentioned, Ephesians presents Christ as the Head both of the cosmos and of the church, but only the latter is His Body, His *Pleroma*. The church is set in a mission that has universal breadth: Christ wants to use Her to bring about His sovereignty in the world. The church becomes mediator of Christ of which it is the *Pleroma*. Let us look at the phrase in Eph 1:22-23a: "[The Father] has put all things under his [Christ's] feet and has made him the head over all things for the church, which is his body." The common translation "and he has made him the *supreme* head"[15*] is not faithful to the original text, which mentions the cosmic supremacy of Christ given to the church. God gave the church a Christ as Sovereign of the universe. As a consequence, there is a new relationship between the church and creation, thanks to the gift of Christ. He, present in the church and in the heart of each believer, is the deep connection between the church and creation.

To expand the Kingdom of Christ, the church should not establish a universal theocracy nor be concerned about extending the proclamation of the gospel to the farthest galaxies. Rather, the church should be open to the Christ present in her and grow in her love toward Him. For the "cosmic" Christ who dwells in the church and in the heart of the individual believers united to the Church, each act of love has cosmic repercussions and brings about concretely in history the universal recapitulation of Christ that has

---

15   * Rossé here refers more specifically to the Italian or French translation of the passage [translator's note].

already taken place in the Risen One. Therefore, the cosmic function of the church is mediated by Christ who dwells in Her.

This connection between church and creation, mediated by Christ, suggested by the Letter to the Ephesians is also an original aspect of Chiara's thought. Consider the following text:

> We will be in the heart of the Bosom of God because we will be in that wound. But we will be also on the outermost surface of God (so to speak) where the root is united, through a mediator who is Nothing, to its Tree.[16] Like this, besides being the Infinitely Small, we will be also the Infinitely Great.[17] We will be God through Jesus, who is among us, who is us.

The Paschal journey of Christ, by participation, becomes for the church both the journey into the bosom of the Father and a mission of universal recapitulation in the world. Chiara writes further: "Having in self . . . the whole of the Word, humankind too will be a mirror of the Universe which is in the Word," mediator for humanity in the universe that He recapitulates. This cosmic-divine breadth mediated by Christ present in the believer is part of Chiara's mystical awareness:

> At Holy Communion Jesus (mirror of the Mystical Body of Christ) entered into me and I, possessing all the Love of the Communion of Saints and more (of all created creatures), said to the Father: "I love you." It was *sincere* love because Love was in me and was Infinite.

The fullness of Christ, universal recapitulator, present in the church, is therefore communicated to the believer, who experiences unity. As daughter in the Son, Chiara addresses the Father with all the richness of the unifying love of Christ. Here is another passage:

> I feel I live in me all the creatures of the world, all the Communion of Saints. Really: because my I is humanity with all the people

---

16. Chiara explains in a note, "We will also be Jesus Forsaken, who is always Jesus. Therefore, we also will be at the periphery, at the surface, where Jesus Forsaken, who is Nothing, is Mediator. Through him the tree, which is humanity and creation, is united to God."
17. During a session of the Abba School, Fr. Foresi commented, "Beyond being infinitely small, we are, through Christ, infinitely great. Through Jesus Forsaken beneath every particular there is the universal."

that were, are, and will be. I feel and I live this reality: because I feel in my soul both the delight of Heaven and the anguish of humanity that is all a great Jesus Forsaken.

Jesus Forsaken, Nothingness, Mediator between God and human beings, is also, because he is Risen, Mediator between the self and the whole of humanity, which he recapitulates. Loving Jesus Forsaken in the heart means realizing in one's own self the eschatological unity between humanity and God, between anguish and fullness of joy. The same concept is found in the following passage:

> Now Jesus makes clear to me that we too must be Wounded: to have in our heart a void, and in the void the whole of Heaven and the earth with all the Children of God and the entire Creation.

The identification with Christ (with the Paschal journey) makes us participate in his reconciliatory mission and at the same time makes us "co-rise and co-seat in Heaven," as it is said in the Letter to the Ephesians. In this regard, Chiara says the following: "to have in our heart the void and in the void the whole of *heaven*." For Chiara, Jesus is always "that Jesus who is the One in whom created and Uncreated converge and are consumed in God." Given Christ who dwells in the heart of the believer who lives out love, each act has an eschatological value: recapitulation of the cosmos and access to the Father.

Chapter Seventeen

Chiara Lubich's Paradise '49 in Light of the Letter to the Ephesians: Jesus Crucified and Forsaken, the Church, and *Agape*-Love[1]

Gérard Rossé

Jesus Crucified and Forsaken

Chiara Lubich's mystical writings, referred to as "Paradise '49," have consistently highlighted the foundation of the unification and divinization that brings all of creation into the Bosom of the Father, namely, Jesus Forsaken and the merit of his death. The cosmic and eschatological significance of the Risen One finds its roots in the cross. In each section of this article, I will first turn to the Letter to the Ephesians and highlight what it reveals about the death of Jesus.

From the Letter to the Ephesians

The author of the Letter to the Ephesians explains the salvific merit in the death of Jesus using strongly Pauline and traditional terminology: redemption-ransom, reconciliation, forgiveness of sins, sacrifice, and so on (Eph 1:7; 2:16; 4:32, etc.). Worth highlighting in the opening blessing of the letter is the shortened statement:

---

1. This article constitutes the final part of a four-part study entitled "Revisiting Chiara Lubich's Paradise'49 in Light of the Letter to the Ephesians." It proposes to collect the points of contact between Lubich's Paradise '49 and the Letter to the Ephesians, and to explore the grand themes of faith that emerge from both of these writings, in particular God, the Word, ecclesiology, and ethics. This fourth article by Rossé was first published in Italian in *Nuova Umanità* 32 (2010): 21-55. It was translated by Giovanna Czander and Jessica Behrend. The four Rossé articles are contained in Section 4 of this volume, "Implications of Paradise '49 for Biblical Studies," pages 241-328.

"God favored us in the Beloved, in whom we have redemption through his blood, the forgiveness of transgressions, in accord with the riches of his grace (Eph 1:6-7)."[2]

The expression "redemption-ransom" has a strong social connotation: It means the freedom of a slave or prisoner through a payment of ransom. Seen as redemption, the death of Jesus means freedom from everything that would tarnish our relationship with God. This freedom comes through the forgiveness of sins, a forgiveness that removes what might be lacking in our relationship with God and brings us into communion with the Father. The traditional expression "through his blood" alludes to a type of violent death that becomes "life-giving." The connotation of the word "blood" is that the death becomes the communication of life. For the author of the letter, as we will see, this reconciliation that is obtained solely by the grace of God is not confined only to the spiritual realm. It also has social and cosmic repercussions. In short, our costly freedom was obtained by the Father's *Beloved*, "and this explains the weight of *agape* in the [salvific] event."[3]

The Letter to the Ephesians reveals how "love" is the key to understanding the event of the cross: the love of a God "rich in mercy, out of the great love with which he loved us" (Eph 2:4). This is a divine love, reflected in Jesus, who "loved us and gave himself up for us, a fragrant offering and sacrifice to God" (Eph 5:2, v. 25). Here, the author links the traditional phrase "Christ gave himself up for us" (Gal 2:20; Mk 9:31, 14:24; 1 Cor 15:3, etc.) to an expression derived from liturgical terminology and presents the death of Jesus as a sacrifice. The death of Jesus as an act of obedient love abolishes forever the sacrifices of the Temple. It is the supreme manifestation of love and is fully accepted by the Father. It reflects the love of the Father, revealing the definitive and unmeasurable "Yes" of God toward humanity.

How is the death of Jesus able to bring about communion with God and make unity among humankind possible? How does the value of such a death have repercussions for the entire universe? To answer these questions, it is important to turn to the central piece of what would be the doctrinal section of the letter, namely, Ephesians 2:11-22 and, more precisely, Ephesians 2:13-18. After addressing the relatively deplorable religious situation of those who in the past had been pagans, the author shifts his emphasis to

---

2. Translators' note: Here, the translation of Rossé's version of this scriptural passage is ours. In all other instances, we use NRSV.
3. Romano Penna, *Lettera agli Efesini* (Bologna: EDB, 1988), 93.

his new and great point: "But now, in Christ Jesus, you who were once far off, have been brought near by the blood of Christ" (Eph 2:13). Note that "Christ" appears twice in the verse. He is the mediator and at the same time the space of relationships. On the one hand, it is "through Christ" that those "far off" together with the Israelites have found a new intimacy with God, who has revealed Godself as the Father of all. On the other hand, it is "in Christ" because of his death on the cross that "Jews" and "non-Jews" have also found themselves in greater fellowship with each other.

The cross gave birth to the unity of peoples. Its reach is broader than one's individual salvation; it embraces the entire social dimension of unity, giving birth to a "new society." The author continues with the verses that form the central section of the letter:

> For he is our peace, in his flesh he has made both groups into one and has broken down the dividing wall, that is, the hostility between us. He has abolished the law with its commandments and ordinances, that he might create in himself one new humanity in place of the two, thus making peace, and might reconcile both groups to God in one body through the cross, thus putting to death that hostility through it. So he came and proclaimed peace to you who were far off and peace to those who were near; for through him both of us have access in one Spirit to the Father (Eph 2:14-18).

"Peace" is the ultimate messianic gift, namely, the state of fullness and happiness that results from a real and lived unity among humanity in the context of the definitive closeness of God. Now it is Christ who is peace. On the cross, he united in one Body Jews and non-Jews, who up to that point had been enemies (v. 16); and he introduced them all into the direct presence of God (v. 18). Therefore, the two categories of peoples, until then symbolizing mutual hatred, have become a united people (while retaining their identities) in the church, where there is no longer Jew nor Greek. They have been introduced into the Bosom of the Father. The cross is the place where the distance between God and humanity, as well as the distance among peoples, is removed.

What happened on the cross? Jesus "put to death hostility in his flesh," breaking down the dividing wall. This dividing wall recalls the wall in the Temple in Jerusalem that prevented non-Jews from coming close to the presence of God. The "wall" also metaphorically recalls judgment, hate, and misunderstandings that Jews and Gentiles inflicted on one another. Concretely, the author blames the Law of Moses (v. 15)! This passage is a criticism of the Torah—the only of its kind in the New Testament—wherein the Law is seen only as a list of commandments that gave birth to numerous prescriptions fostering discrimination, division among peoples, and mutual hate. Jesus needed to suffer this division in his own humanity in order to remove this barrier. In his crucified flesh (that is, in his way of "being" in the state of death),[4] Jesus removed the hatred that divides humanity. He "put to death that hostility in himself." The author does not explicate how Jesus does this. But the concept is clear: Jesus removed all enmity by taking on himself hatred and division, forgiving everything and bringing together these enemies in himself on the cross (Col 2:14), thus opening the way for the divine force of *agape*.

In this obedient love until death, an immeasurable Love breaks forth in his body: the Holy Spirit that definitively surpasses a Law understood as a series of discriminatory prescriptions. On the cross, Jesus gives life to a new Law: to love always and everyone. On the cross, Love moves Jesus to identify himself with the sinner, with that which is division and disunity, to the point of appearing as a sinner even though he was without sin.[5] It is exactly in that Love, the Holy Spirit, that he is united with God the Father. And so, "in Jesus a spiritual space is opened, where God alone reigns without the mediation of the Law; God reigns there by means of His Spirit."[6] Effectively, the cross gives birth to a unity of peoples that, as the church, forms the New Human Being. This is not as a mere sum of different peoples, nor as a mixture, but as a "new creation," already One because it is rooted in the Crucified and carries in itself the face of Christ (being his Body).[7]

---

4. The context shows that "in his flesh" is referring to his death.
5. This thought assumes that the death of the Crucified One is understood as the highest manifestation of love, capable of reaching human beings where they are in their estrangement from God. There is a similar thought, perhaps, in Ephesians 4:9: Jesus "descended into the lower parts of the earth," alluding to his solidarity to the very end with all of humanity, lived out in his death on the cross. In any case, such a thought is also present in the understanding of his death as an act of the highest love and the taking up of division "in his flesh."
6. Robert Baulès, *L'Insondable Richesse du Christ, Lectio Divina 66* (Paris: Cerf, 1971), 35.
7. A similar reality in relationship to the charism of unity is the birth of the "Soul" described by Chiara in "Paradise '49," *Claritas* 1.1 (March 2012): 8. Such a reality is certainly to be placed within the church as its living expression and is not intended as a second church.

In verse 17, Christ, who reconciles through his death the divided parts of humanity, becomes the missionary of his own work for peace. The Risen One universalizes what the Crucified One brought about by his death. By Jesus' resurrection the reconciliation effected on the cross assumes a cosmic dimension. As Baulès writes, "It is not that there is more love in the Risen Jesus than in Jesus as he died; it is the same love, but through the resurrection, this love reigns over the entire universe and conquers hearts."[8]

The text of Ephesians concludes with a striking synthesis: through Christ, and because of the cross, a united humanity gains access to the Father in the one Spirit. Christ is now the Mediator of the gift that is the Holy Spirit, a gift that is the direct avenue for our intimate relationship with the Father and each other. The death on the cross, therefore, gives way to the power of Love that launches our return journey to the Father. Set as Head of the universe, the Risen One has already recapitulated all things in himself and has created universal "peace." He removed the hatred that divides by his death on the cross, and he brought to life the power of Love, the communicated Spirit, that creates harmony and brings humanity together in unity.

The author finds confirmation in what would be the real masterpiece of God's Wisdom, namely, the unity already attained in the church among those who up to that point had been divided enemies (Jews and Greeks) but who are now united into a single New Human Being. This is the visible sign of the cosmic recapitulation brought about by the resurrection, together with the power of freedom that will span history. This is the "unthinkable richness of God" that the apostle needs to proclaim to everyone (Eph 3:8): Humanity and all of creation are called to the "peace" already inaugurated in the Risen One. Erasing enmity, Jesus on the cross generates this unity that he, as the Risen One, extends to the entire universe. He is the universal Mediator of this unity; and as the author points out (in the only occurrence in the New Testament), he is also the author of the new creation (Eph 2:15).

From Chiara Lubich's Writings

For Chiara Lubich, "the love of Christ that surpasses all knowledge" (Eph 3:19) and that was revealed on the cross has a name: Jesus Forsaken. As in the Letter to the Ephesians, Chiara presents a strong understanding that the

---

8. Baulès, *L'Insondable Richesse du Christ,* 47, n16.

death of Jesus, and more precisely his abandonment, is the perennial root of the eschatological event that brings God's plan for humanity and creation to fulfillment. To know Jesus Forsaken is to go to the heart of the love revealed on the cross, a love that makes Christ the universal Mediator.

How can we understand Jesus Forsaken in relation to the eschatological design of God? We read, "In his cry Jesus Forsaken summed the nothingness of things: 'All is vanity of vanities.'"[9] And again, "Jesus Forsaken has destroyed sin and death and put in their place: Love and Life. Jesus Forsaken in fact, summed up in Himself all vanity and filled it with Himself." Or, "Jesus Forsaken breathed into Himself all the vanities, and the vanities became Him and He is God."

Lubich's numerous texts about Jesus Forsaken speak of the fundamental importance of reality for her. Let us try to delve deeper. We read that Jesus Forsaken is nothing, is vanity. How do we understand this "nothing?" Nothing, when it is synonymous with "vanity," conveys the solidarity of Christ crucified with everything that is an "abandonment," everything that is non-God. It is creation as a "vanity" that is not to be understood in a moral sense. Rather, unlike God, it has no stability, it passes away. It is "the nothingness of all that is created; that is, its being is non-being in itself." Vanity as nothingness (that is, the absence of God, the abandonment) is also in reality sinfulness, that is, separation from God as goodness itself: "Having been made sin and so disunity, individuality,[10] as the Forsaken One can be Spouse even of the lowest sinner in the world, even while divided from everyone, because He—as sin—sees Himself in all sinners and all sinners can see themselves in Him." And finally, nothingness seen as "vanity" is also suffering, death, and so on: "Suffering is non-love and therefore, when God (Jesus Forsaken) suffered, He took Love from Himself and gave it to human beings making them children of God."

---

9. An unpublished passage from 1949. Unless otherwise specified, all citations from the writings of Chiara Lubich refer to these unpublished materials, which date to 1949.

10. During a meeting of the Abba School, Chiara commented on this point: "This phenomenon of Jesus in his forsakenness is amazing. This is why Jesus does not say: 'Father, Father, why . . .?' but 'My God, my God, why . . .?' (Mk 15:34; Mt 27:46). He, in fact, having made himself sin (in an ontological sense, not a moral one) is reduced to being simply a human being, to 'individuality.' He is no longer *the* human being, but became a little like Adam who before he sinned was *the* human being having all of humanity in himself) and afterward became an individual."

In addition to this nothingness-vanity that is manifested in the Abandonment, and, with it, the total solidarity of Jesus with everything that is non-God, separation from God, the isolated individual, there is another nothingness. Jesus Forsaken lived another "nothing" within his nothingness. He became the non-existence characteristic of love. The dynamic of love is a total gift of self (a total self-emptying) that fulfills the person who loves by their giving the gift of "pure love" and thereby becomes a fullness of "being love." At the culmination of his death—signified by his abandonment—Jesus lived in a fully human way the nothing of love: non-being as complete openness and gift to the Father and to humanity. In this total love lived on the cross, Jesus experienced "in his flesh" his non-existence as God, his nothingness as the Son in relation to the Father. By doing so, he introduces humanity into the dynamics of the life of God-Love.

Chiara applies the internal dynamics of love (non-being/being) also to the relationship between the Divine Persons: God is Love. In the "Nothing" of God, love and its internal dynamics of non-being/being are lived in complete fullness. Chiara writes, "Three Reals form the Trinity, and yet they are One because Love *is* and *is not* at the same time, but also when it *is not* it is, because it is love.[11] In fact, if out of love I take something from myself and give it (I deprive myself—*it is not*) out of love, I have love (*it is*)." The divine "Nothing," in the logic of being love, corresponds to the *relatio subsistens* (essence signifying relation) of classic theology.

In his abandonment, Jesus lives the non-being of filial love that makes him One with the Father, in the highest solidarity with the non-being of the created world and of sin. In this way, he becomes the transparency of the Father, the point of convergence of God and creation, and the point (i.e., nothingness as empty space) where the Holy Spirit as "Divine Love" springs forth. Some of Chiara's writings shed light on this concept:

---

11. Again, during a meeting of the Abba School, Chiara commented: "Where non-being truly is being, is in the Trinity. The Father, in fact, in begetting the Son out of love, 'loses' himself in Him, lives in Him; he seems thereby to make himself nothing, but precisely in this making himself nothing out of love he is, he is Father. The Son, as echo of the Father, returns to the Father out of love, he 'loses' himself in Him, lives in Him; it seems therefore that he too makes himself nothing out of love, but precisely like this he is, he is Son. Equally the Holy Spirit: in his being mutual love between Father and Son, their bond of unity, He "loses" himself in them, He makes himself nothing, in a certain way out of love, but precisely like this he is, he is the Holy Spirit."

Jesus is Jesus Forsaken. Because Jesus is the Savior, the Redeemer, and He redeems when He pours the Divine upon humanity through the Wound of His Forsakenness which is the pupil of the Eye of God upon the world: an infinite Void through which God looks upon us, the window of God thrown open upon the world and the window of humanity through which we see God.

Therefore, Jesus Forsaken is for humanity the revelation and encounter with God as Love. At the same time in Jesus Forsaken, the Father sees all of created humanity in the Son in that act of recapitulation that transforms the non-being of created humanity into love, that is, into "being." In other words, it is in this "Emptiness" that the marriage takes place (i.e., the definitive communion, the New Covenant) between the Uncreated and the created:

> The Father sent his Son to earth to be intermingled with created things, to sum up and divinize them. Jesus, the Mediator, was the cause of the marriage between the Uncreated and the created, of the unity between the created and the Uncreated, equal to the unity between the Word and the Father.

Jesus Forsaken is "nothingness" in what would be its purest state that can contain the All, God. Jesus Forsaken is the "Pure Act of Love"; *he is God*. Chiara writes:

> Love is to be distilled to the point of being only Holy Spirit. It is distilled by passing it through Jesus Forsaken. Jesus Forsaken is nothingness, is the point and through the point (= Love reduced to the extreme, having given everything) passes only Simplicity that is God: Love. Only Love penetrates.

Jesus Forsaken is then the Mediator, the point where that "dividing wall" vanishes. This dividing wall is between God and non-God that includes the whole of creation and humanity in all the possible situations of separation from God. Jesus Forsaken is the One through whom God recapitulates everything. The Risen One is Jesus Forsaken extended to everything that is non-God.

Chiara Lubich's ingenuity places the mediation of Christ within that "nothingness" where the "vanity" of creation and Trinitarian life can meet and enter each other. In Jesus Forsaken, "Nothingness is so united to the All (God) that what belongs to one belongs to the other and so Nothingness became All: Jesus Forsaken is God." It is important not to forget that the "nothingness" lived by Jesus Forsaken is not a stagnant emptiness. Rather, it follows the dynamics of love. It is this love that has the capacity to transform the non-being of realities into "being" and "relationship."

Chiara (using mystical language) often speaks of a "divinization" that grants to creation a touch of the Eschaton: "Just as He translated pain into love, He translated wretchedness into Mercy. All by him is *divinized*" All negativity, therefore, can be transformed into love, into a Life that remains, transcending the "vanity" as "that which passes." "Jesus Forsaken clothed the All with Nothing[12] to nullify Nothingness and give divine consistency to all that passes: 'All is vanity of vanities' (Eccl 1:2)." Elsewhere, she writes:

> And that Light,[13] received by each one and transforming human nature into divine nature, supernaturalized nature and in humankind all that is created. So that all is going to God and nothing will be lost, for that which is lost will remain in Jesus Forsaken who, by divinizing it gives value, in the eyes of God and of the blessed, to Hell itself.

Therefore, even failures and what is useless are not lost forever. Jesus in his abandonment has saved everything and given everything a meaning. Now the New Creation is seen as more than solely a holy remnant saved from general destruction. It is not even a "new" creation, as it was born from nothing. But it is our nature transformed, where everything that is positive or negative becomes a light and a reflection of the glory of God that shines on the face of Christ.

In Chiara Lubich's thought, therefore, Jesus Forsaken is the key to understanding the depth of Christ's role in recapitulation. Because Jesus is Mediator precisely in his abandonment, the recapitulation of all things is brought about through the dynamics of love lived by the Crucified Man-God—of which the Risen One has given a value that is unchangeable, universal, and definitive. The reality of Jesus Forsaken is not an experience limited to the historical Jesus and therefore relegated to the past. But in Christ Jesus, it has eternal value; it is the eschatological event, where the glorious Christ

---

12. Chiara is thinking of the Nothingness of the Word in the Father and of the Father in the Word. The expression "the All with Nothing" could also have this sense: the Nothingness in all its fullness.

13. During an Abba School meeting, Chiara explained, "That is, the Holy Spirit who springs from Jesus Forsaken."

remains forever the One who was crucified, the slaughtered Lamb. Over time, it is the ever-present way in which Christ acts out in and through the church his role of recapitulation.

Jesus Forsaken: The Role of Mediation of the Church and of Christians

Consistent with Divine Revelation and the Letter to the Ephesians, Chiara Lubich recognizes that the destiny of humanity and creation cannot be separated.

> With that cry he redeemed humanity and made it child of God, God, Trinity, and in it redeemed all that is created, in which the trinitarian trace and life (there we found being and law and life, and all is Love: Father, Son, Holy Spirit) is borne by Jesus Forsaken to the full and complete Trinity.

Here, Jesus Forsaken offers us a completed and full vision that is at the same time:

- *unifying* (the bond between creation and salvation),
- *dynamic* (the bond between redemption and eschatology seen as full participation in the life of God),
- *anthropological* (with humankind as the synthesis of all of creation),
- *Christological* (the place and role of Jesus Forsaken in the plan of salvation-divinization),
- and *Trinitarian* (creation-eschatology as the work of the three Divine Persons).

It is important not to separate the beginning of God's Design carried out "in Christ" from its eschatological and ultimate role in the recapitulation of all things "in Christ." The creation "in Christ" and the universal and eschatological recapitulation are part of the same Design of God. Jesus Forsaken reveals and brings to fruition, even in our own history, both the bond of love that exists between things and the law of the Trinitarian pattern that from the beginning was always underneath creation and is now brought completely to the surface by Eschatology. The universal law or pattern and the relationships among things will turn into beauty, harmony, cohesion, and a reflection of the same Life of their Creator.

As has been observed, the recapitulation of all things in Christ has already been accomplished with the resurrection (see the aorist verb in Eph

1:10). What is the reality within God aims at being accomplished also in history through the church that carries in herself "the Fullness (pleroma) of Christ" (Eph 1:23). What is left is "that through the church the wisdom of God in its rich variety might now be made known to the rulers and authorities in the heavenly places" (Eph 3:10), a step in the plan of salvation that will precede unity. Because of Jesus, humans can be freed from the invisible and hostile powers that dominate them and from the hate that gives birth to division and so can become positive agents in a universe and a history that have universal reconciliation as their ultimate end.

It is the church's mission to irradiate into creation the unifying power of love set into motion by the Crucified One. The church, however, is not an abstract reality. It comes to life in the lives of believers. Therefore, the exhortative section in the Letter to the Ephesians is of great importance. This section seeks to portray the life of unity as a commitment that corresponds to the divine Design already in motion in the church—a living reality that is diverse, dynamic, and constantly growing into its Head, Christ. The desire for unity appears already in the first verses of the exhortative section (Eph 4:1-3) and includes commands that are very concrete and even obvious. We will look more closely into this concept later.

The charism of unity according to the texts of Paradise '49 also goes beyond a mere doctrinal analysis. It leads to the incarnation of the life of unity, inviting us to put it into practice and offering practical solutions for what is faced in daily life. In such texts, specific moral exhortations were not predominant. Instead, the exhortations focused on the mission of universal recapitulation that is entrusted to the church and to which every believer is called to participate. Chiara Lubich does not offer Christians so much a list of prescriptions as the greatness of the God's Design enacted in daily life by their participation in the reality of Jesus Forsaken.

Like Jesus Forsaken, and in communion with the Risen One who lived the abandonment, the Christian is called to bring love to those places where there is none and to give to the "nothing," the eschatological dimension of a divinized reality:

> For every mistake made by my brother or sister I ask forgiveness of the Father as if it were my own because my love takes possession of it. In this way, I am Jesus. And I am Jesus Forsaken always before the Father as Sin and in the greatest act of love for my brothers and sisters and so for the Father.

This text does not mean that one should imitate Jesus Forsaken but rather that one should bring about in history, through communion with the Risen One, the eschatological function of "reconciliation." In a broader sense:

> I understood that *wanting* to communicate with Jesus Forsaken Humanity was like wanting the dreadful pain that circulates in the Mystical Body of Christ[14] and that this communion transmuted the pain into Love (it is always thus in our Ideal) whereby I became: *Christ's Mystical Body*:[15] all clarified by this newest communion.

On this point, Chiara's own experience is quite telling:

> I went into church with a headache, and I said: "Why, my Jesus, do I feel this pain when You have taught me that there *is* only Love? Why can a physical disunity that is not Love make a greater din than health which is Love and so: that which is? I did not understand . . . And yet, I had seen so clearly that only Love *is*!
>
> Throughout the meditation I was in communion with Jesus-Eucharist and with the souls who are me, and I said: "Jesus Forsaken-Love: You are me and I am You" and I thought: "What other Heaven will I be now?" what is the Love of Loves? the Pure Love? and I understood that it is Suffering and that I had become: Jesus Forsaken-Suffering and as such was before God.
>
> It was not enough for God to love in the Uncreated (Trinity) and in the created (with the law of love spread throughout the universe).
>
> He wanted to make of every *disunity: Love*! He made himself human to love in a new form: *with suffering*, to divinize suffering, that is to say, every disunity and he gathered upon himself all the pains of the world, all the disunities of the universe and he made them: Love, God!
>
> Therefore now I can love more than before. I love with Love and I love with Suffering, through Jesus Forsaken divinizing all Suffering.

---

14. Again, at a meeting of the Abba School, Chiara added, "I mean the whole of humanity."
15. Chiara comments, "This means the whole of humanity bought back to Christ."

What value Suffering has! It is an added God; it is the Superlove! And now I am before God as *Love Entire*. I no longer lack anything. I surpass the Trinity and equal Jesus Forsaken. More than this I could not love!

Jesus Forsaken does not strengthen (recapitulate) merely the law of love inscribed by God in creation but also the "negative nothing" (suffering, disunity, death) as an opportunity for salvation: Nothing escapes the salvific love of the God-Man. Therefore, loving in the midst of suffering, loving in a situation of disunity, is not just bearing it but divinizing it: "I, therefore, being Jesus Forsaken Suffering, present myself to God, having in me the Value, that is, the divinization of all the sufferings that were, that are, and that will be." This means bringing to every circumstance of non-being the eschatological dimension of "being." This is a great example not just of the function of recapitulation by Christ ("whatever is assumed is redeemed") but also of the fact that each believer can carry ahead this mission in communion with Jesus Forsaken, that is, with the Risen One who, on the cross, eliminates all divisions.

Joined with Christ, the Christian finds himself or herself wherever the Risen Lord is: in the heart of the world, close to everyone and every situation, since Jesus in his abandonment reached out to everyone, forever. Chiara Lubich is not afraid to write that such love "goes beyond the Trinity," since it is lived in communion with the One who not only is God but also became man in complete solidarity with humanity from within. In fact, concerning soteriology, there is a great consistency between Chiara Lubich's writings and the Letter to the Ephesians.

Redemption is read through the lens of unity (recapitulation, reconciliation) and is perceived in its cosmic and eschatological dimension, to which the understanding of Jesus Forsaken gives all its breadth. Jesus Forsaken also includes the redemption of what is negative and offers a key to a transformed living (the Superlove that can be experienced by anyone as a participation in the mission of the church.

The Church

From the Letter to the Ephesians

I am not setting out to explain all of the ecclesiology in the Letter to the Ephesians. The author has incorporated concepts from tradition (Body of

Christ, Temple of God) and integrated them well in his own vision. I would like to focus on this vision in the aspects where I see the most evident similarities with Chiara Lubich's experience.

The letter is not concerned with the internal organization of the church (though it shows that it is aware of it and mentions it) nor with the church's institutional aspect. Rather the church is seen as a fruit of God's grace, generated on the cross where Jesus abolished all divisions. The church is already an eschatological reality. Since in the church the eschatological reality of unity is already happening, the church is called to bring about in history and in the world this universal reconciliation of which she is a manifestation. To accomplish this calling, it is not necessary to reach out toward the galaxies but, in love, to be introduced into the Divine, where the Risen Lord reigns, where all things are already recapitulated. The previously cited text in Ephesians 2:14ff is key:

> In his flesh he has made both groups into one . . . that he might create in himself one new humanity in place of the two, thus making peace, and might reconcile both groups to God in one body through the cross, thus putting to death that hostility through it.

The church is certainly a social reality, but it was not born through mutual agreements with the purpose of establishing a different nation. The church is a people, but not the people of Israel plus the Gentiles. Rather, it is the "place" where each and all are lifted together to be the New Human Being, that is, already One in its origin. What was born on the cross is a New Creation: a social reality that is also the Body of Christ whose Head already lives in God in the Eschaton and whose Body, nourished by the Head and of the same nature as the Head, in its deepest essence[16] is called to become "the perfectly fulfilled human being" and to achieve the "measure of the fullness of Christ" (Eph 4:13).

Unity manifests the nature of the church. "There is Church wherever there is reconciliation, where the walls of separation are reversed."[17] However, this unity that will become true in the people of God is a gift and belongs to God's Mystery; the deepest identity of the church: Body of Christ. This

---

16. Chiara notes, "We cannot think of a body with a head of one nature, of one brilliance, and the rest of another nature, almost as if the head were of gold and the members of lead."
17. Michel Bouttier, *L'Épître de Saint Paul aux Éphésiens* (Geneva: Labor et Fides, 1991), 284.

unity is essentially an ecclesial experience that starts from Christ and leads to Christ, from the New Human Being (Eph 2:14) to the perfect Human Being (Eph 4:13). It is a story of relationships where Christ is always the origin and ultimate goal. So, the church, which is already "Christ" in her deepest identity (the pleroma), is always journeying toward Him and lives in a constant dynamic of approachment. The church needs to become increasingly, and in always new ways, penetrated and transformed by the presence of the Lord who is her measure, because the Risen Lord is the church's pleroma, the locus of divine Fullness, of her intimacy with God.

It is in the life of unity that Christ, present in the church who is his Body, becomes transparent as fullness received and always goal to be reached. In the unity that leads the church to conformity with its Head, to the perfect Human Being, each one finds one's own fullness and perfection. The Letter to the Ephesians addresses its exhortation to everyone. Each individual is called to find his or her own maturity, that is, perfection and fulfillment in the relational dynamics of the New Human Being who grows toward Christ. As we read in the Letter to the Colossians: "It is he [Christ] whom we proclaim, warning everyone and teaching everyone in all wisdom, so that we may make everyone perfected (fulfilled) in Christ" (Col 1:28).[18] It is in the unity that brings about the New Human Being (= the church) that each person participates in the value of the All, realizing in oneself the growth of the Body toward the Head. The individual receives the value of church and makes visible the dimension of the ecclesial Christ in his or her own existence lived out in love.

From Chiara Lubich's Writings

This reality of church becomes real in the group of people, called "the Soul," who by divine grace decided to put the love of unity as the foundation of their relationships. By "Soul," Chiara Lubich means herself and her companions, who, united to her, shared in the mystical experiences she was having. They felt that they were united as one Soul: "The Soul is the church, but in the sense that by church we mean *Unity* (that is, the New Jerusalem), or better the fullness of Christian life."

This is consistent with Ephesians. To live unity is to live in conformity with the deep essence of the church and let emerge that which constitutes

---

18. The translation of this scriptural passage is ours. [Translators' note]

her identity, the One who makes her One: Christ. The Soul is the manifestation of the church who lives out her own reality of being the Body of Christ. Therefore, each person in this Soul receives also the dimension of the church given him or her by the brothers and sisters in mutual love, therefore by the presence of Christ himself. This close connection between Christ and his Body, lived out in unity by the individual members, is expressed by Chiara as follows:

> Today those who are clarified are living members (with the fullness of Life) of the Mystical Body of Jesus! They are the *same* Jesus, not "another."[19] . . . They are "the same Mystical Body of Christ"[20] and, because thus united, each of them is "the same Christ."

Unity lived out gives to all and each one—they having become Body of Christ—the Christic dimension of the church. This brings about an aspect of God's Design described in the Letter to the Ephesians as making humanity in one Body whose Head is Christ. In Chiara's thought, this reality is inseparable from the other description of the Divine Design: in Christ, the adoption of God's children and the access to the Father, that is, the "Trinitarian" dimension of the life of the church. These two aspects of the great Design of God, namely, Body of Christ and access to the Father, that in Ephesians are at opposite poles are joined into one in the experience of the Soul entering the Bosom of the Father, and therefore are always inseparable in Chiara's thought. This can be summarized in the following way: "We: sons, daughters in the Son in the Father. And Jesus at our side looks and makes us look upon One Alone: the Father. At our side and in us: for through his eyes we look upon the Father."

The reality of church lived out in unity makes individuals similar to the Son in his relationship with the Father. In this above text, Chiara is careful to maintain the distinction of "Jesus at our side." "Being Jesus" in mystical language means to receive from the Spirit Jesus' relationship of sonship, that remains present in one's brother and sister (see Rom 8:29;

---

19. Chiara makes reference here to the unity-distinction in the life of communion, where in any case there prevails the strength that comes from unity ("they are the same").
20. Chiara explains at an Abba School meeting, "They live, that is, the reality of His mystical Body in themselves and among themselves."

Heb 2:11). As Chiara Lubich says, "Whoever lives unity, lives Jesus, and lives in the Father."

Chiara later shared a renewed experience of the Pact[21] that she had on November 10, 1949:

> When Jesus came into my nothingness I clearly heard the voice of the Spirit speaking to my Soul: "What? I have to make a pact with myself? *I* am in your nothingness." And I saw a single Jesus in everyone, and all of us—as if members—uniting to form him, so that in the chapel I seemed to see only him: him with his Head upon the altar and we all members [of his Body].

This experience is a renewal of the ecclesial-Christologic dimension, that is, of being church in her identity of being the Body of Christ. Here, the voice of the Holy Spirit emerges. The Spirit cannot make a pact with himself. The Holy Spirit in "nothingness" is the space for the Divine: "Love is to be distilled all the way to being only Holy Spirit." It is the Holy Spirit present in the "nothingness" of the mutual love that forms the church, who unites individuals with each other so that they are "Body of Christ," since it is the Holy Spirit who is the Relationship of Sonship of Christ with the Father.

Compared to the initial Pact with Foco, here there are new emphases. There is a relationship of identity with Jesus present not only in the tabernacle but also in each person who lives out unity. In unity each one is, for the other, Christ present in the church: "Like this I am Jesus and I live with Jesus." The final impression of this experience is interesting. It is one of identity and not uniformity: "I saw coming out from that little chapel a single Jesus and I thought: 'Whoever meets one of these will meet Jesus! How fortunate they are!' And in us I saw perfect identity." "I saw coming out a single Jesus" is the perception of being One, that is, of living in the dimension of the church with others (the Soul), the presence of Christ as the true Subject of the community: the experience of participating in the church, pleroma of Christ.

A Dynamic Experience of Church in the Letter to the Ephesians

The identification with Christ, experienced in unity, is not static. Participating in the love of unity in the reality of the church, the Body of Christ,

---

21. See Chiara Lubich, "Paradise '49," *Claritas* 1.1 (March 2012): 7–8. See also "The Pact," 113-15 in this volume.

means to participate in a life that entails growth in an increasingly deeper relationship with Christ, the origin and goal of this growth (Eph 2:20f). The goal is to achieve a perfected human being, "to the measure of the full stature of Christ" (Eph 4:13). We need to "act[22] the truth in love," and thus we must grow in every way into Him who is the head, into Christ" (Eph 4:15). "Acting in the truth" means to live the gospel by putting into practice the foundational commandment to love and to live an authentic relationship with the truth contained in love. It is an invitation to live authentically the relationship among brothers and sisters within the community (Eph 4:25). Christ is the goal of this growth. Growth is directed toward Him "in every aspect." Therefore it is not just spiritual growth but also growth that spills over every human activity into all realms of social and individual life, because love wants to inform the whole human person in his or her being and behavior.

The author employs various analogies to express the relationship between the Body and the Head, the church and Christ. From the Head, as source of life, comes the vital energy that permeates the whole Body, nourishes it, and unites it (Eph 4:16; see also Col 2:19). However, this vision that emphasizes Christ as source of life and principle of unity has the negative implication of presenting the church as passive, rather than as a "thou" before Christ. The personal response of the church, who lives her relationship with Christ as a relationship of mutual love, does not always appear. This fact was particularly felt by Chiara: "I understood I had been made Church in order to love Him."

The Letter develops another model present in the biblical tradition: the symbolism connected to the marital relationship between Christ and the church (Eph 5:22ff). In the New Testament, the Letter to the Ephesians is the writing that theologically most develops this marital relationship. One aspect emphasized by the marital reality is the relationship of love between two individuals who give themselves fully to each other. This love has unique qualities: for Christ, marriage-love means "to give oneself up" to the other (Eph 5:25) and thus generate the church as bride. For her part, the love of the church for the Groom (Christ) is expressed as openness and giving (Eph 5:24). And the Groom is always open to the bride, giving His grace at all times. The relationship of the two emphasizes the distinction of two individuals who are *united*. Therefore, there is a vital dynamic in the marriage of Christ and the church, a dynamic where the bride grows in love and unity

---

22. In NRSV, "Speak the truth in love." [Translator's note]

with the Groom, who gives the bride the grace to become a New Human Being. In the words of the letter:

> In the same way, husbands should love their wives as they do their own bodies. He who loves his wife loves himself. For no one ever hates his own body, but he nourishes and tenderly cares for it, just as Christ does for the church, because we are members of his body. (Eph 5:28-30)

In the verses above, the author joined the reality of marital relationship with the one of the Body of Christ, thanks to the term "body," which is synonymous with "flesh" (see Gen 2:24 and Eph 5:30). In the marital union, the two become one flesh and therefore one Body. In the verses under consideration (28-29) the analogy focuses on the love of the husband who sees his wife as another self. "To love one's body," rendered as "loving himself," reminds one of the commandment, "Love your neighbor as yourself." Applied to the relationship of Christ-church, and therefore to the mutual love of the life of unity, this commandment receives its fulfillment, so to speak: "the neighbor and I-myself coincide."[23] This coinciding is something on which Chiara's mystical intuition insists: "I am you, you are me, because on the nothingness of mutual love, we are all Jesus." The author of the letter alludes to this "mystery" by inserting verse 30 "because we are members of his Body." He does not mention the church but talks about "we," and therefore the author shifts from the analogy Christ-church to a level that entails participation that makes one Body out of the two.

The Dynamic Experience of Church as Chiara's Mystical Experience

In Chiara's ecclesiological vision, the relationship between church, Body of Christ, and church-Bride of Christ is relevant to the experience of unity. She and her companions identified first with Christ in the mystical experience of having entered the Bosom of the Father. Therefore, Chiara Lubich emphasized the "same nature" of Head and Body. The Soul-Church (Chiara and her companions as one Soul that is also in that unity the church) lives the fullness of the relationship with Christ as the Bride of Christ: She understood she had been made church in order to love Him. "And so the Word wedded the Soul in a mystical marriage."

---

23. See Bouttier, *L'Épître de Saint Paul aux Ephésiens*, 246.

This experience of the authentic church is remarkable:

- As Bride, the church is a subject capable of loving;

- The fullness of the relationship with Christ is given only to the church, not to an isolated individual except by participation, in unity, to the church. Congar wrote, "All [Christians] are Brides but they are seen and willed to be so by God, as members of the Bride who is the Church."[24]

- The following text by Chiara summarizes well the bridal dimension of the relationship that takes place in a "collective spirituality":

> When any soul, because it is virgin, says that it is the bride of Christ, it lies if that soul is not *Church*. Only now, after our souls, *because of Jesus among them*, have been wedded to one another and are Church (because they are Christ: one Christ and three Christs or as many Christs as souls of ours who in this way are united, one Church and many Churches), can they say, both in unity with the others and *individually* (because each soul has the value of all, that is, of *Jesus* in their midst), that they are brides of Christ. In fact, Jesus can wed only Jesus. For Jesus is not *One* but with Himself.

Here, Chiara does not argue against traditional mysticism, that is, the experience of the individual soul as Bride of Christ, but gives an important criterion for understanding authentic mysticism as well as the life of faith. The spousal experience is possible only because the mystic (the believer) is a member of the Bride, the church who possesses this relationship with Christ. This is what happens in the spirituality of unity.

The church-Bride, whose "I" is Christ present in her, lives the loving relationship with the Groom in more than a sentimental way. Chiara Lubich's whole being was involved in her mystical experience: "My sweetest Spouse. . . . All that is left for me is to swoon into You, to die again into your Heart, consumed by your love!" While this was true, she also emphasized that based on love as expressed in Ephesians 5:24, loving submission to Christ includes: "If you love me, you will keep my commandments" (Jn 14:15).

---

24. Yves Congar, "La personne 'Eglise,'" *Revue Thomiste* 4 (1971): 639.

Therefore, the Word is relevant as the expression of a lived relationship. It is being open to the gospel that nurtures the spousal relationship between the church and Christ and makes her grow. In unity lived out in mutual love, which is the commandment par excellence, the dynamic relationship of the growth of the church toward Christ, between the New Human Being and the Perfected Human Being, is fulfilled:

> To live the reality of the marriage of my Soul with the Word, "Love," who I saw in Paradise after the Father (Infinite Love), I must be only *Word of God*.

> Every instant I live the Word is a kiss upon the Lips of Jesus, which spoke only Words of Life. And from Lips to lips passes the Word; He communicates Himself (who is Word) to my Soul. And I am one with Him! And Christ is born in me.

The Word, the gospel as something to be lived out, is understood not as pure intellectual knowledge but as life that is shared by self-giving through the kiss on the lips, that is, in the very contact with the Person who speaks it. In his Word, Christ brings about his self-giving gift that makes him "alive" in the community and in each member. Another text, also of spousal flavor, confirms this concept:

> Jesus from the tabernacle taught me how I should draw Him to myself with love, almost breathing Him into me, and how He was the Word of Life and how *living* the *Word* I would love Him as Bride and He would be me. . . . *by living the Word in each instant.*

This passage says in different words what Jesus promises in the Gospel of John, "Those who love me will keep my word and my Father will love them and we will come to them and make our home with them" (Jn 14:23). As the commandment par excellence in the Gospel of John is mutual love, it is in the "mutual nothing," and therefore in the life of unity that makes the church, that this relationship is best lived in a spousal manner.

Regarding the growth of the Body of Christ toward Christ and of the spousal relationship between Christ and the church, the Letter to the Ephesians had not yet recognized in the Bride the face of Mary, which later Mariology-ecclesiology developed. On this point, Chiara Lubich makes a Mariological connection that is well attested in theology. However, I would like to offer not just a "reflection" of Chiara Lubich but a mystical experience she had, whose originality is given by the charism of unity. There is a deep consistency here with the ecclesiology in the Letter to the Ephesians:

> One day,[25] one of us suggested consecrating ourselves to Mary, that is to say, consecrating the Soul to Mary. It was the will of all, and in the morning at Holy Communion each of us asked Jesus-Eucharist to consecrate the Soul to Mary, as he intended, asking him to reveal, then, what had taken place in us. As soon as we asked this, the Soul understood that it had become Mary or, better, that it had that same *flesh*, in which she was contained, *immaculatized*. The second rebirth, that of the Spirit, had done so much. Indeed, the Soul understood immediately that our being consecrated by Jesus to Mary was our being *consecrated as Mary*, that is, making us sacred with Mary, like Mary. Our flesh, then, was Marian. The outburst of joy in us was immense.

It was probably the devotion to Mary that suggested this consecration. However, the effects go well beyond devotion and are to be interpreted in light of the charism of unity and, therefore, from the perspective of church. It seems to me that there is an experience of mystical identification with Mary that goes beyond, or is distinct from, the one expressed as "Mary's face of the Church-Bride." In this latter case, Mary's attitude, described in the Annunciation story, is relived by the church and is the typical attitude of the church as Bride, as described in Eph 5:24. It entails submission that is receptive love, made of complete openness to God, of receiving Christ, who communicates himself in the Word and dwelling in the church, temple of the Divine Presence (Eph 2:22).

Now, in Chiara Lubich's case, Christ produced an identification that I would call "existential"—not simply symbolic—with Mary: the experience of having *Marian flesh*. Chiara talks about a "second rebirth, that of the Spirit." This is not the baptismal immaculatization (Eph 5:27) that is the first rebirth but the full accomplishment of the baptismal reality in the life of unity. This experience continues on the following day, July 28, 1949, when it becomes more fully understood:

> But what happened after that was even more marvelous. The following day, we – united – being Mary, the Immaculate, went to Holy Communion, and let Jesus illuminate us on the other mys-

---

25. Probably July 27, 1949.

teries that were happening in us within Paradise. As soon as Jesus had entered into me, I heard distinctly, with the hearing of the soul, a voice: "*Pregnant*," the meaning of which was immediately revealed to me as: "I swathe you within," that is, in your immaculate flesh I now form my Son, or better: your immaculate flesh I transform into divinized flesh, into that of Jesus, in such a way as to make of you "another Jesus" in the truest sense of the word. And I had the impression that Jesus was growing within me to the point of taking my place completely, the place of my immaculate flesh. It was the mystical incarnation!

The experience of having "Mary's flesh" has now a clear purpose: being "pregnant." The Soul that has the *flesh* of Mary is made capable of "generating," of becoming Mother to the mystical incarnation. Through the spousal union, the Soul becomes a tabernacle of Jesus present within her. But the Soul is also Mother, because she is capable of giving Christ to the world by generating him outside of herself, which is possible only if she contains Christ given to the world.

In the maturity of the "second rebirth," the Soul has become capable of offering to the church and the world Jesus generated in the life of unity:

> The Church is Mother because she is not only the recipient nor only the channel of grace but an essential aspect of the grace she receives is that she becomes able to participate to the whole divine life and the communication of this life, because it is the life of *agape*.[26]

The movement expressed in this mystical experience is remarkable: the Soul, being Mary, generates the Son, not as distinct from herself, not by separating herself from him as in any normal motherhood. On the contrary, she becomes the Christ she generates, "your immaculate flesh I transform into divinized flesh, into that of Jesus, in such a way as to make of you 'another Jesus' in the truest sense of the word."

The ecclesiology of the Letter to the Ephesians sheds light on this point: the church, Body of Christ, takes on her universal mission and lives out her vocation not by abandoning her identity of Body of Christ but by growing toward Christ (Eph 1:22ff, 4, 16). Thus, the church becomes increasingly

---

26. Louis Bouyer, *L'Eglise de Dieu* (Paris: Cerf, 1970), 658.

more Christ-like, that is, letting herself be increasingly transformed by the Lord who is generated within her. To reach Christ, the church does not have to go to great distances outside of herself but let herself be "divinized" by Christ, who lives in her deepest recesses. In love, the Body builds itself, says the letter (Eph 4:16). When *agape* is the law of the life of the Soul, the Soul is completely permeated by the pleroma that dwells within her. And thereby the love of Christ, which takes away all divisions (the Crucified one creates unity), can emerge and become a compelling witness.

Chiara Lubich's notes explain that at the beginning of this contemplative period of time, God had given her a magnificent vision of "Mary, Mother of God, God-bearer." Then at a certain point, God gave her what he had already shown her. He gave the Soul with "Mary's flesh" the "true Jesus," that is, the Risen Christ who becomes visible in the "nothingness" of mutual love. The Christ of the "second rebirth" (in the pascal event of death and resurrection) is the true and final "God-with-us." The maternity of Mary is fulfilled in the maternity of the Soul-church: it is "the mystical incarnation." *Unity is the mother of God-with-us.*

Agape-Love

From the Letter to the Ephesians

In the Letter to the Ephesians, the typical sign of the church is the unity already in place between Jews and Gentiles thanks to the Crucified and Risen One who united in one Body these human categories, symbol of a permanent division (see Eph 2:11-12). The parenthetical part of the letter, the exhortations in the second part of the letter, starting from chapter 4, aim at preserving this unity in the daily life of the believers. The exhortation aims at promoting the unity of the Body of Christ among the members. Hence the initial recommendation provides the tone:

> I therefore . . . beg you to lead a life worthy of the calling to which you have been called, with all humility and gentleness, with patience, bearing with one another in love, making every effort to maintain the unity of the Spirit in the bond of peace. (Eph 4:1-3)

Unity[27] is the distinct feature of the church and thus the vocation of every Christian. The author therefore sees in unity the most important task

---

27. In all of the New Testament, the noun "unity" appears only in Eph 4:3, 13.

to carry out. To do this, the author mentions three virtues: humility, meekness, and patience. The context clearly says that these are not qualities that each individual has to develop privately but qualities that are needed to live out the relationship within the community. Humility in the life of unity consists in "being nothingness," which entails deep and complete openness to one's brother or sister and makes room for Christ, who is present in the relationship of mutual love. One who is meek knows to respond with calmness to violence and thus diffuse it. Patience in relationships with brothers and sisters is contrary to intolerance and haste: It is knowing how to make room for the other just as he or she is.

Virtues are therefore unifying qualities of *agape*. Concretely, "bearing with one another" is what is needed. This is at the foundation of life together, the remedy that heals the inevitable conflicts, psychological or of other kinds. This has the purpose of keeping the unity alive that comes from the Holy Spirit. Living unity brings about peace, the eschatological good that envelops the church and all of creation (Eph 1:10). The tone is set, and the letter immediately introduces the reader to a Christian ethics aimed at the life of communion, and therefore at a "collective spirituality" that lives out this communion in the relationships among brothers and sisters in the covenant with God.

From Chiara Lubich's Writings

This logic of Christian ethics is found in Chiara's texts, where she draws a distinction between ethics based on the development of virtues and the "pascal" ethics of the life of unity: "To have God we must lose the virtues: *all of them*. This too is a secret that has burst from the Wound of Jesus Forsaken." Chiara Lubich explains, "Jesus Forsaken teaches us to be nothing and so one has everything, God, who is Love."[28] Chiara Lubich certainly does not question the existence and value of the virtues; rather, she questions an ethics that bases Christian behavior on a planned development of virtues in order to achieve individual perfection: This a self-centered morality. The "nothingness" of love, in the measure of Jesus Forsaken, who has in himself all the eschatological powers of "divinization," includes all the virtues but as expressions of love, therefore as "fruits of the Spirit" (Gal 5:22f). It is not about perfecting one's

---

28. At an Abba School meeting.

ego but about giving oneself to *agape*. In other words, one needs to lose one's ego in the non-being of love and be perfected by God.[29]

For the author of the letter, love, lived out, brings about growth toward Christ (Eph 4:15). The church is herself in as much as, because of mutual love, she lets the face of her Lord shine through her. Chiara Lubich wrote the following on this topic:

> Whoever lives in the brother or sister does not have the virtues as they are normally understood: he or she is *nothing*; and what is nothing has *nothing*: it does not have purity, nor humility, nor patience, nor self-mortification, and so on, because it is nothing. Therefore true purity is the purity of purity, humility is the humility of humility, patience is the patience of patience, and so on. That is, the virtues "in the style of the Trinity," as we put it, which is to say, as they are lived by the Trinity which is Love. Now, a soul in which a particular *virtue* is noticeable, in reality has the opposite vice. In fact, someone who speaks ill of self is spiritually proud, at least unless such speech is used *to love* a neighbor, but then it is not humility, it is charity and to charity everything is permitted.

In this text, *agape* is understood as the "fullness of virtues" (paraphrasing Paul), as their fulfillment that includes and at the same time transcends them. Mortification is there, as well as purity, patience, and the other virtues, which are expressions of the love of neighbor: They are faces of the non-being of love ("purity of purity . . .").

There appears a complete difference between virtue-based morality and unity-based morality (a Paschal morality). Virtue-based morality leads to a virtuous individual who is in control; the unity-based morality leads the individual to being a new creation, a New Human Being. However, as Chiara Lubich reminds us, to become such, one needs to be the "nothing" (the non-being of love), because only then is there room for the Spirit of God that divinizes and unifies. Therefore: "Whoever lives unity has found God as God has never been found before. Going beyond personal perfection (still a seeking after self), he or she *believes all things* and lives Jesus who is in the midst. He or she is Jesus."

---

29. And this perfection lies in the "divinization" that only God can bring about, and in the attainment of one's own vocation, in one's own human-divine design, personal and unique for everyone.

In this "being Jesus" of each person, that is, in reflecting on one's own being the fullness of the presence of Christ in the community (in the unity of two or three . . .), the church is built as the Body of Christ. In the perspective of the letter: In love, each one becomes a channel through which the Life that comes from the Head can obtain the unity of the Body (Eph 4:15-16). All this "morality" is consistent with the life of faith: "Whenever I am weak, then I am strong" (1 Cor 12:10). In the Letter to the Ephesians, as well as for Chiara Lubich, the life of unity is the foundation of Christian ethics. Living the presence of Christ and being church, His Body, are indivisibly connected. Living "in love" brings about both realities in a dynamic of growth that increasingly tends toward elevating and building up the "fullness of Body of Christ" (Eph 4:13). This is the true identity of the church: from the Body, to the dwelling of the Fullness (pleroma) of Christ (Eph 1:23), to the "fullness of Christ" (Eph 4:13).

This ethical-ecclesial concept needs to be included in the broader Design of God on creation, as presented both in the letter and in Chiara Lubich's mystical writings. The invitation to love, to "maintain the unity of the Spirit in the bond of peace" (Eph 4:3), is part of the broader Divine Design that brings it about in history. Knowledge of the "Mystery"—the goal of the letter—leads to contemplation that in turn leads to praise and thanksgiving but also prompts action: It is indispensable in order to accomplish God's universal Design already here on earth. Conversely, this knowledge shapes the actions of each person, whose "love," even if minuscule, is part of the great Divine Design begun with the Risen Crucified Lord: universal recapitulation.

The Use of "In Love" in Ephesians

I would like to conclude by underscoring the relevance of the expression "in love" in the Letter to the Ephesians. The expression appears six times (Eph 1:4; 3:17; 4:2,15,16; 5:2) in the letter and only four other times in the entire New Testament. The expression suggests, and the context confirms this suggestion, that love is not understood as one of the virtues, not even as the greatest of them, nor it is identified with acts of charity, even if they are a natural consequence of love. The author writes, "Be imitators of God, as beloved children, and live in love, as Christ loved us and gave himself up for us" (Eph 5:1-2). "Living in love" is about a way of being that imbues the whole Christian existence and expresses a life whose source and model is God's love, which manifests itself in the Crucified One. "Be imitators of God": this daring expression is unparalleled in the New Testament, though it is a biblical concept (see Deut 5:12-15; Lk 6:36; Mt 5:45; 18:33). It invites one to enter into the perspective of God, who self-revealed as Love.

Love is therefore the foundation of Christian life, the soil in which the life of unity has its roots (see Eph 3:17: "rooted in love"). As such, *agape* is also the unifying force that makes the community grow toward its goal, a growth into a shared nature, which leads the church to be increasingly like Christ, her Beginning. Therefore love brings the great Divine Design to its fulfillment (Eph 4:15, 16).

Finally, when the author of the letter says that the Father "chose us in Christ before the foundation of the world to be holy and blameless before Him *in love*" (Eph 1:4), it is clear that love is not just a means for growth but the very goal. Love is an eschatological reality identified with Life in Paradise, the fullness of life to which we are called. It is "in love" that makes us "holy and blameless," so that we come to participate in the "fullness of God" (Eph 3:19). "The revelation of God in Jesus Christ is the rising of love as universe is destined to be."[30] Whatever is at the origin, what moves God to act is also God's final goal: revealing to all and for all ages that everything is love (Eph 2:4-7). It is *love* as the essential feature of God and of Paradise that strikes Chiara Lubich, and remained consistently present in her experience and reflections. On this Paradise, which is the Divine Design for humanity and creation, I conclude this study comparing the Letter to the Ephesians and Chiara's mystical experience.

---

30. Baulès, *L'Insondable Richesse du Christ*, 102.

Part Five

Implications of Paradise '49
for Humanity and the Church

Chapter Eighteen

Towards an Understanding of the Human Person According to the Mystical Experience of Chiara Lubich in the Paradise of '49

Callan Slipper

Chiara Lubich's mystical experience in what has come to be called the "Paradise of '49" contains a rich and complex structure of thought. In this article I attempt to offer some first notions of an analysis of this thought insofar as it touches upon the human person.

The category "person" is not looked at explicitly by Chiara's[1] mysticism. The word "person" is used principally for two common meanings: for the individual human subject and (with an initial capital letter) for a divine *hypostasis*. Nonetheless the person, meaning by that the deep reality of the human being as seen from the perspective of a philosophical, or perhaps better theological, anthropology, as it emerges in the various genres of writing used by Chiara during that period of particular illumination, is fundamental for understanding her thought. In this sense the category stands beneath and supports Chiara's discourse, implicit and necessary for its coherence, and so it can become a useful tool to assimilate and understand this discourse more fully. To give an example, it is a little like the categories used in Trinitarian theology which are an instrument for understanding the content of biblical discourse even though they are not explicitly present in scripture itself. In the case of the "person," however, the word itself is actually part of the lexicon of the original experience, and it has a sense close, even though only partially so, to its meaning in this study – something that cannot be said of *hypostasis* and *ousia* with regard to the Bible.

This means that this article's methodology is one of an attentive reading of what the author says, in a search to draw out in a systematic manner the theological structure of her thought. Chiara's writings under consideration are not formally "theological," but they contain concepts that have powerful

---

1. Chiara Lubich is universally known simply as "Chiara." I shall follow this practice.

theological impact. This study, therefore, creates a theological "meta-discourse." It is not so much a parallel reflection as an exposition of the presuppositions necessary for the structure of the original discourse. And this implies that the author's mystical language is assumed into a theological discourse that, despite the terminological closeness of the original and of its interpretation, requires hermeneutical mediation.

I think it may be helpful to start with some summary definitions of the "person" as the category emerges in Chiara's writing. The significance of these will become clear as the exposition proceeds:

1) *In brief*
The person is the dynamic in which a specific human being is a created word in the uncreated Word.

2) *Expanded*
The person is the subject where the relational dynamic in which a specific human being—as the image of God and therefore *capax Christi*, making him or herself nothing for love affirms self—is a created word in the uncreated Word. This is exemplified in the Virgin Mary.

3) *In other words*
The person is the capacity of a created being *actively* to welcome God into itself.

To understand the implications of these definitions I shall begin by examining the person's creaturely condition. Just like every other thing in the cosmos, the person is created. It is necessary, however, to distinguish what the person shares in an identical fashion with all other created things and what instead differentiates it from them and is specifically characteristic of the person.

Divine Creativity

The starting point of Chiara's thought is that things, before they are created, that is, before they are given existence in distinction from God, exist as ideas in the mind of God. Here she recovers, certainly in an original fashion, the ancient tradition of the divine ideas. It is not possible within the confines of an article to conduct a comparison of her thought with this rich tradition.[2]

---

2. The tradition has its roots in Plato even though the notion of God having knowledge of created things before their creation or a knowledge of things distinct from

It should be sufficient to say that Chiara uses terminology that recalls this tradition to express her own mystical vision and that she does not in any direct way enter into a philosophical discussion. To understand her thought, however, and in agreement with this tradition, it is possible to assert that "to talk about 'the divine ideas' cannot be taken to refer to realities in God which are in any way distinct either from the divine essence or from one another. If there were any distinction at all, it would be a real distinction; and a real distinction cannot be admitted."[3] Thus, since they are God's ideas, the ideas are not distinct from God. Their being is the same being as God's.

For a Christian vision such as Chiara's, the ideas within the Trinitarian dynamic have their existence in the Word who is God's Idea of Godself. The ideas exist in plurality within the simplicity of God[4] and hence ontological-

---

and determinative of their concrete created existence (sometimes called "exemplarism") is not of itself necessarily Platonic: the notion has the same pattern as Platonism and indeed can use Platonism, but in Christian thinkers such exemplarism is always structured according to a Christian vision of the world. It has been very influential in Christian theology and mysticism, coming via Augustine to the Medieval period in several different versions (see Etienne Gilson, *History of Christian Philosophy in the Middle Ages* [London: Sheed and Ward, 1955]; Frederick Copleston, *A History of Philosophy*, Vol. 3 [London: Continuum, 2003]), ranging from those considered heretical, such as the thought of Duns Scotus Eriugena (see *De divisione naturae*, and also Henry Bett, *Johannes Scotus Erigena, a Study of Medieval Philosophy* [Cambridge: Hyperion Press, 1925]; Dermot Moran, *The Philosophy of John Scotus Eriugena: a study of idealism in the Middle Ages* [Cambridge: CUP, 1989]), to those of recognized doctors of the Church such as Bonaventure of Bagnoreggio (see *Commentary on the Sentences [of Peter Lombard]* and *De scientia Christi* which formed the matrix for his later writing) or Thomas Aquinas, especially in the *Summa Theologica* q. 15 (see Gregory T. Doolan, *Aquinas on the Divine Ideas as Exemplar Causes* [Catholic University of America Press, 2008], Vivian Boland, *Ideas in God According to Saint Thomas Aquinas: sources and synthesis* [Leiden, Netherlands: Brill, 1996]). In the following centuries the tradition was not lost and it appears for example in an English context in the thought of Samuel Taylor Coleridge, (see "On the Divine Ideas," *Opus Maximum*, [Huntington Library MS HM 8195]), and in the Idealism of Berkley, (see Stephen Daniel, "Berkley's Christian Neoplatonism, Archetypes, and Divine Ideas," *Journal of the History of Philosophy* [2001]). For modern examples see also Marc A. Hight, *Idea and ontology: an essay in early modern metaphysics of ideas* (University Park: Pennsylvania State University, 2008), R. Baine Harris, *Neoplatonism and contemporary thought*, Part 2 (New York: SUNY Press, 2002).

3. Frederick Copleston, *A History of Philosophy*, Vol. 3 (London: Continuum, 2003), 88.
4. As Thomas Aquinas demonstrates in the *Summa Theologica* q. 15, a. 2: "Now there cannot be an idea of any whole, unless particular ideas are had of those parts of which the whole is made; just as a builder cannot conceive the idea of a house unless he has the idea of each of its parts. So, then, it must needs be that in the divine

ly they are not distinct from one another because, in the Word, they are not distinct from God. They exist as ideas with the Idea, which is to say as words within the Word, *logoi* within the *Logos*.[5] They are the richnesses, the infinite shades of the beauty of the Word. Referring to these beauties, Chiara uses the expressions "ideas" and "words" in a way that is almost interchangeable, employing, however, each term to underline something in particular. "Ideas" indicate more their existence in the mind of God[6] and "words" indicate their relationship of unity with the Word.[7] Therefore, since it must be affirmed that the Word of God and the ideas-words are one, without difference of separation, it must also be affirmed that, as "words in the Word," the ideas-words are all uncreated and without the limitations of created things; hence they are eternal, each full of the beauty that is the Word.

They are made to have existence distinct from the Word, and hence as different and diverse from the Word, by their creation. They change their ontological state. From being uncreated they pass to being created, with all the limitations of creatureliness, limitations that God, precisely by

---

mind there are the proper ideas of all things . . . . Now it can easily be seen how this is not repugnant to the simplicity of God, if we consider that the idea of a work is in the mind of the operator as that which is understood, and not as the image whereby he understands, which is a form that makes the intellect in act. For the form of the house in the mind of the builder, is something understood by him, to the likeness of which he forms the house in matter. Now, it is not repugnant to the simplicity of the divine mind that it understand many things; though it would be repugnant to its simplicity were His understanding to be formed by a plurality of images. Hence many ideas exist in the divine mind, as things understood by it."

5. Maximus the Confessor says in the *Ambiguum* 7 that before the ages God contains within Godself the *logoi* of all created things. This is a version of the doctrine of the divine ideas and God by means of these *logoi* brings from non-being to being the whole visible and invisible creation. See Torstein Tollefsen, *The Christocentric cosmology of St. Maximus the Confessor* (Oxford: OUP, 2008).

6. As we have seen, speaking of the "ideas," Chiara employs terms and a pattern of thought similar to Plato's. Her vision is not a kind of Neoplatonism, as indeed it was not in the similar case of the Fathers of the Church, such as Augustine, who use Platonic elements to develop their own thought. According to Chiara the ideas exist in the mind of God, which is the Word, and so they are the eternal truth of things. Chiara then, like Thomas Aquinas, associates the idea with the form of a thing. The terminology is derived from the Western philosophical tradition, but in Chiara is given an original interpretation linked specifically to her mystical experience.

7. The use of the term "words" for the truth of things recalls Maximus the Confessor. It is a Christian "exemplarism" that clearly associates the ideas of things with their existence in God's Logos, the eternal Word.

being God, does not have. They have, therefore, characteristics that God in Godself does not have: their creatureliness and the qualities this brings with it, namely, finitude, temporality, incapacity, ignorance, the possibility of suffering. This view is not pantheistic, therefore, because the difference between God and things, as indeed their absolute dependence upon God, is clear. What, in a certain sense, things give to God is the creaturely experience of limitation; that is, an experience outside God of that which God is not, which God, however, in Godself already knows since each thing is an idea of God.

In creation the ideas-words are projected outside God. From being One they pass to being many. Insofar as they are always divine ideas, they remain in God, one with God, but insofar as they are created they are distinct from God and multiple. Their coming out from God, as God's act, takes place according to God's Trinitarian nature, as Chiara puts it:

> When God created, he created all things from nothing because he created them from himself – from nothing means that they did not pre-exist because he alone pre-existed (but this way of speaking is inexact because in God there is no before and after). He, however, drew them out from himself because in creating them he died (of love), he died in love, he loved and so he created.[8]
>
> Just as the Word, who is the Idea of the Father, is God, analogously the ideas of things, which "ab aeterno" are in the Word, are not abstract but are reality: word in the Word.
>
> The Father projects them, as in divergent rays, "outside himself," that is, in a new and different dimension, a created one, where he gives them "Order that is Life and Love and Truth." There is in them, thus, the imprint of the Uncreated, of the Trinity.[9]

These two brief passages summarize how God creates. God's "death" in creating, in fact, replicates the way that God lives eternally in Godself, where each Person gives himself, making himself nothing, to the others. Thus, for example, the Father who is the root of all, gives himself to the Son giving him the whole of himself – if he were to keep anything for himself the Son

---

8. From Chiara Lubich's notes. Unless otherwise stated all references are to these notes from 1949 which are as yet unpublished. Translations of all texts from 1949 are mine.
9. A comment by Chiara at a later date on a passage from 1949.

would not be one with the Father, identical with the Father, but would be something else. Instead, giving everything, and in this sense dying because he keeps nothing for himself, the Father generates in such a way that the Son is truly another self, the perfect Idea of himself.

This dynamic is fundamental to Chiara's thought, rooted in the understanding of the being of God as complete self-noughting,[10] a gift of self to the other which makes the other be; that is, it is love because it empties itself, makes itself nothing for the other (just as we can see illustrated in Jesus who at the climax of his earthly existence, when he is fully himself in the total gift of self – "Although he was a Son, he learned obedience through what he suffered; and having been made perfect, he became the source of eternal salvation for all who obey him" (Heb 5:8-9) – dies forsaken upon the cross (Mt 27:46; Mk 15:34). It is thus a being love that is always dynamic, always in motion, because it always gives itself. And at the same time as it "makes itself the other," noughting itself for the other and bringing the other to be, it affirms itself because it brings itself into existence in relation to the other: the Father generates the Son and is Father because without the Son the Father does not exist.

In creating, God acts in an analogous fashion. The Father, looking at the Son, gives himself, giving his being by participation to the ideas-words (the "words in the Word"), and in that way clothing that which is not, the nothing, with his being, the very being of God. Created things *in themselves are not and remain nothing*, but they have being insofar as it is *given to them by participation*.

This means that creation, even though it is created and distinct from God and always dependent upon God, is, in its being, God. It is an externalized "God," a "God" transferred outside Godself, a "God" that has become other. Certainly things are always nothing in themselves, but insofar as they are, they are constantly created by God. Their being is "God," a "God," so to speak, who is created and so having all the characteristics proper to creatures (finitude, temporality, incapacity, ignorance, the possibility of suffering).

An eschatological perspective can help in understanding things more fully. For if things remain only as they are in creation, they *express* the ideas-words but not *are* them, because in themselves they are nothing. One could say that they are only partially themselves. To be fully themselves they

---

10. The neologism "self-noughting" is used to indicated a dynamic way of taking on nothingness. "Nought" is synonymous with nothing.

would have to be fully their ideas-words, and therefore fully God. They require divinization. To achieve this they have to overcome not only any kind of deviation from the idea-word they express, as is the case in human sinfulness, but in some way they must overcome their creaturely limits, even though in some way retaining them, paradoxically, in that they remain creatures. This can only come about if with their creaturely limitations they participate fully in their ideas-words, being united to the Word who contains all the ideas-words without distinctions in himself. Like this they are united with the Word and between themselves. Therefore, a return to God is implicit in their exit from God. Which is to say that the "divergent rays" must become "convergent rays." Chiara's vision, in fact, is strongly eschatological and normally when she speaks of the divine ideas, she speaks of them in their fulfillment, when all will be returned into God, and God is all in all – which is to say when, even though always remaining creatures, their participation in the divine being is fully realized and they are fully united to their ideas and live the divine life.

The nature of things

a) The Ontological Dynamic of Love

Before their fulfillment in the *eschaton*, in their condition as created and limited (when, that is, they are a nothing only partially united to the all of God), created things reflect the being that God gives them by participation. Their way of being, while having the limitations of creation, and hence also in distinction from God, is according to the nature of the being they participate in, and hence according to the Trinity. The basis for this can already be seen in their existence in God as words in the Word. If when they are expressed these words are each one the expression of what is eternally in the Word, the word of each expression does not lose its identity with the Word, in which it remains contained. Hence the Word contains all and in the all contains all the words that are identical with the all. A specific created thing, therefore, inasmuch as it is an expression of a word in the Word, contains the stars, the mountains, the animals, and all human beings. Thus even if a thing were to attempt to separate itself from other things, it could not do so. No thing exists without all the others. Separation can only exist as an illusion.

Consequently things are in relationship with one another because they only exist together and therefore they make one another exist; that is, one thing depends upon the others, and all things depend upon each single thing and, in this way, each particular, single thing makes the other things exist. It is a gift that each thing gives to the others. In the concreteness of created existence, then, all things make effective the gift that they are in many different manners: co-operating with one another, mutually conditioning one another, dying and dissolving so that they become food or the elements from which others are constituted. In all of this they demonstrate that they are like the Trinity: each for the other, and giving themselves they affirm themselves. Therefore it is possible for Chiara to say:

> On earth all is in relationship of love with all: each thing with each thing. It is necessary to be Love to find the thread of gold among beings.
>
> In fact in Creation all is Trinity: Trinity, things in themselves because their *Being* is Love, is Father; the Law in them is Light, is Son, Word; the Life in them is Love, is Holy Spirit. The All given through participation to the Nothing.

The nothingness of things, therefore, has a double sense. The first is that in itself each thing does not exist and depends radically and totally on God. It exists only because it participates in God in a Trinitarian manner, that is, in each divine Person according to what is specific to that Person. This means that the "*vestigia trinitatis*"—the "traces of the Trinity"—which can be seen impressed upon things, are neither arbitrary nor metaphorical, but are the presence of God, not God in Godself but God shared outside Godself. All creation is God's gift and is given by God's participation precisely in the continuous creative act in which it is given distinct existence by God. Creation has being because the only being is that of the divine, which comes from the source that is the Father; law (or form) because the ideas-words, which give the law (or the form) to things, remain in the Word, that is, in the mind of God; and life because the relating of things to one another, which is the result of the meeting of their being with their law (or form), is a sharing in the One who constitutes the eternal meeting between the source of being and the Word (who is the source's perfect and total expression), that is, the Holy Spirit. The second sense, then, is that things are nothing also because no thing can exist in itself without all the other things. In fact, the dynamic nothingness of being, given by participation from the Father, makes things be projected one towards the other and thus all reciprocally together; and the law of each thing, which is given by participation in the Word, puts each thing in a state of "being for" the other things and so they have no meaning on their own; and the mutual relating that is the life of things, which is a participation in the Holy Spirit, necessarily requires their interdependence. In other words, it could be said that being, form, and life are each one Love and this means that nothing exists on its own, in itself and for itself, and that therefore in itself each created thing is nothing.

What is more, in creation the "dynamic nothingness," the "being for," and the "mutual relating," three Loves that are a single Love and that reflect the Trinity, are affirmed in things supremely in their death, which is the moment of total self-emptying (reflecting the Father's total gift of himself), complete giving (reflecting the deep meaning of every word in the Word), and absolute loss of self in relationship (reflecting the Holy Spirit's being as relationship that keeps nothing for self). Seen like this, death is the climax of love. It is the moment when, since things are Love in its fullest, and hence the words pronounced in them are spoken at their fullest, things are most fully themselves. Making themselves nothing, therefore, they affirm themselves. Their nature thus reflects their origin, God who is One and Three, and it is fulfilled inasmuch as they live the dynamic of God as seen completely displayed in Jesus crucified and forsaken.

This dynamic does not tell us only something about the nature of things. It also expresses something extremely important for our understanding of the human person. Indeed, neither the specific fact of being in relationship, nor participating in the Trinity and the characteristic of having Trinitarian relationships, are definitions of what it means to be a person, because they are characteristic of all things. These things are necessary to be a person, because a person is a created word like all other things, but they are not sufficient. Even if, as we shall see, such things achieve their fullest meaning in the person, they belong in the first place to ontology and the understanding of being as such and not to anthropology and the understanding of what it is to be human.

b) *The Relationship between the Ideas-Words and Their Created Expressions*

This dynamic ontology of love requires a more profound exploration on one precise point: the relationship of created things to the ideas-words of which they are the expressions. A fundamental notion is that the idea-word of each thing is its model. It is for this reason that the idea-word in the Eternal Word is the law or the form of a thing. The model is the universal truth of all its various created expressions:

> Upon earth the plants have no head. There is no model pine. And yet there must be one, for children denote their father. The model pine is in the Word of God, is Word of God.

> At the end of time (and already now for God) the model of every pine, which is beneath each pine, will come into light and simultaneously the particular and the universal will be seen. Now, the head, together with the other models, is there above in the Word of God.

This, however, does not mean that the universal reality of things in the uncreated Word destroys or diminishes or in some way reduces the reality of created things. They are not illusory. God gives them reality precisely because the Word himself is present in the words expressed in creation:

> When I see the water of a lake projected upon the wall by the sun and see the play of the water upon the wall trembling in accord with the quivering of the true water, I think of creation.

> The Father is the true sun. The Word is the true water. The reflected lake is what is created. What is created is nothingness clothed in the Word: it is the Word reflected. Therefore what has "being" in the created is nothing but God. Except that, while the lake on the wall is false, in creation the Word is present and alive: "I am . . . the Life."

> In the created there is unity between God and nothingness. In the Uncreated, between God and God.

As already implicit in what has been said above with regard to how things participate in the Trinity, it can be seen that when God creates, God gives Godself in a real way; therefore things, participating in God, are real. This means that the individuality of the expressions of the Word is also real. Therefore the particular is never destroyed. Indeed, at the end of time when the participation of things in God will be realized:

> There Above will be the Idea and the various ideas of the same Idea; therefore there will be Unity and Trinity (variety). However, (as in the Trinity each one is God) each one of the various Ideas will have the value of the Idea: it will be God.

In a later comment, Chiara underlined the permanent value of every particular: "also the various ideas of the pine tree will be God." And again: "I am thinking for example, of a little bird. In paradise there will be the Idea of the bird and there will be all of its various ideas. It is likely, therefore, that there will also be this little bird 'clarified.'" Everything will be God. Hence things in the *eschaton*, bringing the nothing of their creatureliness, that which God does not have (is not) in Godself, to the model Idea of itself, will reach their fulfillment because the created expression will be permanently united to what it is eternally in the uncreated Word. And, in bringing about this return to the model, each thing will not be lost in a unity without qualifications, a kind of totalizing void, but, returning to the model Idea, the various ideas come back together, in all their variety. And precisely because they are not united only to the original Idea, their return does not happen only in a vertical direction, so to speak, that is, they are not united only to the original idea. To be united to the one model that contains the various ideas, the various expressions must be united among themselves. Among themselves, therefore, they come into a trinitarian relationship, which affirms both the particular and the unity of the particulars: "And they are Trinity among themselves, for the one is Son and Father to the other, and all draw together, loving one another, to the One, whence they came."

We can see, therefore, particular things as members of a "mystical body" of the model Idea. As in a "mystical body," then, all things *together* express the model and at the same time each thing, according to its *particularity*, also expresses the model. What is fulfilled in the *eschaton* thus indicates a relation according to the pattern of a "mystical body" that always exists, that is, which is ongoing from the initial creative act, between the model with its various ideas and the expressions of those ideas united among themselves. Things have a profound relationship with their model because it gives them their Form and they have a profound relationship also with the various ideas of their model because these give things them the specific form with which they express the model Form; and, for this very reason, they have then a profound relationship also with one another because they only exist together and without all the various other expressions no single expression exists. Indeed, all the various things are expressions of the forms of their model Form, and all are necessary to express the model Form. They are all, as it were, ideas in the Idea, which is to say, words in their Word that is originally within the eternal Word. This implies something important for created reality. It means that the structure of the "mystical body" is fundamental for nature and therefore for all created things:

The plants that we see now, such as for example the pines, are "members" of the model pine that is in the Word and hence are destined to be Word. Here too the mystery of the mystical Body in nature.

Clearly if human beings are also created realities, the structure of the Mystical Body, a term that obviously refers in the first instance to their relationship with Christ, is fundamental for them. In reality, as we shall see, this "mystical body" of Christ is essential for any other "mystical body" in nature.[11]

Human specificity

As has already been pointed out, human beings have all the characteristics inherent in created things. They have them, however, in a way that is absolutely distinct, because of their relationship both with nature and with the Word, and in particular with the Word incarnate, Jesus. It is at this point that we can understand their nature as persons.

a) Human Beings as Expression of the Whole of the Word

Human beings have the capability of expressing the whole of the Word. They are made in the image of God (Gn 1:26-27) and reflect the Word, who is the Son who "is the image of the invisible God, the firstborn of all creation" (Col 1:15). Human beings therefore reflect the Son who is incarnate in Jesus. Hence they are like Jesus: the expression of the entire Word. Jesus, however, is the very Word itself become incarnate because in him the Word takes human nature upon itself and with that takes on creatureliness.

---

11. The term "mystical body" used here is an original development within a long tradition that has its roots in one of the fundamental images of the New Testament, present in the Pauline corpus, that speaks of the Church. In 1 Corinthians and in Romans the image is rooted in the Semitic notion of the "body" which indicates the reality of a being in its relation to the world. To say that the Church is the body of Christ, thus, means two things: the identification of the Church with the person of Christ and that the Church is Christ acting today in the world. In the later literature, Colossians and Ephesians, the image undergoes a development and Christ is seen as the head to the Church, which is his body. The term used by Chiara has a wider sense than just the relationship between Christ and the Church; it includes, in a new synthesis, both the Pauline meanings. A "mystical body" has a head with which it is in such radical solidarity as to be the expression of that head in the world of history.

In him the uncreated assumes the created. Jesus, thus, expresses the Word in creation because he is that same Word who becomes a creature. The personal center that acts in him is the Word itself. Human beings, instead, are only the created expressions of the Word; they are not the Word itself present in creation. Jesus is the Word in creation, the Form of all made temporal and spatial, while human beings reflect him. Jesus is the Word who, assuming human nature, is the fulfillment of the human capacity to express the Word, while human beings are created beings who have this capacity but they have not necessarily fulfilled it. This means that human beings find their model, their reality fully expressed, in Jesus: "Jesus," Chiara writes, "is the model for human beings. He is the Human Being."

Hence human beings have a relationship with Jesus like that of the "mystical body" of created things with their ideas-words in the Word. The whole of humanity together and each person as an individual reflect Jesus. When human beings return to the Word, therefore, they do it because they are united to Jesus, becoming "another Son" because they participate in the Son even though they remain distinct from the Son:

> Humankind, instead, being immortal, will return into the Word: as son or daughter in the Son, but will be also distinct from the Son and another son or daughter of God.
>
> Having in self, however, the whole of the Word humankind too will be a mirror of the Universe which is in the Word. . .

Human beings are unique in creation. They reflect Jesus, who, being the Word incarnate, is in created form all that the Word is; for this reason he has in himself also the all the ideas contained in the Word. Every human being, however, is a particular way of being Jesus, that is, a *particular* idea of the *whole* of the Word. According to his or her specificity, then, the human person is one idea that exists in the Word, but according to his or her humanity each person is the whole of the Word, that Word expressed in the variety of the ideas-words projected outside God into creation. Hence, the word in the Word that is the idea of each human being is the entire Word contained in a single, particular word, the whole contained in a detail. For other created things, however, almost the reverse is the case. The ideas of created things are particulars that, through their unity in the Word, contain the whole, that is, all the other ideas to which they are united. But this is only "almost" the reverse, because the same is true of human beings in that they too are particular ideas in the Word. Therefore, they are the whole in a detail that is also a detail that contains the whole. In this way each one is a "version" of Jesus: the whole of the Word like he is, but also a particular idea of the Word expressed in creation. This is fundamental to understanding the person.

But it is necessary to underline something that gives special dignity to human beings. Their Form, their model, does not exist only in the uncreated Word, as is the case with the Forms of other created things. It is the whole of the uncreated Word who has entered into that part of creation capable of receiving him, that is, human nature, because it reflects him and is made according to his wholeness, according to the entire Word. To put it another way, while the models of non-human things, their "heads," exist in the uncreated, the head of the human Mystical Body exists in the uncreated that has become a creature like them.

And since he was always the Word, the Word made creature, Jesus, saw as the Word does. Therefore he was able to see the reality of things. He saw the created expressions and their forms in the Word (that is, in himself), including also the expression of that Form which is the wholeness of himself, human beings:

> At the end of time (and already now for God) the model of every pine, which is beneath each pine, will come into light and simultaneously the particular and the universal will be seen. Now, the head, together with the other models, is there above in the Word of God.
>
> But already now the head is beneath every created being and we do not see it except by faith, by participation in the divine life of Jesus. He sees it because he sees all as redeemed. And just as he sees in each human being the Human Being, that is, himself, the model of the human being, so already beneath the other creatures (such as for instance the pines) he sees the Idea, the Word, which is after all part (= the whole) of him. The human being (made in the image of God) is the whole of him; the plant is part of him (but = to him and it says: the human being (its God) is greater than I).

b) Human Beings as Words in the "Word"

Every person, therefore, as has been said, contains the whole and is also a particular expression of the whole. It is obvious, indeed, that we are not all the same! Particularity is characteristic of creation. In the human person this means that each one, even while containing the whole, is unrepeatable, unique. He or she is a specific Jesus.

Jesus, however, in his being the whole of the Word incarnate, does not cease to be uncreated even though he becomes a creature. The uniqueness of each other human person exists in Jesus because he is the very Word himself and everyone is also an idea in the Word, and remains an idea in the Word, even though, inasmuch as expressed outside God in creation, each one is distinct from God. This uniqueness has profound consequences. It means that persons, in their ideas, are truly words in the Word, and are to be found in the very intimacy of God. To touch a human person, therefore, is to touch the intimacy of God. Then, what happens in their creation is that this uniqueness in the heart of the Godhead comes to be expressed in the multiplicity of things. Consequently, also, it must be said that persons are expressed in the nothingness that creation is in itself and, just as for anything in creation, if persons remain without the being that comes from God, they remain nothing. Thus, just as for anything in creation, they can find their fulfillment only if they are united to their Idea in God; for the human person, this means to be united to his or her model, the Word incarnate in Jesus. If instead a person is not united to Jesus, that person remains empty, remains only a creature that in itself is nothing. If however the person returns to God, being united to his or her model, that person reaches the fullness of his or her reality. The expression is united to the Form, the created to the uncreated. Persons bring to God their creatureliness and now find that their nothing participates in the all of God. And it is precisely to make this possible that Jesus undertook his work of redemption:

> We are, in God, more intimate than God to himself because each of us is Word of God, a Word of God and, as a Word exists in the Word, likewise we are so much in God as to be God's intimate self. He has seen us, he sees us and will see us in the Word, in the heart of the Word, in the intimate self of the Trinity. And whoever touches us touches the Word, just as whoever loves us loves the Word of God. Here we see why the new commandment is to love our brother or sister, because this is to love the intimate self of God, the Heart of God.

> But in each Word is the whole of the Word just as in the Word is each Word.

> Therefore human beings are intimate to God <u>as</u> *God is to himself*. They are God if child of God. They are God through participation and *distinct* from God if living the Life that Jesus brought. If this Life is not lived, they are *God* because they remain Word of God, but not distinct because they do not accept participation. Such a one is a nothing that aspires to all separated from all.

The sorry possibility of hell is underlined in a later observation by Chiara: "Those who go to hell stay just the same in God's the mind, but they do not participate in that reality. Therefore their design, their Word is in God, is God, but they do not participate in it." With this Chiara emphasizes that the word of each person is that person's vocation; it is the person's fundamental reality, his or her deepest self, but it is also what a person must reach.

> I (the Idea of me) is "ab aeterno" [from all eternity] in the Mind of God, in the Word; therefore "ab aeterno" I am loved by the Father and "ab aeterno" I hold the place the Father has assigned me. And it is I there Above, that is, my true "I": Christ in me. There Above I am that Word of God which "ab aeterno" God has uttered.
>
> And I am God. Therefore, even were I not to be saved, God "ab aeterno" and for all eternity would see me and delight in me, just as I ought to have been.

Therefore the idea of a person, which is in God, and the person's "self," the person's "I," coincide; they are not two different things. There is no duality between each person and his or her idea in the Word. It is analogous to what happens in the incarnation, where there is no duality between the Word and Jesus, the "I" of the Word and the Word's reality as something created, human. Hence human persons, even with all the characteristics and the limits of created things, if united to Jesus, are united to their "I" which is an idea in the mind of God, and consequently is God. Jesus, who is in the bosom of the Father, since he is the Word which is always in the Trinity, brings them to be with himself in the bosom of the Father, united to their divine ideas. The vocation of a person, the person's living of his or her "I," therefore, is reached through Jesus, that is, if the person allows Jesus to live within.

This vocation is a process that begins already on this earth and ends only in the *eschaton*. It has, nonetheless, serious implications for life here and now. It means that the true personality of a person, that which is given by being a word in the Word, is Jesus who lives in the person. And if this is true, one's true personality can be achieved only by loving, loving with the same love that can be seen in Jesus, which is a dynamic nothingness since Jesus lives in exactly the same manner as God the Trinity in God's intra-trinitarian relationships.[12] The human person, in a manner analogous to the divine dynamic nothingness – to the extent possible for a creature – affirms his or her true personality, his or her true "I," by losing self out of love.

Still more, in strict relationship with the love that loses everything, there is another highly significant fact. If the true "I" of a person is Jesus, to be it a person can never close in on self, concentrating, as it were, only on his or her specific word without entering into relationship with other words. To do so would be a deformation. Each person, each word in the Word, must be open to all the others for an ontological reason. That is, if the person is not all the words that Jesus is, if the person is not united to the whole of Jesus, the person is not even him or herself. A relationship of unity with the others like him or herself, as for all things which must be united among themselves when they are united to their model, is necessary. One cannot become the model Form without entering into unity with all the other particular forms.

c) Human Beings as "Creation in Miniature"

The fact of expressing, containing in potential, the whole of the Word, who has been expressed also in the projection outside God of the ideas-words in the Word in the entire cosmos, brings with it another aspect, already touched upon, that specifically distinguishes human beings. They recapitulate all things, both as a species, because all together they express the Word, and as individual persons, because the "I" of each person is Jesus, the Word humanized, the model of each one and of the entire species. Therefore "the human being, the last to be created, is also the summary of all creation." This fact implies a key role for human beings in creation. If the entire creation is summed up in human beings, then what happens to them affects the whole of creation. Through them, hence, the whole

---

12. As we have seen, in his own way each divine Person "loses" everything: the Father by giving the whole of his being (if it were not so the Son and the Holy Spirit would not equally be God), the Son because he is the image of the Father (his being is to give himself and he gives himself back to the Father), the Holy Spirit because he keeps nothing for himself but communicates everything to the Son and from the Son to the Father (if there were a limit in what is communicated God would no longer be one).

cosmos can be brought into God. In other words, by means of them the created expressions can be reunited to their uncreated ideas: "Humankind therefore is creation and, when redeemed, all is redeemed." The Mystical Body of human beings with Jesus transforms and fulfills the "mystical bodies" of nature.

What happens is the fulfillment of what is expressed in creation. When the Word is expressed in creation (both as the initial act and as the continuous creative act), what takes place is similar to the incarnation, although creation is not incarnation because the Word in creation does not assume created nature. It is similar in a sense because the contents of the Word, the words in the Word, are expressed outside the Word, given being by the Father. Things pass from being uncreated to being created; in this sense they are the Word "poured out" into creation. This "similarity to the incarnation," however, is only the beginning of the process. In the end, by means of the role of human beings, made possible by the work of the Word incarnate in Jesus, all created things will be reunited to their ideas in the Word and, in that moment, it will be possible to speak in a stronger way of a "similarity to the incarnation" in nature. Things will remain created and yet they will be fully God because, as has already been said, God will be all in all because things will have a threefold participation in God: in God's unlimitedness and hence in the infinity of God's being (patterned on the Father); in their idea-word in the Word, which each is in unity with all the ideas-words in the Word (patterned on the Son); and in the life of love without restrictions (patterned on the Holy Spirit). Human beings are in a key position because, as expressions of the whole of the Word, they contain all that is created and they express also all that is uncreated. In them too, as in the whole of creation, there is something similar, despite the clear difference, to the incarnation, because they are the expression of the entire Word. Consequently, they give the Word a suitable place to become incarnate because humanity is that part of creation which, made in the image of God, already expresses God in a full way; they also sum up all creation. Humankind becomes the point of encounter and transformation for all creation and humankind's becoming Jesus makes all become Jesus.

> Jesus redeems humankind and humankind redeems nature, gives to nature its character, the personality of Christ; and rightly so, because nature is the incarnation of the Word, is the Word incar-

nate.[13] The Word. Since, however, the human being, the last to be created, is also the summary of all creation (and is made in the image of God precisely in being the Word incarnate),[14] the Word was able to be incarnate in humankind alone which, even though a part of creation, is also the whole of creation.

d) Human Beings as "In the Image of God"

The specific nature of human beings could be summarized, therefore, with the bible term "image of God." Being this they are, like their model Jesus, the expression of the whole of the Word and of the entire creation. For the person, however, being the image of God brings with it other important implications in relation to other created things. These implications can be seen perhaps with greater clarity if we recognize that, despite their deep nature, human beings unfortunately do not necessarily live according to their nature. They can, and in the cruelest of ways often do, go against their human-divine model Jesus.

This means that the action of God within creation is not simply to bring all back fully into God, but it is also redemption, that is, a remedy for sin. It is a therapy that heals that way of acting and all its effects, the sin which clings to humanity like an ingrained stain, which goes against God. It is fundamental. Being made in the image of God, persons are created free; for the human person this means that, to be truly free, he or she must have the capacity not to be completely circumscribed by his or her nature. That is, at least so far as the will is concerned, the nature of the person is to be not determined by that nature. Hence to be free the person must be able, at least in a moral sense, to go *beyond* him or herself. This same liberty has, in fact, two faces: to go *against* self in a negative sense, by sinning, or to *rise above* self, in loving. In God, the uncreated, freedom is different. God's uncreated nature is absolute freedom. Whatever God does, and God can do anything, is always the exercise of this absolute freedom; hence God always acts according

---

13. "Here I see nature in the reality of its final fulfillment, when God will be all in all and hence nature will be divinized, that is, Christified and brought by Christ into the bosom of the Father." A comment by Chiara upon this passage.
14. "Humankind is the incarnation, in a manner of speaking, of the Word who wanted it to be 'the image of God' (see Gn 1:26-27), and so humankind, created last, finds itself at the peak of creation and is its summary." A comment by Chiara upon this passage.

to God's nature. God's freedom is completely exercised in God's decision to be love. For a created person, instead, the possibility of choice, falling below or rising above self, gives the possibility of loving actively; not only, as it is for the rest of creation, passively. In the cosmos things are in a relation of love, but they cannot choose. Human beings, on the other hand, can choose and hence can love actively, of their own volition. Since they are able to sin, they can love truly, fully. Thus they can affirm that they have been made in the image of God who is love (1 Jn 4:8 & 16).

The return of creation to God takes place through that part of creation capable of truly loving like God, because it loves freely. As human beings made in God's image, by means of grace, persons renounce sin and live the ontological nothingness of created reality in itself *as a gift of love*, that is, they live the nothingness of their dependence upon the uncreated as a total, faithful openness of God and the nothingness of their interdependence with others as a relationship in which they give themselves, and so, through participation, become God. But it is all gift, all God's work. As Chiara writes:

> God participates in humankind directly, putting in it the soul as his own image and putting it on earth for the adventure of becoming God by returning to the Father who created it, through participation in the divine life, by means of grace.

To have the freedom that can become love, however, it is necessary that the individual person be a self-aware subject, with sufficient consciousness at least to make the choice to love. Here too there is a difference between humanity and the rest of creation. Things—including animals, at least in this way – are not conscious. For this reason human beings are distinguished from the cosmos. They are the part of it that has become aware of itself and therefore, being free, they are distinguished also from God and they can, standing before God, speak to God as his personal interlocutor. They address themselves to God as persons: free, capable of choosing, capable of being love.

Mary

Being the image of God, then, means that human persons, when they love, can fulfill their vocation to be united to Jesus and, in him, with all the ideas in the model Idea. Such a vocation, obviously, is exalted and exacting. It demands everything. It can be seen lived in an exemplary way in the Virgin

Mary. She becomes, thereby, a light on what the person is, in a certain sense, the definition of the person.

a) *The Exemplar*

Mary's characteristic is total openness to the Word ("Here am I, the servant of the Lord; let it be with me according to your word" Lk 1:38). Indeed, she is so open to the Word as to be all word, expression of the Word lived out: "Then I looked above me, where there was a beautiful statue of our Mother, and I understood that She is only *Word of God* and I saw Her as beautiful beyond all telling: all clothed in the Word of God who is the Beauty of the Father, the *Spirit within*." She adheres with the whole of her being to the Word. She chooses, therefore, from the depths of her being, and therefore is free and aware. The act of her freedom and awareness is manifested in placing her center outside herself: Mary is a living Gospel because Jesus *makes her that way*. She is solely a perpetual "fiat" to a will outside herself. In Mary, therefore, can be seen a person who, so to speak, has an ex-centric center, in the will of another—God; just as, in fact, can be seen in Jesus. And given that the openness to this center outside herself takes on the whole of her person, it touches also her bodily dimension, that dimension which she shares also with her Son, Jesus: "The Gospel is Jesus and Jesus is the Word in the flesh of Mary."

Mary, therefore, in the whole of her being, is the full and unimpeded expression of the Form of a human being. She lives creaturely reality to the full and, as a human being, she lives it actively, which is to say that she welcomes her being that comes from the Father, consciously follows her Form that she finds in the Word humanized, her Son Jesus, and she lives the love that comes from the Holy Spirit. She can be seen, therefore, as the most successful example of a creature, where the Trinity expresses itself without any impediment.

And just as every human person should live as the Son of God, according to the model (and by the grace) of Jesus, to be fully the "image of God," Mary is the Daughter of God:

> I saw her – tutored by the Son in loving the Father – loved by the Father as the Son: *the Daughter* par excellence. *The Daughter of God-the Woman of Love*![15] How beautiful she is!

---

15. "It is really beautiful to see Mary like this: the Woman of Love, because the daughter of a Father-Love." A comment by Chiara upon this passage.

Mary is like this because right from the beginning of her created existence she was prepared for what she would do in her life. Her living her creaturely reality with such intensity and completeness is a result of her being full of the presence of God and in no way resists him; thus, in other words, she is all-holy, without sin:

> In fact Mary was conceived without sin because, right from the moment of her conception, in her there was no lack of the presence of God, the presence of the Holy Spirit, which then grew making her: Mother of Jesus and, in her desolation, Mother of Jesus the Mystical Body.

Mary shows the person, therefore, as a creaturely reality full of God, with that fullness among all beings that exist proper to human beings, because they are made in the image of God, creatures capable of being other Christ. While it cannot but be recognized that the rest of humanity struggles and sometimes fails in such a vocation, it is possible to see how Mary, even in all the struggles of her own life, being another Jesus, and so expressing in herself the whole of the Word and summarizing creation, expresses the entire human race in a positive sense. She too has Jesus as her Form, but she lives him perfectly, in a complete way.

> Today I understood that the whole of humanity flowers in Mary. Mary is the Flower of humanity. She, the Immaculate, is the Flower of the Maculate.

> It could not but be like this: according to the Trinity the peak[16] of anything at all is its opposite. The triumph of the green plant is in the flower of another color. Just as the height of Love is Truth.

> Sinful humanity could not but flower in Mary, the all-beautiful!

In Chiara's observation on this passage, which points to the law of the Trinity, there is a useful principle for understanding how Mary can be the expression of the whole of humanity even though, because of her holiness, she is different from other human creatures. In the Trinity the Father expresses himself completely and distinctly from himself in the Son, who is the complete Idea of himself. Therefore the Son is equal to the Father and contains him while he is also his contrary, since he is the Son who receives everything and not the Father who gives everything. Mary, expressed by humanity, is in

---

16. "That is, according to the law of the Trinity." Chiara's observation.

a similar relationship. To use a metaphor, she is like a mirror image that is the reverse expression of its original. She, therefore, is the "reversal" of sinful humanity of which she is the all-holy summary and the crown.

This aspect, because humanity is also the summary and crown of creation, calls attention to something important about Mary. She, like all human beings (individually or together), is the summary and crown of the whole cosmos. Thus Mary "is the entire Creation purified redeemed." She is the person in the state of perfection.

Moreover Mary, being the whole of the Word of God, participates fully in Jesus, the Word incarnate. For this reason she is the perfect person. Therefore in her, through participation, there is the whole of the uncreated and "Mary does not sum up in Herself solely Creation, but the created and the uncreated universe." From Mary, then, Jesus is born; hence what is seen in her as a result of her total welcome of the Word is accomplished also in her physical maternity. She is the *Theotōkos*. She contains God and by this becoming small out of love on the part of God, she even seems bigger than God. Chiara affirms this in a letter:

> Yes, it is true that She is contained by the Trinity, but yesterday I saw her, because the Son showed her to me, as containing within herself the whole of Heaven.

> Outside the sky was of a blue never seen before . . . And so I understood: the sky contains the sun! Mary contains God! God loved Her so much as to make his Mother and his Love made Him become small before Her.

And this means that elsewhere Chiara can also affirm:

> In Her is the entire Trinity with the Creation The Trinity contains. Mary contains Herself in Herself though the Trinity.

> It happens as in those mirrors that, facing one another, project images of each other infinitely and are re-contained in each other through the returning reflection.

All of this, however, is always the outworking of grace and takes place because of "a retroactive action like the Redemption." It is only by means of grace that Jesus has made Mary what she is. And since Mary is the person in the state of perfection, it means that to be person successfully as she is, everyone must reach it via the same grace given by Jesus. In this, Mary, since she is the exemplar of a perfect person, indicates, however, something more: the extremely high vocation of all persons to be so divinized as to contain the God in whom they are contained.

b) The Desolate

All the themes of what it is to be a person that can be found in Mary can be seen especially clearly at the climax of her life, when she stood desolate at the foot of her Son's cross. Here Jesus takes away from her the greatness of being his mother, indicating John instead of himself as her son (Jn 19: 26-27). What it means to be a person according to Mary's example is summed up in this loss:

> But to be Mary it is necessary to be Jesus Forsaken[17] or, indeed, the Virgin desolate: offer oneself to suffer the loss of the Son: rejoice in being without Peace, Joy, Health . . . all that she is: feel ourselves Mary desolate . . .
>
> ". . .because you are desolate": that is, be *only*: Word of God. Hold within yourself only the Word of God.
>
> ". . .and blessed is the fruit of your womb, Jesus . . ."
>
> Giving birth to *Jesus* in oneself (becoming holy for the others = living the Word of God that gives birth to Christ in the entire Soul) for oneself and for the souls.

Here we see that, since Mary in her desolation loses everything, she is absolutely and only the Word, as Chiara observed commenting on this passage: "There is a strong link between the Desolate One and the Word, because truly if we are the Word of God we are no longer ourselves."[18] In an exemplary way, therefore, Mary Desolate adheres to God and so shows herself to be completely free because she carries out, even in the most extreme circumstances, her conscious choice to follow God. In her total making herself nothing out of love, therefore, she is truly the image of God.

---

17. "To be Mary" means to live according to the pattern of Mary and "to be Jesus Forsaken" means to live according to the pattern of Jesus' dereliction upon the cross. The language of "being" is a language of participation that points to how the origin of the ability to live in this way is in the divine action in the life of Jesus.
18. A comment by Chiara.

And it is precisely this self-noughting that makes her able to participate in the action of the dying Jesus. But, paradoxically, it is a participation by means of its opposite. In reality, Jesus excludes Mary from his work when he takes her divine maternity from her and "She was excluded by her Son who alone offered Himself for all, including Her." But in that moment, living out her total self-noughting and letting Jesus enter the absolute self-noughting of his God-forsakenness, where "he had neither Mother, nor Father. He was nothing born of nothing," Mary was also included for the reason that she was excluded: "And at the same time she participated in it with infinite intensity because she was made our Mother precisely there." It was the fulfillment of her role, the full expression of her being *Theotōkos*: "Now, divine Motherhood was hers, hence a Mother not human, but *divine*, infinite. And therefore producing God. Because she was a *divine Mother* she can be Mother of us *all*." Making herself nothing she affirms herself, just as God does, that is, she replicates in herself, in the way a creature can (and as we have also seen is the trinitarian fulfillment of every created thing), the way of being, each according to the specific distinctions of his Personhood, of each of the three divine Persons. Becoming nothing she becomes fully her specific word in the Word; she fulfills God's plan for her.

And here, as a person, she enters into trinitarian relationships, where each one lives at times according to the pattern of the Father and at times according to the pattern of the Son. This is evident because, as a result of her actively living the word expressed by God in her, she has relationships such that those who have given life to her, that is, the whole of humanity (of which she is the summary, the flower), are given life by her:

> ...There came John and with him Humanity. Into Mary's most pure Womb, whence came the Son of God, go back the sons and daughters of humankind to be brought into Godhead via their immaculatization in Mary. She is the Gate of Heaven. One is not Christian if one is not Marian. One is not divine if not immaculate. One does not go to Jesus if not through Mary. One does not possess the Forsaken but through the Desolate.[19]

---

19. A note of caution may be necessary here. Chiara does not mean that anyone without an explicit knowledge or relationship with Mary cannot have a transformative relationship with God. She is indicating the role of Mary, whether we are aware of it or not, in helping human beings come to fulfillment in God. The reason for doing so is to be able to live more fully in the grace of God's action.

The topic of immaculatization deserves a much deeper study than is possible in this article; in this context it emphasizes how Mary, in Jesus and by means of Jesus, has a role according to the pattern of the Father with regard to humanity, because, to make a human being capable of living like her, that is, capable *without putting obstacles in its way* of receiving the Word (both in the sense of the teaching of Scripture and of the Eternal Word in God), she makes the human being capable of "generating" Jesus in self (and also in others).

In Mary Desolate, therefore, can be seen the reality of the person intensified and emphasized. She 1) is a creature, and so a word in the Word, who 2) is human, and so summing up the whole of creation and expressing whole of the Word, who 3) lives her "I" to perfection, choosing absolutely to live in union with the Word humanized, her Son, Jesus, and who 4), as a person, has trinitarian relationships with other persons and with the whole of creation.

Human-divine fulfillment

Living as a person and being in relationship are not independent things. The person does not exist outside of relationships and relationships are the place where persons find their fulfillment as persons. This comes about for two reasons, the functional and the ontological.

Functionally, relationships with others give persons the opportunity for self-noughting. They almost oblige a person to come out of self and, if this happens as the result of a real choice, a person can do this by living the Word which is always love. In that way, in love, he or she lives Jesus and thus lives as a person.

Ontologically, however, if persons are expressions of the model Idea which is Jesus, they must be open one to another in order to be in accordance with the reality of their being. If they were to close themselves in their own word, that word itself would lose its meaning. Therefore if two persons really meet, which is to say if they meet in the mutual self-noughting of love, their words expressed in creation open up to one another. But this opening up is not simply a matter of the words involved, as it were, in the immediate relationship. In fact, it is an opening up to all of the words because in the unity of the Word each word contains all words. The particular contains the universal; or, to say the same thing differently, each human being is an expression of the model, Jesus, so that in his or her particularity are contained also all the other particularities:

> We need to enlarge it [our own heart] to the measure of the Heart of Jesus and love everyone. And as one Sacred Host, from among the millions of hosts on the earth, is enough to nourish us with God, so one brother or sister, the one that God's will puts next to us, is enough to give us communion with humanity, which is the mystical Jesus.

In this mutual opening we open ourselves to the whole of the Word, and thus at the same time to God and the whole of humanity contained in the Word. Such a relationship is an opening, therefore, to the One who is God and is the model of all humanity, that is, the Word humanized, God fully present in creation, Jesus. Human persons in their relating, and by means of their relating, find themselves thus relating to Jesus who is not only in each of them, but goes beyond them, enfolds and transcends them and so is among them.

In this moment they are fulfilled inasmuch as they are words in the Word, because now they are united to all the other words and to their Model Word. They are truly themselves, truly persons. It is something that happens in Jesus, and only by means of a relationship with other human persons; in fact, it could be said that persons become truly persons by means of persons.

This experience is deeply rooted in creaturely being, because in the whole of creation any created word, if united to the other words of its model-Word, discovers its full reality, because it comes into contact with its head that is in the Word who brings with him all the words in the Word. But for human beings there is a further fundamental element. They are subjects made in the image of God; hence they can, indeed they must, choose, so that their task is to be united among themselves by choice of will. Persons can, must, love actively, not merely passively as other things do, and in their loving one another they do what things of their own power cannot: they return already in this present time to their model.

The other things do not have this relationship with their models, because they do not have the possibility in themselves to be united. They are not capable of the full, active love characteristic of persons. Furthermore, they do not have their model in creation because their ideas remain in the Word. Nonetheless, since Jesus is the Word incarnate, these ideas-models are all present in him, and so in him when he is present as "Third" in the midst of human persons. Consequently Chiara can say:

> Looking upon two firs as a unit gives rise to the idea of the model fir. And here is the Gospel of nature. Where two firs are united, there is the idea of the model fir.
>
> Likewise, where two human beings are united in the name of Jesus, there is Jesus; and this because Jesus is the model for human beings. He is the Human Being. And two or more are enough to have present the Idea of him.
>
> The firs are united by the idea of the fir and not by Jesus. However, in the final analysis, they are united in Jesus, since they are united in the idea of the fir that is in the Word. But, since Jesus is the Word Incarnate and contains in his Flesh the whole of nature, the firs are united in Jesus. "For in him all things were created," to form him.

In the experience of being united with Jesus in the midst, therefore, persons, as individual human beings, find themselves made complete because they pass from living united to Jesus in their particularity to being united to the model Ideal that contains all particularities, the entire Jesus. Living Jesus in one's personal particularity, in total love for others, is already a way of being Jesus. Yet to be Jesus fully it is necessary to pass from being in the particularity of a person who loves to having Jesus among persons who love one another:

> You see therefore that for him [Jesus] to be there, it is necessary to love like this. But you know that to love like this means being "another Jesus."[20] Now, for him to be among us, it is necessary before to be him.

Thus, as explained above, if a person loves, making self nothing out of love like Jesus, loving another person who (as a particular expression of the model Jesus) contains all the particular ideas, and is then loved back with the same quality of love, both find themselves together beyond themselves, in Jesus entire. We pass, therefore, from being *in contact* by means of a single person with all his or her particularity, with all the ideas-words of the Word in that single person, to being united to all these particular ideas, to all the

---

20 "It is Jesus, in fact, who loves with the measure of death." Chiara's observation.

ideas-words that the Word contains. That is, we go from loving Jesus (who contains everything) in the other, to together being Jesus (who gives to all the all he contains).

Already in history, therefore, it is possible to have an experience of paradise, where the human being finds realization because he or she experiences the divine who is, in Jesus, fully human and fully divine. In fact, in this way relationships between persons are lived at the highest level even, for example, with regard to human feelings, because all understand one another and each loves and feels loved. It is a mysticism in the social realm that satisfies the created person in his or her individuality, because he or she discovers that trinitarian relationships are not simply about imitating the Trinity but are also a true participation in the life of the Trinity:

> When we are united and he is there, then we are no longer two but *one*. In fact, what I say is not said by me, but it is I, Jesus, and you in me who say it. And when you speak it is not you, but you, Jesus, and I in you. We are a single Jesus and also distinct: I (with you in me and Jesus), you (with me in you and Jesus), Jesus among us in whom I and you are.
>
> And his presence among us is mystical.
>
> And he is in the Father, and so in him the two of us are in the Father and we participate in the Trinitarian Life.

Conclusion

The person is a vocation. Ontology demands life. The deeper being of a member of the human race is in agony until it becomes also a being that is lived. We could say that the God who is already present in a person because of his or her existence must fill every part of that person's existence and make it full of God. It is a process. We, here and now, are at the beginning of the *eschaton*, not at its fulfillment. The pathway towards its realization, however, is clear. Each one, to fulfill the word of which he or she is the created expression, must live the love that is self-noughting. The example of this is Mary. And no one ought or, better, can live loving self-noughting alone. We can reach fullness only through other persons with whom together we can be the Model Word, Jesus.

In all of this we cannot negate the necessity of the work of Jesus. He is the focal point who makes everything work; he with his grace makes divinization possible. He does this above all with his full manifestation of himself in his Forsakenness on the cross.

In fact, behind every element that has emerged as essential to understanding the person, there is a secret. It is this: Jesus Forsaken, the revelation and the fundamental work of Jesus. He is the One who explains the life of God, and hence the being that the Father gives, the Idea that the Word is and the life that the Spirit lives. He, therefore, is the secret of things that in their nothingness participate in the presence of God the Trinity. He is also the internal structure of the relationships that things live with one another. And he, who makes most the radical choice possible of love, and so has the most absolute freedom of an unconditional love, is the incomparable image of God. He therefore is the reality of the person. But he is also the liberator of the person, because he is the reason why persons can be fulfilled, going beyond any limitation. He, then, is the explanation, and the cause of the successful or perfect example of a person, namely, Mary. His Forsakenness is replicated in her Desolation and by a retroactive grace his Forsakenness makes possible Mary's existence as the one who has always been all-holy. And he is the love necessary for his presence, as the Risen One, to be among persons. Jesus Forsaken is the key that opens Chiara's entire thought.

In reality, though, it would be interesting to look in still more detail at each element necessary to understand the person, from the divine creativity to the nature of things in their ontological dynamic of love that expresses the ideas of the Word, to the specificity of what it is to be human, as the expression of the whole of the Word and the summary of the whole of the cosmos, according to which human beings live their creatureliness in the image of God. It would be interesting, next, to look more at Mary and at Jesus in the midst. But I hope that what has been said may have served to show, so far as the notion of the person is concerned, the architecture of thought that undergirds Chiara's mystical experience. Even though she does not use the term "person" in the way it has been explained, the category is fundamental for her vision of what it is to be human.

To grasp what Chiara proposes, therefore, we can never get away from the person seen as the human way of living the Word expressed, a word in the Word, in created terms. It is a way that is always a relational and trinitarian dynamic, as for all things, but that is a dynamic of beings that are unique and unrepeatable and that by making themselves nothing affirm themselves. It is a way in which persons, as well as all things, are fulfilled by being reunited to their Model Idea, which for persons is Jesus; and which is lived most fully when, each one being Jesus, all together they are Jesus and in the midst of them they have Jesus.

Chapter Nineteen

Towards a New Kind of Cognition

Callan Slipper

The importance of the act of knowing cannot be exaggerated. Not only is it fundamental to human survival, it is also basic to every kind of human endeavor. Chiara Lubich offers a form of cognition that builds upon and develops previous forms and this is exemplified in the passage *Look at all the flowers*. To explore Chiara's cognitive proposal, I shall take a phenomenological and interdisciplinary approach as this gives an insight into the experience of cognition and offers a basis for understanding it within the context of human development. In the interests of concision, what I say is necessarily schematic and, of course, reality is more complex and less ordered. Nevertheless, while such a brief study cannot pretend to give an exhaustive account, it may suggest a useful interpretative key.

To begin with a definition: cognition, as I shall speak of it, is the way in which the human subject acquires and uses knowledge. It is thus never passive and merely receptive; it always exists in interaction with reality and it is always within the total context of what it is be human, which means especially the relational dimension.

Three modes of cognition

Looking at how a child develops is, of course, not the only way of looking at human knowing, but it is a strategy for seeing some of the basic forms of cognition present in human beings.[1] While each mode of cognitive growth is in fact discernible once it has been achieved, in life the three

---

1. This kind of psychological approach can also be complemented by philosophical inquiries. For instance, Bernard Lonergan in *Insight: A Study of Human Understanding* (1957) proposed a "generalized empirical method" which he referred to as "critical realism." This approach is indebted to Aristotle and Thomas Aquinas and, "fully cognisant of Hegel and Kant" (Brendan Purcell, *From Big Bang to Big Mystery* (Dublin: Veritas, 2011), 246), it grounds knowing (and valuing) in a critique of the mind similar to Kant's. Lonegan's method could in principle be applied to any of the three proposed modes of cognition.

modes are not discrete compartments and contain considerable variety and complexity.

Somatic or enactive knowledge

The first knowledge a child has of the world is through physical interactions with it: sucking, grasping, tasting, smelling and so on. Jerome Bruner argues that while the initial form of action is "looking at," these other actions allow the child to "objectify" and "correlate" the environment.[2] Thus a cognitive model of the world is constructed through somatic interaction and "Children first understand objects as extensions of their own bodies."[3] Quoting Piaget, Bruner says things are 'lived rather than thought.'[4] The child, then, gradually learns not only to hold things, but to hold them in mind, forming representations or mental models that are either *of something* or, as sensory motor skills develop, *of how to do something* (tying a knot for instance).[5]

Symbolic knowledge

Before complete linguistic mastery is achieved, another set of cognitive capacities begins to develop. These are ways of thinking about the world that represent it, with increasing competency, in symbolic forms: pictorially, mu-

---

2. Jerome Bruner, "On Cognitive Growth" in Bruner, Olver, Greenfield et al., *Studies on Cognitive Growth* (New York: Wiley, 1967), 16. Bruner, following Piaget (see Jean Piaget, *Play, Dreams and Imitation in Childhood*, New York: Norton, 1962) develops a threefold classification of cognitive representation. This is the main source for the threefold schema set out here. As we shall see, it is largely similar to the work of scholars in other fields.
3. Robert M. Bellah, *Religion in Human Evolution* (Cambridge, Massachusetts: Belknap Press of Harvard University Press, 2011), 18. Following Bruner, Bellah proposes three major modes of religious representation, in addition to another mode derived from religious experience, which he calls unitive events.
4. Jean Piaget, *The Construction of Reality in Children* (New York: Basic Books, 1954).
5. These are stored as contrasting and discrete kinds of memory, either of episodes that are recalled in their specifics or in procedures that, as an abstraction from episodes, that recalled as general behavioural patterns. Merlin Donald argues that there are two kinds of memory in early forms of cognitive development, episodic and procedural. "Whereas episodic memory preserves the specifics of events, procedural memory preserves general principles for action, across events. Procedural memories must preserve general principles for action and ignore the specifics of each situation." Merlin Donald, *Origins of the Modern Mind: three stages in the evolution of culture and cognition* (Cambridge, Massachusetts: Harvard, 1991), 150. Fascinatingly these two kinds of memory are stored in different parts of the brain (see Donald.).

sically, poetically and narratively. They both communicate and make sense of experience, as Paul Ricoeur put it "I express myself in expressing the world"[6] and, as such, they generate representations that the mind can use to model reality to itself and that can also create cultural artifacts (paintings, music, poems, stories) conveying these models to others. They are extremely powerful and, each in its own way contains meanings that cannot be fully captured by concepts.[7] This excess of content is present in all forms of symbolic expression, but narrative is capable of explaining intent, motivation, feelings, personal value and individual and collective identity. Each person or community is, as it were, the story about the self or the community.

Theoretic knowledge

From about the age of seven, though not at the same time for all children, conceptual thought begins to emerge. This marks the end of what Piaget calls an "egocentric world" where, since the world and the child are not distinct, all things are understood to happen in relation to and as an extension of the child:[8] the self and other things are now independent elements in the world. This leads to a greater capacity to objectify the world and, with that, the capacity to think abstractly. This is the basis for theoretical thought.

---

6. Paul Ricoeur, *The Symbolism of Evil* (New York: Harper and Row, 1967), 13.
7. Susanne Langer says, "Artistic symbols . . . are untranslatable; their sense . . . is always *implicit*, and cannot be explicated by any interpretation. This is true even of poetry, for *though* the *material* of poetry is verbal, its import is not the literal assertion made in the words, but *the way the assertion is made*, and this involves the sound, the tempo, the aura of associations of the words, the long or short sequences of ideas, the wealth or poverty of transient *imagery* that contains them, the sudden arrest of fantasy by pure fact, or of familiar fact by sudden fantasy, the suspense of literal meaning by a sustained ambiguity resolved in a long-awaited key-word, and the unifying, all-embracing artifice of rhythm." Susanne Langer, *Philosophy in a New Key* (New York: Penguin, 1948), 212.
8. Piaget held a strong view of what, to use Lucien Lévy-Brühl's term, could be called the child's *participation mystique* with the world. Robert Bellah, however, notes: "On the basis of recent research, Piaget's notion of adualism must be qualified, or even perhaps, applied only to the period before birth. George Butterworth has argued that 'a boundary exists in infant perception between infant and the world such that the absolute "adualism" assumed by Piaget is not supported.' But he adds, 'On the other hand, it is clear that the very young infant has no objective, reflective self-awareness.' George Butterworth, 'Some Benefits of Egocentrism,' in *Making Sense: The Child's Construction of the World*, ed. Jerome Bruner and Helen Haste (London: Methuen, 1987), 70-71." Bellah, *Religion in Human Evolution*, note 21, 614.

These modes of knowing have in common several fundamental aspects. Three are significant in our context. Each models the world around it, forming a mental pattern of its knowledge of the environment that is used to interact with it; each is part of a network of relationships with other human subjects in the formation of these mental models, that is, we know as part of a community of knowledge;[9] and each forms representations (via gestures, symbols or theories) which give access to these models, allowing them to be developed, challenged and communicated.

The Evolution of Human Cognition

The three modes of cognitive development suggest ways of understanding the gradual development of human cognition and the culture that accompanies it. Merlin Donald, for instance, posits three stages of cognitive evolution, developing out of pre-human cognitive processes similar to those of the great apes, which generate what he calls "episodic culture."[10] This is followed by the transition to early hominid "mimetic culture" made up of gestures and pre-linguistic vocalizations. Archaeological and anthropological evidence suggest that as brain size grew and body structure altered, from *homo habilis* to *homo erectus*, new skills were being acquired. These show the development of new cognitive abilities in the emergent hominids. Enactment, for example, in the form of mime, can teach how to produce a stone axe, and this implies a mental model not only of what is to be produced but of the procedure to produce it.[11] It is not certain at what point this culture gave place one where mental models were represented by meaningful and syntactically ordered sounds. In *homo erectus* changes in the vocal tract suggest at least the possibility that this species may even have developed language.[12]

---

9. Bruner argues that there are two tenets to what he calls the "instrumental conceptualism" that he and his colleagues propose. The first is that "our knowledge of the world is based on a constructed model of reality, a model that can only partially and intermittently be tested against input." (Bruner, *Studies in Cognitive Growth*, 319). He goes on to say, secondly, that the models contained in this constructed model of reality "develop as a function of the uses to which they have been first put by the culture and then by any of its members who must bend knowledge to their own uses" (Bruner, *Studies in Cognitive Growth*, 320).
10. Donald, *Origins of the Modern Mind*, 124-161.
11. Donald, *Origins of the Modern Mind*, 162-200.
12. For a wide-ranging discussion see Purcell, *From Big Bang to Big Mystery*, 197-206.

Nevertheless, with the advent of *homo sapiens* a cognitive transition has clearly taken place and it is possible to discern in the cultural artifacts produced, the development of a complex culture that uses symbols with semantic content, "mythic culture."[13] In his careful study of human origins and development, Brendan Purcell maintains that it is very likely that what is variously described as a "creative explosion" or a "human revolution" did indeed take place with the arrival of "intentional symbolic activity,"[14] and it would seem that its origins go back as far as about 164,000 years ago in Africa. At this point cognitive development begins to be dominated not so much by biological as cultural change. Mythic culture employs symbolic representations in the context of narratives (*mythos* is Greek for story) and these give human subjects powerful instruments to interpret and interact with the environment.[15] Mythic cognition is not static and it did progress, using its narrative and symbolic methodology, to be self-critical.[16]

This self-criticism became acute in a further transition that took place in several cultures, in particular Greece, ancient Israel, India and China, during what Karl Jaspers called the axial period.[17] The culture that emerged,

---

13. Evidence of this continues to be found. In Europe some of the most impressive creations can be seen, for instance, in the oldest cave paintings currently known at Altamira in Spain. The most ancient of them is a red disk dated at before 4800 BCE, considerably older than the Chauvet paintings in France dated as at least 3700 BCE. The artistry at both sites is superb, demonstrating a complex of skills and also strongly suggesting a socially advanced culture where people could be set aside to develop their artistic talents. See <http://news.nationalgeographic.com/news/2012/06/120614-neanderthal-cave-paintings-spain-science-pike/>
14. Purcell, *From Big Bang to Big Mystery*, 181.
15. The power of story should never be underestimated. One can return again and again to a story, especially if it is a good one, and it will render new insights. Mythic thinking, therefore, can do things that conceptual thought cannot.
16. An example is the first chapter of Genesis, where a story of the one God creating the world he utterly transcends was critical of polytheistic accounts.
17. Jaspers proposed the notion of an axial period in 1949 in his *Vom Ursprung und Ziel der Geschichte* (*The Origin and Goal of History*). He sees it as having taken place "from 800 and 200 BC." (*The Origin and Goal of History*, London: Routledge, 2011, trans. from German by Michael Bullock, 23) Others date it slightly differently; Mormigliano, for instance, puts the axial period in "the classical situation of the ancient world between 600 and 300 BC" (Arnaldo Mormigliano, *Alien Wisdom: The Limits of Hellenization* (Cambridge: CUP, 1975), 8). The idea of the axial period has been further developed by Eric Voegelin, who speaks of "multiple and parallel leaps in being" in the first millennium BCE, in *Order and History*, 5 vols (Baton Rouge: Louisiana State University Press, 1956-1987) and by Shmuel Noah Eisenstadt in "Introduction : The Axial Age Breakthroughs—Their Characteristics

which we are heir to today,[18] can be called, in the pregnant expression of Giuseppe Zanghì, the culture of the *logos*.[19] The *logos* is a form of knowing that attempts to achieve objectivity, that is, to see things without projections from the hopes, fears, fantasies, or preconditioning of the subject. It develops conceptual reasoning that produces theories, and so it corresponds to the acquisition of theoretical knowledge, but the *logos*-word can also be a word of command and so have ethical and existential implications. Furthermore, as the light of understanding it can also mean conscience or a profound spiritual intuition, which attempts to see things as they truly are.[20] As such it is the capacity to engage in what Shmuel Noah Eisenstadt calls "reflexivity" that is, examining one's own assumptions.[21] In Greece, for example, this was undertaken by theoretical discourse in the development of philosophy; the ethical-existential dimension was developed in the light of Transcendence by the Hebrew prophets; a transcendent spiritual intuition (*bodhi*) was at the root of the new conceptual thinking that arose with Buddhism. These are three instances of a cultural shift that privileged a form of cognition that challenged, radicalized and went beyond mythic thought—not that mythic thought disappeared or lost its intrinsic value, but it was reformulated in *logos* culture.[22]

The axial period had a number of emblematic figures: Plato, Isaiah, Buddha, Confucius, Lao Tsu, for instance. Jesus, who is so important for Chiara's life and thought, was outside the axial period as usually defined. Nonetheless, what he brought or, perhaps better in this context, the culture that came about as a result of him, while being a development of the He-

---

and Origins" in *The Origins and Diversity of the Axial Age*, ed. S. N. Eisenstadt (Albany: SUNY Press, 1986).

18. Karen Armstrong, however, argues that a new axial period took place during the enlightenment, in *The Great Transformation* (London: Atlantic Books, 2007). Others say that the modern age displays the characteristics of a new axial period, see Yves Lambert "Religion in Modernity as a New Axial Age: Secularization or New Religious Forms?" in *Sociology of Religion* (1999), 60:3, 303-33.
19. See Giuseppe M. Zanghì, "Quale uomo per il terzo millennio?" in *Nuova Umanità* XXIII (2001/2) 134, 247-77 and "Il pensare come amore. Verso un nuovo paradigma culturale" in *Nuova Umanità* XXV (2003/1) 145, 1-19.
20. It is impossible not to recall the logos in the Prologue of the Fourth Gospel which is said to be "The true light, which enlightens everyone" (Jn 1:9 see also Jn 1:4).
21. See Shmuel Noah Eisenstadt, "Introduction: The Axial Age Breakthroughs."
22. Nothing is ever lost. Somatic forms of cognition also remain, though reformulated in the light of later cognitive evolutions.

brew axial breakthrough, was rooted in a transcendent spiritual intuition that critiqued the culture it developed and laid the basis for a culture that, in dialogue with Greek philosophy, tended to privilege theoretical discourse. As Chiara shows, however, Jesus was more than just a synthesis of what arose with *logos* culture.[23]

Chiara Lubich's Cognitive Proposal

As cognition acquires further capacities, so the relationship of the subject to the known changes. In somatic knowing, present in mimetic culture, the subject sees itself as part of its environment, with only a very limited sense of its distinction from it. A crucial development of selfhood comes with the emergence of symbolic cognition and mythic culture, since the subject becomes aware of the difference between its group and the environment. Nonetheless, here the subject, while it may be aware of its distinction from the group, functions almost exclusively as a member of the group.[24] It thinks in traditional ways, according to symbols and stories that have been handed down. The great acquisition of *logos* culture is awareness of individual selfhood, even at the risk of losing awareness of the subject's participation in its human and natural environments. It is the "objective" stance given by this perception that gives the human subject the acute reflexivity that makes it capable of constructing conceptual theories as mental models to interpret and interact with reality.

Chiara, applying in an original way Jesus' synthesis and challenge to *logos* culture, proposes a different kind of subjectivity. The individual remains but it is now in a relationship of profound mutual involvement with other indi-

---

23. Indeed, Giuseppe Zanghì says, "I have called this cultural paradigm: 'logos,' thinking specifically of the Logos of God. He is, in the Trinity, the one who stands *before* the Father, *before* God, revealing him in himself-Word, in himself-Logos, to be the power that that does not repressively hold on to the other but that distinguishes itself from the other: the Father as Love" ("Il pensare come amore," 9). Translation mine.

24. Giuseppe Zanghì says, "In mythic culture, *who is the thinking subject*? It cannot be the individual as such (the individual is always a 'laceration' of the whole): it is 'the group', with which the individual is identified. And the unity of the group preserves the unity of the Beginning: it is the group which preserves the individual in the divine, in the Origin" ("Il pensare come amore," 4) and "Mythic culture is fundamentally memory of the original unity but wounded by the painful perception of having in some way lost that place" ("Il pensare come amore," 5). Both translations mine.

viduals, a form of recollection both within self and within the other person insofar as empathy, sensitivity and attentive listening and communication (the apotheosis of the *logos*-word) will allow: "We should indeed always recollect ourselves also in the presence of a brother or a sister, but not avoiding the created person, rather recollecting him or her in our own Heaven and recollecting ourselves in the Heaven of the other."

In this context one's individual mental models are challenged, broadened and deepened by contact with the other. While this builds upon the cultural and relational dimension of all cognition, it demands a greater detachment from all mental models than is the case with any of the three modes. In relation to the other person everything can be reframed or rethought; even hard-won theories cannot be defended by the ego that generated them. Gesture, symbol, theory are all offered, not imposed, within the context of a deep meeting. In this way it is the very social nature of this process that offers the participants an intensified reflexivity, an extra possibility of using critical reasoning to challenge their presuppositions. Ideas are seen as instruments of a mutual reflection, engaged in together, so that out of the meeting of persons emerges a new act of cognition, one based on but not bound by any of the previous mental models. It thus has creative potential and is capable of thinking thoughts not had before in an act of cognition that is not closed and which, at least in principle, can be developed in further encounters.

Key to stopping this become a constant change with no fixed points is its openness to transcendence. There is a recognition by all parties that "truth" lies not only in the partial perceptions of individuals, but also beyond them. Dialogue is, in fact, trialogue. It is possible, therefore, to perceive things that have validity outside of or not dependent upon the act of cognition itself. In their mutual openness generated by love, individuals begin to discover another vision. It is what Chiara calls, "the vision of Jesus, of Jesus who, besides being Head of the Mystical Body, is everything: all the Light, the Word, while we are words in the Word."

Indeed, in the experience described by "Look upon All the Flowers," this vision is lived as an opening up to a transcendent experience[25] that is a

---

25. The transcendent experiences of the axial period were manifold. With various intents various taxonomies of mystical, numinous or spiritual experience have been essayed, starting from William James, *The Varieties of Religious Experience: A Study in Human Nature* (London: Longmans, first published 1902) and going to other seminal texts such as Rudolf Otto, *The Idea of the Holy* (Oxford: OUP 1923,

radicalization of the *logos* as spiritual intuition, hence the apt language of "recollection." It is, furthermore, also fully able to use the various forms of somatic, symbolic and theoretical representation (as shown, for instance, in the passage "Look upon All the Flowers" itself). What these things now provide, however, is more than simply enhanced models; rather they convey a sapiential reading of reality: ". . . and the *Light* that you have given me I have given them."[26] This sapiential reading opens up cognitive possibilities beyond the strictly religious or spiritual realm.[27] Meeting together in a shared transcendent experience, the human subjects both feel themselves united with Jesus and find that they are seeing things, as it were, from Jesus.

Chiara's cognitive proposal, therefore, is in continuity with other forms of human cognition, especially as related to non-biological change, but, following Jesus, it radicalizes the cognitive forms of *logos* culture. In doing so it also reframes the context of symbolic and somatic cognition, making them too vehicles of sapiential discourse.

---

first published as *Das Heilige* in 1917) or the work of Robert Charles Zaehner, especially *Mysticism: Sacred and Profane* (Oxford: Clarendon Press, 1957) or of Walter T. Stace, especially *Mysticism and Philosophy* (London: Palgrave Macmillan, 1960) (full text available at http://wudhi.com/mysticism/ws/wts-mp%20-%20index.htm), and more recently Louis Roy, *Transcendent Experiences: Phenomenology and Critique* (Toronto: Toronto University Press, 2001). While different theories can be constructed to relate such experiences to one another and bring them to form a consistent whole, phenomenologically they are distinctive. Using a term like "transcendent experience" does not prejudge their interpretation or presuppose any particular classification.

26. This is how Chiara quotes John 17:22. In fact the text from the Fourth Gospel does not use the word "light" but "doxan" (glory). It is significant because Chiara, in following the Vulgate's "Et ego claritatem, quam dedisti mihi, dedi eis," is highlighting the cognitive aspect of glory.

27. Giuseppe Zanghì puts it thus, "*It is Jesus*, then: the reality thought cannot but be Jesus, the man-God (let us recall St Bonaventure and his sua *reductio artium ad theologiam*!). That Jesus in whom all is recapitulated (see Eph. 1:10). That Jesus in whom the human – every human – and the divine – with all its infinite riches – are One" ("Il pensare come amore," 17). Translation mine.

Chapter Twenty

Look upon All the Flowers
November 6, 1949[1]

Chiara Lubich

Souls in times past sought God within them.

They stood as if in a great garden in full bloom, looking upon and admiring a single flower. They looked upon it with love, both in its details and as a whole, but they did not gaze upon the others.

God asks us to look upon all the flowers because he is in all, and only by gazing upon all of them is he loved more than the single flowers.

God who is in me, who has shaped my soul, who rests there in Trinity (with the saints and the Angels), is also in the heart of my brothers and sisters.

It is not reasonable that I should love him in me alone. Were I to do so, my love would still have something personal, something egoistical: I would love God in me and not *God in God*, while perfection is this: *God in God* (for he is Unity and Trinity).

Therefore my cell, as souls intimate with God would call it and as we [would call it] my Heaven, is in me and, *just as* it is in me, it is in the soul of my brothers and sisters. And just as I love him in me, recollecting myself in this Heaven – when I am alone – I love him in my brother or my sister when they are near me.

And so I will not love silence but the word (spoken or unspoken), the communication, that is, between God in me and God in my brother or my sister. And if these two Heavens meet, there is a single Trinity, where the two are like Father and Son and between them is the Holy Spirit.

We should indeed always recollect ourselves also in the presence of a brother or a sister, but not avoiding the created person, rather recollecting him or her in our own Heaven and recollecting ourselves in the Heaven of the other.

---

1. This passage is taken from the unpublished writings of Chiara Lubich,

And since this Trinity is in human bodies, Jesus is there: the God-who-is-Human.

And between the two is the unity where we are one but not alone. And here is the miracle of the Trinity and the beauty of God who is not alone because he is Love.

And so, when throughout the day the soul has willingly lost God in itself in order to be transferred into God in its brother or sister (for each is equal to the other just as two flowers in that garden are the work of an identical maker), and has done so out of love for Jesus Forsaken who leaves God for God (and precisely God in self for the God present or being born in the brother or sister . . .), when the soul returns to itself or better to the God within (because alone in prayer or in meditation), it will find again the caress of the Spirit who – because he is Love – *is Love* in truth, since God cannot fall short of his word and gives to the one who has given: he gives love to the one who has loved.

Thus disappear darkness and unhappiness with aridity and all the bitter things, leaving behind only the full joy promised to the one who has lived Unity.

The cycle is complete and closed.

We have continually to create these living cells of the Mystical Body of Christ – which are brothers and sisters united in his name – to give life to the whole Body.

To look upon all the flowers is to have the vision of Jesus, of Jesus who, besides being Head of the Mystical Body, is everything: all the Light, the Word, while we are words in the Word. But, if each of us loses ourselves in our brother or sister and forms a cell with them (a cell of the Mystical Body), each becomes the total Christ, Word, the Word. This is why Jesus says, "and *the Light* that you have given me I have given them."

But it is necessary to lose the God in self for God in our brothers and sisters. And this is done only by the one who knows and loves Jesus Forsaken.

And when the tree will have blossomed fully – the Mystical Body will be composed – it will reflect the seed whence it was born. It will be one, because all the flowers will be *one among them* just as each is one with itself.

Christ is the seed. The Mystical Body is the tree's crown.

Christ is the Father of the tree: never was he so much Father as during his forsakenness where he begot us as his children, in his forsakenness where he annihilated himself while remaining: *God*.

The Father is root for the Son. The Son is seed for his brothers and sisters.

And it was the Desolate who, in her silent consent to being Mother of other children, cast this seed into Heaven and the tree blossomed, and blossoms continuously on earth.

Chapter Twenty-One

Transferring Self to Other: Radicalizing Human Being

Jesús Morán

It is always helpful to avoid over-generalization. Nonetheless this should not discourage us from considering the various contemporary analyses of innovative cultural prospects characterized, at least in the West, by a recovery of the original stimuli for philosophical thinking. After centuries of neglect, when there was a monopoly of *logos* understood as rational activity detached from life itself, philosophical discourse speaks again about love or *eros*. Philosophy, it is said, must be again the love of wisdom. It must rediscover, therefore, its creative impulse in love. It comes as no surprise, then, to see expressions summarizing contemporary cultural sensibility as being rather like "a mystical shift in philosophy" or "a theological shift in phenomenology."[1]

This is not a passing phase. It comes from processes of thought over the years that indicates something of the complexity of cultural shifts. For example, we would not be able to speak of a theological or mystical shift in phenomenology without considering the thought of the later Heidegger. This perspective introduces the appeal to transcendence, to "the event" (*Ereignis*), to love, to the body, to life, to poetical thinking and to the divine.[2]

Another characteristic of this new way of facing the human can be seen in the ontological hermeneutics of religious experience. Here too we can recall Heidegger, particularly in his study of the philosophy of religion at Freiburg in the 1920s.[3] At the same time we can recall later developments,

---

1. .L. A. Castrillón, "El posthumanismo del amor: El giro místico de la fenomenología," *Logos* (2012): 68, 73.

2. In these perspectives it is certainly possible to identify some ambiguities or lack of grounding from the point of view of the Christian event as understood by theological thought.

3. Martin Heidegger, *Phänomenologie des religiösen lebens, einleitung in die phänomenologie der religion*; Spanish translation by Jorge Ustescu, *Introducción a la fenomenología de la religion* (Madrid: Ediciones Siruela, 2005); Italian translation by G. Gurisatti, *Fenomenologia della vita religiosa* (Milano: Adelphi, 2003); English trans-

closer to the logic of Christian revelation and its theological understanding, in the hermeneutics of Paul Ricoeur of France and Luigi Pareyson of Turin.[4] In Heidegger's view Christian theology thought of God in "ontic" terms while the next step would be to think "ontologically"—but in this, Heidegger says, poets and mystics see more clearly.[5] The influence of Meister Eckhart's negative and mystical theology on Heidegger cannot be ignored here. As Silvana Filippi affirms:

> [I]t doesn't seem difficult to suppose that such characteristic terms of Eckartian language as *Wesen* (essence), *Grund* (basis), *Abgrund* (abyss that is bottomless or without foundation), *Gelassenheit* (abandonment), *Abgeschiedenheit* (separation, distancing) have some meaning in relation to the same words that appear in the later Heidegger and whose meaning is not of merely secondary importance.[6]

Indeed, in conversation with a group of theologians in Marburg, Heidegger is said to have affirmed that "being" relates to "God" as "thought" relates to "faith."[7] Certainly this relates to Heidegger's particular focus on the "event" (*Ereignis*) of being, that is to the event which is its own source. If there is a relationship between being and *Dasein,* in the same way that theology speaks of the relationship between God and the soul, we must conceive of it as something beyond all words and perhaps all thought (at least all rational thought). Here we see the parallel between Heidegger's *Ereignis* and Eckart's negative theology.

We find a similar relationship, but with a completely Spanish *spirit,* between Maria Zambrano and John of the Cross. Zambrano, a great expert and admirer of the Spanish mystic poet, dedicated an interesting article to the "doctor of the Nada, the Nothing" with the title: "Saint John of the

---

lation by Matthias Fritsch and Jennifer Anna Gosetti-Ferencei, *The Phenomenology of Religious Life* (Bloomington: Indiana University Press 2004).

4. Piero Coda, *Il logos e il nulla. Trinità religioni mistica* (Rome: Città Nuova, 2003), 20, 316–322. Of great interest in this regard is G. M. Zanghì, *Dio che è amore: Trinità e vita in Cristo* (Rome: Città Nuova, 2004).
5. D. Gracia, "Zubiri y la experiencia teologal: La difícil tarea de pensar a dios y la religión a la altura del s. XX," in Brickle, *La filosofía como pasión* (Madrid: Trotta, 2003), 259.
6. Silvana Filippi, "Martin Heigegger y la mistica eckhartiana," *Invenio* (2003): 34.
7. Filippi, "Martin Heigegger y la mistica eckhartiana," 35.

Cross, from Dark Night to Clear Mysticism."[8] She always looked at mysticism from its human, rather than its religious dimension.[9] In a letter to her theologian friend, Agustin Andreu, she expresses her passion for "opening reason, uniting reason and devotion, reason and fundamental sentiment, philosophy and poetry."[10] Or as she also said, "Humanity is the being that suffers its own transcendence."[11] Transcending oneself to fulfill oneself, this is where, Zambrano seems to tell us, human perfection lies.

These remarks were necessary by way of introduction, as they give an idea of current attitudes in the field of philosophical anthropology, and so provide us with background for our consideration of Chiara Lubich's "Look upon All the Flowers." I shall seek to highlight what this passage means for philosophical anthropology, without pretending to exhaust all its implications.[12] In fact, taking into consideration the richness of Chiara's text and the brief scope of this study with its focus upon phenomenological analysis, what is said can only be a few initial comments and they would require further study and elaboration.

---

8   Maria Zambrano, in *La razón en la sombra: Antologica critica*, ed. by Jesús Moreno Sanz (Madrid: Sirucla, 2004), 490–498.

9   In a letter written from Piece in France, where she lived for a few years, to the theologian, Agustin Andreu, she expresses her radical refusal of every anthropology that is closed to the transcendent. It must be said, however, that Zambrano's hermeneutics of John of the Cross is affected by a vision of mysticism that is rooted in the Greek model of exteriority versus interiority in the search for the divine. Zambrano, *Cartas de la Piece: Correspondencia con Agustin Andreu* (Valencia: Pretextos, 2002), 28f.

10 Zambrano, *Cartas de la Piece: Correspondencia con Agustin Andreu*, 195. For Zambrano, mysticism and poetry are linked. For this reason she admired John of the Cross who, the perfect synthesis of mystic and poet, reached the highest peak, non-existence: "His being is finally to manage not to be" (Maria Zambrano, *La razón en la sombra*, 491). He lived out this seeking "not to be" as an imperative that came from life itself. The mystic's revolution is in complete self-alienation, in becoming other, in the complete destruction of self, putting self aside so that another comes to exist in the mystic. Having consumed all the dimensions of being, mental, moral and so on, all that remains is "all-consuming love" (Zambrano, 494). The mystic goes through the door of love to come to naked reality. John chose love and the way of poetry to transcend himself utterly and through this he reached the perfect unity of love and knowledge.

11 Maria Zambrano, *Cartas de la Pièce*, 279

12 It should be said at the outset that Chiara uses brief comparisons not so much to make evaluations as to make herself more aware of the spiritual gift received.

Transcendence and Spirituality of the Human Being

"Souls in times past," Chiara affirms, "sought God within them." If we assimilate the notion of a "soul" to that of a "mystic," in a hermeneutics that sees this as the peak, for any person, of a human being's experience as a human being, we could say that this affirmation of Chiara highlights the search for God that takes place through the human being's self-transcendence. The mystic, insofar as he or she is a creature touched by God, looks for God by being always more immersed in that "wound" of self-transcendence. John of the Cross is the supreme virtuoso in describing this structure of transcendence that starts from the gift of being wounded by God.[13] In the poem, "Transcending All Knowledge,"[14] written after "an ecstasy of profound contemplation," he feels that in this way he reaches the most complete knowledge of God and of himself.

But this is not perfection, Chiara goes on to tell us, for God "is also in the heart my brothers and sisters." Therefore, perfection is not God in me, but "perfection is this: God in God (for he is Unity and Trinity)" The structure of transcendence seems to acquire a new dimension. This is the basis, then, for the joy found in the soul of the other, love for the word more than just silence, experiencing the Trinity, Father, Son, and Spirit, as one but not alone, and the experience of Love. This is the basis for delight instead of darkness with its burden of aridity and bitterness. Furthermore, the experience of the Trinity takes place in human bodies and therefore has meaning and structure that is interpersonal and Christic.

There is no doubt that "souls in times past" also saw God in their neighbors; they communicated their experience of God to others, and they found happiness besides their trials as part of the rigors of an ascetic life. We cannot doubt the Christological value of these experiences, if only because, as we have said, the initiative did not come from them but from a touch that,

---

13. About the beginning of the *Spiritual Canticle* it is said that "God's love not only makes the person leave or put aside the love of other things, but it makes the person come out of self. . . . Without taking anything away from the human effort to purify oneself through the way of love and also to show the need to purify love itself . . . John of the Cross insisted. with equal or even greater strength, on the fact that it is impossible to reach the goal without God's intervention, which is purifying love." J. D. Gaitan, "Dios como amor purificador en San Juan de la Cruz," *Revista de Espiritualidad* 67 (2008): 67.
14. *The Collected Works of St. John of the Cross*, trans. by Kieran Kavanaugh and Otilio Rodriquez (Washinton, D.C.: ICS Publications, 1973), 718–719.

inasmuch as it was divine, could not fail to inflame the heart and fill it with love. This is the nature of Christian mysticism.

Transferring Self to Other

What, then, is specific and original in Chiara's text with regard to what it means to be human? In order to answer this question adequately, we must briefly recall some ideas we explored at the outset. We spoke about the new developments in culture, which Luis Castrillón calls post-humanist, meaning a new humanism "freed from the hegemony of historical context and endowed with a sense of transcendence and interiority."[15] This is a phenomenology that admits a phenomenon's excess in such a way that we are made able to see all that truly appears in a phenomenon because it is what is contained in it. It is a new humanism that tries to go beyond every fragmentation in human intelligence and seeks "to understand a humanity that reveals itself in giving, gratuitousness, and encounter,"[16] seeing as it is, in its body, mind, and spirit.

The fundamental categories present in this reading of the human would seem to be three: transcendence, relationality, and corporeality. It is in the context of these themes that, it seems to me, the contribution of Chiara Lubich's mysticism of unity is to be found in line with the interesting developments we have already mentioned. I will try to make this clear in three steps.

Transcendence

The first step has to do with the concept of *transcendence*.[17] In the impulse to transcend oneself, the emphasis is in the moment of "trans" (from the Latin

---

15. Luis Alberto Castrillón López, "El posthumanismo del amor: El giro mistico de la fenomenologia," *Logos* 21 (1012): 69. This refers to a non-metaphysical humanism, and it is an affirmation that it should be explored in the context of an overview of the state of metaphysics as a discipline. In fact, in principle, a humanism open to the transcendent ought not be contrary to a metaphysical humanism. It all depends upon how metaphysics is conceived.
16. López, "El posthumanismo del amor," 69.
17. I shall use the term "transcend" in its etymological meaning of going beyond what is perceived as real. Regarding the term "transcendental," its meaning, depending on the case, will be identified when necessary. It refers to the Greek medieval conception or that developed by Xavier Zubiri, moving away from Husserl. For Zubiri, the category of the transcendental refers to the purely physical character of reality. This category is not located outside reality but emerges from it. Because of its "trans" character, this transcendental nature or the transcendental structure of

trans + *scandere*, "beyond" + "climb/pass"). In existential logic, this "trans" (beyond) is connected to the "ex" of existence (from the Latin *existere*, composed of *ex* + *sistere*, "remain, stay"). In fact we exist *from* (that is "ex"), pushing *ipseity* from itself towards "trans." Yet, in Heidegger's phenomenological analysis and also in others,[18] we have the impression that the "Trans" remains to some extent closed in *ipseity*, as if it loses its original openness.[19] Jean-Luc Marion denounced this risk of solipsism in Heidegger. In this sense, Chiara's "God in God" seems to be a step of greater radicalness in the understanding of human transcendence, of human ecstasy (Greek *ek-stasis*, out-stand/ place) towards the other. This would be a radical transcendence of self beyond *ipseity*, without denying it, precisely because *it has already been transcended*. It is not that this does not take place in all experiences of interpersonal encounter with the o/Other, but here it would seem to be rendered more effectively explicit.[20]

Relationality

The second step considers the concept of *relation*. The category of relation is fundamental for any kind of philosophical anthropology seeking to see the human as truly open. Nowadays, in an attempt to overcome the possible weaknesses of this concept, there is a preference to speak of *relationality*, precisely to highlight its transcendental character.[21] Here too, the "God in God" of "Look upon All the Flowers" presupposes a step of greater radicalness. In effect, Chiara's expression suggests a dimension anterior to every

---

      reality can be called "metaphysics" (Xavier Zubiri, *Inteligencia sentiente: Inteligencia y realidad* (Madrid: Alianza Editorial, 1998), 113–123.

18. Zubiri, *Inteligencia sentiente*, 85.
19. I am referring to certain currents of existentialism that are based in phenomenology (see Sartre, for example). To some extent, also, Levinas is affected by this kind of turning in upon self.
20. We could say that in mystical experience *ipseity* does not undergo any closing in on self, rather, that the experience inasmuch as it is total ecstasy with God as its source and goal, is actually the highest openness. This is incontrovertible. Perhaps the problem lies in its conceptualization and in its anthropological meaning. This is where we can notice a certain kind of "closure." Hence, not every experience of transcendence necessarily goes beyond *ipseity*, beyond the self, not even in the setting of intersubjectivity.
21. Mauro Mantovani, "Persona e relazione, tra teologia e filosofia," in Manlio Sodi and Lluis Clavel, eds., *Relazione? Una categoria che interpella* (Citta Del Vaticano: Libreria Editrice Vaticana, 2012), 69–82. Relationality can be seen as alongside the classic transcendentals, with all the metaphysical implications.

relation, a dimension that is, we could say, structural, which makes relation possible and gives it a basis. Otherwise, the category of relation would remain subject to external or internal, social or subjective dynamics, which would not touch the personal depths of the human being. The dimension of *transcendental relationality* emerges within the perspective of "Look upon All the Flowers," but this is not in reference to being, and so it does not become a universal and abstract concept (which it risks in Greek-medieval metaphysics). Instead, it refers simply to reality just as it appears (and in this case to human reality). If relations are possible among human beings it is because there is a relational structure. In this sense, relationality is not a concept but a structure of the human person.[22] The person is structurally open, and for this reason has transcendental relationality.

Corporeality

The third step looks at the theme of the body that for decades has been a focus for phenomenological and metaphysical hermeneutics. The attempt is to overcome the dualism pervading Western philosophy and emphasized by modernity insofar as it derived from idealism. Here, we can locate the inquiries of French phenomenology, from Merleau-Ponty with his concept of the *intentionality of the body* or Michel Henry and his theory of the *subjective body*, up to the present, passing through the inquiry of Jean-Luc Marion. Xavier Zubiri distinguishes between *corporeity* and *corporeality*: the latter refers to the material organism, while *corporeity* is the body that is actualized in the person, a type of *personalized body*.[23]

Chiara, in the text that we are considering, says that "this Trinity is in human bodies," and goes on to say that, "Jesus is there: the God-who-is-

---

22. In Zubiri's terms, the transcendental structure of human reality gives a basis to relationality. In this sense, it is possible to speak of transcendental relationality. See Zubiri, *Inteligencia sentiente*, 122.

23. See Xavier Zubiri, "El hombre y su cuerpo," in *Escritos Menores* (Madrid: Alianza Editorial, 2006), 113–16. The observation of V. M. Tirado San Juan is also interesting, with regard to the vision that Zubiri has of the body: "The human being is also nature, but a nature of such an essence . . . that it is transcended in something that is no longer nature, that 'appears of itself' to be an open essence (a *hyper-keimenon*) and, that is, a personal substantiveness which, as such, is not part of the cosmic causal order and follows a different course: the course of freedom." V. M. Tirado, "La encarnación del yo o la inteligencia sentiente: El yo y su cuerpo en Merleau-Ponty y Zubiri. Primera parte: Zubiri," *Cuadernos Salmantinos de filosofía* 25 (1998): 229.

Human." The statement is somewhat bold. The text refers to *trinitarian relationships* assumed into Jesus, so to speak, which implies transcendence and relationality of an unprecedented value. This seems to be a further step with respect to expressions such as *intentional, subjective, or personalized body*.[24]

Trinitarian Foundation of Transferring Self

Having indicated Chiara's contribution in this text to the field of philosophical anthropology, we need now to make explicit the foundation of her radicalization. From the text itself it is clear that it is a *Trinitarian revelation* as unfolded in the Paschal event: "God who is in me," affirms Chiara, "who has shaped my soul, who lives there in Trinity (with the saints and the Angels), is also in the heart of my brothers and sisters."

Emilio Baccarini, in line with the developments in philosophical anthropology we have described, maintains that today it is fundamental to think of the human being in the context of the radicalness of the Christian event.[25] In this sense, the Trinity is a datum that appears as a "fundamental epistemological form."[26] This is connected to the current pressing debate about the possible and necessary relationship between ontology and theology. It would seem that the mysticism of unity, which Chiara's text illustrates, begins with this Trinitarian form of epistemology that presupposes, as pointed out above, a radicalization of the perspectives of openness and transcendence that today permeate inquiries into the nature of what is to be human.

This is how the mysticism of unity translates transcending self into "transferring self" in our brother or sister,[27] and this is nothing other than the active side of "receiving self," another anthropological category with a Trinitarian background. But this self-transcendence is transferring self into "God *in* my brother or sister" (my italics) and not into God *of* my brother or sister, which signals that openness to the other has itself already been

---

24. In other passages, Chiara uses the verb *trinitize* that, since it is used between human persons, includes corporeity.
25. Emilio Baccarini, "Pensare l'uomo a partire dell'evento cristiano," in *Persona, logos, relazione: Uno fenomenologia plurale*, ed., Angela Ales Bello (Rome: Città Nuova, 2011), 472–79.
26. According to Mantovani the expression goes back to the theologian Nicola Ciola: Mauro Mantovani, *Persona e relazione: Tra teologia e filosofia*, 70.
27. Antonio Rosmini uses a similar notion when he speaks of "transporting self into the other" as a movement determined by the personal nature of the human being: Antonio Rosmini, *Teosofia*, n. 872.

transcended. God is not of my brother or sister nor is God mine, but we are in God. What all mystics in history have surely experienced, here seems to be expressed in a way that is closer to reality. At the same time, relationality is not binary or biunique but *Trinitarian relationality or "Trinitarity" given as gift*[28] that, for this reason, is never manipulable but continuously open to the mystery of this gift. In the light of the Trinitarian mystery, reciprocity is thus radically founded.[29]

In Chiara's text, corporeity acquires a fundamental Christological value that suggests the Trinitarian event with powerful social and historical, human-divine implications. It is in this dimension of corporeity and historicity that we need to situate another fundamental meaning of the text: Jesus forsaken as the key of "transferring self," which takes place in what Chiara calls leaving "God for God," a process that leads to discovering the Spirit in God in self, the fullness of Love.[30] Jesus forsaken presents himself as the pattern in the pattern, or the form in the form, of that "*Trinitarity" given as gift*, and in this the text shows us the originality of Chiara's vision of what it is to be human. In this sense, the mystery of Jesus forsaken reveals the face of Love in the dimension of absolute gift and tells us that "transferring self" is nothing other than loving. This form in the form, precisely because it is identified with Jesus forsaken, acquires an inevitably kenotic dimension. It is the *kenotic nature* of giving and of love, without which any hope of meaning for suffering and pain would elude us, as well as any real possibility of understanding love in the human condition.

What does all this mean for an understanding of what it is to be human, seen now not so much as a fundamental form of philosophical anthropology but in its existential repercussions? At the outset I spoke of "a mystical shift in philosophy" and of "a theological shift in phenomenology," and

---

28. This trinitarian nature definitively qualifies transcendental relationality, in the meaning given above, with a radical note of reciprocity. In "trinitarity" reciprocity is also a transcendental.
29. As Piero Coda says, "[R]eciprocity, which is not closed but open, not inclusive but effusive, is the grammar of the origin and the destination of humanity in which the human is written." Piero Coda, "Individuo e comunità: Una prospettiva teologica," in *Persona, Logos, Relazione: Una fenomenologia plural. Scritti in onore di Angela Ales Bello*, eds. E. Baccarini, M. D'Ambra, P. Manganaro, and A.M. Pezzella (Rome: Città Nuova, 2011), 379.
30. Here too we find the same dynamic as seen above in transferring self. Chiara says that in the returning movement the soul does not return into itself, but "to God within."

now we are able to see that *transferring self into the other*, with its Trinitarian radicalization, means avoiding the risk of a spiritualized or individualistic hermeneutics of such a profound anthropological shift—a risk that is very clear, even if paradoxical, in these times of globalization, with all its solitude, intolerance, and depersonalized massification.

Next, Chiara's text urges us towards a more radically relational *praxis*, inasmuch as the proposal goes in the same direction as a continuous *living out of our transferring of self* ("And so, when throughout the day the soul has willingly lost God in itself in order to be transferred into God in its brother or sister. . .") and the living out, in the mutuality, *of welcoming the other*. And here we should emphasize that life lived in this way brings with it in equal measure that fullness of happiness which the experience of a meeting of persons promises in itself and also that communitarian and social commitment which, worked out in history, is implicit in this experience. The heaven of the other is my heaven. In it not only is my heaven not lost, but it is also constantly preserved, rediscovered and enriched as part of a greater heaven which is definitively the heaven of each of us and of all. Therefore the heaven of the other is to be respected, welcomed, guarded, and valued in its uniqueness. This is the basis for active and concrete commitment so the other too may feel that he or she is a heaven.

In short, in the light of Chiara's statement "to look upon all the flowers is to have to vision of Jesus," we can conclude that "transferring self into God in the Other," in its Christological grounding, is not only a mystical experience of tremendous implications for what it is to be human, but it is also a *method* of understanding the divine and the human. It is what Piero Coda calls thinking from and within the Trinity: a form of thinking whereby I transfer myself into the other's thought so as to welcome the other fully in a process in which my own thought is recreated.[31] It is the intellectual aspect of recollecting oneself in the presence of every person without, as Chiara's text says, avoiding the other. After all, this is the experience that with humility, and not without effort, we try to live in the Abba School.

---

31. Piero Coda, *Teologia: La parola di dio nella parole dell' uomo* (Rome, PUL Mursia, 1997), 244; *Dalla Trinità: L'avvento di dio tra storia e profezia* (Rome: Città Nuova, 2011), 584–591.

Chapter Twenty-Two

"When the tree will have blossomed fully...": Reflections on the Church

Brendan Leahy
Hubertus Blaumeiser

In our day, what has happened to that hidden energy of the Good News, which is able to have a powerful effect on man's conscience? To what extent and in what way is that evangelical force capable of really transforming the people of this century? What methods should be followed in order that the power of the Gospel may have its effect? Basically, these inquiries make explicit the fundamental question that the Church is asking herself today and which may be expressed in the following terms: after the Council and thanks to the Council, which was a time given her by God, at this turning-point of history, does the Church or does she not find herself better equipped to proclaim the Gospel and to put it into people's hearts with conviction, freedom of spirit and effectiveness?[1]

These words, written by Pope Paul VI ten years after the conclusion of the Second Vatican Council, are still relevant during the current 50th anniversary of the opening of the Council. They provide a clear indication of how to interpret the Council: it wasn't just about the publication of a series of documents to be put into practice, but about letting the event of Christ and his gospel become present anew in today's world.

In the 1960s the Second Vatican Council was promising. As former Archbishop of Canterbury Rowan Williams commented in October 2012, it "laid out a fresh and joyful vision of how the unchanging reality of Christ living in his Body on earth through the gift of the Holy Spirit might speak in new words to the society of our age and even to those of other faiths."[2]

---

1. Pope Paul VI's Apostolic Exhortation on Evangelization in the Modern World, *Evangelii Nuntiandi* (1975), 4.
2. See Archbishop Rowan Williams' address to the Synod of Bishops on the "New Evangelization for the Transmission of the Christian Faith," Vatican, 10 October 2012.

With its reform in continuity, the Council presented a dynamic vision of the Church: the People of God journeying in history as the "seed" and "beginning" of the Kingdom, the "seed of unity, hope and salvation" (see *Lumen gentium* 5 and 9) that spreads within humanity relationships of mutual giving and receiving rooted in and modelled upon the life of the three divine Persons disclosed to us in Jesus Christ (see *Gaudium et spes* 24).

Fifty years after the Council we realize the task is not easy! With ever new challenges both within the Church and within society, we could easily be tempted either to conform without critical discernment to today's mentality, or else to try and return to the certainty of other times, closing ourselves within a realm of the sacred that is detached from history. But the Church, as Pope Benedict XVI affirmed in *Caritas in Veritate*, "being at God's service, is at the service of the world in terms of love and truth," promoting the full development of humankind (see n.11).

What Chiara Lubich outlines in "Look upon All the Flowers" is an invitation to pursue this pathway; in other words, in order to be in God's service we need to go out to our neighbor.[3] And not simply to help our neighbor, but to let the Kingdom of God occur among us, to let Jesus Christ's dynamic and transforming presence be among us in interpersonal relationships and in the whole of human history. For that to come about we need to "set God aside," as it were, God in oneself – as Chiara explains in the central part of the text – in order to discover him and bring him to light in others.

We won't linger here on this point as others have spoken of this dynamic. Rather, we would like to focus on the final part of the text:

> *And when the tree will have blossomed fully – the Mystical Body will be composed – it will reflect the seed whence it was born. It will be one, because all the flowers will be one among them just as each is one with itself.*
>
> *Christ is the seed. The Mystical Body is the tree's crown.*
>
> *Christ is the Father of the tree: never was he so much Father as during his forsakenness where he begot us as his children, in his forsakenness where he annihilated himself while remaining: God.*
>
> *The Father is root for the Son. The Son is seed for his brothers and sisters.*

---

3. See John Paul II's statement in his first encyclical *Redemptor Hominis*: "Man is the way of the Church" (n. 14).

> *And it was the Desolate who, in her silent consent to being Mother of other children, cast this seed into Heaven and the tree blossomed, and blossoms continuously on earth.*

Given its dense and strongly mystical character, this text is difficult to understand. But we believe that in reading it attentively, referring also to other texts from Paradise '49 as well as to Scripture, it has much to say concerning the life and journey of the Church for the period of history in which we are living.

"*Christ is the seed. The Mystical Body is the tree's crown.*"

Other texts from 1949 help us understand that when Chiara writes of "Mystical Body" here she is thinking not so much of the Church as of the whole of humanity that has already been reached by Christ in his forsakenness, death and resurrection.[4] Following the logic of the text, humanity is called to "blossom," or, in terms found in the Letter to the Ephesians, to grow towards the full maturity of Christ (see Eph 4:13). In other words, it is called to make its own and live the dynamic of giving that we find in the life of Christ, a giving right to the point of self-emptying (*kenosis*—see Phil 2). Not only in relation to God, but also in mutual relationships among people. "To blossom" means that because of Christ (who is the "seed") and through the gift of his Spirit, to establish at all levels and ever more deeply, relationships of unity and distinction that overcome the negative dialectical conflicts that so often characterize human co-existence. It's a question of reproducing (as much as is possible for us human beings), in our mutual relationships, the life of the three divine Persons where each One in full freedom lives *with* the Other, *for* the Other, *in* the Other (see Jn 14-17). As the text states:

> *And when the tree will have blossomed fully – the Mystical Body will be composed – it will reflect the seed whence it was born. It will be one, because all the flowers will be one among them just as each is one with itself.*

The origin of and condition for this "blossoming" of humanity, as the rest of the text makes clear, is the decomposing of the "seed," in other words, the forsakenness of the Son by the Father. Paradoxically, it was precisely in

---

4. See *Gaudium et Spes* 22: "For by His incarnation the Son of God has united Himself in some fashion with every man . . . . [W]e ought to believe that the Holy Spirit in a manner known only to God offers to every man the possibility of being associated with this paschal mystery." See also *LG*, 13-16.

his total human self-emptying and in losing his sense of being God that the Son became "Father" of humanity, filling it with his life of God! He empties himself and yet "remains God," present on earth now not only as the "seed" but as the firstborn among many brothers and sisters (see Rom 8, 26; Heb 1, 6) who form with him and in him one Body (see Col 1, 18; Eph 4, 11-16; 1Cor 12, 12; Rom 12, 4-5):

> *Christ is the Father of the tree: never was he so much Father as during his forsakenness where he begot us as his children, in his forsakenness where he annihilated himself while remaining: God.*

> *The Father is root for the Son. The Son is seed for his brothers and sisters.*

At this point we might ask: between Christ who is the "seed" and humanity as the "foliage" called to "blossom" at all levels in relationships that are not competitive or conflictual but rather "Trinitarian," what is the place and role of the Church? It seems to us that the text we are studying responds in a very succinct manner with the following statement:

> *And it was the Desolate [Mary] who, in her silent consent to being Mother of other children, cast this seed into Heaven and the tree blossomed, and blossoms continuously on earth.*

Let's explore this statement. It is not only dense but, at first glance, rather mysterious. Let's take it step by step, concentrating above all on two crucial moments in the life of Mary, the Mother of the Word Incarnate:

- the moment of the Annunciation when, with her "yes," Mary receives the Word as the divine "seed" and gives him human flesh (see Lk 1:38).

- the moment at the foot of the Cross when, with a new "yes" – the "silent consent" as Chiara puts it – Mary accepts that her God-Son "disincarnates" himself, if we can put it like that, from his particular flesh to take on the flesh of humanity.[5]

---

5. This expression occurs in Paradise '49 and refers to Jesus Forsaken. In a footnote Chiara comments: "As the Word in Jesus became incarnate, so I say the Word in Jesus Forsaken became disincarnate to express the reality of death's climax, forsakenness. I see, that is, something like a disincarnation in the moment when he cried, 'My God, my God, why have you forsaken me?' (Mk 15:34), as if in Jesus God became detached from the human." The theologian S.N. Bulgakov has said something similar: "The Incarnate Son, in his death, forcedly disincarnated himself, as it were . . ."

It's interesting the note the images Chiara uses to describe that moment. At the foot of the Cross Mary, who had received the Word in her womb and given him flesh, "cast this seed in heaven"—in other words, she gave back to God the Son she had conceived, receiving instead John and in him humanity, becoming "Mother of other children." It is with this her "silent consent" that the divine life force – the Spirit – that comes from the "Root" (the Father) pours upon the "flesh" of humanity and shapes humanity according to the Easter life of Christ making it blossom in "Trinitarian" relationships.

In our view, this is a key to understanding both how Mary is model of the Church and also the Marian profile of the Church which John Paul II saw as "the deepest contents of the conciliar renewal."[6]

The Church, in its totality and in each member, is involved in the generation of a renewed and reconciled humanity, one characterized by solidarity. It does so following the example of Mary at the foot of the Cross. On the one hand, the Church is to receive Christ as the divine "seed" that becomes "flesh" in her through the Word and sacraments. On the other hand, however, the Church is called to cast that seed "into heaven" in order to become "mother" of other children; called, that is, to lose God in herself for God present, or to be born, in every man and woman in this world. In other words, the Church is not to be closed in on herself possessing the treasures of grace that she has conceived, as if owning them, but rather she is to open up and go out towards humanity outside herself.

It's a question of being an open and living space in which the kenotic love of Christ, his self-giving to the point of forsakenness, reaches humanity in a concrete-historical way, regenerating it by stamping upon us the character of sonship vis-à-vis God and fraternity among people. This space is

---

(*Agnello di Dio*, Roma 1990, 383). This does not mean – as some of the Gnostics proposed – that the Word of the Second Person of the Trinity was distant from what Jesus was living on the Cross. Rather, here the sense is rather a radicalization of the Incarnation.

6. See John Paul II's *Catechesis on the Signs of the Times* at the General Audience of 25 November 1998. See also his *Address to the Cardinals of the Roman Curia*, 22 December 1987; Benedict XVI, *Homily on the 40th Anniversary of the Conclusion of the Second Vatican Council* (8 December 2005) *and Homily at the Mass with New Cardinals*, 25 March 2006. See further Brendan Leahy, *The Marian Profile of the Church* (Hyde Park, NY: New City, 2000), and Hubertus Blaumeiser and Brendan Leahy, "Prospettive ecclesiogiche a partire da "Gesù in mezzo," in Michel Vandeleene, ed., *Egli è vivo. La presenza del Risorto nella comunità cristiana* (Città Nuova, Rome 2006), 103-29; in particular, 114-22.

relational, one in which the form and the very way of being of Christ and of the uni-Triune God becomes visible and operative. Perhaps we can put it like this: the Church is to be the "womb" of the new humanity in which the Spirit of the Crucified and Risen Christ, in a concrete communitarian context, shapes new men and women who have the form of Christ and of his way of being and acting. It is on account of a Church that is "extrovert" in this sense, directed towards God and towards humanity, that the tree of humanity in its many expressions can "blossom" on earth in a way of relating that is no longer exclusive or conflictual but inclusive and participative—in short, "Trinitarian."

The courageous and new step that the Church is being called to take is to re-live Mary's "yes" at the foot of the Cross in the sense outlined above. The text under consideration, "Look upon All the Flowers," indicates various ways for that to happen:

1. On the *individual* level, it's a matter of "losing God in oneself for God in one's brothers and sisters," that is, of going beyond a search for God that is primarily individual to live an experience of God also in relationship, and ultimately, in society as a whole. The focus, that is, is on Christ not only in the individual but among people, Christ in the midst of us, building up the exterior castle.

2. Similarly, in terms of *each aspect, charism and state of life, parish or religious community of the Church*, it's a question of finding identity by going outside oneself and welcoming others. This is a vital point if we want to be able to reach a deeper and more effective realization of the Church as the People of God in communion. It is vital to achieving a true sense of synodality with all the levels of participation and co-responsibility that this requires. "To be grafted one into another, as are the Persons of the Trinity, in our brother, in our sister we have to lose even God."[7]

3. A third point has to do with *the mission of the Church in the world*. Mission can be understood as expressing and communicating the life of Christ, by placing oneself, in the Spirit of his kenotic love, in an attitude of listening and welcoming that enables God to manifest himself in each person, culture and religion, thereby expanding the spaces in which the presence of the Risen Crucified Christ and his Spirit emerges. It is a presence that draws humanity into the life of mutual giving. This brings about a

---

7. Unpublished text of the Spring of 1950.

manner of living and of inculturation of the Church that paves the way for the explicit proclamation of the truth of the gospel.

But there's another indication provided by the text. Chiara draws our attention to a particular "place," or more precisely a "way," where all of this can and must happen: between two or three who, losing themselves in one another and being consumed in one form a "living cell of the Mystical Body of Christ" capable of gradually reviving the whole Body, the community of the Church and, ultimately, gradually reviving the whole of humanity. It is around such cells in which the Forsaken-Risen Christ releases his kenotic and uniting love, both in the relationships within these cells and in the outreach to others, that the fabric of humanity blossoms. In other words, humanity is "Trinitized," social relations are established, relationships of unity and distinction to the point of mutual immanence.[8]

The way that Chiara lays out for achieving this is a continuous going "beyond," beyond the confines of one's own identity, beyond that of one's own community, beyond every experience of unity with God and others, beyond the Church, in order to be projected towards humanity in an all-around dialogue of life that is not dispersion but rather a way to create ever broader spaces of Trinitarian relationships.

---

8. See also a comment of Chiara Lubich's: "God wants from us that . . . everywhere we bring to life living cells, with Christ in our midst; cells that are ever more ardent, ever more numerous. God wants from us that we light bigger and bigger fires in families, in offices, in factories, in schools, in parishes, in monasteries and convents, to feed the blaze of the love of God in the Church and in society" (*The Key to Unity* [London: New City, 1985], 39). A similar idea is voiced today in many parts of the world in the various forms of small Christian communities. See *Gen's* 49 (2009) n. 3.

As we noted above, it seems this is the step being asked of the Church and of every believer. By way of conclusion, we would like to summarize what we have said in iconic form using two images.

The first image comes from the church of the Savior in Constantinople. The church is called "in Chora," that is, in the countryside. Above the portal of the Byzantine Church there's a depiction of Mary Mother of God *(Theotokos)* with the inscription: "the ground of the Uncontainable" (in Greek: *chora tou achoretou*). This can be translated also as "the womb that contains the Uncontainable." The reference is clearly to the moment of the Incarnation when Mary received the Word in its making itself little, a "seed." It is significant, however, that this image is placed right over the exit of the Church, as the last thing believers see as they leave the sacred building. It's as if to say to them: just like me, you are called to be "the womb of the Uncontainable," you are called to receive Christ and nourish him with your humanity, but then also – and this is the new step – to remind you that he is the "Uncontainable," the One who cannot be kept closed within you but must go outside and shape the reality around you, that is, shape social, political and economic relationships . . . the seed that, in dying, releases all its uncontainable Life by losing it, the Life that is already, in a hidden manner, present in all of creation awaiting to find the conditions for it to sprout and blossom.

The other image is the tree of life depicted in the mosaic in the apse of the Church of San Clemente in Rome. The Crucified Christ is at the center. From him flow rivers of living water – the Spirit – that spray all created reality, depicted both as nature, with plants and animals, and as cultures depicted in symbols that refer to various human activities. Above the Crucified Christ is the hand of God the Father, the One who is the "Root" of the Son. On the left we see Bethlehem and on the right, Jerusalem, the city-symbol of a Trinitarian sociality that is to be lived out throughout the whole of humanity.

We might ask – and where is the Church depicted in this mosaic? On the one hand, it is simply the space, the background, the womb in which all of this happens, as depicted in Mary together with John. With her "silent consent" and with her lived participation, she lets all of this happen. On the other hand, the Church is present in the twelve white doves depicted on the tree of the Cross. They represent the Twelve Apostles. It is there, on the Cross and around the Cross, that the ordained ministers and all the baptized can draw continually upon the source of Easter-Trinitarian relationality that they are called to witness to and bring about in humanity.

To move continuously from the first image to the second, in a constant shift from the religious and ecclesial sphere to the unending sphere of humanity in its lay nature – this is the step which the People of God is called to take and for which a text such as "Look upon All the Flowers" offers important pointers.

Part Six

Implication of Paradise '49 for Society and Culture

Chapter Twenty-Three

The Charism of Unity in Dialogue with Contemporary Culture and the Paradigm of Fraternity

Maria Voce

The title of this article poses a basic question: does the charism of unity, given by God to Chiara Lubich, have something to say to contemporary culture? Right from the beginning of her spiritual and human experience, Chiara intuited that the charism God was giving her had a universal breadth. It was universal in two ways. It had to do with the whole human family in the most diverse geographical and cultural situations. And besides containing a spirituality to be lived, it would be able to have an impact on the different fields of knowledge, as well as the different social, political, and economic realities. This was an intuition that in time revealed itself in history. In order to grasp how much this charism can give to today's cultures, it is important that we focus on its most authentic and innovative content.

The word that God, through Chiara, wished to highlight for humanity today is all contained in Jesus' Testament: "May they all be one" (Jn. 17:21). Chiara's story has a simple flavor, but, at the same time, is also solemn and foundational:

> The war was on. A few girls and I were huddled together in some dark place, perhaps a cellar. By candlelight we were reading the final testament of Jesus. We read through the whole passage. Those difficult words seemed to light up for us, one after another. We felt we understood them. Above all, we felt the solid conviction that what we had before us was the "founding charter" of this new life of ours, and of all that was about to be born around us.[1]

Much later, Chiara explained: "Unity is the word that sums up the life of our Movement. For us it is the word that carries in itself every other super-

---

1. Chiara Lubich, *Essential Writings; Spirituality, Dialogue, Culture* (Hyde Park, NY: New City Press, 2007), 16.

natural reality, every other practice or commandment, every other religious approach."² The charism of unity was thus able to produce a spirituality that is communitarian: "in which love awaits love in return, and giving awaits receivin."³ From this spirituality of unity came forth a current of life and thought that would find both followers and animators in the five continents, in different cultures, in many faiths, and in all expressions of personal and societal life where the needs of humanity show themselves. This current of thought, bears a doctrine and a culture that is innervating the different fields of knowledge and disciplines for a constructive and dialogical rapport in the building of a more human and united world.

Unity can be lived by everyone, really by everyone, on the condition that it be the fruit of love, of what Chiara calls a:

> love that lives deep in the heart of every human being. For the followers of Christ, this love can be a participation in the very love that is the life of God. It is a love that is strong, capable of loving even those who do not reciprocate but instead attack us as enemies. It is a love capable of forgiving."⁴

Love for followers of many faiths is expressed in the Golden Rule: do to others what you would like done to you. It is also a love that for those who do not have religious faith is manifested as solidarity, good will, and nonviolence. Love of God and of neighbor was the initial inspiring spark that was increasingly refined up to the point of discovering anew Jesus' new

---

2. Lubich, *Essential Writings*, 26–27. Father Jesús Castellano, a Discalced Carmelite well-known as an expert of spirituality and mysticism, consultant of various congregations of the Holy See and member of the Abba School, wrote the following: "There is no doubt that a supernatural wisdom, a charism of the Holy Spirit was at the basis of such a new and high discovery, I would say a novelty up to this moment in the Church, even though it is intuited and preached in the Christian spirituality. We can affirm that here we find ourselves in front of a charism born from a page of the Gospel that this time is not the page of poverty, of prayer or works of mercy, but a page that reveals the mystery of unity, the same goal for Christ's coming among human beings, of his death and resurrection. . . . It's a novelty that raises the communitarian and ecclesial spirituality to be a Trinitarian spirituality, a spirituality of unity in which love and therefore the demands of this love, possesses a Trinitarian measure: 'as you in me and I in you.'" (Chiara Lubich, *Unity and Jesus Forsaken*, Hyde Park, NY: New City Press, 1985, 11–12 [editor's translation])
3. Chiara Lubich, Lectio Magistralis in occasion of the conferral of an honorary doctorate by the University of Trnava (Slovakia); June 23, 2003.
4. Chiara Lubich, Speech at the Symposium "Towards a Unity of Nations and a Unity of Peoples," at the UN in New York in 1997. See *Nuova Umanità* XX (1998): 58.

commandment: "This is my commandment, that you love one another as I have loved you" (Jn 15:12).

Latin America: A New Birthplace of Fraternity

Let us go back to the initial question: does the charism of unity have something to say to today's cultures? I think everyone is well aware that in the context of the economic crisis which has especially affected the West, there is the existence of a crisis which is much more profound: that of the European culture. The reflections and research by sociologists reveal the demise of a culture which, after having reached important thresholds, lacked the light of reason due to the weakness and/or incapacity to at least perceive the reality of the light that is the wisdom of God which is able to illuminate and support our quest for the truth.

But in this moment, my attention goes to the Latin American continent, the so-called "continent of hope" that is living a truly extraordinary moment in history. In the context of the celebrations around the independence of South America, the *Roman Observer* recently published an article with a title that seemed very indicative to me: "South America is no Longer the Continent of Lost Opportunities."[5] There is a *kairós* for this continent, an opportune moment in which the virtuous interweaving of various elements is leading it to a full blossoming that was certainly hoped for, but not foreseen so soon. The whole region is for the first time finding its own voice, with an *intercultural identity* that enriches the diverse roots—those of the indigenous peoples, of the Spanish and Portuguese, and of the immigrants coming from all over the world since the end of the nineteenth century—but which at the same time emerges as something new.

The sufficiently clear signs that nourish this hope are: the relative political stability reached by the different democratic systems; the growth of the economy and the social policies that have undoubtedly improved the quality of life of millions of people; a proper system of production that seeks also the integral development of persons; and last but not least the strong tendency towards regional integration, to the unity of the continent:

> Even though pluralistic, South America has powerful roots of unity, like no other region of the world, both for its common origins, events and historical destiny, and for the dominant lan-

---

5. Carriquiry Lecour, *L'Osservatore Romano*, March 8, 2012, 4.

guage and its Catholic tradition, which nourishes a shared sense of solidarity in this enlarged fraternity. What in Bolivar's vision was truly a utopia . . . today begins to decisively take shape and to grow within the internal integrative processes of the last 50 years, which took a leap of quality with the MERCOSUR (Common Market of the South) that, despite all its daily difficulties, broke through the traditional isolation of Brazil with regards to the Hispanic American nations and today emerges also in the UNASUR (Union of South American Nations) and the Community of South American and Caribbean Nations.[6]

In these same signs of hope are hidden the challenges now before the continent: the persistent social inequalities that surface in a deficient "social cohesion"; the more or less profound difference between cities with a high indicator of school enrollment, university culture, research and services and vast peripheral regions with low integral development; the persistence of widespread corruption both at a public and private level. The push to overcome and positively resolve these challenges is found in the very values of the Latin American culture. We said that it is a real and pluralistic culture that also has the instruments to forge corresponding structures for an effective integration.

In 1998, Chiara spent more than a month in Argentina, meeting also with her people who came from Peru, Chile, Uruguay, Bolivia, and Paraguay. It was a memorable month, characterized by events and public and private encounters: the honorary doctorate at the University of Buenos Aires, the proclamation of honored guest by the City Administration of Buenos Aires, the meeting with the Argentinean Episcopal Conference, and the visit to our little town in O'Higgins. Towards the end of the month, she met over 8,000 members of the Movement.

A 360 Degree Dialogue and the Concept of Fraternity

On that occasion, in summing up her encounter with the realities of these lands, she underscored a specific message: It is not enough only to go ahead with the growth of the Movement, but the Movement needs to help make a deeper impact on their social and cultural fabric, on their political and manufacturing sectors. This was sort of an inspiration that was maturing within

---

6. Carriquiry Lecour, *L'Osservatore Romano*, 4.

her while she was in contact with the peoples of Latin America, with their sufferings and their hopes. Chiara explained:

> Here too, something absolutely new was born. This already became clear during the university ceremony. Present there were people of different convictions but also Muslims, Jews, Christians, all united. I said to myself: the charism not only develops Christian people, but it also brings about the universal human family, because it takes in everyone. Therefore, my advice to you here, then, is a 360 degree dialogue, that is, to love everyone. . . .[7]

This underscoring of a dialogue of love by Chiara would then emerge when she continued her trip to Brazil as an appeal addressed to the whole Focolare Movement in the world: to develop, starting from the charism of unity, a doctrine that in the different fields of knowledge would give intellectual and scientific rigor to love in dialogue with culture and different cultures.

In the following years, this dialogue of love was articulated in a concept of *fraternity* that was already present in the early years of Trent[8] but which now was being developed in the most diverse areas of life and of knowledge as an actual social category—that of fraternity—able to address our lives and our attitudes in ways that tend towards unity. Chiara herself deepened this concept at different events and occasions, explaining its application in politics, economy, art, communication, health, the environment, and so forth. She saw fraternity as indispensable for the fulfilment of the common good of the community and of the universal human family.

In a message to politicians and administrators in South America, Chiara said:

> The strong contradictions that mark our era need a *point of reference* that is equally penetrating and incisive, categories of thinking

---

7. Address to the members of the Movement of Argentina, Uruguay, Paraguay, Chile, Bolivia, and Peru in Buenos Aires, April 12, 1998 (unpublished).

8. "Before all else, the soul must always fix its gaze on the one Father of many children. Then it must see all as children of the same Father. In mind and in heart we must always go beyond the bounds imposed on us by human life alone and create the habit of constantly opening ourselves to the reality of being one human family in one Father: God" (Lubich, *Essential Writings*, 17–18). And also later: "Keep your heart open to all of humanity and teach those for whom you are responsible to do the same. May it not be that Jesus came on earth in vain to preach the universal family" (Lubich, *Essential Writings*, 236).

and of actions able to engage every individual person, as well as peoples with their economic, social and political systems. There is a universal idea that is already *an experience in action*, and which is proving to be able to take on this epochal challenge; this idea is universal brotherhood [fraternity].[9]

In a deep dialogue with a prominent North American political leader who founded the "Day for Interdependence," Chiara wrote in a message she sent for the Day for Interdependence celebrated in Philadelphia:

> Without fraternity, no person or people are really truly free and equal. Equality and freedom will always be incomplete and precarious, until fraternity will be an integral part of the political agenda and processes in every region of the world.
>
> Fraternity today can give new content to the reality of interdependence. And fraternity can bring out projects and actions in the complex of the political, cultural and social fabric of our world. It is fraternity that makes us step beyond our isolation and opens the door to development for peoples who are still excluded from it. It is fraternity that indicates how to peacefully resolve the divisions that makes war part of our history books. It is because of fraternity lived out that we can dream and even hope in some form of communion of goods between wealthy and poor nations. . . . The deep need for peace that humanity expresses states that fraternity is not only a value, not only a method, but a global paradigm of political development. This is why a world that is increasingly interdependent needs politicians, business people, intellectuals and artists who place fraternity—an instrument of unity—at the heart of their actions and thinking."[10]

On another occasion, Chiara added:

> [I]nterdependence implies a mutual relationship between two parties who condition one another. This relationship cannot be lived out perfectly between individuals or among nations if not characterized by mutual respect and understanding, by the capac-

---

9. Chiara Lubich, "Cities for Unity," a message at the meeting Ciudades por la Unidad, Rosario, Argentina, June 1, 2005 (unpublished).
10. Chiara Lubich, "Message to the Day of Interdependence," September 12, 2003 (unpublished).

ity to embrace the difficulties and issues each one faces, and by the desire to welcome one another's unique gift. Practically speaking, it requires mutual love as it is lived out among brothers and sisters . . . the choice of respectful dialogue as opposed to hegemony, and the practice of sharing among all as opposed to concentrating resources and expertise exclusively in certain parts of the world. . . . Animated by fraternity, interdependence, beyond being a simple "fact" or "tool," can become the force that drives the process of positive developments.[11]

Fraternity: A Global Paradigm for Unity in Diversity

Upon returning to Rome after her trip in South America in 1998, Chiara decisively launched the "Dialogue with Culture," thus giving life to a Center for the different fields of knowledge, at which dialogue with experts and academicians from the most diverse fields of study, including those of non-religious convictions, could take place. There, the new paradigm of fraternity is beginning to find scientific backing. Through seminars, conferences, study groups, scientific reviews, the charism of unity is taking on a cultural task to penetrate culture from within through a creative dialogue. This cultural proposal is one and also plural. One in its origins and source: the charism of unity. Plural in its dynamic of welcoming and being welcomed in the most diverse contexts, in its many values, in its most distinct applications in personal life and in society. We live in times that are not only very difficult but also particularly complex. Humanity, in its growth curve, is going through a delicate moment: it can take a qualitative step of notable importance, or it could live a static moment, or worse yet, one of involution. The push to aim high and to go ahead can come from every angle.

Chiara's legacy, that which she left to the men and women of our times, is the rediscovery of the gospel as a true propelling force in history, from the small and precious story of each person, as well as the great and equally precious story of peoples, and of all humanity. I think, however, that I cannot keep the key to Chiara's legacy for myself, the secret to every successful unity. Chiara herself did not often speak about it, but she did not remain silent about it. In her talk in 1997 to the UN, after having shown her spirituality as a way and instrument for peace, she added: "Nothing good, nothing

---

11. Lubich, *Essential Writings*, 265–68.

useful, nothing fruitful for the world can be achieved without meeting and accepting weariness and suffering; in a word, without the cross."[12]

The cross is not an assemblage of two crossed pieces of wood, but the wood that carried Jesus, the man-God. Jesus crucified and forsaken covers and takes on all the suffering of the world, and, in a wholly special way, the suffering and sacrifice for which love and unity call. In Chiara's words: "And, to love well, we must not see the difficulties, corruption and sufferings of the world merely as social evils to be resolved. Rather, we must recognize in these the countenance of Christ, who did not disdain to hide himself beneath all human misery."[13] He is also the "place" of the full revelation to us of the love of God for humanity, and the mediator who recomposed our unity with God and among us:

> [E]very physical, moral, or spiritual suffering is nothing other than a shadow of his immense suffering.
>
> Jesus Forsaken is the image of those who feel perplexed, doubtful, of those who ask "why?" Jesus Forsaken is the image of the mute. He can no longer speak.
>
> In a certain sense, Jesus Forsaken is the figure of the blind—he doesn't see; of the deaf—he doesn't hear. He is the exhausted who laments. He seems to be on the edge of despair. He is the one who starves . . . for union with God. He is the image of the disillusioned; he is fearful, bewildered. He appears to have failed. Jesus Forsaken is the image of darkness, melancholy, conflict; the image of all that is indefinable, strange, because he is a God who cries for help! He is non-sense.[14]

It was therefore clear that that immense suffering had something to do with the mystery of unity. Not only, but He, who had not remained in the grip of that infinite suffering but, with a superhuman and unimaginable effort, had re-abandoned Himself to the Father, saying: "Father, into your hands I give up my spirit" (Lk 23:46), was teaching us the way to behave

---

12. Chiara Lubich, Speech at the Symposium "Towards a Unity of Nations and a Unity of Peoples," 58.
13. Chiara Lubich, "For a civilization of Unity." Speech at the Conference on A Culture of Peace for the Unity of Peoples, Castelgandolfo (Rome), June 11–12, 1988 (unpublshed).
14. Chiara Lubich, "Unity and Jesus Crucified and Forsaken: Foundation for a Spirituality of Communion." Speech at the World Council of Churches, Geneva, October 20, 2002; in *Nuova Umanità* XXV (2003): 26–27.

in the midst of different disunities, in the separations, in the abandonments and, therefore, the way to overcome them.[15]

Thus, a 360-degree dialogue exists in full circle with our contemporary cultures. People are together facing and addressing the pressing issues and sufferings facing humankind. Thinking of the projects to promote integration in our continents and between our continents, the charism of unity offers itself to contribute to building a global culture, a global culture that respects the diverse cultures of the world, that finds its paradigm in fraternity.

---

15. Chiara Lubich, "Jesus Crucified and Forsaken: Focal Point for a Spirituality of Communion." Speech to the bishops of Bavaria, April 23, 2003 (unpublished).

Chapter Twenty-Four

Love of All Loves: Politics and Fraternity in the Charismatic Vision of Chiara Lubich

Antonio Maria Baggio

Political reality remains important throughout the reflections of Chiara Lubich. This can be seen in her writings during all periods of her life, both in her private correspondence and in a large number of unpublished notes, up to the great speeches on public occasions given during the last years of her life, especially between 1996 and 2004.

It is a path characterized by various aspects. On the one hand, one cannot speak of her "political thought" in the normal sense of the expression. Chiara does not produce theories or specific political programs. She does not use the technical language of politics. On the other hand, she does address the most important issues of politics and has spoken in such institutions as parliaments and government chambers. Even if her language is full of spirituality and rich with explicit religious references, she is still able to communicate beyond all confessional boundaries. There seems to be originality in the approach which she brings to political reality. It departs, however, from the usual schemes and therefore requires a little effort to grasp its essence.

First, it is important to note the context within which her thought arises, that of the Second World War. War represents the failure of politics and a radical challenge to the cultures and humanism that had preceded it and yet were not able to prevent it. War does not only destroy homes, lives, personal plans, but also collective certainties and great common cultural references. All over the world, but particularly in Europe, the violence of totalitarianism raised questions about the legacy of traditions and about the meaning of the West. This was a time of very serious challenges to thought; and the years of the war saw the publication of relevant philosophical and political reflections that attempted to lay the foundations for the construction of a new society. Within this general rethinking, a burst of feminine genius stands out across the continent and illuminates humanity, carrying out an intellectual and existential search with a radicality proportionate to the evil that caused it. Among other examples we could list: Edith Stein, who fulfilled her fidelity to the truth with the ultimate sacrifice in Auschwitz on August 9, 1942, and Simone Weil, who died on August 28, 1943 of exhaustion while working for the French Resistance in England. It was also during those years—in September 1946—that a new vocation matured for an Albanian nun named Maria Teresa, making her Mother Teresa of Calcutta.

At the Root of Political Thought:
The Tradition of Relational Definitions and Fraternity

It is in the context of such sufferings and amidst such debris that Chiara's search blossoms, in the awareness of the collapse of the theories and the vanity of tired words. An adventure without expectations begins, relying exclusively on the words of the gospels. For Chiara these were the only words capable of passing the test of those difficult times. Chiara, speaking about those days during which her city of Trent was being heavily bombed, explains:

> We had aimed at the poorest areas of Trent, in the effort to kindle the love the Gospel speaks of there, looking after the needy with the help of those who were better off. By doing so, we hoped to bring about equality in fraternity in the city. This activity won the esteem of the local politicians and aroused their desire to do likewise on a larger scale.
>
> Consequently, instead of a vicious circle, mutual love created a virtuous circle which re-established trust, re-opened hope and recomposed the torn personal and civil bonds. In a context of war-caused lawlessness, we started out again from love—the law of laws, the supreme value, the principle and synthesis of all values. This love, capable of re-building community, brought about unity among citizens which is the essential premise of any communal life.[1]

What Chiara describes here is a humanism that reconstructs people and the city, that does not consciously establish political goals for itself, but does fulfill them. Chiara's reflection is not political thought in the ordinary sense,

---

1. Chiara Lubich, "Towards a Politics of Communion," address to the Italian Parliament at Palazzo San Macuto, Rome, December 15, 2000. (Our translation.)

but may be defined as a *charismatic reflection on the city*, on the *polis*. It is drawn from a more profound level than common political thought. It is a "seeing" and a "thinking" that highlights the radical relationship from which *different political thoughts* may be inspired. It is a complete humanism, whose political dimension is only one expression. We note that in the destruction of war, *there was no polis*, in the sense that the specific dimensions of citizenship had degenerated. The humanism triggered by Chiara rebuilds it. It is a combination of constructive thought and the action of the city. Human relationships are rewoven, and this is the premise for the re-establishment of laws and civic virtues; it is the very foundation of citizenship, the unitary condition of any subsequent politics.

Chiara's brief description regarding the action of the first *focolarine* in the city of Trent comes from a talk she gave on June 9, 2000, on the occasion of the first congress of the Movement for Unity in Politics. In explaining this action, Chiara brings together some basic elements: (1) the free decision of the *focolarine* to love; (2) favoring the least who were helped with the goods of the more well-to-do, thus creating bonds of fraternity between the two groups; (3) and thus achieving equality through fraternity. For Chiara, from the very beginning in 1943, these three elements—liberty, equality, fraternity—create the conditions of political life.

In this inaugural talk, Chiara rereads the history of the Focolare Movement and its relationship with politics from the perspective of fraternity, which is proposed as the specific characteristic of the new political Movement for Unity in Politics. So she says:

> What is the specific characteristic of the Movement for Unity in Politics? We know that the redemption brought about by Jesus on the cross transforms from within all human bonds, imbuing them with divine love and making us all brothers and sisters. This has profound meaning for our Movement. If we consider that the great political plan of modernity is summarized in the motto of the French Revolution: "liberty, equality, fraternity." While the first two principles have been partially achieved in recent centuries, despite numerous formal declarations, fraternity has been all but forgotten in the political arena. Instead, it is precisely *fraternity* that can be considered as *what is most specific*

in our Movement. What is more, by living out fraternity, freedom and equality acquire new meaning and find greater fulfillment.[2]

In fact, at that time, to speak of fraternity in the political world, whether at the level of action or in academic reflection, was to risk being misunderstood or mocked. This was and remains a sign of the deep crisis that theoretical and practical politics is going through. We see it when politicians limit their action to the pursuit of the inclinations of the electorate rather than proposing serious and far-reaching programs. We see it when political problems are transformed into issues of law enforcement and public order. We see it when reliance on weapons is preferred over dealing with the real causes of domestic and international injustice. We see it when politics becomes the passive executor of great economic interests and things get out of hand. In each of these cases, politics betrays itself and is reduced to something else, because it no longer knows what it is.

Chiara's approach to politics gives an original contribution within the great tradition of relational definitions of politics, based on the interpretation of the nature of the bond of citizenship starting from the very foundations of political discourse. Aristotle gave rise to this rich and complex tradition, defining the relationship between citizens as friendship based on "utility," where utility is understood as the common good.[3] Aristotle's notion of the common good does not consist only of the availability of material goods, infrastructure, and institutions. It is characterized by a common desire to create the conditions for a happy life, based on the pursuit of what is rational and good. Political friendship is therefore a relationship that requires civic virtues and the ability of each person to set aside his or her private interests in order to attain a good that can be achieved only when pursued together with the others. He also provides other definitions of politics,[4] but the relational type definitions to which he gave rise are genetic and descriptive, showing on what anthropological bases the political society is formed.

---

2. Chiara Lubich, "The Movement for Unity and a Politics of Communion," address to the International Conference of the Movement of Unity in Politics, Castelgandolfo, June 9, 2000. See Chiara Lubich, *Essential Writings* (Hyde Park, NY: New City Press, 2007), 244.
3. Aristotle, *Nicomachean Ethics*, IX, 6, 1167a.
4. Aristotle, *Nicomachean Ethics*, 1094 a–b.

This tradition has provided essential interpretative tools that have served throughout the history of political thought. The relational dimension is decisive, for example, in the political philosophy of Augustine. As is well known, he describes the life of two cities where the relationship among the citizens of one city is very different from the relationship among the citizens of the other. There are two radically different forms of citizenship: the citizenship of the city of God, where citizens are united by social and agapic-love, by the will to do good for each other; and the citizens of the earthly city, characterized by a private and self-love.[5] Throughout history, the two cities are mixed together and it is difficult to distinguish one from the other. In the same parliament we can meet both types of citizens: those who have this social and agapic-love and therefore contribute to the common good, and those who have private and self-love, and whose political activity is really carried out for their own benefit.[6] But according to Augustine, only social love is able to establish true citizenship. The relationship based on private interests is not political; and without social-love there is no real city, there is no *polis*, there is no politics.

Passing on to the modern age, according to Thomas Hobbes the political society is built through a contract in which each person gives up all his or her rights in order to give life to a political institution wherein power is absolute—the Leviathan—precisely to protect each person from the aggressiveness of others. For Hobbes, the essence of human relationality is expressed in aggressiveness, whether this is caused by desire for profit, by the pursuit of personal safety or of glory. In any case, the outcome is destructive and generates a permanent insecurity and fear among citizens for their own lives. The institutions born from such a vision reflects it: humans are subjects rather than citizens.[7]

John Locke adopted a different anthropological vision on the basis of a contract giving rise to political society. Certainly, for Locke there are also other reasons that require the setting up of a political society, especially the element of the defense of property. But even before coming together politically, human beings are linked in society and acknowledge an obligation

---

5. Augustine, *The City of God*, XIV, 7, 2.
6. Augustine, *De Genesi ad Litteram*, 11, 16, 20.
7. Thomas Hobbes, *Leviathan*, I, XIII.

of mutual love.[8] Locke grasps this social vision of human nature from the Bible, of which he was a passionate reader, and from the reflections of the great Anglican theologian Richard Hooker, who considered mutual love not only as a commandment of the gospel, but as a duty that human beings can understand based on natural intelligence.[9] For this reason, according to Locke, human beings already live socially before establishing the political contract. The government that emerges from such an anthropological setting must be based on laws and consensus. In fact, it is the precursor of the modern state of law.[10]

We see then that focusing on the anthropological and relational dimension of citizenship, and using the vocabulary of sociality and love, or their opposites, is not at all improper, but is part of a significant tradition in the history of political thought. Losing it, giving up this kind of language, would mean losing some essential contents of human history. For her part, Chiara recovers this tradition, bringing to light a historical path on which to set one's own thoughts, reinterpreting tradition in order to continue building it.

The Love of All Loves

The relationship of love, the ways to build it and the difficulties it encounters, has great significance in Chiara's reflection on politics. It makes sense that she should try to communicate this fundamental "resource" to those who engage in politics so as to lead them to the source of love itself. For Chiara, this source is God; it is in Christ that it is fully revealed to human beings. Chiara explains: "[Jesus] is the *Human Being*, the perfect human being, who sums up and contains all men and women and every truth and inner urging they may feel to raise themselves to their proper place."[11] But it is not the omnipotent Jesus the miracle worker, or the Jesus who attracts and feeds the crowd, that she feels is closest to the tasks of politicians. For Chiara the greatest love is manifested in Jesus in his abandonment.

---

8. John Locke, *The Second Treatise of Government: An Essay Concerning the True Original, Extent, and End of Civil Government*, II, 5.
9. Richard Hooker, *Of the Laws of Ecclesiastical Polity: Book One*, ed., A. S. McGrade (Cambridge: Cambridge University Press, 2002), 80.
10. Locke, *The Second Treatise of Government* II, 5.
11. Lubich, *Essential Writings*, 240 (translation updated).

In her address at the first congress of the Movement for Unity in Politics,[12] she proposes Jesus forsaken as the model of a politician because he is the one who embraces all divisions, defeats, and separations present in humanity; and he brings them all back to unity with God. Chiara explains that the cry of Jesus forsaken "is the most beautiful Song, because the Love that he gives us is God: his suffering is divine and therefore God is his Love."[13] Politics is also suffering that is transformed into love. It is the choice to devote ourselves to meet the needs of others, to fulfill the rights of human beings. If it were just suffering, it would only turn into resignation or hatred, which are two forms of war: against ourselves or against others. But if suffering is transformed into love, politics takes the place of war, and the united city arises: "Jesus Forsaken [is] the greatest love, the Love of Loves, Unity."[14]

Speaking to a few hundred mayors and administrators of European cities gathered in Innsbruck in 2000, Chiara goes more into this important message. Chiara is realistic in her assessment of the difficulties, conflicts, and tragedies that politics must face and overcome. Therefore, on the one hand, she proposes Jesus forsaken as a model who was able to go beyond conflict, remaining faithful to his duty up to the ultimate sacrifice entrusting himself to the Father. On the other hand, and precisely for this reason, she sees political love not as a sentiment, or a generic love that diverts attention from cruel life, and not even as an ethical reminder that judges the good and evil without considering effective action. Rather it is the specific way in which politics addresses and solves the problems of society. We can understand this better if we follow Chiara along two important pathways.

The first concerns the role of Mary. If Jesus is the model of the politician, for Chiara, Mary is the one who must lead the political movement. She writes:

> It is Mary who sings: "The Mighty One has done great things for me" (Lk 1:49). In her God has deposited his plan for humanity. In her he reveals his mercy for humankind, destroys the false projects of the proud, casts down the powerful from their thrones and lifts up the lowly, reestablishes justice and redistributes riches. Who, then, is more a politician than Mary? The task of the

---

12. Lubich, *Essential Writings*, 242.
13. Chiara Lubich, Unpublished Writings, July 24, 1949.
14. Lubich, Unpublished Writings, July 24, 1949.

Movement for Unity in Politics is to contribute toward fulfilling in human history what Mary announces as already accomplished in herself.[15]

For Chiara, Mary's Magnificat is the summary of the program of the Movement; every word of Mary corresponds to a violated right and a concrete political action to be taken. But Chiara, emphasizing what has "already" been accomplished in Mary, indicates a precise methodology to the Movement: before carrying out something outside, we must have already achieved among us what we want to build for everyone. Mary is the antidote to all ideology.

The second way of understanding the specificity of the political action proposed by Chiara is to carefully examine the words: "Love of all loves." This phrase is often repeated, but not always understood. It is the expression that tradition attributes to Bernard of Clairvaux, to designate the Eucharist,[16] understood as the sacrament which expresses Christ's sacrifice and thus the apex of his love. The phrase enters the tradition of ecclesial thought and perception and remains there up until today.[17] For Chiara, the Love of

---

15. Lubich, *Essential Writings*, 244.
16. The expression "amor amorum" referring to the Eucharist can be found in two texts. Regarding the inauthenticity of the first text, whose author is called Ps. Bernardus, *Sermo de excellentia SS. Sacramenti et dignitate sacerdotum*, n. 10: PL 184, col. 987, we were advised by the editor: "Non est S. Bernardi, sed cujusdam non sacerdotis, ut ex num. 3, 5 et 16 colligitur," ivi, col. 981. The second text, *De coena Domini alius sermo: Opera S. Bernardi*, Basileae 1552, col. 188, does not even exist in the Patrology of Migne. The erroneous attribution can be explained by the existence of a genuine sermon of Bernard of Clairvaux, entitled In *Coena Domini. Sermo de baptismo, sacramento altaris, et ablutione pedum* (PL 183), with which the other two texts, of "unknown author," are commonly confused. The phrase "love of loves" in reference to the Eucharist is attributed to Bernard by many eminent authors such as Francis de Sales (see Letter to Chantal cited by P. G. Galizia, *La vita di S. Francesco de Sales: Vescovo e principe di Geneva, Fondatore dell'ordine della Visitazione*, Venezia, 1762, 367) and Alfonso Maria de' Liguori, *La vera sposa di Gesù Cristo* (1760–1761), XVIII, 235, in *Opere ascetiche*, Vol. XIV–XV. Rome: CSSR, 1935: available in I Edizione IntraText CT, Copyright Èulogos 2007, www.intratext.com; *Pratica di amar Gesù Cristo* (1768), in *Opere ascetiche*, Vol. I, 1–243, CSSR, Roma 1933, available in I Edizione IntraText CT, Copyright Èulogos 2007, www.intratext.com); up to the one closest to us by Annibale Maria di Francia, *A Gesù diletto dei cuor* (1899); in Dattiloscritti, vol. 54, 27; on the official website www.difrancia.net). Such authoritative precedents were taught in many homilies, especially on Holy Thursday where reference to Bernard is usual.
17. It is enough to cite the Post-Synodal Apostolic Exhortation *Sacramentum Caritatis* of the Holy Father Benedict XVI, to the bishops, clergy, consecrated persons and

all loves becomes the Love that embraces suffering and disunity, overcoming them. It therefore retains its Eucharistic meaning and effectiveness; but inasmuch as it is political love, it actively penetrates history laically exercising what is typical of Eucharistic love. Chiara explains:

> In fact, politics seen as love creates and preserves those conditions that allow all other types of love to flourish: the love of young people who want to get married and who need a house and employment; the love of those who want to study and who need schools and books; the love of those who run their own business and who need roads and railways, clear and reliable laws. . . . Thus, politics is the love of all loves, gathering the resources of people and groups into the unity of a common design so as to provide the means for each one to fulfill in complete freedom his or her specific vocation. But it also encourages people to cooperate, bringing together needs and resources, questions and answers, instilling mutual trust among all. Politics can be compared to the stem of a flower, which supports and nourishes the fresh unfolding of the petals of the community.[18]

Here we encounter one of the innovative aspects of the charism of unity: Chiara shares what Bernard said of the Eucharist, but she says the same for politics. For her, politics understood as action and thought of authentic love has similar value to the Eucharist. It is the exercise of the total and splendid priesthood of humanity that loves, of the politician who, in the daily practice of his political profession, offers himself as a sacrifice.[19] On several occasions, in fact, Chiara recalled some examples of politicians who became saints not "in spite of" politics, but through it, among whom there are Robert Schuman, Igino Giordani, and Alcide De Gasperi.

---

    the lay faithful on the Eucharist as the source and summit of the Church's life and mission, Rome, February 22, 2007, where the Eucharist is defined as the "sacrament of love."

18. Chiara Lubich, "A United Europe for a United World," address to One Thousand Cities for Europe, a conference for European mayors, Innsbruck, Austria, November 9, 2001: *Essential Writings*, 254–255.
19. A few years after this talk of Chiara Lubich, Benedict XVI, in the above-cited Post-Synodal Exhortation, would define the "worship pleasing to God" as "Eucharistic consistency"—which is not to be understood only as a private worship—offered by the commitment of politicians in bearing witness to essential human values such political action as specified in the Exhortation: "there is an objective connection here with the Eucharist," no. 83.

The Movement for Unity in Politics

These particular characteristics of the charism of unity have fascinated politicians from the very beginning. It shows Christian life in its fullness, in all of its aspects, a Christian life which does not just descend from the exercise of spiritual life, when one walks out of the focolare or a church to enter the public squares or parliament. From the beginning of the Movement, there have been politicians who experienced, in a small measure through their contact with the Movement, the society they would have wanted to build through their public action. The first among these was Igino Giordani, who Chiara considered as a co-founder of the Movement. Giordani's importance extends beyond the political dimension alone and, together with Pasquale Foresi, takes in all the aspects of the Focolare Movement's social, cultural, and historical commitments. But since he had significant political experience, starting from the *Italian's People's Party (Partito Popolare Italiano)* suppressed by Fascism, and later with the *Christian Democrats (Democrazia Cristiana)* after the Second World War, Giordani helped to nourish Chiara's interest in this aspect and drew various politicians into the Movement. Over the course of decades, they found various positions within the Focolare Movement or they collaborated with it,[20] up until the decisive moment when on March 2, 1996 in Naples, Chiara founded the Movement for Unity in Politics.[21] There she said that she understood this moment as the result of a long journey: "We always gave special attention to the political world because it offered us the possibility to love our neighbor with much greater charity: from interpersonal love to a greater love towards the *polis*. Many of our people have been involved in this, and often in positions of responsibility."[22] The membership of the Movement for Unity in Politics includes parliamentarians, mayors, administrators, diplomats, employees, active citizens, in brief, people committed in many different positions and aspects of political life. Chiara explains "Through their profession and social commitments, members of the Focolare Movement are present in political

---

20. For further information on the development of this story, in addition to where Chiara Lubich mentions it in "The Movement for Unity in Politics," please refer to the study by Tommaso Sorgi, "La citta dell'uomo: L'agire e pensare politico in Chiara Lubich," *Nuova Umanità* XXII (2000): 551–601.
21. In the beginning it was called "Movement for Unity." Later the name was corrected by Chiara herself, explaining that it was a "political" movement, whereas the original name seemed more appropriate for the entire Focolare Movement.
22. Lubich, "The Movement for Unity in Politics," 262.

life, together with many others who know the Ideal of unity and live it, without necessarily belonging to the Focolare."[23] This Movement, therefore, is not a component within the Focolare Movement, but it is a result of the overflowing of the charism of unity outside the structures of the Movement. It is, to use one of Chiara's expressions, an "inundation" which is not left to itself, but assumes the form of a true and proper new Movement endowed with its own structure and culture. Chiara affirms:

> The Movement for Unity in Politics brings with it a new political culture. But its vision of politics does not give rise to a new party. Instead, *it changes the method of political activity*. While remaining faithful to one's own genuine ideals, the politician of unity loves everyone, as we said, and therefore in every circumstance searches for what unites. Today we would like to present a vision of politics perhaps as it has never before been conceived. We would like to give life—forgive my boldness—to *a politics of Jesus*, as he considers it and where he acts through each of us, wherever we are: in national and regional governments, in town councils, in political parties, in various civic and political groups, in government coalitions and in opposition. This unity lived among us, then, must be brought into our political parties, among the parties, into the various political institutions and into every sphere of public life as well as into the relationships among nations. Then people of all nations will be able to rise above their borders and look beyond, loving the others' country as their own. The presence of Jesus will become a reality also among peoples and states, making humanity one universal family.[24]

It would be worth looking further into these words of Chiara. First of all, faced with the many aspects of crisis in politics, the Movement for Unity in Politics acts, with regard to individual politicians who make it up, in a way similar to how the first focolarine acted in bombed-out Trent. On the one hand, the Movement rebuilds the conditions that facilitate dialogue, trust, mutual recognition, and respect for the diversity among those involved in politics. It draws politicians beyond their institutional buildings and parties, and offers them a free space in which to cultivate relationships of fraternity, through which each person can rediscover his or her own original political

---

23. Lubich, "The Movement for Unity in Politics," 243.
24. Lubich, "The Movement for Unity in Politics," 243.

vocation and the best reasons for their own commitment. In this way politicians recover the ability to speak to one another of their differences, without covering up disagreements and possible conflicts, but explaining and clarifying what is positive and constructive in their thought. On the other hand, as Chiara explains, politicians can bring what they have experienced within the Movement for Unity in Politics back into their institutions and parties, into their activities. In this way the Movement can inspire new projects carried out by its members, and sometimes can become the direct promoter of political initiatives of civil, cultural, formative value devoted to the common good. The Movement for Unity in Politics is therefore not an ecclesial nor an institutional subject. It is not a party. Its members however operate and enter into each of these areas. But the Movement as such is a political entity that lives in society, that develops the political dimension of society, which aims at the growth of fraternity understood as the foundation of the bond of citizenship, and at developing all that political theory and practice entail.

Secondly, how are we to understand Chiara's affirmation that the Movement for Unity in Politics wishes to help bring to life "a politics of Jesus," while at the same time remaining a lay reality, open to persons of varying religions and convictions? We can understand Chiara's idea by observing that in her thought there is a constant connection—based on Jesus forsaken—between heaven and earth. In an unpublished note of 1949, Chiara writes: "In fact, those who live Jesus Forsaken live the Gospel and have the hundredfold which is the *earthly Paradise* here below and eternal life which is the heavenly Paradise there Above."[25] Commenting on this thought during a session of the Abba School several years ago, Chiara explained:

> I think that, if all were to live the Gospel, the "earthly paradise" would be a reality. The very issue of poverty would be resolved, throughout the world. We ought to bear this in mind and try to apply it, for example, in politics. But it is necessary to base it, and every other field of knowledge, on the Gospel.[26]

With this, Chiara by no means was thinking of a direct application of religious language or ideas to political realities: there are no fundamentalist leanings in her thought. She continued:

---

25. Chiara Lubich, unpublished writings, July 24, 1949.
26. Chiara Lubich, note to the writing of July 24, 1949.

> It is indeed true that the Gospel contains the solution to every problem. It is also true, however, that once the solution has been found according to the light of the Gospel, it is the various fields of study that have to translate it into the proper know-how and norms of life for various times and cultures.[27]

Inasmuch as the Movement for Unity in Politics is a lay movement expressing itself with the languages of the sciences and of human experience and acting in the social and public arena, it carries out, according to Chiara, precisely that mediation through which the gospel lives in society and in politics, without implying a confessional bond. The root that nourishes this vision for Chiara is very deep:

> It is commonly thought that the Gospel does not resolve all human problems, and that it only brings the Kingdom of God understood strictly in a religious sense. But this is not so. Certainly it is not the historical Jesus or Jesus insofar as Head of the Mystical Body who resolves all problems. It is done by Jesus-us, Jesus-me, Jesus-you, and so on. It is Jesus in human beings, in each particular human being, when his grace is in them, who builds a bridge, constructs a road, and so on. Jesus is the true, deepest personality of each individual. Every human being (every Christian), in fact, is more a child of God (=another Jesus) than a child of his or her own parents. Hence Jesus in each person has the greatest influence on all that he or she does. It is as another Christ, as a member of his Mystical Body, that each person makes a specific and personal contribution in every field: science, art, politics, and so on. Human beings are thus co-creators and co-redeemers with Christ. It is the incarnation that continues, a full incarnation that involves every Jesus of the Mystical Body of Christ.[28]

Therefore, all human beings are part of the Mystical Body of Christ. Every human being is capable of bringing his or her own contribution of love, even those who do not know Jesus Christ. This is why Chiara, in all of her discourses in the context of the Movement for Unity in Politics (1996–2004), never proposed that the politicians she was addressing should *belong*

---

27. Lubich, note to the writing of July 24, 1949.
28. Lubich, note to the writing of July 24, 1949.

to one or another confession. Rather, what she proposed was a way of being human beings and, as a consequence, of living politics.

Fraternity and Politics

We have heard how in the first of her talks to the Movement for Unity in Politics, Chiara affirmed that fraternity is the characteristic of the theory and practice of the Movement itself, and she announced this as something new. While that may be true in terms of her views of politics, as we have seen it is something that was there at the very beginning of the Focolare Movement. Chiara develops the category of fraternity in her political thought. To understand her view, one must look both at the root in the spirituality and at its development in the Movement of Unity in Politics.

To understand this notion better, we should also attend to the way in which she presents the neighbor: (1) seeing Jesus in our neighbor, (2) fraternity lived in mutual love, and (3) the presence of Jesus among his own. These are all aspects central to the spirituality of unity that are constantly present from the very beginning in Chiara's reflections. In particularly important talks, we find expressions such as "peoples who are brothers and sisters,"[29] and references to "the unity of the human family."[30] The idea of universal fraternity (brotherhood/sisterhood), as we can see, appears as soon as Chiara raises her gaze to the worldwide dimension of human problems and relations. We are dealing here not with a generic idea of fraternity, but with a precise one that Chiara expressed many times. We will cite, for its historic and political importance, how she summarizes it in an international conference call with members of the Focolare Movement on December 18, 1989. Referring to the collapse of the socialist regimes of Eastern Europe, Chiara underlined the importance of rooting all ideals in Jesus Christ: ". . . in Him, who preached a society founded upon brotherhood [fraternity] among people, such that it can even be modeled on the life of the most Holy

---

29. Chiara Lubich, "Queen of the World," in *Mary, the Transparency of God*. New York: New City Press, 2003, 104. It is a talk given at Fiera di Primiero (Italy) on August 22, 1959. The term refers only to "Christian peoples," so it does not explicitly mean universal fraternity.
30. For example: Chiara Lubich, "Seeds of a New People," acceptance speech upon receiving the 1996 UNESCO Prize for Peace Education, in *New Humanity Review* 12 (2006): 5–11. "Towards a Unity of Nations and a Unity of Peoples": her address to a Symposium at the United Nations, New York, May 28 1997.

Trinity."[31] For Chiara, fraternity is the name which expresses the Trinitarian relationship, inasmuch as human beings can participate in it. Fraternity is the Love of God that human beings can live amongst themselves. It is only due to linguistic limitations that Chiara uses the masculine expression, using "fraternity or brotherhood." Instead, she means brotherhood and sisterhood, a relation which regards both men and women.[32]

This idea and this life of fraternity always existed in the Focolare Movement. What is new then in the fraternity that Chiara proposes in the year 2000 as the "specific characteristic" of the Movement for Unity in Politics? The important moment in this regard if we follow the order the documents, can be identified in a letter that Chiara wrote on May 7, 1998 from the little city of the Focolare Movement near São Paolo in Brazil. She says that we need to:

> raise the two realities that we have, the Movement for Unity in Politics and the Economy of Communion in society, to true and authentic political and economic movements, with all that entails: first, to possess a true philosophy, a true theoretical and practical political science, a way of being in politics, of doing politics, of looking at the world of politics; to agree among many states to make a new politics; to organize periodic meetings or conferences on politics making use of the media in order to raise awareness; to prepare new politicians . . . knowing that everything cannot but be an expression of the Ideal [of Unity], which is beneath everything. If this will become a great political current that takes you from every side, our people who are called to such an Ideal will have no difficulty in living their "lofty" commitments as expression of a true "vocation."[33]

Two years after the foundation of the Movement for Unity in Politics, Chiara expressed the need to elevate it to an "authentic political current."

---

31. "*Love one another*," in Chiara Lubich, *Cercando le cose di lassù* (Rome: Città Nuova, 165–169 (Our translation).
32. We do not have this problem in some other languages. Spanish, besides the word "Fraternidad," has "hermano" and "hermana," from which comes "Hermandad." German, besides the word "Brüderlichkeit" from bruder (brother), can indicate both "bruder" and "schwester" (sister), by the plural "Geschwister" from which there is "Geschwisterlichkeit" (of brothers and sisters).
33. Chiara Lubich, "Letter to the Little City of Araceli [Brazil]," May 7, 1998 (Our translation.)

To reach this goal, she outlined a two-fold path: one in theoretical research and the other in organization. Work in both areas continues. Within the Abba School, the effort is mainly related to the dimension of political thought. It was there during a session on February 5, 2000 that "fraternity" appears for the first time in its central importance for politics. The Abba School was reading the notes of Chiara concerning the Trinity. The human person is taken within the Trinity because God, Chiara explained, sees humanity in the Word; that is, within the heart of the Trinity. She wrote: "[T]he new commandment is to love our brother or sister, because this is to love the intimate self of God, the Heart of God."[34] From these considerations of Chiara, there emerged the idea of Love as the divine bond which takes in even the human person. Interrupting what we were reading, Chiara said: "What do we ask from the Movement for Unity in Politics? Fraternity. Fraternity is the only bond."

Starting from this first intuition of Chiara, we continued to deepen our research. The first step as we have seen was the congress of the Movement for Unity in Politics held in June of 2000 followed by other inaugural talks by Chiara which from time to time opened up new dimensions of fraternity. Links have been built between scholars throughout the world who, little by little, have joined in the research in a real and truly enlarged Abba School. The first academic books were produced and other schools of thought were met bringing their own original contributions. Political thought on fraternity is such, first of all, in its fraternal methodology. It is not born exclusively within one culture or country, but has from the very beginning grown from the contribution of varying views and different ways of being brothers and sisters. This political thought is spread through books, though these books are always collaborations between more than one author. There is a collaboration of men and women authors thinking together and in different ways, according to their various disciplines and cultures. This work stems from a relational principle that defines what it means to be a human being.

As one can see from the preceding article's introductory review of the scholarship concerning fraternity, the first text of the Abba School was released in Argentina in 2006.[35] Before her death, Chiara could see her thought enter universities through the main door of scientific competence which she

---

34. Chiara Lubich, unpublished writings, October 26, 1949.
35. Antonio M. Baggio, ed., *El principio olvidado: La fraternidad. En la politica y el derecho* (Buenos Aires: Ciudad Nueva, 2006).

considered essential. Courses on, and chairs for, fraternity developed which could begin to educate young people who were not content with what they saw around them. Today these studies on fraternity have reached an impressive level. Let us indicate some of the main sectors of research currently underway, limiting ourselves to the realm of politics and related areas.

Study began on the roles of brothers and sisters in the originating myths of various civilizations. These roles created archetypical behaviors, that is models of relationships that are transmitted to cultures and that are capable of casting light on contemporary behaviors. The philosophical aspects of fraternity are also studied, such as the history of the concept and its relation to other great principles such as liberty and equality which comprise fundamental categories of politics. Considering the triptych of liberty, equality, and fraternity in the wake of two centuries during which liberty and equality have been seen not to work successfully together, allows the development of the perspective of political systems wherein fraternity acts as the regulating principle of the other two. The principle of fraternity is currently being developed within juridical systems—both as the principle of public law as well as in its application to civil and penal law, areas in which the term did not even exist or was unknown because people no longer knew how to interpret the intentions of their Constitutional Fathers. The principle of fraternity supports the concept of "relational justice" and permits the interpretation of political-juridical appeals coming from the experience of a justice that, not limiting itself to punishment, includes remedy and restitution.

The principle of fraternity establishes, at its very least, the equal dignity of brothers/sisters and of their right to be different from one another, as happens in a family. In this sense, fraternity acts as a principle of reality in political theory, because one's brothers and sisters cannot be chosen. Studies focus on the conditions capable of guaranteeing their equality and their difference. Fraternity, that deals in a dynamic way with both freedom and equality, allows the birth of a non-binary logic. A binary logic regards freedom and equality as oppositional along the lines of "friend-enemy," "slave-master," "citizen-foreigner," "with me or against me." These are the ideological thoughts of a conflictual nature that have infested politics over the last two centuries. Instead, we are presented with the possibility of a thought that does not exclude, does not level differences, but instead recognizes and puts them in communion. Fraternity can give life to a thought capable of understanding complexity.

Finally, fraternal behavior in society is itself being studied. There is an attempt to identify the political approaches through which a fraternal society can be encouraged and developed. We are facing the challenge of passing from the philosophical level of principles in political science to the application of fraternity within the empirical sciences. So, today we are studying and living this unique bond of love that Chiara showed to us, one that allows us to free ourselves from all relationships of subordination and injustice, one that permits oppressed peoples to gather their strength and to bring freedom and equality into communion. This bond helps them start again after the violence of nature or of human beings destroys what had been built.

From Chiara, we have learned that fraternity is the bond for the most difficult of moments. But it is also the bond in daily politics because fraternity authorizes the writing of laws, raising up of institutions, and inventing what is new when our brother or sister expresses a need unknown before. We have realized that when the "love of all loves" is lived, when a city is united, when the discourse of its citizens is sincere, and when the common good is desired by all in different but fair ways, then politics seems to disappear. One no longer sees institutions, but persons. We see the open blossom and not the stem alone. This is the moment in which politics is fulfilled; and in this way it spreads and leaves space for beauty.

Chapter Twenty-Five

The Economy of Communion: A Project for a Sustainable and Happy Socioeconomic Future

Luigino Bruni

Introduction:
Global Wealth in the Long Term and World Inequality

Let us begin with some macro scenarios and global issues. The proposed Economy of Communion (EoC) finds its full meaning only within the challenges of our time. If we take a long-term view of global wealth creation, we see immediately that Western economic hegemony is, thus far, but a two-century interlude in Asia's world leadership. As you can see from the following graph,[1] Asia is making a comeback. The world's political and economic arrangements are quickly changing, and new categorizations are necessary to understand and manage these changes.

Distribution (%) of world GDP in 1990, 2008 & 2030 (forecast)

	SHARE (%)		
	1990	2008	2030
Western Europe	22.2	16.9	11.0
USA	21.4	18.6	14.2
Other Western countries	3.2	2.8	2.2
Japan	8.6	5.7	3.3
Rich countries	55.3	44.0	30.6
Eastern Europe	2.4	2.0	1.2
Russia	4.2	2.5	1.8
Other former URSS countries	3.1	1.9	1.1
Latin America	8.3	7.9	7.1
China	7.8	17.5	28.2
India	4.0	6.7	11.3
Other Asian countries	11.4	13.9	15.3
Africa	3.3	3.4	3.5
Rest of the world	44.7	56.0	69.4
World	100.0	100.0	100.0

1. My graph based on data from MOLD Business Index: Posted: November 8, 2010.

Another global issue is inequality. Income distribution is central to our discussion. Global inequality grew between 1988 and 1993 (from 0.84 to 0.87) before decreasing to 0.82 in 2000. Two contrasting tendencies produce this outcome: First, the wealth gap is decreasing between nations (from 78% to 67%) but increasing within nations. Second, people in more equal and just countries enjoy a happier life. There is a much higher correlation between inequality and quality-of-life indicators (lifespan, health, happiness) than between income (defined as the gross domestic product [GDP]) and quality of life.

In capitalist economies, increasing inequality is the major obstacle to socioeconomic development. The wealth that we produce through vicious processes (mainly in the Western world) increases inequality of opportunity, rights, and freedom and does not create jobs or foster true development. In fact, only labor creates jobs; they cannot be created any other way. The seriousness of the inequality in the market economy becomes evident when we analyze the economy's evolution since the Industrial Revolution. In the twentieth century, capitalism managed to reduce inequality in Western economies as they transitioned from feudal social and economic systems to market economies, which were much more dynamic. In the past decades, however, inequality has returned almost to the level it was before the Industrial Revolution. In the United States, the twenty richest hedge-fund managers together earn more than the top five hundred managers, who each make an average of $10 million a year. Furthermore, the level of internal inequality in the United States today is close to that of nations only now overcoming feudal social structures. Thus, as far as inequality is concerned, late capitalism is very similar to late feudalism. Two centuries of economic and legal development have been worth very little or nothing at all.

The detrimental outcomes once produced by a lack of markets are now produced by an excess of markets. This serious and critical fact contradicts reformists' utopian belief in the market as the foundation of the modern political economy. In fact, philosophers of the Enlightenment believed that by developing the market, society would finally overcome feudalism and slowly embrace democracy. It was this democratic spirit that they so craved, the development of which they believed would allow people to live freely and equally. However, four-fifths of the so-called absolute poor (those living on less than two dollars per day) live in medium and high-income countries, not in "poor nations." The dividing line between rich and poor is no longer geographic (North-South) but exists within countries. The new and disturbing fact is that globalization has changed global poverty profoundly.

Gross domestic product (GDP) and well-being indicators are not as connected as we have believed. We are unable to discover much by comparing the relationship between GDP and fundamental human development indicators such as lifespan, children's health, mental disorders, obesity, crime, youth academic achievements, and social mobility. Data from average-and high-income countries are very similar. If instead of GDP we look at inequality indicators such as the Gini index, however, a different picture emerges: fundamental indicators vary significantly *within* countries.

In other words, in terms of lifespan, health, human resources, or capabilities (according to Amartya Sen's theory), the difference between a British employee and an uneducated Caribbean-descended single mother who has an unstable job and lives in a poor neighborhood in London is much greater than between that British employee and a Peruvian worker. This difference between a high-level British manager and a high-level South American manager is even less significant. But it is not only the poor who suffer from inequality. In fact, inequality is a serious public problem that affects the rich as well, since, according to recent statistics, it causes greater social resentment, status competition, insecurity, and wretchedness for all. Therefore, if we wish to work for economic renewal and are committed to the common good, we should not worry so much about GDP. Instead, we should reduce inequality.

The Paradox of Happiness

A third challenge relates to happiness. The "paradox of happiness" triggers a reflection on capitalism. See the following graph.[2]

---

2. My graph based on Richard A Easterlin "Does Economic Growth Improve the Human Lot? Some Empirical Evidence," in Paul A. David and Melvin W. Reder, eds, *Nations and Households in Economic Growth* (New York: Academic Press, 1974), 89-125.

The Economy of Communion

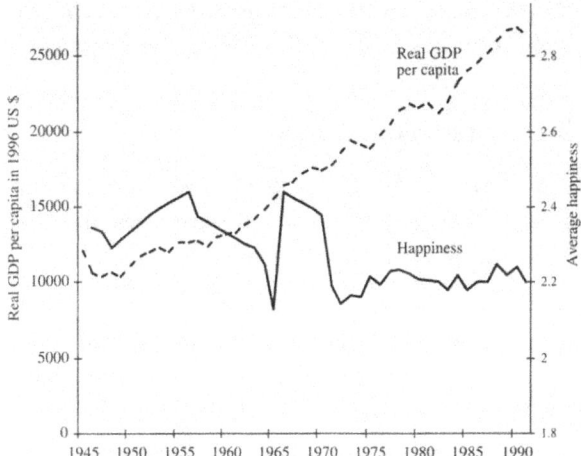

This graph illustrates three important aspects of the nexus of income and happiness:

1. Income growth produces well-being and happiness for poor people and (low-income) poor countries (see the line labeled "Happiness").

2. After a certain threshold, which industrialized countries have already surpassed, income growth no longer produces happiness. Rather it decreases quality of life, as excessive economic growth reduces and "pollutes" important resources such as the environment, social relations, spiritual life, and so on.

3. All of us would be better off if income from the right side of the graph (that originating in the rich and unhappier countries) were shared with the countries on the left side. In that case, all nations would move toward the center where well-being reaches its peak. Unfortunately, we know from history that, besides being very complex to implement, income redistribution has not often happened. Besides, poor countries do not need to receive income; rather, they need the conditions to produce it with equity through common and public goods such as schools, roads, hospitals, public services, and so on.

We may conclude that, according to the inverse relationship between wealth and happiness, beyond a certain threshold, income growth matters very little, while income distribution and other factors, such as relational goods, the environment, communities, and social well-being, are crucial.

Firm Social Responsibility and Shared Values

Up to now we have spoken of macro variables (growth, inequality) and individual variables (happiness). What can we say about businesses? After all, a country's economy and people's jobs ultimately depend on them.

It's crystal clear that a country's welfare depends on the quality of its companies (in sectors such as production, services, agriculture, trade, etc.) and their operation. We have seen varying approaches to the interactions between business and society. Marx's socialism played an important role by revealing how capital exploits labor. Generally speaking, companies would operate in their sphere (the economy or the "market"), while the law would mediate their interaction with the common good. If a company respected the law, then it had no further social duty to which to respond. Common good was a political and civil issue only, so companies helped promote it indirectly and unknowingly by following only their interests (profit optimization) within the limits of the law. In fact, according to the famous metaphor of traditional liberal thought that stretches from Adam Smith to Milton Friedman, the market's "invisible hand" turns entrepreneurs' private interests into national wealth. In recent decades, however, civil society has demanded more from companies, particularly from large companies and multinationals. It has developed a business concept called Corporate Social Responsibility (CSR), a new idea that calls on companies to work voluntarily for social development. Companies have begun promoting and developing social programs for schools, hospitals, low-income residential blocks, and so on, operating in fields that in the past belonged to others (e.g., the state and voluntary service organizations). It is true that the market (companies) and society (the state, civil society) remained separate, but the former began to trespass on the domain of the latter. For example, companies intentionally and voluntarily began to support projects for the protection of animals close to extinction, although this was by definition still a noneconomic activity.

Then in 2006, CSR moved to a new level. In the influential *Harvard Business Review*, American economists Michael Porter and Mark Kramer published "Creating Shared Value," which presents a theoretical framework for the "social business" movement (of which Muhammad Yunus's Grameen Bank in Bangladesh is a well-known example) and other social economic activities located mainly in the United States. What is new in this paper? In an effort to overcome the divide between company and society, Porter and Kramer encouraged entrepreneurs to consider society's shortcomings (poverty, elderly care, etc.) as business opportunities:

> Companies must take the lead in bringing business and society back together. The recognition is there among sophisticated business and thought leaders, and promising elements of a new model are emerging. Yet we still lack an overall framework for guiding these efforts, and most companies remain stuck in a "social responsibility" mind-set in which societal issues are at the periphery, not the core. The solution lies in the principle of shared value, which involves creating economic value in a way that also creates value for society by addressing its needs and challenges. Businesses must reconnect company success with social progress. Shared value is not social responsibility, philanthropy, or even sustainability, but a new way to achieve economic success. It is not on the margin of what companies do but at the center. We believe that it can give rise to the next major transformation of business thinking.[3]

At this point, we can connect two main ideas:

1. Income growth does not increase people's well-being, particularly above a certain national threshold of wealth. Combatting inequality becomes crucial to the process of increasing well-being.

2. Companies' range of actions must expand to include social and community activities not out of legal requirements (taxes, laws) but as new opportunities for economic success (shared value).

The nations of Asia, whose growing economies are led by very talented people, still have a chance to avoid the paradox of happiness and environment that has already ensnared Japan and Western countries, particularly the United States: decades of growth in GDP and decline in happiness and well-being. Since economic growth is not the ultimate goal but a means to achieve a good

---

3. Michael E. Porter and Mark R. Kramer, "Creating Shared Value: How to Reinvent Capitalism and Unleash a Wave of Innovation and Growth," *Harvard Business Review* (January-February 2011): 4.

social and personal life, I propose that Asian nations develop an alternative path to capitalism (or postcapitalism) in which economic growth, social values, equity, and well-being are sustainably reunited. Chiara Lubich's Economy of Communion can help guide Asian nations through this visionary transition.

The Economy of Communion: A Short Walk down Memory Lane

The Economy of Communion (EoC), while still early in its development, nevertheless has already attracted the attention of many intellectuals, cultural personalities, and the Social Doctrine of the Church.[4] It grew from Chiara Lubich's intuitive insights during one of her last trips to São Paulo, Brazil, in May 1991. Shocked by the city's social problems and great inequality, she sought understanding in John Paul II's encyclical *Centesimus Annus*—which views the market and businesses as positive, and reflects on the fall of the Soviet communist system. It was a fruitful but painful visit as her spiritual and "charismatic" view came up against hard evidence of a distorted socioeconomic system that allows skyscrapers (some of which she had noticed from the plane) to stand next to millions of starving and impoverished people. Chiara reacted to this disjuncture by launching a project that encouraged entrepreneurs to engage with three tasks:

1. Contribute to a fair economic system by using profits to promote development programs and by starting companies with goals beyond profit-making. These companies should split their profit into three parts in order to help the poor, create new jobs in the company, and promote the "culture of giving."

2. Create jobs, foster productive inclusion, and support community development (poverty means above all exclusion from productivity, the community, and society).

3. Fight extreme poverty and promote a new "culture of giving." Today there are about 860 EoC companies; most are located in Europe and South America, followed by North America, Asia, and Africa. In the past few years scholars and students have written over three hundred papers about the EoC. The funds raised from profit sharing have financed over one thou-

---

4. *Caritas in Veritate*, n. 46

sand scholarships for young people, various development programs in the southern hemisphere, and the Sophia University Institute. Although these are small numbers, they represent significant experience, because one principle of a charismatic initiative is that, like salt and yeast, it can transform.

What are the Messages of the EoC to the Economy of Today?

If the EoC's messages are well formulated and people are ready to listen, current politics and economies can significantly benefit from them. Among these messages, the following three are particularly relevant today.

Healing Poverty

Poverty, or extreme exclusion (I do not refer here to the charismatic or evangelical sense of the word "poverty" but to humanity's plague), is once again spreading in the world, especially in the West. The word "poverty," however, has not always been considered as solely negative, as are terms such as deception, slavery, and racism. After the life of St. Francis (i.e., after Christianity was consolidated) there was more than one type of poverty; the concept included a broad spectrum of states, from the victims of poverty to the blessing of those who choose freely to be poor in order to help others in need. As long as we fail to embrace the characteristics of freely chosen poverty in a simple and selfless lifestyle, communion, and fraternity, global cultures will not be capable of combating new and old kinds of involuntary poverty. St. Francis reminds us that no one can see nor fight against bad poverty before loving its good form.

As long as the responsibility for implementing governmental or private programs to fight poverty is left to the rich, who can afford to fly from their conferences on poverty to opulent vacations, the study of poverty will continue to be ineffective. As long as poverty serves only as a theme for research and conventions, it will be neither seen nor understood, let alone healed.

In wealthy societies, new kinds of "poverty"—such as those experienced by people excluded from public life, suffering mental disorders, addicted to gambling, and struggling with other addictions such as drugs and alcohol—are joining the old ones. All of these impoverishing states have a common origin. Although sometimes caused by a lack of income and wealth, their origin, and therefore their solution, is not economic but rather relational and social. Since its founding, the EoC has insisted that the first step in addressing poverty is to foster relationships, from those of the family to those of the political sphere. Poverty is not the result of a single problem but of a collection of unhealthy relationships. The first treatment for every form of poverty is to foster fraternity and reciprocity. In simple subsistence economies where people have been able to emerge from forms of endemic poverty, family and community relationships are strong and stable, if often unjust and illiberal (consider the status of women). To enable people to escape the traps of poverty, it is first necessary to increase per capita income, public goods (health, infrastructures, and housing) and meritorious goods (especially schools). Today, such relational goods are fragile and rare. If we do not first heal and rebuild relationships, the necessary interventions in income, public goods, and meritorious goods will remain ineffective. That ineffectiveness marred the many decades of public assistance in Europe. The experience of the EoC, which begins with relationship building as a precondition for every human development project, can serve as an example of how this approach might be changed.

The EoC confirms that before poverty (as an economic state) can exist, poor people must exist. In other words, the economic state of poverty follows from social impoverishment. Without engaging directly with poor people, we cannot hope to end poverty; at most, we will manage poverty by insulating ourselves from it. Only the poor can cure the poor, and therefore charismatic movements are necessary. While the capitalist system has increased the number of institutions for the poor through philanthropy, there is no genuine encounter between helper and helped.

St. Francis embraced the lepers of Assisi and cured their bodies and souls. An embrace is the first part of the cure. Wealthy cultures are suspicious of brotherly relationships and teach us to avoid embraces. St. Francis warns us not to fall into this trap. On the one hand, the number of professionals available to assist and to cure in the numerous institutions created to "heal" poverty has increased, and this is good. On the other hand, the embraces have grown scarcer. "Brotherhood" is another beautiful Franciscan word. It can be measured by the inclusion of the poor in our communities. It turns out that the creation of specialized agencies to care for the poor is often inversely proportional to their inclusion. The commitment of these institutions to "cure the poor" serves an excuse to keep them as far away as possible from our pristine and insulated cities and lives. In the EoC this experience of embracing (as St. Francis embraced the leper) is lived by giving tangible assistance through communitarian experience and, above all, by not resting until the poor are offered jobs in EoC businesses through concrete productive inclusion.

Inequality: Communitarian and, above all, Productive Inclusion is the Answer

Besides poverty, inequality must also be addressed. In the past few decades, inequality has been growing at a greater rate. The EoC calls on companies to share their profits in a daring project to foster a more equal and brotherly economy and society. In fact, true brotherhood or fraternity comes only with an equal distribution of wealth and income, and therefore of capabilities, rights, and freedoms. Businesses and the market, even when they are guided by the principle of community, are not sufficient to build a more equal society. Public and political action is necessary, especially today when people have come to believe that the liberal market has miraculous powers. The market is an expression of freedom and a means for freedom whenever it collaborates with the public sphere and civil society through wealth redistribution and reciprocity, respectively.

Initiatives such as cooperative movements, both past and present, and the (true and good) social economy in Europe should be re-evaluated and held in higher esteem. Europe, up to a few decades ago, managed to sustain growth with low levels of inequality. This equitable growth was not achieved through the welfare state alone, Europe's well-known "social market economy," but through the extraordinary influence of the European cooperative movement. The movement helped develop true democracies while fostering a democratic labor force and economy. The cooperative and social economy movement encouraged people to be productive members of society. They were not miserable employees anymore, dependent on the "generosity" of a few patrons, but workers, partners, and, consequently, better citizens. Today the EoC seeks to reinforce productive inclusion as an effective weapon against exclusion and inequality.

Civil Entrepreneurs and the Crucial Role of Labor

The EoC charges businesses with the mission of fighting exclusion and poverty. Entrepreneurs should not be satisfied merely to pay taxes and respect the law. In these times of crisis, they must use their talents and entrepreneurial vocation to combat poverty and exclusion by creating new forms of work.

When Chiara Lubich proposed businesses that reinvest profits in the business to create new jobs, she was proposing something extremely new. She was saying that businesses can also fight poverty directly by creating jobs that productively include people. This is not primarily about philanthropy. Entrepreneurs are job creators, not philanthropists, and as such they should not give away "slices of pie" to the poor (as other institutions do). Instead, they should create dynamic "new slices of pie" through building businesses in which the poor "produce" goods so that they do not only "consume" assistance.

I believe it is important to regard business and labor as the core of the EoC. We should not forget that the crisis in which we are living derived not from business profits but from the financial speculation of top managers and protected professionals. This is the cancer in today's economy. Only a new alliance between workers and entrepreneurs can protect the labor market from the overwhelming concentration of income in the hands of so few. The world urges workers and entrepreneurs to work together. This income bubble is drying up the resources necessary to invest in production that would create sustainable jobs. Today, combating poverty means fighting unemployment ("labor poverty"), above all among young people.

Indeed, labor has promoted democracy before, namely, through broad labor movements. Men and (fewer) women became citizens when they were released from their servant status in the rural feudal system and could start to work in factories, workshops, schools, offices, and cooperatives. Servants and slaves cannot bring about democracy, but free workers can. A democratic society is grounded in labor; otherwise society is based on nondemocratic income and privileges.

Conclusion: The Need for Communion

In our capitalist society we are all suffering from a serious "famine of communion." Today, we are at risk of getting used to its absence, of ceasing to long for it. There is a strong link between communion and community. Communion is formed within the community. But there can be, and are, communities that have no communion, where gifts become merely obligations, without freedom, or gratuitousness. Current studies on happiness and subjective well-being tell us very clearly that the main source of people's happiness is a life of communion, starting from that first cell of communion that is the family. Living a good life depends on the quality of communal relationships at all levels, including the fundamental experience of communion in work.

We must not make the mistake of thinking that communion is possible only in intimate relationships or inside the family. Communion is the deepest and truest vocation of human beings in all the areas in which human qualities are exercised. Granted, some dimensions of communion are so intimate and spiritual that to describe them we must appeal to the poetic powers of Dante and his ingenious neologisms, such as "*s'io m'intuassi come tu t'inmii*."[5] But there are other dimensions, no less critical to the quality of our lives, that do not require the mutual indwelling of souls but simply fellow citizens who listen to and consider each other as related to and necessary for their own happiness. The world will continue to suffer until the community embraces communion, too. It is the community that supports the declension of our pronouns: I, you, he, she, we, you, they. Communal declension involves the first person plural, "we." If the first person plural is missing from our syntax, the second person singular, "you," may disappear and with it the face of the other person. Then we may find ourselves in communities inhabited by the anonymous and lonely third person singular, "he" or "she."

Communion, to avoid becoming "communionism," must be lived with equality, freedom, and gratuitousness. Unlike community, communion requires us to move from the communion of goods to communion between people. It is an equality in dignity, a "face to face" recognition, knowing that the other is there, in relationship, because he or she, like me, has freely chosen to be there as an act of gratuitousness. This communion requires the overcoming of status and is not complete until this happens. Communities can exist and endure even in feudal and unequal societies; communion requires much more. When the experience of communion begins inside a nonegalitarian or caste-based community, little by little it will undermine and transform the community from within. This transformation is evident in the early Christian communities and in those born from great religious and secular charismatics; people began as either noble or plebeian but soon found themselves in a new reality of true communion, where there was "neither slave nor free . . . nor male and female" (Gal 3:28). True communion teaches siblings a new fraternity in which they become brothers and sisters outside the family too. Communion is always free, because it is the highest experience of gratuitousness. Wherever this kind of equality, freedom, and gratuitousness is missing, we will know community without communion.

---

5. *Paradiso*, vol. IX, 81: "If I were in you as you are in me."

Our world suffers principally from this lack of communion at all levels, starting at the economic level. Communion is necessary if the serious problems of poverty and exclusion are to be resolved. Philanthropy is not enough, and often it is harmful because it is a one-sided affair. Communion calls for much from all of us, from those who give and from those who receive, because it is a form of reciprocity where everyone gives and everyone receives—and where everyone *forgives*, because communion does not last long without continuous and institutionalized forgiveness.

Communion means happiness, well-being, living a good life. But within and around us is a constant picture of noncommunion. To say that communion is a vocation of humanity requires that we have an idea of the health and diseases of human societies. Judeo-Christian humanism, for example, tells us of the beginning of humanity's communion, a beginning that is also the end of history, the goal toward which we strive. Noncommunion is neither the first nor the last word on the human condition. We might say that communion is health and noncommunion disease, with an idea of some therapy by which to cure ourselves. However, the dominant culture reverses these associations, transforming disease into health every time it says that rivalry, envy and greed, and conquest of the other are the main agents of economic growth and that harmony, generosity, and equality do not increase the GDP.

Whenever those who believe in communion as a vocation of human beings find that it is not being realized, they might recall the words of Italian priest Don Zeno Saltini, "man is different," meaning different from what he or she appears to be. We see in history that humans are greater than the discord that surrounds us. It is the realistic possibility of a "not-yet" universal communion that makes an "already" local communion possible and sustainable. When this broad horizon is rejected as naive utopia, the human factor shrinks. Without this ideal in mind to weather even in the worst situations, politics turns into cynicism, economics into dominance, and sociability into life imprisonment.

The civil, moral, and spiritual quality of the third millennium will depend on our capacity to see more in the human being than what we have seen so far. This means we need to equip ourselves with communal institutions (economic, social, political, cultural, and religious) that promote a communion of peace, harmony, well-being, and the desire to live a good life.

Chapter Twenty-Six

Economy of Communion: A Sociological Inquiry on a Contemporary Charismatic Inspiration in Economic and Social Life

Bernhard Callebaut

"The charismatic economy is often left in the shadow as if only institutional dimensions were relevant to understanding economic and social life."[1] This formulation reminds one of the sociologist Bryan Wilson, who asked himself if charismatic experiences were still possible in contemporary society. He concluded that only feeble charismatics were available, and only on the periphery rather than in the very heart of the dynamics of society and the sectors of society that matter.[2] In my own sociological study of the so-called "Economy of Communion" (EoC), however, I believe that I have found a charismatic economy in the very heart of economic life. EoC, created through the intervention of a contemporary religious leader, aims not at the margins of society, but at its very heart.

The EoC is an initiative of Chiara Lubich (1920-2008), founder of the Focolare Movement. In creating the EoC, she asked people who were competent in business and economics to develop new enterprises in order to increase profits, some of which could be shared with the poor. This proposal was not directed at people on the margins of society, but to the central actors in the entire economic process: entrepreneurs. In doing so, Chiara Lubich proposed that the economic world establish a more direct relationship with the social aspect of life. In this way, the EoC would bring together two major areas of human activity, two fundamental functions of society, namely, the economic and the social. EoC thus aims to mediate in a new way be-

---

1. "The Charismatic Principle in Economic and Civil Life: History, Theory and Good Practice," http://www.iu-sophia.org/public/documents/call_for_paper.pdf.
2. Bryan R. Wilson, *The Noble Savages: The Primitive Origins of Charisma and its Contemporary Survival* (Berkeley: University of California Press, 1975), 131.

tween two symbolic figures: the entrepreneur and the poor. It would seek to link them in a new alliance, a new relationship of practical solidarity.

This being the case, two questions arise: Is this an economic initiative of a charismatic type? How can this possibility be explored following the logic of sociological inquiry? I decided to try to answer these questions by following the sociological approach practiced by Max Weber in his studies on charismatic leadershi [3] Because Weber's work on charismatic leadership presupposes the presence of concrete needs and innovative proposals, the question then arises: Do the projects of the EoC constitute answers to certain needs, and do they entail true innovations?

A Charismatic Leader in Contemporary Society

The very idea of a charismatic economy assumes, at least from a Weberian perspective, that it is a result of a charismatic leader. Chiara Lubich launched the EoC during her visit to Brazil in May 1991.[4]

Up to that point her life had clear elements that correspond to Weber's ideal/type of a charismatic leader. Few in the Catholic Church or elsewhere would dispute her status as an eminent religious figure of the twentieth century.[5] For Weber, a charismatic leader has followers, people who esteem the leader as possessing an exceptional idea or gift and who become "disciples" of the message he or she brings. The Focolare Movement that Chiara Lubich originated is today one of the largest in the Catholic world, counting millions of people as adherents to its spirituality. Its committed members include more than 100,000 adults and young people of every race, nation, and social class. The idea behind this foundation is also original. Its spirituality, called a "spirituality of unity," is not absolutely original since it is based on central gospel texts. Although Lubich cannot be called a pure type of charismatic prophet, neither can what she has inspired be considered a mere expression of current Catholic discourse. In various moments of her life Lubich has demonstrated a unique charismatic capacity to re-interpret creatively Christian spirituality

---

3. Max Weber, *Wirtschaft und Gesellschaft* (Tübingen: Mohr, 1980), 140-42.
4. The speech that launched the EoC was published in Chiara Lubich, *L'economia di comunione: Storia e profezia* (Rome: Città Nuova, 2001), 9-14.
5. See Maria Chiara De Lorenzo, "Hanno detto di Chiara e dei Focolari," in Michele Zanzucchi, ed., *Focolari: La fraternità in movimento* (Rome: Città Nuova, 2009), 136-139.

from the perspective of unity.[6] No other contemporary movement for unity has awakened such a global following at the grassroots level of society.

Lubich is known most of all for her original perspective on unity, based on her understanding of Jesus' cry of abandonment on the cross. In this cry she found the secret for renewing relationships between persons, between persons and God, and between persons and creation itself. Her comprehension of what she called "Jesus forsaken" offers without doubt an original contribution to Christian spirituality.[7] For sociological purposes, it should be noted that this contribution creates linkages that surpass barriers between people that impede universal brotherhood. Notwithstanding the normal difficulties inherent in every social concretization of an ideal concept, the ideal of unity born in the Catholic Church and incarnate in the lifestyle of the Focolare not only inspires and unites Catholics as well as Catholics and other Christians, it also builds unity with persons of other religions and persons without any religious commitment.

Many people consider Chiara Lubich to be a prophet of unity because of the extensive dialogues she established with many religious personalities and currents. But from a sociological point of view, it is also fascinating to see how she was able to promote bonds of fellowship and build bridges between parts of society that typically oppose one another. But a sociological study made over several years has convinced me that, in the Weberian way of speaking, Lubich is a religious leader with recognizable characteristics typical of a prophetic charismatic. This is particularly the case if we look at how her Movement develops myriad social projects that aim to create bridges between different social worlds in ways that contribute to a broad culture of fellowship. This fact, in turn, suggests another question: Is the launching of the EoC itself a charismatic moment?

---

6. John Shotter, *Social Accountability and Selfhood* (Oxford: Blackwell, 1984).
7. For an overview of Chiara Lubich's life and thought see: *Essential Writings: Spirituality Dialogue Culture* (Hyde Park, NY: New City Press, 2007). For an exegetical reflection see Gérard Rossé, *Il grido di Gesù in croce: Una panoramica esegetica e teologica* (Rome: Città Nuova, 1984). For a theological approach see Stefan Tobler, *Jesu Gottverlassenheit als Heilsereignis in der Spiritualität Chiara Lubichs: Ein Beitrag zur Überwindung der Sprachnot in der Soteriologie* (Berlin: Walter de Gruyter, 2002); and Florence Gillet, *La scelta di Gesù Abbandonato, nella prospettiva teologica di Chiara Lubich* (Rome: Città Nuova, 2009). For a sociological approach, see Bennie Callebaut, *Tradition, charisme et prophétie dans le Mouvement international des Focolari:Analyse sociologique* (Paris: Nouvelle Cité, 2010).

The Social Context

Chiara Lubich launched the EoC project on May 29, 1991 during a trip to Brazil, where the Focolare Movement had been present since 1958. In just over three decades, it has developed rapidly all over this immense country. There were certain expectations concerning possible results of Lubich's first visit in twenty-five years. This was especially true since it may well have been the last for the founder of the Focolare Movement. Therefore, many hoped she would propose something decisive for the future development of the Focolare in Brazil. In particular, it was hoped that the founder would address the problem of social inequality in the context of an economy that had the potential to become one of the most important in the world.

There is a history behind this hope. When the Focolare arrived in Brazil in the late 1950s, those involved were clearly convinced that in order to spread the gospel, they needed to give priority to the situation of social injustice. But they found that it took all their energies to spread their spirituality, with the hope that one day they would have enough people to address this social goal. They also realized that the Church's "preferential option of the poor" did not in itself suggest how they could contribute to the achievement of social justice. At the same time, Brazilian society operated under the political rule of a military regime determined to maintain the social status quo, with its deep inequality between rich and poor. In this context, the Church in Brazil evolved and eventually embraced the preferential choice in favor of the poor. The Focolare agreed with this option and supported it through a number of specific projects around the country. However, their unique contribution towards realizing this choice remained open.

In the 1960s, the Theology of Liberation and the birth of the Ecclesial Base Communities (CEB's) had enriched the ecclesial panorama and pushed the Brazilian Church forward toward a more engaged presence in the public square. This situation brought reprimands against some of the ecclesial movements of European origin that had come to flourish all over Brazil. The critique was that they privileged middle class people, were not reaching the poor, and therefore did not realize in some way the preferential option in favor of the poor.[8] In the Focolare's case, there were in fact a large number of poor persons in the Movement in Brazil. The middle class members shared in a communion of goods, but it was not enough to meet

---

8. For a synthesis of the situation at the time, see José Comblin, "Os 'movimentos' e pastorale latino-americana," *Revista Eclesiastica Brasileira* 170 (1983), 239-267.

the needs of the poor within the Movement. So by the time Chiara Lubich visited Brazil in 1991, there was a large consensus that this communion of goods and the social projects they had founded could not solve the social problem of poverty within the Focolare communities, let alone the entire nation. Within this context, it was hoped that during her 1991 visit Lubich would address the problem in a larger and more innovative way.

At the time of her visit to Brazil, Chiara Lubich had reflected on the Berlin Wall being pulled down, and the fall of real socialism in Europe. She also reflected on the conclusions of the recent papal encyclical *Centesimus Annus*, written one hundred years after the first papal social encyclical, *Rerum Novarum*. In the recent encyclical, the pope made clear that any evolution in the economic field had to take into account the freedom of the entrepreneur, that economic creativity demands space for liberty. These reflections were reinforced by her experience of the actual economic dynamics of the city of São Paulo, where she stayed. Although the city was the economic heart of Brazil, Lubich noticed the enormous circle of slums (*baraccopoli* or *favelas*) that to her seemed like a "crown of thorns" around the heart of the city. In her diary for May 15, 1991, Lubich reaffirmed that poverty constituted one of the biggest and most tragic problems on earth. She prayed to God for a new insight on how to act. A few days later, an idea emerged.

The Proposal of an "Economy of Communion in Freedom"

Max Weber had the following conviction about prophets: "An authentic prophet generally proclaims, creates, or brings about new offerings."[9] He continues his analysis, affirming that the root meaning of "charism" suggests an inspiration for a concrete call to change that the community of believers recognize as original.[10] In the introduction to her formal presentation of the EoC, Chiara Lubich says: "Here, now . . . is born an idea: God asks our Movement in Brazil that counts some 200,000 people . . . to create a communion of goods that engages the Movement as a whole."[11]

---

9. Weber. The original text says: "der genuine Prophet . . . überhaupt verkündet, schafft, fordert neue Gebote," 41.
10. Weber, *Wirtschaft und Gesellschaft:* "im ursprünglichen Sinn des Charisma: kraft Offenbarung, orakel, Eingebung oder: Kraft konkretem Gestaltungswillen, der von der Glaubens-, Wehr-, Partei-oder anderer Gemeinschaft um seiner Herkunft willen anerkannt wird," 141.
11. The Economy of Communion is described in an address by Chiara Lubich during the conferral of an honorary doctorate in Economics at Sacred Heart Catholic Uni-

No authority asked Chiara Lubich to propose the EoC. And while Lubich never said that this was more than an idea, to her it seemed to be a call for change that came directly from God. She never specified that it was an "inspiration" and she used the more neutral term of "idea." But she clearly considered it something to be accomplished because it was according to God's will. Lubich used language such as this in other similar situations. She never "played" the prophet, even if she realized the gravity of the occasion. But for Weber, the one who offers the idea is not the only important factor in this regard. It is also important that the persons being addressed believe that what is proposed is in line with a charism, part of the broader message already offered by the charismatic figure.

What then was the precise proposal launched by Chiara Lubich? She reasoned that it was not enough to exercise acts of charity, works of mercy, or the "communion of goods" between individual persons. The key people to whom she directed her speech were entrepreneurs capable of managing profitable companies efficiently. The innovation she proposed was that the profits be put in common.[12] She also proposed that the profits be divided into thirds. One part would go to the enterprise itself, one to the poor, and one would be invested in programs that promote education in support of building a "culture of communion." The actual amount of the profits going to each of the three would depend on the needs of the company and those working in it, the needs of the poor, and the potential of the educational programs being proposed.

What's new about all this? Chiara Lubich makes no appeal to traditional ways of doing business that owners and managers were used to practicing. She did not give a traditional speech about profit sharing within companies, or contributions to charity outside companies. Sociologically speaking, Lubich's proposal was a "relative, socially-situated innovation." At the same time, she was speaking from the very heart of Christian tradition. The idea of putting things in common is as old as the first Christian community, as described in the Acts of the Apostles. Looking at the innovative ways of adapting this early communion of goods in the history of Christianity, the original text from Acts "is necessarily always reinterpreted by the mediation of the socio-cultural coordinates of the times, of the place, and of

---

versity, Piacenza, Italy, 29 January 1999. See *Essential Writings*, 274-78.

12. Pino Quartana, "L'economia di comunione nel pensiero di Chiara Lubich," *Nuova Umanità* 80-81 (1992), 16.

the tradition lived by the group. It is by this particularization, differentiation, and conditioning that the adaption is in fact innovative."[13] It is also true that in her legitimation of the practice of the communion of goods in the Movement, Lubich always called attention to the experience of the first Christians. But now she applied the communion of goods to a new field, to companies and enterprises. Here is the real innovation.

It is important to point out here that Lubich's proposal not only addresses a social problem (the poor being marginalized from the normal labor circuit), but does so not with an answer made in religious terms (charity or a communion of personal goods) but in economic terms that go straight to the heart of the economy. The answer for Lubich consists in creating new companies that decide from the beginning to share their profits. The answer is an economic one, with the first part of the profits going to the companies themselves to help the business expand and hire new workers. The second part goes to help people in need, giving them the possibility to live a dignified life while looking for work or by offering them work in the business itself. Finally, the third part provides for the cultural support the business needs in order to grow.

This third aspect of the proposal may not be obvious. But if a leader is charismatic, he or she is so because people believe in the message, and this is true also for social movements. The possibility for success is not great without a group that supports an initiative. But once a significant group exists, and here the group supporting the EoC is the whole Focolare Movement, the potential for success is increased. In the case of the Focolare's support for EoC, Lubich understood that it was necessary that the personal and collective lifestyle of this group become a "culture," a consistent pattern of human behavior expressing a commonly held conviction. Realizing any level of culture requires cultivation, or education in values, Lubich saw the need to cultivate a culture of giving: "I give, therefore I exist" would become one of the popular slogans of this cultural program, a clear alternative to the reigning slogan in the consumer culture: "I buy, therefore I exist."

On the other hand, it is important to urgently note that Chiara Lubich does not oppose the free-market system. Indeed, she understands that a viable solution to the urgent problem of poverty depends upon an economic proposal that produces profits. Her goal is to cultivate successful entrepre-

---

13. Jean Séguy, *Conflit et utopie: ou réformer l'Église* (Paris: Cerf, 1999), 129 (my translation).

neurs who can participate with dignity in a new type of economy, and to cultivate a culture of giving that will provide the support such an economy needs. Most social activists look at entrepreneurs with suspicion, as being part of those who exploit rather than as part of those working in favor of the poor.[14] Therefore, the EoC proposal includes a call to change the way people think about business and social justice—thus the need for education.

Catholicism and Economic Theory

How is this proposal situated in the relationship between modern Catholicism and economics? Émile Poulat, a well-known French sociologist of contemporary Catholicism, identifies three kinds of relationships between modern Catholicism and the economy: struggle without rest (traditionalism), upgrading and fighting (progressivism), and accommodation (modernism). As a matter of fact, none of the three approaches account for the way that EoC integrates respect for existing free market economic logic with solidarity-based evolutionary change.

The fundamental question here is: Down through the centuries, how has the Church been doing in regard to economics? Poulat synthesizes his own research into the reaction of the Church to economic thought in the conviction that it "was always the Achilles heel of the Catholic Church. She [the Church] produced social thought, but never possessed realistic economic thought."[15] The result has been that Catholics active in the economic world have lived in ways that have not been guided by Church doctrine. They have not been preoccupied with theories presented in specific Church social doctrines that do not seem to relate to their life experience. Poulat's explanation, which takes in the period of time from the Middle Ages until now, includes a triple separation.[16] First is the separation between the social teachings of

---

14. It is necessary to understand precisely what sociologists mean when they speak of social realities. Usually, they seek to analyze and to understand society as a large set. But here, they are using the term more in the sense used when talking about economics and social policy. So the term has a narrower scope; it considers the distribution of wealth in the same way that the economy takes care of the production of wealth.
15. Émile Poulat, "Pensée chrétienne et vie économique," *Les Cahiers de l'Unité* 16 (1988), 50.
16. Poulat explains, using the situation during Medieval times as a starting point: "Within the moral battle that placed the Church in opposition with the commercial sphere, the mutual lack of comprehension obscured a mental transformation

the Catholic magisterium and the reality of life lived by Christian people. Second is the separation between economics and religion, similar to that between religion and science. Economics constituted itself outside the Church and did not ask anyone in the Church for the principles of their own development. Third is the separation between economic and the social thought. There has been something like a division of labor—for entrepreneurs it was the economy, for the workers it was the social aspect of life. This artificial division positioned the Church on the side of the social aspect, reinforcing the two other separations.[17]

There is another significant quotation from Poulat:

> Everything started with the long conflict between holy poverty [the Catholic approach, symbolized by Saint Francis] and holy enrichment [Calvin and the bourgeois of Geneva], where pastors and theologians thought they were working in their own religious fields. When holiness disappeared, there remained two naked forces face to face. The question for Catholic thought remains how to understand what the Church can really do in her own terms for this [purely secular economic] topic.[18]

To this end, the Church in recent decades has invested in a more systematic thinking on economics, the famous letter of the Bishops of the United States on the economy (1983) being the most famous example.[19] However, this recent effort cannot hide the fact that the Catholic world has had

---

> that was operating: money didn't have the same scope any more. In other times one lent money to the poor; now one lends money to the rich. We are at a crossroads in ways of acting economically. The moralists didn't catch this transition; they missed the train as it left the station, which in the meantime accelerated at a faster and faster pace. Wealth poses all kind of problems connected with modern capitalism, from industrial development to the internationalization of the economy. We can't delude ourselves: integral [an opposite to liberal Catholicism, in the sense Poulat uses the term] Catholicism concentrated on the social aspect where it already had some leverage, because the Church couldn't make any real impact on the economic side of life where liberalism reigned sovereign. Here, her doctrines touched upon one of her most severe limitations." Émile Poulat, *Le catholicisme sous observation: Entretiens avec Guy Lafon* (Paris: Le Centurion, 1983), 105.

17. Poulat, "Pensée chrétienne et vie économique," 54.
18. Poulat, "Pensée chrétienne et vie économique," 55.
19. United States Catholic Bishops, *Economic Justice for All: Pastoral Letter on Catholic Social Teaching and the U.S. Economy,* 1986: http://www.usccb.org/upload/economic_justice_for_all.pdf.

serious and enduring problems in thinking about the economy from its own perspective. Therefore, the initiative of the EoC stimulates the Catholic world to foster new ways of interpreting of the economy based on this vital initiative from within the economic world itself.

The proposal of Chiara Lubich comes from a non-economist, a non-professional who has nothing to do with the economic sector and who obviously also is a non-entrepreneur. It is even more surprising that she adopts an approach to economics not really taken in the social teachings of the Church, as mentioned above. But she does use the economy as her principal leverage for social change. Certainly this is nothing more than an intuition; it is not a scientifically articulated and validated economic position. One might object that this intuition is more of a mystical type than of an economic type. But one can reply that with the vigor of a prophet, she defines what constitutes the very heart of economic acting. Such economic action, she contends, should ultimately be "love," articulated as concrete "reciprocity" or "communion." Or one could paraphrase Poulat's "holy sharing" as "solidarity." This definition engages the symbolic figure of the modern economic world, the entrepreneur. In so doing, Lubich wants to support enterprises in functioning according to the logic of entrepreneurship so as to produce more goods and services. Therefore, it is not surprising that this approach has awakened interest in the academic world, and that she was awarded a doctorate *honoris causa* in economics at Piacenza in 1999.[20] In his social encyclical *Caritas in veritate* (2009), Pope Benedict XVI refers explicitly at n°39 to the kind of experiences the EoC brings about.

The Economy of Communion and the Charismatic Practice of Economics

There is another way to illustrate the innovative nature of Lubich's May 1991 proposal. The Weberian approach touches also on the charismatic fulfillment of needs. Jean Séguy, discussing the connection between religious institutes and charismatic economics, affirms that there can be certain elements of

---

20. Beginning in 1998, Chiara Lubich asked scholars in economics to direct their studies so that the Economy of Communion "becomes a truly scientific discipline, giving dignity to those called to demonstrate the theory in practice, a true 'vocation' for those involved in it in any capacity" (see *Essential Writings*, 285). The serious studies generated in response to this call have led to numerous scientific and academic initiatives and publications. See www.edc-online.org, as well as the worldwide archive of theses related to the Economy of Communion: www.ecodicom.net.

charismatic economy in contemporary modernity.[21] Séguy notes that Weber, in his notion of charismatic economy, distinguishes two possible types:

> Those that correspond to the pure type – the ones that consider the fulfilment of needs with an answer that includes only a charismatic way, outside of all rational economies; and the ones that conform less to the pure type but in certain instances are very near to a pure charismatic economy. The latter is the case with a minimally or relatively administered charismatic economy that introduces a certain degree of daily economic rationalization that does not impede or dominate the whole process. He [Weber] stresses the fact that many religious institutes do not have anything more urgent than to produce a surplus—in part by following an ascetic rationality—in order to escape . . . from accumulation and the need for investment, which means, from the very logic of the capitalistic market.[22]

The regular economy of the Focolare Movement is founded partly on the professional labor of the members who live in community, partly on the communion of goods of the whole Movement according to the members' free choices, and partly on Providence. The latter is an important part, estimated a few years ago as half of the Movement's entire economy. Thus the Focolare economy can be said to be at least partially charismatic, with one part that is foreseeable and another part that is always a surprise. The companies that began to adopt the EoC way of conducting business according to the distribution of profits obey rational economics and thus submit to the logic of capitalistic markets. But at the same time, out of a charismatic logic, they allow part of their profits to "escape." So here we are not talking about the logic of a pure type of charismatic routine, but about a rational economy that is charismaticized only in part.

The EoC possesses an undeniably innovative aspect. It is not a project run by monks or nuns who administer the enterprises of an abbey or of a

---

21. Séguy defined rational economic practice in the sense of the capitalist economy as a rationality of "accumulation, from the investment of capital in the market, of a return on the investment and the profit of modern daily life." For him, the charismatic economy functions with "the gift, the sharing, the ascetic motivations, gratuity, the non-daily exceptional." Jean Seguy, "Instituts religieux et économie charismatique," *Social Compass* 39 (1992): 48.
22. Seguy, "Instituts religieux et économie charismatique," 35-51.

religious institute; it is run by laypeople who act as entrepreneurs.[23] Considering the three nouns in the expression "Economy of Communion in Freedom" (the full title of the EoC project), on the one hand the company is integrated in a free-market economy, but on the other the charismatic inspiration it receives from the Focolare provides an impulse towards communion. Thus, an enterprise that integrates into the free-market system can be managed according to a charismatic logic of relationality, gift, gratuity, and ascetic motivation, together with a heightened acute sense of the exceptional outside the daily routine of modern economic life.

Innovation in the Role of Classical Distribution

The EoC project introduces within the economy a charismatic logic related to distribution. This raises the question whether this charismatic logic aligns itself more with the authentic logic of human and economic acting than with the logic that dominates economics today. An example of this kind of critical questioning can be seen in an observation by the Italian economist Stefano Zamagni, who critiques the paradigm of competition that is invading other spheres of associative life:

> If the rules of social life become competitive, the other becomes my adversary, someone with whom I must fight. And that is the paradox: We know we need each other. You cannot be happy on your own. How can one attain happiness if the rules by which human relations are organized tend to see the other as a rival?[24]

For Zamagni, the EoC reinforces "interpersonal relationships by the concrete demonstration that one can stay within the market and be competitive without undergoing the conditioning that derives from the motivational structure which considers that the only reason to act in the economy is purely for the maximization of profit."[25]

---

23. Séguy observes that for religious institutes, internal cohesion is a consequence of putting profits in common. The firms which practice the EoC undergo an analogous evolution. The operation of distributing the profits is perceived as an ethically and religiously valorizing element. Séguy concludes: "It allows the interested people to be free of the feeling of guilt that eventually emerges because of the obligation to produce capital for purposes that are beyond their will, and so to risk the rupture or the weakening of the solidarity *ad intra*." Seguy, "Instituts religieux et économie charismatique," 47.
24. Benedetto Gui, "Intervista a Stefano Zamagni," *Economia di Comunione* 14 (2000), 10.
25. Gui, "Intervista a Stefano Zamagni," 10.

Zamagni raises another point about the EoC worth considering. The desire of the EoC to produce in order to distribute profits also goes against current economic thinking. He says,

> Everyone who understands how the economy functions is aware that at least for the last 150 years the basic idea was this: The market is the place where wealth is produced; and as for what concerns distribution (to counter all kinds of injustice, inequalities, etc.), that is for the State to think about. The State has to determine redistribution with the help of well-known instruments, among which taxes come first. This economic model thereby also provides the logic for a dichotomy between market and State. It seems to me that the EoC project challenges this model and its logic, because it uses the market itself not only to produce wealth, but also to realize objectives of the redistribution . . . of income and wealth.[26]

For Zamagni, the EoC represents an innovation in economic theory that stands in clear contrast to the founding practices of Western liberal-capitalistic society. Above all, as a consequence it gives a whole piece of the economy the responsibility not only to produce wealth but also to distribute wealth.

The Poor and the Entrepreneur Pericoretically at the Center

Many times, scholars have difficulty forming perspectives of social movements and, most of all, reflecting theoretically on a possible role for the middle class in addressing the conditions of the poor. My study of the EoC and its innovative character, as well as notes I took during a trip to Brazil in 1988, some years before the birth of the EoC, suggest how to address this difficulty. Among the people I met there was the well-known theologian Leonardo Boff, one of the most prolific authors of the Theology of Liberation and a highly regarded participant-observer of the life and projects of the Ecclesial Base Communities (CEB). At the end of a long conversation at his home in Petropolis, he said that the Theology of Liberation and the CEB had made a relatively small impact on Brazilian society because they did not engage the middle class. As a sociologist, I could accept this as a reason

---

26. Stefano Zamagni, "Economia e relazionalità," in Vita Moramarco and Luigino Bruni, *l'Economia di Comunione: Verso un agire economico a misura di persona* (Milan: Vita e Pensiero, 2000), 57.

without difficulty. At that time, I was already aware that a society is more socially balanced when it develops a strong middle class that assures social mobility from the bottom to the top and a good rate of return from its elites. The middle class also assures the development of small-and medium-sized enterprises, which often are a sign of a country's economic health.

This meeting with Boff came to my mind when EoC emerged. Although she was not a specialist in economic and labor sociology, in her religious "philosophy" and her evangelical "instinct" Chiara Lubich counted on the middle class to be important actors in bringing about the EoC. In this regard, she appealed directly to entrepreneurs. She wanted them to use their own talent—economic entrepreneurship—to serve the poor. A careful reading of Lubich's talks at that time reveals that for her the core question was the situation of the poor. They were the center of her attention as she sought to realize the dream of equality in the evangelical sense, where all are sons and daughters of God. It was for this end that the EoC was brought to life. Here we find the very heart of the preferential option for the poor made by the Latin-American Church. But Lubich adds a surprising charismatic innovation to this option: giving a central place to the entrepreneur, and therefore not exclusively to the poor. She seeks to put the dynamism of entrepreneurs at the service of this "cause" in a way that gives them a new social and religious dignity and motivation for doing their work.[27] Miles N. Hansen has also commented on this point: "The ideological and religious values—in other times underestimated as irrational, suspected, or estimated only negatively relative to economic growth—could in numerous cases be utilized as fundamental motivations for rational economic action."[28]

The atypical construction whereby Chiara Lubich puts both the poor and the entrepreneur at the center of the EoC project is also significant. This will not surprise those who know about the fundamental way in which Lubich has built bridges, has built reciprocity between diverse people and situations. Lubich's spirituality itself is built on a Trinitarian ex-

---

27. It helps them acquire a capital of social prestige. Jean Séguy, discussing religious institutes, said this about the theme of social capital: "The religious acquire prestige (in religion as well as in modernity) by practicing a poverty that is partially adapted to the modern daily economy; transferring via ascetic conduct the products of the ordinary capitalist market rationality into another market that has its is own logic, the one of the social economy, based on humanitarian and religious motivations" (Séguy, "Instituts religieux et économie charismatique," 47).

28. Miles N. Hansen, "The Protestant Ethic as a General Precondition for Economic Development," *Canadian Journal of Economics and Political Science* 29 (1963): 473.

perience that seeks unity in diversity. During the early Christian era, the Greek concept of *perichoresis* was used in Trinitarian theology. It signifies that "two realities can exist one within the other, without confusing them and maintaining (and even expressing better in a certain way) their proper identity: united without confusion and distinct without being divided."[29] Keeping in mind the obvious distinctions that must be made in this kind of comparison, *perichoresis* suggests that an important aspect of the EoC's search for a more solidarity-oriented economy is the realization of the religious significance of linking at a deep level the two figures—the poor and the entrepreneurs. This relationship tends toward the pericoretical. Significantly, as far back as 1964, when she was in Recife, Chiara Lubich explained to Focolare leaders in Brazil that the Movement was present there in order to serve the poor. At that time, the common incapacity of Brazilian society to bridge the social gap between rich and poor not only revealed a lack of concern for the poor in the daily life of the nation, but also suggested a closed mentality in the rich. Lubich saw a need not only to free the poor but also to free the rich, because—in the Trinitarian view that she held—true liberty is found in real social relationships. With charismatic intuition, the founder of the Focolare saw the difficulty that Boff formulated for me so clearly twenty-four years later.

Conclusion

The EoC project represents something new in the Weberian ideal type of a charismatic economy by identifying a need and addressing it in an innovative way. The need: increasing social justice, offering poor people the opportunity to find work and an entry into the social life of Brazil (or elsewhere). The innovative way: helping businesses successfully complete their usual scope of economic action so as to build profits in order to be able to distribute more. It is clear that the EoC presents at least three economic innovations: (1) engaging the middle class in an active role; (2) providing a distributive role for economic production rather than leaving it only to state agencies; (3) offering a charismatic role to the world of free enterprise by integrating religious motivations and actions into a more finely-tuned sense of the exceptional social potential of the economic process. The EoC project innovates in this sense by stimulating ecclesial reflection on economics itself,

---

29. Enrique Cambón, *Trinità, modello sociale* (Rome: Città Nuova, 2009), 31.

not just on certain social aspects of economic life. In this innovation, Lubich adds a fourth dimension to the framework of the Focolare Movement's economy—labor, communion of goods, and Providence. In this way she puts "holy enrichment" at the service of the poor by practicing a new form of "holy poverty." Lubich brings together the middle class and the poor by bringing together Francis and Calvin.

Part Seven

Implications of Paradise '49
for Interreligious Dialogue

Chapter Twenty-Seven

The Mystical Theology of Chiara Lubich: A Foundation for Interreligious Dialogue in East Asia

Donald W. Mitchell

Chiara Lubich's Spirituality and Interreligious Dialogue

Chiara Lubich understood that the cry of Jesus crucified, "My God, my God, why have you forsaken me?" (Mt 27:46) was intimately related to Jesus' last prayer, "May they all be one" (Jn. 17:21). At the moment of his cry on the Cross, Jesus experienced the separation of humankind from God in order to fill that gap and reunite us as one human family in God. His prayer for the oneness of humanity suffering from cultural, racial, political, religious, and personal divisions of all kinds found its answer in the cry of forsakenness. Chiara's spirituality is based on a spiritual union with Jesus Forsaken for the healing of divisions and on a unity of humankind that reflects the unity of the Trinity. Human beings living the Trinitarian life as much as possible is the core of Chiara's spirituality. In the words of Piero Coda, her spirituality is based on "the existential understanding, in light of Jesus Forsaken, of the Trinitarian love between the Father and the Son in the communion of the Holy Spirit."[1]

The *kenosis* (self-emptying) of Jesus on the Cross, as presented in Philippians 2:7, is not only a kenotic love for humankind bringing a new unity to the human family. It is also a self-revelation of the inner Trinitarian *kenosis* of mutual indwelling (perichoresis). This fact would become clear to Chiara during her mystical illuminations in Paradise '49, which we will discuss later. For now, it is important to note that her spirituality of unity, which is based on this kind of kenotic love and perichoretic unity, animates the interreligious dialogues of the Focolare Movement.

---

1. Piero Coda, "Introduction," Chiara Lubich, *Essential Writings* (Hyde Park, NY: New City Press, 2007), xix.

The loving dialogical dynamism of Chiara's relational charism with its thrust toward unity could not be contained within the Catholic Church alone. Chiara describes her first realization of this fact during an encounter in 1966:

> The first major experience we had with brothers and sisters of other religious faiths was with the Bangwa, a tribe in the Cameroons, which follows a traditional religion. . . . One day the king, the Fon, and thousands of his people were gathered in a large clearing in the middle of the forest for a celebration in which they offered us their songs and dances. All at once, I had a strong impression of God, like a huge Sun, embracing all of us, we and they, with his love. For the first time in my life, I intuited that soon we would be involved also with people of non-Christian traditions.[2]

The event that formalized this involvement and dialogue took place in 1977 in London, when Chiara was awarded the Templeton Prize for Progress in Religion. Chiara notes:

> I gave a talk and when I was leaving the hall, the first to greet me were Jews, Muslims, Buddhists, Sikhs, Hindus. . . . It was clear to me that we needed to be involved not just with our own and other churches, but also with these brothers and sisters of other faiths. So began our interreligious dialogue.[3]

In the years after that event, Chiara traveled the world in dialogue with Muslims from North Africa to New York City, with Jewish leaders from Israel to Argentina, with Hindus in India, and Buddhists in East Asia. In all of these encounters, she modeled the way of dialogue that derives from her spirituality. She followed the example of Jesus Forsaken by stripping away all the riches of her own tradition in a *kenosis* of love that made herself one with all she met. She entered their worlds, their hearts and minds, and found brothers and sisters, fellow pilgrims in the religious life. She found herself enriched by the deep realities of other religions and would reflect on how what she found related to her personal experiences. She was fascinated with the similarities while always stressing the unity that is possible even

---

2. Chiara Lubich, "The Focolare Movement's Experience of Interreligious Dialogue," *Essential Writings*, 344.
3. Lubich, "The Focolare Movement's Experience of Interreligious Dialogue," 344.

with differences. For example, here is Chiara's description of her experience of being in dialogue with Jewish leaders in Argentina:

> First there is a desire to get to know you . . . and begin a relationship with you precisely as brothers and sisters. . . . This is what happens when after a long time, brothers and sisters meet again and discover they are brothers and sisters; they love one another. . . . Could it not be that the Lord is beginning to manifest his will clearly that we establish a fraternal relationship among us . . . and offering through our profound communion, through our working together, fresh hope to the world.[4]

About the process of discovering our brothers and sisters in other religions through dialogue, of loving each other in fraternal relationships, and of building a communion and working together to give hope to the world, Chiara writes:

> It brings together, like a real family, people of different languages, races, cultures, nations and also faiths . . . in order to build fraternity among all . . . [with a] vision of all humanity as one family. . . .
>
> It requires that we "make ourselves one" with others, that "we live the others" in a certain way, that we share their sufferings, their joys, in order to understand them to serve and help them in an effective, practical way. . . .
>
> It demands that we empty ourselves completely, that we put aside from our minds our ideas, from our hearts our affections, from our wills everything we would want to do, in order to identify with the other person.
>
> It is a matter of momentarily putting aside even the most beautiful and greatest things we have: our own faith, our own convictions, in order to be "nothing" in front of the other persons, a "nothingness of love." By doing so we put ourselves in an attitude of learning, and in reality we always do have something to learn. . . . We enter their world, in some way we become inculturated in them and we are enriched. This attitude enables us to contribute to making our multicultural societies become intercultural, that

---

4. Lubich, "With our Elder Brothers," *Essential Writings*, 333–34.

is, made up of cultures open to one another and in a profound dialogue of love with one another. . . .

Real, true, heart-felt fraternity is, in fact, the fruit of a love capable of making itself dialogue, relationship, that is, a love that, far from arrogantly closing itself within its own boundaries, opens itself toward others and works together with all people of goodwill in order to build together unity and peace in the world.[5]

"Love capable of making itself dialogue!" The kind of love that Chiara sees as having this capacity is kenotic love, the love of Jesus Forsaken who gave up all to become one with all in order to realize the prayer he made to his Father, "that they all be one." It is Jesus Forsaken in the heart of Chiara as her spiritual spouse who is not only a model for dialogue but also is *love making itself dialogue*. Therefore, this love can achieve the answer to Jesus' prayer: unity. Again in Chiara's words, the goal is "that of restoring unity to the human family, because the Holy Spirit is present and active in some way in every religion, and not just in the individual members, but also within the religious tradition itself."[6]

Persons of different religions who are in dialogue with the Focolare Movement often say that the unity they find through this dialogue of life makes them better Muslims, Buddhists, Jews, Hindus, and so on. One Jewish leader in the United States said that the loving fellowship at a Focolare center in Rome gave her a deep sense that she was living the spirit of the Sabbath as she would at home. A Tibetan Buddhist leader visiting a Focolare center in Los Angeles said that he "felt at home." A Muslim woman from the Philippines who had been traveling for some time said with a deep sigh upon sitting down on a chair at the Chicago Focolare center, "Now I feel I am home again." Once when I was eating dinner with a group of Hindus visiting the Focolare in Italy, there was a long silence and then the elder said, "I feel the presence of God here." All the other Hindus in the group nodded.

This kind of "homecoming" experience goes both ways. To a Muslim's question about what establishing relationships with people of other religions was like, Chiara responded:

---

5. Lubich, "With the World Religions," *Essential Writings*, 338–41.
6. Lubich, "The Focolare Movement's Experience of Interreligious Dialogue," *Essential Writings*, 347.

> I have always felt very comfortable! Because even if our religions are different we have much in common and this unites us. . . . Therefore, I am happy for two reasons: because I come to know new things and enter into another's culture; but also because I come to know brothers and sisters who are the same as me insofar as we believe in so many of the same things.[7]

When asked to say more about what she "feels" when she is with a brother or sister of another religion, Chiara said: "I feel a great desire to relate with them as with members of the same family, to enter immediately into a fraternal relationship, to make unity. . . . I feel that there is a pre-existing bond that was there already."[8]

Feeling "comfortable," "at home," like "brothers and sisters," like "family," like there is a "pre-existing bond"—these feelings are for Chiara the work of the Holy Spirit bringing to earth a taste of the Trinitarian life. Chiara's charism lived out in dialogue brings something of this spiritual reality to people of all religions. In experiencing it, people of other religions do not lose their diverse identities but find a unity that embraces the diversity of brothers and sisters. Christians do not lose their identity but find it set within a broader horizon, like under the "huge Sun" Chiara experienced that embraced everyone in the jungle of the Republic of Cameroon.

I think that this life of dialogue, based on the charism given to Chiara for the good of the church and the world, represents two paradigm shifts. The first shift is away from the primacy of a religiosity that focuses on the individual and his or her own religious practice. Such an individual religiosity stresses the personal devotional aspects of a particular religion that take place within a church, monastery, ashram, mosque, synagogue, at home, or in a retreat or pilgrimage setting. For Chiara, this aspect remains necessary but insufficient. In line with Vatican II, she stresses the importance of a balance between the personal and the communal, which she does not see as competing sides of religious life. In fact, she would often say that by living in deeper communion with others and following the model of the Trinity as best we can, we will find that our personal spiritual life has deepened within us. And prayer, meditation, devotion, and scripture can strengthen the basis for our unity with others.

---

7. Lubich, "With Muslims," *Essential Writings*, 349.
8. Lubich, *Essential Writings*, 350, 354.

The second paradigm shift is away from a vision of one's religion as an enclosed home with locked doors and toward that of an open journey where we find fellow pilgrims of different religions and cultures. This is the path where true dialogue takes place, where we discover we have a bond that unites us as brothers and sisters, and where we are comfortable and at home with each other. In this journey, we can dialogue more deeply, share the treasures of our traditions, build a greater unity, and collaborate for peace and justice in our world. Chiara would say that our world is experiencing a cultural "dark night" involving a fragmentation into different tribes, even within the same religion, that do not listen to but turn to violence against each other. As John Paul II said, this is an evil with a capital "E." We need dialogue to open the hearts and minds of humankind to our spiritual brotherhood and sisterhood, to a life of unity and peace.

Chiara relates this experience of a cultural dark night to the time of St. Augustine.[9] People from the North and the East were migrating to Europe, and the Roman Empire was falling into division and chaos. Augustine had the grace to see that the hatred and violence of that time was not the end of the world but the birth pains of a new world. Today, the way forward into a new and more united and peaceful global culture is dialogue. This is one reason that those of us who are academics in the Focolare Movement have founded a new journal, *Claritas: Journal of Dialogue and Culture*.[10] We believe that fraternal dialogue can contribute the clarity needed to build a culture of unity.

Chiara Lubich's Mystical Insights, East Asian Buddhism, and Confucianism

In this section, I will discuss what I see as possible future points for dialogue between four East Asian religious and philosophical traditions and the mystical thought of Chiara Lubich. The first is the tradition of Emptiness, as presented in Mahayana thought beginning in India and becoming a foundation of East Asian Buddhism in general. The second is the Mahayana tradition's identity of samsara and Nirvana, suffering existence and nirvanic liberation, which also emerged in India and then became foundational to Buddhism in East Asia. The third is the notion of the interpenetration and mutual indwelling of all things, as developed in the Chinese Huayan tradi-

---

9. Lubich, "With World Religions," 337.
10. See: https://claritas.sophiauniversity.org/

tion and considered by many to be the high point of East Asian Buddhist thought. Finally, the fourth is a set of notions presented by Zhu Xi in the Chinese Neo-Confucian tradition, which has had great influence in the rest of East Asia. In all four cases, I will point out both similarities and differences that can inform future dialogue.

Emptiness and Creation

The Mahayana Buddhist notion of Emptiness expands the Buddha's teaching of the dependent arising of the universe in such a way that all beings are interrelated and "lack" or are "empty" of the independence we attribute to them. Emptiness is the matrix, the interconnected wholeness of life found in the penetrating insight of enlightened wisdom. When wisdom penetrates Emptiness, one discovers one's true self, one's Buddha-nature, and Emptiness empties out in one's heart as compassion. One finds that all things are compassionately connected in a harmony from beginningless beginning to endless end.[11]

Chiara Lubich writes about her own mystical experience of creation and of nature during Paradise '49:

> I remember that during those days, nature seemed to me to be enveloped totally by the sun; it already was physically, but it seemed to me that an even stronger sun enveloped it, saturated it, so that the whole of nature appeared to me as being "in love." I saw things, rivers, plants, meadows, grass as linked to one another by a bond of love in which each one had a meaning of love with regard to the others.[12]

> On earth all is in relationship of love with all: each thing with each thing. It is necessary to be Love to find the thread of gold among beings.[13]

---

11. Donald W. Mitchell, *Buddhism: Introducing the Buddhist Experience* (New York: Oxford University Press, 2008), 106-110.
12. Chiara Lubich, "Paradise '49," *Claritas: Journal of Dialogue and Culture* 1 (2012): 7.
13. Quoted by Callan Slipper, "Towards an Understanding of the Human Person According to the Mystical Experience of Chiara Lubich in the Paradise of '49," *Claritas: Journal of Dialogue and Culture* 1 (2012): 30 (translation revised).

In a talk in 1999, Chiara elaborates on this experience:

> When we arrived in the mountains . . . I felt that I could discern, because of a special grace from God, the presence of God beneath things. Because God is present, sustaining all things. Therefore, if the pine trees—which I saw—were golden by the sun, if the brooks flowed into the glimmering falls, if the daisies, other flowers and the sky were all decked in summer array, stronger than all this was the vision of a Sun beneath all creation. In a certain sense, I saw, I believe, God who supports, who upholds things. God was preparing me for what would happen. And the fact that God was beneath things meant that they were not as we see them; they were all linked to one another by love; all, so to speak, in love with one another. So, if the brook flowed into the lake, it was out of love. If the pine tree stood high next to another pine tree, it was out of love.[14]

In a talk two years later, Chiara says that she and her companions felt a "fire" at the time she was experiencing God "beneath" creation:

> This fire that we felt—which we never felt again afterwards—was also outside of us. So we saw, I saw and then I communicated it to the others who then saw it with me—we saw that beneath the things of the world, like the meadows, the stars, the sky, the flowers, the waterfalls, there was Someone who linked them all together, a light that linked everything: it was the presence of God in things.[15]

Chiara experienced a divine "Sun" or "Fire," which she refers to as the love of God, that gives life to all beings through the Word of God. All things in creation exist together in an interrelatedness, in a "bond of love," each being a gift for the others. This interrelatedness of all things expresses in creation "traces" of the Trinity. Chiara saw the cosmos as saturated with a divine love wherein all beings are linked. It is very interesting that Chiara, later commenting on this experience, saw a similarity between this Trinitarian vision of creation and the Buddhist understanding of the cosmos.[16]

---

14. Chiara Lubich, Unpublished Talk at Castel Gandolfo, December 20, 1999.
15. Chiara Lubich, Unpublished Talk at Castel Gandolfo, February 23, 2001.
16. Chiara Lubich, Unpublished Talk to the Gen, December 20, 2003.

Chiara goes on in her talk to discuss how she experienced the relationality of creation:

> During those days everything contributed to creating "Paradise" inside and outside of us, almost as if the elements, people and events themselves were actors in the divine drama that held our soul for a long time. It was as if one divine Wisdom ordered all things in ever new scenarios.[17]

In other words, her previous experience of the "bond of love" uniting all beings in creation was deepened as she experienced the luminous "divine Wisdom" bringing about the harmony or order in creation. In the "ever new scenarios" of creation, all beings that had been seen as, in essence, gifts for each other were seen as harmonized by divine Wisdom. While Buddhism penetrates the interdependence of Emptiness with a "perfection of wisdom," Chiara's mystical experience penetrates divine Wisdom as the very cause of the interrelated harmony of all things.

Concerning this harmony of creation, Chiara notes that Francis of Assisi did not call the sun his brother and the water his sister out of sentimentality but in order to capture the real unity of the universe: "And having discovered the Creator of all things who is the father of each one, he sees them all, though in different ways, related to one another."[18] Chiara also notes that from her Trinitarian vision, one sees "in this world everyone is at the center, because the law of everything is love."[19] Here, Chiara is saying that since each being is fully a gift for all other beings, each is the center of the cosmos and the receiver of the gifts of all entities in the cosmos. In other words, all beings affirm in kenotic love each being, making each the center of creation.[20]

---

17. Lubich, Unpublished Talk to the Gen.
18. Marisa Cerini, *God Who is Love: In the Experience and Thought of Chiara Lubich* (New York: New City Press, 1992), 64–65.
19. Cerini, *God Who is Love*, 65.
20. For a comparative essay on this aspect of Chiara's experience of creation, see Donald W. Mitchell, "The Trinity and Buddhist Cosmology," *Buddhist-Christian Studies* 18 (1998): 169–80.

Suffering and Peace

Related to the Buddhist notion of Emptiness is the Mahayana teaching that "samsara is Nirvana, Nirvana is samsara." Seeing the suffering world through the perfection of wisdom discloses a nirvanic dimension. With our senses and ordinary mind, we see and experience samsara. But with enlightened wisdom, we discover a Higher Truth where one can live out the peace and compassion, joy and loving kindness of Nirvana in one's daily life.[21]

In some of Chiara's writings from before 1949, she describes her experience of a supernatural love, peace, and joy found in the suffering world. For example, Chiara notes in a letter written in 1948:

> This presence [Jesus Forsaken] . . very soon becomes *felt,* so that throwing ourselves into a sea of suffering we discover ourselves in a sea of love, of complete joy . . . and the soul feels itself refilled with the Holy Spirit, who is joy, peace, serenity.[22]

In another letter, Chiara refers to this experience as a movement "beyond the wound":

> that is having embraced Jesus forsaken totally, so that we found ourselves beyond pain, in love we felt like we were contemplating the immense love which God has poured out over the world . . . we were merged with love and shared in its light: the light of Love.[23]

Chiara describes this experience as "a sort of Easter," a "Passover" that seemed to her like "the triumphal entry of God" into the soul.[24]

These two letters indicate experiences that are similar to the Buddhist view that the discovery of Emptiness entails "Emptiness emptying out as the Great Compassion." In this discovery, one finds that Nirvana is samsara and that unmovable peace is found in the sea of suffering. For Chiara, this kind of Passover of the mind and heart from suffering into the freedom of love, peace, and joy is due to the sea of love that is God's embracement of creation. To explain the Trinitarian source of the sea of love, Chiara and the

---

21. Mitchell, *Buddhism,* 139–46.
22. Chiara Lubich, *Unity and Jesus Forsaken* (Hyde Park, NY: New City Press, 1985), 67–68.
23. Lubich, *Unity and Jesus Forsaken,* 70–71.
24. Lubich, *Unity and Jesus Forsaken,* 69.

Abba School, like in Buddhism, use the philosophical categories of "being" and "nonbeing." For example, Chiara says in two places:

> Love is not only an attribute of God: it is his very Being. And because he is Love, God is One and Triune at the same time: Father, Son and Holy Spirit. . . . The Father generates the Son out of love; he loses himself in the Son, he lives in him; in a certain sense he makes himself "non-being" out of love, and for this very reason, he *is,* he is Father. The Son, as echo of the Father, out of love turns to him, he loses himself in the Father, he lives in him, and in a certain sense he makes himself "non-being" out of love; and for this very reason, he *is,* he is the Son. The Holy Spirit, since he is the mutual love between the Father and the Son, their bond of unity, in a certain sense he also makes himself "nonbeing" out of love; and for this very reason, he *is;* he is the Holy Spirit. He is the "emptiness of love" in which the Father and Son are one.

> If we consider the Son in the Father, we must think of the Son as a nothingness (a nothingness of love) in order to think of God as One. And if we consider the Father in the Son, we must think of the Father as a nothingness (a nothingness of love) in order to think of God as One. There are three in the Most Holy Trinity, and yet they are One because Love is not and is at the same time. . . . Each one is complete by not-being, indwelling fully in the others, in an eternal self-giving. . . . Herein lies the dynamics of life within the Trinity, which is revealed to us as unconditional, reciprocal self-giving, as mutual loving, self-emptying out of love, as total and eternal communion.[25]

We are here reminded of another Buddhist notion, namely, "Emptiness as non-being empties out as Wondrous Being." For Chiara, it is the Trinitarian nonbeing of love that "pours over the world" a sea of peace and joy in which we find Wondrous Being.

---

25. Piero Coda, "The Experience and Understanding of the Faith in God-Trinity from Saint Augustine to Chiara Lubich," *New Humanity Review* 15 (2010): 37–38. Translated from Piero Coda "L'esperienza e l'intelligenza della fede in Dio Trinita' da Sant'Agostino a Chiara Lubich," *Nuova Umanità* 167 (2006): 527–52.

Mutual Penetration and Mutual Indwelling

In the Chinese tradition of Huayan Buddhism, there is a profound notion concerning the relation between particular things in the world. Phenomena "mutually interpenetrate" so as to be present within each other in a kind of "mutual containment." This does not mean all things are physically present in other things; the metaphor used by the Huayan Master Fazang is a mirror containing the reflections of other mirrors. This "mutual indwelling" of things does not destroy their freedom. Rather the matrix of this mutual penetration is called "the realm of the non-obstruction between phenomena." To discover this realm enables one to "enter" and "identify" himself or herself with all things in the universe while not obstructing freedom and personal uniqueness.[26]

For Chiara, Trinitarian experience involves the mutual indwelling of the Persons of the Trinity and a reflection of that mutual indwelling among all things. This reality can be realized by those who live the life of unity by emptying themselves though a nonbeing of love into the lives of others. Chiara's Trinitarian experience of mutual indwelling is only now being published by the Abba School.[27] For example, in a recent article, Anna Pelli, a member of the Abba School, quotes Chiara's unpublished writing in which she uses a Huayan-like metaphor of a mirror to explain mutual indwelling:

> It happens as in those mirrors that, looking at one another, project themselves infinitely into one another and re-contain themselves through the reflection that returns. . . . Each particular, then, even though distinct from the others, contains in itself the universal. And since the all, the universal in itself is unity, each particular in itself is "a harmony = a *unity*," and in unity is composed "the harmony of harmonies."[28]

---

26. Mitchell, *Buddhism*, 213–19. See Donald W. Mitchell, "The Trinity and Buddhist Cosmology," 169–82.
27. The best source in English so far for this aspect of Chiara's experience is an above-quoted article by Callan Slipper, "Towards an Understanding of the Human Person According to the Mystical Experience of Chiara Lubich in the Paradise of '49," 24–45.
28. Anna Pelli, "Going from the Pact to the Soul: Exploring a Metaphysical Journey," *Claritas: Journal of Dialogue and Culture* 2 (2013): 17, 20.

Pelli reflects on this statement in the following way:

> Mutual indwelling of subjects, *according to the pattern of the Trinity* . . . leads to refinding oneself in a mirror-like presence of otherness, in a being-more that does not simply exceed these things . . . but that, while it contains them, is, at the same time, contained by them. . . . The individual is the whole, the whole is the individuals. In other words, each one (the particular, the finite) . . . bears in itself the reality of the all, of the one.[29]

The basis of Chiara's thought here is her experience of the divine ideas in the Word. The ideas of all particulars in creation preexist in the Word of God as ideas in the Idea, words within the Word, *logoi* within *Logos*. They are uncreated without the limitations of material, created things—the eternal form of each thing in creation. In the process of creation, they change their ontological state and take on the limitations of finitude. Chiara says:

> When God created, He created all things from nothing because He created them from Himself—from nothing means that they did not pre-exist because He alone pre-existed. . . . He drew them out from Himself. . . . The Father projects them, as in divergent rays, "outside himself," that is, in a new and different dimension, a created one, where he gives them "Order that is Life and Love and Truth." There is in them, thus, the imprint of the Uncreated, of the Trinity.[30]

In explaining this notion of creation, Callan Slipper says the following:

> In creating . . . the Father, looking at the Son, gives himself, giving his being by participation to the ideas-words (the "words in the Word"), and in that way "clothing" that which is not, the nothing, with his being, the very being of God. Created *things in themselves are not and remain nothing*, but they have being insofar as it *is given to them by participation*.[31]

All created things are united to the Word who contains all the ideas-words united in himself. This unity with the Word that contains all

---

29. Pelli, "Going from the Pact to the Soul," 19.
30. Slipper, "Towards an Understanding of the Human Person," 27 (translation revised).
31. Slipper, "Towards an Understanding of the Human Person," 28.

things as ideas and as created particulars of those ideas means that each thing contains all other things; thus the mutual indwelling of creation. Slipper notes, "A specific created thing, therefore, inasmuch as it is an expression of a word in the Word, contains the stars, the mountains, the animals, and all human beings."[32] Here we see a mutual indwelling of particulars similar to that of Huayan.

For Chiara, while human beings have in relation to the divine ideas all the characteristics of other created things, they are distinct in their unique relation to the Word. The Word became a human, Jesus. So, humans have the capacity to express the whole Word-Jesus, not just the divine idea of themselves. In other words, while the divine ideas in the Word provide the model for other creatures, it is Jesus the Word who provides the model for human beings and the basis for our potential relational unity.[33] Chiara says:

> Looking upon two firs as a unit gives rise to the idea of the model fir. And here is the Gospel of nature. Where two firs are united, there is the idea of the model fir.
>
> Likewise, where two human beings are united in the name of Jesus, there is Jesus; and this because Jesus is the model for human beings. He is the Human Being. And two or more are enough to have present the Idea of him.[34]

The Principles in Taiji and the Divine Ideas in the Word

How does all this relate to Confucianism? Here, I want to present a continuation of what has been discussed above as it relates to the philosophy of Zhu Xi, perhaps the greatest of the Neo-Confucian thinkers. Zhu Xi posits certain "principles," "forms," or "laws" (*li*) that exist "above shapes" and "within shapes." Within shapes or things, these formative principles or ordering laws constitute the nature of a thing. But before they are within a thing, they exist beyond the physical universe. They exist in ultimate reality, *Taiji*. In the creation of a thing, the formative principles become immanent in the individuals, and so does *Taiji*. The latter is said to be like the whole moon shining in a lake or a drop of water. Also present in *Taiji* is the source

---

32. Slipper, "Towards an Understanding of the Human Person," 29.
33. For Chiara, this last fact, that Jesus is the basis for human mutuality-unity, is experienced as Jesus present and making them one, what Chiara called Jesus in the midst.
34. Slipper, "Towards an Understanding of the Human Person," 43.

of materiality, called *qi*, which the principles form into things. Zhu Xi sees this process as a kind of "condensation" of *qi* in accordance with the eternal principles, *li*. Finally, these principles determine not only the nature of things but also their proper relationships. They include principles of moral behavior, the root of all virtues being "humanheartedness" (*ren*).

We can see similarities between Zhu Xi's philosophy of principles (*li*) and Chiara's mystical insights about the divine ideas. Cerini writes about Chiara's Trinitarian vision: "[Chiara perceived] the 'trinitarian mark of the Creator' which is present in the entire universe in the vital interrelationships of the basic elements that constitute it."[35] Cerini then provides an example of what Chiara meant by "basic elements," namely, matter, order, and life.[36] Matter is the result of the Trinitarian Love of the Father in the creative act. It is like the *qi* condensing as matter from *Taiji*. The act of creation is through the Word that contains the divine ideas of God, the "forms" that, like *li*, order and provide laws for the created material things of the cosmos. Life is the result of the matter the Father creates, the ordering forms of things found in the Son, the Word, and their unity in the life-giving Holy Spirit.

Similarly, for Zhu Xi, the ordering principles (*li*) and the source of matter (*qi*) are both in *Taiji*. For Chiara, matter and order do not exist apart from each other, just as the Father who originates matter and the Word who orders matter do not exist apart from each other. Life is a consequence of the unity of matter and ordering laws (forms). Here, Cerini says, even the very elements of creation are a "reflection" of the unity/distinction of the Trinity. Slipper describes this understanding of the elements of creation in this way:

> Creation has being because the only being is that of the divine, that comes from the source that is the Father. It has law (or form) because the ideas-words, that give the law (or form) to things, remain in the Word, that is in the mind of God. Creation has life because the relating of things to one another, that is the result of the meeting of their being with their law (or form), is sharing in the One who constitutes the eternal meeting between the source of being and the Word . . . that is, the Holy Spirit.[37]

---

35. Cerini, *God Who is Love*, 62.
36. Chiara's words during Paradise '49 are: "So I see in nature the imprint of the Trinity, an imprint that elsewhere is described as matter-law-life, following the pattern of Father, Son, Holy Spirit."
37. Slipper, "Towards an Understanding of the Human Person," 29.

Cerini calls matter "the mysterious expansion of the free self-giving of Trinitarian Love 'outside'" of the Trinity in the creative act in space and time.[38] Matter is formed by the divine ideas in the Word of God both in what material things are and how they relate:

> Being, made visible through the universe . . . is what Chiara highlights when she recognizes that love is the essence of all things: of the uncreated, of the created, *and* [italics mine] of the very relationships between the uncreated and the created. . . . God-Love sustains all things by his continuous creative act. He orders and moves them in a wondrous unity that preserves distinction, not only between the uncreated and the created, but among all things themselves.[39]

Chiara understood that when persons realize this reality,

> They discover the divine plan which God "designed for us and for our brothers and sisters, where everything falls into a splendid scheme of love," where "a mysterious bond of love links persons and things, guides history, orders the destiny of peoples and individuals, while respecting their freedom to the full."[40]

Or in Chiara's words from her experience of Paradise '49, "the whole of humanity therefore—*and in humanity the cosmos* [italics mine]—[are] eternally present in the Word, . . . which is in the bosom of the Father . . . the starting point and, so to say, the ultimate end of all divine creative action."[41]

Since the divine ideas of all creation and their relationships have eternally been present and united by Love in the Word, when one is *in* unity with others, he or she discovers himself or herself to be *gift for* others in creation. He or she also discovers his or her true personhood as uniquely created by God as a distinct gift for all others. Chiara wrote during Paradise '49, "I felt that I have been created as a gift for the one next to me and the one next to me has been created by God as a gift for me. As the Father in the Trinity is all for the Son and the Son is all for the Father."[42]

---

38. Cerini, *God Who is Love*, 62.
39. Cerini, *God Who is Love*, 63-64.
40. Cerini, *God Who is Love*, 65, quoting Chiara.
41. Slipper, "Towards an Understanding of the Human Person," 25.
42. Cerini, *God Who is Love*, 52. This passage is from the text of Paradise '49 dated September 2, 1949 (translation revised).

This realization opens one to a deeper understanding of the moral and social life to which we are called based on the love present in each person, like the "seed of humanheartedness," to use Meng Zi's notion, that makes us gift for the other. This being a gift of love for others is the basis for what Cerini calls the "horizontal *perichoresis*," the ideal moral and social mutual indwelling that "reflects" the perichoresis of the Trinity. In this horizontal perichoresis, true and distinctive humanhearted or compassion personhood is discovered, refined, and perfected. For Chiara, this is possible since the true identity of each person is already perfect in the Word and therefore in the perichoresis of the Trinity. One needs only to become existentially what he or she already is essentially. In Cerini's words:

> It is possible, therefore, to have a perichoresis among [people], even though it is imperfect, through the vertical perichoresis, so to speak, that exists between them and the Trinity by way of Christ in the Holy Spirit. . . . Unity among human persons "as" among the divine persons, can occur only in God. . . . Only God can produce it. It is his gift. That is why Jesus asks the Father for it: "That they may be [one] in us."[43]

I would add one final remark since I have raised the notion of a vertical *perichoresis* between persons and the Trinity. In Chiara's unpublished writings, she notes a number of times that all of creation flows out of God through the Word *and* that all of creation flows back into God through the Word. In both cases, there is an interrelatedness between all beings as they come forth from God, abide in creation together, and return together into God through the Word. In the Word after death, they are divinized, progressively becoming what they truly are in the mind and heart of God. All parts of creation are like rays of light diverging from the Word and then converging back—always in a relatedness of interdependence, love, and gift for each other.

Final Reflections on the Mystical Thought of Chiara Lubich as a Foundation for Future Interreligious Dialogue in East Asia

I believe it is clear that there are strong similarities between the mystical insights of Chiara Lubich and both the Buddhist and Confucianist traditions of East Asia. It also should be clear that there are differences as well. One

---

43. Cerini, *God Who is Love*, 51.

question that Buddhism has addressed since its beginning in India is the question of causation. For example, what is it that makes the world a matrix of interdependence? Why is it this way and how does it come about? The typical answer is karma. Some Buddhist philosophers claim that karma does the work that in Christianity is deemed to be God's work. Certainly Chiara's Trinitarian experience was of an interrelatedness in nature that derived from a divine source: God's creative Love that through the Word brings the dynamic interdependent order or harmony of things as gifts for each other. The immanent horizontal *perichoresis* in creation is based on a transcendent vertical *perichoresis*. While Buddhists do not posit such a transcendent cause, there is here a foundation for future Buddhist-Christian dialogue.

The relationship between suffering and freedom, samsara and Nirvana, being and nonbeing is essential to both Buddhist epistemology and Buddhist ontology. Chiara's mystical experience of nonbeing in the very heart of the Trinity as eternal Love, and its being lived out by persons in their relationships following the model of Jesus Forsaken, touches on these issues in Buddhism. The discovery of peace, joy, and freedom in this mystery of the Cross resonates with the identity of samsara and Nirvana, but with a personal texture. This personal Trinitarian dimension of nonbeing and being presents another opportunity for in-depth dialogue.

A comparison of Chiara's experience of the mutual indwelling with Huayan's notion of mutual penetration and containment shows how the dialogue can be enriching in both directions. Certainly the "non-obstruction between phenomena" in the Huayan vision touches the mystery of a unity that preserves distinction and freedom. Many of the metaphors and terminology of Huayan can be rich resources for Christian Trinitarian theology. And Chiara's experience of the containment of the cosmos in all things can be a resource for Buddhists as well.

Finally, Christian dialogue with Confucianism often occurs at the level of ethics and social thought. Chiara's ontological insights into the Trinitarian aspects of the creative act—namely, matter, order, and life—however, provide a basis for a deeper interreligious conversation about the fundamental origin of the universe. Also, unlike Buddhism, the Neo-Confucianism of Zhu Xi posits a transcendent reality that includes suggestive parallels to Chiara's experience of the divine ideas that determine the nature of things as well as moral relationships.

In short, I believe that as more of Chiara's mystical writings are published, we will find new horizons for the Catholic Church's dialogue with the religious traditions of East Asia. In so doing, the philosophy of the church may find categories other than those received from the ancient Greeks, the scholastics, and modern European thought that promise to make the Church more global. Chiara's charism in the dialogue of life has built bridges of unity between peoples around the world, bringing them together in a "home" where all "feel comfortable." In that universal home, that "focolare," we will have much to discuss for our mutual enrichment, understanding, and appreciation. This dialogue, I think, will contribute to a global culture of harmony, peace, and good will to all beings.

Chapter Twenty-Eight

Dazzling Darkness: Buddhism and Chiara Lubich's Mystical Writings

Donald W. Mitchell

Buddhism

Let me begin with some historical reflections about Buddhism. Among the earliest *sūtras* of the Mahāyāna tradition are the Perfection of Wisdom *Sūtras* (*Prajñāparamitā-Sūtras*).[1] A central teaching in these texts is that from a higher wisdom, one can realize that all aspects of existence are "empty of own-being" (*svabhāva-śūnya*). As the Heart *Sūtra* states, "Hear, O Śāriputra, form is emptiness, emptiness is form." In other words, all beings do not exist as we ordinarily see them, namely, as substantial independent entities. They exist in an interrelated nexus of all existences. Nāgārjuna,[2] the great philosopher who later reflected on this early teaching, taught that being empty of own-being, or "emptiness," means that all things arise and exist interdependently; they have no substance that makes them independent: "We declare that whatever is dependent arising is emptiness." Here, Nāgārjuna emphasizes one of the Buddha's key teachings: "dependent co-origination" (*pratītya-samutpāda*). All things arise and exist co-dependently. This dynamic of emptiness, of co-arising, is the true nature of existence.

After Nāgārjuna, several Mahāyāna texts were written that looked at this co-arising from a more positive point of view. For example, in India between 250 and 350 CE, a number of *sūtras* were written about the *Tathāgata-garbha*, the womb or embryo of the Buddha. This literature, which became quite influential in East Asia, taught that all beings contain an inner realty like a "womb" of the "embryo" of Buddhahood. This inner essence of Buddhahood, referred to in East Asia as "Buddha-nature," is said to be pure and

---

1. These texts began to be written by the first century BCE.
2. He lived between 150 and 250 CE.

luminous. Therefore, they stressed that while all beings are empty of "own being," the True Body of the Buddha that contains all things in the cosmos (the *Dharmakāya*) is also contained *in* all things. As one *sūtra* says:

> Like a Buddha in a faded lotus flower, like honey covered by bees, like a fruit in its husk, like gold within its impurities, like a treasure hidden in the dirt . . . like a valuable statue covered with dust, so is the Buddha Embryo/Womb within all beings.[3]

> The Body of perfect Buddhahood *irradiates* everything . . . so at all times do all living beings have the Embryo/Womb of the Buddha within them.[4]

In many of these texts, that which "irradiates" everything and is within all beings is described as pure and luminous, shining brightly like a "jewel." This Buddha-nature is dazzling with light from within. And, like many faceted jewels, all beings shine, reflecting all other beings. So, returning to Nāgārjuna, Mahāyāna Buddhism concludes that the world of suffering, called *saṃsāra,* is at the same time Nirvana: "Nothing distinguishes *saṃsāra* from Nirvana; and nothing distinguishes Nirvana from *saṃsāra*. Between even the extremities of *saṃsāra* and Nirvana, one cannot find even a subtle difference."[5] While the world is full of suffering and darkness, it is also "irradiated" by the dazzling luminosity of Nirvana.

In East Asia, Tianti Buddhism[6] uses the metaphor of water and waves to help explain this relation of suffering existence to Nirvana. In their view, the water does not obstruct the waves and the waves do not obstruct the water. While the waves are constantly in motion (*saṃsāra*), the water below (Nirvana) is always unmoved. The water represents the unmoved inner essence of Buddha-nature, while the waves represent the movement of suffering caused by the winds of the world.

Huayan Buddhism[7] takes this a step further. They teach that not only is Buddha-nature with its Nirvanic essence within all beings, but also all beings exist such that they "mutually penetrate" each other and "mutually indwell" in each other. A metaphor for this identity of *saṃsāra*/suffering and

---

3. Ratnagotra-vibhaga I: 154.
4. Ratnagotra-vibhaga I, I: 40, (italics mine).
5. Mulamadhyamaka-karika, XXV: 19–20.
6. Founded around 550 CE by Huiwen.
7. Founded by Dushun (557–640 CE).

Nirvana is a round tower of mirrors wherein the mirrors line the inside of the tower, and at the center of the tower on the ground is a Buddha statue.[8] The Buddha statue luminously shines an image of itself in all the mirrors. The mirrors represent beings, and the Buddha image in them represents their Buddha-nature. Also, all the mirrors are located on the walls of the tower in such a way that they reflect into each other both themselves and the image of the Buddha contained in them. This metaphor explains how the whole universe can be in each of its parts, and at the same time each of its parts contains the same Buddha-nature. For example, the whole universe is in each being (like a banana leaf), and all things, even in the darkness of suffering, shine with the inner light of their Buddha-nature.

The Mystical Experiences of Chiara Lubich

Chiara Lubich experienced a period of mystical insight in 1949, so this period is referred to as "Paradise '49."[9] There are many profound dimensions to her experiences, but here I will limit my remarks just to her experiences that relate to the teachings of Buddhism mentioned above. But before I do, I should point out that in Trinitarian theology, eternally within Godself is the Word (*Logos*) in which God forms what are called the "divine ideas" of all that will be created in the cosmos. The following is how this is stated in the Prologue to John's Gospel in the New Testament:

> In the beginning was the Word, and the Word was with God, and the Word was God. All things came to be through him and without him nothing came to be. What came to be through him was life, and this life was the light of the human race: the light shines in the darkness, and the darkness has not overcome it. (Jn 1:1–5)

In her mystical experience, Chiara found herself in God the "Father." In what she calls "the Bosom of the Father," she says it is like being inside an "infinite Sun of light and love." It was there that she experienced the Word of God, the Son of God:

> Perhaps on the third day, as we remained in the Bosom of the Father, we had the manifestation of the Son. I remember that it had

---

8. The Third Patriarch of Huayan, Fazang (643–712) built such a tower of mirrors to teach Empress Wu about this concept.
9. For Chiara Lubich's introduction to this period, along with a contextual essay, see the first issue of *Claritas: Journal of Dialogue and Culture* (March 2012).

an extraordinary light. . . . I only know that from the walls inside the Sun, the Father pronounced the Word: Love, and this Word, concentrated in the heart of the Father, was his Son.

Outside in the evening, a majestic sunset displayed by nature, rendered more beautiful by the enormous Sun shining in us, seemed to confirm this "vision." And so far as I now recall, if I recall it correctly, the long rays of the sun, that like arrows of light caressed the blue sky after the sun's disk had gone down, gave us an idea of the Word, as the light of the Father, the splendor of the Father.[10]

Notice that in both John's Gospel and this text by Chiara, the reality of God found in the Word is described as "Light that shines in the darkness and the darkness has not overcome it" or as "an extraordinary light . . . concentrated in the heart of the Father . . . the enormous Sun shining in us . . . the long rays of the sun . . . like arrows of light."

In Trinitarian theology, the Father conceives in the Word—in his Love— his divine and loving ideas of all the beings that will be created from the beginning to the end of creation. Chiara notes that when God then creates beings out of the Word, they are all "linked together in his love."[11] She also writes[12] that the beings in this interrelated creative process of generating the universe are in each moment flowing out of the Word with each other in light and love. This is also true of beings as they exist in the cosmos; namely, they all exist in relations of interrelatedness. And when beings die, they return, interrelated with other beings that die at that time.

Chiara gives examples of how she saw this luminous interdependence in nature during Paradise '49:

I remember that during those days, nature seemed to me to be enveloped totally by the sun; it already was physically, but it seemed to me that an even stronger Sun enveloped it, saturated it, so that the whole of nature appeared to me as being "in love." I saw things, rivers, plants, meadows, grass as linked to one another by a bond of love in which each one had a meaning of love with

---

10. Chiara Lubich, "Paradise '49," *Claritas: Journal of Dialogue and Culture* (2012): 9.
11. Much of the text of Paradise '49 is unpublished. Where I have quotations and no footnotes, the quoted text is unpublished.
12. Unpublished text.

regard to the others. It was something similar, but universalized, to what I had experienced while walking down from the Franciscan Institute when I was twenty years old. . . . I seemed to see the blossom of a horse chestnut tree alive with a higher life that sustained it from beneath so that it seemed to be coming out towards me.

When we arrived in the mountains . . . I felt that I could discern, because of a special grace from God, the presence of God beneath things. Because God is present, sustaining all things. Therefore, if the pine trees—which I saw—were golden by the sun, if the brooks flowed into the glimmering falls, if the daisies, other flowers and the sky were all decked in summer array, stronger than all this was the vision of a Sun beneath all creation.

In a certain sense, I saw, I believe, God who supports, who upholds things. . . . And the fact that God was beneath things meant that they were not as we see them; they were all linked to one another by love; all, so to speak, in love with one another. So, if the brook flowed into the lake, it was out of love. If the pine tree stood high next to another pine tree, it was out of love.[13]

On earth all is in a relationship of love with all: each thing with each thing. It is necessary to be Love to find the thread of gold that links beings.[14]

In a talk two years later, Chiara says that she and her companions felt a "light" at the time she was experiencing God "beneath" creation and in all things:

We saw that beneath the things of the world, like the meadows, the stars, the sky, the flowers, the waterfalls, there was Someone who linked them all together, a *light that linked everything: it was the presence of God in things*.[15]

---

13. Chiara Lubich, unpublished talk at Castel Gandolfo, December 20, 1999.
14. Quoted by Callan Slipper, "Towards an Understanding of the Human Person According to the Mystical Experience of Chiara Lubich in the Paradise of '49," *Claritas: Journal of Dialogue and Culture* (2012): 30 (translation revised).
15. Chiara Lubich, unpublished talk at Castel Gandolfo, February 23, 2001 (italics mine).

Note that for Chiara, the "Sun"—God who brings all things into being—is the "higher life that sustained" them "from beneath." The interdependent origination flowing forth in the process of creation, sustaining it in life with light and love, and bringing all things back to their Source is not "descending" from the heavens but is "arising" from a "higher life" beneath creation.

In one passage in the Paradise '49 text, Chiara writes, "The super natural is the Nature of nature." And in a footnote to this sentence she writes, "In other words, that which is 'beneath' nature. . . . There have been some sages, some people of wisdom, who . . . recognized that there was a living presence beneath it." Here, Chiara confirms that the wisdom of other religions provides true insight into this Ultimate Reality.

Now that we can see how Chiara understands the interrelated linkage of all beings on the foundation of the luminous presence of God below and in all things, it is important to look at how she sees each being as containing all other beings. Here, it is important to note that for Chiara, all beings are like "words" of the Word. Therefore, all beings (words) have within them the Word, and the Word within them contains all the words—all the beings in existence, past, present, and future. Hence, the banana leaf contains all the universe because it is a word that contains the Word that contains all things. This applies to all beings, both animate and inanimate. When I pick up a rock, I am holding the entire universe in my hand.

In Chiara's unpublished writings, she uses a Huayan-like metaphor of a mirror to explain this mutual indwelling:

> It happens as in those mirrors that, facing one another, project images of each other infinitely and are re-contained in each other through the returning reflection. . . . Each one of us will be a Word, but, since each Word is the whole Word, each one of us will be the Word, will be a harmony = a unity. The new song is the harmony of harmonies![16]

Anna Pelli reflects on this statement in the following way: "The individual is the whole, the whole is the individuals. In other words, each one (the particular, the finite) . . . bears in itself the reality of the all, of the one."[17]

---

16. Anna Pelli, "Going from the Pact to the Soul: Exploring a Metaphysical Journey," *Claritas: Journal of Dialogue and Culture* (2013): 17, 20 (translation revised).
17. Pelli, "Going from the Pact to the Soul," 19.

The question now is: How are Chiara's experiences related to suffering and to the dazzling darkness we have discussed in the section on Buddhism? First, it is important to note how Chiara always mentions "light" in reference to the Love that is God below and in all creation: for example, "Sun beneath all creation" and "a light that linked everything: it was the presence of God in things." Certainly, this is a nirvanic reality that is the foundation of the interrelatedness between all beings and in all beings in this world of suffering; it is Love, God-Love.

But for Chiara, there is something else involved in this identity between suffering and Love/light. Returning to John's Gospel, after John writes "this life was the light . . . the light shines in the darkness and the darkness has not overcome it," he goes on to say:

> The true light, which enlightens everyone, was coming into the world. He was in the world and the world came to be through him. . . . And the Word became flesh and made his dwelling among us, and we saw his glory, the glory as the Father's only Son, full of grace and truth. (Jn 1: 9–10, 14)

Chiara affirms this understanding of John about the Word, the "true light" coming into the world as Jesus Christ. In terms of Jesus' relation to the suffering of all beings past, present, and future, she turns to his passion, his death on the cross. At the height of his suffering, Jesus cries out to the Father, "My God, my God, why have you forsaken me?" (Mt 27:46) This cry is seen by Chiara as the moment when Jesus took upon himself the sufferings of the world from its beginning to its end. This means that he, as the incarnate Word of God full of Love and light, "emptied himself . . . becoming obedient to death, even death on a cross"[18] where he bore the sins and suffering of all humanity.

Chiara refers to this presence of Jesus suffering with all humanity as "Jesus Forsaken." Whenever she and her companions suffered, they would turn into their hearts and embrace him who takes on our suffering out of an infinite Compassion, where the word "com-passion" means "to suffer with." The result of this embrace, Chiara says, is that: "This presence [Jesus Forsaken] . . . very soon becomes felt, so that throwing ourselves into a *sea*

---

18. Philippians 2:7, 8.

of suffering we discover ourselves in a *sea of love, of complete joy*. . . . And the soul feels itself refilled with the Holy Spirit, who is joy, peace, serenity."[19]

Here, I see a similarity with a passage from the Buddhist writer Śāntideva: "May as many beings as there are who are suffering pain in body or mind find, through my merits, *oceans of happiness and joy* . . . As long as there is space, and as long as there is the world, for that long may my life *be* tending to the sufferings of the world.[20]

In another letter, Chiara refers to her experience as a movement "beyond the wound":

> Having embraced Jesus forsaken totally, so that we found ourselves beyond pain, in love we felt like we were contemplating the immense love which God has poured out over the world . . . we were merged with love and shared in its light: the *light of Love*.[21]

Note that the final words say that they "were merged with love and shared in its light: the light of Love." In Jesus Forsaken, the darkness of suffering existence is identified with the light of God/Love. In Chiara's text on Paradise '49, she writes: "Suffering is love." She underlines "is" for emphasis. It is an ontological statement that Jesus Forsaken takes on the reality of all suffering, so that each suffering "is" Love and light. Here is a uniquely Christian statement that is similar to yet different from the Buddhist statement that "*sam. sāra* is Nirvana."

For Chiara, this is not just an inner Christian spiritual experience, but a transformation of one's life by participation in this inner reality of Jesus Forsaken. As Paul says about Jesus Crucified: "I have been crucified with Christ; yet I live no longer, but Christ lives in me" (Gal 2:19–20). For Chiara, Jesus Forsaken is the Compassion or Mercy of God, and so those who embrace him participate in Jesus Compassion/Mercy/Love for all humanity that lives within them. This reminds me of a time I was walking with Katagiri Roshi at my university. He had just done an act of compassion for a troubled student. I said to him, "That was truly an act of compassion for said that He student." As I walked, I noticed that he had stopped. I turned

---

19. Chiara Lubich, *Unity and Jesus Forsaken* (New York: New City Press, 1985), 67–68 (italics mine).
20. Bodhicaryāvartāra, X: 2, 55 (italics mine). Śāntideva lived in India in the eighth century CE.
21. Chiara Lubich, *Unity and Jesus Forsaken*, 70–71 (italics mine).

and walked back to him. to me very seriously, "I do not *do* compassion. I *am* Compassion!"

Conclusion

Pope Benedict asked the church to develop what he calls a "dialogue of truth." Indeed, *Nostra Aetate* 2 teaches that there are elements of the truth in all cultures and faiths that Catholics have a responsibility to "recognize, preserve, and promote." In the subtitle of then Cardinal Ratzinger's 1998 document entitled "Interreligious Dialogue and Jewish-Christian Relations," he wrote: "The religions can encounter one another only by delving more deeply into the truth." This "deep dialogue" is more of a journey than an event. It is exploring together in dialogue *over time* as fellow pilgrims in an *ongoing* journey to a fuller understanding of the truth. May the life and light of Chiara Lubich's Christian spirituality and the life and light of Buddhist spirituality be sources of an ongoing dialogue of truth.

Chapter Twenty-Nine

Christian and Hindu Dialogue

Cherylanne Menezes

Christian-Hindu dialogue is a complex, challenging, and important frontier. From its beginnings, Focolare founder Chiara Lubich was quick to attribute the Movement's involvement in interreligious dialogue to a plan from God, one for which she considered herself to be a simple instrument.[1] She often wrote of her wonder in seeing how the charism of unity at the heart of the Movement's spirituality was able to bring together and provide points of encounter for members of the great religions, and to do so in ways that fostered understanding, friendship, and respect for one another.[2] Focolare's mode of dialogue, rooted in a charism of unity at the heart of the Movement's life, has generated interest and appreciation not only from Hindus but also within the Catholic Church, of which Chiara Lubich and the Movement are an expression. [3]

---

1. "I feel a wave of emotion, if I think only for a moment at what I have in front of me: a new world born from the Gospel, spread throughout the world, an immense work that no human effort could have brought about. In fact, it is a 'work of God,' for which I was the first one chosen to be his 'useless and unfaithful' instrument," *Vita Trentina* newspaper on the occasion of the 60th anniversary of the Focolare Movement's birth in Trent, Italy. Published November 24, 2003.

2. "The Focolare Movement, which I represent, has sixty years of experience, and yet we are always amazed to see that God has led us along a spiritual pathway that intersects with all the other spiritual ways of Christians as well as faithful of other religions. . . . While maintaining our own identity, it enables us to meet and come to a mutual understanding with all the great religious traditions of humanity." Excerpted from Chiara Lubich's talk, "Can Religions Be Partners in Peace Building? How to face a World of Terrorism and Violence," at an interreligious seminar sponsored by Initiatives of Change in association with the World Conference on Religion and Peace (WCRP) at Caux (Switzerland) on July 29, 2003, and published in *New Humanity Review* 11 (2005): 5–18.

3. Writing to Chiara after her return from her first trip to India, Cardinal Francis Arinze, then the president of the Pontifical Council for Interreligious Dialogue, wrote: "The meetings so rich in harmony and friendship that you have had with Hindu representatives will not fail to bring about good results in the future for a dialogue ever more characterized by understanding and respect." Cardinal Joseph Ratzinger, then prefect of the Congregation for the Doctrine of Faith, also

Interreligious Dialogue, Chiara Lubich, and the Focolare Movement

Before delving into the Movement's journey of dialogue with persons of the Hindu tradition, we will look briefly at the broader milestones of interreligious dialogue in Chiara Lubich's life and that of the Movement as a whole, which preceded later encounters with the Hindu world.

Chiara's initial intuition that the Movement would have something to do with persons of other religious traditions came in 1966, during a trip to the remote African village of Fontem in the heart of the Cameroon jungle. On that occasion, she met with persons from the Bangwa tribe who practiced traditional religious beliefs of the region and with whom there was already a powerful rapport.[4] Reflecting later on that moment, she spoke of a personal and powerful perception of God as a huge sun that enveloped all of humankind in love. It was an insight that would remain with her during the years that followed and was an intuition whose significance she did not yet fully understand, nor what was to later come about.[5]

The visible "founding event" that marked the beginning of the Movement's engagement in interreligious dialogue came more than a decade later, at the 1977 conferral of the Templeton Prize for Progress in Religion to Chiara Lubich. She later wrote:

> After my speech at the Guildhall in London, in front of qualified representatives of the great world religions, I had, for a second time, that same profound feeling that all of us present, although of different faiths, were enveloped by a huge sun, by the love of

---

expressed: "I am delighted with the positive results and for the promising dialogue established with significant Hindu representatives. These are signs of hope brought forward with untiring zeal." See Michele Zanzucchi, *Mille Lune: In India con Chiara Lubich* (Rome: Città Nuova, 2001), 6, n4.

4. References on the history of the rapport with Fontem can be found in "You did it to me," Fontem's Story as narrated by Chiara Lubich, available at http://www.focolare.org/en/news/2013/02/10/lhai-fatto-a-me-storia-di-fontem-narrata-da-chiara-lubich/; see also: http://www.focolare.org/en/focolare-worldwide/africa/camerun/.

5. Roberto Catalano, *Spiritualità di comunione e dialogo interreligioso* (Rome: Città Nuiova, 2010), 49.

God. When I came out of that hall, the first people who came to greet me were Buddhists, Sikhs, Hindus, Muslims, Jews.⁶

In another context, she repeated the experience to others, recounting, "The differences disappeared, and it seemed, for a moment, as if that hall was a realization of Jesus' dream: 'That all may be one!' Perhaps, because there was a profound faith in God. . . . It was as if we were all enveloped by His presence."⁷

After that moment, there was no turning back. New relationships and collaboration with representatives of different religions began to develo In 1979, just two years after the Templeton Prize, Lubich met with Rev. Nikkyō Niwano, founder of Risshō Kōsei-kai, a worldwide Japanese Mahayana Buddhist movement.⁸ Close ties were established and the friendship between these two organizations continues today.

Between 1981 and 1985, Chiara Lubich established the Movement's office for Interreligious Dialogue under the direction of two of her early companions, Natalia Dallapiccola and Enzo M. Fondi. The first school for the study of Asian religions also formed during this period in the Philippines as an experience of life, dialogue, and study between persons from Risshō Kōsei-kai and the Focolare Movement.⁹

Contacts with other schools of Buddhism also occurred during this period, including warm, constructive, and ongoing relationships with a number of followers of Theravada Buddhism through Phra Thongratana Thavorn, a Buddhist monk and his Great Master, the Venerable Ajaan Tong. The latter invited Chiara to Thailand in 1997 to meet with 800 students at the Buddhist Mahajularacha University and 170 Buddhist monks and nuns at Wat Rampoeng monastery. The Great Master introduced Chiara as a Christian, a woman, and a layperson, saying: "The wise person is neither man nor wom-

---

6. See "The Interreligious Dialogue of the Focolare Movement (Part I)," an excerpt from a talk by Chiara at Aachen (Germany), November 13, 1998, available at www.centrochiaralubich.org.
7. Catalano, *Spiritualità di comunione e dialogo interreligioso*, 50.
8. Rev. Niwano was among the most distinguished promoters of interreligious dialogue and cooperation of the twentieth century and one of the founders of the World Conference on Religion and Peace. He was invited by Paul VI to attend the opening session of the Second Vatican Council. To read about his movement, visit http://www.rk-world.org/
9. Paolo Frizzi, *Cristianesimo e religioni nel '900: l'intuizione e la Vicenda di Chiara Lubich, Storia Teologia, Società* (Rome: Città Nuova, 2014), 204–5.

an. When someone lights a light in the darkness, one does not ask whether the one who lit it was a man or a woman. Chiara is here to give us the light she has experienced."[10]

In 1996, Lubich was awarded the UNESCO Prize for Peace Education. Then, in 1997, during a trip to the United States for the conferral of an honorary doctorate from Sacred Heart University in Fairfield, Connecticut, she accepted the invitation extended by Imam Warith Deen Mohammed to speak at the Malcolm Shabazz Mosque in Harlem, New York, to nearly two thousand African American Muslims. Although she had been in contact with the Islamic world in Algeria since the 1970s, this marked the first time Chiara was invited to speak in a mosque. It was also historic in that it was the first time a white woman, of European Catholic descent, had spoken in that renowned place of worship about her Christian experience. Three years later, in November 2000 in Washington, at a follow-up gathering of Muslims and Christians with both leaders present, Imam Mohammed responded to Chiara's words, saying: "I read in the Bible that when Jesus Christ, peace be upon him, invited his followers to wash each other's feet, I think that's just what we are doing. We are washing each other's feet."[11]

Chiara also made deeper contact with the Jewish world during this time, especially with the Argentinian Jewish community of B'nai B'rith, which Chiara visited personally in 1998.

Christian-Hindu Dialogue

The Focolare Movement's dialogue with Hindus had its early roots in a cordial relationship built over several years between Indian statesman and Shanti Ashram founder Dr. M. Aram and one of Chiara's early collaborators, Natalia Dallapiccola. Aram and Lubich were both honorary presidents of the World Conference on Religion and Peace (WCRP), and Dallapiccola had frequently represented Lubich at interreligious gatherings in the years before Lubich's first visit to India. Then, through these contacts, the Movement's community in India (which had been present in the country since the 1980s) also established personal contact with Dr. Aram. He deeply de-

---

10. Piero Coda, *Viaggio in Asia con Chiara Lubich in Thailandia e Filippine* (Roma: Città Nuova, 1997), 54.
11. Amelia J. Uelmen, "Chiara Lubich: A Life for Unity," *Logos, A Journal of Catholic Thought and Culture* 8 (2005): 58, http://mirrorofjustice.blogs.com/mirrorofjustice/uelmen/alifeforunity.pdf.

sired to spread Lubich's vision and understanding of God to many in India. In the years before his death in 1997, Aram would organize informal gatherings at his New Delhi home, bringing together his friends, associates, and local Focolare members.

Dr. Aram and Chiara Lubich would have their first and only personal encounter at the Sixth World Assembly of the WCRP, held at the Vatican in 1994. He greatly appreciated Focolare's collaboration with WCRP and hoped one day to welcome Chiara to India and honor her work for peace and unity among religions. On his return to India that year, he expressed this desire to his wife and collaborator, Minoti Aram, his daughter Vinu Aram, and other close Gandhian associates.[12]

In October 2000, to the surprise of many, and with just a few months' notice, Chiara announced her intention to visit India in early January 2001. Although in India the Movement had spread within the Christian world and in various parts of the country, contacts with Hindus were still relatively limited.

When the Aram family heard of Chiara's desire to visit India, Mrs. Minoti Aram immediately saw it as an occasion to fulfill her husband's dream of honoring Chiara in a Gandhian way and to introduce the charism of unity to a wide swath of Gandhian friends and collaborators. This resulted in an invitation to Chiara to visit Coimbatore to receive the prestigious Defender of Peace Award. Chiara willingly accepted this invitation.

The Focolare community in India thus began to prepare for this seemingly unprecedented event in the journey of dialogue with Hindu brothers and sisters. With the support and guidance of the Catholic Church, the Focolare had spread, touching a number of persons in various regions; as is typical of the charism of unity, these included laypeople, religious, priests, and even some bishops. The community's strongest presence was in Mumbai, Goa, and Bangalore. Thus, news of Chiara's upcoming visit spread in a number of Christian communities and resulted in an invitation to address the Conference of Catholic Bishops of India (CCBI) as well.

One particularly providential contact came through the Pontifical Council for Interreligious Dialogue undersecretary, Rev. Felix Machado (now archbishop of India's Vasai diocese), who was instrumental in a later encounter between Chiara Lubich and Dr. Kala Acharya, director of the

---

12. Catalano, *Spiritualità di comunione e dialogo interreligioso*, 62-63.

K. J. Somaiya Bharatiya Sanskriti Peetham, an institute of Indian culture and research at the Somaiya University Campus in Mumbai. Acharya had been the institute's director since 1989 and represented Hinduism in a number of international, interreligious meetings organized by the Pontifical Council for Interreligious Dialogue and was later an ambassador to the Parliament of the World's Religions. Dr. Acharya was happy to know about Chiara Lubich and would travel to Coimbatore for the award function that took place there.

Another deeply spiritual Hindu personality who was open to dialogue was Prof. S. A. Upadhyaya, director of the (Sanskrit studies and research) Bharatiya Vidya Bhavan. After hearing about Chiara Lubich through some Focolare members who were studying with him to learn Indian culture and Sanskrit, he too wanted to meet her.

Dr. M. Aram had also introduced members of the Focolare Movement to Mr. Rajmohan Gandhi, grandson of Mahatma Gandhi. Mr. Gandhi had met Chiara before her visit to India, and that encounter had profoundly touched Lubich. She had asked Rajmohan Gandhi for his thoughts as she prepared for her visit to India. Rajmohan had advised her to "listen," saying that when a person is in India they must listen. Lubich was very struck by this and felt urged to follow this counsel. In fact, her profound attitude of listening touched many hearts during those days of encounters, as many were also well aware that Chiara herself would have had much to share.

The Defender of Peace Award was presented by two Gandhian-inspired movements, Shanti Ashram and the Sarvodhaya Movement (in collaboration with Gandhigram Rural University and Bharatiya Vidhya Bhavan) in the state of Tamil Nadu.[13] Chiara accepted the invitation to be present for the award ceremony and on December 29, 2000, embarked on her first trip to India. It turned out to be an extraordinarily important moment in the Movement's work for Christian-Hindu dialogue and would bring the foundress back to India in 2003. Chiara herself would follow this dialogue and the relationships she built with various of her "Hindu brothers and sisters" in the years that followed, up until her death in 2008.

Even before her departure at the end of December 2000, Chiara wrote of this first India trip to Focolare Movement members throughout the world, recounting her various preparations, to ensure that all participated and be-

---

13. Catalano, *Spiritualità di comunione e dialogo interreligioso*, 62–63.

came protagonists with her in this important journey. Excerpts from her diary offer a glimpse of her attitude and approach to the various encounters she would have in this completely new culture. Her journal entries provide insight into both the charism of unity and the way Lubich lived interreligious dialogue on a personal level. In particular, one notes in her writings: 1) an attitude of humility and profound respect for a different tradition, 2) a recognition of the richness contained within Hindu teachings and philosophy, 3) an openness to learning from the other by building authentic relationships, and 4) a readiness to offer her authentic Christian experience as a reciprocal gift.

Rome, December 29, 2000:

> I have left Rome for Mumbai. . . . In my soul, a single idea: to love. . . . To love, to love every neighbor. . . . Because: "In the world is buried a God who wants to rise up through love." To this end, I will meditate daily on love. If I do this, I'll return home from India having "grown" (from this experience). This is what I want to do, what I must do: to keep improving, because those who do not go ahead, go backwards.[14]

Mumbai, December 30, 2000:

> We landed last night at Mumbai airport. . . . [In] Rome, whenever I looked at a map of India, it always seemed very, very far away from me. But, today it's as if we walked through a door from one room into another. . . . I've come here to learn about this land by remaining in silence as much as possible: I've been told it is a necessary attitude for those coming to India. In fact, I spent almost the entire day studying the materials that were prepared for us.[15]

Mumbai, January 2, 2001:

> We've only been here a few days. But the more we enter into contact with India, the more it reveals itself to us as an immense world with a multitude of realities and its own unique hallmark, one which is not easy for Westerners to decipher. It's a world that presents a picture of unity in all its richness, in all its diversity. It's as if a jewelry box were laid open before us, filled with spiritual treasures.

---

14. Zanzucchi, *Mille Lune*, 12.
15. Zanzucchi, *Mille Lune*, 13.

One is attracted by its mysticism that encompasses the whole of human nature, a mysticism which is most certainly not extraneous to God's work. But this box can only be opened by those who approach it with respect, love, and above all with a conviction that God has much to tell us through this ancient culture. In our difficult and tormented world of today, this culture has an essential and vital message to offer, one which highlights the primacy of the interior life. It has caused me to reflect: What would happen if India were to encounter that Jesus offered by the Charism of Unity?[16]

On January 4, Chiara traveled to Coimbatore, a large, vibrant city in the southern Indian state of Tamil Nadu. She had an immediate rapport with the family of Dr. Aram and his Gandhian friends. His wife, Minoti Aram, commented: "For a long time, I prayed for this day to come true. In spirit we are one family: you on a big scale, we on a small one, to carry out the same mission. The only thought that animates us is to overcome violence and to sow the seeds of peace. . . . Chiara will find peace and serenity here. She will bring us unity."[17]

The Defender of Peace Award, which honors people actively involved in promoting nonviolence and peace, was jointly conferred by the Shanti Ashram and Sarvodhaya Movements.[18] The ceremony, on January 5 in the presence of important dignitaries and media figures, began with an introduction by Shri Krishnaraj Vanavarayar, local president of the Bharatiya Vidhya Bhavan educational trust. He spoke of Chiara as "a person who paves the way to overcome division and hate" and who has the strength needed to realize this dream, a strength that comes from her experience of God.

In presenting the award to her, the president of Sarvodaya Association, Dr. Markandan, asked Chiara to give particular priority to her work in in-

---

16. Zanzucchi, *Mille Lune*, 24–25.
17. Zanzucchi, *Mille Lune*, 32–33.
18. Shanti Ashram (literally, a community of peace) was founded in 1986 by Dr. Aram. His mottos "Think globally and act locally" and "Spiritually motivated and socially active" are the ideas behind Shanti Ashram. It is a social center formed according to Gandhian principles and is dedicated to the aid and development of women and children in the villages. Today, it works on an International level with UNDP, UNESCO, WCRP, GNRC, Focolare, and so on. Sarvodaya (well-being for all) is the name of the institution founded by Mahatma Gandhi. It is present all over India and works for the development of the lower strata of society at different local levels and also on an international level.

itiating dialogue with Hinduism in Coimbatore, much as she'd done with Buddhist leader, Nikkyo Niwano, in Japan. He asked her to affirm and sustain those spiritual values that are still present in India but are now also threatened by rampant consumerism and technology.

He read the award citation aloud, which began with the words: "Chiara Lubich, using the most powerful human force of love and a strong faith in the unity of all humankind as espoused in the teachings of Jesus Christ, has been chosen to play a tireless role in sowing the seeds of peace and love among all peoples."[19] It was a particularly significant occasion that served to deepen the rapport between the Focolare Movement and the Gandhian family. In the years that followed, this rapport would become a powerful witness of vibrant dialogue and collaboration in the journey toward peace and universal brotherhood.

On January 6, Chiara wrote in her diary:

> To love, to love all those I will meet today so that the love of God may burn in my heart. This is my resolution. I was very struck by a phrase from a philosopher, a non-believer, who defines love as "the capacity to discover similarities in the dissimilar" (Adorno). Could our dialogue, then, be one of the most beautiful expressions of love?[20]

While in Coimbatore, Chiara also had an important encounter with traditional orthodox Hinduism, meeting with two swamis (priests) in the region, His Highness Santhalinga Ramaswami Adigalar and Maruthachala Adigalar of the Perur Pateeswarar Hindu Temple, and with members of Yoga International. Particularly noteworthy was the fact that these two important swamis had accepted the invitation, signifying each one's readiness to travel outside the confines of their own, respective temples to encounter Lubich. It was their first such meeting with the Catholic Church.[21]

Another significant milestone for Christian-Hindu dialogue also occurred during those days in Coimbatore. In a meeting between Chiara Lubich and Dr. Kala Acharya, who had attended the award ceremony, there was an immediate sense of understanding.

---

19. Zanzucchi, *Mille Lune*, 42.
20. Zanzucchi, *Mille Lune*, 47.
21. Zanzucchi, *Mille Lune*, 62–65.

Years later, Dr. Acharya described her personal experience of that first encounter:

> When I was introduced to her, (Chiara) said, "I see God's design in you." These words ignited a blazing flame in me—a radiant flame constantly illuminating my actions, in its light I reflect: whatever I do is a divine plan. So, my actions must be good, worthy and free from any selfish motive; they should be for the good of many.[22]

Dr. Kala returned to Mumbai after that first meeting. With Dr. S. K. Somaiya, head of K. J. Somaiya College, and himself at the forefront of interreligious dialogue, in five days they managed to quickly plan and organize a campus convention, to which they invited Chiara. When she accepted, they titled the convention "Spirituality for Universal Brotherhood by Chiara Lubich." Chiara was warmly welcomed by approximately six hundred participants.

During a first initial exchange of introductions, Chiara had humbly expressed her ignorance of many Hindu teachings and her need to grow in this mutual understanding of one another. Dr. Somaiya replied:

> No, Chiara, I understood it in your eyes. There are leaders who know how to communicate their thoughts. You have a great ideal. Just one person like you can move an entire society. You are one of those very few persons. On our campus not everyone is committed to true religion because we don't have a "Chiara" among us.[23]

Dr. Kala, in introducing Chiara Lubich and the charism of unity within the context of God's plan for humanity, said, "There is only one God, only one purpose in the world. . . . Then we will be one, and we shall live in peace, fraternity and in harmony, it is written in the Vedas. What Chiara says, shows us an anticipation of what this moment will be like."[24] Dr. Kala's

---

22. From the intervention of Dr. Kala Acharya, "Dialogue with Chiara Lubich," at the International Convention, Chiara and Religions, "Together Toward the Unity of the Human Family," Castel Gandolfo March 17–20, 2014, marking the sixth anniversary of Chiara Lubich's death. See also: *Chiara and the World Religions: Together Towards the Unity of the Human Family*, Conference Proceedings Castel Gandolfo, Rome, March 17–20, 2014, ATC, India 2017.
23. http://whydontwedialogue.blogspot.it/2011/01/sk-somaiya-and-chiara-lubich.html. Blog Spot of R. Catalano (acc. on 10/28/2019).
24. Zanzucchi, *Mille Lune*, 97. My ellipsis.

words shed light on the novelty of Chiara's thought and experience of unity in God offered in the "here and now" as it relates to the Hindu concept of oneness in the afterlife. It was a concept that was appreciated and welcomed by Hindus.

Chiara's message and the testimonies by Focolare Movement members were received with admiration and openness by professors, students, and attending dignitaries. In his concluding words, Dr. Somaiya called the encounter "a unique experience" and "very elevating spiritually"; "It greatly served the purpose for which this campus originated. . . . My hope is that this movement will grow always more, because it is needed in our Indian society."[25]

Two interesting comments[26] made by dignitaries present at the event express the particular interest that Hindus have in the ideas proposed by Lubich:

> Although we underline these values in our religion too, there is a difference. Chiara wants us to put these principles of love into practice. . . . Whatever she speaks about she has already lived. That's why people follow her . . . not only Christians but also members of other religions. One beautiful thing is that she does not oblige anyone to change their religion. . . . She only expects you to follow two principles: the love of neighbor and universal brotherhood.[27]

and

> We believe in the unity and in the diversity of religions and cultures, but the concept that underlies everything is unity and universal brotherhood. Chiara Lubich emphasized very clearly the ideas that we already have in this country. This will be greatly appreciated by the great masses of people in our country because our people believe in this philosophical concept.[28]

---

25. See http://whydontwedialogue.blogspot.it/2011/01/sk-somaiya-and-chiara-lubich.html.
26. Zanzucchi, *Mille Lune*, 100–01.
27. Zanzucchi, *Mille Lune*, 100–01.
28. Zanzucchi, *Mille Lune*, 100–01.

In their words, we see the value placed both on the concrete aspect of a life of love and unity proposed by the charism of unity and on its relational dimension of unity, which invites reciprocity.

Chiara also met with the Christian world while in India, addressing the Catholic Bishops' Conference of India and speaking to the Sisters of Charity at their motherhouse, both in Calcutta. In Mumbai, she met with Cardinals Ivan Dias and Simon Pimenta, as well as with members of the Focolare Movement in India. At the end of this rich and important visit, we can intuit the fruits of those days in Lubich's later journal entries:

> Mumbai, January 14, 2001:
>
> We left Rocca di Papa (Italy) for India with a single idea: "To love, love, love." Doesn't it seem to have been a suggestion from the Holy Spirit? This love towards everyone that we tried to live has increased our union with God. Our prayer life has improved, which is useful here in India, because beyond any doubts we might have, here we are in a nation imbued with an inner life. God is present, although at times obscured.[29]

The Ongoing Journey of Hindu Dialogue and Encounter

Of the various types of dialogue[30] lived by persons of the Focolare Movement with members of different religions, the primary type is a *dialogue of life*. As the name suggests, it is rooted in a daily effort of living out dialogue in one's life (living the Golden Rule, getting to know others and their respective activities and projects, promoting collaboration and cooperation on shared endeavors, sharing each one's unique religious experience, and so on). Among the fruits of this dialogue was a joint effort to promote deeper theological and academic exchange through "Hindu-Christian symposiums." The purpose of these Christian-Hindu symposiums, first proposed by Dr. Acharya and immediately supported by Lubich, is to provide an encounter between religious traditions and doctrines in the same spirit of brotherhood and love that marks the dialogue of life. The first symposium took place in June 2002 at the Focolare Movement's International Meeting Centre in Castel Gandolfo, Italy, and was titled "Bhakti: Way of Love To-

---

29. Zanzucchi, *Mille Lune*, 14.
30. See "I tipi di dialogo della Spiritualità di comunione," in Catalano, *Spiritualità di comunione e dialogo interreligioso*, 101–32.

wards God and our Neighbors; Devotion in the Hindu Tradition, and in the Christian Experience of the Spirituality of Communion."[31] Participants included more than a dozen Hindu scholars primarily from Mumbai University, Somaiya Sanskriti Peetham in Mumbai, Bharatiya Vidhya Bhavan, Shanti Ashram, and Ghandigram University in Tamil Nadu and a similar number from the Focolare Movement's interdisciplinary Abba School study center[32] along with several other Focolare members working in interreligious initiatives.

Notwithstanding their highly intellectual nature, these symposiums are unique for each participant's commitment to live concretely the pact of reciprocal love proposed by Lubich during the very first symposium in 2002. From that first symposium, one could sense the commitment to reciprocal love being lived out, both through the efforts made to deeply listen to one another during session presentations and through the respect with which observations, questions, and comments were exchanged. In fact, such a dense, supernatural atmosphere was created that, at the request of the scholars present, Lubich spoke of the mystical and intellectual experience she lived during the summer of 1949. Before that symposium, this experience had been shared only with the closest members of the Movement.

The symposium allotted much time for dialogue and communion, as well as for moments of clarification on aspects of faith. So profound was the dialogue, for example, that Prof. Sureshchandra Upadhyaya[33] asked Chiara to shed further light on the reality of Jesus Crucified and Forsaken. Upadhyaya spoke of his own difficulty in understanding how Jesus, as God, could have felt abandoned. Because this feeling of abandonment is a central point of the charism of unity, Chiara embraced the occasion to present the Christian mystery of the Incarnation and offer her personal

---

31. "I tipi di dialogo della Spiritualità di comunione," in Catalano, *Spiritualità di comunione e dialogo interreligioso*, 128–29.

32. The Abba School, which began in 1990, is a fruit of the awareness, in the words of Lubich herself, "that the charism of unity brings its own culture, which is at one and the same time a child of traditional Christianity and through the light brought by the charism, something new. The growth ... beyond the confines of the Focolare Movement, has highlighted the specifics of this culture, and made deeper study necessary: theological, philosophical, political, economic, psychological, artistic and so on. This is what we are doing within what we call the 'Abba School.'"

33. Sureshchandra Upadhyaya is the director of the Bharatiya Vidhya Bhavan, Mumbai, a prestigious institution of Indian Culture and study with about 119 branches in India and seven abroad.

discovery of Jesus Forsaken. For the Hindu scholars present, it proved to be a fundamentally important and welcome introduction into a mystical dimension of Christianity.[34] At the end of the 2002 symposium, Dr. Acharya concluded by saying:

> We did not aim at a pure academic exercise. Ours was a spiritual experience. . . . For any other seminar, people will speak about their topic; they discuss and debate and leave without a spiritual experience. Normally, a spiritual experience is not the focus. We instead, all together, really underwent a spiritual experience.[35]

Acharya's words confirm one characteristic of the charism of unity that is at the heart of the Focolare's spirituality: its capacity to generate a lived, shared spiritual experience between Christians and Hindus, even within the structure of a formal symposium composed of discourse and discussion.

Another Hindu-Christian symposium at the Focolare Movement's Center in Rome followed one year later, in 2003, and Chiara Lubich made a second trip to India that year. During this trip, several important meetings took place. Through the Catholic Church, programs were organized in Mumbai by Cardinal Ivan Dias and in Delhi by Archbishop Vincent Concessao, who also organized an interreligious meeting. This second trip also strengthened contacts with the Hindu world, including encounters with the widespread Swadhyay Family of Pandurang Athavale and Didi Athavale, whom Lubich had first met at the 2002 Assisi Day of Prayer for Peace. The trip also included meetings in Coimbatore and at the Somaiya Campus in Mumbai.

Among the most anticipated appointments during Lubich's second trip to India was a post-symposium meeting with twenty participants, including eleven Hindu participants from the first symposium in 2002. Having requested that Chiara continue to share with them the illuminations she received in 1949, she spoke again of her Christian experience and the mystical and intellectual intuitions from that period, particularly those related to unity and the Trinity, the Word of God, Mary, creation, and heaven and hell.[36] "We had an experience of Paradise, thanks to Chiara's vision," said

---

34. "Simposio indù-cristiano. Si spalancano gli orizzonti" in *Mariapoli, notiziario interno del movimento dei focolari*, XIX (2002/6), 11; Also see Chiara's answer to Dr. Upadhyaya in R. Catalano, *Spiritualità di comunione*, 208-210.
35. Catalano, *Spiritualità di comunione e dialogo interreligioso*, 129.
36. See "India, nuove luci per la fratellanza universale," in *Mariapoli* XX (2003/1-2): 5.

Dr. Lalita Namjoshi, assistant director at K. J. Somaiya Bharatiya Sanskriti Peetham. "What has deeply touched our hearts was the fact that we share the same Divine experience, the same divine inheritance and in spirituality, we stand together."[37] Similarly, Dr. Upadhyaya commented, "It is something unusual and rare that Chiara has communicated her personal mystical experience in such beautiful words; things like these are normally not discussed, they are experienced."[38] Likewise, Dr. Raja Lingam of the Gandhigram Rural University in Madurai noted: "You have to empty yourself in order to comprehend the spiritual and mystical experiences."

Through these comments, one sees the importance that Hindus place on a lived, spiritual experience in dialogue as well as their profound awareness of the need for a disposition of self-emptiness.

Two other symposiums have since taken place, one in 2008 and another in 2011. Both of these encounters enjoyed the participation of additional Hindu scholars who, in connecting with the charism of unity and the Movement's way of dialogue, expressed a desire to be a part of this ongoing experience and exchange between Hindus and Christians. Through the following comments of a few of those scholars, one sees the continuity of the experience of dialogue that was lived out in earlier symposiums. Dr. Uma Vaidhya, from the University of Mumbai and a participant in the 2008 gathering, reflected, "We were all like small candles which could potentially be lit. While dialogue was in progress, I felt that the attitude of love of those who were posing questions and those who gave answers, lit those candles."[39]

There was a continuous emphasis placed on the novelty of a lived experience of unity between Hindus and Christians based on a commitment to reciprocal love, which in turn illuminates faith and urges each to put into practice this experience of dialogue in their own lives. Dr. Shashi Prabha Kumar from Jawaharlal Nehru University in New Delhi reflected at the conclusion of the 2008 seminar:

> In the Vedas there are expressions about being together, walking together, chanting together. I found these feelings expressed in a much better way in the experience of this symposium. It was a

---

37. Transcribed from the audio-visual documentary "In the Light of the Charism, Chiara's Visit to India 2003," by Margaret Coen, for internal use of the Focolare Movement.
38. "In the Light of the Charism."
39. "In the Light of the Charism," 5.

help to live the abstract aspect of culture together with the concrete dimension.⁴⁰

Bharatiya Vidhya Bhavan, a professor of Indology from Mumbai, spoke in a similar fashion:

> Chiara and the Focolare Movement have taught me to live simultaneously the abstract and the concrete aspects of culture. This is very important for us, because we study, we learn, we teach, but we do not practice what we teach: the holistic approach is important. Certainly, I will carry this experience, everything that I learnt, to my students, my colleagues, the institution, wherever I go and in whatever I do. If whatever we do is done with love and brotherhood, I'm sure we can truly create Heaven on this earth. It is our responsibility to take ahead this civilization of love, and we will have a life of peace.⁴¹

This dialogue of life between Hindus and members of the Focolare Movement has continued on fronts other than the symposiums. In 2014, at the interreligious convention marking the sixth anniversary of Chiara Lubich's death, Mumbai university educator Dr. Madhavi Narsalay spoke of the novelty of an experience of interfaith dialogue in light of a charism of unity. In her talk titled "The 'Different' and the 'Opposite': Constraints in Interfaith Dialogue," she spoke of a "sense of love, unity, harmony, peace and accommodative spirit of inquiry inculcated by members of the Focolare. The differences, which I mentioned at the beginning [of my talk] . . . were really experienced by me, and Focolare has helped me to give answers to those dilemmas."⁴²

On the same occasion in 2008, Dr. Kala Acharya, in an interview with Vatican Radio, used an interesting analogy to speak of Chiara Lubich and the role of the charism of unity in interreligious dialogue:

---

40. Editorial of Roberto Catalano in "God, Man and Nature in the Hindu and Christian Traditions," published papers of the Hindu-Christian Symposium in Rome, May 26–29, 2008 (Mumbai: St. Paul Press), 6 (for private circulation only).
41. Catalano, *Spiritualità di comunione e dialogo interreligioso*, 161–62.
42. Madhavi Narsalay, "The 'Different' and the 'Opposite': Constraints in Interfaith dialogue in Chiara and Religions," at the International Convention Chiara and Religions. "Together Toward the Unity of the Human Family," Castel Gandolfo, March 17–20, 2014, to mark the sixth anniversary of Chiara's death (in press).

> Chiara's spirituality is always accompanied by action, action that for her signified to love humankind. . . . And that is why she has expressed this love she had for mankind through dialogue: a type of dialogue that is new, unusual. . . . She wanted that all the people she met could benefit from this spirituality. She was like the string of the necklace: in the necklace we have pearls, but if there is no string, the pearls are lost. She was like that string of a necklace, which brought thousands of people to live together.[43]

The journey of Hindu-Christian dialogue continues between the Sarvodaya and the Focolare Movement. Roundtables have also taken place and are born from the desire to deepen the roots of Gandhian spirituality and the Focolare's charism of unity for the purpose of living together what each has in common with the other as well as what is different. In this way there may be reciprocal enrichment. Twelve such meetings have taken place to date. Additionally, in a very concrete way and with the strong support of Shanti Ashram, there is now a focus on exposing the younger generations to this way of dialogue. A number of youth exchange programs have been organized between the two movements, including an International Super Congress for teenagers in 2009 in Coimbatore that involved more than a thousand teens from India and abroad. It was a concrete witness to dialogue between the two movements.

We have glimpsed the beginnings of Christian-Hindu dialogue as both a fruit and an effect of the charism of unity given to Chiara Lubich and the Focolare Movement. Deep bonds of friendship, as well as experiential and intellectual collaboration on a number of levels, have continued to develop since Lubich's death in 2008. Unity, as a central concept of Hindu philosophy and experience, will be discussed in greater detail in a future study

---

43. Vatican Radio website with embedded interview links, accessed October 28, 2019: http://www.archivioradiovaticana.va/storico/2014/03/19/250_membri_di_diverse_religioni_in_dialogo_a_castel_gandolfo/it1-782885

Chapter Thirty

Spiritual Friendship and Interreligious Dialogue: The Experience of Chiara Lubich and Nikkyō Niwano[1]

Roberto Catalano

Introduction

The relationship between Niwano and Lubich, as it was noted by Archbishop Marcello Zago, then Secretary of the Secretariat for Relations with Non-Christians – later renamed Pontifical Council for Interreligious Dialogue – has been characterized as multi-faceted. Apart from the obvious protocol type of rapport, Lubich and Niwano developed a spiritual friendship that activated growing and fruitful collaboration in favor of the welfare of humanity with a special commitment to the cause of peacebuilding. In the course of time, they inspired joint social projects and were able to see the positive role religions could play in safeguarding the environment. All this cannot be properly understood and valued unless we look into the nature of the spiritual relationship which Lubich and Niwano were able to build and which they succeeded in handing over to their collaborators and followers. The rapport of spiritual friendship between these two religious leaders offers evidences to the fact that "dialogue of experience has an irreplaceable role, as it succeeds in opening people's hearts, whose deep conversation is the foundation for any growth and transformation."[2]

---

1. This paper was presented at a conference of the Ecclesiological Investigations Research Network at Ming Hua Theological College, Hong Kong, July 20-24, 2016. It will later be published with the proceedings of the conference by Palgrave Macmillan.
2. Marcello Zago, "Introduction" in Chiara Lubich, *Incontri con l'Oriente* (Rome: Città Nuova, 1987), 7-8

The Phenomenon of Religious Renewal Movements

The second part of last century witnessed the birth and development of spiritual renewal movements, within Christianity as well as within other religions. Socio-cultural conditioning and religious sensitiveness sometimes prevent people from making positive comparisons between these movements. Nevertheless, as well will see, the fact remains that there are similarities and commonalities between these movements that are not marginal.[3] It is also true that while each movement offers significant new contributions to there religions at the spiritual, anthropological, and religious levels, these new movements have also become effective vehicles for favoring encounters between people of different cultures and religions. Among these movements, a pivotal dialogical role is the one played by the Focolare Movement and the Risshō Kōsei-kai, founded respectively, by Chiara Lubich and Nikkyō Niwano.

The Focolare Movement is one the first expressions of the phenomenon known as "new movements and ecclesial communities" that characterized the Catholic Church in the years immediately before and, above all, in the decades after the Second Vatican Council. These movements and ecclesial communities share common characteristics that make them protagonists of a large phenomenon within the Catholic Church. They are all inspired by charismatic founders and largely formed and animated by laypeople, but often with a remarkable presence of clergy and consecrated men and women. They are deeply committed to living the words of the gospel and are usually engaged in social issues. They represent one the most innovative and vibrant aspects of the Catholic Church in the course of the last five decades, while also creating complex situations within the traditional structures of parishes and dioceses.[4] In this context, the Focolare Movement, born in 1943, represents one of the early expressions of the movements phenomenon within the Catholic Church. Inspired by Chiara Lubich and a group of young companions, this movement's rapid growth remained centered on the commitment

---

3. On this point see Roberto Catalano, "Gülen, Focolare, and Risshō Kōsei-kai Movements: Commonalities for Religious and Social Renewal" in *Claritas: Journal of Dialogue & Culture*, 4 (2015/1): 42-61.
4. Recently the Vatican Congregation for the Doctrine of the Faith has published "*Iuvenescit Ecclesia*," a document addressed to the bishops of the Catholic Church on the relationship between hierarchical and charismatic gifts for the life and the mission of the Church. (see https://press.vatican.va/content/salastampa/en/bollettino/pubblico/2016/06/14/160614a.html.)

in living the Gospels with a special emphasis on all words that had a connection with love and charity as ways to achieve unity. This ensured that the Focolare Movement developed a "robust spiritual of communion," in the words of St. Pope John Paul II. The Movement spread within a few decades to all continents and among people of all walks of life, different cultures, church denominations, religious traditions, and even those who claim not to have any religious belief.

Also the Risshō Kōsei-kai was born in Japan just a few years before the Second World War.[5] It is part of a large spiritual phenomenon which characterized the Asian country between the turn of the 19th century and the first half of the 20th century. In those decades, about two thousand renewal movements or "new religions" were born as promoters of spiritual guidance for those who expressed some interest in religious issues.[6] In their complexity, these movements and new religions offer a stimulating ground for reflection, since these phenomena were not doctrine based, but were characterized by a great enthusiasm and emotional involvement. Moreover, they were rooted in the ancient religious traditions of Japan and referred to common religious scriptures such as the *Lotus Sutra*.[7] The Risshō Kōsei-kai, one of the most successful and influential of these movements, teaches its members to follow the *Lotus Sutra* tradition to achieve the fullness of Buddhahood by helping everyone, especially the beings who suffer, on the way towards the perfect Awakening. In order to achieve this ideal, it is fundamental to practice the ten virtues (*pāramitā*) of the Bodhisattva Path to the point of achieving the full awareness of *Śūnyatā*, the Absolute Emptiness in which

---

5. The Japanese Movement started in 1938 while the Focolare Movement originated in Trent during the Second World War, in 1943.
6. See Peter Nemeshegyi, "New Religions in the Cultural Context of Japan" in Michael A. Fuss, ed., *Rethinking New Religious Movements* (Rome: Pontificia Università Gregoriana 1998, 470.
7. For instance, Kurozumikyo, Konkōyō and Tenrikyō were all born in the 19th century and carry a clear Shintoist dimension, while other movements founded last century – like Reiyūkai, Sōka Gakkai and Risshō Kōsei-kai are more Buddhist in nature. The Buddhists renewal movements are often based of the *Lotus Sutra* and more specifically to the interpretation given to this sacred text given by the 12th century monk Nichiren. Nichiren presented the *Lotus Sutra* as the text which contains the teachings of all other *sutras* and proposed it as the real and true way to salvation. In more recent years, the Risshō Kōsei-kai has focused on the Tendai Buddhist tradition that preceded Nichiren in the Lotus tradition in Japan. See Cinto Busquet, *Incontrarsi nell'amore: Una lettura Cristiana di Nikkyō Niwano*, (Rome: Città Nuova, 2009), 37.

all things interrelated and that generates the Great Compassion for all living beings enabling people to attain Buddhahood.

Nikkyō Niwano and Chiara Lubich

The two founders of the Focolare and of the Risshō Kōsei-kai met for the first time in Rome on February 20, 1979. Their Movements were already well established and the two founders were figures with global reputations. For example, both received the Templeton Prize for Progress in Religion that Lubich received in 1977 and Niwano later in the course of 1979. Their attitudes towards people of different faiths and religions were open but also marked by their respective cultural and religious backgrounds.

Since the beginning of the Focolare Moviment, Lubich inspired her companions and followers towards developing an attitude of fraternity and a sense of universal brotherhood/sisterhood. She also considered every man and woman as a candidate for the evangelical love which she rediscovered in the Gospels. In the late forties she emphasized this perspective with a sentence written to some of her companions which would remain as the *Magna Charta* of her approach to dialogue that developed decades later:

> Always fix your gaze on the one Father of many children. Then you must see all as children of the same Father. In mind and in heart we must always go beyond the bounds imposed on us by human life alone and create the habit of constantly opening ourselves to the reality of being one human family in one Father: God.[8]

Notwithstanding this early vision, she never thought she would ever work for interreligious or ecumenical dialogue. Until the end of her life, she remained surprised about the unexpected and innovative development of interfaith dialogue that started with her receiving the *Templeton Price* and meeting Niwano in 1979:

> We are always surprised to see that God has led us along a spiritual pathway that intersects with all the other spiritual ways of Christians, but also of the faithful of other religions. In practice, we became partners along the journey of brotherhood and peace. While maintaining our own identity, it enables us to meet

---

8. Chiara Lubich, *The Art of Loving* (Hyde Park, NY: New City Press, 2005), 29.

and come to a mutual understanding with all the great religious traditions of humanity.[9]

On his part, Niwano progressively committed to the cause of dialogue given his growing awareness of the importance of peacebuilding after World War II. In fact, one of the fundamental goals of Risshō Kōsei-kai is to engage in contributing towards fulfilling Buddha's teaching concerning keeping peace in the family, in society, and in the world.[10] From this conviction, Niwano's engagement for peace developed into the creation of a world assembly of religions which was established in 1970 as the World Conference on Religion and Peace, today known as Religions for Peace. Already in 1963, the Risshō Kōsei-kai's founder was part of a delegation of Japanese religious leaders, all committed to the abolition of nuclear weapons, that visited Rome and briefly met Pope Paul VI. Niwano, in fact, grew in the certainty that people of religions have to get together to contribute to the welfare of the entire human race and universe.[11] Moreover Niwano always said that the decisive moment for his commitment to interreligious dialogue came in 1965 when he met Pope Paul VI on the occasion of the opening ceremony of the 4th sessions of the Second Vatican Council.[12] The founder, after being deeply struck by the Pope's words to the great assembly of more than two thousand bishops,[13] had the opportunity to meet Paul VI personally.

> We met in a marble-walled room. The pope, who was again clothed in white, rose upon seeing me enter and welcomed me by name. I replied by saying that I was honored to be with him. I raised my hands and the prayer beads I was holding in a Buddhist

---

9. Chiara Lubich, "Can Religions be Partners in Peace Building?" Paper presented at the Assembly of "Initiatives of Change" (Moral Re-armament), Caux, Switzerland), July 29,2003. (Unpublished text)
10. Nikkyō Niwano, *A Lifetime Beginner* (Tokyo: Kosei, 1994), 192.
11. See Nikkyō Niwano, "Opening Speech and Keynote Address to the Ist General Assembly of WCRP," T*he Annals of WCRP General Assemblies: Sekai Shukyōsha Heiwa Daiikai Sekai Taiki,,* (Tokyo, WCRP Japanese Committee, 1970), 62. Quoted in Cinto Busquet, *Incontrarsi nell'amore*, 63.
12. The 4th sessions of the Vatican Council opened on September 14, 1965, and Niwano personally met the Pope the following day, thanks to Cardinal Paolo Marella, President of the recently established Secretariat for non-Christians.
13. This view of St. Peter's Basilica filled with two thousand bishops listening to Paul VI reminded Niwano of the scene of the first chapter of the *Lotus Sutra* which describes the coming together of a multitude of living beings eager to listen to the Buddha. (see Nikkyō Niwano, *Kono Michi*, (Tokyo: Kosei, 1999),123.

greeting. Then the pope extended his hand, shook mine and finally took it between his, where it remained throughout the audience. "I know what you are doing for interreligious cooperation. It is very wonderful. Please continue to promote this wonderful movement," the pope said to me. As he spoke he looked in my eyes. His voice was low, calm and grave. Continuing he said "In the Vatican too, the attitude toward non-Christian religions is changing. It is important for people of religion not to cling to factions or denominations but recognize each other and pray for each other." "I shall exert my best efforts for the sake of world peace" I said to the pope. He replied: "God will surely bless you in the noble work you have undertaken."[14]

This meeting with the Pope gave Niwano a "budding faith in the realization of my dream."[15] From here he drew the strength in his work for World Conference on Religion and Peace and for facilitating the encounter among religious leaders.

Working Together for the Common Good of Humanity

With these respective backgrounds, when Niwano and Lubich met in Rome in 1979, they immediately understood each other. Their conversation concentrated on a few topics: (1) the commitment in living, and not only in reading or meditating, their respective religious scriptures; (2) the urgency of forming new generations of youth; (3) the centrality of "love" and "compassion" as ways to help people to meet and understand each other; (4) the ecumenical nature of the Focolare Movement and the engagement of Risshō Kōsei-kai in the World Conference on Religion and Peace, and (4) the common lay characteristic of the two movements.[16] These topics will largely remain the points of convergence for their following meetings in Japan in 1981 and 1984.

---

14. Nikkyō Niwano, *A Lifetime Beginner*, 224.
15. Niwano, *A Lifetime Beginner*, 225.
16. For a detailed chronicle of the meeting see Chiara Lubich and Nikkyō Niwano, "Youth and Religion" in *Dharma World* 6.2 (1979): 11-18.

In December 1981, the Catholic leader was expected to start her first journey to Asia[17] with a visit to the small Focolare community in Tokyo. She was invited by President Niwano to visit the Risshō Kōsei-kai's headquarters and address several thousand Buddhist members of the Japanese organization. The conversation between the two leaders revolved again on the same points they touched upon in Rome. But something new emerged: there was a shared awareness of some commonalities between the two movements. For instance, both noticed with surprise and pleasure that in both of their organizations, members have the practice of sharing their own life experiences and that this is a powerful means to create community life.

While Niwano was struck by these commonalities too, Lubich was also amazed by the fact that: "Buddhists mentioned that they felt as they were enveloped by God's love. They were moved."[18] The same impression was shared by many of the thousands of members who listened to Lubich's speech in the Great Sacred Hall, where on December 28, 1981 she presented her personal experience of a relationship with God and with men and women, which can been identified with the birth and development of the Focolare Movement. Lubich concluded her presentation summing up her life in the following words: "The core of my experience is this: the more you love others the more you find God. The more you find God the more you love others. [In living this perspective] it is possible to walk side-by-side while cooperating all united with God for the common good of humanity."[19]

Niwano and Lubich met again in Tokyo in November 1985; and their conversation was a kind of evaluation of the growing collaboration among the two movements. The Focolare had started working within the World Conference on Religion and Peace, and groups of youth had exchanged visits and organized several common events in Asia and in Europe. What was evident in the course of this conversation was the fact that two leaders had reached a deep spiritual sharing. A gesture was particularly significant in this regard. Niwano gifted the Italian Catholic leader with a precious large hand-fan carrying two words written on it: *Ichinen Sanzen*, ("Three thousand worlds in one single thought.") "It means," Niwano explained, "that a single thought relates to three thousand other things. . . .

---

17. Between December 1981 and February 1982, she visited Japan, South Korea, the Philippines, Australia, Hong Kong, and Thailand.
18. Chiara Lubich, *Colloqui con l'Oriente* (Rome: Città Nuova, 1987), 55.
19. Lubich, *Colloqui con l'Oriente*, 25.

[U]nless like-minded people take a hand in a given situation, little good can be done."[20] The following day, on the occasion of the celebration for the 80th birthday of the Japanese leader, Lubich opened a window on the spiritual dimension of this relationship:

> How to express in a few words the long years of the spiritual striving of his soul towards what is perfect? How to describe very briefly one entire life like yours which is burning with passion for Truth, for the Eternal Law and humanity's happiness? It is a life that gives rises to admiration and gratitude. How to express a life which has been and still is a search for unity with all persons who love Truth?[21]

The last meeting between Lubich and Niwano took place in the Fall of 1994 on the occasion of the General Assembly of the World Conference on Religion and Peace held at the Vatican in Rome and in Riva del Garda, Northern Italy. In the following years, the two leaders continued their vast correspondence that characterized their rapport shown by four earlier letters[22] that appeared in some ways prophetic. They discussed in those letters: the goal of world peace and security, the preservation of the environment, care for and formation of youth, the necessity for human beings to be aware of their interdependence with each other and with all creatures, and the centrality of religious scriptures to find adequate answers to life's questions. To the Buddhist perspective offered by Niwano in these letters, Lubich never fails to reply with the Christian perspective, often respectfully presenting God as Love as the center of the Christian message and the figure of Christ as its full expression. The exchange of letters between the two founders ended some time before Niwano's death in 1999.

The Spiritual Dimension of the Lubich-Niwano Friendship

In order to delve into the spiritual dimension of this relationship between the Catholic and the Buddhist leaders, we can begin by examining the mes-

---

20. Chiara Lubich and Nikkyo Niwano, "Religious Unity for World Peace" in *Dharma World*, Vol. 13 (1986/2), 18-19.
21. Lubich, *Colloqui con l'Oriente*, 201.
22. The letters were written by Niwano on March 15, 1987 and on September 25, 1989; and the replies by Lubich are dated, respectively, October 3, 1987 and March 9, 1990. They are kept in the Archives of the International Centre of the Focolare Movement in Rocca di Papa, Italy.

sage Lubich wrote on November 15, 1991. It was written on the occasion of the handing over of the presidency of the Buddhist Movement to his son, Nichiko Niwano. The foundress of the Catholic movement writes a sort of final evaluation of her personal relationship with the founder and of the cooperation between the members of the two movements. The two aspects come clearly into evidence in the following words:

> I wish to retrace along with you the different stages of friendship and collaboration which have given us all the time a great sense of joy and surprise. There is no greater joy that then one God makes flourish in our heart when He favor our meetings as brothers and children of the same Father.[23]

The same dimensions of friendship and collaboration are addressed in Niwano's response:

> I am grateful that you and others of the Focolare have come all the way from Rome to visit our organization. I have looked forward to meeting you and talking with you because when we have met in the past I have found that our ways of thinking agree. I think world peace can only be achieved through interreligious cooperation, with people if all religions reconciling their ideas. By combining, the Focolare and the Risshō Kōsei-kai's influence for inducing other religious organizations to join in interreligious cooperation can be tripled or quadrupled, and more people of other religions will see that achievement of world peace is possible, though it seems hard.[24]

A second element that Lubich underlines in her letter is the fact that this friendship has given the possibility of mutually discovering in each other what she calls the "divine nature," or "the supernatural element that is present in each of us and which can be express and communicated through love, the gift of oneself."[25] It is this kind of interreligious discovery in the other that characterizes the relationship between Lubich and Niwano, and has been a constant surprise. As Lubich note, it is a "discovering of always

---

23. Chiara Lubich, *Lettera a Nikkyo Niwano in occasione del passaggio della Presidenza al figlio Nichiko.*, November, 15 1991. (Unpublished letter maintained in the General Archives of the Focolare Movement, Rocca di Papa, Italy.
24. Chiara Lubich and Nikkyo Niwano, "Religious Unity for World Peace," 15.
25. Chiara Lubich, *Lettera a Nikkyo Niwano in occasione del passaggio della Presidenza al figlio Nichiko.*

new avenues of collaboration, new stimulus to deepen and appreciate our religious experiences which carry many convergences and commonalities."[26]

This feeling of surprise always accompanied the relationship between the two founders and leaders. Neither of them initially seemed to have any plan. This is evident from the Lubich's reaction to those who, before her first trip to Japan in 1981, asked her what her expectations were. She replied that she was completely unaware of what God wanted from that experience. When asked this question by the Japanese journalist for the Vatican Radio, she said: "I go in order to understand what God wants from our encounter, from the relationship which we will be able to establish with brothers and sisters of other religions . . . .I do not know. When I will come back I will tell you."[27] She herself noted on her diary: "Koichiro Taneda who belongs to the Risshō Kōsei-kai Movement and studies our religion in Rome . . . shared with me his certainty that a sort of unity will happen between our two Movements. For this reason, he prays to God and Buddha. We shall see."[28]

Another aspect to the spiritual friendship that comes into evidence over time was the growing awareness that this meeting between a Catholic leader and a Buddhist leader was part of a plan guided by a higher power. Niwano acknowledged that he met the Catholic woman without pre-established plans:

> According to Buddha's teachings all men and women can draw closet to one another fulfilling a sharing of life. When, for the first time, I met Chiara Lubich I gained the impression of her openness and loyalty. She speaks of God with great clarity. Later I discovered in her movement many contacts points with ours.[29]

Lubich, on her part, has been always convinced of being part of a great plan guided by God, and she never missed any opportunity to underline this conviction. In December 1981, a few days after their second encounter and her experience of addressing thousands of Buddhists in Tokyo, Lubich stated:

---

26. Lubich, *Lettera a Nikkyo Niwano*.
27. Interview to Vatican Radio: "Un nuovo passo verso l'unità e la pace," broadcast on December 14, 1981; quoted in Cinto Busquet, *Incontrarsi nell'amore*, 200.
28. Chiara Lubich, *Colloqui con l'Oriente*, 37.
29. Extract from the Vatican Radio interview: "Un nuovo passo verso l'unità e la pace," in Cinto Busquet, *Incontrarsi nell'amore*, 203.

> [D]versity made us understand that the points we share in common are not the result of a human effort or project . . . .Rather they are a supernatural endeavor by God himself, for a goal that He has thought for us and which is still unknown to us.[30]

Lubich had the opportunity of sharing her conviction with Niwano himself during her third encounter in Tokyo in 1985:

> We find true brothers and sisters in Risshō Kōsei-kai members, wherever we meet. We like to say that there is something supernatural, something which is above us. Probably our encounter is part of God's plans, a plan from God's Providence. It cannot be explained in human terms.[31]

Niwano agreed with Lubich's viewpoint. In fact, during the same conversation, he stressed the very same aspect from a Buddhist perspective:

> Our encounter was part of God's plan long before we were born. Unless like-minded people take a hand in a given situation, little good can be done, so I thought I was bound to meet such a person . . . . I felt I was bound to meet with like-minded people, though it was sometime before I met you. After hearing that I was to be awarded the Templeton Prize, when I met you in Rome I thought: What a person . . . that this kind of person should appear before me.[32]

On the other hand, it is important to note that this attitude of being open to God's plans, which prevents from forcing pre-defined projects while remaining docile to accept whatever events and encounters may arise, remained a basic characteristic of Lubich's attitude until the end of her life. In one of the last occasions where she could speak to an interreligious audience, she affirmed clearly:

> Even after more than sixty years of experience, we are surprised to see how the spiritual path that God has traced for us intersects

---

30. Chiara Lubich, *Incontri con l'Oriente*, 77.
31. Extract from an unpublished recording of the encounter, maintained at the Archives of the International Centre of the Focolare Movement, Rocca di Papa, Italy, in Cinto Busquet, *Incontrarsi nell'amore,* 211.
32. Chiara Lubich and Nikkyō Niwano, "Religious Unity for World Peace," 18-19.

with all the other spiritual paths, even those of the faithful of other religions.[33]

Going back to the letter written by Lubich to Niwano in November 1991, we should not ignore another important element which was part of the relationship between the two leaders: the common search for Truth. Lubich writes:

> Your words and your attitude gave me the opportunity to appreciate your great interior freedom in search for the Truth and in achieving that virtue and that serene detachment from all things, which flows from a life which is entirely dedicated to the great values and religion and peace.[34]

Obviously Lubich and Niwano have two different perspectives regarding the Truth. Speaking of the Truth, Niwano refers to the "Wonderful Law" (*saddharma*). In this context, the Truth is identified with the "Law," the real state of all thing that exists in the universe and of all events which occur in the world. Secondly, it means also the Truth which penetrates all things. This Truth is the Buddha and also the Law that rules the relationships between all things, including human beings. Buddha, Truth. and Law are one and same thing. The Truth is the Buddha, and all the functions of the Buddha can be expressed with the Law.[35]

Lubich herself has been constantly in search for the Truth. This has been one of the fundamental aspects of her life, well expressed in one of her most poetic passages:

> I am a soul passing through this world. I have seen many beautiful and good things and I have always been attracted only by them. One day (one indescribable day) I saw a light. It appeared to me as more beautiful than the other beautiful things, and I followed it. I realized it was the Truth."[36]

---

33. Chiara Lubich, *Can Religions be Partners in Peace Building?*
34. Chiara Lubich, *Lettera a Nikkyo Niwano in occasione del passaggio della Presidenza al figlio Nichiko.*
35. Nikkyō Niwano, *Buddhism for Today. A Modern interpretation of the Threefold Lotus Sutra* (Tokyo: Kosei, 1980), 23.
36. Chiara Lubich, *Essential Writings* (Hyde Park, NY: New City Press, 2007), xvii.

This love for Truth which constantly accompanied the Catholic leader along her life, had emerged in the encounter she had with founder Niwano. Recalling some previous meetings of representatives of the two organizations,[37] Lubich commented that on both sides there was a desire to achieve a certain degree of unity. She underlined the common "efforts . . . to seek out the truths we have in common, which already unite us and to live them together."[38]

Finally, the text of the 1991 letter evidences how the relationship between Niwano and Lubich, as well as among the members of the two Movements, is not an end in itself but opens up towards the common welfare of the human family, especially through a concrete commitment towards peacebuilding and dialogue.

> A special mention is deserved for all the initiatives which have seen our youth working together, one next to the other, with enthusiasm and dedication for peace and understanding among peoples . . . and we have fully shared the conviction that only men and women who are animated by a great religious respect towards other human beings and towards creation can truly contribute to the progress of the human family.[39]

In fact, in her letter the foundress of the Focolare quotes in a significant way the Buddhist monk Chih-I (Zhiyi), of whom Niwano had spoken to Lubich: "If my desire is truly according to God's heart, then He will make a multitude be born from the very same desire."[40] Niwano, in fact, spoke to Lubich of his belief in the truth of the statement of the great Chinese priest: "Three Thousand Realms in One Mind."[41] Looking at the two Movements, taking into account their spreading, their numbers, and their commitment

---

37. In fact, the first encounter between Lubich and Niwano was preceded by several meetings of members, especially youth, of the Focolare and Risshō Kōsei-kai. Towards the end of 1975, a delegation of youth leaders of the Japanese Movement travelled to Rome to attend some events at the conclusion of the Holy Year. After attending Christmas Midnight Mass in St. Peter's Basilica and meeting with Vatican officials, they greeted Pope Paul VI and later travelled to Assisi and to the Focolare community of Loppiano (close to Florence) where they had an exchange with about 400 youth of the Catholic Movement. (See "Youth Mission to the Vatican" Dharma World, Vol.3 (1976/2): 6-9.
38. Chiara Lubich and Nikkyō Niwano, "Youth and Religion," 15.
39. Chiara Lubich, *Lettera a Nikkyō Niwano in occasione del passaggio della Presidenza al figlio Nichiko.*
40. Lubich, *Lettera a Nikkyō Niwano.*
41. Chiara Lubich and Nikkyō Niwano, "Religious Unity for World Peace," 18-19.

for high goals such as justice and peace and a value-oriented education for young generations, it can be concluded that this saying of Mahāyāna Buddhist wisdom was embodied by both of the founders.

From Spiritual Friendship to Common Commitment

On the occasion of their first encounter in Rome in 1979, Niwano spoke to Lubich about the World Conference on Religion and Peace as a way to foster collaboration among leaders of different religions towards justice and peace. After their meeting in 1981 in Tokyo, Lubich decided to commit the Focolare to the World Conference on Religion and Peace, and ever since the Catholic Movement has been active in their projects and in participating at the different Assemblies which took place in several parts of the world.[42] Lubich herself was appointed an Honorary President of the organization.[43] Niwano as one of the inspiring and founding fathers of this ground-breaking interreligious organization, was always convinced that if religious people committed themselves to working hard for world peace, the only way to achieve this goal is through interreligious dialogue:

> I think world peace can only be achieved through interreligious cooperation, with people of all religions reconciling their ideas. By combining the Focolare and the Risshō Kōsei-kai's influence we will induce other religious organizations to join in interreligious cooperation, and our efforts can be tripled or quadrupled and more people of other religions will see that achieving world peace is possible, though it may seem hard.[44]

The experience of collaboration within World Conference on Religion and Peace has been very fruitful and significant for Lubich and the Focolare as well:

> It is very useful to have a goal like peace. This offers the motivation for meeting each other, for knowing one another, sharing

---

42. Though the official commitment of the Focolare in the *World Conference on Religion and Peace* started only in 1982, a Focolare delegation participated in the General Assembly held at Princeton University in 1979.
43. More recently, at the General Assembly held in Vienna in November 2013, Maria Voce, the first President of the Focolare Movement after Lubich's death, has been appointed among the Presidents.
44. Chiara Lubich and Nikkyo Niwano, "Religious Unitiy for World Peace," 15.

spiritual goods. Another goal is to commit to work together for humankind's welfare, for instance for the Third World, as we do in the Philippines and we would like to do in Africa. Finally, as I think God prompted our encounters, let us leave to Him to arrange our programs as we go ahead.[45]

A second commitment of this fruitful collaboration between the two movements is towards the education and formation of young generations. Already before the two leaders met in Rome, groups of youth from the two movements had the opportunity to meet together and both leaders had received very positive feedback about these experiences. That is why their conversation in 1979 addresses extensively their work with younger generations. Actually, this was the first question Niwano asked Lubich. He wanted to know what the Focolare Movement was doing to educate and form youth.[46] Both leaders shared the conviction that if young people deeply understood the significance of the words of Jesus or the Buddha, and if they made the choice to live them, they would experience a deep and profound change in their lives. Lubich, while sharing about this view, said that she was inspired by the feedback she received regarding the initial meetings of youth of the two religions. She confirmed that: "our young people feel the desire to be together in loving God. And so when our youth live together the truths that we have in common, we are already one in some way."[47] Even in the letter of 1991, which traces an evaluation of the two decade friendship, Lubich mentioned this collaboration among youth as one of the most fruitful experiences between the two movements.[48]

Conclusion

The spiritual friendship between Niwano and Lubich opened unexpected opportunities for interreligious dialogue between Buddhists and Christians as well as fruitful collaborations for peacebuilding projects and youth exchange programs. All these activities continue today with positive and new results. It is important to note that when these encounters and friendship began, little had been done to engage religions in peacebuilding processes.

---

45. Chiara Lubich, *Incontri con l'Oriente*, 232.
46. See Chiara Lubich and Nikkyo Niwano, "Youth and Religion," 11.
47. Lubich and Niwano, "Youth and Religion," 15.
48. Chiara Lubich, *Lettera a Nikkyo Niwano in occasione del passaggio della Presidenza al figlio Nichiko.*

In fact, as far as interreligious dialogue was concerned, the initiatives taken at that time were often at the theological level of discussions. The more engaged dialogue among Catholics and Buddhists took form in the inter-monastic dialogue between monks and nuns. Lubich and Niwano were the two laypersons who introduced a type of interreligious dialogue of spiritual friendship among the laity, especially the youth, rooted in a living experience of spiritual encounter open to projects of mutual cooperation. This fact is acknowledged also by Archbishop Michael Fitzgerald, President of the Pontifical Council for Interreligious Dialogue. He said of the two founders: "they were animated by a similar spirit, and friendship grew between them and the two movements which has proved to be extremely fruitful in the field of interreligious cooperation."[49]

These encounters and cooperation have been vehicles for facilitating a meeting ground not only between members of these two movements, but also with Buddhists of other linages and Catholics of other religious movements and orders. This fact was underlined by Niwano in 1985: "The example of Focolare members' activities and pure Christian faith has greatly encouraged other Japanese religionists in their attitude toward interreligious cooperation."[50] The importance of this dialogue on the Catholic side was underlined by Hans Urs Von Balthasar who commented very positively regarding Lubich's first trip to Japan and her meeting with several thousand Buddhists:

> I wish to prove my point with an example. And there is one worthy being mentioned. It pertains to Chiara Lubich. She travelled to Japan where she addressed Buddhists who understood her. Self-denial, egoism negation, self-renunciation: this is the center of Buddhism. . . . In this way the wise man reaches the point of self-denial and he attains a sense of peace where there is no longer concupiscence. There is a sort of benevolence towards whatever exists. If you say to this wise man: "*We have to deny ourselves. I have to overcome the concupiscence of being myself, because I belong to Another one, another one who loves me,*" then he will understand. He will see that there is a link between Buddhism and Christianity. This is exactly what Chiara Lubich did. I believe this

---

49. Michael Fitzgerald, "The Venerable Nikkyō Niwano and Interreligious Dialogue" in *Dharma World*, Vol. 33, (2006/4): 10-11.
50. Chiara Lubich and Nikkyo Niwano, "Religious Unity for World Peace," 17.

can be a model for dialogue and dialogue with Buddhism may be the most difficult one.[51]

Finally, in the course of these decades, the role that religions and spiritual people can play for ensuring peace or facilitating peace keeping processes has become increasingly clear. In recent times, political scientists have turned to examining the role that religious movements have played, and are still playing, in these increasingly complex contexts. They appreciate the fact that "religions may have a transformative effect on individuals and communities and no doubt encounter one another within an increasingly global civil society."[52] One important conclusion is that:

> Dialogue . . . is not solely or even primarily about theological matters. It involves members of different religious communities speaking out of their own traditions in an effort to better understand and more effectively navigate inevitable cultural, ethical, and political differences. Dialogue can have a strategic dimension; it can serve to preserve and extend the size of one's own community. But its primary aims are not to prevail over the other but to reduce conflict and promote understanding and cooperation across issues of common concern.[53]

---

51. Hans Urs von Balthasar, "*Il Sabato:*" 14 giugno 1986, quoted by Enzo Maria Fondi, "The Focolare Movement: A Spirituality at the Service of Interreligious Dialogue," *Pro Dialogo Bulletin*, 89 (1985/2): 158.
52. T. Banchoff, "Interreligious Dialogue and International Relations" in T. S. Shah, A. Stepan, and M. Duffy Toft (eds.), *Rethinking Religion and World Affairs* (Oxford: Oxford University Press, 2012), 204.
53. Banchoff, "Interreligious Dialogue and International Relations," 204.

Chapter Thirty-One

A Buddhist-Catholic Dialogue of Life in Japan: Finding Shared Values for Global Collaboration for the Common Good

Cinto Busquet

Interreligious cooperation is based on the dialogue of life: a grassroots, living dialogue between persons of different religions. The dialogue of life between people and communities uncovers common values that are necessary for interreligious collaboration for the common good. Given the global issues facing the world today due to factors such as multiculturalism and globalization, this search for shared values can no longer be regarded as optional. This is not only true from a practical point of view, but also for theoretical reflection on global issues. Nisshō Takeuchi, a Japanese monk and a scholar of the Nichiren School, participated in a Christian-Buddhist Symposium held in Osaka and on Mount Hiei in April 2006 sponsored by the Buddhist Japanese association Risshō Kōsei-kai and the Catholic-based Focolare Movement in collaboration with other Buddhist institutions. After the encounter, Takeuchi affirmed:

> In this twenty-first century, humanity has to face a great variety of very complex problems. The natural and human sciences have to give answers to very serious issues; but it is as if they find themselves up against a wall which they cannot climb over. There is need for a global vision which gives light to the individual questions, and which harmonizes the overall vision with the concrete issues in the various fields. The integration of knowledge is an urgent need. This is the direction towards which Christian theology and Buddhist philosophy must work so as to give a substantial contribution to the twenty-first century. Science alone cannot give the answers, it needs religions. . . . I think that Christianity and Buddhism together, in a harmonious way, like two wheels moving in the same direction, can engage the civilizations of East

and West in profound dialogue and assist humanity in progressing towards a future where the differences are integrated from the very roots in order to reach unity.¹

The encounter between Buddhism and Christianity in Japan has recently been seeking common values in order to address global problems. This is not the encounter between doctrines or religions in the abstract, but it is carried out when Buddhist practitioners and Christian believers meet each other with reciprocal interest and esteem. In this sense, I think the relationship that St. Francis Xavier established in Japan in 1549 with a Buddhist monk in the very first period of the Christian mission is emblematical. A few weeks after landing in Kagoshima, in a letter sent from that city he writes:

> I spoke many times with the wisest of the bonzes, especially with one for whom all of those living here have great respect, for his scholarship, his life and the dignity he possesses, as well as for his venerable age of eighty years; he is called Ninshitsu which in the Japanese language means "Heart of Truth". . . . It is wonderful to behold how this Ninshitsu is a great friend of mine. Many people, lay and monks, are very happy in our company and they are astonished to see that we come from countries which are very far away—Portugal and Japan are six thousand leagues apart—just to speak about the things of God.²

Returning to today, I think it is significant that many Japanese Buddhist leaders were present in the Interreligious Day of Prayer for Peace in Assisi in October 1986. The following year, in August 1987, inspired by the prophetic gesture of Pope John Paul II, the late Venerable Etai Yamada, head of the Tendai Buddhist sect, convened a Religious Summit on Mount Hiei that gathered religious men and women from all over the world. Just a few months before this summit, I had arrived in Japan and I remember how impressive that event was for me. Rev. Yamada quoted Saichō (767–822), the Buddhist monk who founded the Tendai School on Mount Hiei at the beginning of the ninth century, where Saichō explained the expression *Mōko-rita*, "to forget oneself, to benefit the others," in this way: "Take upon yourself that which is bad and pass on to the others that which is good.

---

1. Unpublished interview recorded in Osaka, Japan, by C. S. Chiara Productions (Rocca di Papa, Italy), April 27, 2006.
2. S. Francesco Saverio, *Le lettere e altri documenti* (Rome: Città Nuova, 1991), 325.

Forget yourself and do good to others; this is the supreme expression of compassion."³ According to Etai Yamada, in these few words we can grasp the very essence and the heart of Buddhist values and of any true religious commitment.

John Paul II himself quoted and commented on this passage by Saichō during his meeting in Tokyo with the representatives of the different religions in February 1981.⁴ Indeed, as the Second Vatican Council declares:

> [T]he Church exhorts her sons, that through dialogue and collaboration with the followers of other religions, carried out with prudence and love and in witness to the Christian faith and life, they recognize, preserve and promote the good things, spiritual and moral, as well as the socio-cultural values found among these men" (*Nostra Aetate* 2).

The Catholic Church, therefore, encourages Christians to affirm every positive value found anywhere and to establish sincere bonds of friendship with the followers of other religious traditions in search for the common good.

Buddhists and Christians in Japan Seeking Unity for the Common Good

During the past half century in Japan, there have been many examples of dialogues of life both on the institutional level as well as from private initiatives. I would like to examine one such example, namely, the dialogue between the Risshō Kōsei-kai and the Focolare Movement based on recent research.⁵ Nikkyō Niwano (1906–99) founded the Risshō Kōsei-kai as a Japanese lay Buddhist association in 1938. Niwano was very active in the interreligious field from the early 1960s. Rooted in the universalistic approach of the *Lotus Sūtra*—one of the most important scriptures of Mahāyāna Buddhism in the Japanese context—Niwano recognized and stressed the positive significance of all religious traditions. Moreover, he was particularly open to Christianity

---

3. Etai Yamada, *Onore wo wasurete ta wo risuru* (Tokyo: Kōsei, 1994), 38. This title is modern Japanese for the original expression explained by Saichō.
4. John Paul II, *Address to Representatives of Non-Christian Religions*, Tokyo, February 24, 1981, n. 3.
5. Cinto Busquet, *Incontrarsi nell'amore: Una lettura cristiana di Nikkyō Niwano* (Rome: Città Nuova, 2009).

and he maintained many contacts with the Catholic Church. One such contact in particular was influential in his quest for building global peace.

In September 1965, Nikkyō Niwano was invited to attend the opening ceremony of the fourth and last session of the Second Vatican Council. On September 14, he was probably the only Buddhist in Saint Peter's Basilica. Niwano was very impressed by the whole event, but in a special way he was struck by the following words of Paul VI on universal brotherhood and love:

> The love that animates our communion does not set us apart from other men and women . . . does not make us exclusivists or egoists. On the contrary, because it is a love that comes from God, it gives us a universal dimension; our Truth leads us to Charity. . . . While other currents of thought and action proclaim quite different principles for building human society—power, wealth, science, class struggle, vested interests, or other things—the Church proclaims love. The Council is a solemn act of love for humanity.[6]

In response, Niwano writes in his *Autobiography*:

> The love of God of which the Pope had spoken in his opening message to that session of the Second Vatican Council is the same thing as the compassion advocated by Buddhism. The Pope insisted that the love for the neighbor taught by the New Testament must be interpreted to mean love for peoples everywhere, no matter what their nationality or race. Śākyamuni taught the same thing about compassion.[7]

Here we have already a strong link between Buddhist and Christian life: the fundamental value given to charity or compassion that leads to the ethical commitment to work for the common good. The day after attending the ceremony in the basilica, Niwano was received in a private audience by the pope. He explains that on this occasion Paul VI said to him:

> I know what you are doing for interfaith cooperation. It is wonderful. Please continue to promote such a wonderful movement. In the Vatican, too, the attitude toward non-Christian religions

---

6. Paul VI, Opening Address—Fourth Session of the Second Ecumenical Vatican Council, September 14, 1965.
7. Nikkyō Niwano, *Lifetime Beginner: An Autobiography* (Tokyo: Kōsei, 1978), 225.

is changing. It is important for people of religion not to cling to factions or denominations but to recognize each other and pray for each other.[8]

Many times Niwano said that he could not forget the "warm hands" of Pope Paul VI and that he believed that their firm handshake "put blood into the cooperation, friendship, and mutual understanding between Christianity and Buddhism."[9] From that encounter, Niwano deepened his "determination to be a bridge between the two religions, and to extend this bridge to various others religions, as well."[10]

Nikkyō Niwano met Chiara Lubich, founder of the Focolare Movement, in Rome in 1979. Lubich and Niwano found a common spiritual bond with each other and Niwano invited Lubich to Japan twice, in 1981 and 1985. After Chiara Lubich's second trip to Japan, Hans Urs von Balthasar answered a journalist's question about dialogue among Christians and Buddhists in this way:

> If we question ourselves on the meaning of good, we arrive at the definition of love, which is more than only justice. . . . If you speak about love and you bring it to its extreme consequences, you are speaking as a Christian because God is love. I would like to show you what I mean by giving an example. And I have one which deserves to be known. I am referring to Chiara Lubich. She went to Japan and spoke to Buddhists, and they understood. The negation of self, the negation of egoism, self-denial: this is the center of Buddhism. . . . By doing so, the wise man arrives at self-negation . . . and enjoys a peace in which there is no longer concupiscence but a kind of benevolence towards all that exists. But if you say to this wise man: "Yes, it's true, we must deny ourselves. . . . Yes, I must overcome the concupiscence of being myself, but . . . because I belong to Another, because there is Another who loves me." If you tell him this, he will understand. He will begin to see that there is a link between Buddhism and Christianity. Chiara Lubich did this. I believe it can be a model of dialogue.[11]

---

8. Nikkyō Niwano, *A Buddhist Approach to Peace* (Tokyo: Kōsei, 1977), 87.
9. Niwano, *A Buddhist Approach to Peace*, 87.
10. Niwano, *A Buddhist Approach to Peace*, 88.
11. Enzo Fondi, "The Focolare Movement: A Spirituality at the Service of Interreligious Dialogue," *Pro Dialogo* 89 (1995): 158.

Hence, the dialogue established between the Risshō Kōsei-kai and the Focolare by their founders is not about comparing beliefs or religious practices, but involves living radically according to one's own religion and being attentive to and interested in the other's. In her diary written during her stay in Japan, Chiara Lubich says, "If the Buddhists have the extinguished candle as their symbol, a sign that all desires have been extinguished, we Christians have the lighted candle because we are the followers of Love. In fact we have another light in us which must live; it is the light of God in us. If it lives, it is also the extinction of the self."[12]

Interaction between members of the Focolare and the Risshō Kōsei-kai based on generous religious commitments and profound spiritualities has always been a two-way street that brings further light and love to both sides. Being faithful and consistent to one's own religious convictions while remaining radically open to the other's is what assures that from their dialogue of life these Christians and Buddhists discover shared values on which to build a collaboration that is open to the world and to finding solutions to the global issues we all face today.

Truth and the Value of Openness

In the dialogue between the Risshō Kōsei-kai and the Focolare in Japan, Buddhists and Christians have many things to learn from each other's visions of life and shared values in building unity for collaboration for the common good. They do not see themselves as religious competitors in the marketplace of spiritual supplies. All are seekers and witnesses of the truth. For the Focolare members, Jesus Christ is the truth itself. Living their spirituality in this light means, in part, to live such that Christ is within and among them giving them his spirit and guiding them to the fullness of truth if they persevere in his love. In doing so, they are open to finding truth lived out by persons of other religions.

Śākyamuni Buddha, explains Nikkyō Niwano, "advocated flexibility when he taught that one must be candid and open and obedient to the truth.... One must be ready to accept new truths when they are discovered. ... There can be no absolute incompatibility among human beings. This is a truth to which we must all become enlightened.... To follow the way of

---

12. Chiara Lubich, *Incontri con l'Oriente* (Rome: Città Nuova, 1986), 75.

truth is to have spiritual and mental flexibility. The person who has these traits can grow in all directions."[13]

Romano Guardini also wrote about the initiator of the Buddhist path using the following words:

> There is only one individual who could be placed in a position close to Jesus: the Buddha. This man is a great mystery. He stands there in a frightening, almost supra-human freedom, at the same time he demonstrates a goodness, mighty as a world power. Maybe Buddha will be the last with whom Christianity will have to argue. What for Christians he signifies, nobody has pronounced so far. Perhaps Christ did not have only one precursor in the Old Testament, John, the last prophet, but also one at the bottom of antique culture, Socrates, and a third one who has spoken the ultimate word of eastern-religious knowledge and overcoming, Buddha.[14]

Given the shared value of openness to the truth in the visions of the other, the dialogue of life and collaboration between the Risshō Kōsei-kai and the Focolare in Japan advanced greatly. As a Christian theologian, I would like to explore what other shared values were discovered in this dialogue of life based on openness to the other that in turn have contributed to a long and fruitful collaboration between the Risshō Kōsei-kai and the Focolare. In doing so, with emphasis on Nikkyō Niwano's Buddhist vision of the truth, I will also describe the substantial insights behind these values that contributed to interreligious unity and to successful collaboration for the common good.

Fundamental Unity and the Value of Peacebuilding

Speaking about why interreligious cooperation is essential, Nikkyō Niwano says:

> In its essence religion does not reject others but instead allows us to think of others with the same regard as we have for ourselves. The oneness of self and others is fundamental to religion. Thus even when it is fractured into different sects and groups, it is not natural that they should fight one another. People of religion

---

13. Nikkyō Niwano, *The Richer Life* (Tokyo: Kōsei, 1979), 34–35.
14. Romano Guardini, *Il Signore* (Brescia: Morcelliana, 2005), 404.

should, rather, study each other's doctrines and practices, discuss issues of religious faith that are of mutual concern, and on that basis, work together to establish world peace.[15]

In these words, we find a very important truth: the fundamental unity and equality of human beings. Although it may be interpreted and explained with different categories, we can consider it a common ground of Buddhism and Christianity. For Buddhism, everything and everyone are linked in an interrelatedness of causes and effects, in a continuous interaction among all the elements of the phenomenal world. That is the "Dharma," the Law of dependent arising or the interdependence of all that exists. Nothing exists in or for itself, everything exists in relation to all that exists. Every human being is called to awake to this Universal Law that sustains the whole universe. In every person the same Dharma is at work. If we were to summarize the Buddhist vision of the world and of human existence in a few words, we could possibly express it in this way.

For Christianity, there is also an essential unity and equality between all human beings. It is based on their common dignity, having been created in the image and likeness of God. Jesus reveals the face of God as a loving Father who cares for every man and woman with infinite love; as a logical consequence of this faith, Christianity teaches that all human beings must live as brothers and sisters, as children of the same heavenly Father. The Gospel according to John tells us that the day before his death on the cross Jesus prayed for the perfect unity of his disciples: "That they may all be one, just as you, Father, are in me, and I in you, that they also may be in us, so that the world may believe that you have sent me" (Jn 17:21). Jesus is one with the Father. In the Christian faith, he is the Son of God: God who gives himself completely to humankind in the humanity of Christ. As God is one and humankind is created in God's image, humanity is called to realize this fundamental oneness or unity in God. Humankind is called to be perfect in unity, to be one family where reciprocal love renders our fundamental oneness real and tangible, a oneness that embraces all creation.

These notions of a fundamental unity that embraces all beings provides, in part, the shared value of peacebuilding. Both the Risshō Kōsei-kai and the Focolare give Buddhists and Christians a living experience of a unity that embraces all creation. Chiara Lubich says of her own experience, "[All

---

15. Nikkyō Niwano, "Why Interreligious Cooperation is Essential," *Dharma World* 33 (2006): 33.

things] are linked one to another by a bond of love in which each one [has] a reason for loving the other."¹⁶ Here, a hidden unity gives reason for loving others, for peacebuilding, for the ideal of working together for a more united and peaceful world. This shared value has contributed to a collaborating by the Risshō Kōsei-kai and the Focolare for peace though the World Conference on Religion and Peace (WCRP), of which Nikkyō Niwano is a founder and Chiara Lubich was an honorary president.

Universal Truth and the Value of Compassion

Mahāyāna Buddhism proposes a "Great Vehicle," a path to reach enlightenment suitable for everyone. Within Mahāyāna, the Lotus tradition speaks of *ekayāna* (*Ichijō* in Japanese): the "One Vehicle." This concept, central in the *Lotus Sūtra* and quite popular in Japan, can be understood in an exclusivist way, or, on the contrary, from an inclusive and comprehensive outlook. Usually, Buddhist tradition interprets it from a holistic and all-encompassing point of view: eternal and universal truth must be above every particular expression of it, and at the same time many paths can lead to it. Niwano asserts:

> The *Lotus Sūtra*, in its deepest meaning, is not a proper noun but a common noun meaning the highest and most real teaching, which teaches the truth of the universe to all human beings and leads them to the true way of living. But the real and the highest teaching can never be two. Though it can be expressed in various ways, in its fundamental meaning it is one.[17]

The Zen Master Rempō Niwa, abbot of Eiheiji, the main monastery of the Sōtō Zen School, during the 1986 Interreligious Meeting of Prayer for Peace convened by John Paul II in Assisi, said:

> Generally the faith of human beings is universal: beyond race, sex, or social class. . . . The life of people who communicate intimately in a religious mode is equal without any distinction of rank. . . . Universal truth is reflected in a different way in the diverse religious teachings; fundamentally all the religions are connected with one another.[18]

---

16. Chiara Lubich, "Paradise 1949," *New Humanity Review* 15 (2010): 9.
17. Niwano, *A Buddhist Approach to Peace*, 68.
18. Michael Fuss, Jesús López Gay, and G. Pietro Sono Fazion, *Le grande figure del Buddhismo* (Assisi: Cittadella Ed., 1995), 342–43.

This deep interconnection between different religious traditions is what is meant in the Japanese expression *Bankyō Dōkon*, "all religions spring from the same root." It is a key notion to understanding the basic Japanese approach to religious diversity and pluralism. As Niwano states, it is universal and it is a way of life, a way of living "truly" as a human being.

The Catholic Church professes her faith in Christ as "the way, the truth, and the life" (Jn 14:6) in whom men and women may find the fullness of life and in whom God has reconciled all things to himself. At the same time, as the Second Vatican Council declared, "the Catholic Church rejects nothing that is true and holy" in other religions and "regards with sincere reverence those ways of conduct and of life, those precepts and teachings which, though differing in many aspects from the ones she holds and sets forth, nonetheless often reflect a ray of that Truth which enlightens all men" (*Nostra Aetate* 2). Here too we find truth referred to as a "ray" of light that "enlightens" people so they can discover a way of living that is "true and holy."

According to Niwano, what is the final, the profound truth? For him, "it is the finding of the infinite life of humankind within the eternal life-force of the universe."[19] True human nature, in its union with the eternal life-force of the universe, is called "Buddhanature." All beings possess this potential for enlightenment and for Mahāyāna the noblest form of Buddhist practice is the way of the *bodhisattva,* who devotes himself or herself to attaining enlightenment not only for oneself but for all sentient beings. The motivation behind this devotion to the needs of others is compassion. Compassionate care for those in need defines the true way of living in light of the truth.

For Risshō Kōsei-kai members, this compassion is a fundamental value based on one universal truth as understood in the *Lotus* tradition of Buddhism. For Focolare members, love as charity is a fundamental value based on the truth that "God is love" (1 Jn 4:8). Chiara Lubich often notes that the love of God is most clearly revealed in the moment on the cross when Jesus cries out "My God, my God, why have you forsaken me?" (Mt 27:46). At that moment, he became so one with a lost and suffering humanity that he did not sense the presence of God. His compassion as a "suffering with" all humankind in this moment became for Chiara and her followers in the Focolare the ideal model for loving others.[20] In the Focolare's living out this ideal of love, and in the Risshō Kōsei-kai's living out the *bodhisattva* ideal of

---

19. Nikkyō Niwano, *Shakyamuni Buddha* (Tokyo: Kōsei, 1980), 113.
20. Chiara Lubich, *The Cry* (New York: New City Press, 2001).

compassion, the two movements find another shared value in their dialogue of life on which to build their collaboration for the common good.

Ultimate Reality and the Value of Harmony

Niwano explains that the *Lotus Sūtra* expounds the idea that every person is the child of the Buddha:

> The Buddha in this sense means the great life of the universe, which is the very root of all phenomena. In other words, the *Lotus Sūtra* teaches that even though the individual person appears to live a detached existence, fundamentally everybody is an offshoot of the one great life of the universe.[21]

Niwano was convinced that "the basis of all religions is the belief that all human beings are the children of the Buddha or of God" and that "all religions must transcend the limits of individual organizational differences in order to achieve the goal of religion itself."[22]

The Buddha that Nikkyō Niwano speaks about is not simply the historical Buddha. It is the Original and Eternal Buddha, the personification of the Eternal Dharma that can be recognized in the historical Śākyamuni Buddha. In the Mahāyāna tradition, Ultimate Reality is represented by the image of the Buddha, but it remains something formless beyond any conceptualization and any personified image. Niwano writes:

> There are many ways of naming this biggest, most absolute thing. Some call it the Law that creates and moves the universe. Others call it Truth or universal life-force. No matter how it is called, the absolute is the basic force or rule that makes our existence possible and that gives us life. . . . The universal Law . . . controls the lives of all things and does not, therefore, give special treatment to any one living creature or any one human being. Managing everything in the universe means maintaining harmony among all things, all of which are constantly and dynamically in action.[23]

As it is clearly expressed in this quotation, Ultimate Reality in Niwano's understanding remains the Dharma that gives harmony to the whole uni-

---

21. Niwano, *A Buddhist Approach to Peace*, 77.
22. Niwano, *Lifetime Beginner*, 261–62.
23. Niwano, *The Richer Life*, 104–5.

verse. It is not a personal ontological entity that brings the world and human beings into existence as it is in Christianity and in other Western monotheistic traditions. Rather, Niwano says that religion "is what enables human beings, living in the relative world of things, to perceive the world of the absolute. Religions make the world of the absolute the mainstay of our hearts, allowing us to walk the path of life with sure-footed confidence."[24] Walking ahead on this inner journey toward the deepest layer of their own existence, human beings are set free from the illusion of their independent and possessive self and become radically aware of their interdependent and relational nature. Here one discovers the value of harmony.

From a Christian point of view, in our earthly journey, all of us are travelers, "fellow pilgrims," related in a profound sense. We are all children of the same Father, we are all brothers and sisters, and we must go forward helping each other to advance more and more toward that infinite fullness that abides only in God. In the spirituality of Chiara Lubich, one is called "to walk toward God in unity."[25] Living that unity, Lubich says, one discovers "the magnificent design of [God's] love in all its splendor. . . . this design would be interwoven with other designs, those of the lives of all the other people . . . and the whole pattern would be the work of God . . . [bringing] them harmoniously together."[26] This value of living together in harmony becomes a touchstone in the Focolare for interreligious collaboration for the good of all peoples, nations, and cultures.

At the same time it is important to note that for his disciples, Christ is not just a historical figure of the past to whose teachings we listen. He is the Risen Lord who promised to be with us always until the end of the world. Therefore, even though only in a spiritual way, we can really meet him on the road. The Christian experience is well symbolized in the scene of the disciples of Jesus who were going from Jerusalem to the village of Emmaus and met Jesus on the road, as described in the last chapter of Luke's Gospel.

The Mystery of Life and the Value of Gratitude

The basic expression of Buddhist commitment, common to all Buddhist schools, is to take refuge in the Three Treasures: the Buddha, the Dhar-

---

24. Niwano, *The Richer Life*, 80.
25. Chiara Lubich, *Essential Writings* (Hyde Park, NY: New City Press, 2007), 31.
26. Chiara Lubich, *May They All Be One* (Hyde Park, NY: New City Press, 1995), 41.

ma (interpreted as the Buddhist Doctrine concerning the Universal Law), and the Saṅgha (the Buddhist community). According to Nikkyō Niwano, taking refuge in the Buddha means "attaining a selfless state and entering directly into union with the great life" of the universe. The profound meaning of taking refuge in the Dharma "is the casting off of the ego to reach a state of complete accord with the Truth and the Law of the universe." The meaning of taking refuge in the Saṅgha is "to revere harmony as the highest virtue in human society, to rely on it in one's own life, and to devote one's body and mind to trying to bring it to real life."[27] A primary aim of the Buddhist path for Niwano is to be liberated from the illusion of the self and to become fully aware of being called to express in our lives the cosmic harmony in which we exist.

In general, the Buddhist religious experience does not usually reach the point of experiencing the Transcendent as a personal God with whom we can establish a personal relationship, as Someone to whom we are invited to open our hearts, to listen to, and to whom we can pray and entrust ourselves as it is in the Christian experience of faith. In the Buddhist religious path, the practitioner is not led to meet the One who is the source of existence and to enter into dialogue with Him, but he or she is trained to become aware of the Oneness in which he or she exists and to reach the wisdom of a non-self-centered insight that guides him or her to a compassionate life. For example, Genkai Sugimoto, a Japanese Zen monk who participated in the East-West Monastic Exchange program between European Catholic monks and Japanese Buddhist monks in the 1980s, wrote the following about his experience in the Benedictine Monastery of Montserrat in Catalonia (Spain):

> I think that one of the essential differences between the two religions consists in the fact that the Buddha was a human being, not God. Through his own efforts Buddha reached a state of peace which was fully realized. And he lived as a master who guides others to reach this state of peace. . . . Instead, in the monastery I saw how the Catholic monks diligently endeavor to become humble and obedient before God, praying and praising his holy name. Their greatest concern is God, while ours is our own hearts.[28]

---

27. Niwano, *The Richer Life,* 138–39.
28. Genkai Sugimoto, "Japanese Buddhists in the Monastery of Montserrat," *Buddhist-Christian Studies* 10 (1990): 202.

Nevertheless, in Niwano's writings based on the *Lotus Sūtra* tradition, we can sometimes detect a personalistic approach to the Ultimate Reality. He affirms, for instance:

> If one knows the personal experience of being together with God or the Buddha at all times, waking and sleeping, of maintaining a constant dialogue with either of them in one's heart, of being certain that they support one's life, then can we say one is unhappy? Certainly not. . . . This is because either God or the Buddha fills the universe with his reality. They are the basis of life, the truth. By experiencing unity with them, by always knowing that one is together with them, one is assured of great cheer and courage and of great peace.[29]

In this English translation of Niwano's words, the use of the word "God" and the word "Buddha" in parallel can easily lead to some misunderstanding. In Niwano's mind, they are not separate realities as in a polytheistic comprehension of the divine sphere, but just different ways of referring to the same Ultimate Reality. The melding of Shinto and Buddhist categories in the Japanese religious experience throughout the almost fifteen centuries of the coexistence of Buddhism and the traditional religion of Japan on its soil has produced a manifold and typically Japanese way of describing the realm of the Sacred. The word *shinbutsu*, for instance, is written with two ideograms that mean *kami*, the Japanese word used to refer to the Shinto divinities and the "superior spirits," and *hotoke*, the Japanese word for Buddha. This very characteristic Japanese word *shinbutsu* refers indistinctly to the Transcendent without specifying a specific religious comprehension of it. This sense of the Sacred remains strong in Japanese religiosity but rather indistinct and undefined, as Saigyō, a twelfth-century Japanese poet, very well expresses when he describes his feelings while being in a Shinto shrine: "I don't know what mystery inhabits this place, but I cannot refrain from weeping in gratitude for it."

In the Risshō Kōsei-kai, one finds deeply sincere gratitude for the "Eternal Buddha" being expressed in ritual as well as daily life and community meetings. In the Focolare, one also finds a deep sense of gratitude toward God for his love and toward Jesus Christ for the new life he has brought. In both, the mystery of the Sacred is expressed in life and gratitude extends to

---

29. Nikkyō Niwano, *The Wholesome Family Life* (Tokyo: Kōsei, 1982), 20–21.

other persons and to nature as well. For the Risshō Kōsei-kai, the Buddha is the personal expression of the "eternal life force of the universe." For the Focolare, everything that happens in life is linked by a "thread of gold" that expresses God's love. The shared value of gratefulness inspires both Buddhists and Christians to collaborate for the common good of humankind and for the environment.

Religious Values for Dialogue and Collaboration

My own experience and study of interreligious dialogue in Japan confirms that Saigyō's verse represents a deeply Japanese approach to religion. While Buddhism has its different ways of understanding Ultimate Reality, the import of being religious, of the religious life, has much to do with the value implications of that understanding. The values addressed above of openness, peacebuilding, compassion, harmony, and gratitude lived in dialogue by members of the Risshō Kōsei-kai and the Focolare provide a shared basis for collaboration. When a Buddhist encounters a Christian who also lives these values, he or she finds a spiritual friend with whom he or she can live these shared values. Let me cite two quotations taken from Niwano's writings that confirm this fact:

> Caring or worrying about someone else, or being cared or worried about, is what gives happiness in human life. . . . With this caring, we communicate heart to heart, and such an exchange engenders a profound sense of belonging, of oneness. In the Buddhist canon there is a definition of humanity as that which lives between one person and another. The true meaning of this is not what exists merely physically between people but what moves from heart to heart, what thrives on mutual help and a feeling of solidarity. And this, I believe, is the first key to unlocking the mystery of human happiness.[30]

> Christ said that he came not to be served but to serve. In the Sermon on the Mount he said, "Always treat others as you would like them to treat you" (Mt 7:12). This is known as the Golden Rule and is a guiding principle for human harmony. Some proclaim that the golden age of humanity will arrive when the Golden Rule is always observed. Serve others. Be kind. Help those in need.

---

30. Niwano, *The Wholesome Family Life*, 17.

The practice of helping others is in the end the fastest means of making oneself happy.[31]

It is precisely when they put into practice these shared values in the dialogues of life and collaboration that members of the Risshō Kōsei-kai and the Focolare recognize each other as religious people and are able to encounter each other's traditions more profoundly. Moreover, they support each other in their shared responsibility to promote these values in society, to educate people in the ideals of solidarity, mutual understanding, and respect, and to work together for the common good and for world peace. Addressing the Bishops of Thailand in 2008, Pope Benedict XVI said:

> The coexistence of different religious communities today unfolds against the backdrop of globalization. Recently I observed that the forces of globalization see humanity poised between two poles. On the one hand there is the growing multitude of economic and cultural bonds which usually enhance a sense of global solidarity and shared responsibility for the well-being of humanity. On the other there are disturbing signs of a fragmentation and a certain individualism in which secularism takes a hold, pushing the transcendent and the sense of the sacred to the margins and eclipsing the very source of harmony and unity within the universe.
>
> The negative aspects of this cultural phenomenon . . . in fact point to the importance of interreligious cooperation. They call for a concerted effort to uphold the spiritual and moral soul of your people. In concordance with Buddhists, you can promote mutual understanding concerning the transmission of traditions to succeeding generations, the articulation of ethical values discernable to reason, reverence for the transcendent, prayer and contemplation. Such practices and dispositions serve the common well-being of society and nurture the essence of every human being.[32]

To use Benedict XVI's words, the dialogue of life between members of the Risshō Kōsei-kai and the Focolare Movement is an interreligious example of probing the insights of each tradition concerning "the very source of harmony and unity within the universe." In this joint endeavor, one finds how these insights contribute to the ethical values and dispositions that

---

31. Nikkyō Niwano, *Invisible Eyelashes* (Tokyo: Kōsei, 1994), 137.
32. Benedict XVI, *Address to the Bishops of Thailand*, May 16, 2008.

"serve the common well-being of society and nurture the essence of every human being." Based on this dialogue of life and the values they uncover, many activities of interreligious collaboration between members of both organizations have been carried out in Japan and other parts of the world for the well-being of all humankind and the environment in which we live.

In conclusion, to understand the Buddhist life of wisdom and compassion in depth requires an understanding of the experience that transformed Siddhartha Gautama into the Buddha, the Enlightened One, 2500 years ago. To understand what is at the core of the Christian life of faith and love, we are required to look at Jesus of Nazareth, who gave his life on the cross out of love and who is professed as the Risen Lord by his disciples. But this will not become possible merely with individual, rational effort of intelligence, but rather through vital and spiritual life encounters among truly committed followers of the Buddha and of the Christ. Interreligious dialogue is ultimately not about exchanging information and knowledge, but about communion of hearts in the deepest layer of human existence. It is a shared experience that transforms us into brothers and sisters living together for the common good—for the "common well-being" of all humankind and the natural world.

Authors

Antonio Maria Baggio received degrees in philosophy at the University of Padua and the Pontifical Gregorian University. His doctorate in philosophy is from the Pontifical University of Saint Thomas in Rome. He was professor at the Pontifical Gregorian University from 1992 to 2008. Presently He is professor of political philosophy at the Sophia University Institute. Baggio is author of eight books and numerous articles on political thought.

Hubertus Blaumeiser is a German Catholic priest from the Diocese of Augsburg. He is a theologian and ecumenist who received his doctorate on Luther and the Reformation from the Gregorian University. He is a noted scholar on Martin Luther and author of many books and articles on Luther and the spirituality of the Reformation. He has been consultant for the Vatican's Congregation for Catholic Education and is a member of the Abba School.

Luigino Bruni is professor of economics at the LUMSA University in Rome, and at the Sophia University Institute. He received his doctorate in economics at the University of East Anglia, and his doctorate in the history of economic thought from the University of Florence. For the last fifteen years his research and publishing has covered areas ranging from microeconomics and ethics to happiness in economics.

Cinto Busquet received his doctorate in fundamental theology at the Lateran University and taught at the Urbaniana University before moving to Japan. There, he taught at Sophia University in Tokyo. In Japan, he was active as a theologian in Buddhist-Christian dialogue. He has written books and articles on dialogue with the Rissho Kosei-kai. Presently he serves on the Catholic Advisory Council for Religious Dialogue in Spain.

Bernhard Callebaut received his doctorate in social sciences from the Faculty of Social Sciences at the Pontifical University of Saint Thomas (Rome). He was professor at the Antwerp University Saint-Ignace and the Pontifical University of Saint Thomas. He is now associate professor of social sciences at the Sophia University Institute. He has published extensively on religious charisms.

Roberto Catalano earned a doctorate in theology of religions from the Urbaniana University. He was actively involved in interreligious dialogue in

India for twenty-eight years, organizing several symposia and events in India and in Rome between Hindus and Christians He currently is co-director of the Focolare Movement's International Office for Interreligious Dialogue. He is the author of many articles and books on interreligious dialogue.

Piero Coda received his doctorate at the Pontifical Lateran University where he went on to be full professor of theology. He was president of the Italian Theological Association from 2003 to 2011 and secretary prelate of the Pontifical Academy of Theology from 2003 to 2008. He is an emeritus member of the Abba School and past president of the Sophia University Institute. He is author of many publications including *Dalla Trinità*, which is being translated into English and published by Catholic University of American Press.

Brendan Leahy is bishop of Limerick, Ireland. Before his episcopacy, Leahy received his doctorate from the Gregorian University, and was professor of systematic theology at St. Kieran's College and at the National Seminary at St. Patrick's College in Ireland. A noted scholar on Has Urs Balthasar, he has published ten books and many articles.

Cherylanne Menezes is an advisor to the National Youth Commission of the Conference of Catholic Bishops of India and was an invited auditor at the October 2018 Vatican Synod on Youth. She holds MA degrees in Trinitarian ontology and cultural studies from Sophia University Institute. She presently teaches Christian mysticism at the University of Mumbai, is a member of the Hindu-Christian dialogue in Mumbai, and a member of the Interfaith Dialogue Committee of the Focolare Movement in India.

Donald W. Mitchell is professor emeritus of Asian and comparative philosophy and religion at Purdue University, and a permanent visiting professor at Sophia University Institute. He specializes in Buddhist-Christian dialogue and is one of the founders of the Society for Buddhist-Christian Studies, director of the International Buddhist-Christian Theological Encounter, and advisor to the Vatican's Pontifical Council for Interreligious Dialogue, the U.S. Conference of Catholic Bishops, the Monastic Interreligious Dialogue, and the Catholic Association of Diocesan Ecumenical and Interreligious Officers. Mitchell has published numerous books and articles on dialogue and is author of Oxford University's textbook on Buddhism.

Jesús Morán received degrees in philosophy at the Autonomous University of Madrid, and in dogmatic theology at the Pontifical Catholic University of Chile. He is author of numerous articles on theological anthropology.

Presently, he is a member of the Abba School in Rome and Co-President of the Focolare Movement.

Thomas Norris, a priest of the Diocese of Ossory, Ireland, received his degrees from St Kieran's College, Kilkenny, the Lateran and Gregorian Universities, Rome, and at the National University of Ireland, Cork. He is former professor of systematic theology at St Patrick's College, Maynooth. More recently, he has been Paluch Professor of Theology at Mundelein Seminary, Chicago. and is a member of the International Theological Commission. Presently He is spiritual director at the Pontifical Irish College, Rome. He has authored ten books and many articles.

Anna Pelli is professor of philosophy at the Sophia University Institute. She received degrees in philosophy from the University of Florence and in theology from the Pontifical Lateran University. She is also a member of the Abba School, working on the texts of Paradise '49.

Judith Povilus has served as provost of the Sophia University Institute in Florence, Italy. She received an MA from DePaul University, Chicago, and an MS from the University of Illinois, both in mathematics. Her doctorate in theology is from the Pontifical Lateran University in Rome. She has authored books and articles as a member of the Abba School.

Brian K. Reynolds graduated in Italian and history from University College, Dublin and carried out postgraduate studies at Trinity College, Dublin. He taught in both of these universities as well as in the Università degli Studi, Bari, Italy, before moving to Taiwan, where he is on the faculty of the Department of Italian Language and Culture, Fu Jen Catholic University, Taipei. He has written widely on the patristic and medieval periods with a focus on Marian doctrine and devotion.

Gérard Rossé is professor of biblical studies at Sophia University Institute. He studied biblical theology at the Pontifical Lateran University and the Pontifical Biblical Institute. He taught biblical theology at the University of Fribourg, Switzerland, and has published six books and five biblical commentaries.

David L. Schindler received his doctorate at the Claremont Graduate School and went on to be professor of metaphysics and fundamental theology at the University of Notre Dame. He is Dean Emeritus and Edouard Cardinal Gagnon Professor of Fundamental Theology at the Pontifical John Paul II Institute. He has published widely and is editor of *Communio: International Catholic Review* (American Edition).

Callan Slipper is an Anglican priest living in the Ealing Focolare, London, England. His doctorate is from Lancaster University with a focus on philosophy of religion and the comparative study of cognitive aspects of mystical experience. He is now on the faculty of the Sophia Institute for Culture and is a member of the Abba School. He sits on national ecumenical committees of the Church of England, is involved in interreligious dialogue

Maria Voce was elected President of the Focolare Movement on July 7, 2008, the first successor to the founder, Chiara Lubich. Prior to her election she completed her studies in theology and canon law at the University of Calabria, Italy. She spent ten years in Istanbul where she established ecumenical ties with the Patriarch of Constantinople, Demetrius I. Returning to Rome, she was a member of the Abba School, and worked directly with Chiara Lubich. As President, she participated in and spoke at a Synod of Bishops, delivered lectures at the World Council of Churches, and to the bishops of Bavaria. She is Consulter for the Pontifical Council for the Laity.

New City Press

New City Press is one of more than 20 publishing houses sponsored by the Focolare, a movement founded by Chiara Lubich to help bring about the realization of Jesus' prayer: "That all may be one" (John 17:21). In view of that goal, New City Press publishes books and resources that enrich the lives of people and help all to strive toward the unity of the entire human family. We are a member of the Association of Catholic Publishers.

www.newcitypress.com
202 Comforter Blvd.
Hyde Park, New York

Periodicals
Living City Magazine
www.livingcitymagazine.com

Scan to join our mailing list
for discounts and promotions
or go to www.newcitypress.com
and click on "join our email list."

www.ingramcontent.com/pod-product-compliance
Lightning Source LLC
Chambersburg PA
CBHW070158240426
43671CB00007B/479